CONGRATULATIONS!

As a student purchasing *Valuation: The Art and Science of Corporate Investment Decisions,* **you are entitled to six months of prepaid access to the book's Companion Website.**

The Companion Website features:

- Spreadsheet examples from the text
- Case listings

To access the *Valuation: The Art and Science of Corporate Investment Decisions* **Companion Website for the first time:**
You will need to register online using a computer with an Internet connection and a Web browser. The process takes just a couple of minutes and only needs to be completed once.

1. Go to **http://www.aw-bc.com/titman_martin**
2. Click the **Register** button.
3. Use a coin to scratch off the gray coating below and reveal your student access code.* Do not use a knife or other sharp object, which can damage the code.

4. On the registration page, enter your student access code. Do not type the dashes. You can use lowercase or uppercase letters.
5. Follow the on-screen instructions. If you need help at any time during the online registration process, simply click the **Need Help?** icon.
6. Once your personal Login Name and Password are confirmed, you can begin using the *Valuation: The Art and Science of Corporate Investment Decisions* Companion Website!

To log into this Website after you've registered:
You only need to register for this Companion Website once. After that, you can access the site by going to **http://www.aw-bc.com/titman_martin**, clicking **Student Resources**, and entering your Login Name and Password.

*Important: The Access Code on this page can only be used once to establish a subscription to the *Valuation: The Art and Science of Corporate Investment Decisions* Companion Website. This subscription is valid for six months upon activation and is not transferable. If this access code has already been scratched off, it may no longer be valid. If this is the case, you can purchase a subscription by going to **http://www.aw-bc.com/titman_martin** and clicking **Get Access**.

VALUATION

THE ADDISON-WESLEY SERIES IN FINANCE

Berk/DeMarzo
*Corporate Finance**

Copeland/Weston/Shastri
Financial Theory and Corporate Policy

Dufey/Giddy
Cases in International Finance

Eakins
Finance in .learn

Eiteman/Stonehill/Moffett
Multinational Business Finance

Gitman
*Principles of Managerial Finance**

Gitman
*Principles of Managerial Finance—Brief Edition**

Gitman/Joehnk
*Fundamentals of Investing**

Gitman/Madura
Introduction to Finance

Hughes/MacDonald
International Banking: Text and Cases

Madura
Personal Finance

Marthinsen
Risk Takers: Uses and Abuses of Financial Derivatives

McDonald
Derivatives Markets

Megginson
Corporate Finance Theory

Melvin
International Money and Finance

Mishkin/Eakins
Financial Markets and Institutions

Moffett
Cases in International Finance

Moffett/Stonehill/Eiteman
Fundamentals of Multinational Finance

Pennacchi
Theory of Asset Pricing

Rejda
Principles of Risk Management and Insurance

Solnik/McLeavey
Global Investments

Titman/Martin
Valuation: The Art and Science of Corporate Investment Decisions

*denotes myfinancelab titles. Log onto www.myfinancelab.com to learn more.

VALUATION

The Art and Science of
Corporate Investment Decisions

SHERIDAN TITMAN
University of Texas at Austin

JOHN D. MARTIN
Baylor University

PEARSON
Addison
Wesley

Boston San Francisco New York
London Toronto Sydney Tokyo Singapore Madrid
Mexico City Munich Paris Cape Town Hong Kong Montreal

Publisher: *Greg Tobin*
Editor in Chief: *Denise Clinton*
Executive Editor: *Donna Battista*
Director of Development: *Kay Ueno*
Executive Development Editor: *Mary Clare McEwing*
Editorial Assistant: *Kerri McQueen*
Managing Editor: *Nancy H. Fenton*
Senior Production Supervisor: *Kathryn Dinovo*
Supplements Coordinator: *Heather McNally*
Senior Media Producer: *Bethany Tidd*
Senior Marketing Manager: *Roxanne Hoch*
Marketing Assistant: *Ashlee Clevenger*
Senior Prepress Supervisor: *Caroline Fell*
Rights and Permissions Advisor: *Shannon Barbe*
Senior Manufacturing Buyer: *Carol Melville*
Cover Design: *Gina Hagen Kolenda*
Production Coordination, Text Design, and Composition: *Elm Street Publishing Services, Inc.*

Cover image: © 2007 Jupiterimages Corporation

Many of the designations used by manufacturers and sellers to distinguish their products are claimed as trademarks. Where those designations appear in this book, and Addison Wesley was aware of a trademark claim, the designations have been printed in initial caps or all caps.

Library of Congress Cataloging-in-Publication data

Titman, Sheridan.
    Valuation: the art and science of corporate investment decisions/Sheridan Titman, John D. Martin.
        p. cm. — (Addison-Wesley series in finance)
    Includes bibliographical references and index.
    ISBN-13: 987-0-321-33610-1 (single volume edition)
    ISBN-10: 0-321-33610-0

    1. Valuation. 2. Capital investments. I. Martin, John D., 1945- II. Title. HG4028.V3T58 2008
658.15'22—dc22   2007024317

ISBN-13: 978-0-321-33610-1
ISBN-10: 0-321-33610-0

1 2 3 4 5 6 7 8 9 10—CRW—11 10 09 08 07

To my parents, wife (Meg), and sons (Trevor, Elliot, and Gordon)
—S. T.

To the Martin women (Sally and Mel), men (sons David and Jess),
and boys (grandsons Luke and Burke)
—J.D.M.

About the Authors

SHERIDAN TITMAN holds the McAllister Centennial Chair in Financial Services at the University of Texas. He has a B.S. from the University of Colorado and an M.S. and Ph.D. from Carnegie Mellon University. Prior to joining the faculty at the University of Texas, Professor Titman was a Professor at UCLA, the Hong Kong University of Science and Technology, and Boston College and spent the 1988–89 academic year in Washington, D.C., as the special assistant to the Assistant Secretary of the Treasury for Economic Policy. In addition, he has consulted for a variety of financial institutions and corporations. He has served on the editorial boards of the leading academic finance and real estate journals, was an editor of the *Review of Financial Studies,* and was the founding editor of the *International Review of Finance.* He has served as a director of the American Finance Association, the Asia Pacific Finance Association, the Western Finance Association, and the Financial Management Association and as the President of the Western Finance Association. Professor Titman has published more than 50 articles in both academic and professional journals and a book entitled *Financial Markets and Corporate Strategy*. He has received a number of awards for his research excellence and is a Fellow of the Financial Management Association and a Research Associate of the National Bureau of Economic Research.

Sheridan and Meg live with their three sons and dog (Mango) in Austin, Texas.

JOHN MARTIN holds the Carr P. Collins Chair in Finance in the Hankamer School of Business at Baylor University where he teaches in the Baylor EMBA programs. Over his career he has published more than 50 articles in the leading finance journals and served in a number of editorial positions including the co-editorship of the FMA *Survey and Synthesis Series* for the Oxford University Press. In addition, he has co-authored the following books: *Financial Management,* 10th edition (Prentice Hall Publishing Company); *Foundations of Finance,* 6th edition (Prentice Hall Publishing Company); *Financial Analysis* (McGraw Hill Publishing Company); *The Theory of Finance* (Dryden Press); and *Value Based Management* (Harvard Business School Press/Oxford University Press).

John and Sally have two wonderful sons, the world's finest daughter-in-law (their youngest son isn't married), and two beautiful grandsons who visit them often on their ranch outside of Crawford, Texas, where they raise Brangus cattle and miniature donkeys.

Brief Contents

Detailed Contents

Preface

PROJECT AND ENTERPRISE VALUATION

Most valuation books focus on the valuation of entire businesses, or *enterprise* valuation. But by far the greatest application of valuation methods today is aimed at individual investment projects. With this in mind, we have developed a book that is designed for readers interested in *project* as well as *enterprise valuation*. This broader focus better fits the economic realities of the modern corporation, which acquires productive capacity in one of two basic ways—through internal growth, which requires the evaluation of project value, and through acquisitions of operating business units, which requires the evaluation of business or enterprise value.

We see our potential audience comprised of two key groups:

- **Business professionals** who because of their business needs want a state-of-the-art book on the practical implementation of advanced valuation methods.
- **Students** in MBA and upper-division undergraduate finance elective courses that focus on the valuation and analysis of investment opportunities. Such courses may be lecture/problem- or case-based. Our book would be appropriate as the primary information source for the former and as a supplement for the latter.

VALUATION IN TODAY'S CHALLENGING BUSINESS ENVIRONMENT

In the last decade an unprecedented number of corporate bankruptcies have emerged from some of the largest global companies. Although the fraudulent accounting activities of Parmalat, Enron, and WorldCom have taken center stage in the courtroom and the press, another story lurks beneath the headlines: What created the need for these firms to cover up so much red ink in the first place? In many cases, a history of an undisciplined approach to the evaluation of investment opportunities was the real culprit.

The more stringent reporting and governance requirements resulting from the passage of Sarbanes–Oxley[1] help to ensure the accurate disclosure of financial information for public companies. However, these new policies only address the symptoms rather than the causes of the problem, whereas improved project

---

[1] Sarbanes–Oxley Act of 2002. Section 406, "Code of Ethics for Senior Financial Officers."

and enterprise valuation methods can prevent problems from occurring in the first place. However, Sarbanes–Oxley creates new legal responsibilities to ensure not only that public firms comply with accounting rules but also that their financial statements "fairly and accurately" reflect the overall financial position of the firm. Fulfilling this responsibility requires more rigorous valuation analysis across the firm's entire portfolio of investments. In this book we provide a disciplined approach that can be used for reporting as well as decision making.

A Holistic Approach to Valuation

Our vision for this book is to provide an up-to-date, integrated treatment of the valuation of investment opportunities that seriously considers industry practice as well as recent advances in valuation methods. We understand that investments cannot be valued in a vacuum, and wise investment decisions must account for how the investments relate to the firm's current and future strategies along a number of dimensions:

- What are the relevant risks of the project and can the firm hedge these risks?
- How can the investment be financed, and how does financing contribute to its value?
- How does the investment affect the firm's financial statements?
- Will the investment initially improve the firm's earnings per share, or will it lead to a short-term reduction in earnings?
- Is there flexibility in the way that the project can be implemented, and how does this flexibility contribute to value?
- If we choose to delay the initiation of the investment, will the opportunity still be available in the future?
- Do they exploit the firm's existing comparative advantages, and do they create new comparative advantages that will generate valuable projects in the furure?

In addition to these dimensions, we offer a broad spectrum of valuation approaches. Although financial economists and business practitioners recognize that evaluating investment opportunities requires much more than just discounting cash flows, they often pay little attention to other elements of the valuation process. Our focus is multi-faceted in that we amplify important areas that often receive short shrift in the valuation process.

Pedagogical Features

This book incorporates a number of pedagogical features that should help the seasoned financial analyst as well as students develop a framework for evaluating the simplest to the most complex valuation problems.

Realistic Assumptions

Valuation principles are best illustrated and learned in the context of realistic situations in which decisions are actually made. Thus, we ground our examples in practical settings to give a sense of the context in which decision making takes place. Without delving into theoretical arguments, we rely on the recent work of financial economists who provide the theoretical underpinnings for the practice of finance in a "messy" world where conditions often deviate from the idealized world of classical finance. We also acknowledge the limitations of the models we use and give recommendations on how they can be applied in practice.

Extensions and Insights

A number of special features enrich the text presentation.

- *Industry Insights* delve more deeply into how the tools developed in the book are used in practice.
- *Technical Insights* provide further explanations of mathematics, methodologies, and analytical tools.
- *Behavioral Insights* focus on irrational choices and biases that affect how investment choices are made in practice.
- *Practitioner Insights* provide perspective from a broad spectrum of professionals who use the various valuation methodologies discussed in the text.
- *Did you know?* side comments provide little slices of interesting financial lore.

End-of-Chapter Problems and Mini-Cases

Each chapter contains a generous number of problems designed to review the materials discussed in the chapter and to allow readers to solidify their understanding of key concepts. These exercises are intentionally practical and range in difficulty from brief problems designed to illustrate a single point to mini-cases in selected chapters to moderate-length case studies with multiple parts designed to delve more deeply into issues.

Spreadsheet Usage and Support

The majority of the end-of-chapter problems require the use of spreadsheet software, as do the examples used throughout the book. We provide a complete set of spreadsheets that replicate the in-chapter examples, and we include templates for use in solving end-of-chapter problems. These examples and templates can be found on the Web site accompanying this book at http://www.aw-bc.com/titman_martin.

Use of Simulation Software

Where applicable, we use Monte Carlo simulation. Although the book can be used without this feature, the value of the learning experience will be greatly enriched if the reader works directly with this tool. To facilitate the use of Monte Carlo simulation, an access code to Crystal Ball software has been included with this text. Crystal Ball is an add-in to spreadsheet software that allows you to perform Monte Carlo simulations by automatically calculating thousands of different "what if" cases, saving the inputs and results of each calculation as individual scenarios. Analysis of these scenarios reveals to you the range of possible outcomes, their probability of occurring, which input has the most effect on your model, and where you should focus your efforts. Alternatively, readers already familiar with other simulation packages (e.g., @Risk) may use those instead.

SUPPLEMENTS

We provide a number of ancillary materials for the instructor, student, and practitioner.

Excel solutions are available to instructors for end-of-chapter exercises, in addition to the spreadsheet models that are used. The solutions will be provided on an instructor's resource disk for adopters of the text. Online *PowerPoint Lecture Outlines* set out major points for the entire text, along with slides of figures and tables in the book. A dedicated Web site, http://www.aw-bc.com/titman_martin, contains spreadsheets for in-chapter examples and templates for end-of-chapter problems, plus recommendations for case studies.

STRUCTURE OF THE BOOK

Chapter 1 provides an aerial view of project evaluation and sets out a roadmap for the remaining chapters. We use Chapter 1 to launch a discussion of our view of the art and science of valuation in general, with an emphasis on the need for a rigorous decision process.

Chapters 2 through 12 are divided into four parts. Part I (*Project Analysis Using Discounted Cash Flow*) is comprised of Chapters 2 and 3. In Chapter 2 we set out the basic tool of discounted cash flow analysis and extend the analysis to other models in Chapter 3. Discounted cash flow (DCF) analysis has been the mainstay of financial analysis since the 1950s and continues to be what most financial analysts think of when they think about project or enterprise (business) valuation. However, DCF analysis is often oversimplified in classroom presentations, so that when the various nuances of practical applications are encountered in the real world, the proper application of DCF is often confusing—even for seasoned professionals. We focus on a three-step approach to DCF analysis that entails a careful definition of cash flow estimation, matching cash flows with the proper discount rate, and using the right mechanics to estimate present value.

Part II (*Cost of Capital*), consisting of Chapters 4 and 5, discusses how to estimate the cost of capital, which is an essential building block in the valuation process. The cost of capital can be viewed as the opportunity cost of financing the investment which, in turn, is the appropriate discount rate for valuation analysis. We evaluate the cost of capital for the firm as a whole and for individual investment proposals or projects. The former is the discount rate used to value an entire business enterprise, while the latter is the discount rate for valuing an individual investment.

In Chapters 6 through 9 of Part III (*Enterprise Valuation*), we examine the challenging task of estimating the value of a business enterprise. These chapters combine the DCF methodology developed in earlier chapters with the analysis of various accounting ratios. We consider the value of an ongoing business from the perspective of the firm's stockholders as well as from the perspective of the acquiring firm. In addition, we look at the value of the firm through the eyes of the private equity investor, including both the venture capitalist and the LBO firm. In Chapter 9 we look at the problem of performance measurement and the influence of an investment on the firm's earnings.

Part IV (*Futures, Options, and the Valuation of Real Investments*) features a three-part treatment (Chapters 10–12) of real options. In these chapters we demonstrate how options are used at both the nitty-gritty level where the value of project cash flows are estimated and also at the strategic level where new businesses are evaluated. In Chapter 10 we note that the rapid development of markets for financial derivative products related to basic commodities, foreign exchange, and interest rates has opened the possibility for firms to "lay off" significant risk exposures through hedging transactions and that this opportunity has changed the way we think about valuation. Chapter 11 covers the central issue in real option analysis: The valuation of investments when management has flexibility in how the investment is implemented. In Chapter 12 we use the concepts developed in Chapters 10 and 11 to analyze the value of business strategies.

We also include an Epilogue that discusses the disconnects we have observed between valuation theory and industry practice, and we make a few predictions about the extent to which such gaps may be reduced in the future.

Acknowledgments

We would particularly like to thank the following reviewers and colleagues, whose insights were of immense value as we developed this book.

Andres Almazan, *University of Texas*
Aydogan Alti, *University of Texas*
Christopher Anderson, *University of Kansas*
Sugato Bhattacharyya, *University of Michigan*
Elizabeth Booth, *Michigan State University*
Luiz Brandao, *Catholic University, Rio De Janeiro*
Soku Byoun, *Baylor University*
Su Han Chan, *California State University, Fullerton*
Ryan Davies, *Babson College*
Carlos T. de Arrigunaga, *Golden Gate University*
Ben Esty, *Harvard Business School*
Scott Fine, *Case Western Reserve University*
Sharon Garrison, *University of Arizona*
Scott Gibson, *College of William & Mary*
Todd Houge, *University of Iowa*
Keith Howe, *DePaul University*
Dawny Huh, *Baylor University*
Zeigham Khokher, *University of Western Ontario*
Robert Kieschnick, *University of Texas, Dallas*
Lloyd Levitin, *University of Southern California*
Per Olsson, *Duke University*
Chris Parsons, *McGill University*
Bill Petty, *Baylor University*
Julia Plotts, *University of Southern California*
Robert McDonald, *Northwestern University*
Steve Rich, *Baylor University*
Betty Simkins, *Oklahoma State University*
Colette Southam, *University of Western Ontario*
Mark Stohs, *California State University, Fullerton*
Alex Triantis, *University of Maryland*
Chishen Wei, *University of Texas*
Zhewei Zhang, *Baylor University*

Among our academic reviewers a special note of thanks goes to the following: Scott Gibson, Edie Hotchkiss, Julia Plotts, and Betty Simkins who not only reviewed and class tested the book but also contributed many of the mini-case problems you will find at the end of the chapters. We also want to recognize the students at both Baylor and Texas who suffered through early drafts of the book's chapters and who offered invaluable comments. Among this group a special word of thanks goes to the 2006 EMBA classes at Baylor (Austin and Dallas) who read and used virtually the entire book in their summer finance classes. Finally, we recognize the collaboration of Ravi Anshuman, Indian Institute of Management at Bangalore, who read and commented extensively on the entire book through its many drafts. Ravi is a co-author with us on a forthcoming emerging markets valuation book (Addison Wesley, 2008).

We also want to express our thanks to the many business professionals who were kind enough to provide us with the wisdom of their experiences in the form of the Practitioner Insight boxes. These include the following:

Jim Brenn, CFO, Briggs and Stratton Corporation, Milwaukee, Wisconsin

Kevin Cassidy, Moody's Investors Service, Vice President/Senior Analyst, New York, New York

Keith Crider, New Product Finance Manager, Frito-Lay, Dallas, Texas

Joe Cunningham, MD, managing director for Sante' Health Ventures, Austin, Texas

Jack D. Furst, co-founder of Hicks, Muse, Tate & Furst in 1989 (renamed HM Capital Partners in 2006) and now a Senior Advisor and member of the firm's investment committee

Trevor Harris, Managing Director at Morgan Stanley and co-director of the Center for Excellence in Accounting and Security Analysis at the Columbia University School of Business

Jonathan Hook, Associate Vice President and Chief Investment Officer for the Baylor University Endowment Fund, Baylor University, Waco, Texas

Roger Ibbotson, founder and former Chairman of Ibbotson Associates, Inc.

Vince Kaminski, Professor in the Jesse H. Jones Graduate School of Management, Rice University, Houston, Texas

Steven McColl, Strategic Transactions Coordinator, ConocoPhillips, Houston, Texas

Justin Petit, Partner, Booz Allen Hamilton, New York, New York

Jeffrey Rabel, Vice President—Global Financial Sponsors, Lehman Brothers, New York

J. Douglas Ramsey, Ph.D., Vice President & CFO, EXCO Resources, Inc., Dallas, Texas

Bennett Stewart III, Founding partner of Stern-Stewart and Company, New York, New York

We also appreciate the substantial help we received from a terrific Addison-Wesley editorial support group. This group was led by our very capable friend, Mary Clare McEwing, who managed the entire development process for the book. Along the way, she became the godmother to one of John's calves (who is named—appropriately—Mary Clare Martin). Ann Torbert, our developmental editor, endured the reading of our first draft and guided us as we shaped that effort into the book that you see, and last but far from least, we would like to thank our editor, Donna Battista, who helped shape the initial vision that developed into this book.

S.T.
J.D.M.

Overview of Valuation

Chapter Overview

C hapter 1 focuses on the inherent challenges that arise in the valuation of investments, from large capital budgeting projects to the acquisition of stand-alone businesses. First, we review the notion of project valuation in terms of its anticipated impact on the wealth of the firm's owners. Second, using a case study involving a large investment made by a group of multinational oil companies, we highlight five key challenges that can arise in valuing a major investment proposal.

To deal effectively with the challenges involved in valuing major investments, firms must have a disciplined approach, founded on a sound evaluation process. We present a three-phase investment evaluation process to address this need. This process begins with the identification of an investment idea and ends with the final approval. This process does not eliminate all bad investments, for investing is inherently risky. However, it does help ensure that the firm does not fall victim to decision errors based on flawed analysis.

1.1 INTRODUCTION

While the ultimate success or failure of a firm depends on a lot of different things, management's ability to evaluate and select profitable investments is certainly a key contributor. The investments that we have in mind can include major capital investments, such as Intel's decision to build a new fabricating plant or Wal-Mart's decision to install an automated inventory management system in its regional distribution centers. The investments can also include the acquisition of entire businesses, such as Google's acquisition of YouTube or Ebay's acquisitions of Shopping.com and Skype.com. What these decisions have in common is the fact that the firms must

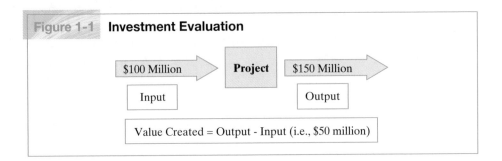

Figure 1-1   **Investment Evaluation**

expend significant resources, both management time and money, for the opportunity to receive an uncertain payoff in the future.

Depending on its stage of development, a firm's investment expenditures can be a substantial portion of the firm's total value. For example, in 2004 Netflix, Inc. (NFLX) spent $117.93 million on assets needed to support its DVD rental business, which represented 47% of its total assets (Company 1OK, 2004). The more mature firm, Home Depot invested $3.9 billion in capital expenditures and about $2.5 billion in acquisitions, which amounted to only 14.4% of its total asset base at the end of 2005.[1]

Throughout most of this book we will assume that the firm's objective is to create wealth by initiating and managing investments that generate future cash flows that are worth more than the amount invested. On the surface the process appears quite simple. Consider the illustration in Figure 1-1: A firm has the opportunity to invest $100 million today in a project that generates a stream of cash flows that are valued at $150 million. By making the investment, the firm generates an incremental $50 million in wealth for its shareholders. In the language of the financial analyst, the firm expects the project to be worth $50 million more than it costs (in today's dollars), which in the jargon of finance, means that the project has a *net present value (NPV)* of $50 million.[2]

It is, however, an unfortunate fact of life that over half of all large investment projects fail to achieve their hoped-for results.[3] The record of merger and acquisition performance is even more problematic, as exemplified by Daimler-Benz's sale of Chrysler Corporation for less than $7.4 billion in 2007 after having paid $36 billion for the company in 1998. If project evaluation is as straightforward as depicted in Figure 1-1, then why do so many big investments fail?

One possible explanation for failed investments is simply that firms invest in risky projects, and we should not expect them to be right all the time. Using a sports analogy,

---

[1]http://ir.homedepot.com/downloads/HD_2005_AR.pdf (as accessed on January 8, 2006).

[2]You will recall that NPV is equal to the difference between the value of expected future cash flows derived from an investment and the cost of making the investment.

[3]Nadim F. Matta and Ronald N. Ashkenas, 2003, Why good projects fail anyway, *Harvard Business Review* (September), 109–114.

when you swing for the fences, you can expect to strike out a lot. However, we will contend throughout this book that there is more than investment risk and bad luck at work here. The fact is that analyzing capital expenditure choices can be both complex and tedious, and managers must make their investment decisions on the basis of incomplete information about uncertain future events. In the face of this complexity and uncertainty managers often just "go with their gut," and initiate the investments that feel right.

We agree that managers with reliable intuition (that is, a discriminating gut) and the experience to make sound judgments will—and should—be ultimately making the major corporate investment choices. However, analytical tools, as well as sophisticated, yet inexpensive and user-friendly computer software, can help managers see through the complexity, as well as work through the tedium, inherent in the evaluation of a major investment. It is our belief that by using these tools and taking a more disciplined approach to valuation, managers' judgment will be enhanced and they will make better investment choices.

1.2 THE NATURE OF MAJOR INVESTMENT DECISIONS

Firms grow and expand their operations in one of two ways: They acquire productive capacity by assembling the necessary assets, or alternatively, they acquire the productive assets of an existing firm. In the case of a firm assembling the necessary assets itself, the valuation problem is called **project valuation.** In the case of a firm acquiring productive assets by purchasing an existing firm, we refer to the valuation problem as one of **enterprise valuation.**

In this section we consider examples of both project and enterprise valuation and provide a common set of underlying principles that can be used for both types of analysis.

Project Valuation—Investing in the Caspian Sea Oil Fields

To gain an appreciation for the complexity encountered when evaluating whether to commit funds to a large investment project, consider the decision faced by a group of multinational oil companies in the early 1990s. Take yourself back in time and imagine that you are sitting at the table when the analysis begins, and are trying to get a handle on the risks and potential rewards that might accrue to your firm if it undertakes the investment.

The investment opportunity involved the development of the Caspian Sea oil fields in Azerbaijan, a newly independent country that once was part of the Soviet Union.[4] The investment involved the formation of a joint-venture consortium comprised of 11 oil companies. The consortium, known as the Azerbaijani International Oil Consortium, includes the state oil company of Azerbaijan, British Petroleum,

---

[4]Benjamin Esty and Michael Kane, BP Amoco (B): Financing Development of the Caspian Oil Fields, *Harvard Business School Press*, Case #9-201-067, 2001.

Figure 1-2	Stages of Investment in the Caspian Sea Oil Development Investment
1998–1999	**Early Oil Project**
	■ Develop Chirag field by refurbishing offshore drilling platform and drilling new wells. ■ Construct undersea oil pipeline to terminal (105 miles). ■ Rebuild two export pipelines (total of 1,300 miles). ■ Estimated cost = $1 billion.
Beginning in 2000	**First-Stage Development**
	■ Develop the Azeri field. ■ Estimated cost = between $2.6 and $3.1 billion.
Beginning in 2002	**Second-Stage Development**
	■ Develop the deepwater Gunashli field. ■ Estimated cost = $3 billion.
Beginning in 2003–2004	**Third-Stage Development**
	■ Additional development of the Azeri field. ■ Estimated cost = $2 billion.

Amoco, the national oil companies of Russia and Turkey, and several other foreign oil companies. The 11 oil companies jointly have the right to develop three oil fields in the western part of the Caspian Sea that were estimated to contain 4.5 to 5 billion barrels of oil.[5]

The right to develop the three fields would be subject to certain conditions. The consortium would complete a seismic survey, an environmental impact study, and drill a series of test wells. It then would have to submit a development plan to the state oil company of Azerbaijan, outlining the development of the fields based on its preliminary findings. Following the initial work, the consortium eventually submitted a plan, involving four stages, summarized in Figure 1-2. Both the state oil company of Azerbaijan and the consortium had the right to approve each step in the process based on the results of the prior stage. Furthermore, a production-sharing agreement defined the revenue-sharing agreement for the output from the investment, if it were successful.

---

[5]"Azerbaijan-Pipeline Knocked Back," *Project Finance International,* (March 24, 1999), p. 45.

As the results of each stage of the project became known, the management of the state oil company of Azerbaijan and the consortium were faced with the decision of whether they should enter the next phase of the project. In essence, if the decision were made to proceed with the early-stage investment, the consortium acquires the *option* to make successive investments in each of the three subsequent stages of the development process. Furthermore, assuming that all stages of the investment were successfully executed, the fact that the consortium had developed expertise in the region would make it possible for each member of the consortium to compete on favorable terms with would-be competitors for future investment opportunities.

Issues to Consider When Valuing an Investment

The Caspian Sea oil field development project illustrates the complexities of the environment in which companies make investment decisions. In any situation in which a company must value a major new investment, five key issues arise. Figure 1-3 highlights these issues, which we discuss below.

Issue #1: Does the "Story" Make Sense?

Before the firm makes any investment, the investment story or strategy must be plausible to decision makers. By "make sense," we mean that management must be convinced that the potential gains from the investment are large enough to warrant initial investigation. Also, management must believe that the firm's management team possesses (or can acquire) the expertise required to reap the rewards of investing. In the terminology of economics, the issue is *competitive advantage*. Specifically, does the firm have an advantage due to specialized knowledge or circumstance that allows it to capture the benefits of the investment?

The ultimate success or failure of an investment is largely driven by the capabilities of the firm that undertakes the investment in comparison to other firms. This notion is captured in the concept of *comparative advantage*. In addition, the value that the firm is able to capture for itself is affected by the actions and reactions of competitor firms. Therefore, a complete analysis of an investment must address the following strategic issues as part of its "story": Does the firm, and does this project, provide any comparative advantage(s) relative to other firms and existing projects?

Figure 1-3   **Important Issues to Think About When Making a Major Investment**

1. Does the "story" make sense?
2. What are the risks involved in undertaking the investment?
3. How can the investment be financed?
4. How does the investment affect near-term earnings?
5. Does the investment have inherent flexibilities?

Are the firm's comparative advantages sufficient to deter competitors from making similar investments?

Issue #2: What Are the Risks Entailed in the Investment and How Can They be Assessed and Dealt with in the Analysis?

The old adage "look before you leap" is good advice when evaluating investment opportunities. Specifically, a careful assessment of *what might go wrong* is perhaps even more important than an analysis of what we hope will go right. For example, international investment projects that are made in underdeveloped parts of the world expose the investing company to a myriad of risks.

Here are some questions that often come up in evaluating and managing risk: What are the underlying risks associated with the investment? How should these risks be incorporated into the project analysis? Do the investment risks affect the rate of return that should be used in evaluating whether to undertake the investment? Are there governmental programs (domestic or foreign) that can insure the investment in the event of political instability? How does the ability of the firm to transfer investment risk affect the financing of the project and the project's valuation?

Issue #3: How Can the Investment be Financed?

There are a variety of ways to fund a major investment project. Moreover, the ability to secure attractive financing is a key determinant of the value of the investment. For example, sometimes firms can obtain debt subsidies in the form of governmental guarantees or credit enhancements, especially when international investments are involved. In other cases, firms might raise private equity and new debt financing to fund off-balance-sheet investments known as special-purpose entities (SPEs).

Specifically, the evaluation of financing opportunities addresses issues such as the following: How do the characteristics of the firm and the project (e.g., the extent that the risks of the project can be managed by transferring the risk to another party via a financial contract) affect how it is financed? How does the financing of the project affect how the project can be valued? We will have more to say about the relation between financing and value in Chapter 4.

In addition to asking how much debt to use, the firm also should discuss the type of debt to use. Should the project be financed on the firm's balance sheet or should it be financed off the balance sheet with nonrecourse debt (i.e., project financing)?[6]

Issue #4: How Does the Investment Affect Near-Term Earnings?

Investors and equity analysts use the firm's reported earnings as an indicator of the firm's success or failure. When considering a large investment, managers will be keenly

---

[6]*Nonrecourse* or project financing refers to debt for which only the investment or project is responsible. That is, the debt is to be repaid out of the cash flows generated by the project, and there is no recourse to the company sponsoring the investment.

aware of its effect on earnings. They will ask whether a project is likely to *dilute* (reduce) or *accrete* (increase) the firm's earnings per share. For example, a major oil project like the Caspian Sea project can often dilute the firm's earnings in the early years because of the considerable up-front expenses and deferred cash flows. However, earnings should increase over time, as the future benefits from the project materialize.

A project's effect on earnings can be important in determining whether managers are willing to initiate an investment for a variety of reasons. For example, if company executives are being paid on earnings-based performance measures, or if they believe that investors focus on earnings per share, then they may be reluctant to invest in a project that negatively affects the firm's earnings. Thus, accounting and the design of pay-for-performance policies often influence a firm's investment decisions. Chapter 9 delves into the potential importance of earnings on a firm's investment decisions, as well as how residual income (or Economic Value Added™)[7] can be used to help resolve the problems associated with earnings as a performance metric.

Issue #5: Does the Investment Have Inherent Flexibilities That Allow the Firm to Modify It in Response to Changing Circumstances?

Firms make investments expecting that a particular set of outcomes will guide the investment toward a particular result. However, uncertain future events make it particularly important that the project provide opportunities to react and adapt the investment to changing circumstances. Specifically, these include the following.

Can the investment be staged?   Often, as in the Caspian Sea oil fields case, firms undertake very large investments in stages. Staging allows the firm to manage its risk exposure by making a series of successively larger commitments based upon the success of the prior investment. This is clearly the case with large oil-development projects: They typically have an early stage that provides information about the size of the oil reserves before the firm initiates later development stages. This is also true for many new products or services for which the test-marketing phase reveals important information about their sales potential.

When the firm invests in the initial stages, it essentially acquires the "option" to invest in later stages of the project (if the intermediate investments prove fruitful). The flexibility to delay implementation of a project, to cut one's losses and abandon a project, or to expand a successful investment are examples of optionality that can add considerable value to a project. We will have more to say about the evaluation of such options in Chapter 11.

Decision makers should be aware that in some instances, what appears to be an option turns out to be an obligation. Specifically, if there is no real possibility that an option will *not* be exercised, then it's not an option at all. In the Caspian Sea case, for example, it may turn out to be very difficult for the consortium members to back out after stage 1.

---

[7]Economic Value Added or EVA™ is a registered trademark of Stern Stewart and Company.

Does the investment offer the opportunity for follow-on investments?   The opportunity to invest in a new product, market, or technology can provide valuable "follow-on investment" opportunities. Most new investment opportunities arise out of previous investments that the firm has made. In the Caspian Sea case there are likely to be additional oil and gas deals, or even the opportunity to enter the petrochemical business in central Asia. Consequently, the valuation of investments with follow-on opportunities requires consideration of *two sets* of cash flows: the cash flows provided by the immediate opportunity, as well as the cash flows from the possible subsequent projects. The fundamental issue is this: How should the company value these follow-on opportunities and incorporate them into the analysis of the initial decision to invest? We will have more to say about this in Chapter 12.

Does the investment provide production or marketing synergies with existing products?   To the extent that the new investment shares existing production and/or marketing resources, the opportunity exists to gain a comparative advantage over the firm's competitors.

Enterprise Valuation—Mergers and Acquisitions

The five basic issues encountered in analyzing the Caspian Sea investment project also apply to *enterprise valuation*—the valuation of an entire firm. From the financial analyst's perspective, the fundamental question is the same: What is the investment worth, and how does this compare to its cost?

Cisco Systems (CSCO) is noted for its policy of acquiring existing firms. This strategy of expansion through acquisitions entails the same problems that we encountered in the Caspian Sea project valuation. For example, on March 20, 2003, Cisco announced plans to acquire The Linksys Group, Inc., of Irvine, California, for a total purchase price of approximately $500 million. Although we do not have detailed information concerning Cisco's analysis of the acquisition, the following discussion (based on a company press release)[8] highlights how Cisco described its assessment of the five basic issues identified earlier.

Issue #1: Does the "story" make sense?

"Fueled by consumer broadband adoption, the home networking space has experienced mass market acceptance. Linksys has captured a strong position in this growing market by developing an extensive, easy-to-use product line for the home and small office."[9] The acquisition is an example of Cisco's strategy to broaden its end-to-end portfolio of network solutions into high-growth markets such as wireless, voice-over IP, and storage area networking.

---

[8]Cisco Systems press release, dated March 20, 2003 (http://newsroom.cisco.com/dlls/corp_032003.html).

[9]News Release, "Cisco Systems Announces Agreement to Acquire the Linksys Group, Inc.," March 20, 2003.

Issue #2: What are the sources of risk in the investment, and can these risks be managed?

An important source of risk to the investment relates to technological risks. For example, are there wireless technologies that might develop that would render Linksys's products noncompetitive? This risk is very real for technology-based companies; however, Cisco has partially mitigated this risk by acquiring the recognized industry leader. The challenge facing Cisco in the future will be to maintain Linksys's competitive edge while operating the company as a division of a much larger firm.

Issue #3: How can the investment be financed?

"Under the terms of the agreement, Cisco will issue common stock with an aggregate value of approximately $500 million to acquire the Linksys business and to assume all outstanding employee stock options."

Issue #4: What is the short-term effect of the investment's acceptance on the firm's reported earnings?

"Exclusive of acquisition charges, Cisco anticipates this transaction will add approximately $0.01 to its FY2004 pro forma EPS. The transaction will be accretive to both GAAP and pro-forma earnings thereafter."

Issue #5: Does the investment have inherent flexibilities that allow the firm to modify it in response to changing circumstances? In particular,

Can the investment be staged?

■ Cisco's acquisition of Linksys is another step in a broad strategy to expand its home and small office product line aimed at developing a dominant position in the home and small office networking market.

Does the investment offer the opportunity for follow-on investments?

■ "This acquisition represents Cisco's entry into the high-growth consumer/SOHO [small office, home office] networking market. Home networks allow consumers to share broadband Internet connections, files, printers, digital music, photos, and gaming, all over a wired or wireless LAN (local area network)."

Does the acquisition offer production and/or marketing synergies with existing products?

■ Clearly Linksys offers products that can be marketed using similar channels of distribution to those already in place at Cisco. In addition, similarities between small business and home applications should provide synergies with Cisco's existing marketing assets.

1.3 DEALING WITH COMPLEXITY—PROCESS AND DISCIPLINE

Whether an investment is like the Caspian Sea investment or like Cisco's acquisition of The Linksys Group, its evaluation can become very complex. To address this complexity in a disciplined way, firms develop policies and procedures that prescribe how to evaluate new investment opportunities. The purpose of these procedures is to ensure that projects receive a thorough analysis and that the project selection process is not subverted by the special interests of one or more managers.

The Investment Evaluation Process

Figure 1-4 summarizes an **investment evaluation process.** This three-phase process captures the critical elements of project *or* enterprise evaluation, beginning with idea generation and ending with a final go–no go investment decision. The process is very general, and illustrates how investments are evaluated across a wide variety of industry settings and sizes of firms. Be aware that in this discussion, the phases can be broad enough to cover enterprise evaluation or narrow enough to cover project valuation.

Figure 1-4	Three-Phase Investment Evaluation Process—Covering All the Bases
PHASE I	**Investment (Idea) Origination and Analysis**
Step 1:	Conduct a strategic assessment.
Step 2:	Estimate the investment's value ("crunch the numbers").
Step 3:	Prepare an investment evaluation report and recommendation to management.
PHASE II	**Managerial Review and Recommendation**
Step 4:	Evaluate the investment's strategic assumptions.
Step 5:	Review and evaluate the methods and assumptions used to estimate the investment's NPV.
Step 6:	Adjust for inherent estimation errors induced by bias, and formulate a recommendation regarding the proposed investment.
PHASE III	**Managerial Decision and Approval**
Step 7:	Make a decision.
Step 8:	Seek final managerial and possibly board approval.

Phase I: Investment (Idea) Origination and Analysis

Firms learn about major investment opportunities from a variety of sources. A common source of ideas is the firm's employees and customers. Another source is outside organizations that bring proposals to the firm's attention, such as investment bankers and other firms that want to buy or sell specific assets.

This initial phase of the analysis includes three activities:

Step 1: Conduct a strategic assessment. Every investment opportunity has an underlying strategy ("value proposition") that provides the basis for making the investment. The initial screening of investment proposals begins with an assessment of the soundness of this underlying strategy. Members of the firm's business development group often do this screening. If the investment (project or enterprise) looks promising after the initial review, then an investment evaluation team further investigates the opportunity and makes a recommendation to management.

Step 2: Estimate the investment value ("crunch the numbers"). The objective of the estimation part of the process is to determine whether the investment has the potential to create value for the firm's stockholders. Traditionally this analysis involves applying valuation models such as discounted cash flow and market-based multiples (e.g., market to book, price to earnings). However, when the investment's potential to create value has multiple sources, the evaluation can involve many other types of analysis. These include analyses of (a) projected cash flows from existing or proposed operations; (b) built-in project flexibility that enables management to modify the investment over its life in response to changing market conditions (i.e., real options); (c) opportunities to manage (i.e., control or even eliminate) some of the investment's inherent sources of risk; (d) the ability to structure the organization (align decision authority and compensation policies) to enhance the investment's value-creation potential; (e) financing alternatives; and (f) the effect of the investment on the firm's near-term earnings.

Step 3: Prepare the investment evaluation report and recommendation to management. Combining the strategic and quantitative analyses from Steps 1 and 2, the investment analysis team prepares a report summarizing its recommendation to the managerial oversight committee. At a minimum the report will contain (a) an assessment of the investment's strategy for creating shareholder value, (b) an estimate of the value of the investment (net present value), and (c) the supporting information and assumptions used in the analysis.

Phase II: Managerial Review and Recommendation

Managerial review serves a control function: It screens the initial analysis for potential sources of errors and investment-selection bias. A different group of employees, ones who did not perform the original analysis, review the new investment proposals. Typically, firms use an investment review committee (sometimes known as the *strategic planning committee*) to review new proposals.

The fundamental responsibility of the investment review committee is, as the name implies, to review the recommendation of the initial investment analysis team. The review committee will make sure that the assumptions of the initial evaluation team are reasonable and that nothing has been forgotten in the analysis. If the review process recommends the investment to management, the review committee also assesses how much to invest. The investment review committee provides a system of checks and balances designed to weed out bad investments and flawed investment analysis.

Phase II involves the activities of Steps 4 through 6:

Step 4: **Evaluate the investment's strategic assumptions.** The review process, like the initial investment screening (Step 1), begins with an assessment of the investment's value proposition or strategy. Does the story underlying its value-creation potential make sense to the managerial review committee? Do the hedging opportunities offer sources of value to the firm? Do investment-specific financing alternatives make sense, and do they have a reasonable prospect of adding value?

Step 5: **Review and evaluate the methods and assumptions used to estimate the NPV of the investment.** The committee evaluates the quantitative analysis conducted in Step 2. Are the assumptions that underlie earlier price, cost, and quantity estimates reasonable in light of observed market prices and the market shares of competitor firms and products? Are there any additional options (follow-on investments and other important sources of value creation) inherent in the proposal that were not considered in the earlier report? Finally, are there opportunities to expand or contract the scope of the investment (even abandon it altogether)? Although it can be very difficult to estimate their value, it is critical that the firm consider these options in order to properly value the investment.

Step 6: **Adjust for inherent estimation errors induced by bias, and formulate a recommendation regarding the investment.** The origination process can be fraught with the potential for biased estimates of an investment's value. After making appropriate adjustments, the managerial review committee passes its recommendation along to the executive responsible for making a final decision.

Phase III: Managerial Decision and Approval

The final responsibility for making the investment rests with an executive in the firm who possesses the appropriate level of authority. Typically, the larger the financial commitment an investment requires, the higher the level in the management hierarchy that is required for commitment approval. Consequently, in the final phase of investment evaluation, the recommendations of the review and evaluation team go to the firm's management team. The management team approves or rejects the proposed investment, and seeks board approval if necessary.

Phase III entails the final two steps in our eight-step investment evaluation process:

Step 7: **Make a decision.** Combining top management's sense of the firm's overall business strategy with the recommendation of the investment review committee, the executive with the appropriate level of authority makes a decision. The choices are to reject the proposal outright or to accept the proposed investment for immediate or deferred implementation.

Step 8: Seek final managerial and possibly board approval. If the decision is to undertake the investment, then the decision maker seeks final approval from the firm's management team and possibly from the board of directors.

The three-phase investment evaluation process provides a complete and integrated analysis of all facets of investment valuation, while maintaining the critical control features. However, as firms implement this process in real-world cases, a range of issues can arise to bias the results. To demonstrate the use of this evaluation process and show some of the complexities that can arise, we will conclude the chapter with a brief case study.

1.4 CASE STUDY—CP3 PHARMACEUTICALS LABORATORIES INC.

Figure 1-4 presented a three-phase, eight-step process for carrying out a disciplined approach to the investment evaluation and decision process. The need for such an approach was evident in the very large and complex Caspian Sea investment project. Firms can—and should—use the same basic approach for making smaller and more focused investments, as well as for acquiring entire enterprises.

In this section, we will use a hypothetical example to walk through a typical investment evaluation for a relatively small project. It involves the desire of CP3 Pharmaceuticals Laboratories Inc. (a fictional name for a real company) to invest $547,000 to install a new materials-handling system. The example begins with the identification of the idea and concludes with the final go–no go decision.

As you read the description of the decision-making process, keep in mind the three-phase, eight-step investment evaluation process outlined in Figure 1-4. CP3's investment decision-making process does not line up exactly with the process. Such differences are not unusual, since firms often modify their processes to fit their own particular needs. However, the process does touch on each step.

Example: Investing in a New Materials-Handling System

Business practice often deviates from theory for reasons that are understandable. As you read through the following fictional account of an investment by the CP3 Pharmaceuticals Laboratories Inc., focus on the process and not the numbers (that's the subject of much of the rest of this textbook). Note specifically how the investment is being analyzed. If you have studied finance in the past, you may even observe some instances where the theory you have been taught conflicts with practice.

Susan Chambliss is a vice president for business development at CP3 Pharmaceuticals Laboratories Inc., located in Austin, Texas. The members of CP3's business development group scout for new investment opportunities for the company on an ongoing basis. Most firms of any size have such a group. Investment opportunities for CP3 could include new products or new markets for existing products. Therefore, it is not at all unusual that someone from this group, Susan in this instance, identifies a promising investment opportunity.[10]

CP3 operates a medical-packaging operation at its Austin facility that has significant costs from product waste. Susan has identified a new materials-handling system that offers the potential for substantial cost savings through waste reduction, reduced head count in the manufacturing area, and savings through plastic recycling. Figure 1-5 provides details of the proposed project, in the format of the company's capital expenditure request form.

Before initiating a formal analysis of the proposed investment, however, Susan engages in informal discussions with senior executives on CP3's strategic planning committee. This committee reviews all major investment proposals that the firm undertakes and makes a recommendation to the firm's management as to whether a project is viable or not. The makeup of this committee at CP3 is typical of such committees at other companies: It includes the company treasurer, the chief financial officer (CFO), the chief operating officer (COO), and the chief executive officer (CEO).

Since Susan will ultimately need the approval of this committee, it makes sense that she begin by floating her idea, while still in the formative stage, by one or more of the members. Given the time and effort associated with the analysis of a new investment opportunity, she will want a preliminary indication that the project has a reasonable chance of approval before going forward. For example, it might be that company executives are considering the possible closure or sale of the medical-packaging operations. If so, then it clearly would not make sense for Susan to invest time or energy to form a working group to explore her idea further.

After several informal discussions, Susan concludes that the new materials-handling system has promise, so she initiates the study. For a project as small as this one, Susan simply assigns the project to a single financial analyst. For very large and complex projects, she might form a team consisting of several people who possess the requisite skills to understand and evaluate the investment opportunity.

Susan asks the analyst to prepare a report for formal submission of the project to the strategic planning committee. The information in Figure 1-5 is an abbreviated version of a firm's typical investment evaluation report. The report provides a thorough analysis of the project. It begins with a list of the various reasons why the group believes the project is likely to be successful. In addition, it includes summary measures of project value, reported in the measures the company uses—in this case, net present value, internal rate of return, and payback. (These are all concepts that we review in later chapters.) The financial analyst who prepared the analysis also included specific cost and cash flow projections to back up the summary analysis.

---

[10]This does not mean that all investment ideas originate out of business development. To the contrary, in a healthy firm, investment ideas come in from all over the firm. However, at some point, if the investment is significant, the business development group will get involved.

Figure 1-5 Capital Expenditure Request Form

1. Executive Summary

CP3 Pharmaceuticals Laboratories' Austin, Texas, plant is requesting $547,000 to purchase and install a new scrap materials-handling system for its medical-packaging operations. Purchasing the new system will allow the plant to meet the following objectives:

- Reduce waste in the firm's packaging operations, for savings of $300,000 per year.
- Reduce head count from the test area. Estimated savings of $35,000 per year.
- Recycle plastic materials that historically were part of waste, with disposal cost of $8,800 per year.
- Earn a 20% rate of return on invested capital.

2. Proposal and Justification

CP3's medical-packaging unit is expected to produce over 400 million vials of over-the-counter drugs this year. The packaging of these vials will generate 1.5 million pounds of scrap plastics. Of this total, one-third can be re-cycled, and the remainder becomes scrap. Under the present method the scrap is collected at the end of each of six production lines in scrap bins. The bins are then collected every 15 minutes and transferred to a grinding room where the scrap is either ground for resale or transported to trash. At present, the disposal cost for the 1 million pounds of scrap plastic is $8,800 per year.

The proposed scrap materials-handling system involves placing a small grinder at the end of each production line that can grind the plastic, then send it via vacuum tubes to a scrap collection site in another part of the plant. The ground-up scrap can then all be sold for $300,000 per year while eliminating the scrap disposal cost of $8,800 per year.

3. Financial Analysis

	2005	2006	2007	2008	2009	2010
Capital spending	(547,000)					
Impact on revenue/(expense)						
Scrap revenue		300,000	300,000	300,000	300,000	300,000
Labor savings		35,000	35,000	35,000	35,000	35,000
Reduced recycle costs		8,800	8,800	8,800	8,800	8,800
Total impact		343,800	343,800	343,800	343,800	343,800
Less: Depreciation (5 years)		(109,400)	(109,400)	(109,400)	(109,400)	(109,400)
Net operating income b/tax		234,400	234,400	234,400	234,400	234,400
Less: Taxes (40%)		(93,760)	(93,760)	(93,760)	(93,760)	(93,760)
Net operating profit after tax		140,640	140,640	140,640	140,640	140,640
Plus: Depreciation expense		109,400	109,400	109,400	109,400	109,400
Less: Capital expenditures	(547,000)	—	—	—	—	—
Project free cash flow (PFCF)	(547,000)	250,040	250,040	250,040	250,040	250,040

Net present value (NPV)	$200,773
Payback (in years)	2.19 years
Internal rate of return (IRR)	35.8%

4. Risks

The grinders and vacuum transport systems have been tested for over a month with only two minor failures. The failures relate to stoppages at the end of line 4, which carries some of the larger scrap pieces. This problem has been addressed by increasing the size of the grinder on that line and by installing sensors to provide an alert that a stoppage is about to occur so the operator can stop the process and clear the grinder and vacuum tubes.

5. Project Timeline

It will take three months to get the new system up and running since the installation must work around production shifts already in place.

These estimates span a period of five years ending in 2010. (Detailed estimates are found in Problem 2-6 at the end of Chapter 2.)

If this project were larger, the report would probably address several other important issues as well. For example, it might include any or all of the following: an estimate of the expected impact of the investment on CP3's reported earnings for several future quarters; an analysis of various scenarios involving key cost and revenue drivers, to highlight the risks inherent in the investment; and a discussion of how the firm can finance the project, as well as risk-management issues.

Once the project analysis report goes to a strategic planning committee, this group will often have another analyst prepare an independent assessment of the proposal's merits. This review checks the assumptions and methodology of the original project valuation estimate. A key concern with regard to the integrity of the investment evaluation process is that the project review and analysis group be truly independent of the analysts who prepared the initial project report and of the analysts assigned to review it by management. Furthermore, the strategic planning committee must be given the authority and funding needed to perform an independent appraisal of the project.

Addressing the Possibility of Decision Bias

Biases of various sorts can enter into the analysis of new investment proposals. Using the CP3 case as an example, Susan and members of the project analysis team may be biased if they have *incentives* to get the deal approved. Indeed, it is Susan's job to identify good opportunities for the firm, and her bonus and her ability to keep her job may depend on her ability to get her ideas approved. Bias may also enter the process simply because of *human nature:* Psychologists have found that individuals tend to be overconfident and overly optimistic about their own ideas.

The Role of the Strategic Planning Committee as the Skeptical Boss

In light of the potential for bias in favor of new investments that make their way up to the strategic planning committee for review, it becomes the task of this committee to play the role of a skeptical boss. Very simply, this committee has the task of reviewing major investment proposals and attempting to ferret out any bias in their analysis that arises out of the natural tendency for project champions to be overconfident and overly optimistic.

The members of the strategic planning committee are experienced in evaluating projects. They understand that projects are often completed at 50% over budget and are rarely completed by more than 10% under budget. They also understand that realized rates of return are almost always lower than projected rates of return. With this in mind, the strategic planning committee's role requires that they carefully work through the assumptions and the analysis and that they question everything. If the controls in the firm are functioning properly, the strategic planning committee must sign off on the analysis before it can go forward.

Although the strategic planning committee will carefully review the analysis on which the project is based, its members also may have a broader perspective. They may consider issues that go beyond the attributes of this specific project. For example, they might be considering the possibility of moving the business offshore and closing down the Austin plant, in which case the new project makes little sense.

Finally, the strategic planning committee is likely to carefully consider the firm's alternatives for financing the project. If the project can be easily funded internally, it is more likely to be approved than if it requires external funding. If the project were so big that it would require the firm to issue equity, the ultimate approval for the project may depend on whether the firm's top management believes this is a good time to issue equity—a decision that has nothing to do with the particular attributes of the project.

If the strategic planning committee approves the project, it then sends the proposal to the executive who has sign-off authority on the capital expenditure required to fund the project. In the case of the scrap materials-handling system, CP3's CEO is the decision maker. The CEO is likely to consider the same issues that the strategic planning group considered. He or she will, of course, have less time to review the specifics of the proposal than the strategic planning committee and will rely on the analysis done for that group.

If the project is so large that it requires approval by the board of directors, the CEO will then take the project to the board. Generally, if the project has the backing of the firm's executive, the board is unlikely to turn down the project, but board members may question some of the aspects of the contractual structure. For example, directors may question the compensation and governance structure of the deal. They may also question how the project is financed, particularly if the project requires an external-equity issue.

1.5 SUMMING UP AND LOOKING FORWARD

Final Comments—The Investment Decision-Making Process

Our discussion of the investment decision-making process gives rise to a number of important observations that will influence the content and structure of the rest of this book:

- *The process can be very costly.* The process of project origination, evaluation, and approval is expensive and time-consuming. Of course, skimping on the analysis of major projects can be even more expensive if it leads to project failures or missed opportunities.
- *The process can be subject to biased estimates of project value arising out of conflicts of interest and incentive problems.* Individuals within the process often have conflicting motives. For example, it is natural for members of the team that champions a proposal through the approval process to become personally

committed to the success of the project, and as a result their analyses may become biased. Furthermore, there is often a financial incentive attached to getting the project approved. For example, year-end bonuses may be tied to getting "deals done." This incentive can easily lead employees to portray a project's prospects in a more optimistic way than may be warranted. On the other hand, the members of the various units within the firm who must analyze and "sign off" on the project are often skeptics. They typically are staff personnel whose role is to ferret out bias in the investment analysis and provide a control over overzealous project champions. Members of the internal control group are not rewarded for deal completion but may suffer consequences when they sign off on a project that fails.

■ *The process is affected by problems arising out of differences in the information available to project champions and the internal review or control group (the strategic planning committee in our earlier example).* Specifically, the control group in Phase II of the process is generally less well informed about the project's inner workings than the project proponents from Phase I. In the interest of efficiency, this situation would ordinarily support delegation of decision-making authority to the managers and project champions who know the most about the project. However, in reality, incentive issues and the natural bias that project champions often exhibit require that some type of control system (such as the strategic planning and review committee) be put in place, and this is exactly what we see in business practice.

An unbalanced emphasis on any one of the three phases of project evaluation shown in Figure 1-4 can have disastrous effects on the firm. For example, too much emphasis on the investment origination (idea) phase, to the detriment of managerial review, can lead to the firm adopting questionable project investments that have a low probability of success. Equally dangerous is overemphasis on the managerial review (Phase II) relative to the investment origination phase. In this instance, excessive caution keeps the firm from undertaking promising new investments. Finally, overemphasis on the final phase of the analysis can result if executives try to micromanage the firm. This can stifle the initiative of employees working in the origination and review phases. In an extreme case, the origination and review phases become nothing more than attempts to "second-guess" the preferences of the firm's top manager(s).

Looking Forward—The Structure of the Rest of the Book

Academics who study finance sometimes strip away some of the complexities of corporate investment decisions in an effort to focus on the heart of what determines value. However, by doing this, we can create a disconnect between what *should* be done in theory, and what *is* in fact done in practice. For example, academics have very well-developed theories that describe how firms should determine the **discount rates** that they use to evaluate investment projects. To a large extent corporate executives are aware of these theories, but have corporate **hurdle rates** (i.e., the minimum rate of return on acceptable projects) that often greatly exceed the discount rates suggested by academic theories. These high hurdle rates may be used to counteract the overoptimism of the managers or they may provide ambitious targets that serve to motivate the managers. Throughout this book, we will emphasize *both* the fundamentals of valuation, as described by academic theories, and the real-world complexities that make their actual implementation somewhat different.

Our approach to the study of valuation integrates the analysis of individual projects and entire enterprises along two dimensions. As demonstrated in the discussions of the investment evaluation process in this chapter, we recognize that project and enterprise valuation both build upon the same theoretical base. In Chapters 2 and 3, we introduce valuation concepts within the context of the simpler of the two applications, *project valuation.* Essentially, project valuation arises out of a firm's decision to grow internally. We then move on to an analysis of *external growth,* or the acquisition of entire businesses, first in the analysis of the cost of capital in Chapters 4 and 5, and then in the valuation of the business enterprise in Chapters 6 through 9.

The last three decades have provided a number of advances in the understanding of the economic forces that drive investment valuation. While we will be providing recent advances in a variety of aspects of investment valuation we will pay particular attention to how recent innovations in the valuation of derivative securities, like options, are used to value real investment projects and investment strategies. We discuss these recent developments in Chapters 10 through 12.

1.6 SUMMARY

Valuation is more than discounting cash flows. The evaluation of new investment opportunities, ranging from the smallest capital budgeting exercise up to the acquisition of an entire firm, has come a long way since the early days in which the focus was solely on the present value of estimated future cash flows. Although the importance of net present value (NPV) has not changed, analysts now consider a broad set of factors. For example, when a firm analyzes whether to make a significant new investment it will generally consider the following issues:

- *Cash flow estimation.* The first step in valuing an investment is to estimate future cash flows. One must ask how certain these cash flow estimates are as well as how sensitive the estimates are to the unexpected changes in the economic environment.
- *Risk assessment.* Major new investments by multinational firms often involve committing funds to underdeveloped regions of the world. Such investments typically come with significant additional risks—political risk, commodity price risk, interest rate risk, and exchange rate risk. Risk must be assessed as well as managed, and

plays an important role in determining the rate at which cash flows are discounted as well as the financing of the investment project.

■ *Financing opportunities.* Financing can offer an important source of value for an investment project and can be a key determinant of the investment's cost of capital.

■ *The effects on the firm's near-term earnings.* Although the value of an investment is created by the cash flows generated by the investment, managers are keenly aware of how a project affects earnings. In practice, an investment's effect on the earnings of a firm will have a large influence on whether the investment is ultimately taken.

■ *Staged investments.* The decision to initiate an investment essentially involves acquiring the "option" to invest in later stages of the project (assuming the intermediate stages prove fruitful). Thus, analysts can use option valuation techniques to evaluate whether to postpone, speed up, or cancel future investments.

■ *"Follow-on" investment opportunities.* Previous investments are a primary source of new investment opportunities. Thus, it is important that we consider the impact of major investment projects on future opportunities.

We recognize at the outset that the analysis of investments is difficult to get right. Even well-intentioned managers can make mistakes, either because of psychological biases that tend to make them overly optimistic, or because project valuations pose difficult problems that are not always well understood. Consequently, it is essential that the firm have in place a well-designed process that incorporates appropriate decision-making checks and balances. Moreover, we emphasize the need to continually push for quantification, even in the face of difficult issues that make measurement difficult.

PART I

Project Analysis Using Discounted Cash Flow (DCF)

The critical insight that underlies the application of discounted cash flow (DCF) analysis to project and firm valuation is that cash flows received at different times have different values, and they can only be aggregated after properly adjusting for the time value of money. This core concept in the theory and practice of valuation must be mastered before we can proceed with more sophisticated valuation concepts. The roots of DCF analysis extend back into antiquity at least until the time of the ancient Greeks, who calculated and used the concepts of simple and compound interest. The modern-day application of DCF can be traced to the seminal work of Irving Fisher[1] and Joel Dean, who popularized the application of discounted cash flow analysis in capital budgeting.[2]

In this section (Chapters 2 and 3) we discuss the fundamentals of DCF analysis, which has been the mainstay of financial analysts

---

[1]Irving Fisher, *The Nature of Income and Capital* (New York: Macmillan, 1906), *The Rate of Interest: Its Nature, Determination and Relation to Economic Phenomena* (New York: Macmillan, 1907), and *The Theory of Interest: As Determined by Impatience to Spend Income and Opportunity to Invest it* (New York: Macmillan, 1930).

[2]Joel Dean, *Capital Budgeting* (New York: Columbia University Press, 1951).

since the 1950s and continues to be what most practitioners think about when they think of project and enterprise valuation. Although DCF analysis is often oversimplified in classroom presentations, in practice the proper application of DCF can get confusing because of complexities that arise in calculating cash flows. Chapter 2 discusses the problems encountered in defining and estimating cash flows and reviews the standard "textbook" approach to DCF. Chapter 3 provides a detailed analysis of the estimation of future cash flows. We utilize two basic approaches that can be used to evaluate the uncertainty in future cash flows. These include breakeven sensitivity analysis and Monte Carlo simulation.

Forecasting and Valuing Cash Flows

Chapter Overview

Discounted cash flow (DCF) analysis is a key building block for a valuation course. This chapter, which introduces the process for applying DCF analysis, describes the relation between cash flows and numbers from the firm's financial statements. We first define cash flow to the equity holders and then cash flow available for distribution to both creditors and owners. After defining cash flows, we present a comprehensive cash flow forecasting example that focuses on the process that one goes through to link units sold, unit costs, and unit revenues to investment cash flows. Finally, the chapter introduces the mechanics of discounting investment cash flows to estimate project value.

2.1 DISCOUNTED CASH FLOWS AND VALUATION

The idea behind **discounted cash flow (DCF) valuation analysis** is simple: The value of an investment is determined by the magnitude and the timing of the cash flows it is expected to generate. The DCF valuation approach provides a basis for assessing the value of these cash flows, and consequently is a cornerstone of financial analysis.

How does DCF analysis fit into the overall investment evaluation process laid out in the previous chapter? You may recall that we discussed the investment valuation process in terms of three phases of analysis that can be broken down into eight key steps (summarized in Figure 1-4). The focus of this and the next chapter is on Step 2 of the first phase—estimating the investment's value, or "crunching the numbers."

The popularization of DCF for project analysis is generally attributed to Joel Dean (1951). However, the roots of DCF analysis go back much further. For example, financial mathematics can be traced back to the early writing of Leonardo of Piza (also known as Fibonacci) in 1202. Generations of business school graduates have made DCF one of the most widely used tools in the arsenal of today's finance professional.

Example—Car Wash

To illustrate the role of DCF valuations in analyzing an investment opportunity, let's assume that you invest in a car wash. The car wash generates *cash inflows* each time a customer purchases a wash and *cash outflows* when the business purchases supplies, pays taxes and wages, and so forth. In addition, there will be times when you have to make repairs to the equipment, resulting in nonroutine cash outflows.

Let's now assume that you open a bank account for the business, and the cash receipts flow into the account and cash disbursements come out of it. After a year of operations you have built up a cash balance of, say, $10,000 after paying all your bills (including any repairs to your equipment). If we assume for the moment that you have not borrowed any of the money used to invest in the car wash, then you have $10,000 that you can distribute to yourself as sole owner of the car wash. This is money you can spend right now, at the end of the first year of operations. Looking forward to years two, three, and so forth and performing a similar computation, we can determine future cash flows—calculated after paying all the firm's operating expenses and making any added capital expenditures. These cash flows are the key element that determines the value of the business.

The Three-Step DCF Process

From this simple example of the car wash, we can develop a DCF process that takes into account the timing of cash flows. Specifically, the use of DCF valuation entails a three-step process as depicted in Figure 2-1: The first step involves forecasting the amount and timing of the anticipated receipt (or payment) of future cash flows. Here the basic issue is, "*How much* cash is the project *expected* to generate and *when?*" This step is the primary focus of this chapter and Chapter 3. The real "heavy lifting" in project evaluation occurs here, for the future can never be known with certainty and forecasts must often be made with little or no historical data to guide the analysis.

Second, the analyst must determine the appropriate discount rate for use in discounting future cash flows back to the present. The fundamental issue here is, "*How risky are the future cash flows?*" This topic is a central focus of finance, and we address it in Chapters 4 and 5. We capture the idea of risk in the discount rate—the rate used to calculate the present value of future cash flows—but for now, we will simply assume that discount rates are known.

Figure 2-1	Steps in Performing a Discounted Cash Flow Analysis
STEPS	**INVESTMENT VALUATION**
Step 1: Forecast the amount and timing of future cash flows. *"How much cash is the project expected to generate and when?"*	Forecast project free cash flow (PFCF).
Step 2: Estimate a risk-appropriate discount rate (covered in Chapters 4 and 5). *"How risky are the future cash flows, and what do investors currently expect to receive for investments of similar risk?"*	Combine the debt and equity discount rate (weighted average cost of capital, WACC).
Step 3: Discount the cash flows. *"What is the present value 'equivalent' of the investment's expected future cash flows?"*	Discount PFCF using WACC to estimate the value of the project as a whole.

Finally, Step 3 involves the mechanical process of discounting future cash flows back to the present. Although we leave the rudiments of this analysis to more introductory finance textbooks,[1] we do offer a brief review in Section 2.4.

2.2 DEFINING INVESTMENT CASH FLOWS

Arriving at an estimate of the value of an investment using DCF analysis requires that the analyst have a good understanding of the investment's cash flows. In this section we discuss three key issues related to the proper definition of investment cash flows:

1. What cash flows are relevant to the valuation of a project or investment?
2. Are the cash flow forecasts either conservative or optimistic?
3. What is the difference between equity and project cash flows?

---

[1]For example, Arthur J. Keown, John D. Martin, J. William Petty, and David F. Scott, Jr., *Financial Management: Principles and Practices*, 10th ed. (Upper Saddle River, NJ: Pearson Prentice Hall, 2005), Chapter 5.

Failure to address each of these issues has led to a great deal of confusion in the application of DCF analysis.

Relevant Cash Flows

As the first step in determining an investment's value we must determine the relevant cash flows. These are often referred to as incremental cash flows, since they are the additional cash flows to the firm that are generated by the investment. These include the cash flows directly generated by the investment as well as the indirect effects that the investment may have on a firm's other lines of business. For example, when Frito-Lay evaluates the introduction of a new flavor of Doritos® brand Tortilla Chips (e.g., lime flavored), the projected revenues and costs of the new product are critical to the analysis. However, the extent to which the new product's sales may cannibalize, or source sales from, other existing products (such as DORITOS NACHO CHEESE® Flavored Tortilla Chips or DORITOS COOL RANCH® Flavored Tortilla Chips) is equally critical, since the true net or incremental cash flows are the new product cash flows net of cannibalization. See the Practitioner Insight box for a look at Frito-Lay's three-step incremental cash flow analysis.

A common mistake in the calculation of incremental cash flows has to do with what are known as *sunk costs*. Sunk costs are expenditures that either have already been made or must be made regardless of whether the firm proceeds with the investment. As a result, sunk costs are not incremental costs and should thus be ignored in the investment analysis.

For example, suppose that Merck previously invested $10 million in the research and development of a new methodology for extracting stem cells from adult donor cells that does not require the use of embryos. The procedure looked very promising for the development of cancer treatments; however, it failed to deliver any significant improvements over less expensive and more conventional treatments during clinical trials. Suppose that subsequent Merck researchers develop a way to apply the new procedure to more efficiently carry out embryo transplants in beef and dairy cattle. In calculating the value of an investment associated with commercializing this procedure, how should Merck treat the original $10 million R&D expenditure?

In general, the research and development costs (incurred in the past) should be viewed as sunk costs and should not be relevant to the analysis of the value of marketing the process to the cattle embryo transplant project. However, the past research would become relevant if Merck receives an offer from Pfizer to acquire the technology for $8 million under the proviso that Merck gives up all rights to the further development and applications of the technology. In this instance, the relevant cost to Merck of using the technology to develop its application to the cattle embryo transplant market is now equal to the $8 million offer from Pfizer (assuming this is the highest bid received), but not the $10 million Merck invested in R&D to develop the methodology. The reason for this is that the original $10 million has been spent and cannot be recovered.

PRACTITIONER

INSIGHT

**Relevant Cash Flows and
Revenue Cannibalization**

Frito-Lay, one of four divisions of PepsiCo, Inc., is currently the market leader for potato chips and other salty snack products. Consequently, when Frito-Lay evaluates a new salty snack product, they realize that a portion of the new product sales will come from the lost sales from existing products (i.e., revenue cannibalization). Such as challenge is common in mature firms with large market share. The evaluation of incremental cash flows is thus an extremely important issue for Frito-Lay and has led the company to develop a formal approach to the incremental effects of new product offerings on the firm's cash flows.

At Frito-Lay they use the following three-step approach when estimating incremental cash flows:

Step 1: Estimate the total revenue that will be generated by the product.
Step 2: Estimate what percent of the revenue is true incremental revenue.
Step 3: Estimate the incremental cash flow.

To estimate the percent of the revenue that is incremental, we classify new product offerings into one of three types. The first type contains projects that have a high likelihood of cannibalizing existing product sales. Examples of this would include products such as a new flavor of Doritos® brand Tortilla Chips. The expectation here is that a low percentage of the sales of this type of product can be viewed as incremental sales from the product, with the remainder coming from reductions in existing product sales. The second type of products provides the potential for additional store shelf space because they provide some new benefit (e.g., baked chips). For this type of product, Frito-Lay assigns a higher percentage of the revenue as true incremental sales. Finally, the third type of product, such as Frito-Lay's natural line, provides the opportunity to enter new channels and/or develop new shelf space in a different part of the store. These products carry the lowest risk of cannibalization and are therefore assigned the highest percentage of incremental sales.

*Based on interview with Keith Crider, New Product Finance Manager, Frito-Lay, Dallas, TX.

However, if Merck proceeds with plans to apply the technology to the embryo transplant market, it must forgo the opportunity to sell the technology to Pfizer for $8 million. Clearly, the $8 million represents an opportunity cost to Merck.[2]

---

[2] One easy way to trap incremental costs is to take the difference between cash flows that would arise if the project is taken up and the free cash flows that would arise if the project is rejected. For instance, the $10 million R&D expense would occur in either case (project take up or rejected), whereas the $8 million opportunity loss (cost) would arise only if the project is rejected (and the technology is sold to Pfizer).

Did you know?

Men tend to be more overconfident than women.

Psychologists have shown that men tend to be more confident than women in a number of settings, including those involving financial forecasts. A study by Barber and Odean* shows that among individual investors, men tend to trade more than women (showing more confidence) but perform worse!

*Brad M. Barber and Terrance Odean, "Boys Will Be Boys: Gender Overconfidence and Common Stock Investment," *The Quarterly Journal of Economics,* February 2001.

The determination of relevant cash flows can sometimes be very difficult, as we have just illustrated. However, it is critical that only the incremental revenues and incremental costs that are a direct result of the firm's decision to undertake the investment be considered in performing the valuation of the project.

Conservative and Optimistic Cash Flows

When academics talk about valuing an investment by discounting cash flows, they generally assume that the cash flows represent "expected cash flows." In the statistical sense they assume that managers estimate the cash flows that the firm *expects* to realize in various scenarios, and sum these cash flows after weighting them by their probabilities of occurrence. For example, if a firm's manager expects to generate a cash flow of either $50,000 or $100,000, each with a 50% probability, the expected cash flow is $75,000. In theory, the firm should discount these expected cash flows, as we noted in Figure 2-1, using a risk-adjusted rate of interest that reflects the risk of the cash flows. (We will have more to say about how these rates are estimated in Chapters 4 and 5.) In practice, however, the cash flow forecasts that managers use are frequently not the same as the expected cash flows that the academics describe in their theories. Depending on the situation, the cash flow forecasts of managers may be either too conservative or too aggressive. Sometimes these biases exist because of managerial incentives and at other times an optimistic bias arises because of managerial overconfidence. (See the Behavioral Insight entitled "Overconfidence").

In order to understand how managers make cash flow forecasts in practice, it is useful to reconsider the investment process described in Chapter 1 and to consider the incentives of the various players that are involved in making the forecasts. Suppose, for example, that you are proposing an investment that you will be managing, and that your cash flow forecasts will serve as future targets that will influence your future bonuses. If this is the case, then you might choose relatively conservative forecasts. Now consider a situation where you get a bonus for identifying a promising investment opportunity that the firm initiates. When this is the case, you might choose relatively optimistic forecasts.

We believe that top executives may encourage their managers to develop forecasts that represent *hoped-for* rather than expected cash flows, because they provide future targets that may serve as motivation when the project is implemented. We also observe management cash flow forecasts that are based on the reasoning: "If all goes as planned, these are the cash flows that we expect to achieve." These optimistic cash flows ignore various unanticipated glitches that may arise when the project

B E H A V I O R A L   I N S I G H T

Overconfidence

Psychological studies show that most people are overconfident about their abilities, and tend to be optimistic about the future. For example, one study found that most people claim to be better-than-average drivers, yet we know that by definition half are above average and half are below average.* Are corporate executives likely to be more or less optimistic and overconfident than the average individual? We would argue that they are likely to be more optimistic and overconfident. Psychologists claim that individuals tend to be subject to what they call self-attribution bias, which means that they want to attribute good things that happen to them to their own efforts and ability. This suggests that top executives are likely to attribute their success to their own abilities, rather than being in the right place at the right time, and may thus be overconfident about their success going forward. It's also likely to be the case that the most optimistic managers work the hardest (because they place a high value on being promoted), which suggests that optimistic people are more likely to be promoted. What this means is that even well-intentioned executives who set out to estimate true expected cash flows may end up with cash flow forecasts that are overly optimistic.

*Ola Svensson, "Are we all less risky and more skillful than our fellow drivers?" *Acta Psychologia* 47 (1981), 143–148.

is implemented. When evaluating hoped-for cash flows, firms should use very high discount rates to adjust for the difference between dreams and reality.

Two examples where we tend to observe what are clearly hoped-for rather than expected cash flows are in emerging markets and venture capital investments. In both cases the firm may have a strategic partner, i.e., the government of a developing country in one case and an entrepreneur in the other case, who may prefer a business plan that is not so specific about possible negative events that may occur. For example, in a proposed joint venture with the government of Venezuela, you might not want to explicitly account for the possibility of a collapse in the current regime. You may prefer to calculate hoped-for cash flows and account for the risk of collapse with an adjustment in the required discount rate. Similarly, as a venture capitalist you may not want to explicitly express a lack of confidence in the viability of the entrepreneur's new product, but may again adjust for the optimistic hoped-for cash flows by requiring a very high discount rate to adjust for the difference between dreams and reality. We return to our discussion of hoped-for cash flows in Chapter 8; for the balance of this chapter, we will assume that all cash flow estimates represent *expected* cash flows.

Equity versus Project Free Cash Flow

Keep in mind that an investment project's cash flow is simply the sum of the cash inflows and outflows from the project. However, as we have already noted, analysts typically structure their analysis of investment cash flows using projected financial statements, commonly referred to as pro forma statements, for the project or firm being valued. That is, they develop their cash flow analysis by first projecting the income or earnings consequences of the project (following accrual accounting—see the Technical Insight box), and then use this information to calculate the project's cash flows.

Two fundamental definitions of cash flow are used in project valuation, and we consider both in the pages that follow. The first, **equity free cash flow (EFCF),** focuses on the cash flow that is available for distribution to the firm's common shareholders. Consequently, EFCF is used to value the equity claim in the project. The second cash flow definition is **project free cash flow (PFCF).** This definition combines the cash flows available for distribution to both the firm's creditors and equity holders. PFCF becomes the basis for estimating the value of the project as a whole (both equity and debt claims combined). The distinction between estimating EFCF and PFCF is crucial, and analysts frequently use the wrong cash flow definition. We will return to this distinction time and again throughout the book.

T E C H N I C A L	
I N S I G H T	**Accrual and Cash-Basis Accounting**

Accounting *income* is not the same as cash flow since it is calculated using the accrual basis of accounting. Unlike cash accounting, **accrual accounting** distinguishes between the recording of costs and benefits associated with economic activities and the actual payment and receipt of cash. For example, under accrual accounting, revenues are recognized (recorded) *when earned*, not when cash actually changes hands. Likewise, under accrual accounting, expenses are matched to the revenues they helped generate, rather than being recorded when cash is actually paid.

Why accrual rather than cash accounting? Investors' demands for *periodic financial reports* that can be used to assess performance during the period (e.g., quarter or year) gave rise to the need for the accrual system. The problem with cash-basis accounting is that cash expenditures made in one period may have an impact on revenues and profits over multiple future periods. Accrual accounting is designed to match expenses with revenues. For example, the cost of a piece of capital equipment that will be productive over many years is spread over multiple years, rather than being expensed entirely in the period of the purchase. Cash-basis accounting would expense the equipment cost, which would distort the performance of the firm's operations during the period.

Equity Free Cash Flow (EFCF) for an All-Equity-Financed Project

To simplify our discussion, we begin by evaluating the cash flow generated by a project that is wholly financed by the owner—that is, a project that is all-equity-financed, or unlevered.[3] The project will not incur any cash inflows from the proceeds of debt offerings, nor will it be required to make principal and interest payments in the future.

From this point forward, we attach the modifier *free* in front of our cash flow definitions. The idea is *not* that the cash flow is in any sense free of cost. Instead, *free* refers to the fact that the cash flow under discussion is available—not needed for any particular purpose. The cash flow equals the amount of cash left over after paying all expenses, including any additional investments in the project. The firm, then, can distribute the remaining cash since it does not, by definition, need it. Consequently, our cash flow calculations result in a cash flow figure that is *free* of any encumbrances or commitments and can therefore be distributed to the sources of capital used to finance the investment. **Equity free cash flow (EFCF)** therefore represents the cash produced by the project that can be distributed to the firm's equity holders or owners. These distributions can take the form of cash dividends or share repurchases.

Using the accounting income statement, we can calculate EFCF for an all-equity-financed project, as shown in Figure 2-2. The resulting EFCF for the unlevered firm represents the residual cash flow after paying the firm's operating expenses and taxes, as well as any new investments in plant and equipment (CAPEX) and changes in net working capital (WC). Note that, since the firm is unlevered, interest expense as well as principal payments and the proceeds from debt issues are all equal to zero.

Alternatively, we can write an equation to calculate EFCF *for the unlevered firm* as follows:

$$EFCF_{\text{Unlevered Firm}} = EBIT(1 - T) + DA - WC - CAPEX \qquad (2.1)$$

Acronym	Definition
EBIT	Earnings before interest and taxes
EBIT(1 − T)	After-tax operating income or net operating profit after tax (NOPAT)
T	Tax rate
DA	Depreciation and amortization expense
WC	Change in net working capital
CAPEX	Capital expenditures for property, plant, and equipment

---

[3]The use of debt financing is commonly referred to as *financial leverage* in the United States and as *gearing* in Great Britain. The idea behind the use of these terms comes from the fact that debt financing magnifies the return earned on the equity investment, increasing the equity return when the project does well and decreasing it when the project does poorly. We illustrate this in the Technical Insight box on page 43.

Figure 2-2	Calculation of Equity Free Cash Flow (EFCF) for an All-Equity-Financed Project, Using the Income Statement
	Revenues
Less:	Cost of goods sold
Equals:	*Gross profit*
Less:	Operating expenses (excluding depreciation and amortization expense)
Equals:	*Earnings before interest, taxes, depreciation, and amortization (EBITDA)*
Less:	Depreciation and amortization (DA)
Equals:	*Earnings before interest and taxes (EBIT)*
Less:	Interest expense **(equal to zero for an unlevered project)**
Equals:	*Earnings before taxes (EBT)*
Less:	Taxes
Equals:	*Net income (NI)*
Plus:	Depreciation and amortization (DA)
Less:	Capital expenditures (CAPEX)
Less:	Increases in net working capital (WC)
Less:	Principal payments on debt **(equal to zero for an unlevered project)**
Plus:	Proceeds from new debt issues **(equal to zero for an unlevered project)**
Equals:	*Equity free cash flow (EFCF)*

You will recall many of the inputs to Equation 2.1 based on your understanding of a firm's income statement. However, some entries deserve further explanation. We explain these inputs to the EFCF definition in the sections that follow.

Depreciation and amortization expense (DA)   As you know from your accounting courses, depreciation and amortization expenses do not represent out-of-pocket cash payments. Rather, they arise out of the matching principle of accounting, which dictates that expenses be matched with revenues whenever it is reasonable and practicable to do so. Therefore, firms use *depreciation expense* to match expenditures made for long-lived assets (such as plant, machinery, and equipment) against the revenues they help generate. However, the actual expenditure of cash may have taken place many years earlier when the assets were acquired. Thus, *the allocation of the original cost against revenues in the form of depreciation or amortization expenses does not represent an actual cash payment.*

Since the Internal Revenue Service requires that expenditures for long-lived assets be offset (i.e., depreciated or amortized, depending on the type of asset) against revenues throughout their useful life and since these expenses are tax deductible, we include them in our calculation of free cash flow. First we subtract them in calculating taxable income, and then we add them back to after-tax income to calculate cash flow. The net result is that we add an amount back to the EFCF equal to the tax savings on the depreciation expense.[4]

Capital expenditures (CAPEX)   To sustain a firm's productive capacity and provide for growth in future cash flows, the firm must periodically make investments in new long-lived assets that are typically referred to as property, plant, and equipment. This includes such things as expanding plant capacity and replacing old equipment. These expenditures are referred to as *capital expenditures* with the acronym *CAPEX*.

CAPEX can be calculated by analyzing how net property, plant, and equipment (net PPE) on the balance sheet changes over time; e.g., consider the change in net PPE from 2006 to 2007:[5]

Net PPE (2006)

Less: Depreciation expense for 2007

Plus: CAPEX for 2007

Equals: Net PPE (2007)

Therefore, CAPEX for 2007 can be calculated as follows:[6]

$$\text{CAPEX for 2007} = \text{Net PPE (2007)} - \text{Net PPE (2006)} \\ + \text{Depreciation Expense for 2007}$$

Based on the above relationship, it is obvious that the capital expenditure for a particular year is related to the firm's depreciation expense for the year, but the amounts will not generally be the same. Why are they different? Depreciation expense is determined by a firm's prior expenditures on plant and equipment, which are amortized or expensed against firm revenues over the life of the plant and equipment. The amount of the depreciation expense is determined both by the amount the firm has spent in the past and by accounting (and tax) rules. Capital expenditures, on the other hand,

---

[4]Defining EBITDA as earnings before interest, taxes, and depreciation or EBIT + DA, we can restate the EFCF formula from Equation 2.1 as follows:

$$\text{EFCF}_{\text{Unlevered Firm}} = (\text{EBITDA} - \text{DA})(1 - T) + \text{DA} - \text{WC} - \text{CAPEX}$$

or, rearranging terms,

$$\text{EFCF}_{\text{Unlevered Firm}} = (\text{EBITDA})(1 - T) + T \times \text{DA} - \text{WC} - \text{CAPEX}$$

where $T \times \text{DA}$ represents the tax savings that accrue to the firm from depreciation and amortization expense.

[5]Net property, plant, and equipment is equal to the difference in the accumulated cost of all property, plant, and equipment (gross PPE) less the accumulated depreciation for those assets.

[6]To predict CAPEX using this relationship requires that we estimate the change in net PPE for 2007 and depreciation expense. Typically the former involves relating changes in net PPE and predicted changes in project revenues.

reflect current period expenditures for new property, plant, and equipment.[7] The amount of CAPEX in any given period reflects the amount of plant and equipment that physically wears out and needs replacement in combination with the demands of growing revenues, which require added plant and equipment capacity. For example, when a firm anticipates growth opportunities, it spends more on long-lived assets than the amount it depreciates on older assets. The amount of CAPEX also may exceed depreciation expense if the cost of new assets is rising or if existing assets are depreciated at a rate that is slower than the actual rate at which the assets physically deteriorate. Similarly, there are situations in which CAPEX may be less than depreciation expense. Thus, in general, we should not expect CAPEX to equal the firm's depreciation expense.

Changes in net working capital (WC)   Just as the firm must invest in property, plant, and equipment as it grows, it must also invest in current assets such as inventories and accounts receivable.[8] However, the additional investment in inventories and receivables is partially financed by increases in the firm's trade credit that arise naturally in the course of the firm's purchases from its suppliers. The end result is that the firm incurs an outlay for working capital equal to what we will refer to as the change in **operating net working capital.** We define operating net working capital as follows:

$$
\begin{aligned}
\text{Operating Net Working Capital} = & \left[\left(\begin{array}{c} \text{Current} \\ \text{Assets} \end{array} \right) - \left(\begin{array}{c} \text{Cash and} \\ \text{Marketable Securities} \end{array} \right) \right] \\
& - \left[\left(\begin{array}{c} \text{Current} \\ \text{Liabilities} \end{array} \right) - \left(\begin{array}{c} \text{Current Portion of} \\ \text{Interest-Bearing} \\ \text{Debt/Notes} \end{array} \right) \right]
\end{aligned}
$$

The cash flow impact of any additional investment the firm must make in working capital then is measured by the *change* in operating net working capital. For any arbitrary year t, the change in operating net working capital is calculated as follows:

$$
\begin{array}{c} \text{Change in} \\ \text{Operating Net} \\ \text{Working Capital}_t \end{array} = \left(\begin{array}{c} \text{Operating} \\ \text{Net Working} \\ \text{Capital} \end{array} \right)_t - \left(\begin{array}{c} \text{Operating} \\ \text{Net Working} \\ \text{Capital} \end{array} \right)_{t-1} \qquad (2.2)
$$

---

[7]A distinction is sometimes made between depreciation as the cost of maintenance of existing assets, whereas CAPEX represents expenditures on capital and equipment required to support anticipated growth.

[8]This can also include cash and marketable securities where the growth requires that the firm hold more liquidity. However, this is typically not as important as inventories required to support additional sales revenues and the accounts receivable that arise naturally out of credit sales.

We used *change* in operating net working capital rather than *increase* since the change can be both positive and negative. For example, as a firm's or project's revenues grow, it usually will have to invest more in working capital such that the change will be positive (representing a cash outflow). However, as a project winds down and revenues stabilize and then decline, the firm's need for working capital will decrease, which means that the change in operating net working capital becomes negative. When this happens, the change actually results in a net inflow of cash.

Note that failure to consider the firm's needs for additional working capital and the funds required to finance those needs will result in an overestimate of the value of the firm. This is especially true for high-growth projects that require frequent infusions of added capital to finance the growing need for inventories and accounts receivable.

Example—equity free cash flow (EFCF) for an all-equity-financed project   To illustrate the calculation of EFCF, we will look at the investment being considered by JC Crawford Enterprises, a privately held firm located in the suburbs of St. Louis, Missouri. The firm is a holding company for six franchise businesses, each selling and supporting a different franchise. JC Crawford has grown rapidly from revenues of $16.5 million and 101 employees in 1999 to more than $150 million and 500 employees today.

In the fall of 2006, JC Crawford's management was considering the construction of a regional distribution center for its franchise business devoted to appliance repairs, Mr. Fix–it–up. There are 50 Mr. Fix–it–up franchisees located in and around Miami, Florida, and the regional distribution center is needed to reduce the time and cost of supplying the franchisees throughout southern Florida.

Panel a of Table 2-1 lists a total of 14 assumptions and predictions that underlie JC Crawford's cash flow calculations for the regional distribution center. We have simplified the analysis by aggregating various items in the income statement and balance sheet into a single line item (e.g., total operating expenses are combined into a single ratio of operating expenses—net of depreciation—to sales). In practice, analysts often include much more detail (i.e., more line items in the financial statements) than we have done in Table 2-1.

The proposed investment requires an initial investment of $550,000, comprised of $400,000 in plant and equipment (line 10) and an additional $150,000 in working capital (line 11).[9] JC Crawford expects the project to generate $1 million in revenues during the first year of its operation (line 7). This figure is expected to grow at a rate of 10% per year over the five-year life of the investment (line 1). As project sales grow, the firm's needs for both capital assets (plant and equipment) and working capital will grow by an amount equal to 40% and 15% of the growth in sales, respectively (lines 5 and 6). JC Crawford Enterprises pays taxes at a rate of 30% (line 4), depreciates

---

[9]The working capital is actually "operating net working capital," as defined earlier.

Table 2-1 **Estimating Equity Free Cash Flows (EFCFs)
for an All-Equity-Financed Project**

Panel a. Assumptions and predictions

1. Sales growth rate	10%
2. Gross profit margin = Gross profit/Sales)	30%
3. Operating expenses (before depreciation)/Sales	20%
4. Tax rate	30%
5. Capital expenditures/Sales	40% (of predicted change in sales)
6. Net working capital/Sales	15% (of predicted change in sales)
7. Base-year sales for 2007	$1,000,000
8. Depreciable life of plant and equipment (CAPEX)	10 years
9. Depreciation method	Straight line
10. Initial investment in plant and equipment	$400,000
11. Initial new working capital requirements	$150,000
12. Target debt/assets ratio	0.0%
13. Interest (borrowing) rate	10%
14. Residual values (working capital and plant and equipment)	Book value in year 2011

Panel b. Pro Forma Income Statements

Income Statement ($000)	2007	2008	2009	2010	2011
Sales	$1,000.00	$1,100.00	$1,210.00	$1,331.00	$1,464.10
Cost of goods sold	(700.00)	(770.00)	(847.00)	(931.70)	(1,024.87)
Gross profit	300.00	330.00	363.00	399.30	439.23
Operating expenses before depreciation	(200.00)	(220.00)	(242.00)	(266.20)	(292.82)
Depreciation expense	(40.00)	(44.00)	(48.40)	(53.24)	(58.56)
EBIT	60.00	66.00	72.60	79.86	87.85
Interest expense	—	—	—	—	—
Earnings before taxes	60.00	66.00	72.60	79.86	87.85
Taxes	(18.00)	(19.80)	(21.78)	(23.96)	(26.35)
Net income	$ 42.00	$ 46.20	$ 50.82	$ 55.90	$ 61.49

Table 2-1 *continued*

Panel c. Pro Forma Balance Sheets

Balance Sheet ($000)	2006	2007	2008	2009	2010	2011*
Net working capital	$150.00	$165.00	$181.50	$199.65	$219.62	$219.62
Gross plant and equipment	400.00	440.00	484.00	532.40	585.64	585.64
Less: Accumulated depreciation	—	(40.00)	(84.00)	(132.40)	(185.64)	(244.20)
Net plant and equipment	400.00	400.00	400.00	400.00	400.00	341.44
Total assets	$550.00	$565.00	$581.50	$599.65	$619.62	$561.05
Interest-bearing debt	$ —	$ —	$ —	$ —	$ —	$ —
Equity	550.00	565.00	581.50	599.65	619.62	561.05
Total liabilities and equity	$550.00	$565.00	$581.50	$599.65	$619.62	$561.05

Panel d. Equity Free Cash Flows (EFCFs)—All-Equity-Financed Project

EFCF ($000)	2006	2007	2008	2009	2010	2011
Net income	$ —	$42.00	$46.20	$50.82	$55.90	$ 61.49
Plus: Depreciation and amortization	—	40.00	44.00	48.40	53.24	58.56
Less: Capital expenditures**	(400.00)	(40.00)	(44.00)	(48.40)	(53.24)	341.44
Less: Changes in net working capital**	(150.00)	(15.00)	(16.50)	(18.15)	(19.97)	219.62
Less: Principal payments	—	—	—	—	—	—
Plus: Proceeds from new debt issues	—	—	—	—	—	—
Equals: Equity free cash flow	$(550.00)	$27.00	$29.70	$32.67	$35.94	$681.11

*At the end of 2011 we assume that the project life is over and the company will liquidate the assets (net working capital and net plant and equipment). As a result, the balance sheet shown here for 2011 is pre-liquidation. Since there is no gain on the sale of assets in 2011, there are no taxes owed.

**The EFCF for 2011 incorporates the balance sheet book values of both net working capital and net plant and equipment as cash inflows. This reflects the "release" of cash corresponding to the termination of the investment in 2011.

its investments using straight-line depreciation over a 10-year life (lines 8 and 9), and does not plan to borrow money to finance the investment (line 12).[10]

---

[10]Straight-line depreciation, you will recall, involves allocating an equal amount of the cost of the asset over its life. For example, the $400,000 CAPEX made in 2003 will lead to depreciation expenses of $40,000 per year over the next 10 years, such that the assets acquired are expected to be worthless at the end of the 10-year period.

Panels b and c show pro forma income statements and balance sheets; Panel d reports EFCF estimates. Note that the project produces positive expected net income beginning in 2007 (the first year of its operation) and has positive profits each year through 2011. The investment's cash flows are negative, however, in 2006, reflecting the $550,000 investment made in capital equipment and working capital. The sizeable positive cash flow in 2011 reflects the proceeds from the sale of the project's plant and equipment and the liquidation of the accumulated investment in working capital over the life of the investment.

Equity Free Cash Flow (EFCF) for a Levered Project

When a firm uses debt to partially finance its investments, there are two cash flow consequences. First, when the debt is issued there is a cash inflow equal to the net proceeds from the issue. Second, the firm must make cash outlays for principal and interest payments throughout the life of the loan. Since interest expense (not principal) is tax deductible, it reduces the taxes the firm has to pay. Consequently, we can calculate EFCF for a levered project as shown in Figure 2-3.

Alternatively, we can express the EFCF for a levered project as follows:

$$EFCF = (EBIT - I)(1 - T) + DA - CAPEX - WC - P + NP \qquad (2.3a)$$

Figure 2-3   Calculation of Equity Free Cash Flow (EFCF) for a Levered Project, Using the Income Statement

	Revenues
Less:	Cost of goods sold
Equals:	*Gross profit*
Less:	Operating expenses (excluding depreciation and amortization expense)
Equals:	*Earnings before interest, taxes, depreciation, and amortization (EBITDA)*
Less:	Depreciation and amortization (DA)
Equals:	*Earnings before interest and taxes (EBIT)*
Less:	Interest expense **(nonzero for a levered project)**
Equals:	*Earnings before taxes (EBT)*
Less:	Taxes
Equals:	*Net income (NI)*
Plus:	Depreciation and amortization (DA)
Less:	Capital expenditures (CAPEX)
Less:	Increases in net working capital (WC)
Less:	Principal payments on debt **(required principal repayments on debt financing, P)**
Plus:	Proceeds from new debt issues **(net proceeds from new borrowing, NP)**
Equals:	*Equity free cash flow (EFCF)*

Acronym	Definition
$(EBIT - I)(1 - T)$	Net income after taxes
$EBIT$	Earnings before interest and taxes
$EBIT(1 - T)$	After-tax operating income or net operating profit after tax (NOPAT)
T	Tax rate
DA	Depreciation and amortization expense
WC	Change in net working capital
$CAPEX$	Capital expenditures for property, plant, and equipment
P	Principal payments on the firm's outstanding debt
NP	Net proceeds from the issuance of new debt

Rearranging terms to isolate interest expense, we get:

$$EFCF = EBIT(1 - T) - I(1 - T) + DA - CAPEX - WC - P + NP \qquad (2.3b)$$

This relationship highlights the fact that the effect of interest expense on EFCF is equal to the after-tax cost of interest, $I(1 - T)$. This is a consequence of the fact that the Internal Revenue Service allows the firm to deduct its interest payments from its taxable income (unlike dividends, which are paid after taxes have been calculated).

Example—EFCF for a levered project   To illustrate the calculation of EFCFs for a project that is partially financed by borrowing, we can return to our JC Crawford Enterprises example, found in Table 2-1. This time we assume that JC Crawford finances 40% of the total investment in the project by borrowing. A quick comparison of the EFCFs in panel d of Table 2-1 (no debt financing) and Table 2-2 (40% debt financing) reveals the consequences of using debt on investment cash flows. First, with debt financing the initial cash outflow for 2006 is only $330,000, compared to $550,000 in the no-debt financing case. The difference, of course reflects the $220,000 net proceeds realized from borrowing 40% of the initial cash outlay.[11] The annual cash flows (EFCFs) in panel d of Table 2-2 are also smaller than those in panel d of Table 2-1. Once again, the differences reflect the fact that in the latter case the firm is paying interest and repaying principal on debt.

---

[11]The firm maintains the debt-to-asset ratio at 40% of assets in each year. This target debt level implies that new debt is issued so long as assets are growing and that debt is retired toward the end of the project's life when assets begin to shrink. For example, in 2007 the addition to total assets is $565,000 - 550,000 = $15,000; thus, new debt proceeds of $.4 \times \$15,000 = \$6,000$ are required. In 2011 assets drop from $619,620 to $561,050; therefore, the firm must retire 40% of the decrease in total assets in order to maintain the target 40% debt-to-assets ratio.

Table 2-2 Estimating Equity Free Cash Flows (EFCFs) for a Levered Project

Panel a. Assumptions and Predictions

1. Sales growth rate	10%
2. Gross profit margin = Gross profit/Sales	30%
3. Operating expenses (before depreciation)/Sales	20%
4. Tax rate	30%
5. Capital expenditures/Sales	40%
6. Net working capital/Sales	15%
7. Base-year sales for 2007	$1,000,000
8. Depreciable life of plant and equipment (CAPEX)	10 years
9. Depreciation method	Straight line
10. Initial investment in plant and equipment	$400,000
11. Initial new working capital requirements	$150,000
12. Target debt/assets ratio	40%
13. Interest (borrowing) rate	10%
14. Residual values (Working capital and plant and equipment)	Book value in year 5

Panel b. Pro Forma Income Statements and Balance Sheets

Income Statement ($000)	2007	2008	2009	2010	2011
Sales	$1,000.00	$1,100.00	$1,210.00	$1,331.00	$1,464.10
Cost of goods sold	(700.00)	(770.00)	(847.00)	(931.70)	(1,024.87)
Gross profit	300.00	330.00	363.00	399.30	439.23
Operating expenses before depreciation	(200.00)	(220.00)	(242.00)	(266.20)	(292.82)
Depreciation expense	(40.00)	(44.00)	(48.40)	(53.24)	(58.56)
EBIT	60.00	66.00	72.60	79.86	87.85
Interest expense*	(22.00)	(22.60)	(23.26)	(23.99)	(24.78)
Earnings before taxes	38.00	43.40	49.34	55.87	63.06
Taxes	(11.40)	(13.02)	(14.80)	(16.76)	(18.92)
Net income	$ 26.60	$ 30.38	$ 34.54	$ 39.11	$ 44.14

The fact that the cash flows in the 40%-debt case are lower than in the all-equity case does not mean the project is less valuable. Remember that we are measuring the cash flows to the equity holders in the project, and in the all-equity case there is more equity invested than in the 40%-debt case.

Table 2-2   continued

Panel c. Pro Forma Balance Sheets

Balance Sheet ($000)	2006	2007	2008	2009	2010	2011**
Net working capital	$150.00	$165.00	$181.50	$199.65	$219.62	$219.62
Gross plant and equipment	400.00	440.00	484.00	532.40	585.64	585.64
Less: Accumulated depreciation	—	(40.00)	(84.00)	(132.40)	(185.64)	(244.20)
Net plant and equipment	$400.00	$400.00	$400.00	$400.00	$400.00	$341.44
Total assets	$550.00	$565.00	$581.50	$599.65	$619.62	$561.05
Interest-bearing debt***	$220.00	$226.00	$232.60	$239.86	$247.85	$224.42
Equity	330.00	339.00	348.90	359.79	371.77	336.63
Total liabilities and equity	$550.00	$565.00	$581.50	$599.65	$619.62	$561.05

Panel d. Equity Free Cash Flows (EFCFs)–Debt-and-Equity-Financed (Levered) Project

EFCF ($000)	2006	2007	2008	2009	2010	2011
Net income	$ —	$26.60	$30.38	$34.54	$39.11	$ 44.14
Plus: Depreciation and amortization	—	40.00	44.00	48.40	53.24	58.56
Less: Capital expenditures****	(400.00)	(40.00)	(44.00)	(48.40)	(53.24)	341.44
Less: Changes in net working capital****	(150.00)	(15.00)	(16.50)	(18.15)	(19.97)	219.62
Less: Principal payments*****	—	—	—	—	—	(224.42)
Plus: Proceeds from new debt issues	220.00	6.00	6.60	7.26	7.99	—
Equals: Equity free cash flow	$(330.00)	$17.60	$20.48	$23.65	$27.13	$439.42

*We assume that interest payments in the levered firm are based on begining-of-year debt values.

**At the end of 2011, we assume that the project life is over and the firm liquidates the assets (net working capital and net plant and equipment). However, the balance sheet shown in Panel c for 2011 is pre-liquidation.

***Debt is issued and retired so as to maintain a constant debt-to-asset ratio of 40%.

****The EFCF for 2011 incorporates the balance sheet or book values of both net working capital and net plant and equipment as cash inflows. Since no gain or loss is realized in 2011, there are no tax consequences.

*****The principal payment for 2011 equals the net amount of interest-bearing debt outstanding at the end of the year, as shown in the firm's 2011 balance sheet.

Financial Leverage and the Volatility of EFCFs

When a firm borrows a portion of the funds it uses to finance an investment, we say that it has employed *financial leverage*. The notion of leverage comes from the fact that borrowing costs are generally fixed. As the firm's profits rise and fall, the borrowing costs do not change, which means that all of the risk associated with the uncertain cash flows must be absorbed by the equity holders. This in turn implies that the share-holders' cash flows become more volatile with the use of financial leverage (see the Technical Insight box on financial leverage). To see this, compare the growth in EFCFs of the JC Crawford Enterprise investment for 2007 and 2010:

Unlevered Equity (Table 2-1) ($000)

	2007	2010	Percent Change
EBIT	$60.00	$79.86	33.1%
EFCF	27.00	35.94	33.1%

Levered Equity (Table 2-2) ($000)

	2007	2010	Percent Change
EBIT	$60.00	$79.86	33.1%
EFCF	17.60	27.13	54.1%

Over the period 2007–2010, earnings before interest and taxes (EBIT) increased 33.1% for both the unlevered and levered firm. The increase is the same for both levered and unlevered firms because neither interest nor principal payments affect EBIT. The effect of financial leverage is evident in the growth or change in EFCF. For the unlevered firm, EFCF increases by the exact same percentage, 33.1%. However, for the levered firm, EFCF increases 54.1% based on the same 33.1% increase in EBIT! This added volatility in EFCF is a direct result of the fact that the creditor return is fixed. Thus, as the project's EBIT grows larger, a larger fraction of the higher EBIT goes to the firm's shareholders.

Financial leverage will not necessarily cause cash flows to increase more quickly—if the project's operating results deteriorate, the levered project's cash flows experience a *far worse decline* than they would if the project were unlevered. To illustrate, just switch the dates for the two EFCFs in the above example. Assuming that EBIT declines by 33.1%, the levered firm's EFCF *drops* by 54.1%, whereas the unlevered project's EFCF declines by only 33.1%.

The effect of financial leverage, then, is to reduce the required investment by equity holders and at the same time increase the risk of the shareholder's investment. Because of the higher risk, shareholders require higher rates of return to entice them to invest in levered projects, other things remaining constant.

Project Free Cash Flow (PFCF)

To this point we have defined cash flow in terms of the cash available for distribution to the equity holders, or EFCF. Although this concept is used in some applications, the more common definition of cash flow for purposes of evaluating investment opportunities focuses on the cash flow available *from the project* that can be distributed to *both* creditors and owners. We refer to this notion of cash flow as **project free cash flow (PFCF).**

Using Financial Leverage to Enhance Equity Returns

Financial leverage has the potential to increase the residual returns earned on equity capital. When a firm borrows a portion of the capital needed to make an investment at rates lower than the rate earned on the investment, the excess goes to enhance the equity return. For example, assume we borrow $500 at a rate of 7% and invest that and another $500 in equity funds in an investment that earns 10% a year. Is the rate of return earned on the owner's investment equal to 10%? Due to the leverage, the rate of return is even higher: It is equal to 13%. Here's how it works:

Invested Capital			
Debt (7%)	$500		
Equity	500		
Total	$1,000		

Return on invested capital	10%	5%
Operating earnings	100	50
Less: Interest	(35)	(35)
Net income	$65	$15
Return to equity holders	13.0%	3.0%

In the above example we ignored taxes and calculated the return earned on the equity in the $1,000 investment. When the project earns 10%, it provides "favorable" financial leverage effects; that is, it earns more than the 7% cost of borrowing. This, in turn, results in a return on the equity capital that is pushed to 13% ($65 ÷ $500). (Remember that you pay the debt holders only 7% regardless of what the investment earns, and the remainder goes to the equity holders.)

However, when the investment earns only 5%, the effects of financial leverage are "unfavorable," since the creditors must get their 7% return before the equity holders are paid anything. The return on equity thus turns out to be only 3% ($15 ÷ $500). The shortfall in earnings has to come out of equity's return.

Calculating PFCF

Project free cash flow (PFCF) combines the cash flow available for distribution to all the firm's sources of capital (e.g., creditors, preferred equity holders, and common stockholders). We can calculate PFCF in one of two equivalent ways: The first involves summing the cash flows that accrue to each of the project's claim holders (debt and equity), as we see in the following formula:

Claimant	Cash Flows
Common stockholders (EFCF)	$NOPAT + DA - I(1 - T) - P + NP - WC - CAPEX$
Creditors (net of tax savings)[12]	$I(1 - T) + P - NP$
Sum: Project free cash flow (PFCF) =	**$NOPAT + DA - WC - CAPEX$** (2.4)

Acronym	Definition
NOPAT	Net operating profit after taxes = $EBIT(1 - T)$
EBIT	Earnings before interest and taxes
T	Tax rate
DA	Depreciation and amortization expense
I	Interest expense
P	Principal payments on outstanding debt
NP	Net proceeds from newly issued debt
WC	Change in net working capital
CAPEX	Capital expenditures

Alternatively, we can think of the PFCF as the sum of all the cash flows from the project's operations, *after* meeting operating expenses, taxes, and new investments in working capital and CAPEX, but *before* any payments are made to the project's claim holders (stockholders and bondholders). This sum, outlined in Figure 2-4, is equal to the sum of the cash flows to the two types of claim holders.

Notice that we refer to a project's after-tax income using the term *net operating profit after tax* and the acronym NOPAT. We do this to recognize *explicitly* that we are not actually calculating taxes as the project would owe them but "as if" the project were financed with no debt and consequently had no interest expense. Thus, the after-tax income estimated above is actually after-tax operating income. In essence, *PFCF is simply EFCF for a project that has been all-equity-financed.*

JC Crawford Enterprises example   Table 2-3 contains PFCF calculations for the JC Crawford Enterprises investment opportunity we analyzed earlier in Tables 2-1 and 2-2. A quick comparison of the PFCFs and EFCFs for an all-equity-financed project

---

[12]The creditor's cash flow equals $I + P - NP$, and the tax savings from the government equal $(T \times I)$ such that the net payment to the creditors is $I(1 - T) + P - NP$.

TECHNICAL INSIGHT

Primer on Discount Rates and Cash Flows

To this point we have not attempted to value the investment opportunity faced by JC Crawford Enterprises. However, we can make an important observation about the type of discount rate that JC Crawford should use. If we are valuing EFCFs, then the discount rate should correspond to an equity holder's required rate of return. If we are valuing PFCF (which, as we've seen, is the sum of the EFCF and after-tax cash flows to the firm's creditors), we should use a discount rate that reflects an aggregation of the equity holder's required rate of return and the expected rate of return of the firm's creditors. In Chapter 4 we define the latter as the weighted average cost of capital.

(Table 2-1) reveals that they are identical, as we expect. Remember that PFCF is the same as EFCF *when no financial leverage is used* (because no interest is paid). Moreover, in Panel b of Table 2-3 we see that the difference in PFCF and EFCF for the levered project (project financed with 40% debt) is attributable to the after-tax cash flows paid to the firm's creditors (i.e., interest expense *less* the tax savings on interest *plus* any new debt issues *less* principal payments).

Figure 2-4	Calculation of Project Free Cash Flow
	Revenues
Less:	Cost of goods sold
Equals:	*Gross profit*
Less:	Operating expenses (excluding depreciation and amortization expense)
Equals:	*Earnings before interest, taxes, depreciation, and amortization (EBITDA)*
Less:	Depreciation and amortization (DA)
Equals:	*Earnings before interest and taxes (EBIT)*
Less:	Taxes
Equals:	*Net operating profit after taxes (NOPAT)*
Plus:	Depreciation and amortization (DA)
Less:	Capital expenditures (CAPEX)
Less:	Increases in net working capital (WC)
Equals:	***Project free cash flow (PFCF)***

**Table 2-3   Estimating Project Free Cash Flows (PFCFs)
for an Investment Project**

a. Calculation of PFCFs—Direct Method

($000)	2006	2007	2008	2009	2010	2011
Earnings before interest and taxes (EBIT)	$ —	$60.00	$66.00	$72.60	$79.86	$ 87.85
Less: Taxes	—	(18.00)	(19.80)	(21.78)	(23.96)	(26.35)
Net operating profit after taxes (NOPAT)	$ —	$42.00	$46.20	$50.82	$55.90	$ 61.49
Plus: Depreciation expense	—	40.00	44.00	48.40	53.24	58.56
Less: Capital expenditures (CAPEX)	(400.00)	(40.00)	(44.00)	(48.40)	(53.24)	341.44
Less: Changes in net working capital	(150.00)	(15.00)	(16.50)	(18.15)	(19.97)	219.62
Equals: Project free cash flow (PFCF)	$(550.00)	$27.00	$29.70	$32.67	$35.94	$681.11

b. Calculation of PFCFs—Indirect Method

($000)	2006	2007	2008	2009	2010	2011
Equity free cash flow	$(330.00)	$17.60	$20.48	$23.65	$27.13	$439.34
Plus: Interest $(1-T)$	—	15.40	15.82	16.28	16.79	17.35
Plus: Principal payments*	—	—	—	—	—	224.42
Less: New debt issues	(220.00)	(6.00)	(6.60)	(7.26)	(7.99)	—
Equals: Project free cash flow (PFCF)	$(550.00)	$27.00	$29.70	$32.67	$35.94	$681.11

*The principal payment for 2011 equals the net amount of interest-bearing debt outstanding at the end of the year, as shown in the firm's 2011 balance sheet. No principal is repaid until 2011.

2.3 COMPREHENSIVE EXAMPLE—FORECASTING PROJECT FREE CASH FLOWS

Forecasting cash flows for prospective investments is not an exact science, but is rather a mixture of science, intuition, and experience. To illustrate the techniques that firms can use to make cash flow forecasts, we analyze an investment involving a high-tech product—liquid crystal display (LCD) panels for big-screen television sets.

By the close of 2003 it was obvious that flat-panel, wall-hanging TVs were fast becoming the preferred format for high-end TVs. Plasma-screen models were the most popular technology for monitors larger than 30 inches diagonally. However, when plasma screens are compared to LCDs, they have some rather serious limitations, including a shorter life span (30,000 hours compared to 50,000) and screen "burn in." With plasma screens, if the TV was left on with a channel with a logo or other fixed image displayed for many hours, "burned-in" images sometimes appeared as shadows on the screen. The LCDs, on the other hand, tended to have superior resolution in daylight hours and did not suffer from burn-in problems. However, the technology for making LCDs larger than 30 inches was only then being developed.

Lecion Electronics Corporation has been involved in the manufacture of flat-panel LCDs for use as computer monitors for 10 years. The company possesses some of the leading technology for both the design and manufacture of large-screen LCDs. The firm is currently considering the cash flow consequences of an investment of $1.75 billion in a new fabrication plant in South Korea that can produce 42-inch LCDs over the next 20 quarters (five years) using the firm's proprietary technology. The investment would almost overnight make Lecion a major supplier of large-screen LCDs for sale in the home-entertainment market. Lecion's marketing group believes the firm can capture an estimated 20% market share once the plant is in full production.

Lecion's Strategic Assessment of the Opportunity

Very early in the project evaluation analysis Lecion Electronics Corporation will need to engage in a thorough assessment of the proposed strategy. This **strategic assessment** process centers on "the story" that underlies the investment. Specifically, we need to answer one overarching question: What are the specific capabilities of the firm and the competitive circumstances that allow it to realize this positive-NPV opportunity?

In trying to address this question, it helps to have a systematic approach that incorporates all the fundamental questions that a firm should answer each time it contemplates a project. One critical aspect of a strategic assessment is that we *explicitly state* the assumptions underlying the investment plan. Lecion's project management team addressed the potential strategic implications of the new investment (using the strategic assessment questions set forth in Chapter 1). They came to the following conclusions:

■ *Assumptions regarding competitor responses.* At present, four major manufacturers have the technological expertise and capacity to compete in the large flat-screen market. Each is expected to continue its efforts to compete for market share. However, the recession following the meltdown of the dot-com market in 2000 led the manufacturers to cut back on their development programs; Lecion has taken a clear technological lead that is expected to hold up for at least a year and possibly two. Furthermore, Lecion's management feels that its technological edge will allow the firm to capture a position of leadership in the industry over the first 12 months of production. The market share the firm anticipates capturing during this period will help it weather any storm of competitor products over the five-year projected life of the investment project being contemplated.

■ *Assumptions regarding producers of complementary products.* Lecion has worked closely with producers of high-end audio products to ensure the compatibility of its LCDs with all their newest product offerings. The firm continues to monitor developments in new wireless technology that will greatly reduce the cost of installing home-theater systems. The firm expects to grow its share of the home-theater market as its LCDs grow in popularity.

■ *Assumptions regarding customer responses.* The early demand for the 42-inch LCDs is expected to come from customers in the upper tiers of consumable income who are not expected to be particularly price-sensitive. This will eventually change over the five-year life of the project, and the firm's estimate of the price per unit of its LCDs incorporates consideration for this declining product price.

■ *Assumptions regarding how employees will respond.* With the economy having moved out of a recessionary period and employment levels growing, Lecion expects that the job market will become increasingly more competitive and tight. As a consequence, they anticipate having to pay higher wages to their employees. However, since the plant is located in South Korea, where wage costs are substantially lower than in the United States, the pressures of wage inflation are not considered to be a significant factor driving the economics of the new plant investment.

The key point to make before we embark on our analysis of "the numbers" is that they must rely upon and be consistent with the strategic assessment story that underlies the investment. If the story is inconsistent with the forecasts that serve as the basis for the cash flow estimates, then the analysis is fatally flawed. The strategic analysis process is necessarily subjective and appears unsophisticated in comparison with the apparent precision of the cash flow numbers. However, it is crucial that both the story and the numbers build upon one another if the project analysis is to produce the information required to make a good decision about the project.

Estimating the Investment's Project Free Cash Flow (PFCF)

Our earlier description of the calculation of PFCF for any period t can be restated in equation form as follows:

$$\text{PFCF}_t = \left[\left(\begin{array}{c} \text{Firm} \\ \text{Revenues}_t \end{array} \right) - \left(\begin{array}{c} \text{Cost of} \\ \text{Goods Sold}_t \end{array} \right) - \left(\begin{array}{c} \text{Operating} \\ \text{Expenses}_t \end{array} \right) - \left(\begin{array}{c} \text{Depreciation} \\ \text{Expense}_t \end{array} \right) \right]$$
$$\times \left(1 - \begin{array}{c} \text{Tax} \\ \text{Rate} \end{array} \right) + \left(\begin{array}{c} \text{Depreciation} \\ \text{Expense}_t \end{array} \right) - \text{CAPEX}_t - \begin{array}{c} \text{Change in} \\ \text{Working Capital}_t \end{array} \quad (2.5)$$

Viewed in this way, it is apparent that the firm's cash flow forecasting problem involves developing estimates for *each* of these components of PFCF for *each year* of the project's anticipated life. Throughout our discussion we will refer to these key components as value drivers since they determine the investment's value.

Forecasting Incremental Revenues

The first value driver found on the right-hand side of Equation 2.5 is firm revenues. Here we refer to the incremental revenues that result from undertaking the LCD investment. Since the LCD investment will only provide revenues if the investment is undertaken, all of the plant's revenues are incremental to Lecion and are therefore relevant to our analysis.

To develop our forecast of revenues from the investment in the new LCD fabrication plant (or simply fab), we begin by defining the key cash flow drivers for firm revenues. To keep matters as uncluttered as possible, we will assume that Lecion's new plant will produce a single product (42-inch LCD panels). This means that the plant's revenues for any given period are equal to the product of the volume of units sold by the firm times the market price received for each unit sold. Additionally, it is often helpful to think of the firm's units produced and sold as a fraction of the total number of units of the product sold by all firms.

In our example, Lecion's revenues for the period are equal to the product of total unit sales for all firms in the industry times Lecion's projected market share multiplied by the market price per unit. Thus, we define Lecion's revenues for period t as follows:

$$\begin{array}{c} \text{Lecion's} \\ \text{Revenues}_t \end{array} = \left(\begin{array}{c} \text{Total} \\ \text{Units Sold}_t \end{array}\right) \times \left(\begin{array}{c} \text{Lecion's} \\ \text{Market} \\ \text{Share}_t \end{array}\right) \times \left(\begin{array}{c} \text{Market} \\ \text{Price per} \\ \text{Unit}_t \end{array}\right) \qquad (2.6)$$

Table 2-4 contains projected revenues for Lecion's LCD plant spanning the 20 quarters beginning with the first quarter of 2004. To generate the forecast of plant revenues, we need to estimate the total units sold of 42-inch LCDs by all manufacturers, the firm's share of those total units, and the price per unit. Although we do not present the details underlying these projections here, the estimates resulted in the set of market demand numbers found in the second column of Table 2-4.

Next, the project management team estimates Lecion will maintain a market share of 20% of total industry sales of 42-inch LCDs in each quarter. Obviously, this fraction is subject to a high level of uncertainty, and some type of sensitivity analysis on this variable would be appropriate. (We return to this point in Chapter 3 when we simulate investment cash flows.)

The final element of the revenue forecast is the price forecast for the 42-inch LCDs. The team predicts that the price of these panels will be $9,995 in the first quarter of 2004 and that this price will drop to $4,094 by the end of the 20-quarter forecast period (Qtr 4 2008). This forecast reflects the use of a *price decay function*, which is commonly used in evaluating prices of high-tech products such as computer semiconductors. In this instance, the decay function assumes a rate of price decay of 15%. This means that every time the cumulative market volume of LCDs produced and sold doubles, the price of an LCD drops by 15%. This relationship is sometimes referred to as the *experience curve*. This functional relationship between product price and cumulative market units produced and sold has been observed over and over in a wide variety of high-tech products.[13]

Estimating Cost of Goods Sold and Operating Expenses

To estimate the Lecion plant's cost of goods sold and operating expenses, we first combine both these expenses, and then the project management team will decompose

---

[13]For example, Lee et al. (1997) observed that a 20% price decay function explained over 88% of the variation in unit semiconductor prices for a major supplier of microprocessors during the early 1990s (Winyih Lee, John Martin, and Hirofumi Matsuo, 1997, "Valuing investments that reduce time-to-market in the semiconductor industry," *Advances in Financial Planning and Forecasting*, 7: 19–23).

Table 2-4	Market Demand and Revenue Projections for Lecion's LCD Fabricating Plant			
Quarter	Total Units Sold (Market)	Firm Units Sold (Total Units × Market Share)	Price/Unit	Firm Revenues
Qtr 1 2004	753,000	150,600	$9,995	$1,505,289,075
Qtr 2 2004	984,000	196,800	8,216	1,616,945,553
Qtr 3 2004	1,193,000	238,600	7,268	1,734,176,681
Qtr 4 2004	1,380,000	276,000	6,639	1,832,430,542
Qtr 1 2005	1,545,000	309,000	6,179	1,909,311,468
Qtr 2 2005	1,688,000	337,600	5,823	1,965,720,217
Qtr 3 2005	1,809,000	361,800	5,536	2,003,063,962
Qtr 4 2005	1,908,000	381,600	5,301	2,022,674,378
Qtr 1 2006	1,985,000	397,000	5,102	2,025,688,587
Qtr 2 2006	2,040,000	408,000	4,934	2,013,044,041
Qtr 3 2006	2,073,000	414,600	4,789	1,985,500,412
Qtr 4 2006	2,084,000	416,800	4,663	1,943,664,577
Qtr 1 2007	2,073,000	414,600	4,554	1,888,012,263
Qtr 2 2007	2,040,000	408,000	4,458	1,818,905,071
Qtr 3 2007	1,985,000	397,000	4,374	1,736,603,080
Qtr 4 2007	1,908,000	381,600	4,301	1,641,273,530
Qtr 1 2008	1,809,000	361,800	4,237	1,532,996,051
Qtr 2 2008	1,688,000	337,600	4,182	1,411,764,732
Qtr 3 2008	1,545,000	309,000	4,134	1,277,487,125
Qtr 4 2008	1,380,000	276,000	4,094	1,129,980,055

them into their variable and fixed components. Thus, we define the sum of the firm's cost of goods sold and operating expenses for the period as follows:

$$\begin{matrix} \text{Cost of Sold}_t \text{ plus} \\ \text{Operating Expenses}_t \end{matrix} = \begin{pmatrix} \text{Variable} \\ \text{Cost per} \\ \text{Unit}_t \end{pmatrix} \times \begin{pmatrix} \text{Total} \\ \text{Units Sold}_t \end{pmatrix}$$

$$\times \text{ (Lexion's Market Share}_t) + \text{(Fixed Cost per Quarter}_t) \qquad (2.7)$$

**Salvage Values and
Terminal Values**

The terms *salvage* and *terminal value* are often used interchangeably when referring to the final cash flow that is realized at the end of the period used to value an investment (i.e., the analysis period). However, we want to draw a subtle but meaningful distinction between these terms for purposes of discounted cash flow analysis. Specifically, when valuing individual projects that have a finite life (as is the case in Chapters 2 and 3), we use the term *salvage* value to refer to the disposal value of the project assets at the end of the term of our analysis. This value is typically what the term *salvage* connotes, in that we dispose of the project assets and the proceeds make up the terminal value of the investment.

However, in some very long-term investments, where the productive life of the project assets is expected to continue indefinitely, the terminal value represents the present value of all investment cash flows beyond the end of the analysis period. In Chapters 7 and 8, when we evaluate the value of a firm, the terminal value estimate is critical for it can often contain the majority of the value of the enterprise. For our purposes in this chapter and the next, however, we will assume that the analysis period is equal to the productive life of the investment such that the terminal value of the project is actually the salvage value of the investment assets.

In Equation 2.7 we need to forecast variable cost per unit and the firm's total fixed operating expenses per quarter. (We have the other amounts from our previous discussion.) Lecion estimates the variable cost per unit using its current estimates of the $11,752 out-of-pocket costs of manufacturing an LCD panel (see Table 2-5), combined with the anticipated benefits from reductions in cost per unit as the firm produces more and more units.

In this particular instance, Lecion's analysts estimate that the variable cost per unit will decline by 22% each time the cumulative volume of production doubles. In this case, the cost estimate reflects a 78% *learning curve model*.[14] That is, each time production volume doubles, Lecion estimates that per unit variable cost will drop to 78% of the variable cost per unit corresponding to half the current volume. For example, if variable costs were $10,000 for 500,000 units, then Lecion would expect them to

---

[14]Willyard and McClees (1987) provide some empirical evidence that in high-tech applications the learning curve reflects about 78 percent (Charles H. Willyard and Cheryl W. McClees, 1987, "Motorola's technology roadmap process," *Research Management*, September-October, Vol. 30, No. 5, pp. 13–19).

Table 2-5	Variable and Fixed Costs per Unit Estimates for the Lecion LCD Plant				
Quarter	Firm Units Sold	Variable Cost per Unit	Fixed Cost per Unit	Depreciation Expense per Qtr.	Total Expenses
Qtr 1 2004	150,600	$(11,752)	$(166)	$(87,500,000)	$(1,882,285,054)
Qtr 2 2004	196,800	(8,698)	(127)	(87,500,000)	(1,824,244,347)
Qtr 3 2004	238,600	(7,206)	(105)	(87,500,000)	(1,831,753,190)
Qtr 4 2004	276,000	(6,271)	(91)	(87,500,000)	(1,843,268,600)
Qtr 1 2005	309,000	(5,616)	(81)	(87,500,000)	(1,847,863,819)
Qtr 2 2005	337,600	(5,127)	(74)	(87,500,000)	(1,843,225,936)
Qtr 3 2005	361,800	(4,745)	(69)	(87,500,000)	(1,829,161,574)
Qtr 4 2005	381,600	(4,438)	(66)	(87,500,000)	(1,806,043,235)
Qtr 1 2006	397,000	(4,186)	(63)	(87,500,000)	(1,774,356,588)
Qtr 2 2006	408,000	(3,976)	(61)	(87,500,000)	(1,734,557,877)
Qtr 3 2006	414,600	(3,798)	(60)	(87,500,000)	(1,687,030,778)
Qtr 4 2006	416,800	(3,646)	(60)	(87,500,000)	(1,632,077,013)
Qtr 1 2007	414,600	(3,515)	(60)	(87,500,000)	(1,569,918,085)
Qtr 2 2007	408,000	(3,402)	(61)	(87,500,000)	(1,500,699,830)
Qtr 3 2007	397,000	(3,305)	(63)	(87,500,000)	(1,424,496,656)
Qtr 4 2007	381,600	(3,220)	(66)	(87,500,000)	(1,341,314,295)
Qtr 1 2008	361,800	(3,147)	(69)	(87,500,000)	(1,251,090,564)
Qtr 2 2008	337,600	(3,084)	(74)	(87,500,000)	(1,153,693,877)
Qtr 3 2008	309,000	(3,030)	(81)	(87,500,000)	(1,048,919,235)
Qtr 4 2008	276,000	(2,985)	(91)	(87,500,000)	(936,481,297)

drop by 22% to $7,800 when the cumulative volume produced reached 1,000,000 units. Of course, there's nothing magical about the notion of a learning curve. It simply represents a tool for describing the effects of learning and continuous improvements on the manufacturing process over the life cycle of the product. Such learning, in turn, lowers the variable costs of production.

Lecion's analysts have made four simplifying assumptions in compiling investment cash flow estimates: First, they have assumed that no new investments in net working capital will be required over the life of the project. Second, they have assumed that plant and equipment will be depreciated using straight-line depreciation resulting in a zero estimated salvage value. Third, the plant is analyzed as if it had no continuing

Table 2-6 Estimated Project Free Cash Flow for the Lecion LCD Investment

Quarter	Firm Revenues	Firm Expenses	Net Operating Profit after Tax	Depreciation Expense	PFCF	Contribution Margin
Qtr 1 2004	$1,505,289,075	$(1,882,285,05)	$(263,897,18)	$(87,500,00)	$(176,397,186)	–17.6%
Qtr 2 2004	1,616,945,553	(1,824,244,347)	(145,109,156)	(87,500,000)	(57,609,156)	–5.9%
Qtr 3 2004	1,734,176,681	(1,831,753,190)	(68,303,556)	(87,500,000)	19,196,444	0.9%
Qtr 4 2004	1,832,430,542	(1,843,268,600)	(7,586,641)	(87,500,000)	79,913,359	5.5%
Qtr 1 2005	1,909,311,468	(1,847,863,819)	43,013,355	(87,500,000)	130,513,355	9.1%
Qtr 2 2005	1,965,720,217	(1,843,225,936)	85,745,997	(87,500,000)	173,245,997	12.0%
Qtr 3 2005	2,003,063,962	(1,829,161,574)	121,731,671	(87,500,000)	209,231,671	14.3%
Qtr 4 2005	2,022,674,378	(1,806,043,235)	151,641,800	(87,500,000)	239,141,800	16.3%
Qtr 1 2006	2,025,688,587	(1,774,356,588)	175,932,399	(87,500,000)	263,432,399	18.0%
Qtr 2 2006	2,013,044,041	(1,734,557,877)	194,940,314	(87,500,000)	282,440,314	19.4%
Qtr 3 2006	1,985,500,412	(1,687,030,778)	208,928,744	(87,500,000)	296,428,744	20.7%
Qtr 4 2006	1,943,664,577	(1,632,077,013)	218,111,295	(87,500,000)	305,611,295	21.8%
Qtr 1 2007	1,888,012,263	(1,569,918,085)	222,665,924	(87,500,000)	310,165,924	22.8%
Qtr 2 2007	1,818,905,071	(1,500,699,830)	222,743,669	(87,500,000)	310,243,669	23.7%
Qtr 3 2007	1,736,603,080	(1,424,496,656)	218,474,497	(87,500,000)	305,974,497	24.5%
Qtr 4 2007	1,641,273,530	(1,341,314,295)	209,971,464	(87,500,000)	297,471,464	25.1%
Qtr 1 2008	1,532,996,051	(1,251,090,564)	197,333,841	(87,500,000)	284,833,841	25.7%
Qtr 2 2008	1,411,764,732	(1,153,693,877)	180,649,599	(87,500,000)	268,149,599	26.2%
Qtr 3 2008	1,277,487,125	(1,048,919,235)	159,997,523	(87,500,000)	247,497,523	26.7%
Qtr 4 2008	1,129,980,055	(936,481,297)	135,449,131	(87,500,000)	222,949,131	27.1%

or terminal value. This is probably an overly conservative assumption since the plant is likely to have some value either as scrap or possibly as a plant site for a later technology fab. Nonetheless, for purposes of the analysis carried out here, the estimated salvage value is zero. Finally, investment income is assumed to be taxed at a constant rate for all periods and all levels of income.

A review of the PFCF estimates found in Table 2-6 indicates that Lecion's analysts expect the project to have a positive cash flow by the end of Quarter 3 and to remain positive throughout the project's remaining life. Moreover, the contribution margin in the final column of Table 2-6 reveals a growing margin of profits over the project's life. (Contribution margin is defined as price per unit less variable cost per unit divided by price per unit.) These forecasts are, of course, predictions and subject to forecast error. We return to a discussion of forecast error in Chapter 3. For now, with the forecasts of the PFCF in hand, we focus on the process of valuing Lecion's expected future cash flows as a next step.

2.4 VALUING INVESTMENT CASH FLOWS

Once the analyst has estimated the future cash flows from an investment, it is time to value them. As you learned in your basic finance course, the value of the future cash flows is equal to the present value of the forecasted cash flows. Very simply, we need to discount the forecasted future cash flows back to the present time using a discount rate that properly reflects the anticipated risks of the future cash flows.

Figure 2-1 (page 25) summarized the DCF process. Up to this point we have dealt *only* with Step 1, which involves estimating investment cash flows. For now, for convenience, we will assume that we have performed Step 2 and that we know the appropriate discount rate for use in calculating the present value of future cash flows.[15]

Example—Valuing Lecion's Project Cash Flows

To illustrate the procedure used to carry out Step 3 of the DCF valuation process, we will value the PFCFs estimated for the Lecion LCD project found in Table 2-6. Below, we provide a quick review of the mathematics of discounting for those who need it. (See the discussion found in the Technical Insight box (p. 60) on the mechanics of time value of money calculations.) However, we will not devote additional space to the topic; if you need more of a brushup, consult one of the many excellent treatments of the subject in introductory finance textbooks.

We assume that the opportunity cost of capital for the Lecion project is 21.55% per year, or 5% per quarter since the cash flows are received quarterly.[16] The discount factor for each quarterly cash flow is defined as follows:

$$\text{Discount Factor for Quarter}_t = \left(\frac{1}{1 + .05} \right)^t$$

The present value of each quarterly cash flow is simply the product of the cash flow and a discount factor for the quarter. Summing the present values of the cash flows generated by the project in each quarter of the project's operations (Quarters 1 through 20,

---

[15]We discuss the choice of the proper discount rate and the calculation of the cost of capital in Chapters 4 and 5.

[16]The formal equivalence of 5% compounded quarterly and 21.55% compounded annually is based on the equality:

$$(1 + .2155) = \left(1 + \frac{\text{Quarterly}}{\text{Compound Rate}} \right)^4 = (1 + .05)^4$$

found in Table 2-6), Lecion estimates the value of the investment to be $2,113,170,300.

Using NPV and IRR to Evaluate the Investment

If Lecion invests $1.75 billion in the project, as indicated in Table 2-7, then the project will produce $363,170,300 more, in present value terms, than it costs.[17] This difference in the present value of the project's expected future cash flows and the initial cost of making the investment is commonly referred to as the **net present value,** or simply NPV.

Another popular indicator of the anticipated wealth created by an investment is the **internal rate of return,** or IRR, of the project. We define the IRR as the compound rate of return earned on the investment, and we calculate it by solving the following expression:

Do corporate executives use DCF?

When asked whether they always or almost always use IRR, 75.7% of corporate CFOs responded in the affirmative. Similarly, 74.9% said they always or almost always used NPV. These results, came from a survey of 392 CFOs done by John Graham and Campbell Harvey,* and reveal a dramatic increase in the reliance on NPV compared to IRR. In a survey completed in 1977, fewer than 10% of the respondents relied on NPV as their primary method, while more than 50% said they relied primarily on IRR.**

*John Graham and Campbell Harvey, "The Theory and Practice of Corporate Finance: Evidence from the Field," *Journal of Financial Economics,* 60 (2001).

**L. Gitman and J. Forrester, Jr., "A Survey of Capital Budgeting Techniques Used by Major U.S. Firms," *Financial Management* (1977), pp. 66–71.

$$\text{Investment Outlay}_0 = \sum_{t=1}^{N} \frac{PFCF_t}{(1 + IRR)^t} \qquad (2.8)$$

Solving Equation 2.8 for the quarterly IRR (since the cash flows are quarterly), Lecion's analysts get 6.55% per quarter.[18] Annualizing this rate, they estimate that the LCD investment will produce a return of 28.91% per year.[19] Comparing the 28.91%

---

[17]For simplicity, we have assumed that the total investment in the project is made immediately. Obviously, this cannot be the case as it would take some period of time for new plant facilities to be constructed and equipment to be ordered and put into operation. Furthermore, firms typically "stage" investments of the magnitude considered in this book. For example, they might commit the minimum amount of money required to capture the investment opportunity and begin the project, but reserve judgment on successive stages of investment until certain milestones have been reached.

[18]Solving for IRR can be quite laborious if done without the help of a calculator or spreadsheet. In Excel there is a built-in IRR function that can be used, and almost all business calculators have a similar feature. If you are relying on these tools you should be aware, however, that multiple IRRs can and often do exist and these built-in functions will not tell you that there is more than one IRR. See the Technical Insight box (p. 58) on multiple internal rates of return for a discussion of this issue.

[19]Are you wondering why 28.91% is not equal to 4 × 6.55%? The reason is compounding of the intermediate (quarterly) cash flows. The investment actually earns an annual compound rate of return of $(1 + .0655)^4 - 1 = 28.91\%$.

Table 2-7   Valuation and Discounting Cash Flows

Quarter	Estimated Cash Flow PFCF = EFCF	Discount Factor	Present Value
0	($1,750,000,000)	1.0000	($1,750,000,000)
1	(176,397,186)	0.9524	(167,997,320)
2	(57,609,156)	0.9070	(52,253,202)
3	19,196,444	0.8638	16,582,610
4	79,913,359	0.8227	65,744,919
5	130,513,355	0.7835	102,260,628
6	173,245,997	0.7462	129,278,830
7	209,231,671	0.7107	148,697,042
8	239,141,800	0.6768	161,860,584
9	263,432,399	0.6446	169,810,873
10	282,440,314	0.6139	173,393,852
11	296,428,744	0.5847	173,315,747
12	305,611,295	0.5568	170,175,805
13	310,165,924	0.5303	164,487,612
14	310,243,669	0.5051	156,694,135
15	305,974,497	0.4810	147,178,965
16	297,471,464	0.4581	136,275,105
17	284,833,841	0.4363	124,272,061
18	268,149,599	0.4155	111,421,697
19	247,497,523	0.3957	97,943,174
20	222,949,131	0.3769	84,027,183
Project value (present value of cash flows for qtrs 1–20) =			$2,113,170,300
Initial cost (expenditure for qtr 0) =			($1,750,000,000)
Net present value =			$363,170,300

IRR to the 21.55% cost of capital we used as our discount rate in calculating the value of the investment, Lecion concludes that the investment should be viewed favorably.

Both the NPV and IRR of the investment indicate that the investment creates value. Does this imply that Lecion should commit to the project and invest $1.75 billion over the coming year? In a world of certainty, where forecasts are made without error, the answer is an unqualified yes. However, in this particular case the analysis is based on very uncertain cash flow estimates. When uncertainty is present, there will be estimation error, and this estimation error can lead to systematic errors in decision making.

It is possible that overconfident managers have provided optimistic forecasts rather than true expected cash flows. Alternatively, the cash flow numbers may have been generated by managers with a vested interest in getting the project approved. As a consequence, firms generally will not accept projects simply because they have positive NPVs or because they have IRRs that exceed the appropriate cost of capital. For these reasons, it is important to dig deeper to understand the uncertainties that underlie both the assumptions and forecasts made in generating the NPV estimate before making the final decision. In Chapter 3 we discuss two different forms of sensitivity analysis that are very helpful in this regard.

Mutually Exclusive Projects

Up to this point in our analysis we have been evaluating one project or investment by itself. Often the analysis will entail consideration of multiple alternatives or competing projects, where the firm must select only one. We refer to these alternatives as **mutually exclusive investments** since the selection of one precludes investment in the others.

When Duke Energy is faced with the opportunity to construct a new power plant, the firm has a number of choices it can make regarding the fuel that is to be used in firing the plant (e.g., natural gas, fuel oil, nuclear, coal, or some mixture of the preceding). Each technology has its particular advantages and disadvantages, but ultimately Duke must select one and only one. When ranking the alternatives, the NPV still provides the best metric, as it measures the expected contribution of the project to the value of the equity of Duke Energy. However, in some cases firms need to choose between competing (mutually exclusive) investments because their ability to finance new investments is limited. In this situation the NPV criteria is not necessarily the best way to evaluate the choice between the investments, and the firm may also want to consider the rate of return or IRR of the investments as well as how quickly the projects can be paid off, so that the capital can be recycled and invested in additional projects.

Many investment opportunities provide their own mutually exclusive alternative in the form of delayed execution or implementation. For example, Lecion's LCD investment opportunity was analyzed as if it had to be implemented immediately or the opportunity would be lost. It is often the case, however, that the firm that possesses the technological advantage may have some degree of flexibility as to how quickly it

Did you know?

Excel's NPV function does not calculate net present value.

Excel includes an NPV function with the following arguments:

$$NPV(rate, value1, value2, \ldots)$$

where rate is the discount rate and value1, value2, and so forth are cash flows received 1, 2, and more periods in the future. Consequently, the NPV function calculates the present value of a stream of future cash flows, with the first being received one period hence. Net present value, on the other hand, incorporates consideration for an initial outlay in the current period that is not discounted at all. Therefore, we can use the NPV function to calculate net present value as follows:

Net Present Value =
$NPV(rate, value1, value2, \ldots)$
$- \text{Initial Cash Outlay}_0$

TECHNICAL
INSIGHT
Multiple Internal Rates of Return (IRRs)

The IRR is defined simply as the compound annual rate of return earned on an investment. In introductory analyses of investment projects, we generally assume that the negative cash flows associated with a project, such as the development costs, come early in the project's life, and then the positive cash flows come later. In reality, it is often the case that positive and negative cash flows are interspersed. When this is the case, there can be multiple rates of return or IRRs that make the NPV of the investment positive.

We can use the net present value (NPV) profile (a graph of NPV for various discount rates) to illustrate the problem. First, consider a typical investment with the following cash flow pattern:

Year 0	Year 1	Year 2	Year 3
$(500)	$400	$300	$50

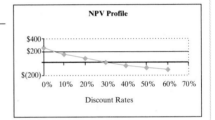

The IRR for these cash flows is 31.44%, which is readily identifiable in the project's NPV Profile, found right:

Now consider the following set of project cash flows:

Year 0	Year 1	Year 2	Year 3
$(200)	$1,200	$(2,200)	$1,200

Note that these cash flows change sign from year to year on three occasions. It turns out that this fact drives the result that there are up to three different IRRs (see right):

In this example there are three IRRs that make the NPV equal to zero: 0%, 100%, and 200%.

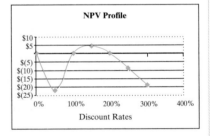

There are instances where no IRR can be computed. We leave the illustration to the reader. Consider the following pattern of cash flows:

Year 0	Year 1	Year 2
$100	$(300)	$350

What is your estimate of the IRR for this stream of cash flows?

INDUSTRY INSIGHT

The Payback Model

Although it is widely derided among academic scholars, the payback model is often used in corporate practice as a tool for evaluating new investments.* The method is straightforward and involves estimating the number of years of expected future cash flows that are required to sum to the investment's initial outlay. For example, a $4 million investment today that produces annual cash flows of $1 million per year over a seven-year period has a payback period of four years.

Payback has three well-known drawbacks. First, it does not account for the time value of money. Second, it ignores the value of cash flows received after the payback period. Finally, the cutoff is not tied to market conditions. It depends on the manager's biases and may often be outdated.

To respond to the first issue, some calculate a discounted payback by using cash flows that are discounted to account for the time value of money. For example, using a 10% discount rate and the earlier example, discounted payback would be calculated as follows:

	Years						
	1	2	3	4	5	6	7
Project free cash flow (PFCF)	$1,000,000	$1,000,000	$1,000,000	$1,000,000	$1,000,000	$1,000,000	$1,000,000
Present value of PFCF	909,091	826,446	751,315	683,013	620,921	564,474	513,158
Cumulative present value	$ 909,091	$1,735,537	$2,486,852	$3,169,865	$3,790,787	$4,355,261	$4,868,419
Discounted payback	—	—	—	—	—	5.63	—

The discounted payback is 5.63 years, rather than 4 years when the time value of future cash flows is ignored.

Although it is never optimal to ignore future payouts, payback may provide a simple screen for project risk since a quick payback means that the firm's investment is at risk for a shorter period of time. Along these lines, it is not uncommon for firms to adopt a screening standard for new projects that precludes consideration of projects with payback periods longer than some threshold, such as three years.

*Over 55% of the CFOs who responded to a study by John Graham and Campbell Harvey ("The Theory and Practice of Corporate Finance: Evidence from the Field," *Journal of Financial Economics* 60 [2001]) indicated that they either always or mostly always used payback when valuing new capital expenditure proposals.

Quick Review of the Mechanics of Time Value of Money Calculations

The majority of the projects that we analyze in this book are *long-lived,* in the sense that they provide cash flows over many years. Thus, an important step in the valuation of such projects involves collapsing these future cash flows down to their present value, so that we can compare that amount to the cost of making the investment. The present value of a future stream of cash flows is the equivalent sum in today's dollars to the set of future cash flows promised by the project.

To illustrate, consider a project that offers three years of future cash flows: C_1, C_2, and C_3. If we assume that the cash flows are risk free, then the appropriate discount rate for the three cash flows is the rate of interest corresponding to a one-, two-, and three-year risk-free security. These rates can be "inferred" from market prices of one-, two-, and three-year risk-free bonds as follows:

$$P_{1-\text{Year}} = \frac{\text{Face}_{\text{Year 1}}}{(1 + r_1)^1}, \quad P_{2-\text{Year}} = \frac{\text{Face}_{\text{Year 2}}}{(1 + r_2)^2}, \quad \text{and} \quad P_{3-\text{Year}} = \frac{\text{Face}_{\text{Year 3}}}{(1 + r_3)^3}$$

where P represents the current market values of the one-, two-, or three-year discount bond, r represents the current market rates of interest on the bonds, and Face is the maturity or face value of the bond that is paid to the holder at the end of each year. Note that the discount bonds pay no interest but simply return their full principal amount (Face) at maturity.

Using the risk-free rates for years one through three, we find the value of the three-year investment by the following formula:

$$PV = \frac{C_1}{(1 + r_1)^1} + \frac{C_2}{(1 + r_2)^2} + \frac{C_3}{(1 + r_3)^3} \tag{2A.1}$$

moves to capitalize on that advantage. If, for example, Lecion could delay initiation of the LCD fab for up to one year, the information gained about market acceptance for similar products and the rate of price decay may make the project even more valuable to Lecion. Consequently, the firm's analysts should not only consider alternative technologies to be mutually exclusive but also delayed execution of the investment. We return to a discussion of the option to delay or defer investing when we discuss real options in Chapter 11. But for now, it is critical that the analyst consider whether or not the firm indeed has a viable option to delay, and if so, what the firm might learn by deferring the initiation of the investment that would make the valuation more concrete.

The problems encountered when analyzing the possibility of delaying project initiation provide an opportunity to emphasize an important fact of life that analysts face daily.

Note that we have specified a different discount rate for each annual cash flow. To simplify matters and since we are dealing with estimates, it is customary to use the same discount rate, r, for all future periods. That is,

$$PV = \frac{C_1}{(1 + r)^1} + \frac{C_2}{(1 + r)^2} + \frac{C_3}{(1 + r)^3} = \sum_{t=1}^{3} \frac{C_t}{(1 + r)^t} \qquad (2A.2)$$

The single discount rate assumption is particularly convenient where we consider the problems associated with estimating the appropriate discount rate for risky projects. (We discuss the cost of capital for risky projects in Chapter 5.)

A popular variant of Equation 2A.2 describes the present value of a stream of cash flows that grow at a constant rate g such that $C_2 = C_1(1 + g)^1$ and $C_3 = C_1(1 + g)^2$. If g is less than r, then we can rewrite Equation 2A.2 as follows:

$$PV = \left(\frac{C_1}{r - g}\right)\left(1 - \frac{(1 + g)^2}{(1 + r)^3}\right) \qquad (2A.3)$$

If the number of periods in which cash flows are received gets very large, then Equation 2A.3 is approximated by:

$$PV = \left(\frac{C_1}{r - g}\right) \qquad (2A.4)$$

Equation 2A.4 is commonly referred to as the **Gordon growth formula** after Myron Gordon, whose name is generally associated with it.[20]

---

[20]The Gordon growth model is another well-known DCF relationship in finance and represents the sum of the following geometric progression:

$$\sum_{t=1}^{\infty} \frac{C_0(1 + g)^t}{(1 + r)^t} = C_0 \sum_{t=1}^{\infty} \frac{(1 + g)^t}{(1 + r)^t},$$

which can be reduced to

$$C_0\left(\frac{1 + g}{r - g}\right) \quad \text{or} \quad C_1\left(\frac{1}{r - g}\right),$$

where $r > g$, and C_1 is equal to $C_0(1 + g)$.

That is, no matter how sophisticated the tools that are brought to bear on the valuation problem, there is always a need to exercise judgment. The point of the analysis is to inform the analyst so that ultimately he or she can make a better decision.

2.5 SUMMARY

The value of an investment project is determined by the cash flows it produces. In this chapter we have discussed valuing investment opportunities using discounted cash flow (DCF) analysis incorporating the three-step process outlined below:

Steps	Project Valuation
Step 1: Forecast the amount and timing of future cash flows.	Forecast project free cash flow (PFCF).
Step 2: Estimate a risk-appropriate discount rate (covered in Chapters 4 and 5).	Combine the debt and equity discount rate (weighted average cost of capital, WACC).
Step 3: Discount the cash flows.	Discount PFCF using the WACC to estimate the value of the project as a whole.

The main focus of this chapter is on identifying and forecasting the *incremental* revenues and costs that are required to estimate expected cash flows. Although cash flow analysis is a key element in investment valuation, the process used to make forecasts is necessarily subjective and fraught with potential estimation errors. Consequently, cash flow forecasting is part art and part science. This does not mean that the analyst should simply throw caution to the wind and engage in crystal ball gazing, for good forecasting is grounded in sound economic analysis and rigorous attention to the details of proper cash flow definition.

A key learning point from this chapter is that forecasting is hard work and is subject to potentially very large errors. To minimize the effect of these forecast errors, good analysts follow a three-pronged approach: First, they take the forecasting problem very seriously and utilize all the information and technology they have at their disposal to arrive at their forecast. Second, as we discuss in Chapter 3, they do post-forecast risk analysis that helps them prepare for a wide range of possible outcomes. Finally, to the extent possible, they try to maintain flexibility in how the investment is implemented so that they can respond to unforeseen future events. We will have more to say about this latter point in Chapter 3 and again in Chapter 11.

PROBLEMS

2-1 CALCULATING PFCF   In the spring of 2007, Jemison Electric was considering an investment in a new distribution center. Jemison's CFO anticipates additional earnings before interest and taxes (EBIT) of $100,000 for the first year of operation of the center in 2008, and over the next 5 years the firm estimates this amount will grow at a rate of 5% per year. The distribution center will require an initial investment of $400,000 that will be depreciated over a five-year period toward a zero salvage value using straight-line depreciation of $80,000 per year. Furthermore, Jemison expects to invest an amount equal to the firm's annual depreciation expense to maintain the physical plant. These additional capital expenditures are also depreciated over a period of five years toward a zero salvage value. Jemison's CFO estimates that the distribution center will need additional net working capital equal to 20% of new EBIT (i.e., the change in EBIT from year to year).

Assuming the firm faces a 30% tax rate, calculate the project's annual project free cash flow (PFCF) for each of the next five years.

2-2 CALCULATING EFCF   Calculate EFCF for the next five years for the distribution center project found in Problem 2-1. Assume that the firm's interest expense for each of the next five years is based on a rate of 10% of the firm's debt that is outstanding at the end of the year. (That is, all borrowing and repayment are assumed to occur at the beginning of the year.) The firm's current borrowing total is $120,000. This debt requires principal payments of $15,000 per year over each of the next five years. Furthermore, the firm plans to borrow an additional $10,000 per year in order to make the required principal payments. The borrowing rate on new debt is 10% per year.

2-3 COMPREHENSIVE PFCF   TCM Petroleum is an integrated oil company headquartered in Fort Worth, Texas. Income statements for 2005 and 2006 are found below ($ millions):

	Dec. 06	Dec. 05
Sales	$13,368.00	$ 12,211.00
Cost of goods sold	(10,591.00)	(9,755.00)
Gross profit	2,777.00	2,456.00
Selling, general, & administrative expense	(698.00)	(704.00)
Operating income before depreciation	2,079.00	1,752.00
Depreciation, depletion, and amortization	(871.00)	(794.00)
Operating profit	1,208.00	958.00
Interest expense	(295.00)	(265.00)
Nonoperating income or expense	151.00	139.00
Special items		20.00
Pretax income	1,064.00	852.00
Total income before taxes	(425.60)	(340.80)
Net income	$ 638.40	$ 511.20

In 2005 TCM made capital expenditures of $875 million followed by $1,322 million in 2006. TCM also invested an additional $102 million in net working capital in 2005, followed by a decrease in its investment in net working capital of $430 million in 2006.

a. Calculate TCM's PFCF for 2005 and 2006. TCM's tax rate is 40%.

b. Estimate TCM's PFCF for 2007–2011 using the following assumptions: Operating income continues to grow at 10% per year over the next five years, CAPEX is expected to be $1,000 million per year, new investments in net working capital are expected to be $100 million per year, and depreciation expense equals the prior year total plus 10% of the prior year's CAPEX. Note that since TCM is a going concern we need not be concern about the liquidation value of the firm's assets at the end of 2011.

2-4 INTRODUCTORY PROJECT VALUATION   Steve's Sub Stop (Steve's) is considering investing in toaster ovens for each of its 120 stores located in the southwestern United States. The high-capacity conveyor toaster ovens, manufactured by Lincoln, will require an initial investment of $15,000 per store plus $1,500 in installation costs for a total investment of $1,860,000. The new capital (including the costs for installation) will be depreciated over five years using straight-line depreciation toward a zero salvage value. In addition, Steve's will also incur additional maintenance expenses totaling $120,000 per year to maintain the ovens. At present firm revenues for the 120 stores total $900,000,000 and the company estimates that adding the toaster feature will increase revenues by 10%.

a. If Steve's faces a 30% tax rate, what expected project free cash flows (PFCFs) for each of the next five years result from the investment in toaster ovens?

b. If Steve's uses a 9% discount rate to analyze its investments in its stores, what is the project's NPV? Should the project be accepted?

2-5 INTRODUCTORY PROJECT VALUATION   South Tel Communications is considering the purchase of a new software management system. The system is called B-Image, and it is expected to drastically reduce the amount of time that company technicians spend installing new software. South Tel's technicians currently spend 6000 hours a month on installations, which cost South Tel $25 per hour. The owners of the B-Image system claim that their software can reduce time on task by at least 25%. The system requires an initial investment of $55,000 and an additional investment of $10,000 for technician training on the new system. Annual upgrades will cost the firm $15,000 per year. Since the investment is comprised of software, it can be expensed fully in the year of the expenditure (i.e., no depreciation). South Tel faces a 30% tax rate and uses a 9% cost of capital to evaluate projects of this type.

a. Assuming that South Tel has sufficient taxable income from other projects so that it can expense the cost of the software immediately, what are the project free cash flows (PFCFs) for the project for years 0 through 5?

b. Calculate the NPV and IRR for the project.

2-6 INTRODUCTORY PROJECT VALUATION CT Computers is considering whether or not to begin offering customers the option to have their old personal computers recycled when they purchase a recycling system. The recycling system would require that CT invest $600,000 to purchase grinders and magnets to use in the recycling process. The company estimates that for each system it recycles, it would generate $1.50 in incremental revenues from the sale of scrap metal and plastics. The machinery has a five-year useful life and will be depreciated straight line toward a zero salvage value. CT believes that in Year 1 it will recycle 100,000 personal computers and that returns will grow by 25% each year over the next five years. The company uses a 15% discount rate to analyze its capital expenditures and faces a 30% tax rate.

a. What are the project free cash flows (PFCFs) for this project?
b. Using NPV and IRR, should CT invest in this project?
c. Judy Dunbar, the manager for the project, is worried that CT will only have returns of 75,000 units in Year 1. If she's right, and assuming a growth rate of 25%, should CT still consider investing in the project?

2-7 PROJECT VALUATION Glentech Manufacturing is considering the purchase of an automated parts handler for the assembly and test area of its Phoenix, Arizona, plant. The handler will cost $250,000 to purchase plus $10,000 for installation and employee training. If the company undertakes the investment, it will automate a part of the semiconductor test area and reduce operating costs by $70,000 per year for the next 10 years. However, five years into the investment's life, Glentech will have to spend an additional $100,000 to update and refurbish the handler. The investment in the handler will be depreciated using straight-line depreciation over 10 years, and the refurbishing costs will be depreciated over the remaining five-year life of the handler (also using straight-line depreciation). In 10 years the handler is expected to be worth $5,000, although its book value will be zero. Glentech's tax rate is 30%, and its opportunity cost of capital is 12%.

Exhibit P2-7.1 contains cash flow calculations for the project that can be used in performing a DCF evaluation of its contribution to firm value. Answer each of the following questions concerning the project:

a. Is this a good project for Glentech? Why or why not?
b. What can we tell about the project from the NPV profile found in Exhibit P2-7.1?
c. If the project were partially financed by borrowing, how would this affect the investment cash flows? How would borrowing a portion of the investment outlay affect the value of the investment to the firm?
d. The project calls for two investments: one immediately, and one at the end of Year 5. How much is Glentech earning on its investment, and how should we account for the additional investment outlay in our calculations?
e. What are the considerations that make this investment somewhat risky, and how would you investigate the potential risks of this investment?

Exhibit P2-7.1 Glentech Manufacturing Company Cash Flow Estimates

	0	1	2	3	4	5	6	7	8	9	10
Investment Outlays											
Equipment purchases	(250,000)										
Installation costs	(10,000)										
Initial outlay	(260,000)					(100,000)					
After-tax salvage value											3,500
Free Cash Flows											
Operating exp. savings		70,000	70,000	70,000	70,000	70,000	70,000	70,000	70,000	70,000	70,000
Less: Depreciation exp.		(26,000)	(26,000)	(26,000)	(26,000)	(26,000)	(26,000)	(26,000)	(26,000)	(46,000)	(46,000)
Added oper. income		44,000	44,000	44,000	44,000	44,000	44,000	24,000	24,000	24,000	24,000
Less: Taxes		(13,200)	(13,200)	(13,200)	(13,200)	(13,200)	(7,200)	(7,200)	(7,200)	(7,200)	(7,200)
NOPAT		30,800	30,800	30,800	30,800	30,800	16,800	16,800	16,800	16,800	16,800
Plus: Depreciation		26,000	26,000	26,000	26,000	26,000	46,000	46,000	46,000	46,000	46,000
Less: CAPEX	(260,000)	—	—	—	—	(100,000)	—	—	—	—	—
Free cash flow	(260,000)	56,800	56,800	56,800	56,800	(43,200)	62,800	62,800	62,800	62,800	66,300

NPV Profile

Net Present Value axis: 300,000; 250,000; 200,000; 150,000; 100,000; 50,000; —; (50,000); (100,000); (150,000); (200,000)

Discount Rates axis: 0%, 10%, 20%, 30%, 40%, 50%

2-8 PROJECT VALUATION   HMG is considering the manufacture of a new chemical compound that is used to make high-pressure plastic containers. An investment of $4 million in plant and equipment is required. The firm estimates the investment will have a five-year life, using straight-line depreciation toward a zero salvage value. However, the investment has an anticipated salvage value equal to 10% of its original cost.

The projected numbers of pounds of the chemical compound that HMG expects to sell over the five-year life of the project are as follows (in millions): 1, 1.5, 3, 3.5, and 2.

Exhibit P2-8.1   HMG Project Analysis

Givens:

Investment	4,000,000					
Plant life	5					
Salvage value	400,000					
Variable cost %	45%					
Fixed operating cost	1,000,000					
Tax rate	38%					
Working capital	10%	Change in revenues				
Required rate of return	15%					

	0	1	2	3	4	5
Sales volume		1,000,000	1,500,000	3,000,000	3,500,000	2,000,000
Unit price		2.00	2.00	2.50	2.50	2.50
Revenues		2,000,000	3,000,000	7,500,000	8,750,000	5,000,000
Variable operating costs		(900,000)	(1,350,000)	(3,375,000)	(3,937,500)	(2,250,000)
Fixed operating costs		(1,000,000)	(1,000,000)	(1,000,000)	(1,000,000)	(1,000,000)
Depreciation expense		(800,000)	(800,000)	(800,000)	(800,000)	(800,000)
Net operating income		(700,000)	(150,000)	2,325,000	3,012,500	950,000
Less: Taxes		266,000	57,000	(883,500)	(1,144,750)	(361,000)
NOPAT		(434,000)	(93,000)	1,441,500	1,867,750	589,000
Plus: Depreciation		800,000	800,000	800,000	800,000	800,000
Less: CAPEX	(4,000,000)	—	—	—	—	248,000
Less: Working capital	(200,000)	(100,000)	(450,000)	(125,000)	375,000	500,000
Free cash flow	(4,200,000)	266,000	257,000	2,116,500	3,042,750	2,137,000
Net present value	419,435					
Internal rate of return	18.01%					

To operate the new plant, HMG estimates that it will incur additional fixed cash operating expenses of $1 million per year and variable operating expenses equal to 45% of revenues. Furthermore, HMG estimates that it will need to invest 10% of the anticipated increase in revenues each year in net working capital. The price per pound for the new compound is expected to be $2 in years 1 and 2, then $2.50 per pound in years 3 through 5. HMG's tax rate is 38%, and it requires a 15% rate of return on its new product investments.

Exhibit P2-8.1 contains projected cash flows for the entire life of the proposed investment. Note that investment cash flow is derived from the additional revenues and costs associated with the proposed investment.

a. Does this project create shareholder value? How much? Should HMG undertake the investment?

b. What if the estimate of the variable costs were to rise to 55%? Would this affect your decision?

2-9 PROJECT VALUATION   Carson Electronics is currently considering whether or not to acquire a new materials handling machine for its manufacturing operations. The machine costs $760,000 and will be depreciated using straight-line depreciation toward a zero salvage value over the next five years. During the life of the machine no new capital expenditures or investments in working capital will be required. The new handler is expected to save Carson $250,000 per year before taxes of 30%. Carson's CFO recently analyzed the firm's opportunity cost of capital and estimated it to be 9%.

a. What are the annual project free cash flows for the project?

b. What are the project's net present value and internal rate of return? Is the project one that Carson should accept?

c. Carson's new head of manufacturing was concerned about whether the new handler could deliver the promised savings. In fact, he projected that the savings might be 20% lower than projected. What are the NPV and IRR for the project under this scenario?

CHAPTER 3

Project Risk Analysis

Chapter Overview

In this chapter we investigate the sources of *uncertainty* in forecasts of future cash flows. Although the presentation of project cash flows is based on accounting income statements, these are not historical statements. They are pro forma, or forecasted, statements and are thus highly uncertain. This chapter also describes the various approaches that are used to analyze risk and deal with uncertainty. Specifically, under the broad umbrella of sensitivity analysis, we consider scenario analysis, breakeven sensitivity analysis, and Monte Carlo simulation. Finally, we provide an initial discussion of the role investment flexibility can have on expected cash flows and the role that decision trees can play in organizing the analysis of decision flexibility. We pick up this discussion again in Chapters 11 and 12, where we consider real option analysis.

3.1 INTRODUCTION

The use of discounted cash flow (DCF) analysis to evaluate major, long-term investments is now accepted practice throughout the world. In its simplest form, analyzing capital expenditures using DCF involves estimating a single stream of expected cash flows, discounting them, and then making a decision based on a single estimate of the investment's NPV. In practice, however, investment decisions take place in a world of uncertain future outcomes, where there are more things that *can* happen than *will* happen, which makes investment analysis considerably more complex.

In this chapter we explicitly confront the challenge of uncertainty and focus on investment risk analysis. In particular, we will consider various techniques that financial analysts use to learn more about an investment's primary value drivers, and the risks that they generate.

To understand how uncertainty is accounted for in an investment analysis, we find it helpful to think about how financial analysts evaluate new investment opportunities in terms of two phases:

- In *Phase I* the analyst tries to envision the possible outcomes from an investment and to come up with an estimate of what he or she *thinks* or *expects* will happen. This analysis forms the basis for estimating an expected value for the investment along with NPV, IRR, and other measures of investment worth.
- In *Phase II* the analyst details the underlying sources of risk. This involves identifying the investment's value drivers and the uncertainty that characterizes each. Once these risks are identified, the analyst will seek ways to mitigate some of those risks while recognizing the firm's exposure to others and the need to monitor them carefully throughout the life of the project.

The challenge to the financial analyst in implementing DCF analysis, then, is twofold: First, the analyst must make all the forecasts and assumptions necessary to generate an estimate of the investment's NPV—as we illustrated in Chapter 2. Second, the analyst must perform an in-depth analysis of the assumptions used when estimating NPV to come to grips with what might happen to the project when (not if) things do not go as planned. In this chapter we describe a variety of tools that analysts can use to test and probe their estimates of the expected NPV of a proposed project. These tools include scenario analysis, breakeven sensitivity analysis, and Monte Carlo simulation.

The tools of investment analysis that we discuss in this chapter may give an impression of a high level of scientific precision. However, the underlying basis for using them is inherently subjective, as it relies on the judgment of the individual(s) performing the analysis. Realization of this fact is often disconcerting to "number-focused" financial analysts who look for answers in techniques and tools. So a key learning point of this chapter involves coming to grips with the inherently subjective nature of the investment evaluation process and the critical role that judgment and experience must play.[1]

3.2 UNCERTAINTY AND INVESTMENT ANALYSIS

Our discussion throughout this chapter focuses on **project valuation**—the evaluation of investments in projects that an individual or firm might consider. However, the tools and discussion apply equally well to **enterprise valuation**—the evaluation of acquisitions of entire firms, which we discuss in Chapters 6 and 7.

---

[1]We often advise our more "technique"oriented students that if there were no need for human judgment, there would be no need for financial analysts!

The Investment Process with Risky Cash Flows

The approach taken in Chapter 2 involved the use of a three-step valuation process:

1. Estimate the amount and timing of future cash flows for each year of the proposed investment's life.
2. Identify a risk-appropriate discount rate.
3. Calculate the present value of future cash flows. If the expected net present value (NPV) of the project's cash flows is positive after considering all the relevant cash inflows and outflows, then the firm should undertake the project.

While in theory, this approach provides the best estimate of the value created by the investment project, in practice the cash flow estimates are at best educated guesses and at worst out-and-out fiction. Hence, the initial DCF analysis should be viewed as only the first phase of the valuation process. This calculation is followed by Phase II, in which the analyst performs a form of "exploratory surgery" on the initial estimate. The object of this "follow-on" analysis is to explore the investment's value drivers—those factors that are most critical to the project's success. The analyst cannot eliminate uncertainty, but can better understand the relative sensitivity of the project's NPV to different key variables.

As an illustration, consider the following investment opportunity in an organic fertilizer product.

Example—The Earthilizer Proposal

CSM, Inc., is considering an investment in a project that requires an initial investment of $580,000 to produce and market a new organic fertilizer made from dairy farm waste. The product, Earthilizer, has been developed by CSM's agricultural division over the past three years in response to two factors: First, there is a growing demand from organic farmers and, second, dairy farmers face increasingly more restrictive environmental rules regarding the disposal of cattle manure. In combination, CSM's management feels that these forces of change present a very promising investment opportunity.

CSM has tested the product extensively as a liquid fertilizer replacement for the more expensive and conventional chemical fertilizers that farmers and ranchers have used since the Second World War. The product will be marketed in a concentrated form, with one gallon of Earthilizer producing about 100 gallons of usable fertilizer.

Not only is the product wholly organic, but it is also cheaper to use than chemical fertilizers. Traditional chemical fertilizers are made from petroleum and cost approximately $25 an acre for grass and hay production; Earthilizer utilizes dairy waste and costs less than $20 per application, with no more applications required over the growing season.

CSM's analysts estimate that an initial investment of $580,000 will put the Earthilizer project in place. This investment is comprised of $250,000 in working capital plus $330,000 in plant and equipment.

Estimating Earthilizer's Project Free Cash Flows (PFCFs)

If the project is approved, the agricultural division of CSM plans to begin construction on the new facilities immediately. The manufacture and distribution of Earthilizer will be "up and running" by the end of 2007, with the project's first year of revenues in 2008. Table 3-1 contains a set of financial projections for the project. These consist of pro forma income statements (Panel a), balance sheets (Panel b), and cash flows (Panel c) spanning the five years used by CSM to evaluate the investment. Of course, if the project is successful, it could operate for many years. However, it is standard practice among many firms to select an arbitrary investment life and analyze the investment as if it will be shut down at the end of that period.

CSM, Inc., is a very conservatively financed firm that finances all its investments out of internally generated cash flows (i.e., the firm does not borrow to obtain funds for new investments). Consequently, the project is all-equity-financed, as evidenced by the fact that there is no interest expense in the income statements (Panel a of Table 3-1), nor is there any debt financing in the pro forma balance sheets for the project (Panel b).

Panel c of Table 3-1 details management's estimates of project free cash flows. Note that CSM's management expects the project to be cash flow positive in 2008, which is the first year of operations, and every year thereafter.

The cash flow calculations for 2008 to 2012 are based on a number of key estimates and assumptions:

■ These estimates assume that the project will require an initial investment of $580,000 at the end of 2007, which includes $250,000 in net working capital and $330,000 in property, plant, and equipment.

■ Sales revenues are expected to be $1,000,000 in 2008 and are expected to grow at an annual rate of 10% throughout the five-year planning period (Panel a).

■ Cost of goods sold is equal to 67.40% of sales,[2] while operating expenses before depreciation are 10% of sales revenues plus a fixed component equal to $115,000 per year (Panel a).

■ The firm uses straight-line depreciation, where plant and equipment is assumed to have a 10-year life and a zero salvage value (Panels a and b).

■ A 30% tax rate is used in the analysis (Panel a).

■ For 2008 through 2012, the firm estimates that its net working capital requirements will equal 25% of Earthilizer's sales. CAPEX is assumed to be $330,000 in 2007 and zero in all future years[3] (Panel c).

---

[2]Note that this ratio implies a gross profit margin of 32.6% = 100% − 67.4%.

[3]Note that we are assuming that no new plant capacity is required over the five-year planning period. CSM simply spends $330,000 in 2007.

Table 3-1 CSM, Inc., Earthilizer Investment Project

Panel a. Pro Forma Income Statements ($000)

Income Statements	2008	2009	2010	2011	2012
Sales (10% growth per year)	$1,000.00	$1,100.00	$1,210.00	$1,331.00	$1,464.10
Cost of goods sold	(674.00)	(741.40)	(815.54)	(897.09)	(986.80)
Gross profit	326.00	358.60	394.46	433.91	477.30
Operating expenses before depreciation	(215.00)	(225.00)	(236.00)	(248.10)	(261.41)
Depreciation expense	(33.00)	(33.00)	(33.00)	(33.00)	(33.00)
Earnings before interest and taxes	78.00	100.60	125.46	152.81	182.89
Interest expense	—	—	—	—	—
Earnings before taxes	78.00	100.60	125.46	152.81	182.89
Taxes	(23.40)	(30.18)	(37.64)	(45.84)	(54.87)
Net income	$ 54.60	$ 70.42	$ 87.82	$ 106.96	$ 128.02

Panel b. Pro Forma Balance Sheets ($000)

Balance Sheets	2007	2008	2009	2010	2011	2012
Net working capital	$250.00	$250.00	$275.00	$302.50	$ 332.75	$ 366.03
Gross plant and equipment	330.00	330.00	330.00	330.00	330.00	330.00
Less: Accumulated depreciation	—	(33.00)	(66.00)	(99.00)	(132.00)	(165.00)
Net plant and equipment	$330.00	$297.00	$264.00	$231.00	$ 198.00	$ 165.00
Total	$580.00	$547.00	$539.00	$533.50	$ 530.75	$ 531.03

Panel c. Expected Project Free Cash Flows ($000)

	2007	2008	2009	2010	2011	2012
EBIT	$ —	$ 78.00	$ 100.60	$ 125.46	$ 152.81	$ 182.89
Less: Taxes	—	(23.40)	(30.18)	(37.64)	(45.84)	(54.87)
NOPAT	$ —	$ 54.60	$ 70.42	$ 87.82	$ 106.96	$ 128.02
Plus: Depreciation expense	—	33.00	33.00	33.00	33.00	33.00
Less: CAPEX	(330.00)	—	—	—	—	—
Less: Changes in net working capital	(250.00)	—	(25.00)	(27.50)	(30.25)	(33.28)
Plus: Liquidation of net working capital						366.03
Plus: Liquidation of PPE						165.00
Equals: Project free cash flow (PFCF)	$ (580.00)	$ 87.60	$ 78.42	$ 93.32	$ 109.71	$ 658.77

CSM assumes that it will terminate the project in 2012, at which time it produces a terminal cash flow of $692,050. This terminal cash flow is equal to the sum of NOPAT plus depreciation expense for 2012 (i.e., $128,020 + 33,000 = $161,020) plus the liquidating value (which is expected to equal the book value) of the firm's investment in net working capital (i.e., $366,030 in Panel b) and the book value of plant and equipment at the end of 2012 (i.e., $165,000 in Panel b).[4]

Of course, the project may not operate for the full five years, or it may operate for more years. Our analysis follows industry practice, which "assumes" a termination date for the project and estimates the cash flows that would be realized from either liquidating or selling the business. We will discuss the estimation of what is generally referred to as *terminal value* in more detail in Chapters 6 and 7. However, to simplify our analysis of the Earthilizer investment, we assume that the terminal value for the Earthilizer assets is equal to their liquidation value (i.e., working capital plus net property, plant and equipment, PP&E), which we assume to be equal to their book value.

Valuing Earthilizer's PFCFs

Our estimates of the expected project free cash flows (PFCFs) generated by the Earthilizer proposal are found in Panel c of Table 3-1. Now it is time to evaluate their present value. To do this, we discount the expected values of the PFCFs using a discount rate that reflects the operating risk characteristics of the project and the fact that the project is all-equity-financed. For now, we assume that the appropriate (risk-adjusted) discount rate for the unlevered PFCFs is 13.25%.[5] Using this rate to discount the PFCFs found in Panel c of Table 3-1, we estimate the present value of the *expected project free cash flows* to be $623,070:

$$\$623,070 = \frac{\$87,600}{(1 + .1325)^1} + \frac{\$78,420}{(1 + .1325)^2} + \frac{\$93,320}{(1 + .1325)^3}$$

$$+ \frac{\$109,710}{(1 + .1325)^4} + \frac{\$658,770}{(1 + .1325)^5}$$

The Decision to Invest (or Not)—NPV and IRR

If the proposed project is worth $623,070, should it be undertaken? The quick answer is yes. We have estimated a value for the project's future cash flows that exceeds the $580,000 initial cost associated with making the investment. In net present value (NPV) terms, the project offers an NPV equal to the difference in the expected value we have placed on it (its DCF value estimate equals $623,070) and the cost of making the investment ($580,000), or $43,070.

---

[4]We assume that when the project is shut down CSM will realize a cash flow equal to the book values of its investments in the project's net working capital and property, plant, and equipment. If the firm has better estimates of the values of these assets, then they (and the taxes on any gains or losses from those assets) should be used to estimate the terminal cash flow from the investment.

[5]We discuss the estimation of the discount rate in Chapters 4 and 5.

A second metric that managers use to evaluate an investment is the project's *rate of return*. In Chapter 2 we defined the *internal rate of return,* or *IRR,* as the discount rate that will result in a zero NPV for the investment. In the above example, we estimated the IRR to be 15.36%. Hence, if the required rate of return is 13.25%, the investment earns an excess rate of return of 2.11%, which, like the positive NPV calculated above, suggests that the investment should be accepted.[6]

It should be emphasized, however, that this analysis does not mean that we are *guaranteed* a net present value of $43,070 or that the return on the investment will be 15.36%. Since this is a risky project and things will not go exactly as planned, CSM needs to learn more about the project to get a better understanding of how confident we should be about the NPV estimate.

3.3 SENSITIVITY ANALYSIS—LEARNING MORE ABOUT THE PROJECT

Phase I of our analysis is now complete: We have an estimate of the NPV of the Earthilizer investment. But how confident can we be that the project will unfold as we expect? What are the key value drivers of the project that the firm should monitor over the life of the investment to ensure its success? We now enter Phase II, where we use a variety of tools to address these concerns. Specifically, we will discuss three such tools: scenario analysis, breakeven sensitivity analysis, and simulation analysis.

Scenario Analysis

Scenario analysis is a technique that helps analysts explore the sensitivity of an investment's value under different situations or scenarios that might arise in the future. Here we use the term *scenario* to refer to different sets of assumptions about the realized values of each of the value drivers.

For example, we might ask what would happen to the value of the Earthilizer project if the initial sales level were to drop to the marketing department's most pessimistic estimate of only $500,000. In this case the DCF value of the project drops to $342,790 and the project becomes a negative-NPV investment, since the investment requires an initial commitment of $580,000 (i.e., the project NPV drops to $342,790 − $580,000 = −$237,210). We could also analyze scenarios involving *multiple sets* of changes in assumptions and forecasts. For example, we might evaluate the project first using the most optimistic estimates for the value drivers and then the most pessimistic estimates. Although scenario analysis is very useful, there is no systematic

---

[6]We noted in Chapter 2 that the IRR is not always unique since there can be as many IRRs as there are changes in signs in the cash flows. For the Earthilizer project there is only one change in sign (i.e., the initial outlay is negative and all the remaining PFCFs are positive); thus, there is only one possible IRR.

B E H A V I O R A L   I N S I G H T

Scenario Analysis as a Strategic Planning Tool at Shell

Shell Oil (RDS) found that scenario analysis was a valuable exercise to help its executives avoid thinking that was constrained by what Warren Buffet refers to as "the institutional imperative." This is the tendency for firms to resist change even in the face of overwhelming evidence that pursuing the current strategy is misguided.

Scenario analysis can enable key executives to prepare a carefully crafted story about the future. The process of writing such a story provides an opportunity for executives to learn about what can happen to an investment, and in so doing, to prepare for the future accordingly. The idea is not so much that you become a better forecaster. Instead, the value of the process is that managers will make themselves aware of potential problems and opportunities, so they can be prepared to take advantage of them when and if they arise. The very act of identifying conditions under which the plug should be pulled on a project can make managers aware of when and why it should be done.

Sources: Shell.com, March 2004, and P. de Geus, "Planning Is Learning," *Harvard Business Review,* March-April 1988.

way to define the scenarios. The number of possible scenarios is limited only by the imagination of the analyst performing the analysis. One approach that is often used to systematize the sensitivity analysis is something called *breakeven sensitivity analysis.*

Breakeven Sensitivity Analysis

In **breakeven sensitivity analysis,** we ask the question: "What is the critical value of a particular value driver that pushes the NPV down to zero?" Although we could use the trial-and-error analysis of a spreadsheet model to determine the critical values that answer this question, it is much easier to use the Goal Seek function in Excel or Backsolver in Lotus 1-2-3.[7]

To illustrate, consider the analysis presented in Table 3-2. The first column of the table identifies six key variables that are important for determining the NPV of the Earthilizer investment opportunity. The second column contains the expected values for each of the value drivers that we used in our analysis of the project's expected NPV. The third column contains the critical or breakeven values for each of the value drivers that result in a zero NPV for the project. The final column of the table compares the expected and critical values for these variables; it calculates the "% Change" in

---

[7]Excel contains a tool called "Goal Seek" under the "Tools" menu that makes this type of analysis very easy to do once the cash flows and NPV have been modeled. See the Technical Insight box on page 78.

Table 3-2	Breakeven Analysis of the Assumptions and Forecasts Underlying the CSM, Inc., Earthilizer Project			
Variable—Forecast or Assumption **(1)**	**Expected** **Value** **(2)**	**Critical** **Value*** **(3)**	**% Change** **(4)**
Sales growth rate	10.00%	5.66%	−43.40%
Gross profit margin = Gross profit/Sales	**32.60%**	**31.12%**	**−4.54%**
Operating expenses (before depreciation)	**10.00%**	**11.48%**	**14.80%**
Tax rate	30.00%	40.14%	33.80%
Net working capital/Sales	25.00%	33.40%	33.60%
Base-year sales for 2008 ($000)	**$1,000,000**	**$923,171**	**−7.68%**

*Critical value for each variable is the value of that variable that would, holding all other variables equal to their expected value, result in a zero NPV. This critical value is more descriptively called the breakeven value since it produces a zero NPV.

each variable from its expected value required to produce a zero NPV. This analysis suggests that three variables are particularly critical to the outcome of the Earthilizer investment, in that very slight deviations from their expected value have a significant impact on project NPV:

- gross profit margin (% change for breakeven = −4.54%)[8]
- operating expenses as a percent of sales (% change for breakeven = +14.80%)
- base-year sales for 2008 (% change for breakeven = −7.68%).

For example, if the gross profit margin declines to 31.12%, which is only 4.54% below the expected value of 32.60%, the project's NPV will drop to zero. Similarly, if operating expense as a percent of sales rises to 11.48% from the expected level of 10%, or if the initial year's sales are only $923,171 rather than the projected $1 million, then the NPV will drop to zero.

Knowing that these three value drivers are critical to the Earthilizer investment's success allows CSM's management to explore additional information regarding the likely values of each. Moreover, if the firm undertakes the investment, management can monitor each of these value drivers very closely, so as to be ready to take corrective actions quickly if the drivers deteriorate.

---

[8]Gross profit margin is technically an indicator of success or failure that is driven by two important value drivers: cost of goods sold and the markup the firm is able to charge over its costs. So when we analyze the gross profit margin as a determinant of value, we are implicitly evaluating the combined effects of the cost of goods sold (cost leadership) and the price markup over cost (product differentiation).

T E C H N I C A L

I N S I G H T   **Using Microsoft Excel's
                                 "Goal Seek" Function**

Goal Seek is a function within Excel (found under the "Tools" tab) that provides a powerful tool for performing "what if"–type analysis. For example, when you know the desired result of a single-cell formula (e.g., NPV = 0) but do not know the input value the formula needs to determine this result (e.g., revenue growth rate over the project's life), you can use the Goal Seek feature to find the critical value of the input variable. In this example, Goal Seek iterates the value of the revenue growth rate until NPV is equal to zero.

The "Solver" tool in Excel is even more general than Goal Seek. Specifically, Solver allows us to solve maximization, minimization, or breakeven analysis problems in the presence of multiple constraints.

Figure 3-1 contains an NPV breakeven chart that illustrates the critical importance of gross profit margin to the success of the Earthilizer project. Our analysis assumes that the gross profit margin remains constant throughout the life of the project, and a gross profit margin of 31.12% in each year of the project's life produces a zero NPV. Note that even very modest changes in the gross profit margin can have

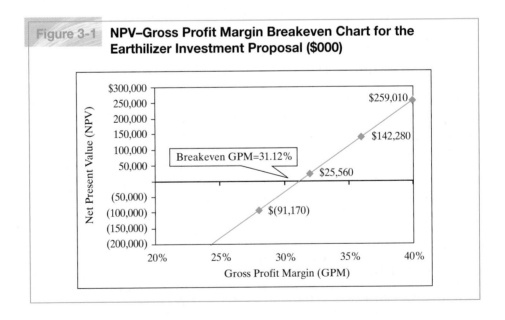

**Figure 3-1   NPV–Gross Profit Margin Breakeven Chart for the
Earthilizer Investment Proposal ($000)**

dramatic effects on the project's NPV. For example, if CSM, Inc. is successful in achieving a 36% gross profit margin (less than a 10.43% increase over the projected 32.6%), the estimated NPV for the project will more than triple in value to $142,280. Unfortunately, similar changes in NPV occur if gross profit margins *drop* below the anticipated level. The clear message to the analyst is that gross profit margin is one of the most critical success factors for the project.

Although breakeven sensitivity analysis can be very helpful in identifying value drivers that are critical to project success, it has its limitations. First, this type of analysis considers only *one* value driver at a time, while holding all others equal to their expected values. This can produce misleading results if two or more of the critical value drivers are correlated with one another. For example, if the gross profit margin and the initial sales level both tend to be lower (higher) than their respective expected values at the same time, then the breakeven sensitivity analysis will understate the true risks of the project.

Second, we don't have any idea about the probabilities associated with exceeding or dropping below the breakeven value drivers. For example, what is the probability that the gross profit margin will drop below 31.12%, or that the initial sales level for the first year of the project will be $923,171 or less? It would be very helpful to have some idea as to the likelihood of missing the key driver "targets."

Finally, we do not have a formal way of incorporating consideration for interrelationships among the variables. For example, gross profit margins and the operating expense to sales ratio are almost surely inversely related. It is important that we be able to consider this, and other interrelationships between the value drivers, in our analysis of the likely outcome from investing in the project.

To gain some insights into the distributions of possible valuation outcomes, we turn to simulation analysis, which offers analysts the ability to address all three of the above shortcomings of breakeven analysis.

Simulation Analysis

Monte Carlo simulation provides a powerful tool that can help the analyst evaluate what *can happen* to an investment's future cash flows and summarize the possibilities in a probability distribution.[9] Simulation is particularly helpful in project analysis since the outcomes from large investment projects are often the result of the interaction of a number of interrelated factors (or value drivers). This setting makes it very difficult to determine the probability distribution of a project's cash flows directly or analytically. However, we can simulate the distribution quite easily, as we illustrate in this section.

---

[9]The term "Monte Carlo" as a form of simulation comes from the famous gambling casinos in Monaco. Gambling, in its pure form, is of course based on the rules of chance or probability, as is simulation.

Using Scenario Analysis as a Prelude to Building a Simulation Model

Scenario analysis and simulation can be complementary tools since a scenario analysis can be an important prelude to the construction of a simulation model. Note that scenario analysis depends solely on the intuition of the decision maker; it helps the analyst think through the possible project outcomes and identify the key value drivers.

Preparing and Running a Simulation

Figure 3-2 outlines the simulation process in three steps. In Step 1 we prepare a spreadsheet model that defines the investment's cash flows. In Step 2 we characterize each of the value drivers using a probability distribution. For example, we might ask the marketing department to describe its optimistic, most likely, and pessimistic estimates for the annual sales growth rate. The response might be that the highest annual growth rate (optimistic estimate) for the Earthilizer investment is 30% per year, the

**Two Popular Probability
Distributions for Use in
Simulation Models: The Uniform and Triangular Distributions**

Among the set of distributions that can be used to model the uncertainty inherent in an investment, the uniform and triangular distributions are among the most popular. An important reason for this is that the variables that are needed to define the shape of both these distributions (known as their parameters) are very intuitive. Consequently, when the financial analyst is trying to elicit information about the proper distribution to use, he or she can ask straightforward questions of individuals who understand the underlying randomness of the variables that are being modeled.

A second reason for the popularity of these distributions relates to the fact that, although simple, they are very flexible and can be used to capture the essence of the randomness of lots of random variables. This is particularly true of the triangular distribution in that its form can be shaped and stretched (by adjusting the parameter values) to capture both symmetric and skewed distributions.

For example, in the uniform distribution, all values between the minimum and maximum are equally likely to occur. Consequently, the only things we need to know in order to completely define a uniform distribution (i.e., the parameters) are the minimum and maximum values that the random variable can take on. The mean of the uniform distribution is simply the sum of the maximum and minimum values divided by 2, since all values in the distribution have an equal probability of occurring. The upper figure on the following page depicts a uniform distribution for Sales with a minimum value of $90 and a maximum of $110.

lowest possible (pessimistic estimate) growth rate is −10%, and the most likely growth rate is +10%. This "intuitive" information fully describes a triangular probability distribution (see the Technical Insight box on two popular probability distributions for simulation).

To illustrate how this analysis might be carried out, in Table 3-3 we provide a set of hypothetical assumptions for the probability distributions used to describe the key value drivers in CSM's Earthilizer investment proposal. Specifically, there are eight value drivers that underlie the uncertainty in the investment outcome. These include (1) base-year sales, (2–5) annual rates of growth in revenues for 2009 through 2012 (four random growth rates), (6) the gross profit margin, (7) operating expenses (before depreciation expense) to sales, and (8) the 2012 terminal value, which is a multiple of the book value of the capital invested in the project. Everything else in the model is assumed to be fixed.

The triangular distribution, on the other hand, can be described by the minimum, maximum, and most likely values. The mean of the triangular distribution is equal to the sum of the minimum, most likely, and maximum values divided by 3. The lower figure depicts a triangular distribution for Sales where the minimum value is $90, the most likely value is $100, and the maximum value is $210.

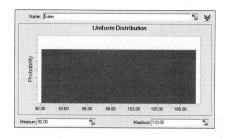

Note that the triangular distribution presented here is highly skewed towards larger values. However, the triangular distribution is very flexible and can be skewed in either direction and can also be symmetrical. For example, if you can imagine what would happen to the graph if you were able to grasp the peak of the triangle and stretch it to the right or left (within the minimum and maximum bounds of the distribution), you can envision the flexibility of the triangular distribution to reflect both skewed and symmetric probability distributions.

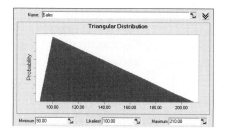

Figure 3-2   Steps in Running a Simulation Using the Earthilizer Example

Step 1: Prepare the spreadsheet model in Excel.

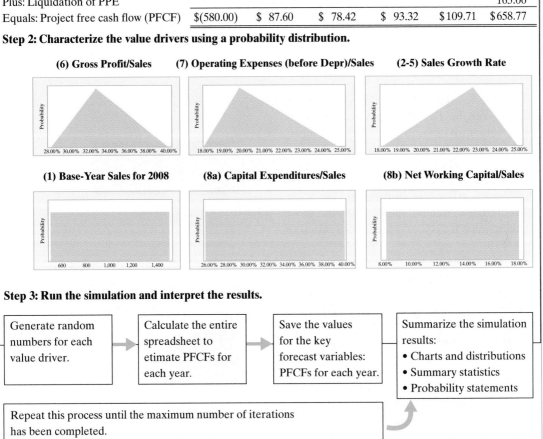

($000)	2007	2008	2009	2010	2011	2012
EBIT	$ —	$ 78.00	$ 100.60	$ 125.46	$ 152.81	$ 182.89
Less: Taxes	—	(23.40)	(30.18)	(37.64)	(45.84)	(54.87)
NOPAT	$ —	$ 54.60	$ 70.42	$ 87.82	$ 106.96	$ 128.02
Plus: Depreciation expense	—	33.00	33.00	33.00	33.00	33.00
Les: CAPEX	(330.00)	—	—	—	—	—
Less: Changes in net working capital	(250.00)	—	(25.00)	(27.50)	(30.25)	(33.28)
Plus: Liquidation of net working capital						366.03
Plus: Liquidation of PPE						165.00
Equals: Project free cash flow (PFCF)	$(580.00)	$ 87.60	$ 78.42	$ 93.32	$ 109.71	$ 658.77

Step 2: Characterize the value drivers using a probability distribution.

(6) Gross Profit/Sales

(7) Operating Expenses (before Depr)/Sales

(2-5) Sales Growth Rate

(1) Base-Year Sales for 2008

(8a) Capital Expenditures/Sales

(8b) Net Working Capital/Sales

Step 3: Run the simulation and interpret the results.

Generate random numbers for each value driver. → Calculate the entire spreadsheet to etimate PFCFs for each year. → Save the values for the key forecast variables: PFCFs for each year. → Summarize the simulation results:
• Charts and distributions
• Summary statistics
• Probability statements

Repeat this process until the maximum number of iterations has been completed.

Table 3-3	Monte Carlo Simulation Assumptions for the CSM, Inc., Earthilizer Investment		
		Distributional Assumption	
Variable	**Expected Value**	**Distribution**	**Parameter Estimates**
Base-year sales for 2008	$1,000,000	Uniform	Min = $500,000 and Max = $1,500,000
Sales growth rates (2009–2012)*	10.0%	Triangular	Max = 30%, Most likely = 10%, and Min = −10%
Gross profit margin = Gross profit/Sales	32.6%	Triangular	Max = 40%, Most likely = 32.6%, and Min = 28%
Operating expenses (before depr.)/Sales	10.0%	Triangular	Max = 15%, Most likely = 10%, and Min = 15%
Terminal value multiple of book value	1.00	Uniform	Min = .5 and Max = 1.5

*There are actually four growth rates, one for each year, beginning with 2009 and ending with 2012.

We have purposefully limited ourselves to the use of the *triangular* and *uniform* distributions. The parameters of both distributions are very intuitive, thereby facilitating their estimation (see the Technical Insight box on choosing a probability distribution). We use the triangular distribution to characterize the sales growth rate, gross profit margin, and operating expense to sales ratio. The parameters of the triangular distribution are the minimum, most likely, and maximum values for the underlying variable. We use the uniform distribution to characterize the base-year sales for 2008 and the terminal value multiple. The parameters of the uniform distribution are simply the minimum and maximum values.[10]

Simulating project revenues The annual cash flows of the Earthilizer investment are determined largely by the project's revenues, which we have modeled using two important drivers: the initial sales level for 2008 and the growth rates in revenue for 2009 through 2012. The initial sales level for 2008 has an expected value of $1 million. However, since sales revenues for the project are subject to a high level of uncertainty, we assume that the sales level follows a uniform distribution with a minimum value of $500,000 and a maximum value of $1.5 million. These estimates are just that,

---

[10]Note that the parameter estimates for both the triangular and uniform distributions are consistent with the expected value used in the deterministic analysis of the investment. You can verify this by calculating the expected value for the triangular distribution as the sum of the minimum, most likely, and maximum values divided by 3, and for the uniform distribution the mean is simply the sum of the minimum and maximum values divided by 2.

TECHNICAL

INSIGHT

Choosing a Probability Distribution

When building a simulation model it is necessary to not only identify the sources of randomness (uncertainty) that are the key value drivers in the model but also to identify an appropriate probability distribution to describe the randomness and estimate the parameters of that distribution. This is a daunting task, but there are some basic rules of thumb that can help the analyst:

■ *First, if you have relevant data, then by all means use it.* Although we will not utilize the *distribution fitting* capability of Crystal Ball in this book, the more advanced user will find this an excellent way to take advantage of historical data related to the distributions being estimated.

■ *Second, does the variable you are modeling only assume discrete values?* For example, if the variable you are estimating can only be zero or one (or yes or no), then a discrete distribution constructed using the custom category in Crystal Ball will work for you.

■ *Third, select distributions that fit the wisdom of the experts from whom you will elicit parameter estimates.* For example, if your experts can only tell you the maximum and minimum values of a variable you are estimating, then the uniform distribution may be a reasonable choice since it assigns the same probability to each value between a minimum and a maximum value. Alternatively, if your expert is willing to estimate a minimum and maximum as well as a most likely value, then the triangular distribution will be a good candidate for you. In this distribution the probability associated with all values below the minimum or above the maximum value is zero, and the probabilities in between the maximum and minimum increase in a linear fashion from either extreme up to the most likely value (thereby forming a triangle).

■ *Fourth, if there are theoretical reasons for selecting a particular distribution then certainly do so.* For example, it is common practice to use a lognormal distribution to characterize market prices for financial securities.

■ *Finally, the KISS principle (Keep It Simple, Stupid) is always appropriate.* Remember that the analyst must elicit information from experts regarding the nature of the distribution to select and for parameter estimates. Since this may often require having discussions with individuals not well versed in the language of probability and probability distributions, it is probably best to err on the side of oversimplification rather than precision and sophistication.

estimates, and in most cases would come from the intuition and experience of the firm's marketing staff.

The sales level for 2009 is estimated using the simulated 2008 revenue number multiplied by one plus the rate of growth in revenues for 2009. We assumed that the rate of growth in revenues for 2009 comes from a triangular distribution with a minimum value of -10%, a most likely value of 10%, and a maximum value of $+30\%$. The dispersion in the minimum and maximum growth rates reflects the degree of uncertainty the analyst has about sales growth. Revenues for 2010–2012 are estimated in a similar fashion.

Forecasting project cash flows Once we have forecasts of annual revenues, we calculate project cash flows by constructing a set of pro forma financial statements such as those presented earlier in Table 3-1. Note that the gross profit margin and operating expense to sales ratios are random variables (described in Table 3-3) that are determined in each of the iterations of the simulation. Based on the estimated revenues, the gross profit margin, and the operating expenses we can calculate the project's pro forma income statement (found in Panel a of Table 3-1).

To complete our estimate of project free cash flow, we must estimate any new investment that might be needed for capital equipment (i.e., CAPEX) and net working capital. CSM's management estimates that after the initial capital expenditure of $330,000, the project will not require any more CAPEX over the period 2008–2012. However, as firm revenues change over time, they estimate that the project's need for net working capital will also rise and fall. Specifically, CSM estimates that the project requires net working capital equal to 25% of firm sales revenues. To accommodate this required investment, we include 25% of the revenues for 2008 as part of the initial investment outlay for 2007. In 2008 we adjust net working capital to equal 25% of realized (simulated) sales. Similarly, in 2009–2012 we set the project's net working capital requirement equal to 25% of simulated sales for the year.[11]

Project free cash flows are then calculated following the method found in Panel c of Table 3-1. Specifically, for 2008 through 2011, we add depreciation expense back to net operating profit after taxes (NOPAT) and subtract the added investment in net working capital. Recall that CAPEX is assumed to be zero. The 2012 cash flow calculation involves one additional step—adding back the estimated terminal value of the Earthilizer project's assets.

---

[11]We set the 2007 investment in net working capital equal to 25% of expected sales for 2008. In 2008 we simply adjust net working capital to reflect 25% of actual revenues. A more involved procedure would also accommodate an estimate of expected needs for net working capital for 2009. However, we have opted for simplicity in the model presented here and make the adjustments to net working capital at the end of the year when we know what annual sales for the period turned out to be. The effects of accommodating expected working capital needs have very little impact on the model outcome in this example.

T E C H N I C A L

I N S I G H T

**Simulation "Add-ins"
for Excel**

There are two principal competing tools for adding easy-to-use simulation capabilities to your spreadsheet program. These include **@Risk** from the Palisade Corporation (http://www.palisade.com/) and **Crystal Ball Professional Edition** from Decisioneering, Inc. (http://www.crystalball.com/). Both software packages offer similar capabilities; we have selected Crystal Ball for all our illustrations. If you are not familiar with Crystal Ball, you will find the short video presentation found on Decisioneering's website very helpful in getting started.

Liquidating the investment and the terminal value The cash flow in 2012 includes both an operating component (just like 2008–2011) plus a terminal value component. The latter deserves a bit of added explanation. We assume that in 2012 when the project is shut down, its accumulated working capital (current assets less current liabilities) plus the property, plant, and equipment can be sold for a multiple of their book value. This multiple is assumed to be a random variable that has a uniform distribution with a minimum value of .5 and a maximum value of 1.5 (this implies an expected value of 1.0). Note that if the terminal value multiple is equal to 1, then there is no taxable gain or loss realized on the sale of the assets. However, in the event that the multiple is greater than 1, then the sale creates a taxable gain that is taxed at the firm's 30% tax rate. Should the assets be sold for a multiple less than 1, the resulting loss offsets taxable income in 2012 and results in a tax credit to CSM.

Simulation software The simulation analysis is carried out for the Earthilizer example using a spreadsheet "add-in" program known as **Crystal Ball Professional Edition.** (See the Technical Insight box on simulation "add-ins" for Excel.) There are a number of other options available, including @Risk as well as proprietary simulation software written for use in specialized applications of a given firm. A brief Appendix is found at the end of the chapter which summarizes the use of Crystal Ball Professional Edition for the beginner.

Interpreting Simulation Results

The simulation uses 10,000 iterations to produce estimates of the distributions of PFCFs for 2008–2012. To illustrate the nature of the simulation results, consider

Panel a of Figure 3-3, which contains the distribution of simulated PFCFs for 2008, as generated by Crystal Ball. The frequency distribution reflects 10,000 PFCF values characterized both in terms of the frequency with which they occurred (measured on the right-side vertical axis) and the corresponding probability of occurrence (measured on the left-side vertical axis).

The simulated distribution of PFCFs for 2008 (found in Panel a of Figure 3-3) provides some interesting insights into the prospects of the investment. First, there is substantial dispersion in the simulated cash flows for 2008, ranging from a minimum of ($29,140) up to a maximum of $161,760 with a mean value of $87,680. The "Certainty" cell found at the bottom of the graph indicates that 99.47% of the total area under the frequency distribution of PFCFs lies above $0.00 (i.e., the simulated PFCFs were positive 99.47% of the time). Although we do not display them here, the PFCF distributions for the remaining years of the project exhibit similar characteristics to those described above for 2008.

From the simulated cash flows in each year we calculate the mean or average cash flow for each year from 2007 to 2012. These expected cash flows are found below ($000):

	2007	2008	2009	2010	2011	2012
Expected PFCF (from the simulation)	$ (580,000)	87,680	78,150	93,460	109,740	660,970
Expected value of the project	$624,218.13					
Expected NPV	$ 44,218.13					
Expected IRR	15.42%					

Discounting the expected cash flows at the 13.25% cost of capital produces a $624,218.13 present value, and subtracting the $580,000 initial cost of the project in 2007 produces an expected NPV of $44,218.13. Finally, based on the future PFCFs and initial investment, we calculate an expected IRR of 15.42%. Note that the expected values of the NPV and IRRs calculated using the simulation differs slightly from our earlier estimates of NPV equal to $43,070 and IRR equal to 15.36%. These differences reflect the fact that the simulated values converge to, but will not necessarily equal, their expected values.

To this point we have simply replicated our analysis of project valuation by simulating the distributions of cash flows that underlie the expected values reported earlier in Table 3-1. But this is just the beginning of our analysis. Let's now look to see what we can learn about the project by analyzing the simulated distributions of NPV and IRR.

Analyzing the Distributions of NPV and IRR

By simulating the distributions of NPV and IRR, we can calculate the probability that the investment will indeed realize an IRR that exceeds any given hurdle, like the firm's cost of capital or the risk-free rate. To estimate these values we treat the

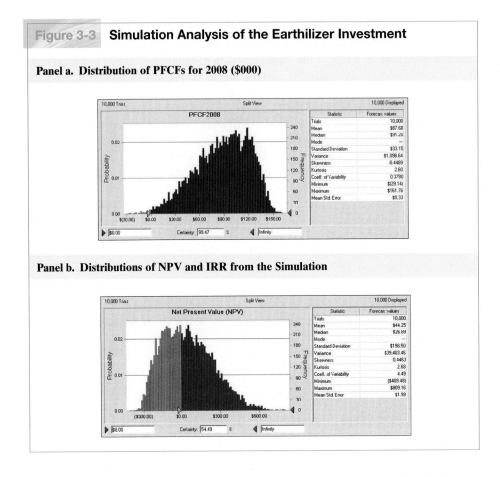

Figure 3-3   **Simulation Analysis of the Earthilizer Investment**

Panel a. Distribution of PFCFs for 2008 ($000)

Panel b. Distributions of NPV and IRR from the Simulation

yearly cash flows from 2008 to 2012 from each of the iterations in the simulation as a possible realization of project free cash flows, and calculate the realized IRR and NPV, given these cash flows.[12] Hence, if we do this simulation 10,000 times, we will have a distribution of 10,000 realized NPVs and IRRs.[13]

---

[12]The NPV and IRR for each of the iterations are part of the same simulation experiment that created the distributions of PFCFs. We simply calculate a value for the NPV and IRR for each simulated set of PFCFs.

[13]We need to be a bit careful here in the way that we interpret the distributions of NPV and IRR. The reason is that the mean of the distribution of NPV and IRR that we simulate and report in Panel b of Figure 3-3 is *not* equal to the NPV of the expected cash flows. The divergence in these numbers comes from something called Jensen's inequality. The issue of Jensen's inequality applies to nonlinear functions of random variables. Therefore, if the uncertainties arise in multiplicative form (for instance, Sales (t) is Sales $(t-1)(1+g)$, where both Sales $(t-1)$ and growth are random variables—as in the case of the Earthilizer problem), Jensen's inequality will matter. Now PFCF and NPV will be nonlinear functions of underlying random variables. The key thing to remember is that we have already estimated the expected NPV and IRR from the simulated distributions of cash flows for the project. From this point forward we are simply investigating the underlying determinants of NPV and IRR (not their expected values).

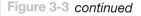

Figure 3-3 *continued*

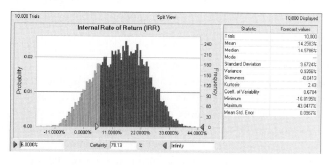

Legend:

 # Trials—the number of iterations in the simulation.

 # Displayed—the number of iterations actually reflected in the frequency distribution. In the above analysis, all 10,000 iterations are included. However, the default in Crystal Ball is to omit outliers such that the number of observations displayed is often less than the number of trials.

Split View—combines the frequency distribution with descriptive statistics. In addition to this view, a number of options are available, including cumulative frequency plots.

Probability—left-side vertical axis describes the simulated values in terms of their appearance as a fraction of the 10,000 iterations.

Frequency—right-hand vertical axis describes the simulated values in terms of the number of occurrences.

Certainty—displays the % of the area either above or below the critical value selected. In Panel a, the critical value is a PFCF of $0.00 and in Panel b, it is an NPV of 0 and an IRR equal to the risk-free rate of 6%.

Panel b of Figure 3-3 presents the distributions of NPV and IRR generated from such a simulation. From these simulated values we see that there is a 54.49% chance that the investment will generate cash flows that are sufficient to make the investment a positive-NPV investment at the firm's cost of capital (see the "Certainty" box at the bottom of the frequency distribution found in Panel b of Figure 3-3).[14] However, this also implies that there is a 45.51% chance that the realized NPV of the project will be negative. It is also the case that there is a 78.13% probability of realizing an IRR that exceeds the risk-free rate of 6%.[15] This indicates that the investment does have some risk, because there is a nontrivial probability that this risky investment will return less than the return on a perfectly safe investment like Treasury bonds.

---

[14] An observant reader will notice that the average IRR in this simulation is not equal to the IRR of the investment calculated using expected cash flows. The reason for this is the same as discussed in the previous footnote.

[15] We deliberately selected the risk-free rate as the "bar" over which we are asking the project to leap since this analysis is designed to explore risk, not value the project. We did the latter when we calculated the expected NPV and expected IRR using the expected PFCFs from the simulation.

What we have learned in the simulation does not provide a clear go–no go choice for CSM with regard to the Earthilizer project. However, we can further explore the sensitivity of the project NPV to each of the random variables in the model using a tool known as a tornado diagram.

Using the Tornado Diagram to Perform Sensitivity Analysis

Earlier, we used breakeven sensitivity analysis to analyze the importance of the value drivers in a simple setting, where we analyzed possible changes in the value drivers one at a time. We now introduce a more powerful tool that combines scenario analysis and simulation to provide a systematic way to analyze how changes in each of the investment's value drivers impact the project NPV. Specifically, we can evaluate the sensitivity of the project valuation to variation in each of the value drivers using the **tornado diagram** found in Figure 3-4. The chart places the assumptions that have the greatest impact on project NPV at the top of the diagram and successively smaller ones down the figure, creating a funnel-shaped diagram, thus the name *tornado diagram.* (See the Technical Insight box on tornado diagrams [p. 92].)[16]

Here is how you interpret the numbers reflected in the tornado diagram. First, not surprisingly, the initial or base-year level of sales for 2008 has the greatest impact on the NPV of the Earthilizer investment. For example, if the 2008 sales level is set equal to its 90th percentile value of $600,000 (the expected value is $1 million), NPV falls to ($181,160). However, if the 2008 sales level is equal to its 10th percentile value, which is $1.4 million, the NPV rises to $267,290. Clearly, the value of the investment is closely tied to the initial customer response to the product, which is critical to its overall success.

Behind the initial sales level in 2008, the next most important variable that drives the success or failure of the Earthilizer investment is the operating expense to sales ratio, followed by the gross profit margin, and the terminal value multiple of the book value of invested assets. These results suggest the following responses:

■ First, to the extent that the viability of the investment is still in question, the analyst might invest additional time and money into learning more about these critical value drivers—specifically, the initial market response that drives 2008 sales. Might CSM take actions to learn more about the potential success of market entry (e.g., hold focus groups with potential customers or engage in pilot programs)? Are there things that CSM might do to ensure that initial sales (market penetration) are maximized? For example, promoting market awareness through an initial advertising campaign may be an effective tool for improving the chances of success of the project.

■ Second, since operating costs are a critical value driver, management should pay particular attention to putting in place processes that can be used to monitor and improve operating efficiency.

---

[16]The tornado diagram provides a "one-at-a-time" form of sensitivity analysis. Crystal Ball also provides a sensitivity analysis tool that uses the simulated values to analyze the rank correction between forecast variables and each of the assumptions.

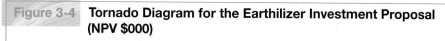

Figure 3-4 **Tornado Diagram for the Earthilizer Investment Proposal (NPV $000)**

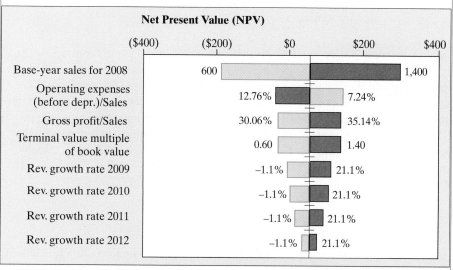

	Net Present Value (NPV)			Input		
Variable	*Downside*	*Upside*	*Range*	*Downside*	*Upside*	*Base Case*
Base-year sales for 2008	($181.16)	$267.29	$448.44	600	1,400	1,000
Operating expenses (before depr.)/Sales	$123.72	($37.59)	$161.31	12.76%	7.24%	10.00%
Gross profit/Sales	($31.14)	$117.27	$148.41	30.06%	35.14%	32.60%
Terminal value multiple of book value	($29.60)	$115.74	$145.34	0.60	1.40	1.00
Rev. growth rate 2009	($1.83)	$87.96	$89.79	−1.1%	21.1%	10.0%
Rev. growth rate 2010	$9.29	$76.85	$67.56	−1.1%	21.1%	10.0%
Rev. growth rate 2011	$20.08	$66.05	$45.97	−1.1%	21.1%	10.0%
Rev. growth rate 2012	$30.57	$55.56	$24.99	−1.1%	21.1%	10.0%

Legend:

Tornado chart—measures the input of each variable one at a time, independently, on the target forecast (NPV in this example).

Range bars—illustrate the impact of each of the input variables (Gross profit/Sales, and so forth) on NPV when the input variables are set equal to their 10th and 90th percentile values. For example, if the Gross profit/Sales ratio drops to its 10th percentile value of 30.06%, then NPV is equal to ($31,140). Alternatively, if the Gross profit/Sales ratio is equal to its 90th percentile value of 35.14%, then NPV rises to $148,410. The color of the bar indicates whether the change in the input is positive or negative. For example, an increase in the Gross profit/Sales ratio produces a positive effect on NPV, whereas an increase in the Operating expenses (before depr.)/Sales ratio results in a decline in NPV. The order of the input variables in the chart ranks them from the greatest to the least impact on NPV.

Tornado Diagrams

The **tornado diagram** can be used to evaluate each assumption's relationship to the forecast variables. In Figure 3-4 the assumptions are set equal to, say, their 10th and 90th percentile values and these extreme values are used to calculate the forecast variable of interest (e.g., project NPV or IRR). Note that the value of the forecast variable is read along the horizontal axis at the top of the diagram, and the 10th and 90th percentile values of the assumption are printed at the end of the bar that identifies their impact on the forecast variable. The assumptions that have the greatest impact on the forecast variable are placed at the top of the diagram, followed by the assumptions that have the next largest impact.

Summing Up the Simulation Results

So what have we learned from the simulation analysis about the Earthilizer investment? First and foremost, the project is likely to be a wealth-enhancing venture (i.e., it has a positive expected NPV). However, the outcome is far from certain. In fact, based on our analysis it appears that there is a 78.13% chance that the project will return more than the 6% rate of return on risk-free Treasury bonds (a 21.87% chance that it will earn less). In addition, we learned that the key value drivers are the initial sales level for 2008, the operating expenses to sales ratio, the terminal valuation multiple for the working capital and fixed assets that are sold at the end of the project's life, and the gross profit margin. Consequently, a key determinant of the success or failure of the investment will be the ability of the firm's management to market the product aggressively from the outset and contain the manufacturing costs underlying cost of goods sold and the operating costs associated with running the business.

Ultimately, however, the decision to undertake the investment is a matter of judgment, and it will depend on the availability of other projects, the amount of capital at risk, and the individuals involved. Simulation analysis is simply another tool for adding information about the nature of the uncertainty underlying the project and its prospects for success. It should be viewed as a decision tool, not a decision maker that provides clean yes/no criteria. This information emphasizes, once again, the importance of learning as much as we can about the critical value drivers for the project.

Reflections on the Use of Simulation

Building a simulation model requires the analyst to think deeply about the underlying sources of uncertainty that affect an investment's profits and forces him or her to be very explicit about assumptions, which might otherwise be implicit. Consequently,

PRACTITIONER
INSIGHT

Sensitivity Analysis at ConocoPhillips:
A Conversation with Steven McColl*

Sensitivity analysis has been a long-established technique in the oil and gas industry when analyzing multi-million-dollar investments. The construction of simulation models to evaluate investments includes the formation of multidisciplinary teams of engineers, commercial specialists, and finance experts to identify and quantify the risks and uncertainties present in each investment.

ConocoPhillips, like many in its peer group, has developed a process for the evaluation of risks and uncertainties to ensure the validity of the numbers entering the financial models. The overall evaluation process includes:

- Establishing a group of experts to understand the problem framework
- Developing technical and financial models to analyze risk and uncertainties
- Providing insight and understanding from those models to management in order to maximize profit and mitigate risks

Investment analysts at ConocoPhillips use simulation to calculate expected cash flows by incorporating uncertainty ranges for oil and gas prices, capital expenditures, operating costs, the amount of reserves, production rates, and tax regimes. The outputs from these models are expressed as Expected Monetary Value (EMV), IRR, Profitability Index, Period to Payback, and a number of other company- and industry-specific measures that describe the risk and reward from the project.

*Strategic transactions coordinator, ConocoPhillips, Houston, Texas.

there are benefits to simulation analysis that arise from the process itself as well as from the actual output of the simulation.

For example, an analyst could forecast the cash flows generated by the Earthilizer investment without the benefit of a simulation model. These estimates would rely upon estimates of the expected values of each of the value drivers (i.e., sales growth rates, gross profit margins, operating expense ratios, and so forth). However, without the need to model the distributions of the value drivers, the analyst might simply rely upon the "best guess" for their expected values. Such "from your gut" forecasting may work reasonably well for very simple investments, but it is problematic for more complex cases where there are multiple sources of uncertainty that interact with one another to determine the distribution of project cash flows.

It is sometimes argued that the difficulty encountered in making these distributional assumptions is reason enough not to do them. However, the fact is that the analyst who fails to address the underlying complexities of an investment's cash flows explicitly is simply making the assumptions implicit in the analysis. As a general rule, we think that it is better to be as explicit as possible when evaluating major investments.

Extensions of the Earthilizer Model

There are virtually limitless possibilities for refining and modifying the simulation model we used to analyze the Earthilizer investment proposal. An important opportunity for improving our model relates to incorporating consideration for dependence in the sources of randomness that drive the project cash flows. Specifically, there are two forms of dependence that are important in modeling project cash flows. The first relates to dependence that evidences itself over time. For example, if project revenues in 2008 are higher than expected, this may suggest that the project will grow more rapidly than if the initial year's revenue is lower than expected.

The second form of dependence relates to the possibility that within any given year some of the expenses may vary together. For example, cost of goods sold (which are captured in the gross profit margin) and operating expenses as a percent of firm sales may move together. This would be the case if the factors that impinge on the firm's ability to operate efficiently and at relatively low cost (labor cost, and so forth) are also linked to the factors that drive the firm's costs of goods sold.

If dependencies of the types described above are important, then the simulation can be modeled in such a way as to capture them. Although we will not dig deeper into the techniques that might be used, suffice it to say that the analyst can either model the dependence directly by linking the values of one value driver to another or by incorporating correlations into the process using Crystal Ball.

The final modeling extension we mention relates to the notion of **mean reversion** in year-to-year revenue growth rates. By this we refer to the fact that it is quite common for growth rates in revenues and earnings to demonstrate the following behavior. If the growth rate in revenues for 2009 is above the expected rate of growth for that year, the rate of growth in revenues for 2010 is likely to be lower than expected. This particular pattern of growth rates can be induced into the simulation model by incorporating negative correlations between the adjacent year's rates of growth in revenue.

Using Simulations to Estimate an Investment's Contribution to Firm and Market Risk

Simulation provides a powerful tool for learning about the value creation potential of a proposed investment. Specifically, it provides a method for incorporating multiple and interacting sources of uncertainty into the analysis of the distribution of an investment's cash flows simultaneously. Consequently, we can use simulation to solve what would otherwise be very complex estimation problems. We should note, however, that in our example, as well as in most industry applications, project risks are considered in isolation.

To get a more complete picture of an investment's risk, one should do simulations that examine how the risk of the project contributes to the overall risk of the firm, and perhaps also the aggregate economy.[17] For example, one might consider the realization of the firm's overall cash flows in the different scenarios and then use simulations to determine the covariance between the proposed investment cash flows and the overall firm cash flows. An investment with a lower covariance would be deemed less risky, because it helps diversify the firm.

3.4 DECISION TREES—VALUING PROJECT FLEXIBILITY

Up to this point we have assumed that the firm has a set way to implement the investment project and will not deviate from this plan. While this greatly simplifies the analysis, in reality, most investment projects offer the firm some flexibility as to the inputs used or even the final products produced. For example, rather than proceeding with a fixed production schedule, firms tend to expand capacity and thus generate greater cash flows when market demand is higher, and similarly, may cut back on capacity when market demand is lower.

The astute student of finance will recognize that we are talking about *options* associated with investments. We will study these *real options* in Chapter 11, where we will analyze their values in much more depth. For now, we will introduce the topic so that readers can recognize how flexibility in the implementation of an investment affects the expected cash flows that are used in a DCF analysis.

A decision tree is a very useful tool that illustrates the degree of flexibility in a project's implementation, and how future decisions can affect values. For example, the decision tree found in Figure 3-5 describes the consequences of a decision to introduce a new product next year versus now. If the firm delays the product introduction, there is the possibility that a competitor may enter, whereas offering the product immediately reduces the likelihood of competition but also reduces the chances of a successful launch.

Note that the decision tree contains a number of nodes identified by vertical lines, circles, and boxes. The vertical lines denote a terminal node that signals the end of the decision process. The circles signify an event node that represents a point where nature intervenes and something happens that is subject to chance. In this decision tree there are only two possible outcomes (High Demand and Low Demand). Finally, the square at the origin of the decision tree depicts a decision node that represents a point where the decision maker determines what happens. For example, will the new product be introduced immediately or delayed for one year?

Although we do not include additional decision nodes, it is conceivable that there might be many opportunities to make decisions over the life of the investment.

---

[17]By examining how the project cash flows correlate with the aggregate economy, we can indirectly gauge the systematic risk of the project, which is a determinant of its required rate of return. We discuss the relation between systematic risk and required rates of return in Chapter 4.

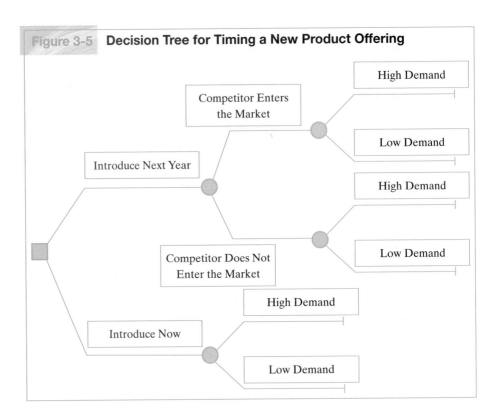

Figure 3-5   Decision Tree for Timing a New Product Offering

For example, if the product is introduced now and the firm faces low demand, it might then face the decision to continue marketing the product or to abandon the investment altogether.

Example—Decision Tree Analysis of the Abandonment Option

To illustrate how we can use decision trees to incorporate flexibility considerations into the analysis of investment projects, consider the following "modification" of the Earthilizer example. Assume that CSM, Inc., faces an EPA test of the runoff effects of Earthilizer on groundwater. If, at the end of one year, the EPA determines that the project poses no hazard, it will give Earthilizer its approval for continued sale in its current form. There will be no effect on project expected cash flows.

If, on the other hand, the EPA finds that Earthilizer has a detrimental effect on groundwater, then further processing will be required that will cost CSM an estimated $80,000 per year in processing costs (after taxes). Based on its own studies, CSM's management "guesstimates" that there is a 20% chance that the EPA will force the company to spend the additional funds.

Evaluating the Revised Earthilizer Project without the Abandonment Option

Let's evaluate the project cash flows and corresponding NPV for the Earthilizer investment, revised to take into account the EPA test. To illustrate the importance of the option to abandon after one year if the EPA ruling goes against the firm, we will first evaluate the revised cash flows assuming the firm continues to operate even if it incurs the EPA costs.

In this case, the expected cash flows are equal to a weighted average of the original cash flows from panel c of Table 3-1 and the revised cash flows. The latter amount is simply the original expected cash flows less the $80,000 in additional processing costs. The weights we apply to the two cash flows equal the probability that the EPA ruling will be favorable and the probability that it will go against the firm (i.e., 1 minus the probability of a favorable outcome). Consequently, for 2008 the revised estimate of the expected PFCF is calculated as follows:

$$\text{Revised PFCF}_{2008} = .8 \times \$87,600 + (1 - .8)(\$87,600 - 80,000) = \$71,600$$

Panel a of Table 3-4 presents the complete set of revised PFCFs for each year. The expected NPV for the Earthilizer project using these revised cash flows is a negative ($12,872). In other words, the risk of having to incur $80,000 in added costs makes the NPV of the project negative. This suggests that the project should not be undertaken at all. Note, however, that we are assuming that the project will be continued for the complete five-year planning period, regardless of what the EPA ruling turns out to be. Let's see the effect of the option to abandon.

The Value of the Abandonment Option

Panel a of Figure 3-6 describes the situation faced by Earthilizer: The firm has the option to abandon after one year should an unfavorable EPA ruling require that the firm spend an additional $80,000 per year (after taxes). If CSM decides to shut down its Earthilizer operations, it anticipates that it can recoup $380,000 of its $580,000 initial investment, plus the first year's expected project free cash flow of $87,600. The character of the investment in Earthilizer changes substantially when we add this additional source of uncertainty to the problem, in conjunction with the potential for shutting down operations and recouping most of the firm's initial investment.

In panel b of Figure 3-6 we evaluate the NPVs of each of the four possible circumstances the firm might face after one year:

- If the EPA ruling is favorable, then operating the Earthilizer project over its full five-year expected life has an NPV of $43,062.
- Moreover, if it abandons the project after one year, it will experience a negative expected NPV of ($167,108).[18]

---

[18]Note that this is the NPV of abandoning at the end of Year 1 whether the EPA rules favorably or unfavorably.

Table 3-4	Revised Cash Flows and NPVs for the Earthilizer Project

Panel a. No Option to Abandon

	2007	2008	2009	2010	2011	2012
Favorable EPA ruling— Expected PFCFs	$ (580,000)	$87,600	$ 78,420	$93,320	$109,710	$658,770
NPV (favorable EPA ruling)	$ 43,062					
Unfavorable EPA ruling— Expected FFCFs	$ (580,000)	$ 7,600	$ (1,580)	$13,320	$ 29,710	$578,770
NPV (unfavorable EPA ruling)	$ (236,608)					
Revised expected PFCFs	(580,000)	71,600	62,420	77,320	93,710	642,770
E[NPV] with no option to abandon	$ (12,872)					

Panel b. Option to Abandon

	2007	2008	2009	2010	2011	2012
Project not abandoned (favorable EPA)	(580,000)	87,600	78,420	93,320	109,710	658,770
NPV (favorable EPA ruling)	43,062					
Project abandoned (unfavorable EPA)	(580,000)	467,600	—	—	—	—
NPV (unfavorable EPA ruling)	$ (167,108)					
E[NPV] with abandonment option	$ 1,028.31					

Obviously, given these two choices, if the EPA ruling is favorable, CSM will want to operate the project. This alternative is highlighted and the inferior alternative (abandoning) is struck out.

What if the EPA ruling is unfavorable? Again, Panel b of Table 3-6 presents the numbers:

■ If the EPA ruling is unfavorable, the expected NPV of continuing operations is ($236,608).
■ The NPV of abandoning the project is only ($167,108).

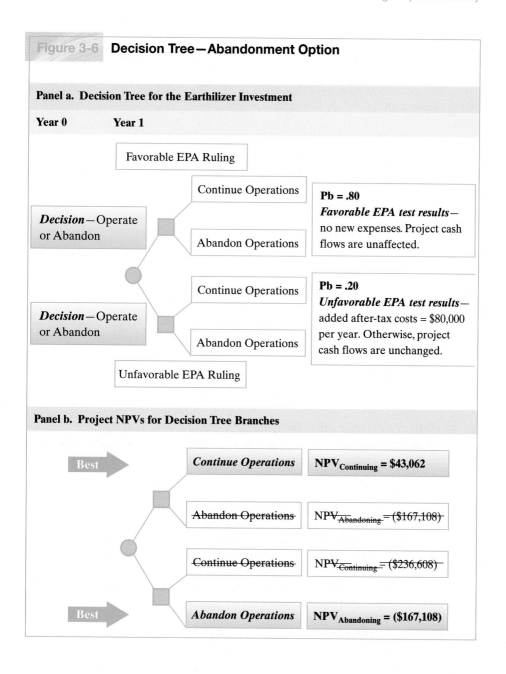

Figure 3-6   Decision Tree—Abandonment Option

Panel a. Decision Tree for the Earthilizer Investment

Year 0   Year 1

Favorable EPA Ruling

Continue Operations

Decision—Operate or Abandon

Abandon Operations

Pb = .80
Favorable EPA test results—
no new expenses. Project cash flows are unaffected.

Continue Operations

Decision—Operate or Abandon

Abandon Operations

Pb = .20
Unfavorable EPA test results—
added after-tax costs = $80,000 per year. Otherwise, project cash flows are unchanged.

Unfavorable EPA Ruling

Panel b. Project NPVs for Decision Tree Branches

Best → **Continue Operations** $NPV_{Continuing} = \$43,062$

Abandon Operations $NPV_{Abandoning} = (\$167,108)$

Continue Operations $NPV_{Continuing} = (\$236,608)$

Best → **Abandon Operations** $NPV_{Abandoning} = (\$167,108)$

So, in the event of an unfavorable ruling, CSM should abandon the project. Once again the superior alternative is highlighted while the inferior alternative is struck out.

If the probability of a favorable ruling is 50%, the expected NPV for the project in the presence of the option to abandon is now:

$$\begin{matrix} \text{Expected} \\ \text{Net Present Value} \\ \text{(with the abandonment option)} \end{matrix} = \begin{bmatrix} \text{Expected Net Present Value} \\ \text{Continue Operations } - \text{ Favorable} \\ \text{EPA Response} \end{bmatrix} \times \begin{bmatrix} \text{Probability} \\ \text{of a Favorable} \\ \text{Ruling} \end{bmatrix}$$

$$+ \begin{bmatrix} \text{Expected Net Present Value} \\ \text{Discontinue Operations } - \\ \text{Unfavorable EPA Response} \end{bmatrix}$$

(3.1)

Therefore,

$$\begin{matrix} \text{Expected} \\ \text{Net Present Value} \\ \text{(with the abandonment option)} \end{matrix} = (\$43{,}062 \times .80) + [-\$167{,}108 \times (1 - .80)] = \$1{,}028.$$

In the event of a negative ruling from the EPA, the option to shut down or abandon the Earthilizer project at the end of Year 1 makes the expected NPV of the project positive. The key here is that the firm can *abandon the project* in order to avoid the losses incurred by operating the project.

Abandonment truncates the lower tail of the distribution of a project's NPV. The truncation eliminates negative NPV outcomes and, as a result, increases the mean of the now-truncated distribution to $1,028. Without the option to abandon, the expected NPV was negative and equal to ($12,872). Essentially, the abandonment option mitigates some of the risk of an unfavorable EPA ruling. Clearly, considering the effects of project flexibility (in this case, the flexibility to reconsider the investment and possibly abandon it should the EPA ruling prove unfavorable) in the analysis of the project has a material effect on project valuation.

Using Option Pricing Theory to Evaluate the Abandonment Option

In Chapter 11 we reconsider the option to abandon an investment in the context of an option pricing model. In our current example we simply assumed that we knew what the project would be worth both with and without a favorable response from the EPA. In Chapter 11 we consider more complex problems in which the investment can be abandoned on a number of future dates. Stay tuned!

3.5 SUMMARY

Determining the value of an investment opportunity is straightforward when future cash flows are known. However, we live in a very uncertain world, and very few investments generate cash flows that can be predicted with any degree of precision. While uncertainty clearly complicates the valuation process, a number of tools help the analyst deal with this complexity more effectively.

This chapter introduced three basic tools that are used to assess the impact of uncertainty on project outcomes: scenario analysis, breakeven sensitivity analysis, and simulation analysis. All three tools provide information that the analyst can use to understand the key factors that drive a project's success or failure. This information helps the analyst develop a better understanding of how confident the firm should be in the project's prospects.

This chapter also introduced the important role played by *project flexibility*. By this we mean the opportunities for the firm to modify an investment over its life in response to changing circumstances and new opportunities. We will discuss real options later in the book, but it is useful to begin thinking now about how flexibility can affect expected cash flows as well as cash flow risks.

PROBLEMS

3-1 BREAKEVEN SENSITIVITY ANALYSIS The Clayton Manufacturing Company is considering an investment in a new automated inventory system for its warehouse that will provide cash savings to the firm over the next five years. The firm's CFO anticipates additional earnings before interest, taxes, depreciation, and amortization (EBITDA)[19] from cost savings equal to $200,000 for the first year of operation of the center, and over the next four years the firm estimates this amount will grow at a rate of 5% per year. The system will require an initial investment of $800,000 that will be depreciated over a five-year period using straight-line depreciation of $160,000 per year and a zero estimated salvage value.

   a. Calculate the project's annual project free cash flow (PFCF) for each of the next five years where the firm's tax rate is 35%.
   b. If the cost of capital for the project is 12%, what is the projected NPV for the investment?
   c. What is the minimum Year 1 dollar savings (i.e., EBITDA) required to produce a breakeven NPV = 0?

---

[19]EBITDA is a widely used measure of firm earnings that we will encounter many times throughout the balance of the book. It is simply earnings before interest or EBIT and taxes plus depreciation and amortization expense.

3-2 PROJECT RISK ANALYSIS—SENSITIVITY ANALYSIS Refer back to the HMG example found in Problem 2-8 (page 67) and answer the following questions:

a. What are the key sources of risk that you see in this project?
b. Use the "Goal Seek" function within Excel to find the breakeven values (i.e., values that force the project NPV to equal zero) for each of the following variables: the initial CAPEX, the working capital percentage of revenue growth, variable cost % of sales, and sales volume. (*Hint:* scale the sales volume for all five years up and down by the same percentage.)
c. Which of the variables analyzed in part b do you think is the greatest source of concern? What, if anything, could you do to reduce the risk of the project?
d. Should you always seek to reduce project risk?

3-3 PROJECT RISK ANALYSIS—COMPREHENSIVE Bridgeway Pharmaceuticals manufactures and sells generic over-the-counter medications in plants located throughout the Western Hemisphere. One of its plants is trying to decide whether to automate a portion of its packaging process by purchasing an automated waste disposal and recycling machine.

The proposed investment is $400,000 to purchase the necessary equipment and get it into place. The machine will have a five-year anticipated life and will be depreciated at a rate of $80,000 per year, toward a zero anticipated salvage value. The firm's analysts estimate that the purchase of the new waste-handling system will bring annual cost savings of $40,000 from reduced labor costs, $18,000 per year from reduced waste disposal costs, and $200,000 per year from the sale of reclaimed plastic waste net of selling expenses. Bridgeway requires a 20% return from capital investments and faces a 35% tax rate.

a. Using the estimates provided above, should Bridgeway purchase the new automated waste-handling system?
b. The manager at the plant where the handling system is being contemplated has raised some questions regarding the potential savings from the system. He asked the financial analyst in charge of preparing the proposal to evaluate the impact of variations in the price of plastic waste materials, which have proven to be volatile in the past. Specifically, what would be the impact of price reductions for the waste that drive the revenues from the sale of waste down to half their estimated amounts in Years 1 through 5?
c. (*Simulation*) Model the new investment whose value is determined by the following random variables: Annual revenues from reclaimed waste in Year 1 follow a triangular distribution with a minimum value of $100,000, a most likely value of $200,000, and a maximum value of $300,000. In Year 2 (and each year thereafter) the distribution is still triangular; however, the most likely value is now equal to the value observed in the previous year, the minimum value is equal to 50% of the observed value in the previous year and the maximum is equal to 150% of

the observed value in the previous year. Furthermore, the revenues from reclaimed waste exhibit a correlation coefficient from year to year of .90. Labor cost savings can be forecast with a high degree of certainty since they represent the savings from one hourly worker that will no longer be needed once the new waste-handling system has been put into place. The reductions in waste disposal costs come from a uniform distribution with minimum value of $15,000 and maximum value of $21,000. The waste disposal costs are assumed to be uncorrelated over time.

  i. What is the probability of a cash flow less than $150,000 in Year 1? In Year 5? (Hint: Define the annual PFCFs for Years 1 through 5 as *forecast* variables. You will use only the Year 1 and 5 cash flow distributions for this question but will use all of them to answer part iii.)

  ii. What are the expected NPV and IRR for the project?

  iii. (Optional) What are the means and standard deviations of the simulated distribution of cash flows for Years 1 through 5? What is the effect of the positive correlation in the underlying determinants of the project's cash flows? (Hint: Look at the standard deviations in annual cash flows through time.)

3-4 PROJECT RISK ANALYSIS—BREAKEVEN SENSITIVITY The TitMar Motor Company is considering the production of a new personal transportation vehicle that would be called the PTV. The PTV would compete directly with the innovative new Segway. The PTV will utilize a three-wheel platform capable of carrying one rider for up to 6 hours per battery charge, thanks to a new battery system developed by TitMar. TitMar's PTV will sell for substantially less than the Segway but will offer equivalent features.

The pro forma financials for the proposed PTV project, including forecasts and assumptions that underlie them, are set out in Exhibit P3-4.1. Note that revenue is calculated as follows: price per unit × market share (%) × market size, and units sold = revenues/price per unit. The project offers an expected NPV of $9,526,209 and an IRR of 39.82%. Given TitMar's stated hurdle rate of 18%, the project looks like a winner.

Even though the project looks very good based on management's estimates, it is risky and can turn from a positive-NPV investment to a negative one with relatively modest changes in the key value drivers. Develop a spreadsheet model of the project valuation and answer the following questions.

  a. If the firm's market share turns out to be only 5%, what happens to the project's NPV and IRR?

  b. If the market share remains at 15% and the price of the PTV falls to $4,500, what is the resulting NPV?

3-5 SIMULATION ANALYSIS Use your model from Problem 3-4 to construct a simulation model for the TitMar PTV. Incorporate two random (i.e., stochastic) variables in

Exhibit P3-4.1   **TitMar Motor Company Personal Transportation Vehicle (PTV) Project**

Assumptions and Predictions

	Estimates
Price per unit	$ 4,895
Market share (%)	15.00%
Market size (Year 1)	200,000 units
Growth rate in market size beginning in Year 2	5.0%
Unit variable cost	$ 4,250
Fixed cost	$9,000,000
Tax rate	50.0%
Cost of capital	18.00%
Investment in NWC	5.00% of the predicted change in firm revenue
Initial investment in PPE	$7,000,000
Annual Depreciation (5-year life w/no salvage)	$1,400,000

Solution

				Cash Flows		
Project Analysis	**Year 0**	**Year 1**	**Year 2**	**Year 3**	**Year 4**	**Year 5**
Investment	(7,000,000)					
Revenue		146,850,000	154,192,500	161,902,125	169,997,231	178,497,093
Variable cost		(127,500,000)	(133,875,000)	(140,568,750)	(147,597,188)	(154,977,047)
Fixed cost		(9,000,000)	(9,000,000)	(9,000,000)	(9,000,000)	(9,000,000)
Depreciation		(1,400,000)	(1,400,000)	(1,400,000)	(1,400,000)	(1,400,000)

	Year 0	Year 1	Year 2	Year 3	Year 4	Year 5
EBT (net operating income)		8,950,000	9,917,500	10,933,375	12,000,044	13,120,046
Tax		(4,475,000)	(4,958,750)	(5,466,688)	(6,000,022)	(6,560,023)
Net operating profit after tax (NOPAT)		4,475,000	4,958,750	5,466,688	6,000,022	6,560,023
Plus: Depreciation expense		1,400,000	1,400,000	1,400,000	1,400,000	1,400,000
Less: CAPEX	(7,000,000)	–	–	–	–	–
Less: Change in NWC	(7,342,500)	(367,125)	(385,481)	(404,755)	(424,993)	8,924,855
Free cash flow	(14,342,500)	5,507,875	5,973,269	6,461,932	6,975,029	16,884,878
Net present value	$ 9,526,209					
Internal rate of return	39.82%					

your model to capture the size of the market for scooters. Each of these variables is modeled differently as follows:

MARKET SHARE. Market share follows a triangular distribution with a most likely value of 15%, a minimum of 10%, and a maximum of 20%.

GROWTH RATE IN MARKET SIZE. The growth rate in market size for Year 1 is assumed to be normally distributed with a mean of 5% and standard deviation of 2%. For Year 2 the expected market size growth rate is equal to the simulated growth rate for Year 1 and has a standard deviation of 2%. The growth rates for Years 3 and beyond follow the pattern described for Year 2.

Run 10,000 random trials and define two output variables—net present value and internal rate of return. What is the probability that the NPV will be zero or lower? What is the probability of an IRR less than 18%?

3-6 DECISION TREE AND BREAKEVEN SENSITIVITY ANALYSIS Reevaluate the Earthilizer decision tree analysis found in Table 3-4, where the abandonment value is only $350,000. What is the expected NPV of the project under these circumstances? What is the minimum abandonment value required to produce an expected NPV for the project of zero with the abandonment option? (Hint: Use the "Goal Seek" function to solve for the abandonment value that produces an expected NPV of zero.)

3-7 INTRODUCTORY SIMULATION EXERCISES Construct a spreadsheet model for each of the following exercises and then use the model to build a simulation model.

a. Jason Enterprises faces uncertain future sales. Specifically, for the coming year the firm's CFO described her sales expectations as follows: "Sales could be as high as $10,000,000 or as low as $7,000,000, but I could not tell you anything more." How would you characterize firm sales using a probability distribution? If Jason's operating earnings are typically 25% of firm sales, what would you estimate earnings to be for next year? Construct a spreadsheet model and incorporate consideration for the uncertainty in future revenues to estimate the expected gross profit for the firm.

b. In the spring of 2008 Aggiebear Dog Snacks, Inc., was estimating its gross profits (revenue less cost of goods sold) for 2009. The firm's CFO had recently attended a two-day seminar on the use of simulation and asked his analyst to construct a simulation model to make the estimate. To help guide the analyst, the CFO prepared the following table:

Income Statement	Variable Description
Revenue	Minimum = $18 million; most likely = $25 million; maximum = $35 million
Cost of goods sold	70% to 80% of revenue

i. Construct a spreadsheet model for Aggiebear's gross profit.

ii. Use the information provided above to convert your spreadsheet model into a simulation model.

iii. Run your simulation model 10,000 iterations. What is the expected level of gross profit for 2008? What is the probability that the gross profit will fall below $3.5 million?

3-8 PROJECT RISK ANALYSIS USING SIMULATION Rayner Aeronautics is considering a $12.5 million investment that has an estimated project free cash flow (PFCF) of $2 million in its first year of operations. The project has a five-year life and Rayner requires a return of 18% in order to justify making the investment.

a. What rate of growth in PFCF for Years 2 through 5 is required for the project to break even (i.e., have an NPV = 0)?

b. Construct a simulation model for the investment opportunity to estimate the expected values of the PFCF for Years 1 through 5. The first year's cash flow is normally distributed with an expected value of $2 million and a standard deviation of $1 million. Moreover, the rate of growth in PFCF for Years 2 through 5 follows a triangular distribution with the following parameter estimates:

Year	Most Likely Growth Rate (ML)	Minimum Growth Rate	Maximum Growth Rate
2	40%	$\frac{1}{2}$ of ML	2 times ML
3	Actual growth rate for the previous year	$\frac{1}{2}$ the actual growth rate for the previous year	2 times the actual growth rate for the previous year
4	Actual growth rate for the previous year	$\frac{1}{2}$ the actual growth rate for the previous year	2 times the actual growth rate for the previous year
5	Actual growth rate for the previous year	$\frac{1}{2}$ the actual growth rate for the previous year	2 times the actual growth rate for the previous year

c. What are the expected NPV and IRR for the project based on your simulation analysis from part b?

PROBLEM 3-9 **MINI-CASE** CONOCOPHILLIPS GAS ACQUISITION PROJECT [20]

ConocoPhillips's (COP's) Natural Gas and Gas Products Department (NG&GP) manages all of the company's activities relating to the gathering, purchase, processing, and sale of natural gas and gas liquids. Chris Simpkins, a recent graduate, was recently hired as a financial analyst to support the NG&GP department. One of Chris's

---

[20]Prepared by Betty Simkins, Oklahoma State University.

Exhibit P3-9.1 **Analysis of the ConocoPhillips Gas Purchase Project**

Year	0	1	2	3
Investment	$1,200,000			
Increase in NWC	145,000			
MACRS depreciation rate (7 year)		0.1429	0.2449	0.1749
Natural gas wellhead price (per MCF)		$ 6.00	$ 6.00	$ 6.00
Volume (MCF/day)		900	720	576
Days per year		365		
Fee to producer of natural gas (per MCF)		$ 3.00	$ 3.00	$ 3.00
Compression & processing costs (per MCF)		0.65	0.65	0.65
Cash Flow Calculations				
Natural gas wellhead price revenue		$1,971,000	$1,576,800	$1,261,400
Lease fee expense		985,500	788,400	630,720
Compression & processing costs		213,525	170,820	136,656
Depreciation expenses		171,480	293,880	209,880
Net operating profit		600,495	323,700	284,184
Less taxes (40%)		(240,198)	(129,480)	(113,674)
Net operating profit after tax (NOPAT)		360,297	194,220	170,510
Plus depreciation		171,480	293,880	209,880
Return of net working capital				
Project free cash flow	**(1,345,000)**	**531,777**	**488,100**	**380,390**

first assignments was to review the projections for a proposed gas purchase project that were made by one of the firm's field engineers. The cash flow projections for the 10-year project are found in Exhibit P3-9.1 and are based on the following assumptions and projections:

■   The investment required for the project consists of two components: First, there is the cost to lay the natural gas pipeline of $1,200,000. The project is expected to

4	5	6	7	8	9	10
0.1249	0.0893	0.0893	0.0893	0.0445		
$ 6.00	$ 6.00	$ 6.00	$ 6.00	$ 6.00	$ 6.00	$ 6.00
461	369	295	236	189	151	121
$ 3.00	$ 3.00	$ 3.00	$ 3.00	$ 3.00	$ 3.00	$ 3.00
0.65	0.65	0.65	0.65	0.65	0.65	0.65
$1,009,152	$807,322	$645,857	$516,686	$413,349	$330,679	$264,543
504,576	403,661	322,929	258,343	206,674	165,339	132,272
109,325	87,460	69,968	55,974	44,779	35,824	28,659
149,880	107,160	107,160	107,160	53,400	—	—
245,371	209,041	145,801	95,209	108,495	129,516	103,613
(98,148)	(83,616)	(58,320)	(38,083)	(43,398)	(51,806)	(41,445)
147,223	125,425	87,480	57,125	65,097	77,710	62,168
149,880	107,160	107,160	107,160	53,400	—	—
						145,000
297,103	232,585	194,640	164,285	118,497	77,710	207,168

have a 10-year life and is depreciated over seven years using seven-year MACRS.[21] Second, the project will require a $145,000 increase in net working capital that is assumed to be recovered at the termination of the project.

---

[21]Modified Accelerated Cost Recovery System (MACRS) uses a shorter depreciable life for assets, thus giving businesses larger tax deductions and cash flows in the earlier years of the project life relative to straight-line depreciation.

■ The well is expected to produce 900 MCF (thousand cubic feet) per day of natural gas during Year 1 and then decline over the remaining nine-year period (365 operating days per year). The natural gas production is expected to decline at a rate of 20% per year after Year 1.

■ In addition to the initial expenditures for the pipeline and additional working capital, two more sets of expenses will be incurred. First, a fee must be paid to the producer consisting of 50 percent of the wellhead natural gas market price. In other words, if the wellhead market price is $6.00 per MCF, 50% (or $3.00 per MCF) is paid to the producer. Second, gas processing and compression costs of $0.65 per MCF will be incurred.

■ There is no salvage value for the equipment at the end of the natural gas lease.

■ The natural gas price at the wellhead is currently $6.00 per MCF.

■ The cost of capital for this project is 15%.

QUESTIONS

1. What are the NPV and IRR for the proposed project based on the forecasts made above? Should Chris recommend that the project be undertaken? Why or why not? What reservations, if any, should Chris have about recommending the project to his boss?

2. Perform a sensitivity analysis of the proposed project to determine the impact on NPV and IRR for each of the following scenarios:
   a. Best case: A natural gas price of $8.00 and a Year 1 production rate of 1,200 MCF per day that declines by 20% per year after that.
   b. Most likely case: A natural gas price of $6.00 and a Year 1 production rate of 900 MCF per day that declines by 20% per year after that.
   c. Worst case: A natural gas price of $3.00 and a Year 1 production rate of 700 MCF per day that declines by 20% per year after that.

3. Do breakeven sensitivity analysis to find each of the following:
   a. Breakeven natural gas price for an NPV = 0.
   b. Breakeven natural gas volume in Year 1 for an NPV = 0.
   c. Breakeven investment for an NPV = 0.

4. Given the results of your risk analysis in Questions 2 and 3 above, do you recommend this project? Why or why not?

PROBLEM 3-10 **MINI-CASE** SOUTHWEST AIRLINES WINGLET PROJECT[22]

As a low-fare airline, Southwest Airlines constantly focuses on ways to improve the efficiency of its operations and maintain a cost structure below that of its competition. In the spring of 2002, Scott Topping, the director of corporate, was approached by Aviation Partners Boeing (APB) regarding an innovative way to save on fuel

---
[22]Prepared by Betty Simkins, Oklahoma State University.

costs—the installation of a new technology known as the Blended Winglet. The winglets, made of carbon-graphite, were designed for the Boeing 737-700 aircraft. Southwest currently had 142 planes of this model in its fleet.

The Blended Winglet system was developed by APB, a joint venture between Aviation Partners Inc. and The Boeing Company. The main purpose of the winglet was to reduce turbulence, leading to higher flying efficiency. As a result, the winglets provided three important benefits that allowed the airplane to extend its range, carry a greater payload, and save on fuel consumption. The winglets accomplish this by increasing the spread of the wing's trailing edge and creating more lift at the wingtips.

To complete his financial analysis, Scott had to verify potential costs and benefits as well as get the approval of the Maintenance Engineering Department, the Flight Operations Department, and the Facilities Department. However, Scott was well aware that regardless of the potential financial benefits, safety was the first priority. This process took several months due to the complexity of the project.

After discussing the project with the requisite departments, Scott made the following estimates of the costs and benefits of the winglet system to Southwest:

- The winglets, which cost $700,000 a pair, could be installed at an additional cost of $56,000 per aircraft. Installation could be scheduled at each maintenance facility to coincide with regular maintenance. As a result, each aircraft was only expected to experience downtime for one extra day at a cost of $5,000.
- After considering the short- and long-term effects of the winglets, the Maintenance Engineering Department estimated that, on average, repair costs would average $2,100 yearly per aircraft due primarily to incidental damage.
- The increased wingspan was expected to allow each of Southwest's aircraft to fly up to 115 nautical miles farther and to decrease fuel usage by 4% to 6%. This meant that Southwest could expect to save 178,500 gallons of jet fuel per airplane per year.
- Flight Operations[23] estimated the additional lift capability provided by the winglet would reduce Southwest's costs of using restricted runways, with an estimated savings of $500 per aircraft per year.
- The Facilities Department assessed the effect of the added wingspan on each of the 59 airports Southwest utilized in its current route structure. The department estimated the necessary facilities modifications could be achieved at a onetime cost of about $1,200 per aircraft.
- The Blended Winglet project qualifies for accelerated tax write-off benefits under the Job Creation and Worker Assistance Act of 2002. With a marginal tax rate of 39% and using a seven-year depreciation schedule (see the table

---

[23]Southwest Airlines estimated the salvage value to be approximately 15% of the winglets' cost; however, this salvage value is very uncertain since this is a new technology with no historical data upon which to base an estimate. Scott felt that the winglets would definitely have some residual value, so 15% seemed like a reasonable salvage value to use based on the limited data available. In the analysis, the winglets should be depreciated to zero and the salvage value in Year 20 should be treated as taxable income.

below), Southwest would be allowed to depreciate an additional 50% of the project in the first year.

	Depreciation Details			
Year	Normal MARCS Table	Normal Table Times 50%	Year 1 (additional 50%)	Total (modified table)
1	14.29%	7.15%	50.00%	57.15%
2	24.49%	12.25%		12.25%
3	17.49%	8.75%		8.75%
4	12.49%	6.25%		6.25%
5	8.93%	4.47%		4.47%
6	8.92%	4.46%		4.46%
7	8.93%	4.47%		4.47%
8	4.46%	2.23%		2.23%

■ The Blended Winglet project is expected to have a life of at least 20 years, at the end of which the winglets are anticipated to have a salvage value of $105,000. Assume a jet fuel cost of $0.80 per gallon and a cost of capital of 9.28% in your analysis. Items other than fuel are expected to escalate at a 3% rate. Conduct the analysis on a "per plane" basis.

Evaluate the project by analyzing the following questions.

a. Estimate the project's annual project free cash flow (PFCF) for each of the next 20 years, as well as the initial cash outflow.

b. Calculate the net present value (NPV) and internal rate of return (IRR) of the Blended Winglet project.

c. What is the breakeven jet fuel cost for the project? What is the breakeven fuel savings in gallons for the project, assuming jet fuel costs $0.80 per gallon?

d. How sensitive is the Blended Winglet project's NPV to changing assumptions regarding expected future fuel costs and fuel savings? Use scenario analysis to analyze a best case scenario (jet fuel price of $1.10 per gallon and fuel savings of 214,000 gallons per year) and a worst case scenario (jet fuel price of $0.50 per gallon and fuel savings of 142,000 gallons per year).

e. What potential risks and benefits do you see that are not incorporated into the quantitative analysis?

f. What is the impact on the project's NPV or IRR if the winglets have no salvage value?

g. Do you suggest Southwest Airlines undertake this project? Why or why not?

An Introduction to Simulation Analysis and Crystal Ball

What Is Simulation?

Simulation refers to the process of constructing a model that imitates a real-life situation: for example, the cash flows resulting from the operation of a power plant.

Why Build Simulation Models?

When cash flows are determined from multiple sources of uncertainty, determining expected cash flows is incredibly complex. In these cases simulation provides a tool that can be used to characterize the solution. Essentially, computer power is used to develop a distribution of possible solutions that reflects the underlying sources of uncertainty in the problem.

What Is Crystal Ball Software?

Crystal Ball is an "add-in" software package that allows you to construct simulation models within Microsoft Excel spreadsheet software. Crystal Ball is a product of Decisioneering, Inc.[24] Although we use Crystal Ball throughout this text, an alternative simulation add-in provided by the Palisade Corporation is called @Risk.[25]

How Do I Build a Simulation Model Using Crystal Ball?

Excel models are **deterministic,** which means that the inputs are fixed (one value to one cell). You can see only one solution at a time. If you want to view alternative results, you need to manually change the inputs in the model. Crystal Ball software

---

[24]http://www.crystalball.com/index.html
[25]http://www.palisade.com/

provides the user with the ability to make changes in the inputs to the model dynamically such that many solutions to the model can be calculated and stored for later analysis. To convert a deterministic spreadsheet model into a dynamic simulation model requires three steps:

- First, we must identify the inputs to the model that are subject to uncertainty and assign each a probability distribution. In Crystal Ball these uncertain or stochastic inputs are called **assumptions.**
- Second, the particular output measures that are important to the analysis of the problem being analyzed must be identified. Crystal Ball refers to these as **forecasts.**
- Finally, once the assumptions and forecasts have been identified (we will talk about how in just a moment), we can start the simulation. This process entails selecting a value for each of the assumptions in the model, calculating the value of each of the forecast variables, and storing the result. This process is repeated for the number of **iterations** you specify.

The output of the simulation experiment consists of all the stored values of the forecast variables (e.g., NPV or IRR). The stored forecast variable data can be summarized using descriptive statistics such as the mean, median, and standard deviation; or by constructing a histogram or frequency distribution.

To illustrate the use of Crystal Ball in a very simple setting, consider the situation faced by WiseData Corp. The firm is evaluating an investment in a new product line that it expects to produce sales revenues for only one year. The firm's management is trying to forecast the gross profit that might be produced by the investment (as part of its analysis of project cash flows). Management's initial estimate of gross profit is $20,000 and is found below in a static Excel model:

	2008
Sales	$100,000.00
Less: Cost of goods sold	$(80,000.00)
Gross profit	$ 20,000.00

However, management realizes that both the level of sales and the cost of goods sold are not known with certainty, such that gross profit is also uncertain. To model gross profit using simulation to evaluate its underlying uncertainty, management has assessed the uncertainty of sales and cost of goods sold as follows:

Variable (Assumption)	Description of Uncertainty	Probability Distribution
Sales	Could be as low as $40,000 or as high as $150,000, but the most likely value is $100,000.	Triangular with minimum value of $40,000; most likely value of $100,000; and maximum value of $150,000.
Cost of Goods Sold	Could be as little as 70% of sales or as much as 90%.	Uniform distribution with a minimum value of 70% and a maximum value of 90%.

Note that the firm's management has identified the variables in the model that are subject to uncertainty, described the nature of the uncertainty (perhaps with the direct input of individuals within the company who are most familiar with the problem), and translated the description of underlying uncertainty into an appropriate probability distribution. Each of these steps requires skill and managerial judgment that can be developed over time with practice.

Crystal Ball adds icons to your spreadsheet toolbar that facilitate the process of defining assumptions and identifying forecasts. The screen containing the final model after placing the cursor on cell C8 (sales) and selecting the ⌂ and entering the minimum, most likely (likeliest), and maximum parameter estimates for the triangular distribution appears as follows:

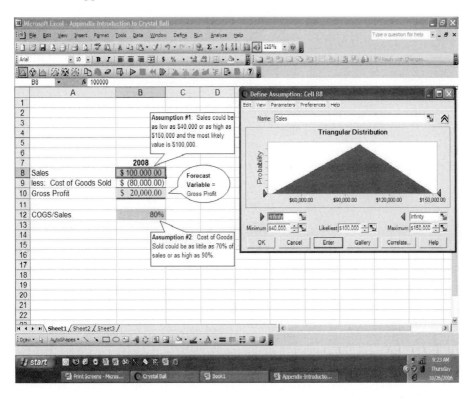

We assign a uniform distribution to cell B8 to make the cost of goods sold to sales ratio stochastic following the same procedure we used in defining sales. Note that in the final model (above) the green shaded cells identify the assumptions (i.e., random or stochastic variables), which include sales and cost of goods sold as a percent of sales, and the blue cell identifies the one output or forecast variable in the model that is also the object of the analysis. To define the forecast variable we select the 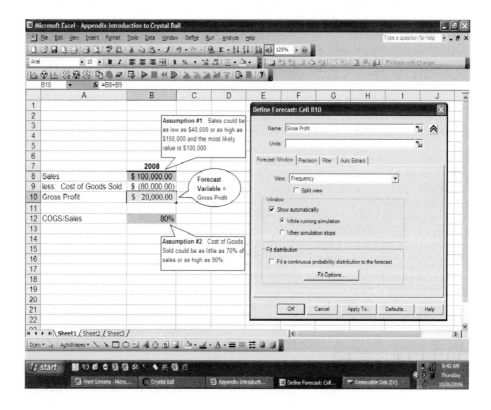 in the toolbar. The Excel screen appears as follows:

The final step before running the simulation involves selecting the 🔲 icon on the toolbar to define the number of iterations we wish to include in the simulation experiment. The Excel screen appears as follows:

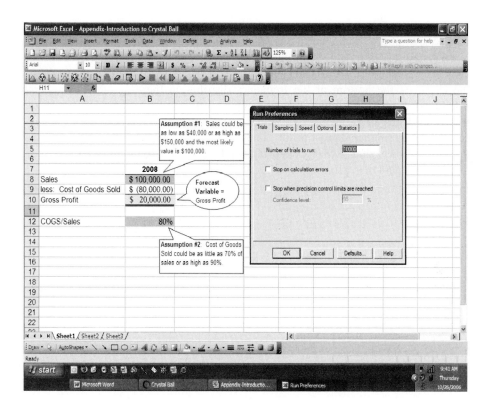

To run the simulation we select the ▷ icon on the toolbar. We ran the simulation 10,000 times (iterations) and Crystal Ball compiled the resulting 10,000 estimates of gross profit into the following histogram (frequency distribution):

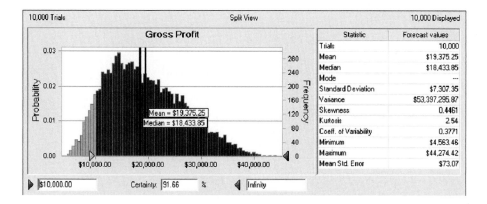

Let's review the basic elements of the histogram of Gross Profit. First, this is the "Split View" of the results, which contains both the frequency distribution and statistics. Crystal Ball offers other options to view the forecast output that we will not review here. Next, there are 10,000 simulation trials and 10,000 iterations displayed in the chart. At the bottom of the frequency distribution there are three numbers: $10,000.00, 91.66%, and Infinity. The first number refers to the truncation point in the frequency distribution that appears above, and the "Certainty" of 91.66% is the percentage of the simulated gross profit values that were above $10,000. In other words, there is a 91.66% chance that gross profit will be at least $10,000 or a 8.34% chance that it will be less than $10,000.

PART II

Cost of Capital

U p to now, our focus has been on estimating cash flows. To value those cash flows we need a discount rate, or a cost of capital that reflects the risks of the cash flows. In this section we introduce the idea of an investment's opportunity cost of capital, which we define as the rate of return that an investor can expect to obtain on an investment in financial securities with equivalent risk characteristics.

Chapter 4 considers discount rate determination and the cost of capital for the firm as a whole. This analysis focuses on the firm's WACC, which is the weighted average of the firm's cost of debt and equity. The firm's WACC provides the appropriate discount rate for valuing an entire firm. However, as we explain, a firm's WACC is not appropriate for determining the cost of capital for individual investment projects the firm might be considering.

In Chapter 5 we address the problem of estimating the cost of capital for an individual project. In theory, each individual investment project can have a unique discount rate that reflects its unique risks. However, in practice, many firms evaluate all of their investment projects with one, firmwide cost of capital. Moreover, firms that use multiple discount rates often use a limited number that correspond to each of the firm's operating divisions. In this chapter we discuss some organizational reasons for why this is the case and offer some basic alternatives that can be used to tailor the cost of capital estimate to the risk attributes of individual projects. These methods balance the organizational costs that can arise in using multiple discount rates against the benefits of using a risk-appropriate opportunity cost of capital for project analysis.

CHAPTER 4

Estimating a Firm's Cost of Capital

Chapter Overview

In earlier chapters we referred to the *discount rate* simply as the interest rate used to calculate present values. To describe the appropriate discount rate that should be used to calculate the value of an investment's future cash flows, financial economists use terms like *opportunity cost of capital* or simply *cost of capital*. In this chapter we focus our attention on the firm's overall weighted average cost of capital (or WACC), which is the discount rate that should be used to value an entire firm. In addition to describing the WACC, we consider the determinants of its various components—the cost of debt and the cost of equity.

4.1 INTRODUCTION

The firm's **weighted average cost of capital** (or **WACC,** pronounced "whack") is the weighted average of the expected after-tax rates of return of the firm's various sources of capital. As we will discuss in this chapter, the WACC is the discount rate that should be used to discount the firm's expected free cash flows to estimate firm value.

A firm's WACC can be viewed as its **opportunity cost of capital,** which is the expected rate of return that its investors forgo from alternative investment opportunities with equivalent risk. This may sound like "finance-speak," but it illustrates a very important concept. Because investors could invest their money elsewhere, providing money to a firm by purchasing its securities (bonds and shares of stock) has an opportunity cost. That is, if an investor puts her money into the stock of Google (GOOG), she gives up (forgoes) the return she would have earned by investing in Microsoft (MSFT) stock. What this means is that if Google and Microsoft have equivalent risks, the expected rate of return on Microsoft stock can be viewed as the opportunity cost of capital for Google and the expected return on Google stock can be viewed as the opportunity cost of capital for Microsoft.

In addition to providing the appropriate discount rate to calculate the firm's value, firms regularly track their WACC and use it as a benchmark for determining the appropriate discount rate for new investment projects, for valuing acquisition candidates, and for evaluating their own performance (we return to this topic in Chapter 9).

4.2 VALUE, CASH FLOWS, AND DISCOUNT RATES

Figure 4-1 reviews the three-step DCF valuation methodology that we described in Chapters 2 and 3. Up until this point we have focused entirely on project valuation (the right-hand column). We now introduce equity valuation (the middle column) and firm valuation.

The key learning point from the second and third columns is that cash flow calculations and discount rates must be properly aligned. If you are trying to estimate the value of the equity invested in the project (i.e., **equity value**) as we do in Chapter 8, then you will estimate equity free cash flows and use a discount rate that is appropriate for the equity investors. On the other hand, if you are estimating the value of an entire firm, which equals the value of the combined equity and debt claims, then the appropriate cash flow is the combination of debt and equity cash flows. In that case, the appropriate discount rate is a combination of the debt- and equity-holder rates, or what we will refer to as the weighted average cost of capital.

It should be emphasized that in all of these cases we are assuming that the estimated cash flows are what we defined in Chapter 2 as expected cash flows. If we are using conservative cash flows, then we would want to use a lower discount rate. Similarly, if the estimated cash flows are really "hoped for" cash flows, then we will need a higher discount rate to offset the optimistic cash flow forecasts.

Defining a Firm's WACC

The **weighted average cost of capital (WACC)** is a weighted average of the after-tax costs of the various sources of invested capital raised by the firm to finance its operations and investments. We define the firm's **invested capital** as capital raised through the issuance of interest-bearing debt and equity (both preferred and common). Note that the above definition of invested capital specifically excludes all non-interest-bearing liabilities such as accounts payable, as well as unfunded pension liabilities and leases. This is because we will be calculating what is known as the firm's **enterprise value,** which is equal to the sum of the value of the firm's equity and interest-bearing

Figure 4-1   Matching Cash Flows and Discount Rates in DCF Analysis

Steps	Object of the Valuation Exercise	
	Equity Valuation	Project or Firm Valuation (Debt Plus Equity Claims)
Step 1: Estimate the amount and timing of future cash flows (covered in Chapter 2)	Equity free cash flow (EFCF)	Project (firm) free cash flow (i.e., PFCF = FFCF)
Step 2: Estimate a risk-appropriate discount rate (covered in Chapters 4 and 5)	Equity required rate of return	Combine debt and equity discount rate (weighted average cost of capital—WACC)
Step 3: Discount the cash flows (covered in Chapter 2)	Calculate the present value of the estimated EFCFs using the equity discount rate to estimate the value of the equity invested in the project.	Calculate the present value of the PFCF (FFCF) using the WACC to estimate the value of the project (firm) as an entity.

liabilities. Note, however, that these excluded sources of capital, (e.g., unfunded pension liabilities and leases) do affect enterprise value, because they affect the firm's future cash flows.

Equation 4.1 defines the WACC as the average of the estimated required rates of return for the firm's interest-bearing debt (k_d), preferred stock (k_p), and common equity (k_e). The weights used for each source of funds are equal to the proportions in which funds are raised. (That is, w_d is the weight attached to debt, w_p is the weight associated with preferred stock, and w_e is the weight attached to equity.)

$$\text{WACC} = k_d(1 - T)w_d + k_p w_p + k_e w_e \qquad (4.1)$$

Note that the cost of debt financing is the rate of return required by the firm's creditors, k_d, adjusted downward by a factor equal to one minus the corporate tax rate $(1 - T)$ to reflect the fact that the firm's interest expense is tax-deductible. Thus, the creditors receive a return equal to k_d but the firm experiences a net cost of only $k_d(1 - T)$. Since the cost of preferred and common equity is not tax-deductible, there is no need for a similar tax adjustment to these costs.

The mechanics of calculating a firm's WACC can be summarized with the following three-step procedure:

- **Step 1:** Evaluate the firm's capital structure and determine the relative importance of each component in the mix.
- **Step 2:** Estimate the opportunity cost of each of the sources of financing and adjust it for the effects of taxes where appropriate.
- **Step 3:** Finally, calculate the firm's WACC by computing a weighted average of the estimated after-tax costs of capital sources used by the firm (i.e., by substituting into Equation 4.1).

As you might suspect, there are some estimation issues that arise with respect to both weights and opportunity costs that need to be addressed. Let's consider each in turn.

Use market weights First, with regard to the capital structure weights, it is important that the components used to calculate the WACC formula reflect the current importance of each source of financing to the firm. Typically this means that the weights should be based on market rather than book values of the firm's securities because market values, unlike book values, represent the relative values placed on the firm's securities at the time of the analysis (rather than at some previous time when the securities were issued).

Use market-based opportunity costs The second estimation issue that arises in calculating the firm's WACC relates to the rates of return or opportunity costs of each source of capital. Just as was the case with the capital structure weights, these costs should reflect the current required rates of return, rather than historical rates, at the time when the capital was raised. This reflects the fact that the WACC is an estimate of the firm's opportunity cost of capital today.

Use forward-looking weights and opportunity costs Firms typically update their estimate of the cost of capital annually or even quarterly to reflect changing market conditions. However, in most cases, analysts apply the WACC in a way that assumes that it will be constant for all future periods. This means that they implicitly assume the weights for each source of financing, the costs of capital for debt and equity, and the corporate tax rate are constant. Although it is reasonable to assume that the components of WACC are constant so long as the firm's financial policies remain fixed, there are circumstances in which financial policies will change in predictable ways over the life of the investment. We encounter one such case in Chapter 8 when we discuss leveraged buyouts, or LBOs. LBO financing typically involves a very high level of debt that is subsequently paid down. In this case we will find it useful to apply another variant of the DCF model (the adjusted present value model), which we discuss in detail in Chapter 7.

Discounted Cash Flow, Firm Value, and the WACC

The connection of the WACC to the discounted cash flow (DCF) estimate of firm value is captured in Equation 4.2 below:[1]

$$\text{Firm Value}_0 = \sum_{t=1}^{N} \frac{E(\text{Firm Free Cash Flow}_t)}{(1 + \text{WACC})^t} \tag{4.2}$$

$E(\text{Firm Free Cash Flow}_t)$ is the expected cash flow earned by the firm in period t where "firm" free cash flow (FFCF) is analogous to "project" free cash flow (PFCF). For our purposes a project can be considered a mini-firm, and a firm is simply the combination of many projects. Consequently, firm and project free cash flows are calculated in exactly the same way.

Equation 4.2 expresses Firm Value with a "0" subscript to indicate that we are determining firm value *today* ("time zero"), based on cash flows starting one period hence. In general, analysts assume that the period length is one year, and they ignore the fact that the cash flow accrues over the course of the year. We will follow this *end-of-year convention* throughout the book; however, we recognize that many financial analysts assume that cash flows arrive at the middle of the year to account for the fact that for most projects cash flows occur throughout the year.

Illustration—Using Discounted Cash Flow Analysis to Value an Acquisition

To illustrate the connection between the WACC and valuation, consider the situation faced by an analyst working for Morgan Stanley, who has a client interested in acquiring OfficeMart, Inc., a retailer of office products. This client is interested in purchasing the entire firm, which means that it will acquire all of its outstanding equity and assume its outstanding debt. Although valuations of company acquisitions can be quite involved, the Morgan Stanley analyst has made a simple "first-pass" analysis of the intrinsic value of OfficeMart following the three-step discounted cash flow process from Chapter 2:[2]

Step 1: *Forecast the amount and timing of free cash flows.* Since we are interested in valuing the firm as an entity (both debt- and equity-holder claims), we estimate firm free cash flows (FFCFs) in the same way that we calculated project free cash

---

[1] Equation 4.2 does not reflect the value of the firm's nonoperating assets nor does it capture the value of the firm's excess liquidity (i.e., marketable securities). We return to the consideration of these points in Chapters 6 and 7.

[2] In Chapters 7 and 8 we delve further into the details of firm valuation.

flows (PFCFs) in Chapter 2. Thus, for the coming year, the Morgan Stanley analyst estimates that OfficeMart's cash flow will be $560,000, as follows:

Sales	$ 3,000,000
Cost of goods sold	(1,800,000)
Depreciation	(500,000)
Earnings before interest and taxes (EBIT)	700,000
Taxes[3] (20%)	(140,000)
Net operating profit after taxes (NOPAT)	560,000
Plus: Depreciation	500,000
Less: Capital expenditures (CAPEX)	(500,000)
Less: Change in net working capital (WC)	(0)
Project (firm) free cash flow (PFCF = FFCF)	$ 560,000

Step 2: *Estimate the appropriate discount rate.* Since we are valuing the entire company (debt plus equity claims), the discount rate we choose should represent a combination of the rates that are appropriate for both debt and equity, or the weighted average cost of capital.

OfficeMart finances 40% of its assets using debt costing 5%; equity investors in companies similar to OfficeMart (both in terms of the industry and their capital structures) demand a 14% return on their investment. Combining OfficeMart's after-tax cost of borrowing (interest expense is tax deductible and the firm's tax rate is 20%) with the estimated cost of equity capital, we calculate a weighted average cost of capital for the firm of 10% (i.e., $5\%(1 - 20\%)0.4 + 14\% \times 0.6 = 10\%$).

Step 3: *Discount the estimated cash flows.* OfficeMart's estimated cash flows form a level perpetuity. That is, each year's cash flow is equal to the prior year's cash flow, or $560,000. Consequently, we can calculate the present value of the firm's future cash flows as follows:

$$\text{Value of OfficeMart, Inc.} = \frac{\$560,000}{.10} = \$5,600,000$$

Thus, this first-pass analysis suggests that the value of OfficeMart is $5,600,000.

---

[3]Recall from our earlier discussion in Chapter 2 that this is *not* the firm's actual tax liability since it is based on earnings before interest expense has been deducted. See the Technical Insight box on interest tax savings.

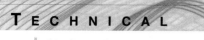

What about Interest Tax Savings?

Note that the taxes in the PFCF and FFCF calculations are based on the level of operating profits or earnings *before* interest has been deducted. In other words, we are calculating the after-tax cash flows of an all-equity firm. However, interest expense and its tax deductibility are not ignored in our valuation. We use the *after-tax* cost of debt when calculating the weighted average cost of capital, which accounts for the tax savings associated with the tax deductibility of interest. For example, if the required rate of return for debt is 7% and the firm pays taxes at a rate of 30%, the after-tax cost of debt is 4.9% — i.e., $.07(1 - .30) = .049$, or 4.9%, while the pre-tax cost of debt is 7%.

Recall that we have estimated firm value, which is the sum of both the firm's debt and equity claims. If we want to estimate the value of the firm's *equity*, we need to subtract the value of its debt claims from the $5,600,000 valuation of the firm. Since OfficeMart has $2,240,000 worth of debt outstanding, the value of the firm's equity is $5,600,000 − $2,240,000 = $3,360,000.

Equity Valuation

But wait a minute. Didn't Figure 4-1 say that the value of the equity could be calculated as the present value of the equity free cash flows (EFCFs)? The calculation we used above solves for equity value simply as what's left over out of firm value after we deduct the amount of the firm's debt.

To estimate the value of the equity in the project, we first estimate the EFCF as follows:

EBIT	$ 700,000
Less: Interest expense	(112,000)
Earnings before taxes	588,000
Less: Taxes	(117,600)
Net income	$ 470,400
Plus: Depreciation expense	500,000
Less: CAPEX	(500,000)
Plus: New debt issues	—
Less: Debt repayments	—
Equity free cash flow (EFCF)	$ 470,400

To value the equity in the project, we discount the EFCF stream (note that the EFCFs are a level perpetuity—a constant cash flow received annually in perpetuity) using the cost of equity capital, which was earlier assumed to be 14%, i.e.,

$$\text{Value of OfficeMart's Equity} = \frac{\$470,400}{.14} = \$3,360,000$$

So the value of OfficeMart's equity is equal to the residual value remaining after the firm's debt obligations are deducted from the value of the firm (i.e., \$5,600,000 − \$2,240,000 = \$3,360,000), and it is also equal to the present value of the equity free cash flows! Whether equity value is estimated directly by discounting EFCFs or indirectly by subtracting the value of the firm's debt from firm value varies in business practice. For example, as we point out in Chapter 8, it is common practice among private equity investors to value equity directly. However, when valuing firms in the context of mergers and acquisitions, the initial valuation generally focuses on the firm as a whole.

4.3 ESTIMATING THE WACC

In this section we introduce techniques for estimating a firm's WACC. In our discussion we will frequently reference the practices of Ibbotson Associates, which is a prominent source of information (see the Practitioner Insight box on page 127). Ibbotson follows the same three-step process we discussed earlier for the estimation of a firm's WACC, but applies the procedure to *industry groups*. The rationale for focusing on the industrywide cost of capital is based on the beliefs that (1) the variance in the cost of capital within industries is modest when compared to the variance between industries, and (2) estimation errors are minimized if we focus on groups of similar firms from the same industry.[4]

Evaluate the Firm's Capital Structure Weights—Step 1

The first step in our analysis of WACC involves the determination of the weights that are to be used for the components of the firm's capital structure. These weights represent the fraction of the firm's **invested capital** contributed by each of the sources of capital. Note that we need to be a bit careful here when talking about invested capital, for it does not include everything on the right-hand side of the firm's balance sheet. Specifically, a firm's invested capital is the sum of *only* the firm's interest-bearing debt, preferred equity, and common equity.

In theory, we should calculate the weights using observed market prices for each of the firm's securities (be they debt or equity), multiplied by the number of outstanding

---

[4]For a complete discussion of its methodology, see Ibbotson Associates, *Cost of Capital—Yearbook.*

P R A C T I T I O N E R

I N S I G H T   **Roger Ibbotson on Business
Valuation and the Cost of Capital***

The appraisal of a firm's value using discounted cash flow is a relatively straightforward process. The standard procedure involves estimating the firm's cost of capital and future cash flows and then discounting the cash flows back to the present using the cost of capital. Unfortunately, estimates of cash flows as well as discount rates are fraught with errors. The potential for estimation errors is probably greatest for cash flow estimates because there are no anchors or boundaries that can be used to provide guidance about what reasonable estimates might be. In contrast, in making cost of capital estimates, the analyst has historical market returns on risk-free securities and common stock (in total and by industry), which provide some indication of the neighborhood in which a firm's cost of capital might reside.

At Ibbotson Associates, we provide historical information about stock and bond returns that indicates appropriate required rates of return on investments with different risks. We also provide alternative models that can be used to calculate the cost of capital. Some of the cost of capital models can seem overly complex when conveyed to upper management, board members, or others who lack financial sophistication. Moreover, estimated costs of capital (particularly equity capital) can, and often do, vary widely. My experience suggests the following guidelines can be useful when addressing the estimation of a company's cost of capital:

■ *Use the simpler models when possible.* Our experience suggests that some of the more sophisticated models of the cost of equity have the highest estimation errors.
■ *Account for company size and industry.* These variables are unambiguously measured and have been reliably demonstrated to be related to the firm's cost of capital.
■ *Calculate the cost of capital using several methods.* Even though you may rely principally on simpler models, each method is informative.

*Roger Ibbotson is founder and former chairman of Ibbotson Associates, Inc. Ibbotson Associates is the largest provider of cost of capital information in the United States. Currently, its *Cost of Capital Quarterly* includes industry cost of capital analysis on more than 300 U.S.–based industries for help in performing discounted cash flow analysis. The data include industry betas, costs of equity, weighted average costs of capital, and other important financial statistics presented by industry.

securities. In practice, however, capital structure weights are typically calculated using market values *only for equity securities* (preferred[5] and common stock). The market prices of equity securities are readily available, so an analyst can simply multiply

---

[5]We use the book value of the firm's preferred stock outstanding, as does Ibbotson Associates. However, where preferred share prices are observable, the market capitalization for these shares should be used.

Estimating the Cost of Debt in Practice

Ibbotson Associates estimates the industry cost of debt using the yield curve for various debt ratings based on the Merrill Lynch U.S. Domestic Bond Indices. As a practical matter, bonds are classified into one of three groups (see Figure 4-2): investment grade (S&P ratings of AAA, AA, A, and BBB), below investment grade (S&P ratings of BB, B, CCC, CC, and D), and not rated. Yields for each group and maturity are then averaged to arrive at an estimate of the yield curve for debt. The average yields for the lower two groups are used as proxies for bonds that are not rated. A weighted average cost of debt can then be calculated for each company in an industry using yields for the firm's debt rating and weights determined by the actual debt maturing in a particular year compared to all debt outstanding. To get an industry cost of debt, the average yields for each company in the industry are averaged. Ibbotson Associates uses debt maturing in each of the next five years, and then assumes that all remaining debt matures in Year 6.

the current market price of the security by the number of shares outstanding to calculate total market values. For debt securities, book values are often substituted for market values, since market prices for corporate debt are often difficult to obtain (see Industry Insight box). However, when market values of debt are available, they should be used in place of book values.

The Cost of Debt—Step 2

In theory, we would like to estimate the expected return that investors require on the firm's debt. In practice, analysts typically use the promised *yield to maturity* on the firm's outstanding debt as their estimate of the expected cost of debt financing.

Yields to Maturity on Corporate Bonds

Estimation of the yield to maturity (YTM) on a corporate bond issue is straightforward when the analyst has access to information regarding the maturity of the bond, its current market price, the coupon rate of interest, and schedule of principal payments. For example, in the spring of 2006 Home Depot (HD) had a bond issue that was due in 2016 (i.e., 10 years to maturity), carried an annual coupon rate of 5.4%, paid semiannual interest and therefore had 20 payments, and had a market price of $968.65. The YTM on the bond issue can be calculated by solving for YTM in the following bond valuation equation:

$$\$968.65 = \frac{(.054/2) \times \$1{,}000}{(1 + \text{YTM})^1} + \frac{(.054/2) \times \$1{,}000}{(1 + \text{YTM})^2} + \frac{(.054/2) \times \$1{,}000}{(1 + \text{YTM})^3} + \cdots$$

$$+ \frac{(.054/2) \times \$1{,}000 + \$1{,}000}{(1 + \text{YTM})^{20}}$$

Figure 4-2   A Guide to Corporate Bond Ratings

Moody's	S&P	Fitch	Definitions
Aaa	AAA	AAA	Prime (maximum safety)
Aa1	AA+	AA+	High grade, high quality
Aa2	AA	AA	
Aa3	AA–	AA–	
A1	A+	A+	Upper medium grade
A2	A	A	
A3	A–	A–	
Baa1	BBB+	BBB+	Lower medium grade
Baa2	BBB	BBB	
Baa3	BBB–	BBB–	
Ba1	BB+	BB+	Noninvestment grade
Ba2	BB	BB	Speculative
Ba3	BB–	BB–	
B1	B+	B+	Highly speculative
B2	B	B	
B3	B–	B–	
Caa1	CCC+	CCC	Substantial risk
Caa2	CCC	–	In poor standing
Caa3	CCC–	–	
Ca	–	–	Extremely speculative
C	–	–	May be in default
–	–	DDD	Default
–	–	DD	
–	D	D	

The semiannual YTM is 2.91%, which converts to an annualized YTM of 5.9%.[6] Based on a marginal tax rate of 35%, the after-tax cost of Home Depot's bond issue is then 3.835% = 5.9%(1 − .35).

Calculating the YTM of a firm's debt is difficult for firms with a large amount of debt that is privately held, and hence does not have market prices that are readily

---

[6]Annual YTM = $(1 + \text{Semiannual YTM})^2 - 1 = (1 + .0291)^2 - 1 = .059$ or 5.9%. This quantity is often referred to as the effective annual rate, or just yield.

Figure 4-3 **Reuters Corporate Spreads (in basis points) for Industrials in 2004***

Rating	1 yr	2 yr	3 yr	5 yr	7 yr	10 yr	30 yr
Aaa/AAA	5	10	15	20	25	33	60
Aa1/AA+	10	15	20	30	35	42	66
Aa2/AA	15	25	30	35	44	52	71
Aa3/AA-	20	30	35	45	52	59	78
A1/A+	25	35	40	50	55	65	85
A2/A	35	44	55	60	65	73	90
A3/A-	45	59	68	75	80	89	110
Baa1/BBB+	55	65	80	90	94	104	123
Baa2/BBB	60	75	100	105	112	122	143
Baa3/BBB-	75	90	110	115	124	140	173
Ba1/BB+	115	125	140	170	180	210	235
Ba2/BB	140	180	210	205	210	250	300
Ba3/BB-	165	200	230	235	235	270	320
B1/B+	190	215	250	250	275	335	360
B2/B	215	220	260	300	315	350	450
B3/B-	265	310	350	400	435	480	525
Caa/CCC	1125	1225	1250	1200	1200	1275	1400

*Methodology—Reuters Pricing Service (RPS) has eight experienced evaluators responsible for pricing approximately 20,000 investment-grade corporate bonds. Corporate bonds are segregated into four industry sectors: industrial, financial, transports, and utilities. RPS prices corporate bonds at a spread above an underlying Treasury issue. The evaluators obtain the spreads from brokers and traders at various firms. A generic spread for each sector is created using input from street contacts and the evaluator's expertise. A matrix is then developed based on sector, rating, and maturity.

available. Because of this, it is standard practice to estimate the cost of debt using the yield to maturity on a portfolio of bonds with similar credit ratings and maturity as the firm's outstanding debt.

Reuters provides average spreads to Treasury data that is updated daily and cross-categorized by both default rating and years to maturity, as found in Figure 4-3. Using our Home Depot bond issue, we can estimate the YTM for a 10-year bond with a default rating of Aa3/AA−. Such a bond has a spread to the 10-year Treasury bond YTM of .59%, or 59 basis points (see boxed number in Figure 4-3). Given that the 10-year Treasury YTM was 5.02% at the time of this writing, this provides an estimate of 5.02% + .59% = 5.61% for the YTM on Home Depot's bonds.

Promised versus Expected Rates of Return

The yield to maturity is calculated using the promised interest and principal payments and thus can be considered a reasonable estimate of the cost of debt financing only when the risk of default is so low that promised cash flows are reasonable estimates of expected cash flow. For lower-rated debt, however, promised and expected cash flows are not the same, and an explicit adjustment for the prospect of loss in the event of default becomes necessary.

To elaborate on the distinction between promised yields and expected returns on debt, consider the calculation of the yield to maturity (YTM) on a bond with one year to maturity, found in Equation 4.3a:

$$\frac{\text{Bond}}{\text{Price}} = \frac{\text{Interest} + \text{Principal}}{(1 + \text{YTM})} \tag{4.3a}$$

Note that the cash flows used to determine YTM are the contractual or promised cash payments, which equal expected cash flows *only* for default-free bonds. For debt with default risk, the expected cash flows must reflect the probability of default (Pb) and the recovery rate (Re) on the debt in the event of default. For our one-period bond issue the cost of debt k_d can be calculated using expected cash flows to the bondholder as follows:

$$\frac{\text{Bond}}{\text{Price}} = \frac{[\text{Interest} + \text{Principal}] \times (1 - Pb) + [\text{Interest} + \text{Principal}] \times Pb \times Re}{(1 + k_d)}$$

$$\tag{4.3b}$$

The expected cash flow to the bondholder is the promised principal and interest payments, weighted by the probability that the debt defaults $(1 - Pb)$, plus the cash flow that is received in the event of default, weighted by the probability of default (Pb). To illustrate this, consider a bond with a $1,000 face value and one year to maturity, which is currently selling for $985.00 and paying a 9% interest payment annually. Using Equation 4.3a, we estimate the bond's YTM to be 10.66%, i.e.,

$$\frac{\text{Bond}}{\text{Price}} = \frac{\text{Interest} + \text{Principal}}{(1 + \text{YTM})^1} = \frac{.09 \times \$1,000 + \$1,000}{(1 + .1066)} = \$985$$

The 10.66% YTM represents the rate of return an investor would realize if the bond does not default. If, however, the probability of default on the bond is 15% and the recovery rate is 75%, the expected rate of return to the investor, using Equation 4.3b, is 6.51%.

In practice, the differences between YTM and k_d are relatively modest for investment-grade debt (i.e., debt rated BBB or higher), and the YTM provides a reasonable estimate of the cost of debt. However, for firms with below-investment-grade debt, there can be a meaningful difference between the *promised yield to maturity* on the debt and the *expected return* or cost of the debt (as we demonstrated in the above example).

There are two ways to estimate the cost of debt for below-investment-grade debt. The first method involves estimating the expected cash flows of the debt using expected rates of default and recovery rates, and using these expected cash flows to calculate the internal rate of return on the debt. We illustrate how this can be done in the Appendix. The second method applies the capital asset pricing model (CAPM), which we discuss in more detail later in the chapter when we discuss the cost of equity capital. Very briefly, the CAPM requires an estimate of the beta of the debt, along with an expected return premium on the stock market. For example, betas of low-rated bonds are approximately .4, while bonds with AAA ratings generally have betas that are about .2. If we assume a market risk premium of 5%, then the spread between the expected returns of a AAA bond and a below-investment-grade bond is approximately $(0.4 - 0.1)$ times 5%, which equals 1.5%. Therefore, if the current yield and expected return on a AAA bond (our proxy for the risk-free rate) is 6%, then the expected return on the lower-rated bond is about 7.5%.

Estimating the Cost of Convertible Corporate Bonds

Convertible bonds represent a hybrid form of financing that is both debt and equity since the holder of the bond can, at his or her discretion, convert the bond into a prescribed number of common shares. Since these bonds have the conversion feature, they typically carry a lower rate of interest and consequently their estimated yield to maturity understates the true cost of debt. This "dual" source of value means that the cost of financing by issuing convertibles is a function of both the underlying security (bond or preferred stock) and the call option. Consequently, the cost of capital obtained by issuing convertible bonds can be thought of as a weighted average of the cost of issuing straight bonds and the cost of the exchange feature (call option), where the weights equal the relative contributions of the two components to the value of the security. We delve into the estimation of the cost of convertible debt in the Appendix.

The Cost of Preferred Equity—Step 2 (continued)

Estimating the cost of straight (i.e., nonconvertible) preferred stock is straightforward, since it typically pays the holder a fixed dividend each period (quarterly), forever.[7] The value of such a stream of dividends can be found as follows:

$$\text{Preferred Stock Price, } P_{ps} = \frac{\text{Preferred Dividend, } Div_{ps}}{\text{Required Return, } k_{ps}} \tag{4.4a}$$

---

[7]We discuss a method for evaluating the conversion feature with respect to corporate bonds in the Appendix. A similar approach can be taken for the evaluation of convertible preferred shares.

Using the preferred dividend and observed price of preferred stock, we can infer the investor's required rate of return as follows:

$$k_{ps} = \frac{Div_{ps}}{P_{ps}} \qquad (4.4b)$$

To illustrate, consider the preferred shares issued by Alabama Power Company (ALP-PP), which pay a 5.3% annual dividend on a $25.00 par value, or $1.33 per share. On May 24, 2006, these preferred shares were selling for $23.35 per share. Consequently, investors require a 5.67% return on these shares, calculated as follows:

$$k_{ps} = \frac{\$1.33}{23.35} = .0567 \text{ or } 5.67\%$$

Note that the preferred dividend is also a *promised* dividend, in the same way that the interest on corporate bonds is *promised* interest, and thus *does not* necessarily represent the dividend that the preferred stockholder expects to receive. This means that the 5.67% return calculated above provides an upper limit on the cost of preferred stock, since the firm may decide to suspend payment or become bankrupt.[8]

The key thing to remember here is that the standard method for estimating the cost of preferred stock using Equation 4.4a is biased upward, yielding estimated costs that are higher than the expected costs. However, it is standard practice to use the promised dividend divided by the price of the preferred stock, as we did in Equation 4.4b.

The Cost of Common Equity—Step 2 (continued)

The cost of common equity capital (k_e) is the most difficult estimate we have to make in evaluating a firm's cost of capital. The difficulty arises from the fact that the common shareholders are the residual claimants of the firm's earnings. That is, the common stockholders receive a return out of what is left over after all other claimants (bondholders and preferred stockholders) have been paid. Hence, there is no promised or prespecified return based on a financial contract (as is the case with both bondholders and preferred stockholders).

The relevant cost of equity is simply the rate of return investors *expect* from investing in the firm's stock. This return comes in the form of cash distributions (i.e., dividends and cash proceeds from the sale of the stock). We review two broad approaches that are each widely used to estimate the cost of equity. The first consists of what financial economists refer to as *asset pricing models*. Specifically, we present three variants of the *Capital Asset Pricing Model (CAPM)*.

---

[8]In contrast to corporate bond interest and principal payments, the issuing firm can suspend payment of the preferred dividend without being forced into bankruptcy. This makes the difference in promised and expected dividends even more dramatic than with bonds, since the issuing firm is less likely to default on interest and principal payments.

The second approach has a much older heritage in finance and comes out of the pioneering work of John Burr Williams (1938) and, later, Myron Gordon (1962).[9] This approach, which is often referred to as the *discounted cash flow approach*, first estimates the expected stream of dividends and then calculates the implied cost of equity capital, or equivalently the internal rate of return, that makes the present value of the dividend stream equal the firm's stock price. This implied return is then used as the firm's cost of equity.

Method 1—Asset Pricing Models

Asset pricing theories entered the finance literature in the 1960s with the introduction of the **capital asset pricing model,** or **CAPM.** The traditional CAPM was followed by a host of modified versions that relaxed some of the more stringent assumptions upon which the original theory was based. We consider three versions: the traditional CAPM, the size-adjusted CAPM, and multifactor models.

The traditional CAPM One of the basic tenets of finance is that if investors are risk-averse, they will require a higher rate of return to hold riskier investments. The important question addressed by the CAPM is how one should measure risk. The basic intuition of the CAPM is that the relevant risk of a stock is determined by how that stock contributes to the overall volatility of a well-diversified portfolio. As it turns out, there are some stocks that are quite volatile, that is, their returns vary a lot from month to month, but despite their volatility they contribute very little to the volatility of a well-diversified portfolio. According to the CAPM, these stocks should require lower rates of return than their counterparts that may be less volatile, but which contribute more to the volatility of well-diversified portfolios.

To understand the relation between risk and return it is useful to decompose the risk associated with an investment into two components. The first component consists of variability that contributes to the risk of a diversified portfolio, and the second source consists of variability that does not contribute to the risk of a diversified portfolio. The first component is generally referred to as either **systematic risk** or **nondiversifiable risk,** and the second source is generally referred to as **nonsystematic risk** or **diversifiable risk.** Sources of systematic risk include market factors such as changes in interest rates and energy prices that influence almost all stocks. The logic of the CAPM suggests that stocks that are very sensitive to these sources of risk should have high required rates of return, since these stocks contribute more to the variability of diversified portfolios. Sources of nonsystematic risk include random firm-specific events such as lawsuits, product defects, and various technical innovations.

---

[9]J. B. Williams, *Theory of Investment Value* (Cambridge, MA.: Harvard University Press, 1938), and M. Gordon, *The Investment, Financing, and Valuation of the Corporation* (Homewood, IL: Irwin, 1962).

The logic of the CAPM suggests that these sources of risk should have almost no effect on required rates of return because they contribute very little to the overall variability of diversified portfolios.

The CAPM can be expressed as the following equation that relates the required expected return of an investment to systematic risk:

$$k_e = k_{rf} + \beta_e(k_m - k_{rf}) \qquad (4.5)$$

where

k_{rf} = the risk-free rate of interest

β_e = the beta, or systematic risk of the company's common equity, which is estimated from a regression of a stock's return minus the risk-free rate on a market return, such as the S&P 500 return, minus the risk-free rate

k_m = the expected return on the overall market portfolio comprised of all risky assets

$(k_m - k_{rf})$ = the expected equity risk premium (the expected return on the overall market minus the risk-free rate)

Figure 4-4 illustrates the connection between systematic risk and the expected rate of return on common equity. For example, to determine the cost of equity to Dell Corporation, let's assume that we estimate its beta coefficient to be 1.20 and the

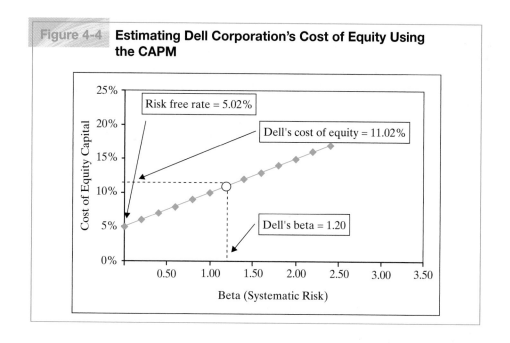

Figure 4-4 **Estimating Dell Corporation's Cost of Equity Using the CAPM**

risk-free rate of interest is 5.02% and the market risk premium is approximately 5%.[10] We can substitute into Equation 4.5 to estimate the expected cost of equity capital for the firm as 11.02%.

We now turn to a more in-depth discussion of the three CAPM inputs: the risk-free interest rate, beta, and the market risk premium.

Selecting the risk-free rate of interest The risk-free rate of interest is the least controversial estimate we have to make for the CAPM inputs. Nevertheless, there are two issues we need to address: First, what is a risk-free security, and second, what maturity should we use? Unfortunately, the CAPM provides little guidance in responding to either of these issues.

Identifying the risk-free rate: Analysts typically use current yields on U.S. Treasury securities to define the risk-free rate of interest when evaluating the cost of capital in the United States.[11] When applying the CAPM in other economies, it is customary to use their domestic risk-free rates so as to capture differences in rates of inflation between the United States and that economy.

Choosing a maturity: As a general rule, we want to match the maturity of the risk-free rate with the maturity of the cash flows being discounted. In practice, maturity matching is seldom done, however. Most textbooks suggest that short-term rates be used as the risk-free rate, since they are consistent with the simplest version of the CAPM. However, because the estimated cost of equity is typically used to discount distant cash flows, it is common practice to use a long-term rate for, say, 10- or 20-year maturities as the risk-free rate.[12] We agree with this practice, however, as we note below, the beta estimate used in the CAPM equation should also reflect this longer-maturity risk-free rate.

Estimating the beta The firm's **beta** represents the sensitivity of its equity returns to variations in the rates of return on the overall market portfolio. That is, if the value of the market portfolio of risky investments outperforms Treasury bonds by 10% during a particular month, then a stock with a beta coefficient of 1.25 would expect to outperform Treasury bonds by 12.5%. A stock's beta should be estimated by regressing the firm's excess stock returns on the excess returns of a market portfolio, where excess returns are defined as the returns in excess of the risk-free return, as shown in the following equation:

$$(k_e - k_{rf})_t = \alpha + \beta_e(k_m - k_{rf})_t + e_t \tag{4.6}$$

---

[10] We discuss the market risk premium in detail later in the chapter.

[11] Because Treasury securities have special appeal to foreign central banks and are exempt from state taxes, we cannot expect a zero-beta stock to have a return as low as the yield on a Treasury security. Because of this one might want to use the AAA corporate bond or equivalent commercial paper rate instead of the Treasury rate. However, we follow industry practice and use the long-term Treasury rate.

[12] For example, Ibbotson Associates uses the long-term government bond yield to approximate the risk-free rate in its cost of capital calculations.

where

k_e = the observed rate of return earned for investing in the firm's equity in period t,

k_{rf} = the risk-free rate of interest observed in period t,

α = a constant (intercept) term,

β_e = the beta for the company's common equity,

$(k_m - k_{rf})$ = the equity risk premium, and

e_t = the error term (that part of the equity return that is not explained by overall market movements)

Note that many analysts make a common mistake. They fail to match the maturity of the risk-free rate, used in Equation 4.6 to calculate beta, with the maturity of the rate used to calculate the equity risk premium. Very simply, if you use a long-term Treasury bond yield as the risk-free rate, then the excess return on the market used to calculate beta should be the excess return of the market portfolio over the long-term Treasury bond return.[13]

Although we typically estimate a company's beta using historical returns, we should always be mindful that our objective is to estimate the beta coefficient that reflects the relationship between risk and return in the future. Unfortunately, the beta estimate is just that—an estimate—and is subject to estimation error. Fortunately, there are a number of ways to address estimation error (see the Industry Insight box [p. 140] on alternative beta estimation methods).

The most common fix involves using an average of a sample of beta estimates for similar companies, which has the effect of reducing the influence of random estimation errors. However, it is not enough just to select similar firms, say, from the same industry. Beta coefficients vary not only by industry (or with business risk) but also by the firm's capital structure. Firms that use more financial leverage have higher betas. Consequently, computing a beta from a sample of similar firms' betas is a multistep process. First, we must identify a sample of firms that face similar business risk (usually from the same industry). For example, in Table 4-1 we use four firms from the drug industry to calculate a beta estimate for Pfizer. Second, we must "unlever" the betas for each of the sample firms to remove the influence of their particular capital structures on their beta coefficients. The relationship between levered and unlevered beta coefficients is defined in Equation 4.7 in Table 4-1. Third, we average the unlevered beta coefficients and finally relever them to reflect the capital structure of the firm in question.

In Table 4-1, the average unlevered beta for Pfizer and the other drug firms is .498. If we relever this average beta (Step 3) using Pfizer's debt-to-equity capitalization ratio

---

[13]It is our understanding that most publicly available betas are estimated with short-term risk-free rates or simply by regressing stock returns on market returns.

Table 4-1 **Estimating the Beta Coefficient for Pfizer Drug Using a Sample of Comparable Drug Firms—Unlevering and Levering Beta Coefficients**

Step 1: Identify a set of firms that operate in the same line of business as the subject firm (i.e., Pfizer). For each, either estimate directly or locate published estimates of its levered equity beta, β_{Levered}, the book value of the firm's interest-bearing debt, and the market capitalization of the firm's equity.[14]

Company Name	Levered Equity Beta	Debt/Equity Capitalization	Assumed Debt Beta	Unlevered Equity Beta
Abbott Laboratories	0.3600	9.66%	0.30	0.3566
Johnson & Johnson	0.3500	1.56%	0.30	0.3495
Merck	0.8100	7.25%	0.30	0.7881
Pfizer	0.7100	6.58%	0.30	0.6939
		6.26%	Average	0.4981

Step 2: Unlever the equity beta coefficient for each firm to get an estimate of the beta for each of the sample firms (including Pfizer) as if it used no financial leverage (i.e., $\beta_{\text{Unlevered}}$), and calculate the average for the five unlevered betas.

We unlever the equity beta coefficient using the following relationship between levered (β_{Levered_j}) and unlevered ($\beta_{\text{Unlevered}_j}$) beta coefficients:[15]

---

of 6.58%, we get a levered beta estimate for Pfizer of .2734. In this calculation we place the same weight on Pfizer that we do on each of the other firms. However, because Pfizer is obviously the best match for Pfizer, the analyst may want to increase the weight assigned to Pfizer, say, to be equal to that of all the other firms. If we use this

---

[14]Typically, debt is estimated using the book value of the firm's interest-bearing liabilities (short-term notes payable, the current portion of the firm's long-term debt, plus long-term debt). Although we should technically use the market value of the firm's debt, it is customary to use book values since most corporate debt is thinly traded if at all. The equity capitalization of the firm is estimated using the current market price of the firm's shares multiplied by the number of outstanding shares. Betas for individual stocks can be obtained from a number of published sources including virtually all online investment information sources such as Yahoo Finance or Microsoft's MoneyCentral Web site.

[15]It should be noted that analysts often apply Equation 4.7 under the assumption that the debt beta is zero.

Table 4-1 *continued*

$$\beta_{\text{Unlevered}_j} = \frac{\beta_{\text{Levered}_j} + \left(1 - \frac{\text{Marginal}}{\text{Tax Rate}}\right)\left(\frac{\text{Book Debt}_j}{\text{Equity Capitalization}_j}\right)\beta_{\text{Debt}}}{1 + \left(1 - \frac{\text{Marginal}}{\text{Tax Rate}}\right)\left(\frac{\text{Book Debt}_j}{\text{Equity Capitalization}_j}\right)} \quad (4.7)$$

where Equity Capitalization$_j$ is equal to the current stock price times the number of outstanding shares of stock. We assume a marginal tax rate of 38% and a debt beta of .30 for all firms.[16]

In the preceding example, the average unlevered beta is .4981.

Step 3: Relever the average unlevered equity beta to reflect the target firm's debt-to-equity capitalization ratio and corporate tax rate.

The process of relevering equity betas is simply the reverse of the unlevering process. Technically, we solve Equation 4.7 for β_{Levered} as follows:[17]

$$\beta_{\text{Levered}_j} = \beta_{\text{Unlevered}_j}\left(1 + \left[\left(\frac{\text{Book Debt}_j}{\text{Equity Capitalization}_j}\right)\left(1 - \frac{\text{Marginal}}{\text{Tax Rate}}\right)\right]\right)$$
$$- \beta_{\text{Debt}}\left[\left(\frac{\text{Book Debt}_j}{\text{Equity Capitalization}_j}\right)\left(1 - \frac{\text{Marginal}}{\text{Tax Rate}}\right)\right]$$

then substitute the average unlevered beta of .4981 and Pfizer's debt-to-equity capitalization ratio of 6.58% and solve for $\beta_{\text{Levered}} = .5061$.

weighting scheme, we get an unlevered beta estimate of .398, which produces a levered beta estimate of .406.

Estimating the market risk premium Determining the market risk premium requires a prediction of the future spread between the rate of return on the market portfolio and the risk-free return. Remember that the discount rate must reflect the opportunity cost of capital, which is in turn determined by the rate of return associated with

---

[16]The beta on debt is in fact close to zero in cases where default is not too likely and when the firm's debt has approximately the same maturity as the maturity of the risk-free debt used to calculate betas. Since most analysts tend to use excess returns using short-term debt to calculate betas, the relevant betas of corporate bonds are between .2 and .4, depending on their default rating and maturity.

[17]If the corporate bond beta is assumed to be zero (as many analysts assume), then the last term on the right-hand side of this expression drops out.

INDUSTRY INSIGHT

Alternative Beta Estimation Methods

The problems we noted with the estimation of beta coefficients from historical return data have led to the development of alternative prediction methods for betas. We will present two of those methods that have gained widespread usage: the BARRA model and the Bloomberg model.

The *BARRA method* is named for its founder, University of California professor of finance Barr Rosenberg. The basic thesis underlying BARRA's methodology is that a stock's beta is not stationary over time, but varies with changes in the fundamental attributes of the firm. Consequently, BARRA developed a forward-looking beta that accounts for current firm characteristics in its beta estimates.

The method is based on research showing that betas estimated from historical returns alone were not as good at predicting future betas as betas that also incorporated consideration for fundamental variables such as an industry variable and various company descriptors. The BARRA method uses an industry variable since it is well-known that some industries (such as agriculture and regulated utilities) are persistently low-beta industries, while others (such as electronics, air transportation, and securities firms) are persistently high-beta industries. Moreover, income statement and balance sheet variables are included in the model as predictors. For example, high dividend payout is predictive of low-beta firms, while high covariability of firm earnings with economy-wide earnings is indicative of higher betas.

A second alternative beta estimation model is used by the Bloomberg investment data company. The Bloomberg model adjusts betas estimated using historical data to account for the tendency of historical betas to regress toward the mean. To adjust for this tendency, the Bloomberg adjusted beta uses the following adjustment:

$$\begin{matrix} \text{Bloomberg} \\ \text{Adjusted} \\ \text{Beta} \end{matrix} = .33 + .67 \begin{pmatrix} \text{Unadjusted} \\ \text{Historical} \\ \text{Beta} \end{pmatrix}$$

The coefficients of the above model are estimated using past values of contemporaneously estimated betas.

investing in other risky investments. If one believes that the stock market will generate high returns over the next 10 years, then the required rate of return on a firm's stock will also be quite high.

Historical Estimates There is no getting around the fact that the market risk premiums that are used in applications of the CAPM are simply guesses. However, they should be educated guesses that are based on sound reasoning.

The approach taken by many analysts is to use past history as a guide to the estimation of the future market return premium. Figure 4-5 contains summary statistics on historical rates of return for U.S. stocks and bonds spanning the period 1926–2005. Note that the geometric averages are always lower than arithmetic averages.[18] Although most textbooks use the arithmetic average, practitioners often prefer geometric averages. (For a discussion of geometric versus arithmetic averages, see the Technical Insight box.)

Historical data suggest that the equity risk premium for the market portfolio has averaged 6% to 8% a year over the past 75 years. However, there is good reason to believe that looking forward the equity risk premium will not be this high. Indeed, current equity risk premium forecasts can be as low as 3%. For the examples in this book we will use an equity risk premium of 5% which is commonly used in practice.

Figure 4-5 **Historical Stock and Bond Returns: Summary Statistics for 1926–2005**

	Mean		Standard Deviation
	Geometric	**Arithmetic**	**Standard Deviation**
Large company stocks	10.4%	12.3%	20.2%
Small company stocks	12.6%	17.4%	32.9%
Long-term corporate bonds	5.9%	6.2%	8.5%
Long-term government bonds	5.5%	5.8%	9.2%
Intermediate-term government bonds	5.3%	5.5%	5.7%
Treasury bills	3.7%	3.8%	3.1%
Inflation	3.0%	3.1%	4.3%

Source: Ibbotson Associates *SBBI 2006 Yearbook.*

---

[18]This reflects the fact that the geometric mean captures the effects of compound interest whereas the arithmetic mean does not.

Geometric versus Arithmetic Mean

Consider the following investment in the stock of Carebare, Inc. On December 31, 2006, the firm's shares were trading for $100 a share. One year later, the shares had dropped to only $50. However, in 2007 the firm experienced a banner year that doubled the share price, leaving it at $100 on January 1, 2008. If you purchased the shares of Carebare on January 1, 2006, what rate of return did you realize when you sold them on January 1, 2008?

The obvious answer (not considering transaction costs) is 0%, since you ended up exactly where you started. That is,

$$\text{Stock Price}_{2008} = \text{Stock Price}_{2006}(1 + \text{HPR}_{2007})(1 + \text{HPR}_{2008})$$
$$= \text{Stock Price}_{2006}(1 + \text{HPR}_{\text{Mean}})^2$$

Thus, the mean annual holding period return (HPR) for the two-year period is found by solving for HPR_{Mean}:

$$\text{Stock Price}_{2006}(1 + \text{HPR}_{2007})(1 + \text{HPR}_{2008}) = \text{Stock Price}_{2006}(1 + \text{HPR}_{\text{Mean}})^2$$

or

$$\text{HPR}_{\text{Mean}} = [(1 + \text{HPR}_{2007})(1 + \text{HPR}_{2008})]^{1/2} - 1$$

It turns out that HPR_{Mean} is the *geometric mean* of the HPRs. For example, we can calculate this return by estimating the geometric mean of the returns earned in 2007 and 2008 as follows:

$$\frac{\text{Geometric}}{\text{Mean}} = [(1 + -.50)(1 + 1.00)]^{1/2} - 1 = 0\%$$

CAPM with a size premium The capital asset pricing model (CAPM) is taught in virtually all major business schools throughout the world. Unfortunately, the theory has only weak empirical support. Indeed, academic research has failed to find a significant cross-sectional relation between the beta estimates of stocks and their future rates of return. Research finds that firm characteristics, like market capitalization and book-to-market ratios, provide much better predictions of future returns than do

On the other hand, the *arithmetic mean* of the HPRs for 2006 and 2007 is calculated as follows:

$$\frac{\text{Arithmetic}}{\text{Mean}} = \frac{-50\% + 100\%}{2} = 25\%$$

The difference in the geometric and arithmetic mean is generally not as stark as in this example, but it serves to emphasize the points we want to make. The geometric mean return is the appropriate way to measure the rate of return earned during a particular historical return sequence. However, the geometric mean is not the best estimator of future returns unless we expect this sample path to be repeated in the future.

When all future sample paths are equally likely, the best estimate of the forward-looking returns is the arithmetic mean. Technically, we are assuming that each HPR is an independent observation from a stationary underlying probability distribution. So, if we observe annual returns of 10%, −5%, 25%, and 20% and these annual rates of return are assumed to represent random draws from a single underlying distribution of annual returns, then the best estimate of the mean of this distribution is the arithmetic mean, i.e.,

$$\frac{\text{Arithmetic}}{\text{Mean}} = \frac{10\% - 5\% + 25\% + 20\%}{4} = 12.5\%$$

Note that we have calculated the expected rate of return for one year (not four years) to be 12.5%. What if we wanted to estimate the annual rate of return expected over the next five years? In this instance we might estimate the annual rate of return realized over the previous five years using the geometric mean for that five-year period, for the five years before that, and so forth. Let's say that you estimated 10 such geometric means for nonoverlapping five-year periods going back 50 years. Now, to estimate the expected annual rate of return over the next five years, we would calculate the arithmetic mean of these five-year geometric rates of return.[19]

The idea again is that the geometric mean is the appropriate way to measure a historical return. However, if returns are drawn from independent and identically distributed distributions, the best estimator of the mean of that distribution is the arithmetic mean.

---

[19]It is obvious that our methodology for estimating five-year returns is limited by the amount of non-overlapping five-year periods from which we have to choose. The problem gets even worse where we try to estimate the distribution of longer-period returns (say, of 10 or 20 years). In practice, analysts restrict their attention to annual holding period returns because of the convention of quoting returns as annual rates.

betas.[20] In response to these observations, academics have proposed modifications of the CAPM that incorporate consideration for differences in stock returns related to these firm characteristics.

To illustrate how a size premium might be added to the CAPM, consider the methodology followed by Ibbotson Associates, in their 2005 yearbook, which divides firms into four discrete groups based on the total market value of their equity: *Large-cap firms,* those with more than $4.794 billion in market capitalization, receive no size premium. *Mid-cap firms,* with between $4.794 billion and $1.167 billion in equity value, receive a size premium of 0.91%. *Low-cap firms,* with equity value between $1.167 billion and $331 million, receive a size premium of 1.70%, and *micro-cap firms,* with equity values below $331 million, receive a size premium of 4.01%. Thus, the expected rate of return on equity using the size-adjusted CAPM can be described in Equation 4.8 below:

$$k_e = k_{rf} + \beta(k_m - k_{rf})$$
$$+ \begin{cases} \text{Large cap: } 0.0\% \text{ if market cap} > \$4.794 \text{ billion} \\ \text{Mid cap: } 0.91\% \text{ if } \$4.794 \text{ billion} \geq \text{market cap} \geq \$1.167 \text{ billion} \\ \text{Low cap: } 1.70\% \text{ if } \$1.167 \text{ billion} > \text{market cap} > \$.331 \text{ billion} \\ \text{Micro cap: } 4.01\% \text{ if market cap is} \leq \$.331 \text{ billion} \end{cases} \quad (4.8)$$

Factor models   A second approach that was introduced in the 1980s is the use of multifactor risk models that capture the risk of investments with multiple betas and factor risk premiums. These risk factors can come from macroeconomic variables, like changes in interest rates, inflation, or GDP, or from the returns of what are known as factor portfolios. Factor portfolios can be formed using purely statistical procedures, like factor analysis or principle components analysis, or by grouping stocks based on their characteristics.

The most widely used factor model is the *Fama-French three-factor model* that attempts to capture the determinants of equity returns using three risk premiums:[21] the equity risk premium of the CAPM, a size risk premium, and a risk premium related to the relative value of the firm when compared to its book value (historical cost-based value). The Fama-French equation for the cost of equity capital includes three factors with their associated risk premiums (thus the use of the term "three-factor model"), found in Equation 4.9:

$$k_e = k_{rf} + b \times (\text{ERP}) + s \times (\text{SMBP}) + h \times (\text{HMLP}) \quad (4.9)$$

---

[20]E. Fama and K. French, "The Cross-section of Expected Stock Returns," *Journal of Finance* 47 (1992), 427–465.

[21]E. Fama and K. French, "Common Risk Factors in the Returns on Stocks and Bonds," *Journal of Financial Economics* 33, 3–56.

where k_e is the required rate of return for the common stock of the firm; k_{rf} is the risk-free rate of interest on long-term government bonds (5.02% on the date of this writing); b, s, and h are estimated coefficients for the particular firm whose cost of equity is being evaluated; ERP is the equity risk premium, equal to the difference in the expected rate of return from investing in the market portfolio of equities and the long-term risk-free-rate of interest (as noted earlier, we use an ERP of 5%); SMBP is the "small minus big risk premium," estimated from historical return differences in large- and small-cap stocks (3.36%); and HMLP is the "high minus low risk premium," estimated as the difference between the historical average annual returns on the high book-to-market (value) and low book-to-market (growth) portfolios (4.4%).[22]

The key to implementing the Fama-French model involves the estimation of the three factor coefficients (i.e., b, s, and h). To do this we use the following multiple regression equation of a firm's common stock returns on the historical values of each of the risk premia variables. We illustrate the use of the Fama-French three-factor model for Dell Computer Corporation. Estimates of b, s, and h are found below, using returns for the 48-month period ending with December 31, 2005, and using the regression model in Equation 4.10.

$$(R_{Dell} - R_f)_t = \alpha + b(R_m - R_f)_t + s(R_S - R_L)_t + h(R_H - R_L)_t + \epsilon_t \quad (4.10)$$

where $(R_m - R_f)_t$ is the market's equity risk premium (ERP) for month t, $(R_S - R_L)_t$ is the difference in returns from portfolios of small and large company stock returns for month t (i.e., SMBP), $(R_H - R_L)_t$ is the difference in returns from portfolios of high and low book-to-market stocks for month t (i.e., HMLP), and ϵ_t is the regression error term. Historical monthly values for the three risk premia variables dating back to 1927 and daily data back to 1963 can be found on Kenneth French's Web site.[23] (See the Technical Insight box on calculating the Fama-French risk premia.)

We estimate Dell's cost of equity by substituting into Equation 4.10 as follows:

Coefficients	Coefficient Estimates	Risk Premia	Product
b	1.1726	5.00%	5.86%
s	0.1677	3.36%	0.56%
h	−0.7085	4.40%	−3.12%
		Risk premium =	3.31%
		+ Risk-free rate =	5.02%
		Cost of equity	8.33%

---

[22] The equity market risk premium (ERP) used here is our estimate, while the two remaining risk premia represent average risk premia as reported in Ibbotson Associates, *Cost of Capital Yearbook for 2005*, p. 40.

[23] http://mba.tuck.dartmouth.edu/pages/faculty/ken.french/data_library.html

Calculating the Fama-French Risk Premia

Annual, monthly, and daily estimates for each of the three sources of risk in the Fama-French three-factor model can be found on Ken French's Web site. Each of the factors is defined as follows:

- $R_m - R_f$, the excess return on the market, is the value-weighted return on all NYSE, AMEX, and NASDAQ stocks (from CRSP) minus the one-month Treasury bill rate (from Ibbotson Associates).

- $R_S - R_B$ is the average return on three small portfolios minus the average return on three big portfolios,

$$R_S - R_B = 1/3(\text{Small Value} + \text{Small Neutral} + \text{Small Growth})$$
$$- 1/3(\text{Big Value} + \text{Big Neutral} + \text{Big Growth})$$

- $R_H - R_L$ is the average return on two value portfolios minus the average return on two growth portfolios,

$$R_H - R_L = 1/2 \,(\text{Small Value} + \text{Big Value}) - 1/2 \,(\text{Small Growth} + \text{Big Growth})$$

See E. Fama and K. French, 1993, "Common Risk Factors in the Returns on Stocks and Bonds," *Journal of Financial Economics* 33, 3–56, for a complete description of the factor returns.

The resulting estimate of Dell's cost of equity in this example is 8.33%, which is very different from the 11.02% we got using the standard CAPM.

To explore differences between the cost of equity estimates using the Fama-French three-factor model and the standard CAPM, we present the cost of equity using each method for a variety of stocks in Table 4-2. A quick review of the two estimates of the cost of equity (Fama-French and the traditional CAPM) found in this table indicates that the estimates are very similar for most firms, but there are notable exceptions. For example, the cost of equity from the three-factor model is somewhat lower for Dell and is somewhat higher for General Motors. These differences reflect the fact that the three-factor model is designed to account for the fact that the CAPM has historically overestimated the returns of growth stocks like Dell and has underestimated the returns of value stocks like General Motors.

Which model provides a better estimate of the cost of equity? The empirical evidence shows that the three-factor model better explains historical returns than the traditional one-factor CAPM, which is not surprising given that the model was designed

Table 4-2   **Fama-French versus CAPM Estimates of the Cost of Equity**

Company Name	Fama-French (FF) Coefficients			FF Cost of Equity	CAPM Beta	CAPM Cost of Equity	CAPM Minus FF Cost of Equity
	b	s	h				
Dell Computers	1.1726	0.1677	−0.7085	8.33%	1.2	11.02%	2.69%
General Motors	0.9189	0.5838	0.9102	15.58%	1.2	11.02%	−4.56%
IBM	1.5145	0.0203	0.3632	14.26%	1.01	10.07%	−4.19%
Merck	0.8035	−1.6398	0.3546	5.09%	0.42	7.12%	2.03%
Pepsico	0.4834	−0.4545	−0.2429	4.84%	0.33	6.67%	1.83%
Pfizer	0.6052	−0.4841	−0.1223	5.88%	0.46	7.32%	1.44%
WalMart	0.6691	−0.2622	−0.0327	7.34%	0.6	8.02%	0.68%

to explain these returns. However, the cost of equity is a forward-looking concept, and we consider historical returns only because they provide some guidance about what we can expect to observe in the future. If we believe that the past is a good indicator of the future, then we should use the three-factor model. However, one might believe that the relatively high returns of value stocks and low returns of growth stocks represent a market inefficiency that is not likely to exist in the future, now that the "value effect" is very well known. In this case, one might prefer the traditional CAPM, which is better grounded in theory.

Limitations of cost of equity estimates based on historical returns The problems that arise with the use of historical returns to estimate the cost of equity relate to the fact that the past returns and, consequently, risk premia are frequently not very reliable predictors of future risk premia. Specifically, there are three fundamental problems associated with using historical returns as the basis for estimating the equity risk premium: (1) Historical returns vary widely over time, resulting in large estimation errors. (2) Recent changes in the tax status of equity returns and the rapid rate of expansion in access to global equity markets are likely to have driven down the equity risk premium. (3) Finally, historical returns over the long term, at least in the United States, may be too high, relative to what we can expect in the future; the U.S. economy did exceptionally well in the last century, and we don't necessarily expect that performance to be repeated.

Historical security returns are highly variable. From Figure 4-5 we see that the average historical return on a portfolio of large stocks over the period 1926 through 2005 was about 12.3%. Over this period, the average long-term Treasury bond return was 5.8%, implying that the excess return on large stocks was about 6.5%. The standard deviation of these returns was 20.2%, which implies that the standard error of the equity risk premium is approximately 2%.[24] What this means is that the 95% confidence interval of the estimate of the equity risk premium is from 2.5% to 10.5%. Clearly, the breadth of this confidence interval suggests that the most prudent course of action is to interpret historical data as *suggestive* rather than definitive.

Market conditions are changing. Looking forward, we can say that there are at least three key market factors that have changed over time and that can potentially lead to an equity risk premium that is lower in the future than it was in the past. The first has to do with taxes; the second, with increased participation in the stock market; and the third, with the increased globalization of security markets.

The tax rate on dividend income, interest income, and capital gains fluctuates over time, making equity more or less tax favored in different time periods. When equity is more tax favored, the return premium on equity should be lower relative to the rates on Treasury bonds. In the U.S., equity is more tax favored today than at any time in recent history. The Jobs and Growth Tax Relief Reconciliation Act of 2003 reduced the maximum tax rate on dividends to 15%. Previously, dividend income was taxed as ordinary income with rates up to 35%. Thirty years ago, dividends were taxed at 70%.

A second change in market conditions that is likely to affect the equity risk premium in the future relates to the growing number of individuals who participate in the equity market either by direct investments or by indirect investing via their retirement fund. Whereas the equity markets were once dominated by a limited number of wealthy investors, this is no longer the case. An important factor underlying this change was the passage of the Employment Retirement Income Security Act (ERISA) in 1974 and the growth in pension plans that ensued. Today, more than half the equity securities in the United States are held by institutional investors, including mutual funds and pension plans. The broadening participation of more individuals in the public equity markets has led to a sharing of the risk of equity ownership and may have driven down the equity risk premium.

Still another factor that can lead to a lower equity risk premium in the future relates to effects of improved investor access to global markets. This increased access tends to drive down required rates of return (and consequently the equity risk premium) due to the increased opportunities for diversification and greater participation by more investors who share the risks associated with equity investments.[25]

Historical returns exhibit survivor bias. The final problem that we encounter when using historical returns to estimate future equity risk premia relates to the fact that historical market returns that are generally available reflect the performance of

---

[24]The standard error of the sample mean return is calculated as follows: $\sigma_{\text{Annual Returns}} \div \sqrt{n-2}$ where the standard deviation in annual returns is 20.2% and n is the number of annual returns in the sample, which here is 78, resulting in an estimate of the standard error of the sample mean of 2.2%.

[25]For example, Rene Stulz suggests that the increased investment opportunity set would reduce the expected risk premium to about two-thirds of the average since 1926 (Rene Stulz, "Globalization of Capital Markets and the Cost of Capital: The Case of Nestle," *Journal of Applied Corporate Finance* 8, Issue 3 (Fall 1995).

stock markets that have done relatively well. That is, only the winners in the financial markets, such as the United States and the United Kingdom, survive to be analyzed and incorporated into the record of historical returns. Indeed, there are very few markets that have an uninterrupted period of surviving for over 75 years. History teaches us that we cannot confidently forecast that the next 75 years will be equally successful.

Method 2—Discounted Cash Flow or Imputed Rate of Return Approaches

Up to this point, we have estimated expected rates of return using the past return history as our guide. However, as the above discussion indicates, past returns may be an overly optimistic indicator of expected future returns. In this section we will describe a method of estimating the return on the market that uses *forward-looking* rather than *historical* estimates of *equity risk premia*.

Our forward-looking approach starts with the familiar discounted cash flow model. However, instead of using the DCF model to determine the value of an investment, the method takes observed values and estimated cash flows and uses the DCF model to estimate the internal rate of return, or the *implied* cost of equity capital. As we discuss below, analysts apply this methodology in two related ways. Some use the method to come up with an estimate of the market return premium that can be used to generate a CAPM-based estimate of the cost of equity. Others use the method to directly estimate a forward-looking cost of equity for individual firms.

Single-stage DCF growth model

We discuss two variants of the discounted cash flow model. The first is the Gordon growth model, which assumes that the firm's dividends grow at a constant rate forever (i.e., that there is a single growth rate or single stage of growth). The resulting single-stage discounted cash flow model of equity value can be easily deduced from the general discounted cash flow model found in Equation 4.11a below:

$$\text{Stock Price}_0 = \sum_{t=1}^{\infty} \frac{\text{Div}_{\text{Year } t}}{(1 + k_e)^t} \qquad (4.11a)$$

where

Stock Price_0 = the current stock price of the firm's shares,
$\text{Div}_{\text{Year } t}$ = expected dividend for year t, and
k_e = the cost of equity capital.

When the firm's dividends are expected to grow at a constant rate, g, forever and this rate is less than the firm's cost of equity capital, the above valuation expression can be reduced to the following:

$$\text{Stock Price}_0 = \frac{\text{Div}_{\text{Year } 0}(1 + g)}{k_e - g} = \frac{\text{Div}_{\text{Year } 1}}{k_e - g} \qquad (4.11b)$$

Consequently, the cost of equity can be found by solving for k_e in Equation 4.11c:

$$k_e = \frac{\text{Div}_{\text{Year } 1}}{\text{Stock Price}_0} + g \qquad (4.11c)$$

Analysts typically solve for k_e by observing the most recent dividend paid over the last 12 months, $\text{Div}_{\text{Year } 0}$, along with the most recent Stock Price$_0$ for the company's shares and using analysts' earnings growth rate estimates to estimate the growth rate in the firm's dividends. Depending on how the cost of equity estimate is to be used, firms will either use dividend growth estimates from stock analysts who cover the firm or will use their own internal estimates.

To illustrate, consider the case of Duke Energy Corporation (DUK). Duke is involved in a number of businesses, including natural gas transmission and electric power production. In 2005 the company paid a dividend of $1.24 per share, and on May 24, 2006, the firm's stock closed trading at a price of $27.50. The analysts' expected rate of growth in earnings for 2007 through 2011 is 5% per annum.[26] Since Equation 4.11c assumes that the firm's dividends grow forever at a constant rate, we use the five-year estimate to estimate Duke's cost of equity capital as follows:

$$k_e = \frac{\text{Div}_{\text{Year } 0}(1 + g)}{P_E} + g = \frac{\$1.24(1 + .05)}{\$27.50} + .05 = .09735 \text{ or } 9.735\%$$

Aggregating the forward-looking equity risk premia The method we have just used to impute the equity required rate of return for one firm can also be used to estimate the market's equity risk premium. The method requires that the equity risk premia for a broad sample of individual firms be estimated and then aggregated across the sample. A number of recent studies have performed this analysis, and the principal feature of the empirical evidence regarding forward-looking equity risk premia is that they are much lower than the estimates based on historical data.[27] In general, most financial analysts who estimate forward-looking equity risk premia find them to be in the 3% to 5% range.

Three-stage growth model The second variant of the discounted cash flow model differs from the first only in that it provides for *three* different growth rates, corresponding

---

[26]Based on the Yahoo Finance five-year earnings growth rate estimate (http://finance.yahoo.com/q/ae?s=DUK)

[27]Specifically, forward equity risk premia estimated in recent years for the U.S. equity market have been 3% or less. Moreover, some researchers have argued that the historical estimates of an 8% equity risk premium (using the Treasury bills to proxy for the risk-free rate) and 5% (where long-term U.S. Treasury bonds are used to proxy for the risk-free rate), have never been realistic except at market bottoms or at times of crisis (i.e., warfare).

BEHAVIORAL   INSIGHT

Managerial Optimism and the Cost of Capital

The tendency for managers to be overly optimistic about their own firm's prospects is a well-documented behavioral bias. However, this bias may not be a serious problem when it comes to the estimation of the firm's cost of capital if a discounted cash flow model such as the Gordon growth model is used. This approach to evaluating a firm's cost of equity has a potentially important side benefit when the cost of equity is estimated by a member of the firm's management. Very simply, overoptimism on the part of a member of the management team in estimating the anticipated rate of growth in the firm's earnings and dividends will lead to an upward bias in the cost of equity and, consequently, the cost of capital estimate.

To illustrate, let's consider the estimate of Duke's Energy Corporation's (DUK) cost of equity from the above example. If Duke's internal analysts are making their own estimates about future growth in the firm's earnings and dividends, they may feel that 7% is a reasonable estimate, whereas market analysts used 5%. The effect of Duke's optimistic estimate of the future rate of growth in earnings and dividends is to increase the cost of equity from 9.735% to 11.825%. This higher discount rate will tend to counter the effects of excessive optimism these same analysts may exhibit when estimating the future cash flows of Duke's investment opportunities.

to three stages of a company's growth. Specifically, this model provides for different dividend growth rates for Years 1 through 5, 6 through 10, and 11 and beyond. The corresponding three-stage growth model can be written as follows:

$$
\begin{aligned}
\text{Stock Price}_{\text{Year}_0} = &\sum_{t=1}^{5} \frac{\text{Div}_{\text{Year }0}(1 + g_{\text{Years 1 to 5}})^t}{(1 + k_e)^t} \\
&+ \sum_{t=6}^{10} \frac{\text{Div}_{\text{Year }0}(1 + g_{\text{Years 1 to 5}})^5(1 + g_{\text{Years 6 to 10}})^{t-5}}{(1 + k_e)^t} \\
&+ \left(\frac{\text{Div}_{\text{Year }0}(1 + g_{\text{Years 1 to 5}})^5(1 + g_{\text{Years 6 to 10}})^5(1 + g_{\text{Years 11 and beyond}})}{k_e - g_{\text{Years 11 and beyond}}} \right) \\
&\times \frac{1}{(1 + k_e)^{10}}
\end{aligned}
\tag{4.12}
$$

Given estimates of the three growth rates ($g_{\text{Years 1 to 5}}$, $g_{\text{Years 6 to 10}}$, and $g_{\text{Years 11 and beyond}}$), the current period dividend ($\text{Div}_{\text{Year 0}}$), and the current stock price ($\text{Stock Price}_{\text{Year 0}}$), we can solve for the cost of equity (k_e).

PRACTITIONER

INSIGHT

Market-Implied (ex ante) Market Risk Premia—An Interview with Justin Petit*

Wall Street analysts estimate the equity risk premium (hereafter ERP) in one of two ways. The ERP is typically estimated using the average spread of historical equity returns over a U.S. Treasury yield. Since this method only uses historical data, we can think of it as the ex post method. The ERP is also estimated using professional analysts' expectations of future performance and the Gordon growth model (see Equation 4.11b), which is the ex ante method.

The Gordon dividend discount model is a single-stage growth model (see Equation 4.11b) that can be rewritten for purposes of estimating the ERP. If we apply the Gordon model to the market for all common equity and then solve for the required rate of return on equity and subtract the risk-free rate of interest, we estimate the ERP as follows:

$$\text{ERP} = \left(\frac{\text{Div}_{\text{Year 0}}\,(1 + g)}{\text{Market Cap}} + g \right) - k_f$$

where $\text{Div}_{\text{Year 0}}$ is the most recent year's annual dividend payment for the market as a whole, Market Cap is the total market value of all equities, and g is the estimated long-term dividend growth rate for all stocks in the economy. Although the constant growth rate assumption of the single-stage Gordon model is problematic for a single company, analysts feel that it is more useful for a broad market.[28]

Analysts typically estimate the growth rate as the product of the average return on equity (ROE) and reinvestment rate for all equities where the reinvestment rate is simply one minus the fraction of firm earnings distributed to shareholders through dividends

The advantage of the three-stage model is its flexibility to incorporate different growth rates over the life cycle of the firm. The corresponding disadvantage, of course, is that it requires that these growth rates be estimated. Ibbotson Associates uses the I/B/E/S expected rate of growth in earnings to estimate the first growth rate, and the average rate of historical growth in earnings for the firm's industry to estimate the second.

---

[28]The ex ante model described here follows a "top-down" approach since it focuses on the aggregate return to the market for equities as a whole. An alternative method that we discuss in the text begins by estimating the ERP for individual stocks and then aggregating them to form an estimate of the ERP for all equities. This is the "bottom-up" approach.

and share repurchases. This is an ex ante approach to estimating future growth rates because it uses current market information to impute the market's expected MRP. For example, a 10% ROE and 65% reinvestment rate implies a 6.5% growth rate. Note that we are using the "distributed" rather than the "dividend" yield for, increasingly, firms pay out cash via share repurchases rather than dividends. Regardless of the mechanism, these funds are not reinvested.

The following table shows a range of potential market risk premia as a function of assumed perpetual growth rates and distributed yields (i.e., ratios of cash distributions through dividends and share repurchases divided by the current market capitalization):

Market Risk Premium	Nominal Perpetual Growth Rate				
	4%	5%	6%	7%	8%
1%	0.3%	1.3%	2.3%	3.3%	4.3%
2%	1.3%	2.3%	3.3%	4.3%	5.3%
Distributed Yield 3%	2.3%	3.3%	4.3%	5.3%	6.3%
4%	3.3%	4.3%	5.3%	6.3%	7.3%

Analysts typically arrive at an estimate of 4% to 5% for the MRP under growth rate assumptions of 5% to 7% and distributed yields of 3% to 4%. The 5% to 7% consensus estimates of long-term sustainable (nominal) growth rates are consistent with expected inflation of 2% to 3% and real GDP growth of 3% to 4%.

*Justin Petit is a Partner, Booz Allen Hamilton, New York, New York.

For the third growth rate, it uses a rate that reflects the long-term rate of growth in GDP and long-term inflation forecast; for 2004, this growth rate was 3%.[29]

To illustrate the methodology, consider Rushmore Electronics, which is a small but fast-growing company headquartered in Portland, Oregon. The firm went public two years ago, and the firm's stock currently sells for $24.00 per share with cash dividends per share of $2.20. Over the past 10 years Rushmore's earnings grew at a compound

---

[29]One further caveat needs to be mentioned with regard to Ibbotson's three-stage growth model. Since many firms do not pay dividends, Ibbotson Associates replaces dividends with cash flow in the first two terms and uses earnings per share before extraordinary items in the third term. In the latter case the earnings substitution for cash flow reflects the assumption that over time depreciation and capital expenditures will be roughly equal, such that cash flow is equal to earnings.

annual rate of 10% per year. Analysts project the firm's earnings will grow at a rate of 14% per year over the next five years. Moreover, the economy is expected to grow at a rate of 6.5%. Substituting into Equation 4.12, we get the following equation, in which the only unknown is the cost of equity, k_e:

$$\$24.00 = \sum_{t=1}^{5} \frac{\$2.20(1 + .14)^t}{(1 + k_e)^t} + \sum_{t=6}^{10} \frac{\$2.20(1 + .14)^5(1 + .10)^{t-5}}{(1 + k_e)^t}$$
$$+ \left(\frac{\$2.20(1 + .14)^5(1 + .10)^5(1 + .065)}{k_e - .065} \right) \frac{1}{(1 + k_e)^{10}}$$

Solving for k_e produces an estimate of Rushmore's cost of equity of 20.38%.[30]

In this example we have followed the Ibbotson Associates approach by making the first two growth periods five years long and by using their prescription for the estimation of stage two and three growth rates. If the analyst has good reason to believe that either the length of the growth periods or the specific growth rates should be different, these estimates should be used.

Calculating the WACC (Putting It All Together)—Step 3

The final step in the estimation of a firm's WACC involves calculating a weighted average of the estimated costs of the firm's outstanding securities. To illustrate the three-step process used to estimate WACC, consider the case of Champion Energy Corporation, which was founded in 1987 and is based in Houston, Texas. The company provides midstream energy services, including natural gas gathering, intrastate transmission, and processing in the Southwestern Louisiana and Texas Gulf Coast regions. As of December 31, 2005, the company operated approximately 5,500 miles of natural gas gathering and transmission pipelines and seven natural gas processing plants.

Evaluating Champion's Capital Structure

A condensed version of Champion's liabilities and owner's equity is found in the first two columns of Table 4-3.

Champion wants to reevaluate its cost of capital in light of its plans to make a significant acquisition to expand its operations in January and needs an additional $1.25 billion. Based on discussions with the firm's investment banker, Champion's management has chosen to increase the firm's debt from the current level of $0.75 billion up to $2 billion. Given current market conditions, they can raise the additional debt at 8.25%. Increasing the firm's use of borrowed funds is appealing to Champion's management since the interest expense offsets taxable income at the 25% tax rate faced by the firm.

---

[30]This problem is easily solved in a spreadsheet using built-in functions (for example, in Excel the function is "Goal Seek").

Table 4-3   Liabilities and Owner's Equity for Champion Energy Corporation

Liabilities and Owners' Capital ($000)	December 31, 2006 Balance Sheet (Book Values)	December 31, 2006 Invested Capital (Market Values)
Current liabilities		
Accounts payable	$ 150,250.00	
Notes payable	—	$ —
Other current liabilities	37,250.00	
Total current liabilities	$ 187,500.00	$ —
Long-term debt (8% interest paid semiannually, due in 2015)	750,000.00	2,000,000.00
Total liabilities	$ 937,500.00	2,000,000.00
Owners' capital		
Common stock ($1 par value per share)	$ 400,000.00	
Paid-in-capital	1,250,000.00	
Accumulated earnings	2,855,000.00	
Total owners' capital	$4,505,000.00	8,000,000.00
Total liabilities and owners' capital	$5,442,500.00	$10,000,000.00

Champion's CFO called in his chief financial analyst and asked that he make an initial estimate of the firm's WACC assuming the firm went through with the $1.25 billion debt offering and assuming that the nature of the firm's operations and business risk are not affected by the use of the net proceeds. The analyst began her analysis by evaluating the firm's capital structure under the assumption that the new debt offering was consummated. Since the effect of the offering on the value of the firm's equity was uncertain, she thought as a first approximation she would just assume that the total market value of the firms' shares would be unchanged. Based on the current market price of $20.00 per share, she calculated the market capitalization of the firm's equity to be $8 billion.

The third column on the right-hand side of Table 4-3 contains the results of the analysts' investigation into Champion's proposed capital structure following the new debt issue. Champion's total invested capital is equal to $10 billion, which includes interest-bearing debt of $2 billion and the firm's equity capitalization of $8 billion ($20.00 per share multiplied by 400 million shares). Consequently, the capital structure weights are 20% debt and 80% equity.

Estimating Champion's Costs of Debt and Equity Capital

Based on current yields to maturity for Champion's new debt offering, we estimate the before-tax cost of debt financing to be 8.25%. Since Champion enjoys an investment-grade bond rating, we can use the yield to maturity as a reasonable approximation to the cost of new debt financing. Adjusting the 8.25% yield for the firm's 25% tax rate produces an after-tax cost of debt of 6.19% = 8.25%(1 − .25).

To calculate the cost of equity, three estimates were used: the CAPM, the three-factor Fama-French, and the three-stage DCF model.[31] The resulting estimates are found below:

Cost of Equity Model	Estimated Cost of Equity
CAPM	8.37%
Three-Factor Fama-French	10.02%
Discounted cash flow (Three-stage)	11.60%

The average of the three estimates of the cost of equity is 10.0%, and the analyst decided to use this as her initial estimate of the cost of equity capital to calculate the firm's WACC.

Calculating Champion's WACC

The WACC for Champion's proposed capital structure is calculated as follows:

Source of Capital	Capital Structure Weight (Proportion)	After-Tax Cost	Weighted After-Tax Cost
Debt	20%	6.19%	0.01238
Equity	80%	10.00%	0.07997
		WACC =	9.23%

Therefore, we estimate Champion's WACC to be 9.23% based on its planned use of debt financing and operating plans.

Taking a Stand on the Issues—Estimating the Firm's Cost of Capital

Our discussion of the estimation of the cost of capital began by enumerating three basic issues that had to be addressed. In the process of reviewing all the ins and outs

---

[31]These cost of equity estimates represent the large industry composite for SIC 4924 (Natural Gas Distribution) as estimated by Ibbotson and Associates, *Cost of Capital 2006 Yearbook* (data through March 2006).

of the estimation process, it is apparent that analysts must make a lot of decisions that can have a material effect on the cost of capital estimate. Here we briefly recap each of the issues that must be addressed and summarize the procedures that we feel represent the best thinking on each issue.

Figure 4-6 compiles a listing of each of the basic issues we have addressed in the estimation of the cost of capital to this point. The salient points are the following:

- Use market value weights to define a firm's capital structure and omit non-interest-bearing debt from the calculations. If the firm plans to change its current usage of debt and equity, then the target weights should replace current weights.
- If the cost of capital is to be used to discount distant future cash flows, then use the yield on a long-term bond in the estimation of the market risk premium, as well as in calculating the excess market returns that are used in the estimation of beta.
- When the firm issues investment-grade debt, use the yield to maturity (estimated using current market prices and promised interest and principal payments) to estimate the cost of debt. However, when the firm's debt is speculative-grade, the yield to maturity on the firm's debt (which represents the promised, not expected, yield on the debt) will overestimate the cost of debt financing.
- Use multiple methods for estimating the cost of equity capital. This is the single most difficult estimate the firm will make. Using both asset pricing models and discounted cash flow models provides independent estimates of the cost of equity.
- Since the cost of capital is used to discount cash flows to be received in the future, the focus of our analysis should be forward-looking. This does not mean that we ignore historical data. However, it does mean that historical data are useful only if they help us better understand the future. Indeed, the equity risk premium for the market is typically estimated as an average of past returns, which implies a market risk premium of 6% to 8%. However, a number of recent studies have utilized the expectations of investment professionals to infer an equity risk premium and found it to be much lower. The estimates for the forward-looking market risk premium are in the 3% to 4% range.

4.4 SUMMARY

A firm's weighted average cost of capital (WACC) provides the rate that is used to discount a firm's future cash flows and determine how it is likely to be valued in the financial marketplace. The estimation of a firm's WACC involves three fundamental activities: evaluating the composition of the firm's capital structure, estimating the opportunity cost of each source of capital, and calculating a weighted average of the after-tax cost of each source of capital.

The WACC is used extensively by firms throughout the world. Firms use their own WACCs to calculate whether they are under- or overvalued. Hence, a firm's

Figure 4-6   Issues and Recommendations on the Estimation of a Firm's Cost of Capital

Topic	Issues	Best Practices
(1) Defining the firm's capital structure	What liabilities should be included in defining the firm's capital structure?	Include only those liabilities that have an explicit interest cost associated with them. Specifically, exclude noninterest-bearing liabilities such as accounts payable.
	How should the various sources of capital in the capital structure be weighted?	Weights should reflect the current importance of sources of financing which, in turn, is reflected in current market values. However, since corporate bonds do not trade often, if at all, and a large component of corporate debt is private debt (i.e., bank loans), which does not have an observable market value, book values are often used.
(2) Choosing the appropriate risk-free rate of interest	What maturity is appropriate for the risk-free government security?	U.S. government debt is the best representation of a risk-free security. However, asset pricing theory provides little guidance as to whether a short-term, intermediate-term, or long-term U.S. Treasury security should be used. Standard practice now is to use a long-term government bond.
(3) Estimating the cost of debt financing	How do you estimate the expected rate of return on investment-grade debt?	Current yields to maturity serve as a reasonable proxy for the expected cost of debt.
	How do you estimate the expected rate of return on speculative or below-investment-grade debt?	Adjustments for the risk of default and recovery rates become important where the prospect of default is significant. The adjustments lead to an estimate of the expected rate of return to the firm's creditors that is based on expected cash flows rather than promised cash flows.
(4) Estimating the cost of equity financing	What model should be used to estimate the cost of equity financing?	Two classes of models are widely used in the estimation of the cost of equity financing: One is based on asset pricing theory, and the other is based on discounted cash flow. Given the inherent difficulties involved in estimating the cost of equity capital, it is wise to use both types of models in an effort to define the potential range of equity capital costs.
	Should historical or forward-looking data be the basis for estimating the cost of common equity?	Historical data are only useful in estimating the cost of capital to the extent that these data are informative about future returns. Thus, in general, forward-looking information is more consistent with the objective of the analysis than are historical data.
	How large is the equity risk premium?	Historical data suggest that the equity risk premium for the market portfolio has averaged 6% to 8% a year over the past 75 years. However, there is good reason to believe that this estimate is far too high. In fact, the equity risk premium according to recent estimates lies in the range of 3% to 4%. We recommend a 5% equity risk premium for the market.

WACC will influence how firms respond to acquisition offers, and because firms are reluctant to issue undervalued securities, the WACC calculation can also influence financing choices. Finally, as we will discuss in Chapter 9, firms often use their WACC to evaluate the extent to which their managers are able to generate returns that exceed their firms' cost of capital.

The main focus in this book is on how firms evaluate investment opportunities. In this regard, the WACC plays a key role. When firms evaluate opportunities to acquire other firms, they calculate the WACC of the acquisition candidate. We will be discussing this in more detail in Chapter 7. When firms evaluate an investment project, they need a discount rate that we will refer to as the project WACC. A discussion of the project WACC is the focus of Chapter 5.

PROBLEMS

4-1 THREE-STEP PROCESS FOR ESTIMATING A FIRM'S WACC Compano Inc. was founded in 1986 in Baytown, Texas. The firm provides oil-field services to the Texas Gulf Coast region, including the leasing of drilling barges. Its balance sheet for year-end 2006 describes a firm with $830,541,000 in assets (book values) and invested capital of more than $1.334 billion (based on market values):

| | December 31, 2006 | |
Liabilities and Owners' Capital	Balance Sheet (Book Values)	Invested Capital (Market Values)
Current liabilities		
Accounts payable	$ 8,250,000	
Notes payable	—	—
Other current liabilities	7,266,000	
Total current liabilities	$ 15,516,000	$ —
Long-term debt (8.5% interest paid semiannually, due in 2015)	$420,000,000	$ 434,091,171
Total liabilities	$435,516,000	$ 434,091,171
Owners' capital		
Common stock ($1 par value per share)	$ 40,000,000	
Paid-in-capital	100,025,000	
Accumulated earnings	255,000,000	
Total owners' capital	$395,025,000	$ 900,000,000
Total liabilities and owners' capital	$830,541,000	$1,334,091,171

Compano's executive management team is concerned that its new investments be required to meet an appropriate cost of capital hurdle before capital is committed. Consequently, the firm's CFO has initiated a cost of capital study by one of his senior financial analysts, Jim Tipolli. Jim's first action was to contact the firm's investment banker to get input on current capital costs.

Jim learned that although the firm's current debt capital required an 8.5% coupon rate of interest (with annual interest payments and no principal repayments until 2015), the current yield on similar debt had declined to 8% if the firms were to raise debt funds today. When he asked about the beta for Compano's debt, Jim was told that it was standard practice to assume a beta of .30 for the corporate debt of firms such as Compano.

a. What are Compano's total invested capital and capital structure weights for debt and equity?

b. Based on Compano's corporate income tax rate of 40%, the firm's current capital structure, and an unlevered beta estimate of .90, what is Compano's levered equity beta?

c. Assuming a long-term U.S. Treasury bond yield of 5.42% and an estimated market risk premium of 5%, what should Jim's estimate of Compano's cost of equity be if he uses the CAPM?

d. What is your estimate of Compano's WACC?

4-2 CALCULATING THE EXPECTED YTM International Tile Importers, Inc., is a rapidly growing firm that imports and markets floor tiles from around the world that are used in the construction of custom homes and commercial buildings. The firm has grown so fast that its management is considering the issuance of a five-year interest-only note. The notes would have a principal amount of $1,000 and pay 12% interest each year, with the principal amount due at the end of Year 5. The firm's investment banker has agreed to help the firm place the notes and has estimated that they can be sold for $800 each under today's market conditions.

a. What is the promised yield to maturity based on the terms suggested by the investment banker?

b. *(Hint: Refer to the Appendix for this analysis.)* The firm's management looked at the yield to maturity estimated above with dismay, for it was much higher than the 12% coupon rate, which is much higher than current yields on investment-grade debt. The investment banker explained that for a small firm such as International Tile, the bond rating would probably be in the middle of the speculative grades, which requires a much higher yield to attract investors. It even suggested that the firm recalculate the expected yield to maturity on the debt under the following assumptions: The risk of default in Years 1 through 5 is 5% per year, and the recovery rate in the event of default is only 50%. What is the expected yield to maturity under these conditions?

4-3 CALCULATING THE PROMISED YTM In 2005 the Eastman Kodak Corporation (EK) had a straight bond issue outstanding that was due in eight years. The bonds are currently selling for 108.126 or $1,081.26 per bond and pay a semiannual interest payment based on a 7.25% (annual) coupon rate of interest. Assuming that the bonds remain outstanding until maturity and the company makes all promised interest and principal payments in a timely basis, what is the yield to maturity to the bondholders?

4-4 CALCULATING THE PROMISED YTM Evaluate the promised yield to maturity for the bonds issued by Ford (F) and General Motors (GM) as of February 2005. (You may assume that interest is paid semiannually. Also, round the number of compounding periods to the nearest six months.)

Ford Motor Co.

Coupon:	6.3750%
Maturity:	02/01/2029
Rating:	Baa1/BBB–
Price:	92.7840

General Motors Corp.

Coupon:	8.375%
Maturity:	07/15/2033
Rating:	Baa2 /BBB–
Price:	106.1250

Noting that both these bond issues have similar ratings, comment on the use of yield to maturity you have just calculated as an estimate of the cost of debt financing to the two firms.

4-5 CALCULATING THE COST OF EQUITY Smaltz Enterprises is currently involved in its annual review of the firm's cost of capital. Historically, the firm has relied on the CAPM to estimate its cost of equity capital. The firm estimates that its equity beta is 1.25, and the current yield on long-term U.S. Treasury bonds is 4.28%. The firm's CFO is currently in a debate with one of the firm's advisors at its investment bank about the level of the equity risk premium. Historically, Smaltz has used 7% to approximate the equity risk premium. However, the investment banker argues that this premium has shrunk dramatically in recent years and is more likely to be in the 3% to 4% range.

  a. Estimate Smaltz's cost of equity capital using a market risk premium of 3.5%.
  b. Smaltz's capital structure is comprised of 75% equity (based on current market prices) and 25% debt on which the firm pays a yield of 5.125% before taxes at 25%.

What is the firm's WACC under each of the two assumptions about the market risk premium?

4-6 THREE-STEP PROCESS FOR ESTIMATING A FIRM'S WACC Harriston Electronics builds circuit boards for a variety of applications in industrial equipment. The firm was founded in 1983 by two electrical engineers who left their jobs with the General Electric (GE) Corporation. Its balance sheet for year-end 2006 describes a firm with $1,184,841,000 in assets (book values) and invested capital of approximately $2.2 billion (based on market values):

	December 31, 2006	
	Balance Sheet	Invested Capital
Liabilities and Owners' Capital	(Book Values)	(Market Values)
Current Liabilities		
Accounts payable	$ 17,550,000	
Notes payable	20,000,000	20,000,000
Other current liabilities	22,266,000	
Total current liabilities	$ 59,816,000	$ 20,000,000
Long-term debt (7.5% interest paid semiannually, due in 2012)	$ 650,000,000	$ 624,385,826
Total liabilities	$ 709,816,000	$ 644,385,826
Owners' capital		
Common stock ($1 par value per share)	$ 20,000,000	
Paid-in-capital	200,025,000	
Accumulated earnings	255,000,000	
Total owners' capital	$ 475,025,000	$1,560,000,000
Total liabilities and owners' capital	$1,184,841,000	$ 2,204,385,826

Harriston's CFO, Margaret L. Hines, is concerned that its new investments be required to meet an appropriate cost of capital hurdle before capital is committed. Consequently, she initiated a cost of capital study by one of her senior financial analysts, Jack Frist. Shortly after receiving the assignment, Jack called the firm's investment banker to get input on current capital costs.

Jack learned that although the firm's current debt capital required a 7.5% coupon rate of interest (with annual interest payments and no principal repayments until 2012), the current yield to maturity on similar debt had risen to 8.5%, such that the current market value of the firm's outstanding bonds had fallen to $624,385,826.

Moreover, since the firm's short-term notes were issued within the last 30 days, the 9% contract rate on the notes was the same as the current cost of credit for such notes.

    a. What are Harriston's total invested capital and capital structure weights for debt and equity? (Hint: The firm has some short-term debt [notes payable] that is also interest bearing.)

    b. Assuming a long-term U.S. Treasury bond yield of 5.42% and an estimated market risk premium of 5%, what is Harriston's cost of equity based on the CAPM if the firm's levered equity beta is 1.2?

    c. What is your estimate of Harriston's WACC? The firm's tax rate is 35%.

4-7 UNLEVERING AND RELEVERING EQUITY BETAS In 2006 the major airline carriers, with the principal exception of Southwest Airlines (LUV) continued to be in dire financial condition following the attack on the World Trade Center in 2001.

    a. Given the following data for Southwest Airlines and three other airlines (for November 28, 2006), estimate the unlevered equity beta for Southwest Airlines using the procedure described in Table 4-1. You may assume a 38% tax rate in your calculations.

Company Name	Levered Equity Beta	Debt/Equity Capitalization	Assumed Debt Beta
American Airlines (AMR)	3.2400	205.16%	0.30
Delta Airlines (DALR.PK)	4.0500	5663.67%	0.40
Jet Blue (JBLU)	(0.1100)	106.22%	0.30
Southwest Airlines (LUV)	(0.0100)	14.93%	0.20

    b. Based on your estimate of Southwest Airlines's unlevered equity beta, relever the beta to get an estimate of the firm's levered beta.

    c. The airline industry is obviously in a very unique position at the end of 2006. Are there any special concerns that you have regarding the estimation of the cost of equity for Southwest Airlines using the procedure described here?

4-8 ESTIMATING THE COST OF EQUITY USING THE FAMA-FRENCH METHOD Telecom services is an industry under rapid transformation as telephone, Internet, and television services are being brought together under a common technology. In the fall of 2006 the telecom analyst for HML Capital, a private investment company, was trying to evaluate the cost of equity for two giants in the telecom industry: SBC Communications (AT&T) and Verizon Communications. Specifically, he wanted to look at two alternative methods for making the estimate: the CAPM and Fama-French three-factor model. The CAPM utilizes only one risk premium for the market as a whole, whereas the Fama-French model uses three (one for each of three factors).

The factors are (1) a market risk premium, (2) a risk premium related to firm size, and (3) a market to book risk premium. Data for the risk premium sensitivities $(b, s,$ and $h)$ as well as the beta coefficient for the CAPM are found below:

Company Name	Fama-French (FF) Coefficients			CAPM Beta
	b	s	h	
SBC Communications (AT&T)	1.0603	−1.4998	1.0776	0.62
Verizon Communications	1.1113	−0.9541	0.639	0.79

The risk premia for each of the risk factors are as follows:

Coefficients	Risk Premia
Market risk premium	5.00%
Size risk premium	3.36%
Market to book risk premium	4.40%

a. If the risk-free rate of interest is 5.02%, what is the estimated cost of equity for the two firms using the CAPM?

b. What is the estimated cost of equity capital for the two firms using the Fama-French three-factor model? Interpret the meaning of the signs $(+/-)$ attached to each of the factors, (i.e., $b, s,$ and h).

4-9 CALCULATING THE COST OF CONVERTIBLE DEBT *(Hint: This exercise is based on the Appendix.)* The Eastman Kodak Corporation has an issue of convertible bonds outstanding in the spring of 2005 that have a $6\frac{3}{4}\%$ coupon rate of interest and sell for $1,277.20 per bond. The interest payments are made semiannually. If the cost of straight debt is equal to the yield to maturity on the bonds described in Problem 4-3 and the cost of new equity raised through the sale of the conversion option is 13.5%, what is the estimated cost of convertible bonds to the company?

4-10 PROMISED VERSUS EXPECTED YTM *(Hint: This exercise is based on the Appendix.)* In May 2005 the credit rating agencies downgraded the debt of the General Motors Corporation (GM) to junk status.

a. Discuss the effect of this drop in credit status on the company's WACC.

b. If you have been using the yield to maturity for the firm's bonds as your estimate of the cost of debt capital and you use the same estimation procedure following the downgrade, has your estimate become more or less reliable? Explain.

Extensions and Refinements of WACC Estimation

Our analysis of WACC in the chapter dealt with the basic issues encountered in a simple setting. In this section we address some problems that arise in the analysis of a firm's WACC that are often overlooked in introductory discussions. Specifically, we discuss: (1) the estimation of the cost of below-investment-grade debt, where the promised yield to maturity is often much higher than the expected cost of the debt; (2) estimation of the cost of convertible debt, which is a hybrid form of financing that contains both debt and equity elements; and (3) the analysis of *off-balance-sheet* sources of financing, including special-purpose entities.

Estimating the Expected Cost of Below-Investment-Grade Debt Financing

We noted earlier in the chapter that the promised yield to maturity (calculated using the promised principal and interest payments) overstates the cost of debt to the company if the debt is below investment grade. To see why this is so, consider how the stated yield to maturity of a bond is calculated. The yield to maturity, as traditionally defined, is simply the internal rate of return earned by purchasing a bond for its current market price, assuming that you receive all of the bond's promised interest and principal payments over the life of the bond. Since this calculation uses *promised* interest and principal payments, and not *expected* cash receipts (which allow for the prospect of default and the recovery of less than 100% of the bond's face value), this computation produces an estimate of the *promised yield to maturity* on the debt,[32] not the *expected yield to maturity*.

---

[32]In Chapter 2 we used the term "hoped-for" cash flows as optimistic cash flows, contrasted with expected cash flows. In essence, the promised principal and interest payments for bonds that are risky (i.e., have a nonnegligible risk of default) are the bondholder's "hoped-for" cash flows. Thus, the term *promised* cash flow is synonymous with *hoped-for* cash flow.

We calculate the promised yield to maturity by solving for the discount rate, $Y_{Promised}$, which satisfies the following discounted cash flow equation:

$$\begin{array}{c} \text{Bond Price} \\ \text{Today} \end{array} = \$1{,}000 = \frac{\text{Promised Principal and Interest in One Year}}{(1 + Y_{Promised})^1}$$

$$= \frac{\$1{,}100}{(1 + Y_{Promised})^1}$$

The $Y_{Promised}$ is 10% in this instance. This promised yield to maturity is equal to the expected return to the investor only when the promised payment of $1,100 is made with certainty. In other words, $Y_{Promised}$ is the investor's expected rate of return (thus the firm's cost of debt capital) only when there is no risk of default.

When a firm's debt is subject to the risk of default, the promised yield to maturity *overstates* the expected yield to maturity to the debt holder. To see how the prospect of default drives a wedge between the promised and expected yields to maturity on debt, consider the simple case of a bond that matures in one year and pays the holder the $1,000 face value of the bond plus $100 in interest. The risky bond has a current price of $800 and promises to pay the holder $1,100 in principal and interest in one year. We calculate the promised yield to maturity by solving for the discount rate, $Y_{Promised}$, which satisfies the following discounted cash flow equation:

$$\begin{array}{c} \text{Bond Price} \\ \text{Today} \end{array} = \$800 = \frac{\text{Promised Principal and Interest in One Year}}{(1 + Y_{Promised})^1}$$

$$= \frac{\$1{,}100}{(1 + Y_{Promised})^1}$$

Solving for the promised yield to maturity, we estimate it to be 37.5%.

Now assume that the likelihood of default by the issuer of the bond is 20% (i.e., there is an 80% probability that the bondholder will receive the full $1,100). Also, in the event of default the debt holder will receive 60% of the promised $1,100 payment, or $660. The expected cash flow then is $(.80 \times \$1{,}100) + (.2 \times \$660) = \$1{,}012$. We can now calculate the expected yield to maturity using this expected cash flow as follows:

$$\begin{array}{c} \text{Bond Price} \\ \text{Today} \end{array} = \$800 = \frac{\text{Expected Bond Payment in One Year}}{(1 + Y_{Expected})^1} = \frac{\$1{,}012}{(1 + Y_{Expected})^1}$$

The estimate of $Y_{Expected}$ is only 26.5%. This represents the expected cost of the firm's debt capital, not the promised yield to maturity of 37.5% calculated above. The difference between the promised and the expected yield to maturity in this example is quite large, because the probability of default is quite high, and the recovery rate is 60%.

Default Rates, Recovery Rates, and Yields on Corporate Debt

In order to determine the expected return on a debt instrument, one needs estimates of both default rates and recovery rates. Moody's Investors Service provides historical research regarding both these rates and forecasts of future rates as well.

For example, Table 4A-1 summarizes the cumulative default rates on corporate bonds over the period 1983–2000. Note that there is a dramatic difference in default risk for investment- versus speculative-grade bonds. In fact, the cumulative default risk for investment-grade bonds is less than 2% even after 10 years, whereas the comparable rate for speculative-grade bonds exceeds 30%.

The important thing to note about Table 4A-1 is the following: For firms that issue investment-grade debt, the risk of default is so low that the difference between promised and expected yields is insignificant for practical purposes. However, for speculative-grade debt, issuers' default is much more likely, and it has a significant effect on the cost of debt capital.

What about bondholder recovery rates in the event of default? Estimates of expected recovery rates (like expected default rates) are based on historical experience, and Moody's maintains records on recovery rates. Moody's approximates the recovery rate using the ratio of the market price to the par value of the bond one month after default. The average recovery rate in 2000 was 28.8% of par, a rate that was down from 39.7% a year earlier and the post-1970 average of 42%.[33]

Complicating the prediction process is the fact that recovery rates are inversely correlated with default rates. Very simply, higher default rates are often associated with lower recovery rates. However, for our purposes in the examples that follow, we assume a constant recovery rate.

Estimating the Expected Yield to Maturity for a Long-Term Bond

To illustrate how we might estimate the expected yield to maturity on a bond that faces the risk of default, consider the example posed in Table 4A-2. The bond has a

---

Table 4A-1 **Average Cumulative Default Rates for 1 to 10 Years—1983–2000**

	Year 1	Year 2	Year 3	Year 4	Year 5	Year 6	Year 7	Year 8	Year 9	Year 10
Investment grade	0.05%	0.17%	0.35%	0.60%	0.84%	1.08%	1.28%	1.47%	1.62%	1.73%
Speculative grade	3.69%	8.39%	12.87%	16.80%	20.39%	23.61%	26.44%	29.04%	31.22%	32.89%

Source: Moody's Investors Service, *Default and Recovery Rates of Corporate Bond Issuers: 2000,* Global Credit Research (February 2001), Exhibit 42, p. 47.

---

[33]D. Hamilton, G. Gupton, and A. Berthault, *Default and Recovery Rates of Corporate Bond Issuers: 2000,* Moody's Investors Service Global Credit Research (February 2001), p. 3.

Table 4A-2 Estimating the Expected Cost of Debt on a Long-Term Bond (Rated Caa/CCC)

Coupon	14%	Bond rating	Caa/CCC
Principal	$1,000.00	10-Year Treasury yield = 5.02%	
Price	$ 829.41		
Maturity	10 years		
Recovery rate	50%		

Year	Default Cash Flows										Promised Cash Flow
	Year 1	Year 2	Year 3	Year 4	Year 5	Year 6	Year 7	Year 8	Year 9	Year 10	
0	(829.41)	(829.41)	(829.41)	(829.41)	(829.41)	(829.41)	(829.41)	(829.41)	(829.41)	(829.41)	(829.41)
1	570.00	140.00	140.00	140.00	140.00	140.00	140.00	140.00	140.00	140.00	140.00
2		570.00	140.00	140.00	140.00	140.00	140.00	140.00	140.00	140.00	140.00
3			570.00	140.00	140.00	140.00	140.00	140.00	140.00	140.00	140.00
4				570.00	140.00	140.00	140.00	140.00	140.00	140.00	140.00
5					570.00	140.00	140.00	140.00	140.00	140.00	140.00
6						570.00	140.00	140.00	140.00	140.00	140.00
7							570.00	140.00	140.00	140.00	140.00
8								570.00	140.00	140.00	140.00
9									570.00	140.00	140.00
10										570.00	1,140.00
Expected yield to maturity if default occurs in this year	−31.28%	−8.23%	0.98%	5.85%	8.80%	10.76%	12.12%	13.12%	13.87%	14.44%	**17.76%**
Probability of default in each year	3.69%	4.70%	4.48%	3.93%	3.59%	3.22%	2.83%	2.60%	2.18%	1.67%	67.11%
Weighted YTM = E(YTM) × Probability of default	−1.15%	−0.39%	0.04%	0.23%	0.32%	0.35%	0.34%	0.34%	0.30%	0.24%	11.92%

Promised YTM → 17.76%

Expected YTM = Cost of debt

12.54% → Average YTM based on expected cash flows

10-year maturity, a 14% coupon rate, and a $1,000 principal amount. This bond, which has a current price of $829.41, has a promised yield to maturity of 17.76%, which is of course substantially higher than the expected yield to maturity of 12.54%, which accounts for the probability of default and less than 100% recovery rate.[34]

To account for the probability of default, we list in the columns the cash flows that the bondholder receives in the event the bond defaults after each year up to 10 years. The probability of default for each of these default scenarios is found below each of the "Year" columns.[35] In addition, we assume that the recovery rate in the event of default is 50%, regardless of the year in which the default occurs. This means that in the event of default the cash flow to the bondholders is $570 (i.e., the product of the $1,140 in promised interest plus principal multiplied by the estimated recovery rate of 50%).

Estimating the expected yield to maturity for the 10-year bond is a two-step process. The first step entails estimating the yield to maturity for the cash flows in each scenario. For example, if the bond were to default in the first year after its issuance, then the bondholder would have received a return one year later of only $570 (50% of the promised principal plus interest), resulting in a rate of return or yield to maturity of −31.28% on his or her $829.41 investment.

Once the yield to maturity for each of the years in which default might occur (i.e., the default scenarios) is calculated, we can combine them to determine the expected yield to maturity for the bond. We consider a total of 11 different default scenarios corresponding to default in Years 1 through 10 plus the no-default scenario. The expected yield to maturity of the bond is equal to a weighted average of these possible yields, where the weights are equal to the probability of default in each year plus the probability of not defaulting at all. The resulting expected yield to maturity for this bond is 12.54%, which is substantially less than the promised yield to maturity of 17.76%.

In our example we assumed a recovery rate of 50%. However, we reported earlier that the average recovery rates have been falling and now are approximately 30%. At this lower recovery rate, the expected YTM is only 9.13%. Consequently, lower recovery rates result in an even more dramatic difference between promised and expected YTM.

Estimating the Cost of Hybrid Sources of Financing—Convertible Bonds

Firms often issue what are referred to as **hybrid securities,** which have the attributes of debt and common equity or of preferred stock and common equity. For example, *convertible bonds and convertible preferred stock* represent a very important class of hybrid securities that give the holder the option to exchange, at his or her discretion,

---

[34]The 17.76% promised YTM is consistent with the 12.75% spread over the YTM on 10-year Treasury bonds (5.02% YTM) for Caa/CCC bonds reported in Figure 4-3.

[35]The probability of default is equal to the incremental percent of below-investment-grade debt that defaults each year, as reported in Table 4A-1.

the bond or preferred stock for a prescribed number of common shares. Although these securities are not major sources of capital for investment-grade companies, they provide an important source of financing for many emerging high-tech companies and other smaller firms.

The value of a convertible security can be viewed as the value of the bond or preferred share plus the value of the conversion feature, which is technically a call option.[36] To illustrate, consider the case of a convertible bond whose value is defined by Equation 4A.1:

$$\begin{array}{c} \text{Convertible} \\ \text{Bond Value} \end{array} = \left(\begin{array}{c} \text{Straight} \\ \text{Bond Value} \end{array} \right) + \left(\begin{array}{c} \text{Call} \\ \text{Option Value} \end{array} \right) \qquad (4A.1)$$

This "dual" source of value means that the cost of financing by issuing convertibles is a function of both the underlying security (bond or preferred stock) and the call option. Consequently, the cost of capital obtained by issuing convertible bonds can be thought of as a weighted average of the cost of issuing straight bonds and the cost of the exchange feature (call option), where the weights equal the relative contributions of the two components to the value of the security.

To illustrate how we might approach the estimation of the cost of convertible debt, consider the convertible debt issued by Computer Associates (CA) that is due March 15, 2007. The bonds sold for $1,066.19 on February 3, 2005, and paid a semiannual coupon payment based on an annual rate of interest equal to 5%. Each bond can be converted into 41.0846 shares of Computer Associates common stock beginning March 21, 2005. The convertible bond issue, like all of the firm's bonds, is rated BB+ by Standard and Poor's.

Before describing how to determine the appropriate cost of capital that should be ascribed to this convertible security, we first note that the promised yield to maturity on the bond, assuming that it is not converted, is only 1.61%. It should also be noted that the promised yield on the firm's straight debt is 4.25%. Clearly, the expected return on the convertible security exceeds the return on the straight debt, but by how much?

To estimate the cost of financing to Computer Associates from the convertible issue, we calculate a weighted average of the cost of straight debt and the cost of raising capital through the sale of the associated call option. We estimate the required rate of return on the convertible bonds using a three-step procedure:

Step 1: *Estimate the component values of the convertible bond issue: straight debt and the conversion call option.* Computer Associates' convertible bonds sold for $1,066.19 on the date of our analysis, so if we value the straight-debt component, we can calculate the value that the market is assigning to the call option component.

---

[36]We discuss options and their valuation in some detail beginning in Chapter 10. However, for now it is sufficient that we understand what a call option represents.

To value the straight-debt component, we need an estimate of the market's yield to maturity for straight debt that Computer Associates could issue today. The firm has a straight-debt issue outstanding with a similar maturity to the convertibles. The straight bond provides a market-based yield to maturity to the bondholders of 4.25%. Consequently, the straight-bond component of the convertible issue can be valued by discounting the promised interest and principal payments using 4.25%:

$$\text{Straight Bond Value} = \frac{\$25.00}{(1 + .0425/2)^1} + \frac{\$25.00}{(1 + .0425/2)^2} + \frac{\$25.00}{(1 + .0425/2)^3}$$
$$+ \frac{\$25.00 + \$1,000.00}{(1 + .0425/2)^4} = \$1,014.24$$

The value of the call option component therefore is $51.95 = \$1,066.19 - 1,014.24$.

Step 2: *Estimate the costs of the straight-debt and option components of the convertible bond issue.* We have already estimated the cost of the straight debt to Computer Associates using the yield to maturity on similarly rated bonds issued by the firm that have a similar term to maturity (i.e., 4.25%).[37] However, estimating the cost of the conversion feature (i.e., the conversion call option component) is more difficult and requires an understanding of call options, which we discuss in Chapter 11. Since the call options can be viewed as a levered version of the firm's common equity, we know that the cost of capital associated with the option component of the convertible exceeds the cost of common equity of the issuing firm. In this example we will assume that the cost of capital on the option component is 20%.

Step 3: *Calculate the cost of convertible debt.* Here we simply calculate a weighted average of debt and equity raised through the conversion feature. The weights attached to each source of financing reflect the relative importance (market values) of each:

	$ Value	% of Value
Straight bond	$1,014.24	95.1%
Conversion option	51.95	4.9%
Current bond price	$1,066.19	100.0%

---

[37]Technically, the 4.25% yield to maturity on Computer Associates' straight debt is the *promised* yield; this rate overstates the expected cost of debt financing, as we discussed earlier.

Assuming the conversion option has a required rate of return of 20% and using the 4.25% cost of straight debt, we estimate the cost of the convertible debt as follows:

	Fraction of Bond Value	Cost of Capital	Product
Straight bond	0.9513	4.25%	0.0404
Equity-conversion option	0.0487	20.00%	0.0097
Cost of capital from convertible bonds =			5.01%

Thus, we estimate that the cost of raising capital with convertible bonds is approximately 5%, which is higher than the cost of issuing debt but lower than the cost of issuing equity. This makes sense because convertibles are less risky than equity but more risky than straight debt.

Off-Balance-Sheet Financing and WACC

Following the high-profile financial scandals of the last decade, analysts have been made painfully aware of the importance of off-balance-sheet sources of financing—that is, sources of financing that are not listed among the firm's corporate liabilities but are nevertheless very real liabilities. Here we discuss special purpose entities.

Special Purpose Entities

The acronym SPE, which stands for special purpose entity, has become synonymous with the wrongdoing that led to the collapse of Enron Corp. Unfortunately, Enron's use of SPEs has besmirched a very worthwhile concept that has been extremely valuable in a wide range of industries. Specifically, an SPE is an entity created by a sponsoring firm to carry out a specific purpose, activity, or series of transactions that are directly related to its specific purpose.[38]

The issue we want to discuss arises out of the fact that many SPEs are not consolidated with the firm's financial statements and, consequently, their assets and financial structures are off balance sheet. Should the capital structures of the off-balance-sheet SPEs be incorporated into the estimation of the firm's WACC? In Enron's case many of the SPEs did not meet the rules prescribed for off-balance-sheet reporting, so the answer to the above question is obviously yes. However, where SPEs are truly separate entities (the technical term is *bankruptcy remote*), then their liabilities do not reach back to the founding firm and consequently are not relevant to the calculation of the firm's WACC.

---

[38]This discussion relies on Cheryl de Mesa Graziano, "Special Purpose Entities: Understanding the Guidelines," *Issues Alert, Financial Executives International* (January 2002).

CHAPTER 5

Estimating Required Rates of Return for Projects

Chapter Overview

The most widely used method for identifying the discount rate for new investments is to use the firm's WACC. However, this approach has some rather severe shortcomings when a firm invests in projects with widely varying risk characteristics. In this chapter we discuss two methods for customizing or tailoring the discount rate to the specific attributes of the project. We begin by considering the divisional WACC. The divisional WACC approach involves estimating a different cost of capital for each of the firm's operating divisions, using a straightforward extension of the firm WACC approach discussed in Chapter 4. The project-specific WACC is the final approach we consider for identifying the discount rate for new investments. This approach focuses on the specific risk attributes and financing components of individual projects. We consider two variants of the project-specific WACC: (1) projects that are the beneficiaries of nonrecourse, project debt financing and (2) projects that are financed using general corporate financing.

Although supported in theory, allowing managers to tailor the cost of capital to their division or to the specifics of a particular project has its cost. Granting managers discretion in the choice of the discount rate provides them with an opportunity to misuse this discretion to pursue their own pet projects. Consequently, in an effort to constrain this incentive problem, many firms allow their managers no discretion and use the same discount rate for all projects (such as the firm's WACC), while others offer limited discretion (e.g., in the form of a divisional WACC).

We close the chapter with a discussion of the concept of a hurdle rate. Some firms require that their investments have an expected internal rate of return that exceeds a hurdle rate which is higher than the firm's WACC.

5.1 INTRODUCTION

In Chapter 4 we introduced the concept of a firm's cost of capital (i.e., the weighted average cost of capital, or WACC). The firm's WACC is a key determinant of the value of the firm, as we discuss in Chapter 7, but also is widely used as an important element in the evaluation of firm performance, as we learn in Chapter 8. In addition, a firm's WACC is often used as a starting point for identifying the discount rates used to evaluate new investments that the firm may be considering. Our focus in the current chapter is on such investment projects.

The discount rates that firms use to evaluate individual investment projects are not necessarily the same as their WACC. Most firms are faced with a variety of investment opportunities, and if these investment opportunities have different risks and can be financed in different ways, then it makes sense that they should be evaluated with different discount rates. In particular, investment projects that are less risky and add more to the firm's ability to raise debt capital should require a lower discount rate. In this chapter we describe how firms can go about determining what these different discount rates should be.

Before proceeding, we should point out that an investment evaluation policy that allows managers to use different discount rates for different investment opportunities is not necessarily easy to implement. Technical issues must be addressed, as well as political issues within a firm's organization that can potentially make the use of multiple discount rates more trouble than it is worth. Perhaps, because of these issues, more than 50% of the surveyed firms in a 2001 study used a *single, companywide discount rate* to evaluate all investment proposals.[1] However, there can be substantial gains associated with using different discount rates for projects with different risks and as we show in this chapter, the technical issues can be addressed. And although we are not experts on the politics of organizations, we believe that well-managed corporations can address the political issues once they are made aware of the problem.

This chapter is organized as follows: Section 5.2 presents the case for addressing differences in project and firm costs of capital when evaluating new investment proposals. Section 5.3 discusses two methods for estimating discount rates that are tailored, to varying degrees, to the specific risks of the projects being evaluated and that also minimize the estimation problems and administrative issues involved in using multiple discount rates. These are the divisional WACC and the project-specific WACC. Section 5.4 discusses hurdle rates and the cost of capital. Finally, Section 5.5 contains summary comments.

---

[1]John Graham and Campbell Harvey, 2001, "The Theory and Practice of Corporate Finance: Evidence from the Field," *Journal of Financial Economics* 60, 187–243.

5.2 PROS AND CONS OF MULTIPLE RISK-ADJUSTED COSTS OF CAPITAL

The decision to use a single, companywide discount rate, versus a more refined estimate that is specifically tailored to the risks of the project being valued, is ultimately a matter of managerial judgment. Each approach has its benefits and costs, and as we now discuss, the benefits and costs will vary from firm to firm.

The Rationale for Using Multiple Discount Rates

Finance theory is very explicit about the appropriate rate at which the cash flows of investment projects should be discounted. The appropriate discount rate should reflect the opportunity cost of capital, which in turn reflects the risk of the investment. The rationale for this approach is intuitive when one views the appropriate opportunity cost as the expected rates of return on publicly traded stocks and bonds. One would not initiate an investment project with expected returns that are less than the returns that can be generated from investments in publicly traded stocks and bonds with equivalent risk. Hence, less risky investments, whose cash flows resemble the cash flows of a portfolio of bonds, will have an opportunity cost of capital that is lower than more risky investments, whose cash flows resemble the cash flows of a portfolio of stock.

Figure 5-1 illustrates that when a single discount rate (firm WACC) is used, the firm will tend to take on investment projects that are relatively risky (Project B), which appear to be attractive because they generate internal rates of return that exceed

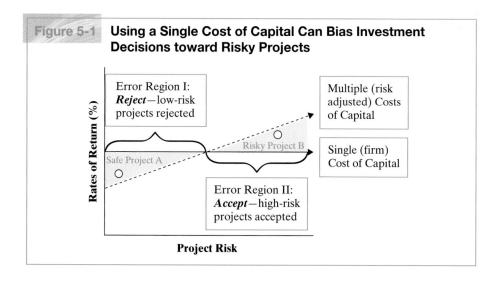

Figure 5-1 **Using a Single Cost of Capital Can Bias Investment Decisions toward Risky Projects**

Error Region I:
Reject—low-risk projects rejected

Multiple (risk adjusted) Costs of Capital

Safe Project A

Risky Project B

Single (firm) Cost of Capital

Error Region II:
Accept—high-risk projects accepted

Rates of Return (%)

Project Risk

the firm's WACC. Similarly, the firm will tend to pass up investment projects that are relatively safe (Project A), but which generate internal rates of return that are less than the firm's WACC. Left unchecked, this bias in favor of high-risk projects will make the firm riskier over time.

Convincing Your Skeptical Boss—Low-Risk Projects Can Be Good Investments

To illustrate the advantages of using multiple discount rates, consider the situation faced by a hypothetical high-tech manufacturing company, Huson Packer Inc., or HPI, which generates most of its revenues from technology-driven products that generate relatively high rates of return. This is a risky business and as such, the firm is all equity financed with a cost of equity and company cost of capital equal to 12%. Some of the firm's engineers have designed a new laser technology and have proposed that the firm invest $300 million to launch a line of laser printers to commercialize the technology. Based on an analysis similar to what was described in Chapters 2 and 3, the engineers estimate that the investment will generate an expected internal rate of return of 10.5%. Although the expected return is lower than the firm's WACC of 12%, it should be noted that the project is also less risky than the firm's core business. In particular, the beta for the printer business is only .80, while the beta of HPI's core business is 1.40.

After reviewing the proposal, HPI's CEO responded, "I can't understand how it makes sense to undertake an investment that generates a 10.5% return when our shareholders expect a return on their investment of 12%." How would you convince your skeptical boss that the investment makes sense? As we explain below, to understand how an investment that returns 10.5% makes sense for a firm with a WACC of 12% we must understand the distinction between the marginal cost of capital and the average cost of capital.

Let's assume that the expected return on the market portfolio is 10% and the risk-free rate is 5%, so that the market risk premium is $10\% - 5\% = 5\%$. Under these conditions, HPI estimates its cost of equity using the CAPM to be 12% (i.e., $5\% + 1.4 \times 5\%$). Now let's assume that the printer business will constitute 20% of the value of HPI if the investment is undertaken. With the printer business, HPI's new beta will become a weighted average of the beta for the printer business and its core business, which will constitute 80% of the value of the new company. Consequently, HPI's beta after investing in the printer business will decline to 1.28 (i.e., $.80 \times 1.4 + .20 \times .8 = 1.28$), and with this lower beta, HPI's required rate of return on its equity (and WACC, since the firm is assumed to be all equity financed) will decline to $5\% + 1.28 \times 5\% = 11.4\%$. (See the Technical Insight box on portfolio betas.)

One way to assess whether the printer business makes sense is to ask whether HPI, with the addition of the printer business, generates an expected rate of return that exceeds the 11.4% rate of return that will be the firm's cost of capital if it enters the printer business. To calculate whether this is indeed the case we combine the 10.5% expected rate of return on the printer business (which was based on the cost of entering into the business) with the expected rate of return on the firm's existing business (which is 12% based on the firm's current market value). With the addition

T E C H N I C A L

I N S I G H T   **Portfolio Betas**

The return to a portfolio is simply a weighted average (reflecting the relative investment amounts) of the rates of return earned by the individual assets in the portfolio. It turns out that the risk of a portfolio, measured by its beta, is also a weighted average of the assets in the portfolio. Consider a simple portfolio of two assets A and B, where each asset constitutes 50% of the value of the portfolio. Asset A has a beta of 1.00 and Asset B has a beta of 2.00. The following figure illustrates how the rate of return each asset is expected to earn varies when the market generates rates of return ranging from −5% to +5%. Note that the portfolio return is more volatile than Asset A but less than Asset B, i.e., the portfolio beta is $1.5 = .5 \times 2 + .5 \times 1$.

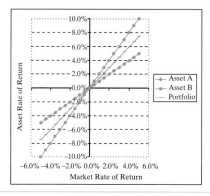

of the new project, the firm will generate an expected return of $.80 \times 12\% + .20 \times 10.5\% = 11.7\%$, which exceeds the required rate of return of 11.4%. This implies that the addition of the printer business will cause HPI's stock price to increase enough to drive down its future expected rate of return to its required return of 11.4%. In other words, the printer business is a value-increasing investment.

In practice, valuing an investment project by calculating the firm's WACC, both with and without the evaluated project, would be quite tedious. However, this is not necessary. One would arrive at exactly the same conclusion by evaluating the project in isolation using a discount rate that reflects the project's beta of .80. Specifically, we should evaluate the project by discounting its expected cash flows at a rate estimated using the CAPM, where the risk-free rate and market risk premium are both equal to 5%, that is, $5\% + .8 \times 5\% = 9\%$.

It should be noted that the preceding example is relatively straightforward because HPI and the printer project are assumed to be all equity financed. Since debt financing, because of the tax advantage, is assumed to be a less expensive source of capital, one also has to account for the extent to which the project contributes to the firm's ability to raise debt financing. As our discussion in the rest of the chapter illustrates, the consideration of debt financing definitely adds a few wrinkles to our analysis.

The Benefits of Using a Single Discount Rate

Despite the aforementioned benefits of using multiple discount rates that more nearly reflect project risk, nearly six out of every 10 firms use a single, companywide discount rate to evaluate all of their investment projects. One reason for this is that many firms engage in a very narrow spectrum of activities, and a single discount rate works pretty well for them. A second reason is that using multiple discount rates is difficult, and up until recently, the benefits of using different discount rates for different investment projects were not well articulated. Finally, as we will discuss in more detail, the use of multiple discount rates poses an administrative cost that can arise when overly optimistic or opportunistic managers have too much discretion in determining the key parameters that determine the valuation of the investment under consideration.

The latter problem arises from the fact that managers have an incentive to get projects approved that benefit them personally. This may, in turn, encourage them to inflate cash flow forecasts and argue for low discount rates for their pet projects. The incentive to inflate cash flow forecasts is mitigated somewhat by the fact that an investment's realized cash flows can later be compared to the forecasts. However, one cannot do an ex post evaluation to determine whether the appropriate discount rate was used when the project was being evaluated. Hence, there is a greater incentive for managers to underestimate project risk (and consequently the cost of capital for the project) rather than to overestimate the cash flows of the investment projects that they propose.

Influence Costs

To get a better understanding of the potential costs associated with using multiple discount rates, it is useful to describe what economists refer to as **influence costs.** (See the Behavioral Insight box on influence costs and managerial discretion.) These added costs include the extra time and effort a project advocate spends trying to justify a lower discount rate, as well as the time spent by the managers charged with evaluating the project, who must figure out the extent of the bias.

To understand the problems posed by influence costs, consider the incentives of a manager who is responsible for developing new investment opportunities in Bolivia. Since the manager benefits personally from having the project accepted, he or she has a clear incentive to put the investment proposal in the most favorable light possible.[2] Hence, in addition to providing optimistic cash flow forecasts, the manager

---

[2]There are a variety of reasons why this may be true, including (1) the manager's compensation is tied to finding profitable investments; (2) the manager develops special skills associated with the project that could enhance the value of his or her human capital; and (3) the manager simply derives utility from managing large projects.

Limiting Managerial Flexibility to Control Influence Costs

Economists refer to influence costs as costs that arise out of the tendency for employees to spend time and effort attempting to persuade top executives to make choices that are beneficial to themselves and their group or division. The benefits of a firm's capital allocation decisions come in the form of augmenting the scope of employees' power, prestige, visibility, and, of course, their compensation. While some of these choices actually create value, much of the time spent lobbying is likely to waste not only the employee's time, but also the time of other employees and top management.[3]

Because of the potential costs associated with influence-seeking behavior, corporations sometimes set rules and procedures that limit managerial flexibility. These rules are often thought of as bureaucratic stumbling blocks that can lead to suboptimal choices. However, by limiting managerial discretion, management's ability to waste time and resources may also be reduced.

has an incentive to *understate risk* in order to justify a lower discount rate that inflates the project's net present value.

The added discretion associated with multiple discount rates can lead to the selection of inferior projects if some managers, because they are either politically better connected within the organization or simply more persuasive, are able to justify lower discount rates for their projects, even when the projects are quite risky. When discount rates are discretionary, it opens up the possibility that "favored" or more persuasive managers will be able to use artificially low discount rates for their projects, perhaps making it relatively easy for them to meet their benchmarks. Such a perceived lack of fairness can be very costly to a firm and can potentially generate infighting and a general lack of cooperation between workers (See the Practitioner Insight box on keeping WACC simple.). Thus, using a single discount rate for all projects may increase the perception that all workers are evaluated fairly, improving employee morale as it removes one source of influence cost.

Weighing the Costs and Benefits of Multiple versus Single Discount Rates

We noted at the outset of this section that there are both pros and cons associated with the use of multiple versus single discount rates that each firm must balance in

---

[3]Influence costs are discussed in detail by Paul Milgrom and John Roberts in their article "Bargaining Costs, Influence Costs, and the Organization of Economic Activity," in *Perspectives in Positive Political Economy,* J. Alt and K. Shepsle, eds. (Cambridge: Cambridge University Press, 1990).

P R A C T I T I O N E R

I N S I G H T

The Importance of Keeping WACC Simple and Understandable—A Conversation with Jim Brenn*

Our firm was a pioneer in the adoption and use of a bonus performance measure based on a comparison of the company's return on invested capital to its cost of capital. When we implemented the system we were very concerned that the rank-and-file employees would trust the system and that it could influence their behavior in ways that contributed to the creation of value for our shareholders. We quickly learned that to be a trusted performance measure, the measure had to be understandable and verifiable.

The importance of making the performance measure and the standard of firm performance (the cost of capital) transparent and understandable meant that we were willing to sacrifice some technical sophistication. For example, we wanted our employees to be able to replicate our estimate of the firm's cost of capital, so we used book value weights based on our most recent balance sheet to calculate the firm's weighted average cost of capital. Had we used the technically correct, market value weights, the cost of capital calculated at any one point in time would reflect current market prices, over which our employees can exercise no control. Therefore, we used book value weights in an effort to provide a stable and easy-to-calculate weighted average cost of capital estimate.

*Chief financial officer for Briggs and Stratton Corporation, Milwaukee, Wisconsin.

---

light of its particular circumstances. The benefits associated with multiple discount rates is most pronounced when the risk attributes of the projects a firm considers vary widely, as is likely to be the case for firms operating in different lines of business or in different countries. For example, firms that operate multiple divisions that face very different risk profiles are obviously better candidates for using multiple discount rates than are firms that operate a single, homogeneous division.

The incentive problems that arise when managers have more discretion to choose discount rates are very real but extremely nebulous and difficult to identify and measure. However, these incentive problems can be mitigated if there is a systematic and verifiable way to estimate the cost of capital. In particular, we recommend that when multiple discount rates are used, the determination of these discount rates should be tied to outside market forces that are not under the control of the managers who may benefit from the investment projects' selection. With this in mind we recommend the following approaches.

5.3 Choosing a Project Discount Rate

Choosing the appropriate discount rate for an investment project can appear to be a daunting task, and there is no getting around the fact that completing the task entails a substantial amount of judgment on the part of the individuals involved. We now discuss three approaches that can be used to select discount rates that reflect differences in project risk levels. All three methods meet the following criteria: They are consistent with financial theory, are relatively easy to understand and implement, and use discount rates based on market returns.

The approaches which are described in Figure 5-2 include: (1) firm WACC (the subject of Chapter 4), (2) divisional WACC, and (3) project-specific WACC. We discuss two variations of a project-specific WACC: one where debt has recourse only to the project's cash flows (project financing) and one where debt has recourse to other assets of the firm (corporate financing).

Method #1: Divisional WACC (Industry-Based Divisional Costs of Capital)

Most investments are financed using corporate finance, which means that the debt used to finance the investment comes from corporate debt issues that are guaranteed by the corporation as a whole. Determining the appropriate discount rate for a project under these circumstances can be somewhat more challenging, as the cost of financing the project cannot be directly identified. The approach taken by most firms that face this situation is to try to isolate their costs of capital for each of their business units or divisions by estimating divisional WACCs. The idea here is that the divisions take on investment projects with unique levels of risk and, consequently, the WACC used in each division is potentially unique to that division. Generally, divisions are defined either by geographical regions (e.g., the Latin American division) or industry lines of business. In the discussion that follows, we will assume that the divisions are defined along industry lines and that the divisional WACCs can be approximated using the average firm WACC within an industry.

The advantages of using a divisional WACC include the following:

- It provides different discount rates that reflect differences in the systematic risk within each of the firm's divisions. The idea here is that the individual divisions take on investment projects with common levels of risk that differ across divisions.
- It entails only one cost of capital estimate per division (as opposed to unique discount rates for each project), thereby minimizing the time and effort of estimating the cost of capital.

Figure 5-2 Choosing the Right WACC–Discount Rates and Project Risk

Method		Description	Advantages	Disadvantages	When to Use
Firm WACC (discussed in Chapter 4)		Estimate the WACC for the firm as an entity and use it as the discount rate on *all* projects	• Is a familiar concept to most business executives • Minimizes estimation costs, as there is only one cost of capital calculation for the firm • Does not create influence cost issues	• Does not adjust discount rates for differences in project risk • Does not provide for flexibility in adjusting for differences in project debt capacities	• Projects are similar in risk to the firm as a whole • Using multiple discount rates creates significant influence costs
Method #1: Divisional WACC		Estimate WACC for individual business units or divisions of the firm. Use these estimates as the only discount rates within each division.	• Uses division-level risk to adjust discount rates for individual projects • Entails minimal influence costs within divisions	• Does not capture intra-division risk differences in projects • Does not account for differences in project debt capacities within divisions • Potential influence costs associated with the choice of discount rates across divisions • Difficult to find single-division firms to proxy for divisions	• Individual projects within each division have similar risks and debt capacities • Discount rate discretion creates significant influence costs within divisions but not between divisions
Method #2: Project-specific WACC	Project financing	Estimate WACC for each individual project using the capital costs associated with the actual financing package for the project	• Provides a unique discount rate that reflects the risks and financing mix of the project	• Market proxies for project risk may be difficult to find • Creates the potential for high influence costs as managers seek to manipulate to get their pet projects accepted • Capital structure weights are problematic, as equity value of the project is unobservable	• The project is financed with nonrecourse debt • The costs of administering multiple discount rates are not too great
	Corporate financing	Estimate WACC for each individual project using the capital costs associated with the debt capacity of the project	• Provides a unique discount rate that reflects the risks and financing mix of the project	• All of the above, plus: • Project debt capacity must be allocated since it is not readily observed	• The project is of such significance that it has a material impact on the firm's debt capacity

■   The use of a common discount rate throughout the division limits managerial latitude and the attendant influence costs.[4]

To see how firms can estimate divisional WACCs, consider the problem faced by ExxonMobil (XOM), a fully integrated oil company. By "fully integrated," we mean that the company is engaged in every activity associated with its product, beginning with finding and producing oil up through pumping gasoline into consumers' automobiles. Table 5-1 describes how the firm divides its businesses into three groups: Upstream, Downstream, and Chemicals. Each has its own special risks, so that the opportunity cost of capital for each is likely to be different.

An approach that can be taken to deal with differences in the costs of capital for each of ExxonMobil's business units involves identifying what we will call **comparison firms** (or comps) that operate in only one of the individual businesses (where possible). ExxonMobil can then use the WACCs for these comparison firms to calculate an estimate of the divisional WACC. For example, to estimate the WACC for its Upstream business unit, ExxonMobil might use a WACC estimate for firms that operate in the Oil and Gas Extraction industry class (SIC 1300). These firms span a wide variety of subindustries related to oil and gas exploration, development, and production.

Table 5-1 ExxonMobil Divisions (Business Units)—2005 Operating Results

	*Upstream—*Oil and Gas Exploration and Development	*Downstream—* Refining Oil and Gas for Energy Use	*Chemicals—* Conversion of Crude into Plastics and Other Nonenergy Products
Earnings	$24.349 billion	$7.992 billion	$3.943 billion
Return on average capital employed[*]	45.7%	32.4%	28.0%
Capital expenditures	$14.47 billion	$2.495 billion	$0.654 billion

Source: ExxonMobil 2005 Annual Report.

[*]Return on average capital employed is a performance measure ratio. From the perspective of the business segments, this return is annual business segment earnings divided by average business segment capital employed (average of beginning and end-of-year amounts). These segment earnings include ExxonMobil's share of segment earnings of equity companies, consistent with our capital employed definition, and exclude the cost of financing.

---

[4]However, we expect that divisional managers may still expend resources to lobby for lower discount rates for their divisions, so the influence costs associated with allowing managers some discretion over what discount rates to use still exist to some extent.

Similarly, analysts could use firms in the Petroleum Refining and Related Industries (SIC industry 2900) to estimate the relevant WACC for the Downstream business unit, and could use firms in Chemicals and Allied Products (SIC industry 2800) to determine the WACC for the Chemicals business unit.

Table 5-2 summarizes the cost of capital for each of these industries using the Ibbotson Associates 2006: *Cost of Capital* quarterly estimates. The procedures used by Ibbotson Associates, which were discussed in Chapter 4, can be briefly described as follows:

■ The cost of equity for each firm in the industry is estimated from five different models. We follow Ibbotson Associates and calculate the median value for the

Table 5-2	**Summary Divisional Costs of Capital Estimates for ExxonMobil**		
	Upstream—Oil and Gas Exploration and Development (SIC 1300)[a]	*Downstream— Refining Oil and Gas for Energy Use (SIC 2900)[b]*	*Chemicals— Production of Plastics and Other Nonenergy Products (SIC 2800)[c]*
Cost of equity[d]	9.96%	9.85%	10.07%
Debt ratio[e]	13.78%	4.66%	10.85%
WACC[f]	9.47%	9.68%	9.65%

Source: Ibbotson Associates, *Cost of Capital: 2006 Yearbook* (data through March 2006).

Legend

[a]SIC 1300—Oil and Gas Extraction. This group of firms is primarily engaged in (1) producing crude petroleum and natural gas; (2) extracting oil from oil sands and oil shale; (3) producing natural gasoline and cycle condensate; and (4) producing gas and hydrocarbon liquids from coal at the mine site.

[b]SIC 2900—Petroleum Refining and Related Industries. This major group includes firms primarily engaged in petroleum refining, manufacturing paving and roofing materials, and compounding lubricating oils and greases from purchased materials.

[c]SIC 2800—Chemicals and Allied Products. This group includes firms that produce basic chemicals, as well as firms that manufacture products by predominantly chemical processes.

[d]Ibbotson reports five different estimates of the cost of equity, as we discussed in Chapter 4. However, we report the return estimate for the large composite sample based on the CAPM.

[e]The debt ratio is equal to the book value of debt divided by the sum of the book value of debt and the market value of the firm's equity. Again, this ratio reflects an average of the firms in the large-composite category.

[f]We report the WACC for the large composite group within the industry that is calculated using the CAPM-based estimate of the cost of equity.

industry using each of the five approaches.[5] For our purposes we use a simple average of the five estimated costs of equity as our estimate of the cost of equity for the division.

■ The cost of debt financing reflects both the current rates of interest and the credit rating of the firm's debt.

■ The debt ratio for the industry reflects the book value of the firm's interest-bearing liabilities (both short-term and long-term) divided by the sum of the book value of the firm's debt plus the market value of the firm's equity. For example, in November of 2006 Valero Energy Corp (VLO) had total debt outstanding of $5.13 billion. The market value of Valero's equity (i.e., its market cap) was $32.18 billion. Thus the debt ratio was $5.13 billion ÷ ($5.13 billion + 32.18 billion) = 13.75%. The debt ratio provides the weight attached to the firm's after-tax cost of debt, and one minus this ratio is the weight attached to the cost of equity to calculate the firm's WACC.

A quick review of Table 5-2 reveals divisional WACCs for ExxonMobil that are very close to one another in this instance, ranging from 9.47% for the Upstream division to 9.68% for the Downstream division. Even so, if the company were to use a single WACC for all divisions it would tend to overinvest in the Upstream division and underinvest in the Downstream division.

Divisional WACC—Estimation Issues and Limitations

Although the divisional WACC approach is generally a significant improvement over the single, companywide WACC, the way that it is often implemented using industry-based comparison firms has a number of potential shortcomings:

■ *The sample of firms in a given industry may include firms that are not good matches for the firm or one of its divisions.* For example, the ExxonMobil company analyst may be able to select a narrower subset of firms whose risk profiles more nearly match the division being analyzed, (e.g., in our ExxonMobil example, the comparison firms for the Upstream division consisted of the 114 companies in SIC 1300, the comparison firms for the Chemicals division included the 293 companies from SIC 2800, and the Downstream division comparison firms included the 15 firms from SIC 2900). The firm's management can easily address this problem by selecting appropriate comparison firms. However, the fact that the selection of different comparison firms affects our estimate of the divisional cost of capital implies that if divisional managers participate in the selection process, they have an opportunity to exercise influence over their own cost of capital.

---

[5]For example, across all firms in the Upstream industry (SIC 1300), the lowest estimate of the cost of equity resulted from the use of the three-stage discounted cash flow model, where the median value was 9.40%. The highest estimate of the cost of equity for the Upstream division came from the single-stage discounted cash flow model (the Gordon growth model described in Chapter 4), which had an industry median value of 18.85%. The latter is not particularly surprising in that this method extrapolates recent growth patterns (which have been very high) into the indefinite future.

- *The division being analyzed may not have a capital structure that is similar to the sample of firms that are used as comps.* The division may be more or less levered than the firms whose costs of capital are used to proxy for the divisional cost of capital. For example, ExxonMobil raises very little of its capital through debt financing, whereas Valero Energy (VLO) has raised 13.75% of its capital with debt.[6]

   Resolving this problem is more difficult than it may appear at first glance: Multidivision firms do not ordinarily allocate corporate debt to individual divisions, so we really cannot identify divisional capital structures. Therefore, using the capital structures of the comparison firms may be as good as the firm can do when attempting to estimate its divisional WACC.[7] Furthermore, attempts to allocate debt to the divisions can give rise to an opportunity for divisional managers to lobby for a larger allocation in the hope that it will result in a reduced cost of capital, thus creating yet another instance in which influence costs can enter into the process of estimating the divisional WACC.

- *There may be substantial differences in project risks for investments within a division.* Firms, by definition, are engaged in a variety of activities, and it can be very difficult to identify a group of firms that are predominantly engaged in activities that are truly comparable to a given project. Even within divisions, individual projects can have very different risk profiles. This means that even if we *are able* to match divisional risks very closely, there may still be significant differences in risk across projects undertaken within a division. For example, some projects may entail extensions of existing production capabilities, while others involve new-product development. Both types of investments take place within a given division, but they have potentially very different risk profiles.

- *Good matches for comparison firms for a particular division may be difficult to find.* The preponderance of publicly traded firms report multiple lines of business, yet each company is classified into a single industry group. In the case of ExxonMobil, we found three operating divisions (Upstream, Downstream, and Chemicals) and identified an industry proxy for each. However, our Downstream industry proxy (Petroleum Refining and Related Industries—SIC 2900) actually contained ExxonMobil, since this is the firm's dominant industry group.

The preceding discussion suggests that although the use of divisional WACCs to determine project discount rates may represent an improvement over the use of a

---

[6]This estimate is based on year-end 2005 financial statements, using book values of interest-bearing short- and long-term debt and the market value of the firm's equity on February 16, 2006.

[7]Even when the firm can allocate its debt to its individual divisions, there still remains the problem of evaluating (allocating) the market value of the firm's equity to the various divisions. The analyst might use multiples of earnings for the division that reflect current market conditions to estimate equity values. However, this methodology is not without its limitations, as it presumes the multidivision firm is valued by the market as the sum of its divisions (i.e., that there are no synergies to the multidivision firm). Furthermore, the more problematic and complex the estimation procedure, the greater the risk that the divisional WACC will become a political football for division managers to use in their attempts to gain larger capital allocations for their division.

companywide WACC, this methodology is far from a perfect solution. However, if the firm has investment opportunities with risks that vary principally with industry-risk characteristics, the use of a divisional WACC has some clear advantages over the use of the firm's WACC. It provides a methodology that allows for different discount rates, and it avoids some of the influence costs associated with giving managers complete leeway to select project-specific discount rates.

Method #2: Project-Specific WACCs

We now consider the estimation of an individual project's WACC. The objective here is to fine-tune our estimate of the cost of capital to reflect the specifics of an individual project, as opposed to a division or the firm as a whole. A project-specific WACC requires the same inputs as a firm's WACC. That is, it requires estimates for the cost of debt, the cost of equity, and the weights for each source of capital. As we will discuss, there are considerable challenges associated with coming up with each of these inputs.

We first consider a situation where the investment is **project financed** using **nonrecourse** debt financing. With nonrecourse debt, the project is the sole source of collateral and the debt holders have no recourse to the sponsoring firm's assets in the event of default. Investments that are project financed are very similar to an independent firm, since lenders loan money based solely on the ability of the project cash flows and assets to repay it. A critical feature of project financing and nonrecourse debt relates to something called *bankruptcy remoteness*, which means that if the borrower were to go into bankruptcy, it's creditors would not have any claim on the assets of the project-financed asset. Although we do not delve into the legal details, we do want to emphasize that lenders are very cautious when offering nonrecourse financing to a project. Specifically, they want to be assured that the project sponsor's creditors have no claim on the assets of the project in the event the sponsor goes into bankruptcy. Remember that the project lenders have no claim on the sponsor's other assets and, likewise, they want the sponsor's creditors to have no claim on the project assets.

Calculating the appropriate project-specific WACC for a project-financed investment is somewhat more straightforward because the sources of financing are specifically defined for the project and can be observed. In particular, a specific amount of debt is attached to the investment, which is not the case when the project is financed on the firm's balance sheet using corporate financing. Knowing the amount of debt attached to an investment is helpful, but as we will discuss, it is not sufficient for determining the weights on the investment's debt and equity financing, since these weights require the market value of equity.

Investments that are financed on the firm's balance sheet add another layer of complexity to the analysis because in this case the financing of the project is intermingled with the financing of the firm's other investments. As we will discuss, determining what we will refer to as the debt capacity of a project that is financed on a firm's balance sheet is not completely arbitrary, but it does require some judgment on the part of the manager.

Example: Determining the Project-Specific WACC for Project-Financed Projects
To illustrate the estimation of the project-specific WACC, we will first consider a project-financed investment being evaluated by the independent electric power producer Catalina, Inc. As shown in Catalina, Inc.'s balance sheet, depicted in Panel a of Figure 5-3, Catalina currently has total assets of $1.2 billion. It is considering the construction and operation of a $200 million major power production facility in south Texas. The project is substantial and will require Catalina to raise $200 million in additional funds.

Panel b of Figure 5-3 highlights the effects of the $200 million investment on the firm's balance sheet if Catalina decides to use corporate financing by borrowing 80% of the funds and raising the remainder using an equity offering. In this case the total assets of Catalina rise by $200 million to $1.4 billion; the firm's debt rises by $160 million to $760 million; and its equity increases by $40 million to $640 million.

Alternatively, Catalina might use project financing, which entails the creation of a new entity, as depicted in Panel c of Figure 5-3. The entity is a new company, Power Project, which owns and operates the project. However, since the $40 million in equity financing comes from Catalina, Catalina's balance sheet shows an increase of $40 million in assets (corresponding to the equity in the project) and an increase of the same amount in Catalina's equity account, reflecting the equity issue used to finance the equity portion of the investment.

Estimating project equity value directly—the flow-through-to-equity model   The focus of project-financed investments is typically on the equity invested in the project, which is valued with the **flow-through-to-equity** approach. This approach is simply a discounted cash flow model that focuses directly on the valuation of the equity invested in the project, rather than the value of the project as a whole. Using this approach we calculate the present value of the equity free cash flows (EFCFs) using the project's cost of equity capital, and compare the estimated equity value with the equity invested in the project.[8] Note that this approach does not require the calculation of the project's WACC but relies on the cost of equity and EFCFs.

We believe that the flow-through-to-equity approach is an appropriate approach for assessing the value of a specific project. However, for the purpose of comparing investments across different lines of business, firms may also want to know the appropriate project WACCs for their different investments. Consequently, we extend our analysis of the value of the equity invested in a project to include the value of the project as a whole, and the corresponding project-specific WACC which, for the special case where project finance is used, we refer to as the **project finance WACC.**

Estimating the cost of equity and project free cash flows   Panel a of Table 5-3 summarizes the assumptions that underlie the cash flow projections for the power generation project. Of particular note is the fact that a consortium of banks has

---

[8]Equity free cash flows were defined in Chapter 2.

Figure 5-3   Project versus Firm Financing

Panel a. Pre-Investment Corporation

Catalina, Inc.
Balance Sheet
December 31, 2007

Assets $1,200 million	Bonds $ 600 million
	Equity 600 million
	Total $1,200 million

Panel b. Alternative #1 — Corporate Finance

Catalina, Inc.
Balance Sheet
December 31, 2007

Assets	$1,200 million	Bonds	$ 760 million
Project	200 million	Equity	640 million
Total	$1,400 million	Total	$1,400 million

Panel c. Alternative #2 — Project-Financing Alternative

Catalina, Inc.
Balance Sheet
December 31, 2007

Assets	$1,200 million	Debt	$ 600 million
Equity$_{Project}$	40 million	Equity	640 million
Total	$1,240 million	Total	$1,240 million

Power Project
Balance Sheet
December 31, 2007

Assets $200 million	Debt	$ 160 million
	Equity	40 million
	Total	$ 200 million

Table 5-3	Projected Earnings and Cash Flows for the Catalina Power Generation Project

Panel a. Assumptions and Forecasts

Initial investment = $200 million in Year 0

Depreciable fixed assets = $200 million

Depreciation is straight line on $200 million of capital
equipment (no working capital), which is depreciated
toward $0.00 in 40 years.

Capital expenditures (CAPEX) = Depreciation expense = $5 million per year

Financing mix: $160 million in debt and $40 million in equity

Debt financing terms and conditions:

   a. Type of debt—nonrecourse project financing

   b. Maturity—infinite

   c. Terms—interest only, forever

   d. Interest rate—6.52%

   e. Beta (debt) = .30

Estimated project operating earnings (EBIT) =
   $20,109.419 per year (Year 1–infinity)

Corporate tax rate = 38%

Capital market estimates and assumptions:

   a. Risk-free rate of return on long-term U.S. government bonds = 5.02%

   b. Market risk premium = 5.00%

offered to loan the project $160 million at a rate of 6.52%, which is 52 basis points over the prime rate, which is currently 6%. Panel b contains the pro forma income statements for the project, which, for simplicity, is expected to operate forever producing a level stream of income. We assume that the entire $200 million investment is comprised of plant and equipment that depreciates straight line over 40 years toward a zero salvage value. In addition, we assume that the firm must spend an amount equal to the depreciation on CAPEX in order to maintain the plant's productive capacity.

The project is expected to produce net operating income (i.e., earnings before interest and taxes) of $20,109,419 per year and will pay $10,432,000 in interest expense. Deducting taxes produces an estimated annual net income of $6,000,000 per year in perpetuity. Since CAPEX is assumed to equal the depreciation expense and there are no principal repayments or new debt issues, equity free cash flows (EFCFs) for the project are estimated to equal $6,000,000 per year (forever). The corresponding project free

Table 5-3 *continued*

Panel b. Pro Forma Income Statements and Cash Flow Projections

Pro Forma Income Statements		Years 1–Infinity
Earnings before interest and taxes (EBIT)		$ 20,109,419
Less: Interest expense		(10,432,000)
EBT		$ 9,677,419
Less: Taxes		(3,677,419)
Net income		$ 6,000,000

Calculation of Equity Free Cash Flow	Year 0	Years 1–Infinity
Net income		$ 6,000,000
Plus: Depreciation expense		5,000,000
Less: CAPEX	(200,000,000)	(5,000,000)
Less: Principal payments	—	—
Plus: Proceeds from new debt offerings	160,000,000	—
Equity free cash flow	$ (40,000,000)	$ 6,000,000

Calculation of Project Free Cash Flow	Year 0	Years 1–Infinity
Earnings before interest and taxes		$ 20,109,419
Less: Taxes		(7,641,579)
NOPAT		$ 12,467,840
Plus: Depreciation expense		5,000,000
Less: CAPEX	(200,000,000)	(5,000,000)
Project free cash flow (PFCF)	$ (200,000,000)	$ 12,467,840

cash flows (PFCFs) are equal to $12,467,840 per year since these cash flows do not reflect the firm's financing mix (i.e., they do not reflect either interest or principal payments).

Estimating the value of the equity and the cost of equity capital using iteration   To this point we have followed a simple three-step procedure for implementing discounted cash flow analysis:

Step 1: Estimate future cash flows.
Step 2: Estimate a discount rate.
Step 3: Calculate the present value of the cash flows using the discount rate estimated in Step 2.

There is, however, a slight wrinkle in this procedure when the discount rate is not known.

The problem that arises when estimating the cost of equity for a project is that the beta of the project, and thus its cost of equity, is determined by the extent to which the project is levered. If the project is more highly levered, the equity beta will be higher, which means the cost of equity is higher, and the value of equity is lower. As a first pass, analysts generally use the amount of invested equity in the project (i.e., the book value of the equity investment) to calculate the project's leverage and the firm's cost of equity. For example, in the Catalina project the analyst would assume an equity value of $40 million and calculate its cost of equity accordingly. As we discuss below, if the value of equity is greater than $40 million, this procedure overestimates the cost of equity and thereby underestimates the value of the project's equity.

The fact that using invested equity rather than the market value of equity can overestimate the risk of a positive-NPV project is not a major problem. First, it will not lead one to incorrectly conclude that a positive-NPV project really has a negative NPV or vice versa. Rather, it leads one to understate the NPV of positive-NPV investments and understate (make more negative) the NPV of negative-NPV investments. Second, as we describe below, a simple iterative procedure can be used to determine the correct NPV.

To understand these issues, we will calculate the value of the Catalina project's equity. As we illustrate in Table 5-4, we start with a sample of comparable firms to estimate unlevered equity betas for power generation projects. You may recall that we used this same process earlier in Table 4-1 to estimate the unlevered equity beta for Pfizer. The process involves first unlevering the equity betas for the proxy firms and then averaging the unlevered betas to use as our estimate of the unlevered equity beta for the Catalina power generation project. The resulting unlevered equity beta estimate for the project is .2755.

To estimate the cost of equity for Catalina's power project, we must relever this unlevered beta to determine the levered beta and cost of equity for the project. As a first step, we substitute the project's book value debt to equity ratio (i.e., $160 million/$40 million = 4) into equation (i) found in Panel c of Table 5-4 to relever the unlevered equity beta. The levered beta estimate is then used to calculate the levered cost of equity, and consequently the value of the project's equity. This analysis generates a cost of equity of 7.33% and an equity value of slightly more than $81 million. Since $81 million is greater than $40 million, we know that the project does create value and, in addition, that the actual levered beta of the project is lower, and the equity value is higher, than is indicated by this calculation.

To get a better estimate of both the cost of equity and the value of this equity investment, we can use the estimated value of the equity ($81 million) in place of the invested equity ($40 million) and repeat the above calculations. By doing this we calculate a slightly lower cost of equity (6.86%) and a slightly higher equity value ($87,526,326). You can then take this new estimate of equity value and again repeat these calculations, calculating a new equity value. You can continue this process, iterating between new equity values and levered betas until the value of the project's cost of equity and equity value converge to a fixed level. A quick review of the results of the iterative process found in Panel b of Table 5-4 reveals that they converge very

Table 5-4 Estimating Project Value and the Cost of Equity for a Power Generation Project

Panel a. Estimating the Unlevered Project Beta Using Proxy Firms

Company Name	Levered Equity Betas	Debt/Equity	Assumed Debt Betas	Unlevered Equity Betas
Ameren Corp.	0.2500	60.95%	0.20	0.2363
American Electric Power	0.3660	85.23%	0.20	0.3086
Dominion Resources	0.3320	65.81%	0.20	0.2937
Exelog Corp.	0.2800	42.52%	0.20	0.2633
PPL Corp.	0.6710	70.32%	0.20	0.5280
			Average	0.2755

Panel b. Iterative Procedure for Estimating the Cost of Equity, Equity Value, Project Value, and Project-Finance WACC

(A) Iteration Steps	(B) Unlevered Equity Beta	(C) Debt/Equity Ratio	(D) Estimated Levered Beta	(E) Estimate of the Cost of Equity	(F) Estimated Equity Value
Book Weights	0.2755	4.0000	0.4627	7.333%	$81,816,334
Iteration #1	0.2755	1.9556	0.3670	6.855%	$87,526,326
Iteration #2	0.2755	1.8280	0.3610	6.825%	$87,909,187
Iteration #3	0.2755	1.8201	0.3607	6.823%	$87,933,190
Iteration #4	0.2755	1.8196	0.3606	6.823%	$87,934,688
Iteration #5	0.2755	1.8195	0.3606	6.823%	$87,934,782
Iteration #6	0.2755	1.8195	0.3606	6.823%	$87,934,787

Legend

Column	Description
(A)	*Iteration steps*—the iteration process begins by substituting the book value debt to equity ratio into equation (i) in Panel c to solve for the levered equity beta for the project.
(B)	*Unlevered equity beta*—this estimate represents the simple average of the unlevered equity betas found in Panel a above.
(C)	*Debt to equity ratio*—a key input into the relevering of beta that should represent market values. Since we do not know the market value of the equity invested in the project, we begin our iterative analysis by using the book value of this ratio.
(D)	*Estimated levered beta*—the project's levered equity beta, estimated using equation (i) from Panel c below.
(E)	*Estimated cost of equity*—calculated using the CAPM found in equation (ii) in Panel c below, and the estimate of the levered equity beta from the current iteration.
(F)	*Estimated equity value*—the value of the equity invested in the project, estimated using equation (iii) found in Panel c below.

(Continued)

Table 5-4 *continued*

Panel c. Equations Used in Estimating Project Value and the Project's Cost of Equity

(i)

$$\beta_{\text{Levered}} = \beta_{\text{Unlevered}}\left(1 + \left[\left(\frac{\text{Book Debt}}{\text{Project Equity Value}}\right)\left(1 - \frac{\text{Marginal}}{\text{Tax Rate}}\right)\right]\right)$$

$$- \beta_{\text{Debt}}\left[\left(\frac{\text{Book Debt}}{\text{Project Equity Value}}\right)\left(1 - \frac{\text{Marginal}}{\text{Tax Rate}}\right)\right]$$

where β_{Debt} is the estimated debt beta for the project.

(ii)

$$\frac{\text{Levered Cost of}}{\text{Equity }(k_e)} = \frac{\text{Risk-free}}{\text{rate }(r_f)} + \left(\begin{array}{c}\text{Levered} \\ \text{Equity} \\ \text{Beta }(\beta_{\text{Levered}})\end{array}\right)\left(\begin{array}{c}\text{Market} \\ \text{Risk Premium}\end{array}\right)$$

(iii)

$$\frac{\text{Project}}{\text{Equity Value}} = \frac{\text{Equity Free Cash Flow (EFCF)}_t}{\text{Levered Cost of Equity }(k_e)}$$

quickly. The project's cost of equity capital converges to 6.82% and the value of the equity converges to $87,934,787 in the sixth iteration. We included six iterations to demonstrate that convergence happens very quickly.

Calculating project value and the project finance WACC   Having calculated the equity value, it is straightforward to value the project by simply adding the estimated value of the project's equity (from the sixth iteration in Panel b of Table 5-4), $87,934,787, to the project's debt, $160 million, to arrive at a project value that equals $247,934,787. Using this value we can calculate the project finance WACC as the weighted average of the after-tax costs of debt and equity using as weights the estimated value of the project's equity and the face value of the firm's debt:[9]

---

[9]Alternatively, the project finance WACC is equal to the discount rate in the following project value equation:

$$\text{Project Value} = \text{Project Equity Value} + \text{Book Value of Project Debt}$$

$$= \frac{\text{Project Free Cash Flow (PFCF)}_t}{\text{Project Finance WACC}} = \$247,934,787 = \frac{\$12,467,840}{\text{Project Finance WACC}}$$

The project finance WACC is 5.03%. Note that if we had solved for the discount rate that makes the present value equal to the $200 million cost of the project (instead of the $247,934,787 value of the project), the result would have been an estimate of the project's IRR, which in this case equals 6.23%.

	Values	Value Weights	Capital Costs	Product
Debt	$ 160,000,000	0.6453	4.04%	2.61%
Equity	87,934,787	0.3547	6.82%	2.42%
	$ 247,934,787	1.0000		

Project finance WACC = 5.03%

Project-Specific WACC with Corporate Financing

Firms finance most of their investment projects on their balance sheets, which can make it especially challenging to come up with an approach for estimating project-specific WACCs. This can be a formidable task, since one must first determine the amount of debt and equity that can be attributed to the project and then estimate the costs of these financing sources. As we mentioned earlier, this is more difficult when the investments are financed on the firm's balance sheet since the financing is commingled with the financing of the firm's other investments. As a result, determining the appropriate weight for each source of capital for a particular investment requires the exercise of managerial judgment.

Project debt capacity—how much debt will the project support? Determining the appropriate weights for a project's sources of financing requires that we first understand the concept of a project's debt capacity. We define the **debt capacity** of a project as the amount of *additional debt* the firm can take on as a result of undertaking the project, without lowering the firm's credit rating. In general, riskier projects will have lower debt capacities since they require more equity to offset their higher risk. For example, an investment in new-product development can be quite risky and provides little, if any, debt capacity. However, renovation of the firm's present facilities that are used to support existing product lines is less risky and thus has a higher debt capacity.

It should be noted that the debt capacity of a project is not necessarily the same as the amount of debt that the firm takes on to finance the project. The actual addition to the firm's debt may have more to do with other investment projects that are initiated at about the same time and whether the firm's executives believe that the firm currently has too much debt or too little debt.

To understand how one can determine the debt capacity of an investment, consider a firm that currently has a BBB+ rating and faces an investment opportunity that requires a $100 million investment. Since the investment is expected to generate positive cash flows, taking the project will enhance the firm's credit rating if it is financed completely with equity. This indicates that the project has at least some debt capacity. However, since the investment is risky, financing it either completely with debt—or, equivalently, by depleting the firm's cash balances—would result in a downgrade in the firm's credit rating. If, for example, the rating agencies indicate that the firm in the above example will suffer a drop in its rating from BBB+ to BBB if it finances its $100 million investment with more than $45 million in debt, then the project's debt capacity is $45 million.

What determines the debt capacity of a project? Probably the first determinant is the volatility of the project's cash flows. Are the project's cash flows more volatile or less volatile than the firm's total cash flows? If they are more volatile, then the project may have less debt capacity (as a fraction of the value of the project) than the firm. In other words, if the firm has a debt ratio of 30%, then the more risky project may have a debt capacity of only 20%. One should also consider the extent to which the investment project contributes to the firm's diversification. If adding the project reduces the volatility of the firm's total cash flows because of the diversification effect, then the project will have a higher debt capacity. Finally, it is worth noting that investments that can be sold easily with minimal loss of value may also have higher debt capacities. Such projects make firms more attractive to rating agencies, since firms can easily convert these assets to cash in the event of financial distress, thereby helping the firm to stave off default and bankruptcy.

It's clear that estimating a project's debt capacity is subjective, but for large investments, firms can get a pretty good idea of the project's debt capacity by consulting their investment bankers or by talking directly to the credit agencies. (See the Practitioner Insight box describing the interaction between borrowers and the credit rating agencies.) If the project is deemed to be very risky, these outsiders may suggest that the firm use more equity and less debt in the financing package, to reduce the potential for a detrimental effect on the firm's credit rating. Alternatively, the bankers and the credit analysts at the ratings agencies may suggest that the project can support additional debt. The important point is that individuals outside the firm who do not have a direct stake in whether or not the project is ultimately accepted can impartially help the firm assess the project's debt capacity.

What are the appropriate costs of debt and equity for an individual project? Our recommended process for determining the project's debt capacity provides the appropriate weights for debt and equity that are used in our WACC formula. We now need to determine the relevant costs of debt and equity for the project. Our solution to this problem is very simple: We recommend calculating the project's WACC using estimates of the firm's costs of debt and equity, but using different weights for debt and equity that reflect the debt capacities of the projects. This is obviously a shortcut, but as we will illustrate, if the debt capacities are chosen appropriately, one gets a reasonable estimate of the differences between the costs of capital of different projects using the same costs of debt and equity for each project. Indeed, this approach provides the correct discount rates if differences in debt capacities across projects fully

---

Did you know?

The history of bond ratings

In 1914 John Moody began expanding his published rating coverage to bonds issued by U.S. cities and other municipalities. By 1924, Moody's ratings covered nearly 100 percent of the U.S. bond market.

In 1916 Standard Statistics (a predecessor of the Standard & Poor's Corporation) began assigning debt ratings to corporate bonds. The firm introduced ratings for municipal bonds in 1940.

The Credit Ratings Process—An Interview with Kevin Cassidy*

The credit rating process begins when a firm requests that its debt be rated by one of the credit rating agencies such as Moody's. Firms typically request a rating either because it is required by a lender or they want to sell their debt in the public markets. Once a firm's debt has received a credit rating, the rating agency continues to monitor the firm's credit on an ongoing basis as information becomes available to determine whether the assigned rating is still valid or should be raised or lowered. At Moody's, credit ratings are determined by rating committees and not by individual analysts. The rating committee composition is based on expertise and diversity of opinion, and its decision is based on a majority vote with each committee member having an equal vote.

In addition to regular reviews, the credit rating agency monitors each of the firms whose debt they rate for special events that might trigger a change in default risk. Examples of such events include the acquisition of another firm or a change in financial policy, such as the institution of a share repurchase program. For example, on November 29, 2006, Moody's Investors Service announced the downgrade of the debt of the Aleris International, Inc.'s ("Aleris") corporate family to a rating of B2 from B1. The announcement stated that the downgrade reflected (1) the substantial increase in debt resulting from the leveraged acquisition of the company, (2) its weakened debt protection metrics, and (3) the execution risks for timely deleveraging, particularly for a company with relatively thin margins and high sensitivity to volume levels (http:www.Moodys.com). The point here is that firms can, and do, take actions that result in a change in their credit rating!

*Kevin Cassidy, Moody's Investors Service, vice president/senior analyst, New York, New York.

reflect differences in systematic risk across projects (that is, projects with more systematic risk have lower debt capacities).

Although this method is an approximation, it does generate higher project WACC estimates for riskier projects that have lower debt capacities, and lower project WACC estimates for less risky projects that have higher debt capacities. To illustrate, suppose that the firm's cost of equity is 12% and its cost of debt is 4%. Assume also that Project #1 is quite risky and has a debt capacity of only 20%, whereas Project #2 is much less risky and has a debt capacity of 60%. Consequently, the WACC for Project #1 is

$$(.20 \times 4\%) + (.80 \times 12\%) = 10.4\% \qquad \textit{Project \#1 WACC}$$

while the WACC for Project #2 is only

$$(.60 \times 4\%) + (.40 \times 12\%) = 7.2\%. \qquad \textit{Project \#2 WACC}$$

As this simple example illustrates, the project-specific WACC approach provides a straightforward way to allow project sponsors to argue for different discount rates for different projects, while at the same time putting constraints on the managers' ability to argue for a low discount rate.

Figure 5-4 illustrates the effects of varying debt capacity on the WACC for projects whose debt capacities range from 0% to 100%. In practice, the range is likely to be much tighter, but the implications are the same. Within these boundaries, the project WACC we calculate is a function of the debt capacity of the project, and of the estimated costs of debt and equity financing for the firm (or division). The key assumption we are making here is that by accounting for differences in the projects' debt capacities, we are fully accounting for differences in project risk.

Summing up—adjusting project WACC using project debt capacity   The key assumption we are making in the approach we have taken in the analysis of the project-specific WACC is that by accounting for differences in project debt capacity, we are fully accounting for differences in project risk. This is a reasonable assumption for projects that are in the same line of business, and are thus subject to the same risk factors, but which have different cost structures and profit margins, and thus different sensitivities to these risk factors.[10] For example, because of improved technology, power plants built with the most recent technology are more fuel efficient and have lower operating costs per kwh than plants built using older technology. Because of this, new-technology power plants have higher profit margins, which make them less risky and give them higher debt capacities.

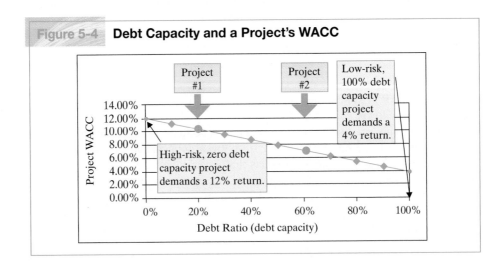

Figure 5-4   Debt Capacity and a Project's WACC

---

[10]Recall from our earlier discussions that firms in the same line of business can have different levels of operating leverage that can cause them to have different levels of risk. In general, firms with higher operating leverage will use less financial leverage.

To illustrate the higher debt capacity provided by the more efficient new plant technology, consider an example in which a firm is considering the construction of a new electric power generation plant with either the newest technology (New Plant) or a more traditional (older) technology (Old Plant). Table 5-5 contains the characteristics of the two plant alternatives. In Panel a we note that both plants have the capacity to produce 1,100,000 kwh per year; however, New Plant incurs total costs of $8,990,000, while Old Plant incurs costs of $10,200,000 to produce the

Table 5-5 Using Debt Capacity to Adjust for Project Risk— New Plant versus Old Plant

Panel a. Operating Costs, Operating Risk, and Debt Capacity

	New Plant	Old Plant
Capacity in kwh per year	1,100,000	1,100,000
Fixed operating costs	$ 8,000,000	$ 8,000,000
Variable operating costs/kwh	$ 0.90	$ 2.00
Total operating costs at capacity	$ 8,990,000	$ 10,200,000

Price/Kwh	Revenues	Operating Income (NOI)		% Change Revenue	% Change NOI	
		New Plant	Old Plant		New Plant	Old Plant
$10.00	$ 11,000,000	$ 2,010,000	$ 800,000			
12.00	13,200,000	4,210,000	3,000,000	20.0%	109%	275%
14.00	15,400,000	6,410,000	5,200,000	16.7%	52%	73%
16.00	17,600,000	8,610,000	7,400,000	14.3%	34%	42%

Panel b. Debt Capacity and Equity Risk

Debt	$25,125,000	$10,000,000
Interest rate	8.0%	8.0%
Interest expense	$2,010,000	$800.000
Tax rate	30%	30%

Price/Kwh	Net Income	
	New Plant	Old Plant
$10.00	$ —	$ —
12.00	1,540,000	1,540,000
14.00	3,080,000	3,080,000
16.00	4,620,000	4,620,000

capacity output.[11] If the per unit price is $12 per kwh, then both plants generate revenues of $13,200,000 per year, with the more efficient newer plant earning $4,210,000 in operating profits compared to only $3,000,000 for the less efficient older plant. Other things being the same, New Plant is clearly more valuable and will have a greater total debt capacity due to its higher value. However, in addition, the new plant will have a greater debt capacity as a percent of its value because its profits are less volatile in response to changes in electric power prices.[12] To see this, consider the effects of a drop in price from $12.00 to $10.00 per kwh (a drop of 16.7%). Assuming both plants continue to operate at capacity, the New Plant's operating profits will drop by 52%, but the Old Plant's will drop by 73%. This greater sensitivity of the older plant to price changes means that its ability to service debt is less than that of the newer plant.

In Panel b of Table 5-5 we assume that the Old Plant is financed with $10 million in debt that carries an 8% rate of interest. Note that if New Plant's debt financing is set equal to $25,125,000 of 8% debt, the New Plant and Old Plant will produce the same level of net income regardless of the price of electric power. Consequently, if this is the case, the equity cash flows to both plants will be the same, which means that the probability of default for both debt issues will be the same and the appropriate cost of both debt and equity will be the same for both plants. However, as we discussed earlier, the project-specific WACCs for the two plants will be different; the new plant will have a lower WACC since, as a proportion of its value, it is financed with less debt.

The preceding example illustrates that the project-specific WACC approach is likely to work very well for projects that are very similar in all respects other than risk. For projects in very different lines of business, however, the approach is clearly imperfect. For example, differences in the debt capacity of an integrated oil company's refinery business and its chemical business may provide a good indicator of differences in its cost of capital. However, it should be emphasized that this is only an approximation, since there may be inherent differences between the betas of chemical and refinery businesses that are not fully captured by differences in their respective debt capacities.

Before concluding our discussion of this approach, it is worth noting that even for firms in only one line of business, the debt capacity of any individual investment project can look very different than the overall debt ratio of the firm. For example, consider a manufacturing firm with a market value of $2.5 billion that owns a number of factories with an aggregate value of $1.5 billion. Why is the market value of the

---

[11]These computations are based on the assumption that both plants incur $8 million per year in fixed operating costs but that the New Plant incurs only $0.90 per kwh to produce power while the Old Plant (which is much less fuel efficient) incurs $2.00 per kwh. Note that we fix output capacity such that the changes in operating profits are driven solely by the price of electric power per kwh, as the total costs of producing the 1,100,000 kwh of electric power are fixed for each plant.

[12]Both plants are assumed to continue to operate at their full capacity in the face of changing power prices.

firm so much higher than the value of its assets? The answer is that the market value of the firm not only reflects the value of the firm's assets, but also the cumulative value of all the firm's future opportunities to take on positive-NPV investments. In this case, $1 billion of the firm's value is represented by the fact that it has opportunities to take on positive-NPV investments in the future.

If the firm has $500 million of debt outstanding, then its debt ratio (in market value terms) is $500 million/$2.5 billion = 20%. When calculating the firm's WACC, we use market value weights of .20 for debt and .80 for equity. However, if each new plant can be financed like the existing plants with 33% debt, then the project-specific WACC would put more weight on debt and would thus be less than the firm's WACC. Put somewhat differently, the firm's growth opportunities may have zero debt capacity, and the debt capacity of the firm's operating assets may be 33%.

5.4 HURDLE RATES AND THE COST OF CAPITAL

In this chapter we have discussed a variety of ways in which firms can determine the cost of capital associated with a given investment project. The traditional theory suggests that to evaluate a project, firms should discount the project's cash flow at the project's cost of capital, and then accept the project if the calculated NPV is positive. In practice, however, firms tend to discount cash flows using discount rates, often referred to as *hurdle rates,* which exceed the appropriate cost of capital for the project being evaluated. For example, it's not unusual to see corporate hurdle rates as high as 15% for firms with WACCs, as well as project WACCs, as low as 10%. In other words, firms generally require that accepted projects have a substantial *NPV cushion,* or margin of safety. For example, most managers are unwilling to invest in a project with an initial expenditure of $100 million if the project's NPV is only $200,000. In theory, this is a positive-NPV project that will add $200,000 to the firm's value. In practice, most managers would consider an NPV cushion of 0.2% of the project's initial expenditure to be too small.

Mutually Exclusive Projects

There are a number of reasons why it makes sense to require either an NPV cushion or, equivalently, a hurdle rate that exceeds the project's cost of capital. The first and probably most important reason is that most firms do not believe that the WACC, which is the opportunity cost that we calculate from the capital markets, is the appropriate opportunity cost. The capital markets provide the appropriate opportunity cost for firms that have no constraints and can implement all positive-NPV investments. However, for firms that have constraints limiting the number of projects that can be accepted, the opportunity cost of capital reflects the return on alternative investments that may have to be passed up. More precisely, the opportunity cost of capital must reflect the rate of return forgone on the next best project that must be rejected if the evaluated project is accepted. For example, suppose a firm is choosing between two projects that are of equivalent risk. Suppose that the first project can generate an expected internal rate of return of 18%. If taking the second project precludes taking the first project, then the appropriate opportunity cost of capital that should be used to evaluate the second project is 18%, not the cost of capital.

High Hurdle Rates May Provide Better Incentives for Project Sponsors

By requiring a high hurdle rate, firms may signal that they have good investment opportunities, which may have the side benefit of motivating project sponsors to find better projects. For example, if top management sets a corporate hurdle rate at 12%, project sponsors may be happy to propose a project with an internal rate of return of 13%. However, with a 15% hurdle rate, the project sponsor will need to put in more effort and negotiate harder with suppliers and strategic partners to come up with an investment plan that meets the higher hurdle. Indeed, we can envision situations where a high hurdle rate actually helps in the negotiation process. For example, suppose that a profitable project requires the participation of two firms that are structuring a deal that, in effect, divides the project's profits. Suppose now that the first firm requires a very high hurdle rate for investment projects, but the second firm does not. In such a situation, the second firm may be willing to make concessions to the first firm to get the project approved.

Accounting for Optimistic Projections and Selection Bias

In general, cash flow forecasts are not very accurate even if they are unbiased estimates. However, the process used to select projects often induces an optimistic bias in the cash flow forecasts for those projects that are eventually selected. As a result, it generally makes sense to use a high hurdle rate to offset the optimistic cash flow forecasts.

To understand how these biases can come about it is useful to consider an investment that a number of firms are competing to acquire. For example, a conglomerate may be selling one of its divisions and will sell to the high bidder. In this situation, we might expect between five and 10 firms to evaluate the division and make a bid that is somewhat lower than their estimated values. In this situation, the highest bidder is likely to have the most optimistic forecast of the division's future cash flows, and thus the highest valuation for the business.

Auction theorists have coined the term "the winner's curse" to convey the idea that the winning bidder, being the most optimistic of all the bidders, is likely to be too optimistic and may thus have overbid. (See the Behavioral Insight box on the winner's curse.) To counteract this tendency to overpay in auction-like settings, auction theorists recommend that firms shade down their bids to reflect the fact that they are likely to be overly optimistic if they do win the bid. One way to accomplish this

B E H A V I O R A L   I N S I G H T

The Winner's Curse

The winner's curse is a thriving part of our culture. This is illustrated in a comment once made by Groucho Marx, "I would never join a club that would have me for a member." Woody Allen (in the movie *Annie Hall*) later applied this same logic to his reluctance to enter a relationship with a woman who would be interested in him. Allen considered this tendency to be one of his many neuroses. However, economists recognize the tendency to devalue those things that are available to us as a rational response to an environment in which we have less than perfect information.

is to require very high hurdle rates when evaluating projects in auction-like settings. For businesses that are more difficult to value and in situations where there are likely to be more bidders, the winner's curse is more severe. In such situations, an even higher hurdle rate is warranted.

A similar situation arises whenever a firm selects from a set of proposed investment projects. In this situation the firm is likely to select those projects that look to be the most attractive; in general, these are likely to be the best projects, but these will also be projects that are likely to be not quite as attractive as they may appear. Again, a high hurdle rate is warranted to offset the fact that the cash flow forecasts of selected projects are likely to be optimistic forecasts.

To understand the importance of this selection bias, consider a college that selects only students with very high SAT scores. On average, the students will be very bright, but perhaps not quite as bright as their SAT scores would suggest. By selecting students based on high SAT scores, the college will get students that are indeed smarter than average, but they will also be somewhat luckier than average. Students with abilities commensurate with a 1525 SAT score, who are unlucky and score only 1450 points, will get rejected, while students with abilities commensurate with a 1425 SAT score, but who are lucky and score 1500, will get selected. Hence, on average the students admitted to this college will tend to have SAT scores that exceed their true abilities. For similar reasons, we expect that selected investment projects will tend to have cash flow forecasts that exceed their true expected cash flows, which in turn suggests that they should be evaluated using a hurdle rate that exceeds the true cost of capital.

5.5 SUMMARY

Discounted cash flow valuation requires two important inputs: estimates of future cash flows and discount rates. In Chapters 2 and 3 we dealt with cash flows, and in Chapter 4 we focused on discount rates that can be used to value entire firms.

This chapter examined the appropriate discount rate that firms should use to value individual investment projects.

In general, project discount rates derived from academic theory deviate substantially from industry practice. Theory suggests that firms should evaluate each investment project with individual discount rates that reflect both the debt capacity and the unique risks of the investment. In practice, firms often use their companywide WACC to evaluate their investments. There are two very practical reasons for this: First, the cost of capital is a subjective concept that is difficult to estimate for publicly traded firms and even more difficult to estimate for an individual project. Second, providing project advocates with latitude in the selection of the appropriate discount rate may create managerial biases that are worse than those created by using just one discount rate. That is, overly optimistic and/or opportunistic managers may waste time and valuable resources to persuade project evaluators to value their projects with lower discount rates that make the projects look better than they really are.

In practice firms use one of three approaches to determine the discount rate to use in valuing investment alternatives. The most common approach involves the use of a single, firmwide WACC for all projects. For firms that operate in multiple divisions whose project risks and financing patterns are unique, a divisional WACC is often used. Finally, some firms estimate a project-specific WACC where the project is of such significance to the firm that the benefits of developing a customized or tailored estimate of the project WACC are warranted. We discussed two important variants of the project WACC: The first involved projects that are financed using project financing (i.e., nonrecourse debt). The second involved projects that were financed out of corporate sources. In the latter case the analyst has the added task of estimating the project's debt capacity.

PROBLEMS

5-1 INVESTOR OPTIMISM AND THE COST OF CAPITAL   Investment projects located in Indonesia and other emerging markets frequently have low systematic risk, implying that the appropriate discount rates for projects are quite low. In practice, most firms (with some notable exceptions) use very high discount rates for these projects. One explanation that has been offered for this practice is that the investing firm uses the high discount rates in an attempt to offset the effects of optimistic cash flow estimates. Is it a good idea to adjust for the risk of overly optimistic cash flow forecasts using changes in discount rates, or should the cash flows themselves be adjusted?

5-2 CALCULATING A FIRM'S WACC AND PROJECT WACC   Amgel Manufacturing Company's current capital structure is comprised of 30% debt and 70% equity (based on market values). Amgel's equity beta (based on its current level of debt financing) is 1.20, and its debt beta is 0.29. Also, the risk-free rate of interest is currently 4.5% on long-term government bonds. Amgel's investment banker advised the firm that, according to its estimates, the market risk premium is 5.25%.

a. What is your estimate of the cost of equity capital for Amgel (based on the CAPM)?

b. If Amgel's marginal tax rate is 35%, what is the firm's overall weighted average cost of capital (WACC)?

c. Amgel is considering a major expansion of its current business operations. The firm's investment banker estimates that Amgel will be able to borrow up to 40% of the needed funds and maintain its current credit rating and borrowing cost. Estimate the WACC for this project.

5-3 CONCEPTUAL EXERCISE   The term "hurdle rate" is often used in the context of project evaluation and sometimes is used to refer to the risk-adjusted discount rate—i.e., the required rate of return on a project with a given level of risk. The risk-adjusted discount rate refers to the cost of capital or opportunity cost of raising money to finance an investment, and hurdle rates are generally higher than the cost of capital. Why might a firm use hurdle rates that exceed its cost of capital?

5-4 CONCEPTUAL EXERCISE   Smith Inc. is a public company but is tightly controlled by Joe Smith, the grandson of the founder. Mr. Smith is quite confident about his ability to evaluate investments in all aspects of the business. The situation at Smith Inc. is quite different than that at Jones Inc., although they share a similar line of business. Jones Inc. has a much less powerful CEO who delegates much more control to the heads of the firm's various business units. In fact, Fred Jones, the company's CEO, meets with the heads of the various business units, and they make capital allocation choices as a group. Discuss how and why Smith Inc. and Jones Inc. might have different approaches for determining the discount rates used to evaluate their projects.

5-5 DIVISIONAL WACC   In 2006 Anheuser-Busch Companies, Inc., (BUD) engaged in the production and distribution of beer worldwide, operating through four business segments: Domestic Beer, International Beer, Packaging, and Entertainment. The Domestic Beer segment offers beer under Budweiser, Michelob, Busch, and Natural brands in the United States in addition to a number of specialty beers including non-alcohol brews, malt liquors, and specialty malt beverages, as well as energy drinks. The International Beer segment markets and sells Budweiser and other brands outside the United States and operates breweries in the United Kingdom and China. In addition, the International Beer segment also negotiates and administers license and contract brewing agreements with various foreign brewers. The Packaging segment manufactures beverage cans and can lids for drink customers, buys and sells used aluminum beverage containers, and recycles aluminum containers. Finally, the Entertainment segment owns and operates theme parks.

In 2005 Anheuser-Busch reported the following segment revenues and net income:

($ millions)	Domestic Beer	International Beer	Packaging	Entertainment
2005				
Gross sales	$ 10,121.00	$ 864.00	$ 1,831.50	$ 904.40
Income before income taxes	2,293.40	70.10	120.40	215.10
Equity income	—	147.10	—	—
Net income	$ 1,421.90	$ 433.70	$ 74.60	$ 133.40

Assume that you have just been charged with the responsibility for evaluating the divisional cost of capital for each of the business segments.

a. Outline the general approach that you would take in evaluating the cost of capital for each of the business segments.

b. Should the fact that $1,156 million of the Packaging segment's revenues come from internal sales to other Busch segments affect your analysis? If so, how?

5-6 PROJECT-SPECIFIC WACC   In 2005, worldwide capacity of wind-powered generators was just under 60,000 megawatts. This constitutes less than 1% of worldwide electricity use, but in Denmark wind power provides over 20% of electricity. Moreover, the use of wind power has grown rapidly in recent years, quadrupling between 1999 and 2005. The key feature of wind power is its heavy capital intensity and low ongoing costs, as the wind is free. Combined with advances in wind-power-generation technology, this alternative power source appears to be one of the most promising clean energy sources for the future.

Gusty Power Company (GPC) of Amarillo, Texas, builds and operates wind farms that produce electrical power that is then sold into the electrical grid. GPC has recently been contacted by the Plains Energy Company of Plainview, Texas, to construct one of the largest wind-power farms ever built. Plains Energy is an independent power producer that normally sells all the electrical power it produces back into the power grid at prevailing market prices. However, in this instance Plains has arranged to sell all of its production to a consortium of electric power companies in the area for a long-term, contractually set price. Assume that the project generates perpetual cash flows (annual PFCF of $8,000,000), debt principal is never repaid, capital expenditures (CAPEX) equal depreciation in each period, and the tax rate is 35%.

The project calls for an investment of $100 million, and Plains has arranged for an $80 million project loan which has no recourse to Plains's other assets. The loan carries a 7% rate of interest, which reflects current market conditions for loans of this type. Plains will invest $10 million in the project, and the remainder will be provided by two local power companies that are part of the consortium that will purchase the electrical power the project produces.

a. What is the project-specific WACC calculated using the book values of debt and equity as a proportion of the $100 million cost of the project? Given this estimate of the WACC, what is the value of the project?

b. Reevaluate the project-specific WACC using your estimate of the value of the project from part a above as the basis for your weights. Use this WACC to reestimate the value of the project and then recalculate the weights for the project-finance WACC using this revised estimate of WACC. Repeat this process until the value of the project converges to a stable value. What is the project's value? What is the project-finance WACC?

c. Reevaluate the project-specific WACC and project value where the contract calls for a 2.5% rate of increase in the project free cash flow beginning in the second year of the project's life.

5-7 PROJECT WACC USING CORPORATE FINANCING In the fall of 2008, Pearson Electronics, which manufactures printed circuit boards used in a wide variety of applications ranging from automobiles to washing machines, was considering whether or not to invest in two major projects. The first was a new fabricating plant in Omaha, Nebraska, which would replace a smaller operation in Charleston, South Carolina. The plant would cost $50 million to build and incorporate the most modern fabricating and assembly equipment available. The alternative investment involved expanding the old Charleston plant so that it could match the capacity of the Omaha plant and modernizing some of the handling equipment at a cost of $30 million. Given the location of the Charleston plant, however, it would not be possible to completely modernize the plant due to space limitations. The end result, then, is that the Charleston modernization alternative cannot match the out-of-pocket operating costs per unit of the fully modernized Omaha alternative.

Pearson's senior financial analyst, Shirley Davies, made extensive forecasts of the cash flows for both alternatives but was puzzling over what discount rate or rates she should use to evaluate them. The firm's WACC was estimated to be 9.12% based on an estimated cost of equity capital of 12% and an after-tax cost of debt capital of 4.8%. However, this calculation reflected a debt-to-value ratio of 40% for the firm, which she felt was unrealistic for the two plant investments. In fact, conversations with the firm's investment banker indicated that Pearson might be able to borrow as much as $12 million to finance the new plant in Omaha but no more than $5 million to fund the modernization and expansion of the Charleston plant without jeopardizing the firm's current debt rating. Although it was not completely clear what was driving the differences in the borrowing capacities of the two plants, Shirley suspected that a major factor was the fact that the Omaha plant was more cost effective and offered the prospect of much higher cash flows.

a. Assuming that the investment banker is correct, use book value weights to estimate the project-specific costs of capital for the two projects. (*Hint:* The only difference in the WACC calculations relates to the debt capacities for the two projects.)

b. How would your analysis of the project-specific WACCs be affected if Pearson's CEO decided to delever the firm by using equity to finance the better of the two alternatives (i.e., the new Omaha plant or the Charleston plant expansion)?

5-8 PROJECT-SPECIFIC WACC USING CORPORATE FINANCING   Lampkin Manufacturing Company has two projects. The first, Project A, involves the construction of an addition to the firm's primary manufacturing facility. The plant expansion will add fixed operating costs equal to $200,000,000 per year and variable costs equal to 20% of sales. Project B, on the other hand, involves outsourcing the added manufacturing to a specialty manufacturing firm in Silicon Valley. Project B has lower fixed costs of only $50,000 per year, and thus lower operating leverage than Project A, while its variable costs are much higher at 40% of sales. Finally, Project A has an initial cost of $3.2 million while Project B will cost $3.4 million.

When the question arose as to what discount rates the firm should use to evaluate the two projects, Lampkin's CFO, Paul Keown, called his old friend Arthur Laux, who works for Lampkin's investment banker.

"Art, we're trying to decide which of two major investments we should undertake, and I need your assessment of our firm's capital costs and the debt capacities of both projects. I've asked my assistant to e-mail you descriptions of each. We need to expand the capacity of our manufacturing facility, and these two projects represent very different approaches to accomplishing that task. Project A involves a traditional plant expansion totaling $3.2 million, while Project B relies heavily on outsourcing arrangements and will cost us a little more up-front, $3.4 million, but will have much lower fixed operating costs each year. What I want to know is how much debt we can use to finance each project without putting our credit rating in jeopardy. I realize this is a very subjective thing, but I know you have some very bright analysts who can provide us with valuable insight."

Art replied:

"Paul, I don't know the answers to your questions right off the top of my head, but I'll put one of our analysts on it and get back to you by the end of the day."

The next day Art left the following voice-mail message for Paul:

"Paul, I've got suggestions for you regarding the debt-carrying capacity of your projects and current capital costs for Lampkin. Our guys think that you've probably got room for about $1,200,000 in new borrowing if you do the traditional plant expansion project, (i.e., Project A). If you decide on Project B, we estimate you could borrow up to $2,400,000 without realizing serious pressure from the credit rating agencies. Moreover, if the credit agencies cooperate as expected, we can place that debt for you with a yield of 5%. Our analysts also did a study of your firm's cost of equity and estimate that it is about 10% right now. Give me a call if I can be of additional help to you."

a. Assuming that Lampkin's investment banker is correct, use book value weights to estimate the project-specific costs of capital for the two projects. (Hint: The only difference in the WACC calculations relates to the debt capacities for the two projects.)

b. How would your analysis of the project-specific WACCs be affected if Lampkin's CEO decided he wanted to delever the firm by using equity to finance the better of the two alternatives (i.e., Project A or B)?

Enterprise Valuation

Estimation of the value of a business enterprise is a challenging task. In Part III of this book we apply a combination of market-based multiples (Chapter 6) and the DCF methodology (Chapter 7), developed in earlier chapters, to estimate enterprise value. In Chapter 8 we look at the problem of enterprise valuation through the eyes of a private equity investor. This includes venture capitalists who are trying to structure a deal with an entrepreneur for capital in exchange for a share of the business, as well as leveraged buyout firms who use substantial amounts of borrowed money in combination with relatively little equity to acquire entire business units. Although there are important differences between all of these approaches, the rationale for each is based on the traditional DCF methodology.

In Chapter 9 we change our focus somewhat and consider the fact that in addition to evaluating investment projects based on NPV analysis, managers frequently consider how a proposed investment project is likely to influence their firm's reported earnings per share. We discuss why managers have an incentive to improve earnings per share rather than long-term value creation, which leads to a discussion of performance assessment. The potential disconnect between long-term value creation and the improvement of earnings per share has long been recognized by consultants who have used the logic of DCF analysis to design methods to evaluate and compensate managers.

CHAPTER 6

Relative Valuation Using Market Comparables

Chapter Overview

In this chapter we discuss *relative valuation,* or valuation using *market comparables*—a technique that is often used to value businesses, business units, and other major investments. We introduce the use of relative valuation in the context of a valuation problem faced by virtually everyone—the valuation of residential real estate. Although this illustration is quite simple, it illustrates the basic tenets of the use of relative valuation. Relative valuation criteria are often viewed as substitutes for the discounted cash flow (DCF) analysis we described in earlier chapters. As the discussion in this chapter illustrates, the DCF approach can be viewed as the conceptual basis for most relative valuation criteria, and the two approaches should be seen as complements.

6.1 INTRODUCTION

Relative valuation uses market prices from observed transactions to impute the value of a firm or investment opportunity. If you are considering the sale of your home, you might estimate the appropriate asking price by looking at **market comparables.** For example, you might calculate the ratio of prices from recent sales in the neighborhood to the square footage of the homes to calculate a price per square foot, and then multiply this number by the number of square feet in your house to get an estimate of what the home should sell for. For income-producing investments, analysts consider additional ratios, which include market values relative to the various earnings and cash flow numbers, sales, or the book value of recent transactions.

Up to this point we have estimated the value of an investment by discounting cash flows, which requires that the analyst develop a forecast of expected future cash flows as well as an appropriate discount rate. As we will illustrate in this chapter, valuing investments using *market comparables* (or *comps*) essentially solves the same problem using different information. Specifically, instead of trying to estimate future cash flows, this approach uses information from the market prices of comparable transactions. The critical assumption that underlies this approach to valuation is that the "comparable" transactions are truly comparable to the investment being evaluated.

Even though the science behind relative valuation is relatively easy to grasp, the successful application of this valuation methodology requires considerable skill. To help you develop that skill, we have organized the chapter as follows: In Section 6.2 we introduce relative valuation using examples from both residential and commercial real estate. Here we present the essential elements of the comparables valuation process, and we demonstrate the link between relative valuation multiples and DCF valuation. In Section 6.3 we discuss the use of comparables to value an entire business or enterprise. Here we learn that one of the most popular valuation ratios is the ratio of enterprise value to EBITDA (earnings before interest, taxes, depreciation, and amortization). In Section 6.4 we illustrate the use of the price–earnings multiple to value a firm's common equity, which is arguably the most common use of relative valuation. Section 6.5 discusses the valuation of a firm's equity when company shares are sold to the public for the first time (i.e., an initial public offering). In Section 6.6 we discuss a number of critical issues that arise in the use of relative valuation using market-based comparables. Finally, Section 6.7 contains summary comments.

6.2 Valuation Using Comparables

Relative valuation using market comparables involves a four-step process. To illustrate the steps, consider the valuation of a service station in Tulsa, Oklahoma.

Step 1: *Identify similar or comparable investments and recent market prices for each.* This is the most critical step in the process; the quality of the resulting estimate of value depends on how carefully matched the comparables are to the investment being valued.

> **Example:** Within the last six months two other service stations in Tulsa have sold. Sales prices and other pertinent information for the sales are available for analysis.

Step 2: *Calculate a "valuation metric" for use in valuing the asset.* This involves identifying a key attribute of the investment being valued and dividing it into the market prices of the comparables to compute a valuation ratio. Examples of attributes that are commonly used include earnings per share (when valuing common stock), the number of square feet (when valuing a home or building), and earnings before interest, taxes, depreciation, and amortization (when valuing a business enterprise). Once we have calculated the valuation ratios for the market comps, we typically average them to calculate the *valuation ratio* used in valuing the asset.

Example: The valuation of businesses like the Tulsa service station typically uses a valuation ratio based on some definition of earnings. For illustration purposes, we will use the operating earnings and define the valuation ratio as the sale or transaction price divided by the station's net operating earnings. For the two service station sales we have identified as market comps, we have the following information:

Station	Sale Price	Net Operating Earnings	Valuation Ratio
A	$ 900,000	$450,000	2
B	$1,200,000	$100,000	12
		Average valuation ratio	7

Step 3: *Calculate an initial estimate of value.* Multiply the valuation ratio (typically the average of a set of market comps) by the key "attribute" of the investment whose value is being estimated.

Example: The operating earnings of the Tulsa service station were $150,000 for the most recent year. Applying the average valuation ratio of 7 to these earnings produces an initial value estimate of $1,050,000.

Step 4: *Refine or tailor your initial valuation estimate to the specific characteristics of the investment.* In "refining the estimate," we analyze, and if need be, adjust the valuation ratio to reflect the peculiarities of the investment being valued.

Example: The immediate concern we have about the initial estimate for the Tulsa service station relates to the dramatic disparity in valuation ratios for the two comparable sales. Why did Station B sell for a multiple of 12 times operating earnings, while Station A commanded a multiple of only 2? At this point we will want to make sure that the numbers used in arriving at the comparable valuation ratios are reasonable. For example, it may be that Station B actually generated operating earnings of only $100,000 in the year of the analysis; however, in the year of the sale the station's earnings were depressed by the partial closure of its main entrance for six months due to road improvements. If we normalized the firm's operating earnings to reflect our estimate of what operating earnings would have been without the construction, Station B would have had operating earnings of $200,000. With the normalized earnings figure, the valuation ratio for Station B would have been only 6 (not 12). Using the revised valuation ratio for Station B and assuming Station A was not similarly affected, we get an average valuation ratio of 4.0 and a value estimate for the station being analyzed of only $600,000 (4.0 × $150,000), which is dramatically lower than the initial estimate.

To gain additional perspective on the issues raised in the service station valuation example, we include two real estate valuation examples. The first entails an analysis of a residence, and the second is a more complicated commercial real estate example.

Valuing Residential Real Estate Using Comparables

Anyone who has ever sold or bought a house through a real estate agent has experienced the use of relative valuation based on the method of comparables. The standard valuation approach for residential housing is to look for the price per square foot at which similar properties have recently sold. Just like our service station example, the valuation of a house begins by looking for comparable sale transactions. Perhaps the best way to gain an appreciation for the nuances of this methodology is by use of a simple example.

Example: Consider the valuation of a home with 3,581 square feet of floor space located in McGregor, Texas (five miles east of President George W. Bush's ranch in Crawford, Texas). The house is only one year old, is situated on an oversized lot, and has a swimming pool. The owner has set an asking price of $385,000 but has indicated a willingness to be flexible. Our problem is to estimate what the house should sell for, given the information on two recent market transactions in the same neighborhood.

The home is located in a popular area where recent sales have been recorded. The subdivision in which the home sits is less than five years old, so all the homes are of approximately the same age and condition. Two sales occurred in the immediate neighborhood over the previous six months. Details on these sales are found below:

	Comp #1	Comp #2
Sale price	$330,000	$323,000
Square footage	3,556	4,143
Selling price/sq. ft.	$ 92.80	$ 77.96
Time on the market	97 days	32 days

We can use the selling price per square foot for the two comps to estimate the value of the home, by multiplying the home's square footage of 3,581 by the corresponding selling prices per square foot for the comps.

Valuation Using Comps	Comp #1	Comp #2	Average
Comparable sq. ft. selling price	$ 92.80	$ 77.96	$ 85.38
Square footage of house being valued	3,581	3,581	3,581
Estimated value	$332,317	$279,175	$305,746

The estimates of the value of the home range from $279,175, based on the sale price of Comp #2, to $332,317, based on the sale price of Comp #1. The average of the two price estimates is $305,746.

Up to now, we have not taken into account two distinctive features of the house we are valuing. Specifically, it is located on a lot that is somewhat larger than the average lot in the subdivision, which may be worth $15,000–$20,000 more than the average lot. In addition, the home has a new swimming pool, which cost about $30,000 to build.

Valuation Using Comps	Comp #1	Comp #2	Average
Estimated value	$332,317	$279,175	$305,746
Adjustments			
Plus lot premium	20,000	20,000	20,000
Plus pool	15,000	15,000	15,000
Estimated market value	$367,317	$314,175	$340,746

To adjust for these two differences, we add a lot size premium of $20,000 plus half the cost of installing the pool, or $15,000. (Not everyone wants a swimming pool, and typically pools increase the price of the home by about half their cost when the home is sold.) This raises our average estimated value of the house to $340,746.

Is the house worth the estimated $340,746? The answer is an emphatic *maybe*. The reason for hesitating is that there are always intangibles that influence the value of a house (or a company, for that matter) that are not captured in the pricing of similar properties (comps). For example, it is not uncommon for houses that are built on premium lots to have special amenities or premium features. Although we do not know whether this is the case here, it is important that we consider the unique attributes of the house before arriving at our final estimate of its value.

This simple housing valuation example illustrates three key points concerning the use of the method of comparables.

- Point #1: *Identification of appropriate comps is paramount.* The valuation estimate is only as good as the set of comparables selected to determine the valuation multiple. Consequently, a real effort should be made to identify appropriate comparables.

- Point #2: *The initial estimate must be tailored to the investment's specific attributes.* The initial value estimate is only the beginning of the analysis. Even carefully selected comparables are almost always imperfect replicas of the investment being evaluated. As a result, the method of comparables requires that the analyst make a number of adjustments. In this case we were able to make adjustments for known differences between the house we are valuing and the comparison homes. Even after this process is complete, however, there are often other intangible differences that can lead to differences of opinion as to the actual value of the house. When a business or a large investment project is valued, these types of adjustments can be extremely important.

- Point #3: *The specific metric used as the basis for the valuation can vary from one application to another.* In our residential real estate valuation example, we used square footage as the comparable "feature," yet we used operating earnings in the service station example. In general, analysts use multiples of cash flows or some measure of earnings when reliable measures are available, but rely on less direct measures of an investment's earnings potential in other cases. In the case of a residential home, the owner receives "housing services," which can be viewed as his or her earnings from the property. When we use square footage (as opposed to cash flows) as the basis for comparing houses, we are assuming that the flow of housing services is directly related to the size of the house. Similarly, when valuing cable companies, analysts often use the number of cable subscribers as the key valuation metric. The important thing is that we select a valuation metric that is closely related to the investment's ability to generate cash flows or other benefits.

Valuing Commercial Real Estate

The residential real estate example involving the house in McGregor, Texas, should provide some feel for how to use the market comparables approach. Let's now consider commercial real estate. Although commercial real estate is often valued with the same multiples or comparables as residential real estate, analysts generally value commercial real estate by evaluating cash flow ratios as well as prices per square foot. As we show below, the cash flow valuation multiples that are used in practice have a direct relationship to the DCF approach that we discussed in the earlier chapters.

Valuation Ratios (Multiples) and DCF Valuation

To illustrate the connection between DCF valuation and relative valuation, let's consider the problem of valuing a perpetual cash flow stream of $100 per year, where the rate used to discount the cash flows is 20%. In Chapter 2 we noted that the present value of this cash flow stream is calculated as follows:[1]

$$\text{Value} = \frac{\text{Cash Flows}}{\text{Discount Rate } (k)} \tag{6.1}$$

Substituting into Equation 6.1, we estimate a value of $500, i.e.,

$$\text{Value} = \frac{\$100}{.20} = \$500$$

With a slight rearrangement of terms, we can express the DCF valuation as the product of the annual cash flow of $100 and a multiple, i.e.,

$$\text{Value} = \$100 \times \left(\frac{1}{.20}\right) = \$100 \times 5 = \$500$$

---

[1]The present value of a level perpetuity with periodic cash flow X and discount rate k can be shown to be equal to X/k. This result is well known in finance and constitutes the sum of the following geometric progression:

$$\sum_{t=1}^{\infty} \frac{X}{(1+k)^t} = X\sum_{t=1}^{\infty}\frac{1}{(1+k)^t} = X\left(\frac{1}{k}\right)$$

This analytical expression has a very intuitive basis. Think of the following situation. You want to generate a cash flow of X each year forever. How much would you have to put in a bank if the interest rate paid is k? The answer is X/k since the interest you earn each year is $k(X/k)$—exactly X. Thus, investing an amount X/k is equivalent to generating a cash flow of X each year forever.

In this form we recognize that the multiplier used to value the stream of $100 cash flows is $(1/.20) = 5$. It is customary when valuing commercial real estate to define what is known as a capitalization or "cap" rate. The **capitalization rate** is the reciprocal of the multiple used to value the property. In this instance, the cap rate is $1/5 = .20$, which in this example (a level perpetuity cash flow stream) is simply the discount rate. However, the cap rate is not always the discount rate; indeed, it is somewhat less than the discount rate when cash flows are expected to grow, and it exceeds the discount rate when cash flows are expected to shrink or decline over time.

To illustrate how the cap rate can differ from the discount rate, let's consider the case where the $100 cash flow grows at a rate of 5% per year forever and the discount rate is 20%. Recall from our earlier discussions in Chapters 2 and 4 that the DCF valuation formula for this situation (Equation 6.2) is known as the **Gordon growth model,** i.e.,[2]

$$\text{Value} = \frac{\text{Cash Flow}_0 \, [1 + \text{Growth Rate } (g)]}{\text{Discount Rate } (k) - \text{Growth Rate } (g)} \tag{6.2}$$

Substituting into Equation 6.2 produces an estimate of value equal to $700, i.e.,

$$\text{Value} = \frac{\$100 \, (1 + .05)}{.20 - .05} = \$700$$

Once again, we can restate the above DCF formula in terms of a multiple of firm cash flows, i.e.,

$$\text{Value} = \text{Cash Flow}_0 \times \left(\frac{[1 + \text{Growth Rate } (g)]}{\text{Discount Rate } (k) - \text{Growth Rate } (g)} \right) \tag{6.3}$$

where the term in parentheses is the valuation multiple that reflects a growing stream of cash flows. Again, substituting into Equation 6.3, we get the following:

$$\text{Value} = \$100 \times \left(\frac{1 + .05}{.20 - .05} \right) = \$100 \times 7 = \$700$$

---

[2]You will recall from our discussion in Chapter 2 that the Gordon growth model is simply the sum of the following geometric progression:

$$\sum_{t=1}^{\infty} \frac{X_0 \, (1 + g)^t}{(1 + k)^t} = X_0 \sum_{t=1}^{\infty} \frac{(1 + g)^t}{(1 + k)^t},$$

which can be reduced to

$$X_0 \left(\frac{1 + g}{k - g} \right) \text{ or } X_1 \left(\frac{1}{k - g} \right)$$

where $k > g$, and X_1 is equal to $X_0(1 + g)$.

The valuation multiple in this example is equal to the ratio of one plus the growth rate in future cash flows, divided by the difference between the discount rate and anticipated rate of growth in future cash flows. In the example of the growing perpetuity calculated above, the valuation multiple is 7. Since the multiple is equal to 7, the cap rate is 1/7 or 14.29%, which is less than the 20% discount rate.

Using the cap rate, we value the growing cash flow stream "as if it were a level perpetuity" as follows:

$$\text{Value} = \text{Cash Flow}_0 \times \left(\frac{[1 + \text{Growth Rate } (g)]}{\text{Discount Rate } (k) - \text{Growth Rate } (g)} \right)$$

$$= \text{Cash Flow}_0 \left(\frac{1}{\text{Cap Rate}} \right) = \$100 \times \left(\frac{1}{.1429} \right) = \$700$$

The difference between the discount rate and the capitalization rate increases with the growth rate anticipated in future cash flows. Table 6-1 illustrates this situation: Panel a includes the valuation multiples corresponding to discount rates ranging from 5% to 22.5% and growth rates ranging from 0% to 5%.[3] Note that only when there is zero anticipated growth in future cash flows (as seen in the first column) are the discount rate and the capitalization rate equal to one another. Moreover, as the rate of growth increases, the divergence between the cap rate and discount rate widens. In fact, the cap rate is approximately equal to the difference between the discount rate (k) and the growth rate (g), but not quite, since the growth rate also appears in the numerator of the valuation multiple, i.e., $(1 + g)/(k - g)$.[4]

Office Building Example

To demonstrate the valuation of an investment with market multiples, let's consider an office building that is currently generating cash flows of $3 million per year. To value the building using the DCF approach, you need estimates of both the expected growth rates of the cash flows (g) as well as the appropriate discount rate (k), neither of which is readily observable. In contrast, the cash flow multiples approach requires only one input that can be inferred from previous transactions. For example, if a similar office building that generated $4 million per year recently sold for $40 million,

---

[3]We include only one case where the discount rate of 5% is equal to the growth rate of 5%. For this case, and whenever the growth rate exceeds the discount rate, the Gordon model "blows up" and indicates an infinite value for the investment opportunity. The Gordon model cannot be applied since the growth rate in cash flows would dominate the effects of discounting. Clearly, this makes little economic sense. In practice, while growth rates may exceed discount rates for temporary periods of very high growth, they will never be greater than the discount rate on a permanent basis, as such a growth rate is not sustainable. The investment would attract new capital, and competition among new entrants would drive down profit margins and consequently growth rates in cash flows.

[4]It is also common to define the Gordon growth model using the projected cash flow for the end of the first period, (i.e., Cash Flow$_1$ = Cash Flow$_0(1 + g)$) in which case the valuation multiple becomes $\left(\frac{1}{k - g} \right)$ and the capitalization or cap rate equals $(k - g)$.

Table 6-1	**Capitalization Rates, Discount Rates, Growth Rates, and Valuation Multiples**

Panel a. Valuation Multiple $= \left(\dfrac{1 + g}{k - g}\right)$

	Growth Rates (g)					
Discount Rates (k)	0%	1%	2%	3%	4%	5%
5.0%	20.00	25.25	34.00	51.50	104.00	infinite
7.5%	13.33	15.54	18.55	22.89	29.71	42.00
10.0%	10.00	11.22	12.75	14.71	17.33	21.00
12.5%	8.00	8.78	9.71	10.84	12.24	14.00
15.0%	6.67	7.21	7.85	8.58	9.45	10.50
17.5%	5.71	6.12	6.58	7.10	7.70	8.40
20.0%	5.00	5.32	5.67	6.06	6.50	7.00
22.5%	4.44	4.70	4.98	5.28	5.62	6.00

Panel b. Implied Capitalization Rate $= 1 \Big/ \left(\dfrac{1 + g}{k - g}\right) = \left(\dfrac{k - g}{1 + g}\right)$

	Growth Rates (g)					
Discount Rates (k)	0%	1%	2%	3%	4%	5%
5.0%	5.00%	3.96%	2.94%	1.94%	0.96%	NM
7.5%	7.50%	6.44%	5.39%	4.37%	3.37%	2.38%
10.0%	10.00%	8.91%	7.84%	6.80%	5.77%	4.76%
12.5%	12.50%	11.39%	10.29%	9.22%	8.17%	7.14%
15.0%	15.00%	13.86%	12.75%	11.65%	10.58%	9.52%
17.5%	17.50%	16.34%	15.20%	14.08%	12.98%	11.90%
20.0%	20.00%	18.81%	17.65%	16.50%	15.38%	14.29%
22.5%	22.50%	21.29%	20.10%	18.93%	17.79%	16.67%

NM = not meaningful.

one could say that the market multiple is 10, and the cap rate is 10%. If the office building in question is truly comparable, you might then say that its value is $3 million times 10, or $30 million. This, of course, is a trivial exercise if the buildings really are directly comparable. The challenge lies in determining the extent to which the buildings really are comparable and in then assessing how their differences should influence the appropriate multiples.

Valuation When the Buildings Are not Identical In practice, no two investments are identical, so you must assess the extent to which the differences are likely to have a material effect on the valuation multiples. To see how small differences between the comps and the investment being valued can be very important, consider the valuation of the two office buildings described below:

	Per Square Foot		Total	
	Bldg. A	**Bldg. B**	**Bldg. A**	**Bldg. B**
Building size	—	—	50,000 sq. ft.	50,000 sq. ft.
Rent	$ 30/sq. ft.	$ 21/sq. ft.	$ 1,500,000	$ 1,050,000
Maintenance	(10.00)/sq. ft.	(10.00)/sq. ft.	(500,000)	(500,000)
Net operating income	$ 20.00/sq. ft.	$ 11.00/sq. ft.	$ 1,000,000	$ 550,000
Selling price information				
Sales multiple for NOI	10/sq. ft.	? /sq. ft.	10	?
Cap rate = 1/Sales multiple	10%/sq. ft.	? /sq. ft.	10%	?
Estimated property value	$ 200/sq. ft.	? /sq. ft.	$ 10,000,000	?

Building A sold for $200 per square foot, or $10,000,000, which reflects a sales multiple of 10 times the building's $1,000,000 annual net operating income (NOI) and a capitalization rate of 10%. The two buildings are identical in size (50,000 square feet) and maintenance costs ($10/sq. ft. or $500,000 per year), but there is one very important difference. The rental rates ($30 versus $21 per square foot) are very different, reflecting their different locations. Building A is in the heart of the down-town business district; Building B is not. However, the local economic factors that drive rental rates affect the two buildings in a similar fashion. Thus, the rental income of each building is similar with respect to *risk and expected growth rates*. This is an important assumption, which we use later.

The two buildings and their operating costs are virtually identical. Since the tenants pay their own utilities and day-to-day operating expenses, the maintenance costs of the building's owner do not vary over time or with swings in occupancy and rental rates. It is tempting to simply apply Building A's NOI multiple (of 10) to Building B, which would produce a valuation of $110 per square foot, or $5,500,000 for the building. But is this valuation correct? Should Building B sell for the same multiple and consequently have the same cap rate as Building A?

At first glance it does appear that the two buildings are very similar; they are the same size, their rental incomes are determined by the same local economic fluctuations,

and both have identical maintenance costs. But, as we now discuss, the different locations of the buildings and the attendant impact of these locations on rental rates have
a significant effect on the operating risk characteristics of the two buildings.
Specifically, since the rents (revenues) are lower for Building B, it has more **operating
leverage,** which means that its cash flows are more sensitive to changes in revenue. As
a result, the risks and the growth rates of the cash flows of the two buildings are not
the same, which in turn implies that the buildings should sell for different multiples of
their cash flows.

Operating Leverage and Investment Risk To understand the differences in operating leverage between the two buildings, note that Building A rents for $30 per square
foot and has maintenance costs of $10 per square foot, while Building B is much
closer to breakeven and rents for only $21 per square foot and has the same $10 per
square foot maintenance costs as Building A. What this means is that Building B has
higher fixed costs relative to revenues, which means that it has substantially higher
operating leverage than Building A. To illustrate how operating leverage affects risk,
look at what happens to the NOI for Building A when its rental revenues increase or
decrease by 20%:

	Building A		
% Change in revenues	−20%	0%	20%
Revenues	$1,200,000	$1,500,000	$1,800,000
Maintenance (fixed cost)	(500,000)	(500,000)	(500,000)
Net operating income	$ 700,000	$1,000,000	$1,300,000
% Change in revenues	**−20%**	**0%**	**20%**
% Change in NOI	**−30%**	**0%**	**30%**

A decrease in revenues of 20% results in a 30% drop in Building A's NOI.
Similarly, when revenues rise by 20%, Building A's NOI rises by 30%. This dynamic
reflects the fact that for Building A the ratio of the % Change in NOI divided by the
% Change in revenues is 1.5. Note, however, that this particular relationship between
the percent change in operating income and revenues is not constant for a particular
investment but varies with the level of firm revenues and NOI. In fact, the closer the
revenue level is to breakeven (i.e., NOI equal to zero), the larger will be this multiple.
The fact that the percent changes in NOI are greater than the corresponding percent
changes in revenues is due to the fact that building maintenance costs do not rise pro-
portionately with revenues. In this particular case, the maintenance costs do not
change as revenues rise and fall.

	Building B		
% Change in revenues	−20%	0%	20%
Revenues	$840,000	$1,050,000	$1,260,000
Maintenance (fixed cost)	(500,000)	(500,000)	(500,000)
Net operating income	$340,000	$ 550,000	$ 760,000
% Change in revenues	**−20.00%**	**0.00%**	**20.00%**
% Change in NOI	**−38.18%**	**0.00%**	**38.18%**

Now let's look at the relationship between revenues and NOI for Building B: For Building B, a 20% decrease in revenues leads to a 38.18% decrease in its NOI; when revenues rise by 20%, the NOI increases by 38.18%. Hence, Building B's operating income is more sensitive to changes in rental revenues than is Building A's. In short, Building B has higher operating leverage than Building A, and as a result, we expect its operating income to be more volatile in response to changes in rental revenues.

Investigating the Determinants of Cash Flows Even though we have established that the two buildings are *not* perfectly comparable, it is still possible to use an adjusted comparable analysis, based on the sale price of Building A, to value Building B. To do this, we need to first get a better feel for what determines the values of the two buildings by digging a bit more deeply into the determinants of their cash flows. Specifically, we can decompose each building's NOI into rental revenues and maintenance costs. In addition, we can also think of distinct *revenue multipliers* and *maintenance-cost multipliers* instead of a composite NOI multiplier. This decomposition helps us analyze how each component of NOI influences the values of the two buildings. Equation 6.4a defines building value based on NOI as the difference between the value of the building's rental revenues and the value of its maintenance costs:

$$\text{Building Value} = \left(\text{NOI} \times \frac{\text{NOI}}{\text{Multiple}} \right) = \left(\text{Rental Revenues} \times \frac{\text{Revenue}}{\text{Multiple}} \right) - \left(\text{Maintenance Costs} \times \frac{\text{Maintenance}}{\text{Multiple}} \right) \tag{6.4a}$$

or, using capitalization rates:

$$\text{Building Value} = \left(\frac{\text{NOI}}{\text{NOI Cap Rate}} \right) = \left(\frac{\text{Rental Revenues}}{\text{Revenue Cap Rate}} \right) - \left(\frac{\text{Maintenance Costs}}{\text{Maintenance Cap Rate}} \right) \tag{6.4b}$$

We use the cap-rate formulation in our analysis and assume that the rates applicable to Building A's maintenance and revenues are also appropriate for Building B. Since both buildings cost the same to maintain, it seems reasonable to use identical cap rates for the maintenance costs. Moreover, since we have assumed that rent revenues for each building are similar in terms of both growth and risk, a single revenue cap rate is reasonable to apply to the rents from both buildings.

If the ratio of rents to expenses were the same for both buildings (resulting in identical operating leverage), then these assumptions would imply that cap rates for each building would also be identical. However, as we will show, when two buildings differ in their operating leverage, they will generally differ in their overall cap rates, even when they have the same revenue and maintenance cap rates. The decomposition method we illustrate here allows the analyst to compare buildings that differ only in their operating leverage. If Buildings A and B differ on more than this dimension, additional analysis is required.

Since we assume the maintenance costs are fixed, they are somewhat easier to value and are a logical starting point of our analysis. Recall that the cap rate and the discount rate are the same for the case of a constant perpetuity. We assume that the discount rate (and cap rate) for maintenance, which is assumed to be certain, is the borrowing rate associated with Building A, which is 8%. Thus we can calculate the value of Building A's maintenance costs using Equation 6.1 as follows:

$$\text{Value of Building A's Maintenance Costs} = \frac{\$500,000}{.08} = \$6,250,000$$

Given the $10,000,000 value of Building A and the above estimate of the value of its maintenance costs, the value of the building's revenues must equal $16,250,000. This amount is the value of the building plus the value of the maintenance costs. This implies a capitalization rate for Building A's annual rental revenues of 9.23% after rounding (since $1,500,000/.0923 = $16,250,000).

We now use the capitalization rates from Building A to value Building B. Specifically, we will use the 9.23% cap rate inferred from the valuation of Building A's revenues to value the revenues of Building B as follows:

$$\frac{\$1,050,000}{.0923076} = \$11,375,000$$

Moreover, we use the 8% cap rate on Building A's maintenance costs to value the costs for Building B as follows:

$$\frac{\$500,000}{.08} = \$6,250,000$$

The resulting valuation of Building B is $5,125,000 (which we calculate as $11,375,000 − $6,250,000). The details of our analysis of Building B are summarized in the table on the next page:

	Per Square Foot		Total	
	Bldg. A	Bldg. B	Bldg. A	Bldg. B
Borrowing rate	8%	8%	8%	8%
Value of maintenance costs	(125.00)	(125.00)	(6,250,000)	(6,250,000)
Implied revenue value	$325.00	$ 227.50	$16,250,000	$11,375,000
Implied revenue multiple	10.833	10.833	10.833	10.833
Implied revenue cap rate	9.23%	9.23%	9.23%	9.23%
Property value	$200.00	$ 102.50	$10,000,000	$ 5,125,000
Implied multiple of NOI	10.000	9.318	10.000	9.318
Implied cap rate of NOI	10.0%	10.732%	10.0%	10.732%

Based on this analysis, we estimate that Building B is actually worth only $5,125,000 rather than the earlier estimate of $5,500,000, which was based on a more naïve application of multiples. The lower value reflects the fact that Building B has more operating leverage and is thus riskier, which in turn implies that it must have a higher cap rate.

Key learning points We can draw two important learning points from the commercial real estate valuation exercise that generalize to almost any investment. The first point is that investments that look very similar on the surface can generate cash flows with very different risks and growth rates, and should thus sell for different multiples. As this example illustrates, operating leverage is an important determinant of value and must be accounted for in choosing comps, and when operating leverage is different, it is important to adjust comps for these differences. Finally, the example illustrates the importance of exercising great care and using creative ways to properly apply the method of market comparables. It is very tempting to assume that since the use of market comparables as a valuation tool appears very simple, the analysis *is* simple. The fact is that valuation using market comparables requires the same diligence and care as discounted cash flow analysis.

6.3 ENTERPRISE VALUATION USING EBITDA MULTIPLES

The most popular approach used by business professionals to estimate a firm's enterprise value involves the use of a multiple of an accounting earnings number commonly called **EBITDA** which refers to earnings before interest, taxes, depreciation, and amortization. Analysts generally view EBITDA as a crude measure of a firm's cash flow, and thus view EBITDA multiples as roughly analogous to the cash flow multiples used in real estate. As our discussion in this section indicates, sometimes the analogy is good and sometimes it is not.

Enterprise Value versus Firm Value

You may recall from our discussion of the firm's cost of capital in Chapter 4 that the enterprise value of a firm is defined as the sum of the values of the firm's interest-bearing debt and its equity minus the firm's cash balance on the date of the valuation. For example, in August 2005 Airgas, Inc., (ARG)[5] had an enterprise value of $2.96 billion, consisting of the following components:

Elements of the Firm's Balance Sheet	Values
Noninterest-bearing debt	$ 669,056,000
Interest-bearing debt (short- and long-term)	808,635,000
Common equity (market value = price per share × shares outstanding)	2,180,000,000
Firm value	$ 3,657,691,000
Less: Noninterest-bearing debt	(669,056,000)
Less: Cash and equivalents	(32,640,000)
Equals: Enterprise value	$ 2,955,995,000

We can calculate the equity value of Airgas, Inc., from enterprise value as follows:

$$\text{Owners' Equity} = \text{Enterprise Value} - (\text{Interest-Bearing Debt} - \text{Cash}) \quad (6.5a)$$

$$= \text{Enterprise Value} - \text{Net Debt}$$

$$\$2.18 \text{ billion} = \$2.96 \text{ billion} - 0.78 \text{ billion} \quad (6.5b)$$

where the term *net debt* refers to the firm's interest-bearing liabilities less cash.

The Airgas EBITDA Multiple

To calculate the Airgas EBITDA multiple, we solve the following equation:

$$\text{Enterprise Value}_{\text{Airgas 2005}} = \text{EBITDA}_{\text{Airgas 2005}} \times \frac{\text{EBITDA}}{\text{Multiple}} \quad (6.6)$$

For example, on August 1, 2005, Airgas's EBITDA was $340 million and its enterprise value was $2,955,995,000; this results in an EBITDA multiple for Airgas of 8.69. In the next section we look at how the Airgas EBITDA multiple, along with multiples of similar firms, might be used to value a privately held company.

---

[5]Airgas, Inc., and its subsidiaries distribute industrial, medical, and specialty gases and welding, safety, and related products in the United States.

Example—Valuing a Privately Held Firm

To explore the use of an EBITDA multiple, we consider the valuation of Helix Corporation, a privately owned company operating out of Phoenix, Arizona, that is a potential acquisition candidate. Since it is privately owned, a potential acquirer cannot observe its market value. However, the acquirer can use similar firms that *are* publicly traded to infer a value for Helix by using the appropriate EBITDA valuation ratio.

We first identify comparable firms from which to calculate an appropriate EBITDA multiple and then apply this multiple to Helix's EBITDA to arrive at an initial estimate of the enterprise value of the firm.[6] The second step in the process involves refining our estimates of both the EBITDA multiple and the firm's EBITDA. This step constitutes a careful assessment of the basic elements of the valuation (EBITDA and the EBITDA multiple or valuation ratio) so as to tailor the analysis to the specific firm that is being valued. We consider each step in the analysis over the next few pages.

We first note that Helix is a regional supplier of specialty gases including nitrogen, oxygen, argon, helium, acetylene, carbon dioxide, nitrous oxide, hydrogen, welding gases, purity grades, and application blends. We identify four national firms that constitute the primary competitors to Helix. These include Air Products (APD), Airgas (ARG), Praxair (PX), and Applied Industrial Technologies (AIT). Consequently, we begin by identifying the EBITDA multiple for these firms.

Table 6-2, which describes financial information about the four public firms that are engaged in a similar business to Helix, reveals that the average EBITDA multiple for comparable firms is 10.48. If Helix anticipates earning $10 million in EBITDA this year, then our initial estimate of the firm's enterprise value is $10 million $\times$ 10.48 = $104.8 million. Helix has a cash balance of $2.4 million and owes interest-bearing debt totaling $21 million. Consequently, we estimate the value of Helix's equity to be $86.2 million.

Table 6-2   Comparable-Firm EBITDA Multiples for Helix Corporation

($ millions)	Air Products	Praxair, Inc.	Applied Industrial Technologies, Inc.	Airgas	Average
Enterprise value	$ 16,100	$ 19,450	$ 10,800	$ 29,560	
EBITDA	1,390	1,810	99	340	
EBITDA multiple	11.58	10.75	10.91	8.69	10.48

---

[6]We are assuming that Helix's EBITDA for the year just ended is known. This would be the case if Helix and Airgas had entered into negotiations.

Figure 6-1   EBITDA and Cash Flow

Comparing the Calculation of FFCF and EBITDA		Difference
Firm Free Cash Flow (FFCF)	**EBITDA**	**FFCF − EBITDA**
EBIT (Earnings before interest and taxes)	EBIT	0
Less: Taxes = T × EBIT	NA	−T × EBIT
Plus: Depreciation and amortization	Plus: Depreciation and amortization	0
Less: Capital expenditures (CAPEX)	NA	−CAPEX
Less: Change in net working capital (NWC)	NA	−NWC
Sum: FFCF	EBITDA	**−T × EBIT − CAPEX − NWC**

Just as we did earlier with our real estate valuation exercises, we must now engage in the second phase of the valuation process, which involves tailoring the analysis to Helix. In other words, we consider the need to make adjustments to both the EBITDA and the EBITDA multiple used in Step 1. To gain some perspective on the issues that arise in the second step of the valuation process, we must first take a detour and review the relationship between EBITDA and free cash flow.

EBITDA and Firm Free Cash Flow

When we opened our discussion of the EBITDA enterprise-valuation approach, we noted that analysts often think of EBITDA as a rough estimate of cash flow. Technically, although the two measures are related, EBITDA is not the same as firm free cash flow (FFCF). Figure 6-1 illustrates the difference between EBITDA and a project's or firm's free cash flow, which can help us understand when the EBITDA valuation approach works well and when it does not. It shows that EBITDA falls short of the firm's free cash flow by the sum at the bottom of the rightmost column of Figure 6-1. Specifically, EBITDA is a before-tax measure and does not include expenditures for new capital equipment (CAPEX) and does not account for changes in working capital (NWC).

EBITDA	$ 10,000,000
Enterprise value = 10.48 × $10,000,000	104,800,000
Plus: Cash	2,400,000
Less: Interest-bearing debt	(21,000,000)
Equity value	$ 86,200,000

Summarizing Figure 6-1, we see that all the items listed here make EBITDA overstate FFCF.

$$\text{EBITDA} = \text{FFCF} + (\text{T} \times \text{EBIT} + \text{CAPEX} + \text{NWC}) \qquad (6.7a)$$

Similarly, solving for FFCF,

$$\text{FFCF} = \text{EBITDA} - (\text{T} \times \text{EBIT} + \text{CAPEX} + \text{NWC}) \qquad (6.7b)$$

What this last expression illustrates is that FFCF is often more volatile than EBITDA. The reason is that FFCF includes consideration for new investments in capital equipment (CAPEX) and working capital (NWC), which are discretionary to varying degrees[7] and vary over the business cycle, rising in good times and contracting in bad times. Thus, in those years when large capital investments are being made, EBITDA significantly overstates the firm's free cash flow, and vice versa.

Why Use EBITDA Multiples Rather than Cash Flow Multiples?

Although EBITDA provides a crude estimate of a firm's cash flows, it does provide a relatively good measure of the before-tax cash flows that are generated by the firm's existing assets. To see this, reexamine Equation 6.6 and assume that the firm will not be paying taxes and will not be investing and growing, and since the firm will not be growing, it will not experience any changes in working capital. Under these assumptions, FFCF will be equal to EBITDA, as can be seen from Equation 6.7b. We can value these cash flows using Gordon's growth model (Equation 6.2), but we must recognize that without new investment, the cash flows from the firm's existing business are likely to diminish over time, as competitors enter the firm's market and as its plant and equipment become obsolete.

Remember, however, since EBITDA measures only the earnings of the firm's assets already in place, it ignores the value of the firm's new investments. This is clearly a disadvantage of this valuation tool. One might think that it would be better to value the earnings potential of the entire firm using an FFCF multiple than to value just its assets in place using an EBITDA multiple. However, as we noted earlier, FFCF for most firms is very volatile since it reflects discretionary expenditures for capital investments and working capital that can change dramatically from year to year. In fact, FFCF is frequently negative, since capital expenditures often exceed internally generated capital. As a result, FFCF multiples are unlikely to be as reliable as multiples based on EBITDA, and for this reason they are not used as often in practice.

---

[7]For example, to the extent that capital expenditures can be delayed or sped up and credit terms allow the firm some discretion over when to pay for short-term credit, these expenditures are under the control of management.

One may ask, however, whether it is reasonable to simply ignore the firm's capital expenditures, which is implicitly being done in the calculation of EBITDA.[8] The answer is that we can ignore capital expenditures if we believe that the firm's investments have zero net present values on average. However, while this might be a reasonable assumption for many mature firms, one certainly does not want to ignore growth opportunities that have positive NPVs. Given this, in any valuation that utilizes EBITDA multiples, it is important to take into account differences between the value of the growth opportunities of the firm being valued (that is, the extent to which the firm has positive-NPV investments) and the growth opportunities of the comparison firms.

In summary, EBITDA multiples provide a good valuation tool for businesses in which most of the value comes from a firm's existing assets. For this reason, in practice we see EBITDA multiples being used primarily for the valuation of stable, mature businesses. EBITDA multiples are much less useful for evaluating businesses whose values come mainly from future growth opportunities.

The Effects of Risk and Growth Potential on EBITDA Multiples

As just mentioned, EBITDA reflects the cash flows generated by the assets that the firm currently owns and operates, and in general, these cash flows are likely to decline over time. However, the decline is likely to be less for some businesses than others, and in some businesses we expect to see increases rather than decreases in cash flows. Consequently, when using an EBITDA multiple, one must consider the growth potential of the firm being valued and select a set of comparable firms to estimate the EBITDA valuation ratio that share similar prospects. In addition, one must consider the risk differences between the firm being evaluated and the comparison firms and determine how these risk differences should be reflected in discount rates and, hence, in multiples.

It is common practice to select firms within the same industry as market comparables, since these are likely to be the most similar to the firm being evaluated.

---

[8]The EBITDA calculation clearly ignores capital expenditures; however, the EBITDA multiple (which reflects prevailing market prices) probably does reflect capital expenditures and their anticipated effects on firm value. For instance, if a firm uses more capital to generate the same EBITDA as another company in the same industry, the former may have a higher multiple. This is because EV (enterprise value) reflects PV(FFCF), which reflects capital expenditures. In fact for consistency, it must be the case. Consider the simple case of constant growth in FFCF. Note that $EV = PV(FFCF_t) = FFCF_0(1 + g)/(k - g)$. Since M (multiple) = $EV/EBITDA_0$, it follows that $M = FFCF_0(1 + g)/[EBITDA_0(k - g)]$ for consistency between the two equations. If the multiple (M) is accurate, it would reflect the capital expenditure (implicit in the growth rate g for this constant-growth-rate simple case). The multiple M is the product of two ratios: $[FFCF_0/EBITDA_0]$ and $[(1 + g)/(k - g)]$.

However, there can be substantial differences in risk characteristics and growth opportunities among firms within an industry, and EBITDA multiples should be adjusted to reflect these differences. To a large extent, differences in firm risk arise because of variations in operating leverage across firms, and as our commercial real estate example illustrated, differences in operating leverage can arise because of differences in profit margins. In addition, differences can arise because of differences between fixed and variable operating costs. Firms that incur higher levels of fixed operating costs but lower variable costs will experience more volatile swings in profits as their sales rise and fall over the business cycle. Differences in expected growth rates tend to be somewhat more subjective; however, analysts can consider past growth rates as indicators of future growth rates.

Although it is generally quite difficult to make objective adjustments to EBITDA multiples to allow for differences in risk and growth opportunities, it is critical that these considerations enter into the selection of comparable firms. Let's return to our earlier analysis of the appropriate EBITDA multiple for the valuation of Helix Corporation to see how we might make such adjustments. We might, for example, want to compare Helix's growth opportunities and risk with each of the firms in Table 6-2. The relatively low EBITDA multiple for Airgas may reflect the fact that its risk (as reflected in the firm's cost of capital) is high and/or its growth opportunities are low when compared to the other firms. This begs the question as to whether Helix is more like Airgas or the remaining comparison firms. Although we cannot answer this question without more information about Helix and the comparison firms, this analysis is exactly what is required to get the best possible estimate of the EBITDA valuation multiple for valuing Helix.

Normalizing EBITDA

We argued earlier that the appeal of EBITDA over cash flow relates to its relative stability when compared to FFCF. However, EBITDA does vary over time, and any given year's EBITDA may be influenced by idiosyncratic effects that need to be accounted for when using the EBITDA valuation model. For example, in the Helix Corporation example, we used the firm's most recent year's EBITDA of $10 million to value the firm. The presumption we made was that this EBITDA was not influenced by any nonrecurring special event during the past year. If the EBITDA was affected by any such event, it would lead us to place a value on Helix that is not reflective of the firm's future earning power. For example, if the 2005 EBITDA for Helix reflected the results of a onetime transaction with a customer, which contributed $500,000 to EBITDA but is not likely to be repeated in future years, we might want to make a downward adjustment to EBITDA to $9,500,000. Similarly, if the 2005 EBITDA reflects extraordinary write-offs of $250,000, then we might want to make an upward adjustment of EBITDA to $10,250,000.

Adjusting the Valuation Ratio for Liquidity Discounts and Control Premiums

It should be noted that the value calculated in the preceding exercise is not necessarily the price a buyer will be willing to pay. A purely financial buyer, that is, a private equity investor or hedge fund, is likely to want a discount from this value. On the other hand, a strategic buyer that can realize synergies by acquiring and controlling the investment may be willing to pay a control premium.

The rationale for the possible discount is that Helix is a privately held firm and the market-based EBITDA multiples we used in our first-pass valuation were based on a sample of publicly held firms. Private companies often sell at a discount to their publicly traded counterparts since they cannot be sold as easily. A discount of 20% to 30% is not unusual in these circumstances, and the discount is typically attributed to the fact that the shares of privately held firms are less liquid (i.e., harder to sell) than those of public firms. Hence, if we apply a 30% discount, our estimate of the enterprise value of Helix is reduced to $73,360,000 = 10.48 \times \$10,000,000 (1 - .3)$. In this case the estimated value of Helix's equity equals $54,760,000, i.e.,

Enterprise value (revised)	$73,360,000
Plus: Cash	2,400,000
Less: Interest-bearing debt	(21,000,000)
Equity value	$54,760,000

If Helix is being acquired by Airgas, which is a publicly traded firm, is the liquidity discount likely to be an issue? Since Airgas is itself a public firm and is unlikely to want to sell Helix, the relevance of a liquidity discount is subject to debate. The actual price that will be paid on this transaction depends on the relative bargaining strengths of the buyer and seller (i.e., how motivated Airgas is to make the acquisition and how interested Helix's owners are to sell). This in turn depends on the synergies and improvements that Airgas expects to achieve when it takes control of Helix.

The Airgas acquisition of Helix might be considered a "strategic acquisition," which is a fancy way of saying that there are benefits (or synergies) from control. In contrast to purely financial acquisitions, which often require liquidity discounts, strategic acquisitions often feature control premiums, which can enhance the value of an acquisition target by 30% or more. Once again, when acquiring a private firm such as Helix, the amount of any control premium paid will depend upon the relative strength of the bargaining positions of the buyer and seller. The point here is that adjustments for liquidity discounts and control premiums will vary from one situation to another.

6.4 Equity Valuation Using the Price–Earnings Multiple

Up to this point our focus has been on the valuation of either major investment projects or the enterprise value of an entire firm. For these applications, it is common for financial analysts to use EBITDA multiples along with the DCF approach. In this section we explore how analysts value a firm's equity.

One approach would be to use EBITDA multiples to estimate enterprise value, as described in the last section, and then subtract the firm's interest-bearing debt to determine the value of its equity. While this approach is used in practice, it is not the main approach that is used when valuing a firm's equity. Instead, equity analysts tend to focus their attention on estimating the earnings of the firms they evaluate, and then use the **price-to-earnings (P/E) ratio** to evaluate the price of the common stock.

The price-earnings (P/E) multiple valuation approach is defined in Equation 6.8 below:

$$\left(\frac{\text{Price per Share for a Comparable Firm}}{\text{Earnings per Share for a Comparable Firm}} \right) \times \begin{array}{c} \text{Earnings per Share} \\ \text{for the Firm Being Valued} \end{array}$$

$$= \begin{array}{c} \text{Estimated Value} \\ \text{of the Firm's Equity} \end{array} \tag{6.8}$$

As we just mentioned, the P/E valuation approach is used to estimate the value of *the firm's equity*. It is not used to find the enterprise value, as we did using the EBITDA valuation method.

Example—Valuing ExxonMobil's Chemical Division Using the P/E Method

To illustrate the use of the P/E ratio valuation approach, let's suppose that Exxon-Mobil (XOM) was considering the sale of its chemical division. Although this is a hypothetical case, it provides a realistic setting in which the use of the P/E multiple valuation approach might prove useful. If the chemical division is sold as an independent company to the public, ExxonMobil could use an initial public offering (IPO) to sell the new company's shares. Alternatively, the division could be sold to another company. In either instance, ExxonMobil needs to place a value on the division.

In 2004 the chemical division of ExxonMobil was the third largest chemical company in the world, ranked behind BASF AG (BF) and DuPont (DD), based on total revenues.[9] The chemical division earned $3.428 billion in 2004, compared to $1.432

---

[9]Not every firm makes its divisional reporting available in its public filings. Where no divisional reporting is available, this type of analysis would be very difficult to carry out by an outside analyst. However, the company could, as we propose here, perform the analysis internally so long as it maintains divisional financial reports.

Table 6-3	Chemical Company Price/Earnings Ratios (August 16, 2005)				
	Share Price	÷	**EPS**	=	**P/E Ratio**
BASF AG (BF)	$ 70.47		$ 5.243		13.44
Bayer AG (BAY)	35.64		1.511		23.59
Dow Chemical (DOW)	47.40		4.401		10.77
E I DuPont (DD)	41.00		2.572		15.94
Eastman Chemical (EMN)	51.69		5.75		8.99
FMC (FMC)	59.52		5.729		10.39
Rohm & Hass (ROH)	45.02		2.678		16.81
			Average		14.28

billion in 2003 and $830 million in 2002. If the company were to consider selling the division via an initial public offering, a key question it would want to answer would be, "How much can we expect to receive for the sale of the equity?" We can get a quick glimpse at the magnitude of this equity value by applying an average P/E ratio of similar firms to the chemical division's earnings. Table 6-3 contains P/E ratios for seven of the largest chemical companies in the world. They have an average P/E multiple of 14.28, which implies that as a first approximation, ExxonMobil's chemical division is likely to be worth about $48.94 billion = 14.28 × $3.428 billion.

To refine the estimate of the value of ExxonMobil's (XOM's) chemical division, we want to more closely scrutinize the market comparables and evaluate the extent to which they are really similar to ExxonMobil's chemical division. For example, we noted above that the revenues of ExxonMobil's chemical division make it the third largest chemical company in the world. If firm size is an important determinant of P/E ratios, then the appropriate comparison group would consist of the very largest firms from the industry. Based on their market capitalizations, which is equal to price per share multiplied by the number of shares of common stock outstanding (found in Table 6-4), the four largest firms include BASF AG, Bayer AG, Dow Chemical, and E I DuPont. The average P/E multiple for these four firms is 15.935, and if we apply this multiple to the valuation of ExxonMobil's equity in the chemical division, our valuation increases the estimate to $54.63 billion. This is a number that ExxonMobil's management would find much more to their liking!

However, there is substantial dispersion in the P/E ratios in this industry. Hence, to value the ExxonMobil chemical division, we must ask whether its risk and growth potential are more like those of Bayer AG, which has a P/E ratio of 23.59, or more like Dow, which has a P/E ratio of only 10.77. A complete answer to this question would require more in-depth analysis of differences and similarities between ExxonMobil's chemical division and each of the comparable firms, which would certainly include an analysis of the growth prospects and the operating leverage of the different firms.

Table 6-4 Market Capitalization and P/E Ratios for the Chemical Industry Comps		
	P/E Ratio	**Market Capitalization (billions)**
BASF AG (BF)	13.44	$38.25
Bayer AG (BAY)	23.59	25.63
Dow Chemical (DOW)	10.77	45.25
E I DuPont (DD)	15.94	40.61
Eastman Chemical (EMN)	8.99	4.10
FMC (FMC)	10.39	2.20
Rohm & Hass (ROH)	16.81	10.01
Average (Big 4)	15.94	$37.44
Average (Small 3)	12.06	5.44

The remainder of our P/E discussion delves into the impact of a firm's growth prospects on its P/E ratio, both in the context of a stable firm that grows at a steady rate forever and for a high-growth-rate firm that enjoys a period of high rates of growth followed by a reduction to a sustainable but lower rate of growth.

P/E Multiples for Stable-Growth Firms

A stable-growth firm is one that is expected to grow indefinitely at a constant rate. The P/E multiple of such a firm is determined by its constant rate of growth, and can be calculated by solving the Gordon growth model applied to the valuation of a firm's equity and found in Equation 6.9 below:[10]

$$P_0 = \frac{\text{Dividend per Share}_0(1 + g)}{k - g} = \frac{\text{Earnings per Share}_0(1 - b)(1 + g)}{k - g} \quad (6.9)$$

where b is the retention ratio, or the fraction of firm earnings that the firm retains, implying that $(1 - b)$ is the fraction of firm earnings paid in dividends; g is the growth rate of these dividends; and k is the required rate of return on the firm's equity. By rearranging the terms in this equation, we can express the P/E ratio as follows:

$$\text{P/E Ratio} = \frac{(1 - b)(1 + g)}{k - g} \quad (6.10a)$$

---

[10]Note that this equation is simply Equation 6.2 applied to the firm's equity rather than enterprise value.

T E C H N I C A L

I N S I G H T

Current versus Forward Earnings and the P/E Ratio

The price–earnings (P/E) ratio is a simple concept: current market price of a firm's common stock divided by the firm's annual earnings per share. Although the current market price is an unambiguous variable, earnings are not. For example, the earnings variable sometimes represents earnings per share for the most recent year. In that case, the P/E ratio is referred to as the *current P/E ratio* or *trailing P/E ratio*. There is yet another commonly used definition of the P/E ratio that defines earnings per share by using analysts' forecasts of the next year's earnings. This is the *forward P/E ratio*.

To illustrate, let's consider the sample of chemical companies used in the valuation example of the ExxonMobil chemical division. The current (trailing) and forward P/E ratios for these firms are found below:

	Share Price	Current EPS	Current/ Trailing P/E Ratio	Forecast EPS	Forward P/E Ratio
BASF AG (BF)	$ 70.47	$ 5.243	13.44	$ 7.27	9.69
Bayer AG (BAY)	35.64	1.511	23.59	2.69	13.27
Dow Chemical (DOW)	47.40	4.401	10.77	5.71	8.30
E I DuPont (DD)	41.00	2.572	15.94	3.04	13.48
Eastman Chemical (EMN)	51.69	5.75	8.99	5.93	8.71
FMC (FMC)	59.52	5.729	10.39	5.66	10.51
Rohm & Hass (ROH)	45.02	2.678	16.81	3.12	14.44
		Average	14.28		11.20

The forward P/E ratios are lower than the current (trailing) P/Es in the six instances where earnings are expected to grow and are higher in the one instance (FMC) in which earnings per share is expected to decline. Although the differences in P/E are not dramatic for these sample firms, they can be dramatic in turnaround situations or in the case of firms that are facing large changes in their earnings prospects for the future. For these cases it is important for the analyst to look beyond the current or trailing P/E when trying to compare the market's current valuation of a share of stock to that of comparable firms.

To look more deeply into the determination of P/E ratios, we first observe that firms are able to grow their earnings by reinvesting retained earnings in positive-net-present-value projects. We will assume that these positive-NPV investments earn a rate of return, which we will denote as r, that exceeds the firm's required rate of return, k. Well-positioned firms with competitive advantages, intellectual property, patents, and managerial expertise are able to generate both higher rates of return on new investment, as well as opportunities to reinvest more of their earnings. It is the combination of the amount by which r exceeds k, and the fraction of firm earnings that can be profitably reinvested each year $(1 - b)$ that determines the firm's P/E ratio.

To illustrate, suppose that a firm with $100 million of invested capital generates returns on invested capital of 20% per year. If the firm pays out 100% of its earnings each year, then the dividend will be $20 million each year. In this case the growth rate of the firm's dividends, g, is zero. Now suppose that the firm pays only 40% of its earnings in dividends and reinvests the remaining 60% in its operations. In this case, the first dividend will be $D_1 = \$100\text{M} \times (.2) \times (.4) = \$8$ million, leaving the firm with a capital base of $112 million. If the firm continues to generate the same 20% return on the larger capital base, and if it continues to pay out 40% of its earnings and retain 60%, its second-year dividend will be $D_2 = \$112\text{M} \times (.2) \times (.4) = \$8.96$ million. Dividends will continue to grow at ($8.96 − $8.00)/$8.00 = 12% annually as long as the dividend payout policy continues, and the firm's return on capital remains equal to 20%.

Under these assumptions, we can express a firm's dividend growth rate as the product of its retention rate, b, and the rate of return it can provide on newly invested capital, r. We can now restate the P/E multiple from Equation 6.10a as follows:

$$\text{P/E Multiple} = \frac{(1 - b)(1 + g)}{k - g} = \frac{(1 - b)(1 + br)}{k - br} \qquad (6.10b)$$

Using Equation 6.10b, we see that for a stable-growth firm, the P/E multiple is determined by the firm's dividend payout policy (i.e., one minus the retention ratio, or $1 − b$); the required rate of return of the stockholders, k; and the rate of return the firm expects to earn on reinvested earnings, r. Thus, we can use Equation 6.10b to explore the relationship between the P/E multiple and each of these key variables.

To illustrate the effect of differences in anticipated rates of growth and retention ratios on the P/E ratio, let's consider the two example firms (A and B) described in Table 6-5. Firm A has the opportunity to create value for shareholders by retaining and reinvesting its earnings. This is reflected in the fact that the firm's return on invested capital, r, is 10%, which is greater than the stockholders' required rate of return, k, of 8%. Firm B, on the other hand, hurts its shareholders if it reinvests since its return on invested capital (10%) is less than the stockholders' required rate of return (12%).

Note that for Firm A, the P/E multiple rises as the fraction of its earnings that can be retained and profitably invested rises. This reflects the creation of shareholder wealth that occurs when a firm with an 8% required rate of return earns 10% on its new investment. The P/E multiple found in Equation 6.10b becomes infinite, however, when the retention ratio hits 80%. At an 80% retention ratio, the firm's growth rate (which equals the product of b and r) equals 8%. A quick glance at Equation 6.10b tells us why this happens: The growth rate and required rate of return on equity are both 8%; thus the value of the firm's equity is undefined. The situation with Firm B is the inverse of that of Firm A: The P/E multiple decreases as the firm retains a larger fraction of its earnings (i.e., as b increases). This, of course, reflects the fact that

Table 6-5	The P/E Multiple and Dividend Policy for a Stable-Growth Firm				

Firm A: $r = 10\%, k = 8\%$			Firm B: $r = 10\%, k = 12\%$		
Retention Ratio (*b*)	Growth Rate (*g*)	P/E Multiple	Retention Ratio (*b*)	Growth Rate (*g*)	P/E Multiple
0%	0%	12.50	0%	0%	8.33
10%	1%	12.99	10%	1%	8.26
20%	2%	13.60	20%	2%	8.16
30%	3%	14.42	30%	3%	8.01
40%	4%	15.60	40%	4%	7.80
50%	5%	17.50	50%	5%	7.50
60%	6%	21.20	60%	6%	7.07
70%	7%	32.10	70%	7%	6.42
80%	8%	Undefined*	80%	8%	5.40
90%	9%	Undefined*	90%	9%	3.63
100%	10%	Undefined*	100%	10%	0.00

Legend

r = return on reinvested earnings

k = stockholders' required rate of return

* These cells have negative P/E multiples. Here the formula for P/E multiple $(1 - b)(1 + g)/(k - g)$ does not apply because for $k < g$, the series (perpetuity) does not converge. Intuitively, this situation implies that the earnings are growing faster than the cost of capital forever. This situation cannot arise in a competitive economy, where free entry will drive down high growth rates to the feasible range (where $k < g$).

the firm is able to earn only 10% by reinvesting the earnings when its stockholders demand a 12% return.

P/E Multiple for a High-Growth Firm

We can relate the P/E multiple for a high-growth firm to company fundamentals in much the same way as we did for a stable-growth firm—with one important difference. Since we do not expect a firm to be able to achieve high growth forever, describing the firm's growth prospects requires two growth periods. We assume that the firm experiences very high growth lasting for a period of *n* years, followed by a period of much lower but stable growth.[11] Equation 6.11 captures

---

[11] You will recall that we are describing a two-stage growth model similar to our discussion in Chapter 4. The difference here is that we define equity value as the present value of expected future dividends (not equity free cash flow).

the valuation of the equity of such a firm:

$$P_0 = \frac{EPS_0(1 + g_1)(1 - b_1)}{k - g_1}\left(1 - \frac{(1 + g_1)^n}{(1 + k)^n}\right)$$

$$+ \frac{EPS_0(1 + g_1)^n(1 - b_2)(1 + g_2)}{k - g_2}\left(\frac{1}{(1 + k)^n}\right) \tag{6.11}$$

In this equation we abbreviate earnings per share$_0$ as EPS_0, and both the retention ratio (b) and the growth rate (g) are now subscripted to reflect the fact that the firm's dividend policy and its growth prospects can be different for the two growth periods.[12]

We can interpret Equation 6.11 as follows: The first term on the right-hand side expresses the present value of a stream of dividends received over the next n years. For the high-growth firm, dividends grow at a rapid rate equal to g_1 for n years, after which time the nth-year dividends grow at a constant (and lower) rate g_2, forever.

We can now solve for the P/E multiple simply by dividing through both sides of Equation 6.11 by EPS_0. The result is found below:

$$\frac{P_0}{EPS_0} = \frac{(1 - b_1)(1 + g_1)}{k - g_1}\left(1 - \frac{(1 + g_1)^n}{(1 + k)^n}\right)$$

$$+ \frac{(1 - b_2)(1 + g_1)^n(1 + g_2)}{k - g_2}\left(\frac{1}{(1 + k)^n}\right) \tag{6.12}$$

Let's analyze the determinants of the P/E multiple for the high-growth firm. Recalling that $g_1 = b_1 r_1$ and $g_2 = b_2 r_2$, we see that the firm's P/E multiple is a function of the firm's dividend policy in the two periods (i.e., b_1 and b_2), the return on equity that the firm earns on its invested capital (r_1 and r_2), and the stockholders' required rate of return (k). Again, the relationship between r (both r_1 and r_2) and k—the return on reinvested earnings and the stockholders' required rate of return, respectively—is the key determinant of the P/E multiple. If $r > k$, the firm's P/E multiple increases, and the amount of the increase is determined by its retention ratio, b.

---

[12]Earnings would grow at g_1 for n years and at g_2 immediately thereafter. In contrast, dividends will grow at g_1 for n years and at a lower g_2 after ($n + 1$) years. But in the intervening period, ($n, n + 1$), there would be a discontinuity in dividend growth, as shown below:

Year	Earnings	Imputed Earnings Growth	Dividends	Imputed Rate of Dividend Growth
$(n - 1, n)$	$EPS_0(1 + g_1)^n$	g_1	$EPS_0(1 + g_1)^n (1 - b_1)$	g_1
$(n, n + 1)$	$EPS_0(1 + g_1)^n (1 + g_2)$	g_2	$EPS_0(1 + g_1)^n (1 + g_2)(1 - b_2)$	$[(1 + g_2)(1 - b_2)]/(1 - b_1) - 1$
$(n + 1, n + 2)$	$EPS_0(1 + g_1)^n (1 + g_2)^2$	g_2	$EPS_0(1 + g_1)^n (1 + g_2)^2 (1 - b_2)$	g_2

To illustrate the use of the P/E ratio for a high-growth firm, consider Google, Inc., which was formed in 1998 and provides Google WebSearch to access Web pages. The company went public in 2004 and by July 11, 2006, its share price was $424.56, giving the firm a P/E multiple of 74.5 based on 2005 earnings of $5.70 per share. To evaluate whether this high P/E ratio can be justified, we will use Equation 6.12, which provides for two growth periods: a finite period of high growth followed by a stable-growth period.

To analyze Google's P/E ratio using Equation 6.12, we use information found in Panel a of Table 6-6, along with estimates of the duration of the high-growth period (n in Equation 6.12), the dividend payout ratio after year n (i.e., $[1 - b_2]$), and the anticipated rate of growth in earnings (g_2) after year n. Recall that the growth rate in earnings after year n can be estimated as the product of the fraction of the firm's earnings that are retained (i.e., that are not paid out in dividends) and the rate of return earned on reinvested earnings, or the return on equity. Thus, the key determinants of Google's P/E are the length of the high-growth period, in combination with the dividend payout ratio and the return on equity during the post-high-growth period. Table 6-6 contains three scenarios that include sets of these key parameters, which each produce the observed P/E of 74.5. Of course, these are not the only possible combinations of these parameters that will produce a P/E ratio of 74.5 for Google. However, they do illustrate the feasibility of obtaining a P/E ratio that is consistent with its observed market P/E.

To determine how one might evaluate the plausibility of these scenarios, let's consider Scenario #1 in more depth. Scenario #1 assumes that Google will be able to reinvest all of its earnings for the next 12 years at its current return on equity of 24.7%. Since the firm retains all of its earnings, the rate of growth in earnings is also 24.7% (recall that the rate of growth is equal to the product of the return on equity and the retention ratio). Thus, in 12 years Google's estimated earnings per share will be $80.61 = \$5.70(1 + .247)^{12}$. At this future date the firm's P/E ratio will be 14.93, which is much lower than its current P/E ratio of 74.5. The reason for the decline in the P/E ratio is that Google's growth rate in this later period drops from 24.7% to only 4.93%. By multiplying this estimate of the P/E ratio in 2018 times the estimate of the future earnings per share, $80.61, we estimate that Google's stock price is expected to appreciate to $1,203.38 at the end of the 12-year period of high growth.

Is it really likely that Google will be able to maintain a 24.7% return on its reinvested earnings for 12 years? If Google can indeed accomplish this, it will earn $24.43 billion in 2018, which would be almost double Microsoft Corporation's 2005 earnings of $13.47 billion. One might decide that this particular set of assumptions is overly optimistic and conclude that Google's stock is overpriced. Alternatively, one might consider whether Scenarios #2 or #3 are more plausible. These scenarios make less optimistic assumptions about the duration of the high-growth-rate period but justify Google's current P/E multiple by assuming a higher long-term growth forecast. For example, in Scenario #2

Table 6-6 Analyzing the P/E Ratio of a High-Growth Firm—Google, Inc.

Panel a. Current Stock Price and Earnings Information

P/E ratio	74.5	Return on equity	24.7%
Beta	0.81	Dividend payout	0.0%
Risk-free rate	5.02%	Cost of equity	9.07%
Market risk premium	5.00%		

Panel b. Scenario Analysis

	Growth Period, n	Dividend Payout $(1 - b_2)$	Return on Equity	Growth Rate, g_2	P/E Ratio	Estimates for 2018			
						EPS	P/E	Stock Price	Net Income
Scenario #1	12	58.94%	12.00%	4.93%	74.484	$ 80.61	14.93	$ 1,203.38	$24,432,218,360
Scenario #2	5	31.98%	12.00%	8.16%	74.484	$ 29.77	38.12	$ 1,135.04	$ 9,023,395,570
Scenario #3	5	58.94%	18.05%	7.41%	74.484	$ 28.35	38.13	$ 1,080.86	$ 8,592,575,505

Google's earnings after 12 years (in 2018) are much lower than under Scenario #1[13] and are less than Microsoft's current earnings, but its P/E ratio is 38.12, which is much higher than the 14.93 P/E under Scenario #1. This difference in P/E ratios reflects the fact that in Scenario #2 Google's earnings during the second growth period are expected to grow at 8.16%, compared to 4.93% for Scenario #1.

As this Google example illustrates, the use of P/E multiples, like all of the approaches we consider, provides equity valuations that are only as good as the judgment of the equity analyst who performs the analysis. The P/E multiples approach provides a useful tool for taking a set of assumptions and translating them into an estimate of stock price. When carrying out a valuation analysis, one should consider a variety of plausible scenarios and determine how sensitive the valuation model's output is to the duration of the period of high growth as well as the reinvestment rate and return on equity that will prevail after the period of high growth.

6.5 Pricing an Initial Public Offering

When a firm sells its shares in the public market for the first time, the process of offering those shares is commonly referred to as an *initial public offering* or *IPO*. As we will briefly discuss in this section, the market comparables approach used in this chapter plays an important role in the pricing of IPOs.

As a first step in the IPO process, the lead underwriter (that is, the investment banker who manages the IPO process for the company that is going public) determines an initial estimate of a range of values for the issuer's shares. The estimate typically is the result of a comparables valuation analysis that utilizes several valuation ratios such as the ones discussed in this chapter. For example, the underwriter may estimate enterprise value using an EBITDA multiple and then subtract the firm's net debt (i.e., interest-bearing debt less the firm's cash reserves) to get an estimate of the issuer's equity value. The price per share then is simply equity value divided by the number of shares the firm is issuing. Given the variety of comparables and valuation ratios typically used in this analysis, this exercise will result in a range of equity prices (say $10 to $15 per share) for the new issue, not a single offering price.

After setting the initial price range, the underwriters go through what is known as a "book-building" process, where they gauge the level of investor interest. Specifically, over the weeks leading up to the offering date, the lead underwriter and

---

[13]In Scenario #2, Google's EPS are assumed to grow at 24.7% for only five years and then at 8.16% thereafter.

company executives travel around the country meeting with potential investors. These visits are known as the "road show." During these visits the underwriter's sales force collects information from potential institutional investors related to their interest in purchasing shares at various prices within the initial valuation range. This information forms the basis for the "book," which contains nonbinding expressions of interest in buying shares of the IPO at various prices, generally within the initial price range.

Finally, during the pricing meeting on the eve of the IPO, the investment banker and company executives meet to decide on the initial offering price. Narrowing the range of prices down to a single price is a result of the judgment of company executives and the following considerations:

- An updated valuation analysis based on that day's pricing information for comparable companies and recent IPO transactions in combination with the most up-to-date measures of company performance (i.e., EBITDA).
- An analysis of the level of interest in the new offering that is determined in the book-building process. Obviously, high expressions of interest will encourage the firm to move the offering price toward the upper end of the initial pricing range and vice versa.
- Finally, the underwriters like to price the IPO at a discount, typically 10% to 25%, to the price the shares are likely to trade on the market. Underwriters argue that this helps generate good after-market support for the offering.

6.6 OTHER PRACTICAL CONSIDERATIONS

In this section we close our discussion of relative valuation by delving into some practical issues that arise when performing a valuation exercise using multiples. Specifically, the first two steps of the four-step procedure are the most critical to the overall success of the effort. These steps involve choices that the analyst must make regarding the set of comparable firms and the particular valuation metric used to determine relative value. In addition, we open a discussion that will continue into Chapter 7 dealing with the use of multiples valuation and DCF valuation.

Selecting Comparable Firms

We now circle back to Step 1—choosing comparable firms—to explore it in more detail. Although it is the first task facing the analyst, it is perhaps the most difficult. Comparable firms share similar operating and financial characteristics. In particular, comparable firms should share similar growth prospects and operating cost structures as well as similar capital structures.

PRACTITIONER
INSIGHT

**The Pricing of New Shares
in an Initial Public Offering
(IPO)—An Interview with J. Douglas Ramsey, Ph.D.***

In 2006 we took EXCO Resources (NYSE: XCO) public with an initial public offering. EXCO had only been a privately held firm since 2003, when we were taken private after being listed on Nasdaq with the help of the private equity firm Cerberus Capital Management, LP. The motivation for going public at this time was to raise capital needed to fund some major acquisitions of oil and gas properties and reduce the amount of debt on the balance sheet. This followed on the heels of an equity buyout several months earlier where certain private equity investors from the 2003 going-private transaction were cashed out. The equity buyout was funded with a combination of debt and new private equity.

The pricing of the new shares is done by the lead investment bank (J.P. Morgan in our case) using market price comparables for similar firms. Specifically, our banker looked at six different ratios equal to enterprise value divided by one of six different valuation metrics that are commonly used in our industry.** This analysis, in combination with the values of EXCO's own valuation metrics, gave us an idea of what type of enterprise value we could expect once the IPO was complete. From this valuation and the number of shares we planned to sell, we could then impute a price for our shares.

The actual price at which the new shares were offered was not determined until the night before the IPO in a pricing meeting. In this meeting our investment banker brought an updated analysis of market comparables along with "the book." The latter is comprised of a listing of the indications of interest in acquiring our shares in the initial offering. This book is built over the weeks prior to the IPO during what is typically referred to as the "road show" where company management and representatives of the joint book runners, in our case J.P. Morgan, Bear Stearns, and Goldman Sachs, barnstorm the country talking to potential institutional investors about the offering.

*Chief financial officer for EXCO Resources, Inc., Dallas, Texas.
**The valuation metrics include company-specific attributes that are believed to be important indicators of the firm's enterprise value. In the case of an E&P company, these typically included such things as the current year's production, proved reserves of oil and natural gas, current-year free cash flow, and estimates of earnings before interest, taxes, depreciation, and amortization plus development and maintenance expenses (EBITDAX) for the next two years.

The typical approach taken when selecting comparable firms entails using firms from the same industry group. This makes sense for a number of reasons. First, firms within a given industry tend to utilize similar accounting conventions, which allow the analyst to directly compare the various accounting ratios. Second, firms in the same industry tend to have similar risks and growth prospects.[14] However, as we have discussed, different firms in the same industry often have very different management philosophies, which lead to very different risk and growth profiles, and in addition, firms often do business in multiple industries, making it difficult to assess to which industry group a firm belongs. For example, in our earlier analysis of ExxonMobil (XOM), we found that it had three operating divisions located in different industries.[15] When this occurs, the analyst may find it necessary to utilize an average of the industry valuation ratios corresponding to each of the firm's operating business units.

Choosing the Valuation Ratio

Although earnings and EBITDA valuation ratios tend to be the most commonly used, some firms have either zero or negative earnings. When this is the case, analysts tend to look to other valuation ratios for guidance. For example, as we discussed earlier, real estate valuations generally include an analysis of the price per square foot of comparable properties. For some businesses, analysts use valuation ratios based on firm sales or book value. Table 6-7 (pp. 250–252) provides a summary list of some of the most popular valuation ratios. Panel a focuses on equity valuation ratios, and Panel b lists some popular enterprise valuation ratios.

Maintaining Consistency when Selecting a Valuation Ratio

A simple but important guide for using valuation ratios is that the numerator and denominator of the ratio should be consistent. By consistent we mean that if the price or value metric in the numerator is based on equity value (e.g., price per share), then the denominator should reflect an attribute of the firm that is directly related to share price. For example, net income per share or earnings per share can be directly linked to share price, since earnings represent the income that is available for distribution to shareholders or reinvested on their behalf. However, on occasion we have seen analysts report share price relative to EBITDA and share price to sales ratios (i.e., price per share divided by sales per share), which are inconsistent ratios, since EBITDA and sales are generated by the entire assets of the firm, not just the equity portion of the firm's balance sheet. Consequently, if one does want to compare firms on the

---

[14]These results are based on a comparison of observed prices to estimated prices (based on the various ways of forming groups of comparable firms and assessing the significance of the absolute deviation, measured as a percent of the observed price). See A. Alford, "The Effect of the Set of Comparable Firms on the Accuracy of the Price–Earnings Valuation Method," *Journal of Accounting Research* (Spring 1992): 94–108.

[15]These divisions included Upstream—oil and gas exploration and development, Downstream—refining oil and gas for energy use, and Chemicals—conversion of crude into plastics and other non-energy products.

basis of a ratio that involves a variable like sales per share, one must be careful to select comparable firms that share similar operating leverage and financial leverage with the evaluated firm.

Dealing with Unreliable Financial Information

In any given year a firm's reported earnings often provide an imperfect measure of the business's ability to generate future cash flows. This is particularly true for young firms that are very far from reaching their potential (i.e., have significant growth potential), or for that matter, almost any firm going through a transition. Under these circumstances, EBITDA or earnings per share are often negative, making it impossible to rely on ratios based on earnings. In other cases, either the accounting is suspect or the business is able to generate value to its owners, perhaps by paying high salaries, in ways that do not show up in the firm's income statements.

For situations like these, the firm's reported earnings are unreliable indicators of the firm's value. In these circumstances the analyst can take one of two possible courses of action. The first involves the use of other valuation ratios that may utilize more reliable measures of the firm's ability to generate future cash flows. Most of these alternatives are measures of the size of the business and are thus analogous to valuing real estate on a price per square foot basis. The most popular size measure is firm revenues or sales, followed closely by the book value of the firm's assets. For example, in Panel a of Table 6-7, the market to book value of equity ratio might be used if the objective is estimating a firm's equity value, or the enterprise value to sales ratio might be used to estimate enterprise value. There are also commonly used measures of size that are unique to particular industries. For example, newspapers, magazines, and cable companies are often valued relative to their number of subscribers, and money management firms and other financial institutions are often valued relative to the amount of assets they manage.

The second course of action open to the analyst who finds corporate earnings are not reflective of the firm's earning potential involves adjusting or normalizing reported earnings so that they provide a more reasonable reflection of the firm's earning potential. For example, when valuing small, family-run businesses, it is not uncommon for the owner to pay himself or herself a noncompetitive salary as a way of extracting additional tax deductible value out of the business.[16] When faced with the prospect of valuing such a business, the analyst must make appropriate adjustments to the firm's earnings before using them to value the enterprise. We will not delve into this process in any detail since there are many excellent books on financial statement analysis that detail the circumstances that give rise to a need to normalize earnings and how to do it.

---

[16]For example, a $500,000 salary costs the business only $350,000 if the firm is in a 30% tax bracket.

Table 6-7 Alternative Valuation Ratios

Panel a. Equity Valuation Ratios

Valuation Ratio	Definition	Measurement Issues	When to Use	Valuation Model
Price to earnings (P/E)	$\dfrac{\text{Price per Share}}{\text{Earnings per Share}}$ Price per share = Market price per share of common stock Earnings per share = Annual net income ÷ Shares outstanding	Price per share—Typically the most recent share price is used. However, if share price is very volatile, a normalized price (e.g., an average of beginning and ending prices for the month) may be used. Earnings per share—Although current-year or annualized current-quarter (trailing) earnings can be used, it is not uncommon to use analysts' expectations of future (leading) earnings. Moreover, earnings are typically measured before extraordinary items and may only include earnings from the firm's primary operations.	Firms with an established record of positive earnings that do not have significant noncash expenditures.	$\text{Estimated Stock Price} = (\text{EPS})_{\text{Firm}}$ $\times \left(\dfrac{\text{P/E}}{\text{Ratio}}\right)_{\text{Industry}}$
Price to earnings to growth (PEG)	$\dfrac{\text{Price per Share}}{\text{Earnings per Share (EPS)}}$ $\div \text{Growth rate in EPS}$ Growth rate in EPS = Expected rate of growth in EPS over the next year	Growth rate in EPS—estimates of growth rates can be made from historical earnings estimates or can be obtained from analysts' estimates.	Firms that face stable prospects for future growth in EPS as well as similar capital structures and similar industry risk attributes.	$\text{Estimated Stock Price} = \left(\dfrac{\text{Growth Rate in EPS}}{\text{EPS}}\right)_{\text{Firm}}$ $\times \left(\dfrac{\text{PEG}}{\text{Ratio}}\right)_{\text{Industry}}$

Market to book value of equity	Market Value of Equity / Book Value of Equity *Market value of equity* = Price per share × Shares outstanding *Book value of equity* = Total assets − Total liabilities	*Market value of equity* — The same issues that arise in selecting a price per share apply here. *Book value of equity* — Although the book value of equity is easy to pull from the firm's balance sheet, differences in the ages of firm assets (when acquired and rates of depreciation) as well as other differences in how various assets are accounted for (fair market value — mark to market — or cost), and the conservatism employed in accounting practices can lead to variation across firms.	Firms whose balance sheets are reasonable reflections of the market values of their assets. Financial institutions are the classic case.	$\text{Estimated Equity Value} = \left(\dfrac{\text{Book Value}}{\text{of Equity}}\right)_{\text{Firm}} \times \left(\dfrac{\text{Market to}}{\text{Book Ratio}}\right)_{\text{Industry}}$

Panel b. Enterprise Valuation Ratios

Enterprise value (EV) to EBITDA	Enterprise Value / EBITDA *Enterprise value* = Price per share × Shares outstanding plus Interest-bearing (short- and long-term) debt less cash *EBITDA* = Earnings before interest, taxes, depreciation, and amortization	*Enterprise value* — EV is typically estimated as the market value of the firm's equity (price per share times shares outstanding) plus the book value of the firm's interest-bearing debt. Consequently, the problems that arise in determining which stock price to use (most recent versus normalized) arise here, too. *EBITDA* — This earnings figure is easily accessed from the firm's income statement. However, cyclical variations in earnings and unusual variations in firm revenues may require some normalization to better reflect the firm's future earnings potential.	Firms that have significant noncash expenses (i.e., depreciation and amortization). Examples include industries with large investments in fixed assets, including health care, oil and gas equipment services, and telecommunications.	$\text{Estimated Enterprise Value} = (\text{EBITDA})_{\text{Firm}} \times \left(\dfrac{\text{EV to EBITDA}}{\text{Ratio}}\right)_{\text{Industry}}$

(Continued)

Table 6-7 *Continued*

Valuation Ratio	Definition	Measurement Issues	When to Use	Valuation Model
Enterprise value (EV) to cash flow	$\dfrac{\text{Enterprise Value}}{\text{Cash Flow per Share}}$ *Enterprise value* = Price per share × Shares outstanding plus Interest-bearing debt *Cash flow* = Firm free cash flow (FFCF)	*Cash flow*—FFCF adjusts EBIT-DA to consider taxes and additional investment required in capital equipment (CAPEX). Consequently, the issues that arise with FFCF include those applicable to EBITDA, plus any normalization of CAPEX required to adjust for extraordinary circumstances in any given year.	Firms with stable growth and thus predictable capital expenditures. Examples include chemicals, paper products, forestry, and industrial metals.	Estimated Enterprise Value $(\text{FFCF})_{\text{Firm}}$ $= \times \left(\dfrac{\text{EV to FFCF}}{\text{Ratio}}\right)_{\text{Industry}}$
Enterprise value (EV) to sales	$\dfrac{\text{Enterprise Value}}{\text{Sales}}$ *Sales* = Firm annual revenues	*Sales*—Firm revenues sit at the top of the firm's income statement. However, they, too, may not be reflective of the firm's earning potential if they are abnormally large or depressed due to nonrecurring factors.	Young firms and start-ups that do not have an established history of earnings.	Estimated Enterprise Value $(\text{Sales})_{\text{Firm}}$ $= \times \left(\dfrac{\text{EV to Sales}}{\text{Ratio}}\right)_{\text{Industry}}$

Valuation Ratios versus DCF Analysis

When valuing major investments, it often makes sense to do both a DCF analysis (which we discuss in detail in Chapter 7) as well as a valuation that employs a number of different comparables-based multiples. Once the analysis is complete, the analyst is still left with the problem of sorting out the various value estimates and using his or her professional judgment to arrive at a final valuation. This judgment will depend in part on the quality of information that is available and in part on the purpose of the valuation.

To understand what we mean by the purpose of the valuation, let's consider an investor with an interest in acquiring coal-fired power plants. Suppose that this particular investor is considering the purchase of a specific plant that is quite similar in both age and technology to five other plants that were sold in the last three months, and two others that are currently for sale. In this situation the quality of the comparables market data is quite good, which means that the acquirer should compare the plants based on valuation ratios, rather than projecting future plant cash flows, estimating an appropriate discount rate, and then performing a DCF analysis. Again, we are assuming that the technologies and the ages of the plants are similar so that their values, relative to their earnings, cash flows, or electricity-generating capacities, should be very similar. In a sense the question being answered in this valuation is, "What should I expect to have to pay for the coal-fired power plant under today's market conditions?"

Although the comparables approach provides the appropriate methodology for evaluating whether a particular power plant is favorably priced, it is much less useful for a firm that wants to evaluate whether or not it makes sense to acquire power plants in general. The basic question in this case is, "What should a coal-fired power plant be worth today in absolute terms?" Note that we are asking a much more basic question here. We no longer just want to know how one coal-fired plant is valued relative to others, but whether coal-fired plants, in general, are good investments. To answer this question we can still envision comparing EBITDA ratios of power plants and oil refineries as a starting point in the evaluation of which type of investment is likely to be more attractive. However, for this more general question, the analyst should rely much more heavily on DCF analysis, which involves making forecasts of future power output, electricity prices, and costs of generation.[17]

6.7 SUMMARY

In this chapter we introduced market-based valuation ratios as an alternative to the discounted cash flow (DCF) method for valuing an investment. Although the

---

[17]Should the company also mine its coal, the health care liability related to black lung disease can be a very important consideration.

DCF approach is generally emphasized by academics, practitioners prefer to use market-based multiples based on comparable firms or transactions for valuing businesses. An important advantage of using valuation ratios is that it provides the analyst with a method for estimating the value of an investment without making explicit estimates of either the investment's future cash flows or the discount rate. However, an even more important reason for using valuation comparables is that it makes direct use of observed market pricing information. Intuitively, it does not make sense to use rough estimates of the discount rate and future cash flows to come up with an estimate of the market value of an investment, if you can directly observe how the market values such an investment with comparable transactions.

The reality is that using comparable transactions is not as easy as it might at first seem. There are two important steps to the application, and each is critical. First, the analyst must identify a set of comparable transactions for which market pricing data is available. The principal weakness of market-based comparables valuation is that we almost never have truly comparable transactions. Investments typically have unique attributes, and in most cases, the investments that are used as comparables are somewhat of a stretch. For this reason it is critical that we think carefully when determining the appropriate multiples to use. For example, we should use higher multiples when the cash flows of an investment are likely to grow faster than those of the comparable investments, and we should use lower multiples when the risk of the investment is higher. In other words, you should use the insights learned from DCF valuation to augment your implementation of the multiples approach.

The second critical step in using market comparables entails the selection of an appropriate valuation ratio or metric. By appropriate, we mean that the value of the investment can be thought of as simply a scaled value of the metric where the investment attribute (e.g., earnings, cash flow, square footage) is the scaling variable. For example, when the P/E ratio is used as the valuation metric, we are assuming that the value of the firm's equity is equal to firm earnings scaled by the ratio of share price to earnings. Or, if we're valuing an entire firm, we might use the enterprise value to EBITDA multiple whereby we scale the firm's EBITDA by the multiple to get an estimate of enterprise value.

PROBLEMS

6-1 VALUING RESIDENTIAL REAL ESTATE Sarah Fluggel is considering the purchase of a home located at 2121 Tarter Circle in Frisco, Texas. The home has 3,000 square feet of heated and cooled living area, and the current owners are asking a price of $375,000 for it.

    a. Use the information provided in the following table to determine an initial estimate of the value of the home Sarah is considering:

	Comp #1	Comp #2
Sale price	#240,000	$265,000
Square footage	2,240	2,145
Selling price/sq. ft.	$107.14	$123.54
Time on the market	61 days	32 days

b. After making her initial estimate of the value of the home, Sarah decided to investigate whether the owner's asking price of $375,000 might be justified based on unique attributes of the home. What types of details might you recommend Sarah look for in trying to justify the price of the home?

c. What if the house Sarah is considering had an asking price of $315,000? What would you recommend Sarah do?

6-2 VALUING COMMERCIAL REAL ESTATE BuildingOne Properties is a limited partnership formed with the express purpose of investing in commercial real estate. The firm is currently considering the acquisition of an office building that we refer to simply as Building B. Building B is very similar to Building A, which recently sold for $36,960,000.

BuildingOne has gathered general information about the two buildings, including valuation information for Building A:

	Per Square Foot		Total Square Footage	
	A	B	A	B
Building size (sq. ft.)			80,000	90,000
Rent	$100/sq. ft.	$120/sq. ft.	$8,000,000	$10,800,000
Maintenance (fixed cost)	(23)/sq. ft.	(30)/sq. ft.	(1,840,000)	(2,700,000)
Net operating income	$ 77/sq. ft.	$ 90/sq. ft.	$6,160,000	$ 8,100,000

Buildings A and B are similar in size (80,000 and 90,000 square feet, respectively). However, the two buildings differ both in maintenance costs ($23 and $30 per square foot), and rental rates ($100 versus $120 per square foot). At this point we do not know why these differences exist. Nonetheless, the difference is real and should somehow be "accounted for" in the analysis of the value of Building B using data based on the sale of Building A.

Building A sold for $462 per square foot, or $36,960,000. This reflects a sales multiple of six times the building's net operating income (NOI) of $6,160,000 per year and a capitalization rate of 16.67%.

a. Using the multiple of operating income, determine what value BuildingOne should place on Building B.

b. If the risk-free rate of interest is 5.5% and the building maintenance costs are known with a high degree of certainty, what value should BuildingOne place on Building B's maintenance costs? How much value should BuildingOne place on Building B's revenues and, consequently, on the firm?

6-3 VALUING A PRIVATELY HELD FIRM The auto parts business has three large publicly held firms: O'Reilly Automotive Inc. (Orly), Advance Auto Parts Inc. (AAP), and Auto Zone Inc. (AZO). In addition to these publicly held firms, Carquest is the largest privately held firm in the industry. Assume that in the summer of 2006 your investment banking firm is considering whether to approach the top management of O'Reilly with a proposal that they consider acquiring Carquest, which owns over 4,000 auto parts outlets in the United States. As a preliminary step in the evaluation of the possible acquisition, you have assembled a team of analysts to prepare a preliminary analysis of acquisition price multiples that might be warranted based upon current market conditions.

The analyst team went to work immediately and compiled the following set of financial information and potential valuation ratios:

Financial Information (millions)	O'Reilly	Advance	Auto Zone
Revenues	$ 2,120.00	$ 4,400.00	$ 5,890.00
EBITDA	321.86	544.38	1,130.00
Net income	171.62	240.16	562.44
Earnings per share	1,507	2.183	7.301
Interest-bearing debt	120.00	560.00	1,720.00
Common equity	1,145.77	939.51	641.16
Total assets	1,713.90	2,615.73	4,401.85
Financial Ratios			
Debt to equity	10.5%	59.6%	269.3%
Gross margins	44.0%	47.3%	49.1%
Operating margins	12.47%	9.42%	16.77%
Expected growth in EPS (5 yrs)	18.5%	16.0%	13.0%

Market Valuations (millions)

Market capitalization	$ 3,240	$ 3,040	$ 6,290
Enterprise value	3,360	3,600	8,010

Valuation Ratios

Enterprise value/EBITDA	10.44	6.61	7.09
P/E ratio (trailing)	19.42	13.30	11.56
P/E ratio (forward)	15.24	11.21	10.21
Beta	1.24	1.79	1.25

a. How would you use this information to evaluate a potential offer to acquire Carquest's equity?

b. What do you think is driving the rather dramatic differences in the valuation ratios of the three firms?

6-4 NORMALIZING EBITDA Jason Kidwell is considering whether or not to acquire a local toy manufacturing company, Toys'n Things, Inc. The company's annual income statements for the last three years are as follows:

	2006	2005	2004
Revenues	$ 2,243,155	$ 2,001,501	$ 2,115,002
Cost of goods sold	(1,458,051)	(1,300,976)	(1,374,751)
Gross profits	$ 785,104	$ 700,525	$ 740,251
General and administrative expenses	(574,316)	(550,150)	(561,500)
Net operating income	$ 210,789	$ 150,375	$ 178,751

a. Jason has learned that small private companies such as this one typically sell for EBITDA multiples of three to four times. Depreciation expense equals $50,000 per year. What value would you recommend Jason put on the company?

b. The current owner of Toys'n Things indicated to Jason that he would not take less than five times 2006 EBITDA to sell out. Jason decided that, based on what he knew about the company, the price could not be justified. However, upon further investigation Jason learned that the owner's wife was paid $100,000 a year for administrative services that Jason thought could be done by a $50,000-per-year assistant. Moreover, the owner paid himself a salary of $250,000 per year to run the business, which Jason thought was at least $50,000 too high based on the demands of the business. In addition, Jason thinks that by outsourcing raw materials to Asia, he can reduce the firm's cost of goods sold by 10%. After making adjustments for excessive salaries, what value should Jason place on the business? Can Jason justify the value the owner is placing on the business?

6-5 OPERATING LEVERAGE AND FLUCTUATIONS IN OPERATING EARNINGS Assume that Jason Kidwell (from Problem 6-4) is able to purchase Toys'n Things, Inc., for $2.2 million. Jason estimates that after initiating his changes in the company's operations (i.e., the salary savings plus outsourcing savings described in Problem 6-4), the firm's cost of goods sold are 55% of firm revenues and operating expenses are equal to a fixed component of $250,000 plus a variable cost component equal to 10% of revenues.

a. Under the above circumstances, estimate the firm's net operating income for revenue levels of $1 million, $2 million, and $4 million. What is the percent change in operating income if revenues go from $2 million to $4 million? What is the percent change in operating income if revenues change from $2 million to $1 million?

b. Assume now that Jason is able to modify the firm's cost structure such that the fixed component of operating expenses declines to $50,000 per year, but the variable cost rises to 30% of firm revenues. Answer Part a above under this revised cost structure. Which of the two cost structures generates the highest level of operating leverage? What should be the effect of the change in cost structure on the firm's equity beta?

6-6 VALUING THE EQUITY OF A STABLE-GROWTH FIRM The Emerson Electric Company (EMR) was founded in 1890 and is located in St. Louis, Missouri. The firm provides product technologies and engineering services for industrial, commercial, and consumer markets worldwide. The firm operates in five business segments: process management, industrial automation, network power, climate technologies, and appliance and tools.

The company has a lengthy history of dividend payments and steady growth. In recent years the firm's dividend payout has averaged 40% of earnings. For 2008 firm earnings are estimated to be $5.69 a share, and on December 7, 2006, Emerson's shares were trading for $86.01, which represents a price–earnings ratio of 19.276. Data for the industry, sector, Emerson, and four competitor firms are shown on page 259.

a. Is Emerson's current stock price reasonable in light of its sector, industry, and comparison firms?

b. Emerson's beta coefficient is 1.27. Assuming a risk-free rate of 5.02% and a market risk premium of 5%, what is your estimate of the required rate of return for Emerson's stock using the CAPM? What rate of growth in earnings is consistent with Emerson's policy of paying out 40% of earnings in dividends and the firm's historical return on equity? Using your estimated growth rate, what is the value of Emerson's shares using the Gordon (single-stage) growth model? Analyze the reasonableness of your estimated value per share using the Gordon model.

Description	Market Cap	P/E	Return on Equity %	Dividend Yield %	Long-term Debt to Equity	Price to Book Value	Net Profit Margin	Price to Free Cash Flow
Sector: Industrial goods		16.606	14.94%	1.48%	0.87	50.471	5.40%	75.481
Industry: Industrial equipment & components		15.900	18.40%	1.41%	0.649	10.11	7.90%	−134.9
Emerson Electric Co.	$34.61B	19.276	23.72%	2.40%	0.494	4.257	9.54%	65.156
Parker-Hannifin Corp.	9.81B	14.150	18.16%	1.20%	0.308	2.298	8.25%	34.392
Roper Industries Inc.	4.44B	24.685	14.27%	0.50%	0.603	3.122	11.89%	232.735
Pentair Inc.	3.23B	17.943	11.56%	1.70%	0.485	1.974	4.48%	147.667
Walter Industries Inc.	2.19B	23.537	15.70%	0.30%	4.036	2.731	7.38%	−10.682

c. Using your analysis in part b above, what growth rate is consistent with Emerson's current share price of $86.01?

6-7 HIGH-GROWTH OR STABLE-GROWTH FIRM? Intel Corporation is a leading manufacturer of semiconductor chips. The firm was incorporated in 1968 in Santa Clara, California, and represents one of the greatest success stories of the computer age.

Although Intel continues to grow, the industry in which it operates has matured so there is some question whether the firm should be evaluated as a high-growth company or stable-growth company from now on. For example, in December of 2007 the firm's shares were trading for $20.88, which represented a price–earnings ratio of only 17.61. Compared to Google, Inc.'s price–earnings ratio of 53.71 on the same date, it would appear that the decision has already been made by the market.

Intel's expected earnings for 2007 are $1.13 per share, and its payout ratio is 48%. Furthermore, selected financial data for the sector, industry, and seven of the largest firms (including Intel) are found in Exhibit 6-7.1

a. Is Intel's current stock price of $20.88 reasonable in light of its sector, industry, and comparison firms?

b. Intel has a beta coefficient equal to 1.66. If we assume a risk-free rate of 5.02% and a market risk premium of 5%, what is your estimate of the required rate of return for Intel's stock using the CAPM? What rate of growth in earnings is consistent with Intel's policy of paying out 40% of earnings in dividends and the firm's historical return on equity? Using your estimated growth rate, what is the value of Intel's shares using the Gordon (single-stage) growth model? Analyze the reasonableness of your estimated value per share using the Gordon model.

c. Using your analysis in part b above, what growth rate is consistent with Intel's current share price of $20.88?

d. Analysts expect Intel's earnings to grow at a rate of 12% per year over the next five years. What rate of growth from Year 6 forward (forever) is needed to warrant Intel's current stock price (use your CAPM estimate of the required rate of return on equity)? (*Hint:* Use a two-stage growth model where Intel's earnings grow for five years at 12% and from Year 6 forward at a constant rate.)

6-8 VALUATION MULTIPLES AND CHANGES IN INTEREST RATES—THOUGHT QUESTION Both EBITDA to enterprise value and P/E ratios can be linked to interest rates through the discount rate used in discounted cash flow valuation. Holding all else equal, when discount rates are higher, valuation ratios are lower. Perhaps, because of this, we tend to see stock prices as well as the value of private business transactions decline when interest rates increase.

Macroeconomists like to describe interest rates as consisting of two components: the real interest rate component and an expected inflation component. In some situations, increases in interest rates are the result of an increasing real interest rate; and

Exhibit 6-7.1 Industry Comparables for Intel Corporation

Description	Market Cap	P/E	Return on Equity %	Dividend Yield %	Long-term Debt to Equity	Price to Book Value	Net Profit Margin	Price to Free Cash Flow
Sector: Technology	5344.81B	27.716	14.77%	1.90%	0.691	5.588	10.39%	55.435
Industry: Semiconductor — Broad line	252.89B	19.9	16.20%	1.30%	0.096	3.42	15.50%	193.3
Intel Corp.	120.51B	17.622	19.63%	1.90%	0.064	3.437	18.72%	121.039
Texas Instruments Inc.	44.62B	11.08	22.94%	0.50%	0.004	3.71	18.67%	-5577.55
STMicroelectronics NV	16.35B	24.959	7.81%	0.70%	0.209	1.764	8.24%	-11.219
Advanced Micro Devices Inc.	11.79B	21.152	12.61%	0.00%	0.138	2.088	10.13%	-58.916
Analog Devices Inc.	11.48B	22.667	15.42%	1.90%	NA	3.342	21.48%	311.392
Maxim Integrated Products Inc.	10.28B	23.025	16.93%	1.90%	NA	3.681	21.39%	NA
National Semiconductor Corp.	8.04B	18.49	25.67%	0.60%	0.012	4.481	22.18%	154.483

in other situations, the cause of an interest rate increase is an increase in expected inflation. How might valuation ratios be expected to respond to an interest rate increase generated by an increase in expected inflation versus an interest rate increase that represents an increase in real interest rates?

PROBLEM 6-9   **MINI-CASE** PRICING SHARES FOR THE
FRAMCO RESOURCES IPO

Framco Resources is an independent oil and natural gas company that engages in the acquisition, development, and exploitation of onshore North American oil and natural gas properties. The company has followed a strategy of growth through the development of its inventory of drilling locations and exploitation projects, and selectively pursuing acquisitions. The firm's current management team first purchased a significant ownership interest in Framco (which was a public entity) in December 1997, and since then has achieved substantial growth in reserves and production. In 2003 the company was taken private through a buyout financed using debt capital and equity capital provided by a private equity partner. Late in 2005 Framco's board decided that the time was right for the firm to once again become a public entity by doing an initial public offering of its shares.

Framco's board selected an investment banker who prepared a preliminary analysis of possible offering prices for Framco's shares, found in Exhibits P6-9.1 and P6-9.2 (p. 263). The valuation analysis utilizes valuation ratios based on the current enterprise values of five independent oil and gas companies and three key valuation metrics that are commonly used in the industry: estimated reserves; estimated earnings before interest, taxes, depreciation and amortization, and maintenance capital expenditures (EBITDAX); and firm free cash flow.

Exhibit P6-9.2 contains estimates of Framco's equity and enterprise valuation that would correspond to different IPO share prices. This analysis is based on the assumption that Framco will sell 51.6 million shares of stock for a price of $20 to $30 per share. To complete the comparative analysis, Framco's CFO provided the investment banker with the necessary estimates of his firm's proved reserves for 2005, EBITDAX for 2006 and 2007, and free cash flow. These estimates are found below:

Valuation Metric	Framco Estimates
2005E proved reserves	$700 million
2006E EBITDAX	$302 million
2007E EBITDAX	$280 million
Firm free cash flow	$191 million

Industry Comparables Used in Framco Resources IPO Pricing Analysis

Company	Firm Characteristics (millions)					Firm Valuation Ratios			
	Enterprise Value	2005E Reserves	2006E EBIT-DAX	2007E EBIT-DAX	Firm Free Cash Flow[1]	2005E Reserves	2006 EBIT-DAX	2007 EBIT-DAX	Firm Free Cash Flow[1]
Company #1	$20,547	7,311	$3,210	$2,873	$2,940	$2.81	6.40	7.15	6.99
Company #2	21,280	7,220	3,806	3,299	3,502	2.95	5.59	6.45	6.08
Company #3	4,781	1,411	601	602	450	3.39	7.96	7.94	10.62
Company #4	2,508	1,222	380	342	252	2.05	6.60	7.33	9.95
Company #5	2,355	798	460	399	241	2.95	5.12	5.90	9.77
Mean						2.83	6.33	6.96	8.68
Median						2.95	6.40	7.15	9.77

[1]Firm free cash flow is calculated in the usual way and includes company estimates of maintenance capital expenditures.

Enterprise Value Estimates for Framco Based on Alternative IPO Share Prices

	Expected IPO Share Price					
	$20.00	$22.00	$24.00	$26.00	$28.00	$30.00
Diluted shares outstanding (millions)	51.60	51.60	51.60	51.60	51.60	51.60
Equity value (millions)	$1,032	$1,135	$1,238	$1,342	$1,445	$1,548
Plus: Net debt (millions)[1]	740	688	637	585	534	482
Enterprise value (millions)	$1,772	$1,824	$1,875	$1,927	$1,978	$2,030

[1]Net debt equals interest-bearing debt less cash ($250,000). The interest-bearing debt total declines with increasing IPO share prices, since half the additional proceeds resulting from a higher price are used to retire Framco's debt.

a. Calculate the valuation ratios found in Exhibit P6-9.1 using Framco's valuation metrics for each of the alternative IPO prices found in Exhibit P6-9.2.

b. Based on your calculations (and assuming the valuation metrics are used by investors to make value comparisons among independent oil and gas firms), what price do you think Framco's shares will command at the time of the IPO?

c. The actual offering price for Framco's shares is not set until the pricing meeting with the investment banker the night before the offering date. At this meeting the investment banker not only has updated comparables data such as that found in Exhibit P6-9.1 but also has indications of interest in purchasing the new shares (the book). At this meeting Framco's investment banker reviewed Framco's most recent estimates of the valuation metrics, which were virtually identical to the estimates found in Exhibit P6-9.1. However, the book was quite strong, indicating an oversubscription for the 51.6 million shares at prices at the upper end of the range of prices found in Exhibit P6-9.2. Should Framco try to raise the offering price outside the original range set forth in Exhibit P6-9.2? Why or why not?

PROBLEM 6-10   **MINI-CASE** VALUING GOOGLE IPO SHARE PRICE[18]

Google, Inc., of Mountain View, California, operates the most popular and powerful search engine on the Web. The company went public using an unconventional Dutch auction method on August 19, 2004. The resulting IPO was the largest Internet IPO ever, raising $1.67 billion and leaving the firm with 271,219,643 shares of common stock.

While Google commands a wide lead over its competitors in the search engine market, it is witnessing an increased pressure from well-funded rival entities. Yahoo! Inc., with a market cap of approximately $38.43 billion, is generally regarded as following a business model very similar to Google's.

a. Using the method of multiples based on both the P/E ratio and the enterprise value to EBITDA ratio, at what price should the stock be offered? Use the data found in Exhibit P6-10.1 for the following companies as comparables in your analysis: Earthlink, Yahoo, eBay, and Microsoft. Compute the IPO value for Google's shares using each of the comparable firms separately, and then use an average "multiple" of the comparable firms. Use the year-end 2003 balance sheets and income statements of the comparable firms to do the analysis. Assume Google's forecasted values at the time of the IPO are as follows: EBITDA is approximately $800 million, cash and equivalents are $430 million, and interest bearing debt (total short-term and long-term) equals only $10 million.[19]

---

[18]Prepared by Betty Simkins, Oklahoma State University.

[19]These estimates for Google are approximate and are based on the prospectus.

Exhibit P6-10.1

Financial Information	Earthlink (ELINK)	Yahoo (YHOO)	eBay (EBAY)	Microsoft (MSFT)
2003 Shares outstanding	159,399,000	655,602,000	646,819,000	10,800,000,000
2003 Fiscal close stock price	$ 10.00	$ 45.03	$ 64.61	$ 25.64
Market capitalization	$ 1,593,990,000	$29,521,758,060	$41,790,975,590	$276,912,000,000
Short-term debt	$ 900,000	$ 0	$ 2,800,000	$ 0
Long-term debt	$ 0	$ 750,000,000	$ 124,500,000	$ 0
Cash & equivalents	$ 349,740,000	$ 713,539,000	$ 1,381,513,000	$ 6,438,000,000
Short-term investments	$ 89,088,000	$ 595,975,000	$ 340,576,000	$ 42,610,000,000
EBITDA	$ 218,100,000	$ 455,300,000	$ 818,200,000	$ 14,656,000,000
Net income	$ (62,200,000)	$ 237,900,000	$ 441,800,000	$ 9,993,000,000
Calculated EPS	(0.39)	0.36	0.68	0.93

b. Which of the four comparable firms do you think is the best comparison firm for Google? Why?

c. How has the stock performed since the IPO? Do you believe Google is currently correctly valued in the stock market? Why or why not?

PROBLEM 6-11   **MINI-CASE** VALUING CONOCOPHILLIPS' ACQUISITION OF BURLINGTON RESOURCES[20]

You have recently been hired as an equity analyst by Wall Street Valuation Consultants and have been assigned the task of valuing the proposed acquisition described in the following press release:

> Houston, Texas (December 12, 2005)—ConocoPhillips (NYSE: COP) and Burlington Resources Inc. (NYSE: BR) announced today they have signed a definitive agreement under which ConocoPhillips will acquire Burlington Resources in a transaction valued at $33.9 billion. The transaction, upon approval by Burlington Resources shareholders, will provide ConocoPhillips with extensive, high quality natural gas exploration and production assets, primarily located in North America. The Burlington Resources portfolio provides a strong complement to ConocoPhillips' global portfolio of integrated exploration, production, refining and energy transportation operations,

[20]Prepared by Betty Simkins, Oklahoma State University.

Exhibit P6-11.1 Income Statement and Balance Sheet Values are in Thousands

	XTO Energy	Chesapeake Energy	Devon Energy	Apache	Burlington Resources
Ticker	XTO	CHK	DVN	APA	BR
PERIOD ENDING	31-Dec-04	31-Dec-04	31-Dec-04	31-Dec-04	31-Dec-04
Income Statement ($ 000)					
Total revenue	**1,947,601**	**2,709,268**	**9,189,0000**	**5,332,577**	**5,618,0**
Cost of revenue	436,998	204,821	1,535,000	946,639	1,040,0
Gross profit	**1,510,603**	**2,504,447**	**7,654,000**	**4,385,938**	**4,578,00**
Operating Expenses					
Selling, general, and administrative	165,092	896,290	1,616,000	173,194	215,00
Depreciation, depleletion, and amortization	414,341	615,822	2,334,000	1,270,683	1,137,0
Others	11,830	—	—	162,493	640,00
Operating income or loss	**919,281**	**992,335**	**3,704,000**	**2,779,568**	**2,586,00**
Income from Continuing Operations					
Total other income/expenses (net)	—	−20,081	64,000	857	—
Earnings before interest and taxes	919,281	972,254	3,768,000	2,780,425	2,586,00
Interest expense	93,661	167,328	475,000	117,342	282,00
Income before tax	825,620	804,926	3,293,000	2,663,083	2,304,00
Income tax expense	317,738	289,771	1,107,000	993,012	777,00
Net income from continuing operations	**507,882**	**515,155**	**2,186,000**	**1,670,071**	**1,527,0**
Nonrecurring Events					
Effect of accounting changes	—	—	—	−1,317	—
Net income	**507,882**	**515,155**	**2,186,000**	**1,668,757**	**1,527,00**
Preferred stock and other adjustments	—	—	−10,000	−5,680	—
Net income applicable to common shares	**$507,882**	**$515,155**	**$2,176,000**	**1,663,074**	**$1,527,00**

Balance Sheet ($000)

Assets

Current Assets					
Cash and cash equivalents	9,700	6,896	1,152,000	111,093	217,900
Short-term investments	14,713	51,061	968,000	–	–
Net receivables	364,836	477,436	1,320,000	1,022,625	994,00
Inventory	–	32,147	–	157,293	124,00
Other current assets	47,716	–	143,000	57,771	158,000
Total current assets	**436,965**	**567,540**	**3,583,000**	**1,348,782**	**3,455,00**
Long-term investments	–	136,912	753,000	–	–
Property, plant, and equipment	5,624,378	7,444,384	19,346,000	13,860,359	1,103,300
Goodwill	–	–	5,637,000	189,252	105,400
Other assets	49,029	95,673	417,000	–	202,000
Deferred long-term asset charges	–	–	–	104,087	–
Total assets	**6,110,372**	**8,244,509**	**29,736,000**	**15,502,480**	**15,744,00**

Liabilities

Current Liabilities					
Accounts payable	425,173	872,539	1,722,000	1,158,181	118,200
Short/Current long-term debt	75,534	91,414	1,378,000	21,273	2,000
Other current liabilities	259	–	–	103,487	41,500
Total current liabilities	**500,966**	**963,953**	**3,100,000**	**1,282,891**	**1,599,00**
Long-term debt	2,053,911	3,076,405	7,796,000	2,619,807	3,887,00
Other liabilities	199,753	107,395	366,000	1,022,880	851,00
Deferred long-term liability charges	756,369	933,873	4,800,000	2,372,481	2,396,00
Total liabilities	**3,510,999**	**5,081,626**	**16,062,000**	**7,298,059**	**8,733,00**

(*Continued*)

Exhibit P6-11.1 Continued

Ticker	XTO Energy	Chesapeake Energy	Devon Energy	Apache	Burlington Resources
	XTO	CHK	DVN	APA	BR
PERIOD ENDING	31-Dec-04	31-Dec-04	31-Dec-04	31-Dec-04	31-Dec-04
Stockholders' Equity					
Preferred stock	—	490,906	1,000	98,387	—
Common stock	3,484	3,169	48,000	209,320	5,000
Retained earnings	1,239,553	262,987	3,693,000	4,017,339	4,163,00
Treasury stock	−24,917	−22,091	—	−97,325	−2,208,00
Capital surplus	1,410,135	2,440,105	9,087,000	4,106,182	3,973,00
Other stockholders' equity	−28,882	−12,193	845,000	−129,482	1,078,00
Total stockholders' equity	**2,599,373**	**3,162,883**	**13,674,000**	**8,204,421**	**7,011,00**
Total liabilities and stockholders' equity	**6,110,372**	**8,244,509**	**29,736,000**	**15,502,480**	**15,744,00**
Other Financial Data					
Exploration expenses (millions)	$599.5	$184.3	$279.0	$2,300.0	$258.0
Shares outstanding (millions)	332.9	253.2	482.0	327.5	392.0
Year-end 2004 closing price	$35.38	$16.50	$38.92	$50.57	
Market capitalization (millions)	$11,778.00	$4,177.80	$18,759.44	$16,561.68	

Brief Company Descriptions

XTO Energy

XTO Energy, Inc., and its subsidiaries, engages in the acquisition, development, exploitation, and exploration of producing oil and gas properties in the United States. The company also produces, processes, markets, and transports oil and natural gas. Its proved reserves are principally located in the Eastern Region, including the East Texas Basin and northwestern Louisiana; Barnett Shale of North Texas; San Juan and Raton Basins of New Mexico and Colorado; Permian and South Texas Region; Mid-Continent and Rocky Mountain Region in Wyoming, Kansas, Oklahoma, and Arkansas; and Middle Ground Shoal Field of Alaska's Cook Inlet. As of December 31, 2005, the company had estimated proved reserves 6.09 trillion cubic feet of natural gas, 47.4 million barrels of natural gas liquids, and 208.7 million barrels of oil.

Chesapeake Energy

Chesapeake Energy Corporation engages in the development, acquisition, production, exploration, and marketing of onshore oil and natural gas properties in the United States. Its properties are located in Oklahoma, Texas, Arkansas, Louisiana, Kansas, Montana, Colorado, North Dakota, New Mexico, West Virginia, Kentucky, Ohio, New York, Maryland, Michigan, Pennsylvania, Tennessee, and Virginia. As of December 31, 2005, the company had proved developed and undeveloped reserves of approximately 7,520,690 million cubic feet of gas equivalent, including approximately 103,323 thousand barrels of oil and approximately 6,900,754 million cubic feet of natural gas. It also owned interests in approximately 30,600 producing oil and gas wells, as of the above date.

Devon Energy

Devon Energy Corporation primarily engages in the exploration, development, and production of oil and gas. It owns oil and gas properties located principally the United States and Canada. The company's U.S. operations are focused in the Permian Basin, the Mid-Continent, the Rocky Mountains, and onshore and offshore Gulf Coast regions; and Canadian properties are focused in the western Canadian sedimentary basin in Alberta and British Columbia. Devon Energy also owns properties located in Azerbaijan, China, and Egypt, as well as areas in West Africa, including Equatorial Guinea, Gabon, and Cote d'Ivoire. In addition, the company markets and transports oil, gas, and natural gas liquids; and constructs and operates pipelines, storage and treating facilities, and gas processing plants. As of December 31, 2005, its estimated proved reserves were 2,112 million barrels of oil equivalent. Devon Energy sells its gas production to various customers, including pipelines, utilities, gas marketing firms, industrial users, and local distribution companies.

Apache

Apache Corporation engages in the exploration, development, and production of natural gas, crude oil, and natural gas liquids primarily in North America. It has exploration and production interests in the Gulf of Mexico, the Gulf Coast, east Texas, the Permian Basin, the Anadarko Basin, and the western Sedimentary Basin of Canada. The company also holds exploration and production interests onshore Egypt, offshore Western Australia, offshore the United Kingdom in the North Sea, offshore the People's Republic of China, and onshore Argentina. As of December 31, 2005, it had total estimated proved reserves of 976 millions of barrels of crude oil, condensate, and natural gas liquids; and 6.8 trillion cubic feet of natural gas.

thereby positioning the combined company for future growth. (Source: http://www
.conocophillips.com/NR/rdonlyres/86E7B7A6-B953-4D0D-9B45-E4F1016DD8FD/0/
cop_burlingtonpressrelease.pdf)

In his letter to ConocoPhillips shareholders contained in the company's 2005 annual report, CEO Jim Mulva described the rationale for the proposed Burlington
acquisition as follows:

> Burlington's near-term production profile is robust and growing, plus Burlington pos-
> sesses an extensive inventory of prospects and significant land positions in the most
> promising basins in North America, primarily onshore. With this access to high-qual-
> ity, long-life reserves, the acquisition enhances our production growth from both con-
> ventional and unconventional gas resources.
>
> Specifically, our portfolio will be bolstered by opportunities to enhance produc-
> tion and gain operating synergies in the San Juan Basin of the United States and by
> an expanded presence and better utilization of our assets in Western Canada. In addi-
> tion to growth possibilities, these assets also provide significant cash generation po-
> tential well into the future.
>
> Beyond adding to production and reserves, Burlington also brings well-recog-
> nized technical expertise that, together with ConocoPhillips' existing upstream capa-
> bilities, will create a superior organization to capitalize on the expanded asset base.
> We do not anticipate that the $33.9 billion acquisition will require asset sales within
> either ConocoPhillips or Burlington, nor should it change our organic growth plans
> for the company. We expect to achieve synergies and pretax cost savings of approxi-
> mately $375 million annually, after the operations of the two companies are fully
> integrated.
>
> We anticipate immediate and future cash generation from this transaction that
> will aid in the rapid reduction of debt incurred for the acquisition and go toward the
> redeployment of cash into strategic areas of growth. Burlington shareholders will
> vote on the proposed transaction at a meeting on March 30, 2006. (Source:
> http://wh.conocophillips.com/about/reports/ar05/letter.htm)

However, at an analysts' meeting, CEO Mulva hinted that the price ConocoPhillips
paid for Burlington might be viewed as high by some:

> In terms of acquisitions, mergers and acquisitions, it really becomes more and more
> of a seller's market and terms and conditions are not that attractive to buyers.
> (Source: http://news.softpedia.com/news/ConocoPhillips-Plans-To-Acquire-Burlington-
> 14628.shtml)

Your task is to answer the following basic question: "Is Burlington Resources
worth the $35.6 billion offered by ConocoPhillips?" Although you are new to the ex-
ploration and production (E&P) industry, you quickly learned that the method of multiples or market-based comparables and, specifically, the ratio of enterprise value (EV)
to EBITDAX are typically used as benchmarks to value E&P companies. EBITDAX
stands for "earnings before interest, taxes, depreciation and amortization, and exploration expenses." EBITDAX differs from EBITDA in that it adds back exploration expenses in addition to depreciation and amortization—hence the term "EBITDAX."

a. Using the method of multiples based on enterprise value to EBITDAX, the P/E ratio, and the enterprise value to EBITDA ratio, what should the acquisition price be for Burlington Resources shares? Use the following companies as comparables for your analysis: Chesapeake Energy, XTO Energy, Devon Energy, and Apache. Year-end 2004 balance sheets and income statement summary information as well as market capitalization data are provided in Exhibit P6-11.1 (pp. 266–269) for Burlington Resources and each of the comparable firms.

b. Which of the four firms used as comparables do you think is the best comparison firm for Burlington Resources? Why?

c. Based on your analysis of comparables, did ConocoPhillips pay too much or find a bargain? Why or why not?

d. What additional information would help you with this analysis?

PROBLEM 6-12   **MINI-CASE** DICK'S SPORTING GOODS IPO[21]

Setting: It is early in October 2002 and your investment bank has been hired by the management team at Dick's Sporting Goods (DKS) to determine a valuation/offering price for their stock's initial public offering (IPO).

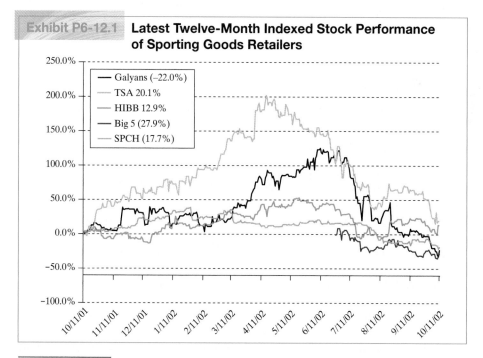

Exhibit P6-12.1   **Latest Twelve-Month Indexed Stock Performance of Sporting Goods Retailers**

_____

[21]Prepared by Julia Plotts, University of Southern California.

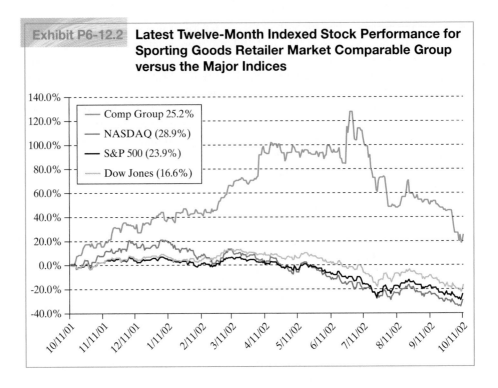

Exhibit P6-12.2 **Latest Twelve-Month Indexed Stock Performance for Sporting Goods Retailer Market Comparable Group versus the Major Indices**

About Dick's Sporting Goods: DKS, headquartered in Pittsburgh, Pennsylvania, was founded when Dick Stack opened his first store in 1948 with $300 from his grandmother's cookie jar. This company is growing rapidly and plans to use the IPO proceeds for store openings and acquisitions. DKS operates more than 130 stores in 25 states, primarily in the eastern United States. The store format is a large "big-box" store containing smaller shops featuring sporting goods, apparel, and footwear for activities ranging from football and golf to hunting and camping. Besides brands like NIKE and Adidas, Dick's carries Ativa, Walter Hagen, and others exclusive to the company. At the time of the IPO, the DKS management team included the founder's son, Ed, who holds 37% ownership in the company, and the investment firm Vulcan Ventures (founded by former Microsoft executive Paul Allen) owns 12% of DKS as a result of a private equity investment.

Industry/Market Overview: Sporting goods retailers were consolidating with the rise of "big-box" retailers. In 1997 and 2001 Gart Sports Company (GRTS) acquired Sport Mart Inc. and OSH Sporting Goods, respectively. Private equity and venture capital firms held equity investments within the industry. DKS was the first retailer to launch an IPO in three months; from the beginning of July 2002 until the time of offering it had been the lowest combined IPO tally since the second quarter of 1978. In

Exhibit P6-12.3	Dick's Sporting Goods Latest Twelve-Month Performance
Dick's Sporting Goods Financial Data ($ millions)	
Revenues	$1,173.794
Gross profit	$298.453
EBIT	$55.899
Depreciation and amortization	$13.499
EBITDA	$69.398
Balance Sheet Data 8/3/02	
Checks drawn	$33.584
Current portion of long-term debt	$0.211
Revolving bank line of credit	$90.299
Long-term debt and capital leases	$3.466
Total debt	$127.560
Cash	$13.874
Stockholders' equity	$78.984

2002 other retail IPOs had mixed success. Big 5 Sporting Goods stock price had declined by 23% since its private equity investor Leonard Green & Partners, LP, raised $105 million in June 2002. Market conditions for equity capital raises were unfavorable and during the DKS road show, many of the institutional investors expressed concerns that the suggested IPO range of $15–$18 per share was too high.

VALUATION ASSIGNMENT

a. Based on the DKS financial data (Exhibit P6-12.3) and sporting goods retailer market comparables valuation (Exhibit P6-12.4), estimate an implied equity valuation for the firm for its initial public offering. Calculate an implied equity valuation range based on the comparable enterprise valuation multiples (EV/Revenue, EV/EBIT, EV/EBITDA). Determine an IPO price range for an estimated 9.4 million shares of equity outstanding.

b. In your opinion, are the selected publicly traded sporting goods companies shown in Exhibit P6-12.4 good choices for market comparables for DKS? Why or why not?

Exhibit P6-12.4   Sporting Goods Retailer Market Comparables Valuation[19, 20]

Sporting Goods Retailers	Ticker	Stock Price 10/9/2002	% Change from 12-Month		Calendar EPS[a]		Secular Growth Rate[a]	Calendar P/E Multiples	
			Low	High	2002E	2003E		2002E	2003E
Galyan's Trading Co.	GLYN	$ 7.25	0.0%	(68.8%)	$1.06	$1.32	23%	6.8×	5.5×
Gart Sports Co.	GRTS	$14.64	20.8%	(61.2%)	$1.80	$2.10	18%	8.1×	7.0×
Hibbett Sporting Goods	HIBB	$18.89	17.1%	(33.7%)	$1.35	$1.62	20%	14.0×	11.7×
Sport Chalet	SPCH	$ 6.12	0.0%	(43.1%)	$0.71	$0.87	14%	8.6×	7.0×
The Sports Authority	TSA	$ 4.15	1.7%	(71.9%)	$0.66	$0.76	13%	6.3×	5.5×
Big 5 Sporting Goods	BGFV	$ 8.60	0.0%	(39.8%)	$1.09	$1.25	15%	7.9×	6.9×
Average			**6.6%**	**(53.1%)**			**17%**	**8.6×**	**7.2×**
Median			**0.9%**	**(52.1%)**			**16%**	**8.0×**	**6.9×**

Sporting Goods Retailers	LTM Ended	Market Value	Enterprise Value	Enterprise Value/LTM			Debt/ Total Cap	LTM Margins		
				Revenue	EBITDA	EBIT		Gross	EBITDA	EBIT
Galyan's Trading Co.	7/02	$123.50	$123.50	0.2×	3.0×	4.6×	6%	30%	8%	5%
Gart Sports Co.	7/02	$178.50	$313.00	0.3×	6.2×	9.4×	44%	26%	5%	3%
Hibbett Sporting Goods	7/02	$189.90	$191.70	0.7×	7.0×	9.2×	6%	31%	10%	8%
Sport Chalet	6/02	$ 40.40	$ 45.60	0.2×	4.0×	7.3×	14%	28%	5%	3%
The Sports Authority	7/02	$136.20	$331.90	0.2×	4.9×	12.4×	59%	2%	5%	2%
Big 5 Sporting Goods	6/02	$186.40	$327.40	0.5×	5.8×	7.0×	105%	35%	9%	7%
Average				**0.37×**	**5.2×**	**8.3×**	**39%**	**25%**	**7%**	**5%**
Median				**0.27×**	**5.4×**	**8.3×**	**29%**	**29%**	**7%**	**4%**

[a] Annualized 3-year EPS growth rate

Legend: LTM = latest 12 months; Gross (LTM) margin = Gross profit/Revenues; EBITDA (LTM) margin = EBITDA/Revenues; EBIT (LTM) margin = EBIT/Revenues

[19] Latest 12 months is most recent for the company as of 10/9/02; EPS and growth forecast per First Call analyst consensus.

[20] Financial data has been normalized for unusual and nonrecurring items.

CHAPTER 7

Enterprise Valuation

Chapter Overview

In this chapter we review the basics of business, or enterprise, valuation. Our focus is on the *hybrid valuation approach* that combines DCF analysis (discussed in Chapters 2–5) with relative valuation (introduced in Chapter 6). We decompose the enterprise valuation problem into two steps: The first step involves the valuation of a business's planning period cash flows spanning a 3- to 10-year period, and the second step involves the calculation of the *terminal value,* which is the value of all cash flows that follow the planning period. Pure DCF valuation models use DCF analysis to analyze the value of the planning period and terminal value cash flows, whereas the hybrid valuation model we discuss utilizes DCF analysis to value the planning period cash flows and an EBITDA multiple to estimate the terminal value.

7.1 INTRODUCTION

In this chapter we focus our attention on what is generally referred to as enterprise valuation, which is the valuation of a business or going concern. The approach that we recommend, which we refer to as the hybrid approach, recognizes that forecasting cash flows into the foreseeable future poses a unique challenge since most enterprises are expected to stay in business for many years. To deal with this forecasting problem, analysts typically make explicit and detailed forecasts of firm cash flows for only a limited number of years (often referred to as the *planning period*) and estimate the value of all remaining cash flows as a *terminal value,* at the end of the planning period.

The terminal value can be estimated in one of two ways. The first method is a straightforward application of DCF analysis using the Gordon growth model. As we discussed in earlier chapters, this approach requires an estimate of both a growth rate and a discount rate. The second method applies the multiples approach we discussed in the last chapter; typically, the terminal value is determined as a multiple of the projected end-of-planning-period earnings before interest, taxes, depreciation, and amortization (EBITDA). When this latter approach is used to evaluate terminal value and DCF is used to evaluate the planning period cash flows, the model is no longer a pure DCF model but becomes a hybrid approach to enterprise valuation.

The enterprise valuation approach described in this chapter is used in a number of applications. These include acquisitions, which we consider in the example highlighted in this chapter; initial public offerings, where firms go public and issue equity for the first time, which we described in the previous chapter. "Going private" transactions (which we will consider in the next chapter); spin-offs and carve-outs (where the division of a firm becomes a legally separate entity); and finally, the valuation of a firm's equity for investment purposes.

In most applications, analysts use a single discount rate—the weighted average cost of capital (or WACC) of the investment—to discount both the planning period cash flows and the terminal value. This approach makes sense if the financial structure and the risk of the investment are relatively stable over time. However, analysts frequently need to estimate the enterprise value of a firm that is experiencing some sort of transition, and in these cases the firm's capital structure is often expected to change over time. Indeed, firms are often acquired using a high proportion of debt, which is then paid down over time until the firm reaches what is considered an appropriate capital structure. In these cases, the assumption of a fixed WACC is inappropriate, and we recommend the use of a variant of the discounted cash flow model known as the *adjusted present value model,* which we describe later in this chapter.

Finally, it should be noted that when firms acquire existing businesses, they typically plan on making changes in the business's operating strategy. This requires that the potential acquirer value the business given both its current strategy as well as the proposed new strategy. Valuing the current strategy can be viewed as a reality check—if the business is not valued appropriately given its current strategy, why not? One could then value scenarios where the firm's operating strategy is changed following the acquisition to determine whether the new strategy creates additional value. To help answer this question, sensitivity analysis can be deployed to determine the situations in which this additional value is indeed realized.

The chapter is organized as follows: Section 7.2 introduces the notion of estimating a firm's or business unit's enterprise value using the hybrid/multiples approach. Section 7.3 introduces the adjusted present value (APV) model, which is an alternative model that does not require that the firm's capital structure remain constant over the foreseeable future. Finally, we close our discussion of enterprise valuation with summary comments in Section 7.4.

7.2 USING A TWO-STEP APPROACH TO ESTIMATE ENTERPRISE VALUE

We noted in the introduction that forecasting firm cash flows into the foreseeable future is a challenging task, and for that reason analysts typically break the future into two segments: a finite number of years known as the planning period, and all years thereafter. (See the Practitioner Insight box, Enterprise Valuation Methods Used on Wall Street.) Consequently, the application of the DCF model to the estimation of enterprise value can best be thought of as the sum of the two terms found in Equation 7.1. The first term represents the present value of a set of cash flows spanning a finite number of years, referred to as the *planning period (PP)*.

$$\underset{\text{Value}}{\text{Enterprise}} = \underset{\substack{\text{of the Planning} \\ \text{Period (PP) Cash Flows}}}{\overline{\underset{\text{Present Value}}{\text{Term 1}}}} + \underset{\substack{\text{of the Terminal} \\ \text{Value in Period PP}}}{\overline{\underset{\text{Present Value}}{\text{Term 2}}}} \qquad (7.1)$$

The second term is the present value of the estimated terminal value (TV_{PP}) of the firm at the end of the planning period. As such, the terminal value represents the present value of all the cash flows that are expected to be received beyond the end of the planning period. As the following Technical Insight box on page 284 illustrates, the terminal value estimate is generally quite important and can often represent over 50% of the value of the enterprise.

Example—Immersion Chemical Corporation Acquires Genetic Research Corporation

To illustrate our enterprise valuation approach, consider the valuation problem faced by the Immersion Chemical Corporation in the spring of 2007. Immersion provides products and services worldwide to the life sciences industry and operates in four businesses: Human Health, Biosciences, Animal Health/Agriculture, and Specialty and Fine Chemicals. The company's overall strategy is to focus on niche markets that have global opportunities, develop its strong customer relations, and enhance its new-products pipeline. In an effort to expand into biopharmaceuticals, Immersion is considering the acquisition of Genetics Research Corporation (hereafter GRC), which will be integrated into Immersion's Specialty and Fine Chemicals division.

Immersion can acquire GRC for a cash payment of $100 million, which is equal to a multiple of six times GRC's 2006 earnings before interest, taxes, depreciation, and amortization (EBITDA). Immersion will also be assuming GRC's accounts payable and accrued expenses, which total $9,825,826, so the book value of GRC acquisition would be $109,825,826 (found in Table 7-1). To finance the GRC acquisition, Immersion will borrow $40 million in nonrecourse debt and will need to raise $60 million in equity.[1] Based on conversations with its investment banker, Immersion's management has learned that the $100 million acquisition cost is well within the range of five to seven times EBITDA that has recently been paid for similar firms. As the analysis below indicates, this price is also in line with Immersion's own DCF analysis of GRC, given cash flow projections based on its current operating strategy.

Table 7-1 contains the pre- and post-acquisition balance sheets for GRC, which indicate that Immersion is paying just over $20 million more than GRC's book value

---

[1] The remaining $9,825,826 represents the value of GRC's accounts payable and accrued expenses, which are assumed by Immersion.

In broad brush terms there are three basic valuation methodologies used throughout the investment banking industry: trading or comparable company multiples, transaction multiples, and discounted cash flows. Emphasis on a particular methodology varies depending on the particular setting or type of transaction. For equity transactions such as the pricing of an initial public offering (IPO), relative valuation based on multiples of market comparables (firms in the same or related industries, as well as firms that have been involved in recent similar transactions) is the preferred approach. The reason for the emphasis on this type of valuation is that the Company will have publicly traded equity and thus investors will be able to choose whether to buy said Company or any of the other companies that are "peers."

A key consideration in relative valuation analysis is the selection of a set of comparable firms. For example, in the Hertz IPO we looked at not only the relative prices of car rental firms (Avis, Budget, etc.) but also considered industrial equipment leasing companies (United Rental, RSC Equipment, etc.) since this was a growing piece of Hertz's business model. We also looked at travel related companies, as a large part of the Hertz rental car business is driven by airline travel. Some also believed that Hertz, because of its strong brand name recognition, should be compared to valuation multiples of a set of companies with strong brand recognition including firms such as Nike or Coke. Obviously selection of a comparable group of firms and transactions is critical when carrying out a relative valuation because different comparable sets trade at different multiples and this affects the valuation estimate.

In merger and acquisition ("M&A") analysis involving a strategic buyer (typically another firm in the same or a related industry) or a financial buyer such as a private equity

for the business. Note that the $20,819,867 difference between the purchase price and GRC's pre-acquisition (book value) total assets is recorded as goodwill on the revised balance sheet.[2] Moreover, GRC's post-acquisition balance sheet contains $40 million in long-term debt (on which it pays 6.5% interest) plus $60 million in common equity (common stock at par plus paid-in capital). The remainder of the right-hand side of the balance sheet consists of current liabilities that consist entirely of payables and accrued expenses, which are noninterest-bearing liabilities. Thus, after it is acquired by Immersion, GRC will have a total of $100 million in invested capital, of which 40% is debt and 60% is equity.

_____

[2]By including all of the purchase premium as goodwill, we are assuming that the appraised value of GRC's assets is equal to their book value.

firm (see Chapter 8 for further discussion) the second type of relative valuation method, transaction multiples, is used in combination with discounted cash flows (DCF). The reason for the focus on a transaction multiple is the fact that transaction multiples represent what other buyers have been willing to pay for similar companies or companies with related lines of business. The transaction multiples are used in combination with the DCF approach as DCF allows the buyers to value the acquisition based on their forecast of its performance under their assumptions about how the business will be run.

DCF valuation methods vary slightly from one investment bank to another; however, the typical approach to enterprise valuation is a hybrid approach consisting of forecasting cash flows to evaluate near-term projections and relative valuation to estimate a terminal value. The analysis typically involves a five-year forecast of the firm's cash flows which are discounted using an estimate of the firm's weighted average cost of capital. Then the value of cash flows that extend beyond the end of the planning period are estimated using a terminal value that is calculated based on a multiple of a key firm performance attribute such as EBITDA. The terminal value estimate is frequently stress tested using a constant growth rate with the Gordon growth model to assess the reasonableness of the implied growth rate reflected in the terminal value multiple.

The final valuation approach we use a variant of the DCF approach that is used where a M&A transaction involves a financial sponsor (generally a private equity firm such as Blackstone, Cerberus or KKR. Financial buyers are primarily driven by the rate of return they earn on their investor's money so the valuation approach they use focuses on the IRR of the transaction. The basic idea is to arrive at a set of short-term cash flow forecasts that the buyer is comfortable with, estimate a terminal value at the end of the forecast period (typically 5 years), and then determining IRRs by varying the acquisition price.

[*]Jeffrey Rabel is a CPA and a Vice President in the Global Financial Sponsors group at Lehman Brothers in New York.

Valuing GRC Using DCF Analysis

In Chapter 2 we laid out the following three-step process for using DCF analysis, which we will now apply to the valuation of GRC:

Step 1—Estimate the amount and timing of the expected cash flows.
Step 2—Estimate a risk-appropriate discount rate.
Step 3—Calculate the present value of the expected cash flows, or enterprise value.

Table 7-2 details our analysis of the DCF evaluation of the enterprise value of GRC under the assumption that the firm's operations continue as they have in the past. We refer to this as the *status quo strategy*.

Step 1.   Estimate the amount and timing of the expected cash flows. In Panels a and b of Table 7-2 we present the pro forma financial statements and cash flow projections for GRC that are required to complete Step 1 of a DCF analysis. The cash flow

Table 7-1	Pre- and Post-Acquisition Balance Sheets for GRC	
	Pre-Acquisition 2006	Post-Acquisition 2006
Current assets	$ 41,865,867	$ 41,865,867
Gross property, plant, and equipment	88,164,876	88,164,876
Less: Accumulated depreciation	(41,024,785)	(41,024,785)
Net property, plant, and equipment	$ 47,140,092	$ 47,140,092
Goodwill	–	20,819,867
Total	$ 89,005,959	$ 109,825,826
Current liabilities	$ 9,825,826	$ 9,825,826
Long-term debt	36,839,923	40,000,000
Total liabilities	$ 46,665,749	$ 49,825,826
Common stock (par)	290,353	400,000
Paid-in capital	20,712,517	59,600,000
Retained earnings	21,337,340	–
Common equity	$ 42,340,210	$ 60,000,000
Total	$ 89,005,959	$ 109,825,826

Legend

Acquisition Financing—

Assumed payables and accrued expenses	$ 9,825,826	
Long-term debt (40% of enterprise value)	40,000,000	
Sale of common stock	60,000,000	
Total	$ 109,825,826	
Shares issued ($1.00 par value)	400,000	
Net proceeds	$ 60,000,000	
Price per share	$ 150.00	

projections consist of planning period cash flows spanning the period 2007–2012, and terminal value estimates based on cash flow projections for 2013 and beyond. In addition, Panel a contains the pro forma financial statements upon which these projections are built. The pro forma income statements assume that GRC maintains its operations as it has in the past (i.e., under a status quo strategy) and reflect an assumed rate of growth in revenues of 4% per year during the planning period.

The asset levels found in the pro forma balance sheets reflect the assets that GRC needs to support the projected revenues. The initial financing for the acquisition was presented earlier in Table 7-1. Any additional financing requirements are

Table 7-2 Estimating GRC's Enterprise Value Using DCF Analysis (Status Quo Strategy)

Panel a. (Step 1) Estimate the Amount and Timing of the Planning Period Future Cash Flows

Planning Period Pro Forma Financial Statements

Pro Forma Income Statements

	Pre-Acquisition 2006	Post-Acquisition 2006	2007	2008	2009	2010	2011	2012
Revenues	$ 80,000,000	$ 80,000,000	$ 83,200,000	$ 86,528,000	$ 89,989,120	$ 93,588,685	$ 97,332,232	$ 101,225,521
Cost of goods sold	(45,733,270)	(45,733,270)	(50,932,000)	(52,629,280)	(54,394,451)	(56,230,229)	(58,139,438)	(60,125,016)
Gross profit	$ 34,266,730	$ 34,266,730	$ 32,268,000	$ 33,898,720	$ 35,594,669	$ 37,358,456	$ 39,192,794	$ 41,100,506
General and administrative expense	(17,600,000)	(17,600,000)	(17,984,000)	(18,383,360)	(18,798,694)	(19,230,642)	(19,679,868)	(20,147,063)
Depreciation expense	(6,500,000)	(6,500,000)	(7,856,682)	(7,856,682)	(7,856,682)	(7,856,682)	(7,856,682)	(7,856,682)
Net operating income	$ 10,166,730	$ 10,166,730	$ 6,427,318	$ 7,658,678	$ 8,939,292	$ 10,271,131	$ 11,658,244	$ 13,096,761
Interest expense	(2,523,020)	(2,523,020)	(2,600,000)	(2,549,847)	(2,453,680)	(2,307,941)	(2,108,865)	(1,852,465)
Earnings before taxes	$ 7,643,710	$ 7,643,710	$ 3,827,318	$ 5,108,831	$ 6,485,612	$ 7,963,190	$ 9,547,379	$ 11,244,296
Taxes	(1,910,928)	(1,910,928)	(956,830)	(1,277,208)	(1,621,403)	(1,990,798)	(2,386,845)	(2,811,074)
Net income	$ 5,732,783	$ 5,732,783	$ 2,870,489	$ 3,831,623	$ 4,864,209	$ 5,972,393	$ 7,160,534	$ 8,433,222

Pro Forma Balance Sheets

	Pre-Acquisition 2006	Post-Acquisition 2006	2007	2008	2009	2010	2011	2012
Current assets	$ 41,865,867	$ 41,865,867	43,540,501.76	45,282,121.84	47,093,406.71	48,977,142.98	50,936,228.70	52,973,677.84
Gross property, plant, and equipment	88,164,876	88,164,876	96,021,558	103,878,240	111,734,922	119,591,604	127,448,286	135,304,968
Less: Accumulated depreciation	(41,024,785)	(41,024,785)	(48,881,467)	(56,738,149)	(64,594,831)	(72,451,513)	(80,308,194)	(88,164,876)
Net property, plant, and equipment	$ 47,140,092	$ 47,140,092	$ 47,140,092	$ 47,140,092	$ 47,140,092	$ 47,140,092	$ 47,140,092	47,140,092
Goodwill	—	20,819,867	20,819,867	20,819,867	20,819,867	20,819,867	20,819,867	20,819,867
Total	$ 89,005,959	$ 109,825,826	$ 111,500,461	$ 113,242,081	$ 115,053,366	$ 116,937,102	$ 118,896,188	$ 120,933,637

(continued)

Table 7-2 Continued

Current liabilities	$ 9,825,826	$ 9,825,826	$ 9,975,651	$ 10,131,469	$ 10,293,520	$ 10,462,053	$ 10,637,327	$ 10,819,613
Long-term debt	36,839,923	40,000,000	39,228,419	37,748,922	35,506,789	32,444,078	28,499,462	23,608,049
Total liabilities	$ 46,665,749	$ 49,825,826	$ 49,204,070	$ 47,880,392	$ 45,800,309	$ 42,906,131	$ 39,136,790	$ 34,427,661
Common stock (par)	290,353	400,000	400,000	400,000	400,000	400,000	400,000	400,000
Paid-in capital	20,712,517	59,600,000	59,600,000	59,600,000	59,600,000	59,600,000	59,600,000	59,600,000
Retained earnings	21,337,340	—	2,296,391	5,361,689	9,253,057	14,030,971	19,759,398	26,505,976
Common equity	$ 42,340,210	$ 60,000,000	$ 62,296,391	$ 65,361,689	$ 69,253,057	$ 74,030,971	$ 79,759,398	$ 86,505,976
Total	$ 89,005,959	$ 109,825,826	$ 111,500,461	$ 113,242,081	$ 115,053,366	$ 116,937,102	$ 118,896,188	$ 120,933,637

Planning Period Cash Flow Estimates

Projected Firm Free Cash Flows

	2007	2008	2009	2010	2011	2012
Net operating income	$ 6,427,318	7,658,678	$ 8,939,292	$ 10,271,131	$ 11,656,244	$ 13,096,761
Less: Taxes	(1,606,830)	(1,914,670)	(2,234,823)	(2,567,783)	(2,914,061)	(3,274,190)
NOPAT	$ 4,820,489	$ 5,744,009	$ 6,704,469	$ 7,703,349	$ 8,742,183	$ 9,822,571
Plus: Depreciation	7,856,682	7,856,682	7,856,682	7,856,682	7,856,682	7,856,682
Less: CAPEX	(7,856,682)	(7,856,682)	(7,856,682)	(7,856,682)	(7,856,682)	(7,856,682)
Less: Changes in net working capital	(1,281,602)	(1,332,866)	(1,386,180)	(1,441,628)	(1,499,293)	(1,559,264)
Equals FFCF	$ 3,538,887	$ 4,411,143	$ 5,318,289	$ 6,261,721	$ 7,242,890	$ 8,263,306

Panel b. (Step 1—continued) Terminal Value Cash Flow Estimate

Method #1—DCF Using the Gordon Growth Model

Terminal Value Multiples from the Gordon Model

	Growth Rates (g)			
Discount Rates	0%	1%	2%	3%
8.3%	12.05	13.84	16.19	19.43
8.8%	11.36	12.95	15.00	17.76
9.3%	10.75	12.17	13.97	16.35
9.8%	10.20	11.48	13.08	15.15

Method #2–Multiples Using Enterprise Value to EBITDA Ratio

Terminal Value Estimates

Enterprise Value		Terminal Value
	EBITDA	
	5.00	$104,767,215
	5.50	115,243,936
	6.00	125,720,658
	6.50	136,197,379
	7.00	146,674,101

Terminal Value Estimates (for FFCFs received in 2013 and beyond)

Discount Rates	Growth Rates (g)			
	0%	1%	2%	3%
8.3%	$99,557,908	$114,327,938	$133,786,865	$160,588,784
8.8%	$93,901,209	$106,999,224	$123,949,596	$146,744,924
9.3%	$88,852,757	$100,553,487	$115,459,897	$135,098,501
9.8%	$84,319,453	$94,840,221	$108,058,622	$125,164,788

Panel c. (Step 2) Estimate a "Risk-Appropriate" Discount Rate

■ *Cost of debt*—Estimated borrowing rate is 6.5% with a marginal tax of 25%, resulting in an after-tax cost of debt of 4.875%.

■ *Cost of equity*—An average industry unlevered equity beta of .89 implies a levered equity beta for GRC of 1.28, assuming a target debt ratio of 40% and a debt beta of .30. Using the capital asset pricing model with a 10-year Treasury bond yield of 5.02% and a market risk premium of 5% produces an estimate of the levered cost of equity of 11.42%.

■ *Weighted average cost of capital* (WACC)—Using the target debt-to-value ratio of 40%, the WACC is approximately 8.8%.

Panel d. (Step 3) Calculate the Present Value of Future Cash Flows

		Present Values of Expected Future Cash Flows			
		Terminal Value		Enterprise Value	
Discount Rate	Planning Period FFCF	Method #1	Method #2	Method #1	Method #2
7.8%	$26,201,884	$78,986,073	$80,112,266	$105,187,958	$106,314,150
8.8%	$25,309,857	$74,729,086	$75,794,582	$100,038,943	$101,104,439
9.8%	$24,461,738	$70,737,378	$71,745,960	$95,199,116	$96,207,698

Terminal Values, Expected Growth Rates, and the Cost of Capital

When estimating value using a planning period and a terminal value, how much of the value can be attributed to each of these components? To answer this question, consider the situation where a firm's free cash flows are expected to grow at a rate of 12% per year for a period of five years, followed by a 2% rate of growth thereafter. If the cost of capital for the firm is 10%, then the relative importance of the planning period cash flows and the terminal value cash flows for different planning periods is captured in the upper figure:

If the analyst uses a five-year planning period, then the present value of the planning period cash flows in this setting constitutes 27.45% of the value of the enterprise, leaving over 72.55% of enterprise value in the terminal value. Similarly, if a three-year planning period is used, then the terminal value constitutes 83.83% of the enterprise value estimate, leaving only 16.17% for the planning period. The key observation we can make from this analysis is that the terminal value is at least 50% of the value for the firm for all commonly used planning periods (i.e., three to 10 years).

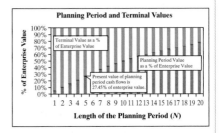

The previous example was obviously a very high-growth firm. It stands to reason, then, that the terminal value may be less important for more stable (low-growth) firms. It turns out (as the lower figure indicates) that even for a very low- and stable-growth firm whose cash flows grow at 2% per year forever, the terminal value is still the dominant component of the enterprise value estimate for the typical three- to 10-year planning period. In this case where the firm has a constant rate of growth of 2% per year for all years, a five-year planning period results in 31.45% of the enterprise value coming from the cash flows in the planning period, which leaves 68.55% of enterprise value in the terminal value.

The message is very clear. The analyst must spend significant time estimating the firm's terminal value. In fact, even for a long (by industry standards) planning period of 10 years, the terminal value for the slow-growth firm above is still roughly half (47%) of the firm's enterprise value.

How important should the terminal value be to the enterprise value of your firm? As the

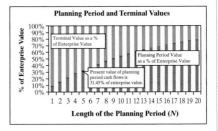

examples we've used above suggest, the answer will vary with the firm's growth prospects and the length of the planning period used in the analysis. In general, terminal value increases in importance with the growth rate in firm cash flows and decreases with the length of the planning period.

assumed to be raised by first retaining 80% of GRC's earnings and then raising any additional funds the firm requires using long-term debt. A quick review of the pro forma balance sheets found in Panel a of Table 7-2, however, indicates that under the status quo strategy GRC's long-term debt actually declines from $40 million at the end of 2006 to $23,608,049 by 2012. This decrease reflects the fact that, given our projections, the firm's retention of future earnings is more than adequate to meet its financing needs, which allows the firm to retire its long-term debt. Finally, GRC's estimated cash flows, also found in Panel a, indicate that from 2007 through 2012 cash flows are expected to grow from $3,538,887 to $8,263,306.

Following the planning period cash flows, Panel b includes two analyses of the terminal value of GRC evaluated in 2012. The first method (Method #1) uses the Gordon growth model (introduced in Chapter 2) to estimate the present value of the firm free cash flows (FFCFs) beginning in 2013 and continuing indefinitely. Specifically, we estimate the terminal value in 2012 using Equation 7.2:

$$\begin{array}{c} \text{Terminal} \\ \text{Value}_{2012} \end{array} = \frac{\text{FFCF}_{2012}\left(1 + \begin{array}{c}\text{Terminal} \\ \text{Growth Rate } (g)\end{array}\right)}{\left(\begin{array}{c}\text{Cost of Capital} \\ (k_{\text{WACC}})\end{array} - \begin{array}{c}\text{Terminal} \\ \text{Growth Rate } (g)\end{array}\right)} \qquad (7.2)$$

To estimate the terminal value using this method, we assume that the cash flows the firm is expected to generate after the end of the planning period grow at a constant rate (g), which is less than the cost of capital (k_{WACC}). Recall from our discussion of multiples in Chapter 6 that Equation 7.2a can be interpreted as a multiple of FFCF_{2012}, where the multiple is equal to the ratio of one plus the terminal growth rate divided by the difference in the cost of capital and the growth rate, i.e.,

$$\begin{array}{c}\text{Terminal} \\ \text{Value}_{2012}\end{array} = \text{FFCF}_{2012}\left(\frac{1 + g}{k_{\text{WACC}} - g}\right) = \text{FFCF}_{2012} \times \left(\begin{array}{c}\text{Gordon Growth} \\ \text{Model Multiple}\end{array}\right) \quad (7.2a)$$

In Panel b of Table 7-2 we report a panel of Gordon growth model multiples that correspond to what Immersion's management thinks is a reasonable range of values of the discount rate and rate of growth in future cash flows. For example, for an 8.8% cost of capital and a 2% terminal growth rate, the multiple for terminal value based on the Gordon growth model, $(\frac{1 + g}{k_{\text{WACC}} - g})$, is 15. Based on the estimated FFCF_{2012} of $8,263,306, this produces an estimate of the terminal value at the end of 2012 of $123,949,596.

In addition to the DCF analysis of the terminal value, Panel b of Table 7-2 provides an analysis that uses EBITDA multiples (Method #2), as shown in Equation 7.3:

$$\begin{array}{c}\text{Terminal} \\ \text{Value}_{2012}\end{array} = \text{EBITDA}_{2012} \times \begin{array}{c}\text{EBITDA} \\ \text{Multiple}\end{array} \qquad (7.3)$$

Multiples ranging from five to seven are reported in Panel b of Table 7-2. Using a multiple of six (which is the multiple reflected in the asking price for GRC) times

EBITDA$_{2012}$ (i.e., the sum of net operating income and depreciation expense for 2012, which equals $7,856,682) produces an estimated terminal value for GRC in 2012 of $125,720,658 = 6 × ($13,096,761 + 7,856,682). It should be noted that the EBITDA multiple and the free cash flow multiple generate very similar terminal value estimates when there are no extraordinary capital expenditures or invest- ments in net working capital. If this were not the case, the analyst would want to double-check his or her assumptions and attempt to reconcile the conflicting terminal value estimates.

Step 2. Estimate a risk-appropriate discount rate. Since the debt financing for GRC is nonrecourse to Immersion, Immersion's finance staff analyzed the cost of capital using the project financing method described earlier in Chapter 5. Details supporting the calculation are provided in Panel c of Table 7-2. The analysis re- sulted in an estimated cost of capital for GRC of 8.8%.

Step 3. Calculate the present value of the expected cash flows, or enterprise value. In Panel d of Table 7-2 we estimate the enterprise value of GRC using the cash flow estimates from Panel a and discounting them with the estimated cost of capital for GRC from Panel c, plus and minus one percent—8.8% (the estimated WACC), 7.8%, and 9.8%. The result is an array of enterprise value estimates reflecting each of the methods used to estimate the terminal value and the range of cost of capital estimates. With the 8.8% cost of capital, the estimate of enterprise value is just slightly higher than $100 million. Indeed, based on the $100 million investment, and the cash flow forecast found in Panel a of Table 7-2, we estimate that the inter- nal rate of return for the acquisition is 9.02% (when the relatively conservative EBITDA multiples are used to compute the terminal value of the cash flows).

Based on this analysis, we can see that the acquisition is fairly priced with an enter- prise value very nearly equal to the $100 million in invested capital. In other words, this is essentially a zero-NPV investment. Given the uncertainties that naturally underlie the cash flow and discount rate estimates, we would not expect Immersion's managers to proceed with this acquisition unless they expect to make changes in the operating strat- egy of the business that will make the investment look more attractive. As we discuss below, Immersion's management does, in fact, wish to consider implementing changes.

Typically, a new owner will consider changes in operating strategies following an acquisition. In this case, Immersion's management is considering a proposal that includes additional expenditures on capital equipment and marketing with the hope of expand- ing GRC's market share. Given the economies of scale associated with manufacturing in this industry, the higher market share will lead to higher operating margins and an enhanced value for the acquired business. The question we need to answer, then, is whether these anticipated changes will, in fact, increase the NPV of the investment.

Valuing GRC under the Growth Strategy

To evaluate the GRC acquisition under the assumed growth strategy, Immersion's analysts carefully revised GRC's projected cash flows and repeated the valuation analy- sis carried out for the status quo case. The results of this analysis are contained in Table 7-3. Panel a of Table 7-3 presents GRC's most recent year's financial statements

Table 7-3 Estimating GRC's Enterprise Value Using DCF Analysis (Growth Strategy)

Panel a. (Step 1) Estimate the Amount and Timing of the Planning Period Future Cash Flows

Planning Period Pro Forma Financial Statements

Pro Forma Income Statements

	Pre-Acquisition 2006	Post-Acquisition 2006	2007	2008	2009	2010	2011	2012
Revenues	$80,000,000	$80,000,000	$86,400,000	$93,312,000	$100,776,960	$108,839,117	$117,546,246	$126,949,946
Cost of goods sold	(45,733,270)	(45,733,270)	(52,564,000)	(56,089,120)	(59,896,250)	(64,007,950)	(68,448,586)	(73,244,472)
Gross profit	$34,266,730	$34,266,730	$33,836,000	$37,222,880	$49,880,710	$44,831,167	$9,097,661	$53,705,473
General and administrative expense	(17,600,000)	(17,600,000)	(21,368,000)	(22,197,440)	(23,093,235)	(21,060,694)	(22,105,550)	(23,233,994)
Depreciation expense	(6,500,000)	(6,500,000)	(7,856,682)	(8,023,349)	(8,190,015)	(8,356,682)	(8,523,349)	(8,690,015)
Net operating income	$10,166,730	$10,166,730	$4,611,318	$7,002,091	$9,597,460	$15,413,791	$18,468,762	$21,781,465
Interest expense	(2,523,020)	(2,523,020)	(2,600,000)	(2,778,968)	(2,887,535)	(2,916,242)	(2,737,729)	(2,453,086)
Earnings before taxes	$7,643,710	$7,643,710	$2,011,318	$4,223,123	$6,709,925	$12,497,549	$15,731,034	$19,328,378
Taxes	(1,910,928)	(1,910,928)	(502,830)	(1,055,781)	(1,677,481)	(3,124,387)	(3,932,758)	(4,832,095)
Net income	$5,732,783	$5,732,783	$1,508,489	$3,167,342	$5,032,444	$9,373,162	$11,798,275	$14,496,284

Pro Forma Balance Sheets

	Pre-Acquisition 2006	Post-Acquisition 2006	2007	2008	2009	2010	2011	2012
Current assets	$41,865,867	$41,865,867	45,215,137	48,832,347	52,738,935	56,958,050	61,514,694	66,435,870
Gross property, plant, and equipment	88,164,876	88,164,876	97,021,558	106,044,907	115,234,922	124,591,604	134,114,953	142,804,968
Less: Accumulated depreciation	(41,024,785)	(41,024,785)	(48,881,467)	(56,904,815)	(65,094,831)	(73,451,513)	(81,974,861)	(90,664,876)
Net property, plant, and equipment	$47,140,092	$47,140,092	$48,140,092	$49,140,092	$50,140,092	$51,140,092	$52,140,092	$52,140,092
Goodwill	—	20,819,867	20,819,867	20,819,867	20,819,867	20,819,867	20,819,867	20,819,867
Total	$89,005,959	$109,825,826	$114,175,095	$118,792,306	$123,698,894	$128,918,009	$134,474,653	$139,395,829

(continued)

Table 7-3 Continued

Pro Forma Balance Sheets

	Pre-Acquisition 2006	Post-Acquisition 2006	2007	2008	2009	2010	2011	2012
Current liabilities	$ 9,825,826	$ 9,825,826	$ 10,214,944	$ 10,628,033	$ 11,067,013	$ 11,533,953	$ 12,031,091	$ 12,471,376
Long-term debt	36,839,923	40,000,000	42,753,361	44,423,608	44,865,262	42,118,906	37,739,792	30,623,656
Total liabilities	$ 46,665,749	$ 49,825,826	$ 52,968,305	$ 55,051,642	$ 55,932,274	$ 53,652,860	$ 49,770,884	$ 43,095,032
Common stock (par)	290,353	340,353	340,353	340,353	340,353	340,353	340,353	340,353
Paid-in capital	20,712,517	38,322,307	38,322,307	38,322,307	38,322,307	38,322,307	38,322,307	38,322,307
Retained earnings	21,337,340	21,337,340	22,544,131	25,078,005	29,103,960	36,602,489	46,041,110	57,638,136
Common equity	$ 42,340,210	$ 60,000,000	$ 61,206,791	$ 63,740,665	$ 67,766,620	$ 75,265,149	$ 84,703,769	$ 96,300,796
Total	$ 89,005,959	$ 109,825,826	$ 114,175,095	$ 118,792,306	$ 123,698,894	$ 128,918,009	$ 134,474,653	$ 139,395,829

Planning Period Cash Flow Estimates

Projected Firm Free Cash Flows

	2007	2008	2009	2010	2011	2012
Net operating income	$4,611,318	7,002,091	$9,597,460	$15,413,791	$18,468,762	$21,781,465
Less: Taxes	(1,152,830)	(1,750,523)	(2,399,365)	(3,853,448)	(4,617,191)	(5,445,366)
NOPAT	$3,458,489	$5,251,569	$7,198,095	$11,560,343	$13,851,572	$16,336,098
Plus: Depreciation	7,856,682	8,023,349	8,190,015	8,356,682	8,523,349	8,690,015
Less: CAPEX	(8,856,682)	(9,023,349)	(9,190,015)	(9,356,682)	(9,523,349)	(8,690,015)
Less: Changes in net working capital	(2,563,203)	(2,768,260)	(2,989,720)	(3,228,898)	(3,487,210)	(3,766,187)
Equals FFCF	$ (104,715)	$1,483,309	$3,208,375	$ 7,331,446	$ 9,364,362	$12,569,912

Panel b. (Step 1—continued) Terminal Value Cash Flow Estimate

Method #1–DCF Using the Gordon Growth Model | *Method #2–Multiples Using Enterprise Value to EBITDA Ratio*

Terminal Value Estimates (for FFCFs received in 2013 and beyond) | **Terminal Value Estimates**

Discount Rates	Growth Rates (g)			
	0%	1%	2%	3%
8.3%	$151,444,722	$173,912,480	$203,512,860	$244,283,194
8.8%	$142,839,909	$162,764,244	$188,548,679	$223,224,298
9.3%	$135,160,344	$152,959,169	$175,634,386	$205,508,084
9.8%	$128,264,408	$144,268,308	$164,375,772	$190,397,196

Enterprise Value	
EBITDA	Terminal Value
5.00	$ 152,356,701
5.50	$ 167,592,441
6.00	$ 182,828,181
6.50	$ 198,063,921
7.00	$ 213,299,661

Panel c. (Step 2) Estimate a "Risk-Appropriate" Discount Rate

Based on the analysis presented in Panel c of Table 7-1, GRC's WACC is estimated to be 8.8%.

Panel d. (Step 3) Calculate the Present Value of Future Cash Flows

Present Values of Expected Future Cash Flows

Discount Rate	Planning Period FFCF	Terminal Value		Enterprise Value	
		Method #1	Method #2	Method #1	Method #2
7.8%	$23,611,874	$129,683,352	$116,502,541	$153,295,226	$140,114,445
8.8%	**$22,600,651**	**$122,694,014**	**$110,223,616**	**$145,294,665**	**$132,824,267**
9.8%	$21,643,890	$116,140,225	$104,335,942	$137,784,115	$125,979,832

289

(for 2006, both pre- and post-acquisition) and pro forma financial statements for the six-year planning period that spans 2007 through 2012.

The growth strategy involves increased expenditures on marketing as well as the addition of new manufacturing capacity. Specifically, the plan calls for spending an additional $3 million per year on advertising, plus an additional $1 million per year on capital equipment throughout the six-year planning period. Immersion's analysts expect the combined effect of these actions to double the planning period rate of growth in sales to 8% per year, compared to only 4% under the status quo strategy. After achieving the higher target market share in 2012, capital expenditures and marketing expenditures are expected to return to the status quo levels, and the expected rate of growth in firm free cash flows for 2013 and beyond is assumed to be 2%, just as in the status quo case.

Comparing the cash flow projections for the status quo strategy found in Panel a of Table 7-2 with those of the growth strategy in Panel a of Table 7-3, we see that the growth strategy has the initial effect of reducing cash flows below status quo levels for 2007–2009. However, beginning in 2010 the growth strategy expected cash flows exceed those of the status quo strategy ($7,331,446 for the growth strategy versus $6,261,721 for the status quo strategy), and continue to be higher for all subsequent years.

Since the growth strategy initially has lower cash flows than the status quo strategy but later generates much higher cash flows, its incremental value will depend on the discount rate that is used to evaluate the strategy. In Panel c of Table 7-3 we initially assume that the cost of capital for the growth strategy is the same as that for the status quo strategy (i.e., 8.8%). In this case, the enterprise value estimates are dramatically higher than under the status quo strategy, producing an expected enterprise value of $145,294,665 when the Gordon growth model is used to estimate the terminal value (Method #1 in Panel d of Table 7-3) and $132,824,267 when a six-times-EBITDA multiple is used to estimate the terminal value.

However, the growth strategy is almost certainly more risky than the status quo strategy and should require a higher cost of capital. To evaluate how a higher cost of capital will affect the value of the growth strategy, Panel d of Table 7-3 presents values of the growth strategy cash flows with alternative discount rates as high as 12%. Although the NPV is reduced, it remains positive even using a 12% discount rate, which represents an increase of over 30% in the 8.8% cost of capital we used to value the status quo strategy.

Sensitivity Analysis

The acquisition of GRC is a risky investment, so it is important that we perform a sensitivity analysis of the proposal. In this instance we will limit ourselves to the use of breakeven sensitivity analysis although, as we illustrated in Chapter 3, it is also useful to examine a simulation model that calculates the influence of the key value drivers.

We consider three important value drivers for the GRC acquisition under the growth strategy. The first relates to the cost of capital for the acquisition and the second and third pertain to determinants of the level of the future cash flows: (1) the estimated rate of growth in GRC's cash flows during the planning period and (2) the terminal value multiple used to value the post-planning-period cash flows. In the risk analysis that follows, we focus our attention solely on the valuation that uses the EBITDA multiple (Method #2) to estimate the terminal value.

Sensitivity Analysis—Cost of Capital

The cost of capital, like all the value drivers, is always estimated with some error. However, in this instance we have another reason to be concerned about the cost of capital estimate. The growth strategy is a more risky strategy than the status quo strategy, which means that the growth strategy cash flows should require a higher discount rate—but how much higher? One approach we can take to addressing this issue is to explore the importance of the discount rate to the valuation of GRC under the growth strategy. To do this, we can calculate the internal rate of return (IRR) of the investment and ask whether it is plausible that the appropriate discount rate exceeds the IRR. Recall that we considered a similar question when evaluating the status quo strategy where the IRR was only 9.02% and the cost of capital was 8.8%. In that instance there was little room for error in estimating the WACC.

We calculate the IRR for the acquisition based on the expected cash flows found in Panel a in Table 7-3 (and a terminal value for 2012 equal to six times $EBITDA_{2012}$) and the $100 million in invested capital reflected in the asking price. Based on these assumptions, the investment has an IRR of 14.28%. Consequently, if the higher cost of capital for the riskier growth strategy exceeds 14.28%, the acquisition should not be undertaken. Although the appropriate discount rate for this investment is likely to be higher than the discount rate for the status quo investment, it is quite unlikely that it exceeds 14.28%. In Panel c of Table 7-2 we noted that GRC's estimated equity beta was 1.28, which generates a cost of equity of 11.42% and a weighted average cost of capital of 8.8%. To generate a cost of capital of 14.28%, GRC's equity beta would have to rise to 3.11, which is highly unlikely.

Sensitivity Analysis—Revenue Growth Rate

Next we consider a breakeven sensitivity analysis of the planning period rate of growth in revenues. This analysis reveals that the 8% expected rate of growth in revenues can be reduced to only 5% (recall that the status quo strategy assumes a 4% rate of growth in revenues) before the acquisition value drops to the $100 million purchase price.[3] The rate of growth in revenues and consequently firm earnings is very important since it not only determines what the annual cash flows will be during the planning period but also has an important impact on terminal value by increasing the level of $EBITDA_{2012}$.

Sensitivity Analysis—Terminal Value EBITDA Multiple

The final value driver we consider is the terminal value multiple (i.e., enterprise value divided by EBITDA) that is used to estimate the terminal value of GRC in 2012. In our earlier analysis we used a multiple of six, which was the purchase price multiple

---

[3]Note that we are holding everything constant except the revenue growth rate in this analysis. For instance, the discount rate is still assumed to be 8.8%.

Immersion must pay for GRC. However, if we reduce this terminal value EBITDA multiple to 4.21, the present value of the acquisition drops to the $100 million acquisition price for GRC.

Scenario Analysis

Up to this point we have considered three value drivers (the discount rate, the growth rate, and the EBITDA multiple at the terminal date)—one at a time. This discussion suggests that our conclusion about the attractiveness of the investment is not likely to change if we alter any one of the value drivers individually. However, there are scenarios in which all three value drivers differ from their expected values that results in a negative NPV for the GRC investment. For example, although we argued that a 14% discount rate is very unlikely, a 10% discount rate is plausible. Similarly, one might assume that the planning period revenue growth rate may be 6% rather than 8%. If these changes are made, then the terminal value EBITDA multiple only has to drop to 5.73 times before the enterprise value of GRC under the growth strategy drops to the $100 million acquisition price.

As the following table indicates, there are a number of plausible scenarios under which the acquisition and implementation of the growth strategy might not be value-enhancing. For example, with a 5.5 EBITDA multiple for our terminal value calculation, the acquisition is worth just over $96 million (i.e., becomes a negative-NPV investment) if we also make slightly less favorable assumptions about the discount rate (10%) and the revenue growth rate for the planning period (6%). As we learned earlier in Chapter 3, reviewing likely, but less favorable, scenarios that can lead to a negative NPV is a very powerful tool for learning about an investment's risk.

Value Driver	Initial Parameters	Breakeven Scenarios			Negative-NPV Scenario
		Scenario #1	Scenario #2	Scenario #3	Scenario #4
Cost of capital	8.8%	10%	**10.72%**	9%	**10%**
Revenue growth rate during the planning period	8%	6%	6%	**5.1%**	**6%**
Terminal value EBITDA multiple	6 times	**5.73 times**	6 times	6 times	**5.5 times**
Enterprise value	$132,824,688	$100,000,000	$100,000,000	$100,000,000	$96,634,832

The scenarios reviewed above are far from exhaustive, and we can always find scenarios under which almost any investment has either a positive or negative NPV. What this means is that the tools that we have developed are just that—decision tools. They provide support and background for the actual decision maker, but they do not

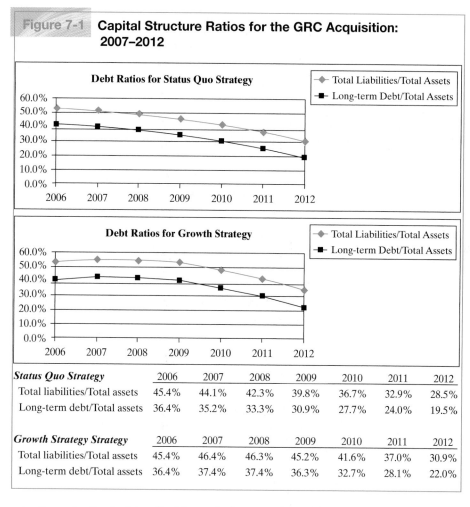

Figure 7-1 **Capital Structure Ratios for the GRC Acquisition: 2007–2012**

Status Quo Strategy	2006	2007	2008	2009	2010	2011	2012
Total liabilities/Total assets	45.4%	44.1%	42.3%	39.8%	36.7%	32.9%	28.5%
Long-term debt/Total assets	36.4%	35.2%	33.3%	30.9%	27.7%	24.0%	19.5%

Growth Strategy Strategy	2006	2007	2008	2009	2010	2011	2012
Total liabilities/Total assets	45.4%	46.4%	46.3%	45.2%	41.6%	37.0%	30.9%
Long-term debt/Total assets	36.4%	37.4%	37.4%	36.3%	32.7%	28.1%	22.0%

actually make the decision. In this particular case, the numbers do not provide a clear picture about whether or not Immersion should go forward with the acquisition. This will generally be the case. The tools provide management with valuable information, but ultimately management must use their judgment to make the decision.

7.3 USING THE APV MODEL TO ESTIMATE ENTERPRISE VALUE

Up to this point we have been using the **traditional WACC approach,** which uses a constant discount rate to value the enterprise cash flows. While this approach makes sense for valuing GRC prior to its acquisition by Immersion Chemical Corporation, the constant discount rate is inconsistent with the projected changes in the firm's capital structure after GRC's acquisition. A quick review of the debt ratios found in Figure 7-1 indicates that the capital structure weights (measured here in terms of book values) are not constant over time for either the status quo or growth strategy. As a result, *the use of a single discount rate is problematic.*

In situations in which the firm's capital structure is expected to substantially change over time, we recommend that the **adjusted present value, or APV approach,** be used.

Introducing the APV Approach

The APV approach expresses enterprise value as the sum of the following two components:

$$\text{Enterprise Value (APV Approach)} = \begin{pmatrix} \text{Value of the} \\ \text{Unlevered Equity} \\ \text{Free Cash Flows} \end{pmatrix} + \begin{pmatrix} \text{Value of the} \\ \text{Interest} \\ \text{Tax Savings} \end{pmatrix} \quad (7.4)$$

The first component is the value of the firm's operating cash flows. Since the operating cash flows are not affected by how the firm is financed, we refer to these cash flows as the unlevered equity free cash flows. The present value of the unlevered equity free cash flows represents the value of the firm's cash flows under the assumption that the firm is 100% equity financed. The second component on the right-hand side of Equation 7.4 is the present value of the interest tax savings associated with the firm's use of debt financing. The basic premise of the APV approach is that debt financing provides a tax benefit because of the interest tax deduction.[4] By decomposing firm value in this way, the analyst is forced to deal explicitly with how the financing choice influences enterprise value.

Using the APV Approach to Value GRC under the Growth Strategy

The APV approach is typically implemented using a procedure very similar to what we did to estimate the enterprise value using the traditional WACC approach found in Equation 7.1 and is described in Equation 7.4a.

$$\text{Enterprise Value (APV Approach)} = \begin{pmatrix} \text{Value of the} \\ \text{Unlevered Equity} \\ \text{Free Cash Flows} \\ \text{for the Planning Period} \end{pmatrix} + \begin{pmatrix} \text{Value of the} \\ \text{Planning Period} \\ \text{Interest Tax} \\ \text{Savings} \end{pmatrix} + \begin{pmatrix} \text{Present Value} \\ \text{of the Estimated} \\ \text{Terminal Value} \end{pmatrix} \quad (7.4a)$$

That is, we make detailed projections of cash flows for a finite planning period and then capture the value of all cash flows after the planning period in a terminal value. From a practical perspective the principal difference between the APV and traditional

---

[4]Technically the second term can be an amalgam that captures all potential "side effects" of the firm's financing decisions. In addition to interest tax savings, the firm may also realize financing benefits that come in the form of below-market or subsidized financing. For example, when one firm acquires assets or an operating division from another, it is not uncommon for the seller to help finance the purchase with a very attractive loan rate.

WACC approaches is that, with the APV approach, we have two cash flow streams to value: the unlevered equity cash flows and the interest tax savings.

Figure 7-2 summarizes the implementation of the APV approach in three steps: First, we estimate the value of the planning period cash flows in two components: unlevered equity (or operating) cash flows, and interest tax savings resulting from the firm's use of debt financing. In Step 2 we estimate the residual or terminal value of the levered firm at the end of the planning period, and finally, in Step 3, we sum the present values of the planning period cash flows and the terminal value to estimate the enterprise value of the firm.

Step 1: Estimate the Value of the Planning Period Cash Flows

The planning period cash flows are comprised of both the unlevered equity free cash flows and the interest tax savings. We value these cash flows for GRC using two separate calculations. Equation 7.5 shows how we value the unlevered equity cash flows for the planning period (PP):[5]

$$\begin{matrix} \text{Value of the} \\ \text{Planning Period} \\ \text{Unlevered Equity} \\ \text{Free Cash Flows} \end{matrix} = \sum_{t=1}^{PP} \frac{FFCF_t}{(1 + k_{Unlevered})^t} \qquad (7.5)$$

Applying Equation 7.5 to the valuation of GRC's operating cash flows for the planning period (2007–2012) for the growth strategy case summarized in Table 7-4, we estimate a value of $21,955,607:

$$\begin{matrix} \text{Value of the} \\ \text{Unlevered Equity} \\ \text{Free Cash Flows} \end{matrix} = \left(\frac{\$(104,715)}{(1 + .0947)^1} + \frac{\$1,483,309}{(1 + .0947)^2} + \frac{\$3,208,375}{(1 + .0947)^3} \right.$$
$$\left. + \frac{\$7,331,446}{(1 + .0947)^4} + \frac{\$9,364,362}{(1 + .0947)^5} + \frac{\$12,569,912}{(1 + .0947)^6} \right)$$
$$= \$21,955,607$$

This valuation is based on an estimate of the unlevered cost of equity equal to 9.47%. We estimate the unlevered cost of equity in Figure 7-3 using the procedure described in Table 4-1 of Chapter 4, where we estimated the firm's WACC, and used again in Chapter 5 to estimate a project's cost of capital. The estimated unlevered beta for GRC is .89, which when combined with a 10-year U.S. Treasury yield of 5.02% and a 5% market risk premium generates an unlevered cost of equity of 9.47%.

Next we calculate the value of the interest tax savings for the planning period as follows:

$$\begin{matrix} \text{Value of the} \\ \text{Planning Period} \\ \text{Interest Tax Savings} \end{matrix} = \sum_{t=1}^{PP} \frac{\text{Interest Expense}_t \times \text{Tax Rate}}{(1 + r)^t} \qquad (7.6)$$

---

[5]Recall from our earlier discussion in Chapter 2 that firm free cash flow (FFCF) is the same as the equity free cash flow for an unlevered firm.

Figure 7-2

Using the Adjusted Present Value (APV) Model to Estimate Enterprise Value

Step 1: Estimate the Value of the Planning Period Cash Flows

Evaluation of Operating (unlevered) Cash Flows

Definition: Unlevered Equity Free Cash Flows = Firm or Project Free Cash Flows

Net operating income

Less: Taxes

Net operating profit after taxes (NOPAT)

Plus: Depreciation expense

Less: Capital expenditures (CAPEX)

Less: Increases in net working capital

Equals unlevered equity free cash flows = FFCF

Formula:

$$\text{Value of Planning Period Unlevered Equity Cash Flows} = \sum_{t=1}^{PP} \frac{FFCF_t}{(1 + k_{\text{Unlevered}})^t}$$

$FFCF_t$ = firm free cash flows (equals equity free cash flows for the unlevered firm)

$k_{\text{Unlevered}}$ = discount rate for project cash flows (unlevered equity)

PP = planning period

Evaluation of the Interest Tax Savings

Definition: Interest Tax Savings

Interest Tax Savings in Year t = Interest Expense in Year t × Tax Rate

Formula:

$$\text{Value of the Interest Tax Saving} = \left[\sum_{t=1}^{PP} \frac{\text{Interest Expense}_t \times \text{Tax Rate}}{(1 + r)^t} \right]$$

PP = planning period

r = firm's borrowing rate

Step 2: Estimate the Value of the Levered Firm at the End of the Planning Period (i.e., the terminal value)

Evaluation of the Terminal Value

Definition: Terminal value of firm is equal to the enterprise value of the levered firm at the end of the planning period.

Assumptions:
- After the planning period the firm maintains a constant proportion, L, of debt in its capital structure.
- The firm's cash flows grow at a constant rate g, which is less than the firm's weighted average cost of capital forever.

Formula:

$$\text{Terminal Value of the Levered Firm}_{\text{PP}} = \frac{FFCF_{\text{PP}}(1 + g)}{k_{\text{WACC}} - g}$$

$FFCF_{\text{PP}}$ = firm free cash flows for the end of the planning period

k_{WACC} = weighted average cost of capital

g = rate of growth in FFCF after the end of the planning period in perpetuity

Step 1: Value of Planning Period Cash Flows

Step 2: Value of the Terminal Period Cash Flows

Step 3: Sum the Estimated Values for the Planning Period and Terminal Period Cash Flows

$$\text{APV Model of Enterprise Value} = \left[\sum_{t=1}^{PP} \frac{FFCF_t}{(1 + k_{\text{Unlevered}})^t} + \sum_{t=1}^{PP} \frac{\text{Interest Expense}_t \times \text{Tax Rate}}{(1 + r)^t} \right] + \left[\left(\frac{FFCF_{\text{PP}}(1 + g)}{k_{\text{WACC}} - g} \right) \left(\frac{1}{1 + k_{\text{Unlevered}}} \right)^{PP} \right]$$

where r is the firm's borrowing rate. Substituting GRC's interest tax savings for the growth strategy (found in Table 7-4) into Equation 7.6 produces a $3,307,031 estimate for the value of its planning period interest tax savings.

$$
\begin{aligned}
\begin{matrix} \text{Value of the} \\ \text{Planning Period} \\ \text{Interest Tax Savings} \end{matrix} &= \left(\frac{\$650,000}{(1+.065)^1} + \frac{\$694,742}{(1+.065)^2} + \frac{\$721,884}{(1+.065)^3} \right. \\
&\left. + \frac{\$729,061}{(1+.065)^4} + \frac{\$684,432}{(1+.065)^5} + \frac{\$613,272}{(1+.065)^6} \right) \\
&= \$3,307,031
\end{aligned}
$$

The combined value of operating cash flows and interest tax savings for the planning period under the growth strategy, then, is $25,262,638 = $21,955,607 + 3,307,031.

Step 2: Estimate GRC's Terminal Value

The terminal value calculation for the APV approach is identical to the calculation we made for our WACC analysis. As we previously stated, at the terminal date, GRC's cash flows are assumed to grow at a constant rate of 2% per year, and its capital structure will revert to a constant mix of debt and equity, keeping the debt-to-value ratio at 40%. Therefore, we can use the Gordon growth model to estimate the terminal value of the levered firm at the end of the planning period (PP) as follows:

$$
\begin{matrix} \text{Terminal Value of the} \\ \text{Levered Firm}_{PP} \end{matrix} = \frac{FFCF_{PP}(1 + g)}{k_{WACC} - g} \qquad (7.8)
$$

GRC's $FFCF_{PP}$ in 2012 (which is the end of the planning period) is equal to $12,569,912 (see Table 7-4), and this FFCF is expected to grow at a rate g of 2% in perpetuity; the

---

Table 7-4   **GRC's Operating and Financial Cash Flows for the Planning Period**

Panel a. Unlevered Equity Free Cash Flows (same as FFCF)

	2007	2008	2009	2010	2011	2012
Status quo strategy	$3,538,887	$4,411,143	$5,318,289	$6,261,721	$7,242,890	$ 8,263,306
Growth strategy	$ (104,715)	$1,483,309	$3,208,375	$7,331,446	$9,364,362	$12,569,912

Panel b. Interest Tax Savings

	2007	2008	2009	2010	2011	2012
Status quo strategy	$ 650,000	$ 637,462	$ 613,420	$ 576,985	$ 527,216	$ 463,116
Growth strategy	$ 650,000	$ 694,742	$ 721,884	$ 729,061	$ 684,432	$ 613,272

Figure 7-3	**Three-Step Process for Estimating GRC's Unlevered Cost of Equity**

Step 1:   Identify a set of firms that operate in the same line of business as GRC. For each market comp, either estimate directly or locate published estimates of its levered equity beta, β_{Levered}, the book value of the firm's interest-bearing debt, and the market capitalization of the firm's equity.[6]

GRC: A review of the specialty chemical industry reveals four firms that are reasonably similar to GRC. Their equity betas (i.e., levered equity betas) range from .88 to 1.45, and their debt-to-equity ratios range from 35% to 80%.

Comparable Firms	Levered Equity Betas	Debt/Equity Ratio	Assumed Debt Beta	Unlevered Equity Betas
A	1.45	0.65	0.30	1.00
B	1.40	0.60	0.30	0.99
C	0.88	0.35	0.30	0.73
D	1.25	0.80	0.30	0.83
Averages	1.25	0.60		0.89

Step 2:   Unlever each of the levered equity beta coefficients and average them to get an estimate of GRC's unlevered equity beta. The unlevering process uses the following relationship:[7]

$$\beta_{\text{Unlevered}} = \frac{\beta_{\text{Levered}} + \left(1 - T \times \dfrac{r_d}{1 + r_d}\right) L \beta_{\text{Debt}}}{1 + \left(1 - T \times \dfrac{r_d}{1 + r_d}\right) L} \qquad (7.7)$$

where $\beta_{\text{Unlevered}}$, β_{Levered}, and β_{Debt} are the betas for the firm's unlevered and levered equity, plus its debt. The cost of debt is r_d, T is the corporate tax rate, and L is the debt-to-equity ratio.

[6]Typically, debt is estimated using the book value of the firm's interest-bearing liabilities (short-term notes payable, the current portion of the firm's long-term debt, plus long-term debt). Although we should technically use the market value of the firm's debt, it is customary to use book values since most corporate debt is thinly traded if at all. The equity capitalization of the firm is estimated using the current market price of the firm's shares multiplied by the number of outstanding shares. Betas for individual stocks can be obtained from a number of published sources, including virtually all online investment information sources such as Yahoo Finance or Microsoft's MoneyCentral Web site.

[7]This relationship captures the effects of financial leverage on the firm's beta coefficient. It is a more general version of a similar formula discussed in Chapter 5. It applies in the setting where the firm faces uncertain perpetual cash flows and corporate taxes, corporate debt is risky (i.e., debt betas are greater than zero), and the firm's use of financial leverage (i.e., the debt-to-equity ratio, L) is reset every period to keep leverage constant. For a derivation of Equation 7.7, see E. Arzac and L. Glosten, "A Reconsideration of Tax Shield Valuation," unpublished manuscript, 2004.

Figure 7-3 *Continued*
GRC: Applying Equation 7.7 to the levered equity betas of the four comparable firms produces an average unlevered equity beta of .89. Note that we have assumed a debt beta of .30 for the debt of all four comparable firms and a corporate tax rate of 25%. Research has shown that debt betas range from .20 to .40 in practice. In addition, we assume that the corporate debt yield for each of the comparable firms is equal to GRC's 6.5% borrowing rate. Where significant differences in debt ratings and consequently borrowing rates are present, we use firm-specific borrowing rates in the beta unlevering process described in Equation 7.7 before.
Step 3: Substitute the average unlevered equity beta into the CAPM to estimate the unlevered cost of equity for the subject firm.
GRC: Substituting our estimate of GRC's unlevered equity beta into the CAPM, where the risk-free rate is 5.02% and the market risk premium is 5%, we get an estimated cost of equity for an unlevered investment of 9.47%, i.e., $k_{\text{Unlevered equity}} = \text{Risk-Free Rate} + \beta_{\text{Unlevered}} \text{(Market Risk Premium)}$ $k_{\text{Unlevered equity}} = .0502 + .89 \times .05 = .09472 \text{ or } 9.47\%$

weighted average cost of capital (k_{WACC}) is 8.8%.[8] Using Equation 7.8 we estimate the terminal value for GRC in 2012 as follows:

$$\text{Terminal Value of the Levered Firm}_{2012} = \frac{\$12,569,912(1 + .02)}{.088 - .02} = \$188,554,340$$

We have one remaining calculation to make in order to value GRC's terminal value. We need to discount the terminal value estimated in Equation 7.8 back to the present using the unlevered cost of equity, i.e.,

$$\text{Present Value of the Terminal Value}_{2006} = \left(\frac{\$12,569,912(1 + .02)}{.088 - .02}\right)\left(\frac{1}{(1 + .0947)^6}\right) = \$131,531,641$$

To complete the valuation of GRC using the APV method, we now sum the value of the planning period and terminal value in the final step.

---

[8] The weighted average cost of capital can also be related to the unlevered cost of equity capital by using the following relationship:

$$k_{\text{WACC}} = k_{\text{Unlevered}} - r(\text{Tax Rate})\frac{L}{1 + L}\left(\frac{1 + k_{\text{Unlevered}}}{1 + r_d}\right)$$

$$k_{\text{WACC}} = .0947 - .065 \times .25 \times \left(\frac{.40}{1 + .40}\right) \times \left(\frac{1 + .0947}{1 + .065}\right) = .088 \text{ or } 8.8\%$$

where L is the ratio of debt to enterprise value for the firm, which is assumed to be 40% in the GRC example.

Step 3: Summing the Values of the Planning Period and Terminal Period

Using the APV approach, we estimate the enterprise value of the firm as the following sum:

$$\text{Enterprise Value} \atop \text{(APV Approach)} = \left[\underbrace{\sum_{t=1}^{PP} \frac{FFCF_t}{(1 + k_{Unlevered})^t} + \sum_{t=1}^{PP} \frac{\text{Interest Expense}_t \times \text{Tax Rate}}{(1 + r)^t}}_{\textbf{Value of Planning Period Cash Flows}} \right]$$

$$+ \underbrace{\left[\frac{FFCF_{PP}(1 + g)}{k_{WACC} - g} \left(\frac{1}{1 + k_{Unlevered}} \right)^{PP} \right]}_{\textbf{Value of the Terminal Period Cash Flows}} \qquad (7.4a)$$

Substituting for the two components, we estimate GRC's enterprise value using the APV model to be \$134,838,672, i.e.,

$$\text{Enterprise Value} \atop \text{(APV Approach)} = \$21,955,607 + \$3,307,031 + \$134,798,673 = \$134,838,672$$

Using an EBITDA Multiple to Calculate the Terminal Value

The preceding application of the APV approach to the estimation of GRC's enterprise value used the discounted cash flow (DCF) approach to value both the planning period value and the post–planning period terminal value. What typically happens in practice, however, is that a market-based multiple is used to estimate the value of the post–planning period cash flows. Equation 7.4b defines the APV approach of enterprise value as the sum of the present values of the planning period cash flows (i.e., both the unlevered cash flows of the firm[9] and the interest tax savings) plus the terminal value of the firm, which is estimated using the EBITDA multiple, i.e.,

$$\text{Enterprise Value} \atop \text{(Hybrid APV Approach)} = \left(\begin{matrix} \text{Value of the Unlevered} & \text{Value of the Planning} \\ \text{Equity Free Cash Flows} + & \text{Period Interest Tax} \\ \text{for the Planning Period} & \text{Savings} \end{matrix} \right)$$

$$+ \left(\begin{matrix} \text{Present Value of the} \\ \text{EBITDA Multiple Estimate} \\ \text{of Terminal Value} \end{matrix} \right) \qquad (7.4b)$$

---

[9]Recall from Chapter 2 that the unlevered cash flows of a firm are simply the cash flows that the firm would realize if it uses no debt financing. Furthermore, these unlevered cash flows are the same as the firm free cash flows (FFCFs) calculated earlier to value the firm using the traditional WACC model. However, in the APV model we discount the FFCFs using the unlevered cost of equity capital (i.e., the equity discount rate appropriate for a firm that uses no debt financing) and then account for the value of the firm's interest tax savings as a separate present-value calculation.

The values of the two planning period cash flow streams for GRC under the growth strategy were estimated earlier using Table 7-4, and equal $21,955,607 for the operating cash flows and $3,307,031 for the interest tax savings. Using the six times multiple of EBITDA from our previous analysis and the estimated EBITDA for 2012 (found using Table 7-4), we calculate GRC's terminal value cash flow as follows:

$$\begin{aligned}\text{Present Value of the} \\ \text{Estimated Terminal} \\ \text{Value}_{2006}\end{aligned} = \frac{\text{Terminal Value}_{2012}}{(1 + k_{\text{Unlevered}})^6} = \frac{6 \times \text{EBITDA}_{2012}}{(1 + .0947)^6}$$

$$= \frac{\$182,828,880}{(1 + .0947)^6} = \$106,248,753$$

EBITDA for 2012 is found using Table 7-3 by summing net operating income, which equals $21,781,465, and depreciation expense, which equals $8,690,015, to get $30,471,480. Multiplying this EBITDA estimate by six produces an estimate of the terminal value in 2012 of $182,828,880. Discounting the terminal value back to the present using the unlevered cost of equity, we get $106,248,753. To complete the estimate of enterprise value using the hybrid APV, we simply substitute our estimates of the values of the cash flow streams into Equation 7.4b as follows:

$$\begin{aligned}\text{Enterprise Value} \\ \text{(Hybrid APV Approach)}\end{aligned} = \$21,955,607 + \$3,307,031 + \$106,248,753$$

$$= \$131,511,391$$

This value is slightly lower than our earlier estimate because in this case the EBITDA multiple provided a more conservative estimate of GRC's terminal value.

Table 7-5 summarizes the APV estimates of enterprise value for the status quo and growth strategies using our two methods for estimating terminal value.

Comparing the WACC and APV Estimates of GRC's Enterprise Value

Table 7-6 combines our estimates of GRC's enterprise value using both the traditional WACC approach and the APV approach. Although the estimates are not exactly the same, they are quite similar. In all cases the GRC acquisition at a price of $100 million appears to be a good investment, and the growth strategy clearly dominates the status quo strategy.

In this particular application of the WACC and APV valuation approaches, the results are for all practical purposes the same. There are cases, however, where capital structure effects caused by very dramatic changes in debt financing over the life of the investment can lead to meaningful differences in the results of the two valuation approaches, and in these instances the APV approach has a clear advantage in that it can more easily accommodate the effects of changing capital structure.

The EBITDA multiple used in the valuation of GRC produced results that were very similar to the DCF estimate, and this is purely an artifact of the particular

Table 7-5   APV Valuation Summary for GRC for Status Quo and Growth Strategies

Panel a. Status Quo Strategy

APV Estimate of Enterprise Value

	Present Values		
	APV Calculation of Planning Period Cash Flows	DCF Estimates of Terminal Values	Total
Unlevered equity free cash flows	$ 24,738,517	$ 72,033,945	$ 96,772,462
Interest tax savings	2,830,870	—	2,830,870
Total	$ 27,569,388	$ 72,033,945	**$ 99,603,332**

Hybrid APV Estimate of Enterprise Value

	Present Values		
	APV Calculation of Planning Period Cash Flows	EBITDA Multiple Terminal Value	Total
Unlevered equity free cash flows	$ 24,738,517	$ 73,060,734	$ 97,799,251
Interest tax savings	2,830,870	—	2,830,870
Total	$ 27,569,388	$ 73,060,734	**$ 100,630,121**

Panel b. Growth Strategy

APV Estimate of Enterprise Value

	Present Values		
	APV Calculation of Planning Period Cash Flows	DCF Estimates of Terminal Values	Total
Unlevered equity free cash flows	$ 21,955,607	109,576,035	131,531,641
Interest tax savings	3,307,031	—	3,307,031
Total	$ 25,262,638	109,576,035	**134,838,671**

Hybrid APV Estimate of Enterprise Value

	Present Values		
	APV Calculation of Planning Period Cash Flows	EBITDA Multiple Terminal Value	Total
Unlevered equity free cash flows	$ 21,955,607	$ 106,248,753	$ 128,204,360
Interest tax savings	3,307,031	—	3,307,031
Total	$ 25,262,638	$ 106,248,753	**$ 131,511,391**

Table 7-6	**Summary of WACC and APV Estimates of GRC's Enterprise Value**	
Status Quo Strategy	**Traditional WACC**	**APV**
DCF estimate of terminal value	$ 100,038,943	$ 99,603,333
EBITDA multiple estimate of terminal value	101,104,149	100,630,121
Growth Strategy	**Traditional WACC**	**APV**
DCF estimate of terminal value	$ 136,276,460	$ 134,838,672
EBITDA multiple estimate of terminal value	132,824,689	131,511,391

Legend

Status quo strategy represents a set of cash flow estimates that correspond to the current method of operations of the business.

Growth strategy represents cash flow estimates reflecting the implementation of an explicit plan to grow the business by making additional investments in capital equipment and changing the current method of operating the firm.

DCF estimate of terminal value is based on the Gordon growth model, where cash flows are expected to grow at a constant rate of 2% per year, indefinitely.

EBITDA multiple estimate of terminal value is based on a six times multiple of EBITDA estimated for 2012 (the end of the planning period).

choices made in carrying out this valuation. Due to the importance of the terminal value to the overall estimate of enterprise value, we recommend that both approaches be used and that when selecting an EBITDA multiple, close attention be paid to recent transactions involving closely comparable firms. The advantage of the EBITDA multiple in this setting is that it ties the analysis of more distant cash flows back to a recent market transaction. However, the EBITDA multiple estimate of terminal value should be compared to a DCF estimate using the analyst's estimates of reasonable growth rates as a test of the reasonableness of the terminal value estimate based on multiples.

A Brief Summary of the WACC and APV Valuation Approaches

The following grid provides a summary of the salient features of the traditional WACC and APV approaches. As we have discussed, the traditional WACC method is the approach that is used in practice. However, when the capital structure of the firm being valued is likely to be changing over time, the APV is the preferred approach.

	Adjusted Present Value (APV) Method	**Traditional WACC Method**
Object of the Analysis	*Enterprise value* as the sum of the values of: ■ The unlevered equity cash flows, and ■ Financing side effects	*Enterprise value* equal to the present value of the firm's capital cash flows discounted using the after-tax WACC
Cash Flow Calculation	■ Unlevered equity free cash flows (i.e., firm free cash flows), plus ■ Interest tax savings	Firm free cash flows (FFCF)
Discount Rate(s)	■ Unlevered equity cash flows—cost of equity for unlevered firm, and ■ Interest tax savings—the yield to maturity on the firm's debt	After-tax weighted average cost of capital (WACC)
How Capital Structure Effects Are Dealt with—Discount Rates, Cash Flows, or Both	*Cash flows*—Capital structure affects the present value of the interest tax savings only. The value of the unlevered firm is not affected by the firm's use of debt financing.	*Discount rate*—The debt-equity mix in the firm's capital structure affects the firm's WACC. However, the mix of debt and equity is assumed to be constant throughout the life of the investment.

Technical Issues—Equations

| **Valuation Models** | *Enterprise Value*

$\text{Enterprise Value} = \text{Value of the Unlevered Firm} + \text{Value of Interest Tax Savings}$

$= \sum_{t=1}^{\infty} \frac{\text{EFCF}_t^{\text{Unlevered}}}{(1 + k_{\text{Unlevered}})^t}$

$+ \sum_{t=1}^{\infty} \frac{\text{Interest} \times \text{Tax Rate}}{(1 + k_{\text{Debt}})^t}$

where
$\text{EFCF}_t^{\text{Unlevered}}$ = equity free cash flows for an unlevered firm (same as FFCF$_t$).
k_u = cost of equity for an unlevered firm | *Enterprise Value*

$\text{Enterprise Value} = \sum_{t=1}^{\infty} \frac{\text{FFCF}_t}{(1 + k_{\text{WACC}})^t}$

where
FFCF$_t$ = firm free cash flow for year$_t$
k_{WACC} = the firm's weighted average cost of capital |

User's Guide

| **Choosing the Right Model** | Although not as popular as the traditional WACC method, this approach is gaining support and is particularly attractive when valuing highly leveraged transactions, such as LBOs, where capital structure is not stationary through time. | Most widely used methodology for valuing individual investment projects (capital budgeting) and entire firms. Since the discount rate (the WACC) assumes constant weights for debt and equity, this method is not well suited for situations where dramatic changes in capital structure are anticipated (e.g., LBOs). |

Estimating the Value of Subsidized Debt Financing

In our preceding example, financing affects firm value only through its effect on in-terest tax savings. However, it is not uncommon for the seller of a business to offer an incentive to the buyer in the form of below-market-rate debt financing. To illustrate how we might analyze the value of below-market financing, consider the $40 million loan offer outlined in Table 7-7. Although the current market rate for such a loan is 6.5%, the loan carries an interest rate of 5%, which implies a 1.5% reduction in the rate of interest charged on the loan. The loan requires that the firm pay only interest, and no principal is due until maturity. Consequently, the required payments consist of $2 million per year in interest payments over the next five years and, in the fifth year (the year in which the loan matures), the full principal amount of $40 million is due and payable.

To value the subsidy associated with the below-market rate financing, we calcu-late that the present value of the payments, using the current market rate of inter-est, is only $37,506,592, which indicates that the financing provides the borrower with a subsidy worth $2,493,407! In essence, the seller has reduced the selling price of the firm or asset being sold by two and a half million dollars as an incentive to the buyer.

Table 7-7   The Value of Subsidized Debt Financing

Given:					
Loan amount	$ 40,000,000				
Current market rate	6.5%				
Cost of debt (subsidized)	5.0%				
Term of loan	5				
Type of loan	Interest only				
	2007	**2008**	**2009**	**2010**	**2011**
Interest payments	$ 2,000,000	$ 2,000,000	$ 2,000,000	$ 2,000,000	$ 2,000,000
Principal payment					40,000,000
Total	$ 2,000,000	$ 2,000,000	$ 2,000,000	$ 2,000,000	$ 42,000,000
Evaluation of Subsidized Loan:					
Cash received	$ 40,000,000				
Present value of payments	37,506,592				
Value of loan subsidy	$ 2,493,407				

7.4 SUMMARY

Using discounted cash flow analysis (DCF) to value a *firm* is a straightforward extension of its use in *project* valuation. The added complexity of firm valuation comes largely from the fact that the time horizon of firm cash flows is indefinite, while project cash flows are typically finite. In most cases, analysts solve this problem by estimating the value of cash flows in what is referred to as a *planning period* using standard DCF analysis, and then using the method of comparables or multiples (as introduced in Chapter 6) to calculate what is generally referred to as the *terminal value* of the investment. In most cases, the planning period cash flows and terminal value estimates are discounted using the investment's weighted average cost of capital.

As we have noted, the WACC approach that we described in the first half of this chapter is widely used throughout industry to value businesses. However, it should be emphasized that this approach requires a number of implicit assumptions, which may be difficult to justify in most applications. In particular, the analysis assumes that the risks of the cash flows do not change over time and that the firm's financial structure does not change. For this reason we would again like to add our usual caveat that the tools that we present are imperfect and should be viewed as providing support for management and not a substitute for management judgment.

The second half of the chapter considered the case where the debt ratio of the acquired business changes over time. When this is the case, the APV approach provides an improvement over the WACC approach. Although this approach is not frequently used by industry practitioners, we expect that over time it will become more popular.

PROBLEMS

7-1 ENTERPRISE VALUATION—TRADITIONAL WACC MODEL   Canton Corporation is a privately owned firm that engages in the production and sale of industrial chemicals primarily in North America. The firm's primary product line consists of organic solvents and intermediates for pharmaceutical, agricultural, and chemical products. Canton's management has recently been considering the possibility of taking the company public and has asked the firm's investment banker to perform some preliminary analysis of the value of the firm's equity.

To support its analysis, the investment banker has prepared pro forma financial statements for each of the next four years under the (simplifying) assumption that firm sales are flat (i.e., have a zero rate of growth), the corporate tax rate equals 30%, and capital expenditures are equal to the estimated depreciation expense. In addition to the financial information on Canton, the investment banker has assembled the following information concerning current rates of return in the capital market.

Canton Corporation Financials

Pro Forma Balance Sheets ($000)

	0	1	2	3	4
Current assets	$ 15,000	$ 15,000	$ 15,000	$ 15,000	$ 15,000
Property, plant and equipment	40,000	40,000	40,000	40,000	40,000
Total	$ 55,000	$ 55,000	$ 55,000	$ 55,000	$ 55,000
Accruals and payables	$ 5,000	$ 5,000	$ 5,000	$ 5,000	$ 5,000
Long-term debt	25,000	25,000	25,000	25,000	25,000
Equity	25,000	25,000	25,000	25,000	25,000
Total	$ 55,000	$ 55,000	$ 55,000	$ 55,000	$ 55,000

Pro Forma Income Statements ($000)

	1	2	3	4
Sales	$ 100,000	$ 100,000	$ 100,000	$ 100,000
Cost of goods sold	(40,000)	(40,000)	(40,000)	(40,000)
Gross profit	$ 60,000	$ 60,000	$ 60,000	$ 60,000
Operating expenses (excluding depreciation)	(30,000)	(30,000)	(30,000)	(30,000)
Depreciation expense	(8,000)	(8,000)	(8,000)	(8,000)
Operating income (earnings before interest and taxes)	$ 22,000	$ 22,000	$ 22,000	$ 22,000
Less: Interest expense	(2,000)	(2,000)	(2,000)	(2,000)
Earnings before taxes	$ 20,000	$ 20,000	$ 20,000	$ 20,000
Less: Taxes	(6,000)	(6,000)	(6,000)	(6,000)
Net income	$ 14,000	$ 14,000	$ 14,000	$ 14,000

■ The current market rate of interest on 10-year Treasury bonds is 7%, and the market risk premium is estimated to be 5%.
■ Canton's debt currently carries a rate of 8%, and this is the rate the firm would have to pay for any future borrowing as well.
■ Using publicly traded firms as proxies, the estimated equity beta for Canton is 1.60.

a. What is Canton's cost of equity capital? What is the after-tax cost of debt for the firm?
b. Calculate the equity free cash flows for Canton for each of the next four years. Assuming that equity free cash flows are a level perpetuity for Years 5 and beyond, estimate the value of Canton's equity. (*Hint:* Equity value is equal to the present value of the equity free cash flows discounted at the levered cost of equity.) If the market rate of interest on Canton's debt is equal to the 8% coupon, what is the current market value of the firm's debt? What is the

enterprise value of Canton? (*Hint:* Enterprise value can be estimated as the sum of the estimated values of the firm's interest-bearing debt plus equity.)

c. Using the market values of Canton's debt and equity calculated in part b above, calculate the firm's after-tax weighted average cost of capital. *Hint:*

$$k_{\text{WACC}} = \frac{\text{Cost of}}{\text{Debt}}\left(1 - \frac{\text{Tax}}{\text{Rate}}\right)\left(\frac{\text{Debt Value}}{\text{Enterprise Value}}\right)$$
$$+ \frac{\text{Cost of}}{\text{Levered Equity}}\left(\frac{\text{Equity Value}}{\text{Enterprise Value}}\right).$$

d. What are the firm free cash flows (FFCFs) for Canton for Years 1 through 4?

e. Estimate the enterprise value of Canton using the traditional WACC model based on your previous answers and assuming that the FFCFs after Year 4 are a level perpetuity equal to the Year 4 FFCF. How does your estimate compare to your earlier estimate using the sum of the values of the firm's debt and equity?

f. Based on your estimate of enterprise value, what is the value per share of equity for the firm if the firm has two million shares outstanding (remember that your calculations to this point have been in thousands of dollars.)

7-2 TRADITIONAL WACC VALUATION The owner of Big Boy Flea Market (BBFM), Lewis Redding, passed away on December 30, 2006. His 100% ownership interest in BBFM became part of his estate, on which his heirs must pay estate taxes. The IRS has hired a valuation expert who has submitted a report stating that the business was worth approximately $20 million at the time of Mr. Redding's death. Mr. Redding's heirs believe the IRS valuation is too high and have hired you to perform a separate valuation analysis in hopes of supporting their position.

a. Estimate the firm free cash flows for 2007–2011 where the firm's tax rate is 25%, capital expenditures are assumed to equal depreciation expense, and there are no changes in net working capital over the period.

b. Value BBFM using the traditional WACC model and the following information:
   i. BBFM's cost of equity is estimated to be 20% and the cost of debt is 10%.
   ii. BBFM's management targets its long-term debt ratio at 10% of enterprise value.
   iii. After 2011, the long-term growth rate in the firm's free cash flow is 5% per year.

7-3 ENTERPRISE VALUATION—APV MODEL This problem uses the information from Problem 7-1 about Canton Corporation to estimate the firm's enterprise value using the APV model.

a. What is the firm's unlevered cost of equity?

b. What are the unlevered equity free cash flows for Canton for Years 1 through 4? (*Hint:* The unlevered equity free cash flows are the same as the firm free cash flows.)

c. What are the interest tax savings for Canton Corp. for Years 1 through 4?

Big Boy Flea Market Financials

Income Statement	Base Year 2006	Forecast 2007	2008	2009	2010	2011
Sales	$ 3,417,500.00	$ 3,700,625.00	$ 3,983,750.00	$ 4,266,875.00	$ 4,550,000.00	$ 4,833,125.00
Depreciation		48,190.60	50,118.22	52,122.95	54,207.87	56,376.19
COGS		1,402,798.69	1,496,881.13	1,590,963.56	1,685,046.00	1,779,128.44
Other operating expenses		1,078,447.38	1,109,874.25	1,141,301.13	1,172,728.00	1,204,154.88
EBIT		$ 1,171,188.34	$ 1,326,876.40	$ 1,482,487.36	$ 1,638,018.13	$ 1,793,465.50
Interest		5,110.00	5,110.00	5,110.00	5,110.00	5,860.00
Earnings before taxes		$ 1,166,078.34	$ 1,321,766.40	$ 1,477,377.36	$ 1,632,908.13	$ 1,787,605.50
Income taxes		291,519.58	330,441.60	369,344.34	408,227.03	446,901.38
Net income		$ 874,558.75	$ 991,324.80	$ 1,108,033.02	$ 1,224,681.10	$ 1,340,704.13
Preferred stock dividends		—	—	—	—	—
Net income to common stock		874,558.75	991,324.80	1,108,033.02	1,224,681.10	1,340,704.13
Common stock dividends		874,558.75	991,324.80	1,108,033.02	1,224,681.10	1,340,704.13
Income to retained earnings		—	—	—	—	—

Balance Sheet	Base Year 2006	Forecast 2007	2008	2009	2010	2011
Current assets	$ 170,630.00	$ 185,031.25	$ 199,187.50	$ 213,343.75	$ 227,500.00	$ 241,656.25
Gross fixed assets	1,204,765.00	1,252,955.60	1,303,073.82	1,355,196.78	1,409,404.65	1,540,780.83
Accumulated depreciation	(734,750.00)	(782,940.60)	(833,058.82)	(885,181.78)	(939,389.65)	(995,765.83)
Net fixed assets	$ 470,015.00	$ 470,015.00	$ 470,015.00	$ 470,015.00	$ 470,015.00	$ 545,015.00
Total assets	$ 640,645.00	$ 655,046.25	$ 669,202.50	$ 683,358.75	$ 697,515.00	$ 786,671.25
Current liabilities	$ 129,645.00	$ 144,046.25	$ 158,202.50	$ 172,358.75	$ 186,515.00	$ 200,671.25
L-T debt	51,100.00	51,100.00	51,100.00	51,100.00	51,100.00	58,600.00
Preferred stock	—	—	—	—	—	—
Common stock	1,000.00	1,000.00	1,000.00	1,000.00	1,000.00	68,500.00
Retained earnings	458,900.00	458,900.00	458,900.00	458,900.00	458,900.00	458,900.00
Total common equity	$ 459,900.00	$ 459,900.00	$ 459,900.00	$ 459,900.00	$ 459,900.00	$ 527,400.00
Total liabilities & equity	$ 640,645.00	$ 655,046.25	$ 669,202.50	$ 683,358.75	$ 697,515.00	$ 786,671.25

d. Assuming that the firm's future cash flows from operations (i.e., its FFCFs) and its interest tax savings are level perpetuities for Years 5 and beyond that equal their Year 4 values, what is your estimate of the enterprise value of Canton Corp.?

e. Based on your estimate of enterprise value, what is the value per share of equity for the firm if the firm has two million shares outstanding? (Remember that your calculations to this point have been in thousands of dollars.)

7-4 APV VALUATION   The following information provides the basis for performing a straightforward application of the adjusted present value (APV) model.

Assumptions

Unlevered cost of equity	12%
Borrowing rate	8%
Tax rate	30%
Current debt outstanding	$200.00

	Years			
	1	2	3	4 & Beyond
Firm free cash flows	$100.00	$120.00	$180.00	$200.00
Interest-bearing debt	200.00	150.00	100.00	50.00
Interest expense	16.00	12.00	8.00	4.00
Interest tax savings	4.80	3.60	2.40	1.20

Legend

Unlevered cost of equity—the rate of return required by stockholders in the company, where the firm has used only equity financing.

Borrowing rate—the rate of interest the firm pays on its debt. We also assume that this rate is equal to the current cost of borrowing for the firm or the current market rate of interest.

Tax rate—the corporate tax rate on earnings. We assume that this tax rate is constant for all income levels.

Current debt outstanding—Total interest-bearing debt excluding payables and other forms of non-interest-bearing debt, at the time of the valuation.

Firm free cash flows—Net operating earnings after tax (NOPAT), plus depreciation (and other noncash charges), less new investments in net working capital less capital expenditures (CAPEX) for the period. This is the free cash flow to the unlevered firm, since no interest or principal are considered in its calculation.

Interest-bearing debt—Outstanding debt at the beginning of the period, which carries an explicit interest cost.

Interest expense—Interest-bearing debt for the period times the contractual rate of interest that the firm must pay.

Interest tax savings—Interest expense for the period times the corporate tax rate.

a. What is the value of the unlevered firm, assuming that its free cash flows for Years 5 and beyond are equal to the Year 4 free cash flow?

b. What is the value of the firm's interest tax savings, assuming that they remain constant for Years 4 and beyond?

c. What is the value of the levered firm?

d. What is the value of the levered firm's equity (assuming that the firm's debt is equal to its book value)?

7-5 APV VALUATION Clarion Manufacturing Company is a publicly held company that is engaged in the manufacture of home and office furniture. The firm's most recent income statement and balance sheet are found below ($000).

Income Statement

Sales	$ 16,000
Cost of goods sold	(9,000)
Gross profit	7,000
Selling and administrative expenses	(2,000)
Operating income	5,000
Interest expense	(720)
Earnings before taxes	4,280
Taxes	(1,284)
Net income	$ 2,996

Balance Sheet

Current assets	$ 5,000	Liabilities[10]	$ 7,000
Fixed assets	9,000	Owners' equity	7,000
	$ 14,000		$ 14,000

a. If Clarion's future operating earnings are flat (i.e., no growth), and it anticipates making capital expenditures equal to depreciation expense with no increase anticipated in the firm's net working capital, what is the value of the firm using the adjusted present value model? To respond to this question, you may assume the following: The firm's current borrowing rate is the same as the 9% rate it presently pays on its debt; all the firm's liabilities are interest bearing; the firm's "unlevered" cost of equity is 12%; and the firm's tax rate is 30%.

b. What is the value of Clarion's equity (i.e., its levered equity) under the circumstances described above?

c. What is Clarion's weighted average cost of capital, given your answers to parts a and b above?

---

[10]All liabilities are assumed to be interest bearing.

d. Based upon your answers to the above questions, what is Clarion's levered cost of equity?[11]

e. If the risk-free rate is 5.25% and the market risk premium is 7%, what is Clarion's levered beta? What is Clarion's unlevered beta?

7-6 TERMINAL VALUE ANALYSIS   Terminal value refers to the valuation attached to the end of the planning period and which captures the value of all subsequent cash flows. Estimate the value today for each of the following sets of future cash flow forecasts:

a. Claymore Mining Company anticipates that it will earn firm free cash flows (FFCFs) of $4 million per year for each of the next five years. Moreover, beginning in Year 6, the firm will earn WACCs of $5 million per year for the indefinite future. If Claymore's cost of capital is 10%, what is the value of the firm's future cash flows?

b. Shameless Commerce Inc. has no outstanding debt and is being evaluated as a possible acquisition. Shameless's FFCFs for the next five years are projected to be $1 million per year and, beginning in Year 6, the cash flows are expected to begin growing at the anticipated rate of inflation, which is currently 3% per annum. If the cost of capital for Shameless is 10%, what is your estimate of the present value of the FFCFs?

c. Dustin Electric Inc. is about to be acquired by the firm's management from the firm's founder for $15 million in cash. The purchase price will be financed with $10 million in notes that are repaid in $2 million increments over the next five years. At the end of this five-year period, the firm will have no remaining debt. The FFCFs are expected to be $3 million a year for the next five years. Beginning in Year 6, the FFCFs are expected to grow at a rate of 2% per year into the indefinite future. If the unlevered cost of equity for Dustin is approximately 15% and the firm's borrowing rate on the buyout debt is 10% (before taxes at a rate of 30%), what is your estimate of the value of the firm?

7-7 ENTERPRISE VALUATION—TRADITIONAL WACC VERSUS APV   Answer the following questions for the Canton Corporation described in Problem 7-1 where firm revenues grow at a rate of 10% per year during Years 1 through 4 before leveling out at no growth for Years 5 and beyond. You may assume that Canton maintains equal dollar amounts of long-term debt and equity to finance its growing needs for invested capital. Also assume that the cost of unlevered equity in this case is 13.84% and the cost of levered equity is 15.28%. The cost of debt remains at 8%. The corporate tax rate is 30%.

a. Calculate the enterprise value using the adjusted present value method.

b. From part a, calculate the value of equity after deducting the value of debt from enterprise value. Use these market values as weights to compute the weighted average cost of capital.

c. Value the firm's free cash flows using the WACC approach.

---

[11]A firm's "levered cost of equity" represents the rate of return investors require when investing in the firm's common equity, given the firm's present use of financial leverage.

d. Compare your enterprise value estimates for the two discounted cash flow models. Which of the two models do you feel best suits the valuation problem posed for Canton?

7-8 TERMINAL VALUE AND THE LENGTH OF THE PLANNING PERIOD   The Prestonwood Development Corporation has projected its cash flows (i.e., firm free cash flows) for the indefinite future under the following assumptions: (1) Last year the firm's FFCF was $1 million and the firm expects this to grow at a rate of 20% for the next 8 years; (2) beginning Year 9, the firm anticipates that its FFCF will grow at a rate of 4% indefinitely; and (3) the firm estimates its cost of capital to be 12%. Based on these assumptions, the firm's projected FFCF over the next 20 years is the following:

Years	Cash Flows (millions)
1	$ 1.2000
2	1.4400
3	1.7280
4	2.0736
5	2.4883
6	2.9860
7	3.5832
8	4.2998
9	4.4718
10	4.6507
11	4.8367
12	5.0302
13	5.2314
14	5.4406
15	5.6583
16	5.8846
17	6.1200
18	6.3648
19	6.6194
20	6.8841

a. Based on the information given and a terminal value estimate for the firm of $89.4939 million for Year 20, what is your estimate of the firm's enterprise value today (in 2006)?

b. If a three-year planning period is used to value Prestonwood, what is the value of the planning period cash flows and the present value of the terminal value at the end of Year 3?

c. Answer part b for planning periods of 10 and 20 years. How does the relative importance of the terminal value change as you lengthen the planning period?

PROBLEM 7-9 **MINI-CASE** APV VALUATION [12]

Flowmaster Forge Inc. is a designer and manufacturer of industrial air handling equipment that is a wholly owned subsidiary of Howden Industrial Inc. Howden is interested in selling Flowmaster to an investment group formed by company CFO Gary Burton.

Burton prepared a set of financial projections for Flowmaster under the new ownership. For the first year of operations, firm revenues were estimated to be $160 million, variable and fixed operating expenses (excluding depreciation expense) were projected to be $80 million, and depreciation expense was estimated to be $15 million. Revenues and expenses were projected to grow at a rate of 4% per year in perpetuity.

Flowmaster currently has $125 million in debt outstanding that carries an interest rate of 6%. The debt trades at par (i.e., at a price equal to its face value). The investment group intends to keep the debt outstanding after the acquisition is completed, and the level of debt is expected to grow by the same 4% rate as firm revenues.

Projected income statements for the first three years of operation of Flowmaster following the acquisition are as follows ($ millions):

	Pro Forma Income Statements		
	Year 1	Year 2	Year 3
Revenues	$ 160.00	$ 166.40	$ 173.06
Expenses	(80.00)	$ (83.20)	$ (86.53)
Depreciation (note 1)	(15.00)	$ (15.60)	$ (16.22)
Earnings before interest and taxes	$ 65.00	$ 67.60	$ 70.30
Interest expense (note 2)	(7.50)	(7.80)	(8.11)
Earnings before taxes	$ 57.50	$ 59.80	$ 62.19
Taxes (34%)	(19.55)	(20.33)	(21.15)
Net income	$ 37.95	$ 39.47	$ 41.05

Note 1—Property, plant, and equipment grow at the same rate as revenues such that depreciation expenses grow at 4% per year.

Note 2—The initial debt level of $125 million is assumed to grow with firm assets at a rate of 4% per year.

---

[12]This problem was written and contributed by Professor Scott Gibson, College of William and Mary, Williamsburg, Virginia.

Burton anticipates that efficiency gains can be implemented that will allow Flowmaster to reduce its needs for net working capital. Currently Flowmaster has net working capital equal to 30% of anticipated revenues for Year 1. He estimates that for Year 1, the firm's net working capital can be reduced to 25% of Year 2 revenues, then 20% of revenues for all subsequent years. Estimated net working capital for Years 1 through 3 is as follows ($ millions):

	Current	Pro Forma		
Net working capital $(t-1)$/Revenues (t)	30%	25%	20%	20%
Net working capital	$ 48.00	$ 41.60	$ 34.61	$ 36.00

To sustain the firm's expected revenue growth, Burton estimates that annual capital expenditures will be required that equal the firm's annual depreciation expense.

Gary Burton had been thinking for some time about whether to use Howden's corporate cost of capital of 9% to value Flowmaster and had come to the conclusion that an independent estimate should be made. To make the estimate, he collected the following information on the betas and leverage ratios for three publicly traded firms with manufacturing operations that are very similar to Flowmaster's:

Company	Leveraged Equity Beta	Debt Beta	Leverage Ratio*	Revenues** ($ millions)
Gopher Forge	1.61	0.52	0.46	$ 400
Alpha	1.53	0.49	0.44	380
Global Diversified	0.73	0.03	0.15	9,400

*The leverage ratio is the ratio of the market value of debt to the market value of debt and equity.

**Revenues are the entire firm's revenues for the most recent fiscal year.

a. Calculate the unlevered equity cash flows (i.e., the firm free cash flows for Flowmaster for Years 1–3).
b. Calculate the unlevered cost of equity capital for Flowmaster. The risk free rate of interest is 4.5% and the market risk premium is estimated to be 6%.
c. Calculate the value of Flowmaster's unlevered business.
d. What is the value of Flowmaster's interest tax savings, based on the assumption that the $125 million in debt remains outstanding (i.e., the investment group assumes the debt obligation) and that the firm's debt and consequently its interest expenses grow at the same rate as revenues?

e. What is your estimate of the enterprise value of Flowmaster based on your analysis to this point? How much is the equity of the firm worth today, assuming the $125 million in debt remains outstanding?

f. In conversations with the investment banker who was helping the investment group finance the purchase, Mr. Burton learned that Flowmaster has sufficient debt capacity to issue additional debt that would have a subordinate claim to the present debt holders carrying an 8.5% rate. The amount of new debt is constrained by the need to maintain an interest coverage ratio (i.e., earnings before interest, taxes, and depreciation divided by interest expense) of five to one. Assuming that Flowmaster's $125 million of 6% senior debt remains in place (and grows at a rate of 4% per year going forward), what is the maximum amount of subordinated debt that can be issued to help finance the purchase of Flowmaster?

g. If the investment group decides to raise the additional subordinated debt (from part f), Gary Burton, CFO, anticipates that Flowmaster's unsecured suppliers will grant less favorable credit terms (note that the amount of subordinated debt that Flowmaster can support will continue to increase along with Flowmaster's EBITDA growth). In fact, he estimated that the decrease in accounts payable will result in an increase in the required net working capital in perpetuity by 20% of anticipated revenues per year. Consequently, the current net working capital balance would increase from 30% of revenues to 50%, or from .3 × $160 million = $48 million to .50 × $160 million = $80 million. Similarly, the projected net working capital balance for the end of Year 1 would increase from 25% to 45% of revenues. For Years 2 and beyond, working capital will increase from the 20% projected earlier to 40% of revenues. Use the APV approach to estimating Flowmaster's enterprise value to determine whether the additional subordinated debt should be issued.

PROBLEM 7-10 **MINI-CASE** TRADITIONAL WACC VALUATION[13]

Setting: It is early January 2007 and as the Chief Financial Officer of TM Toys Inc. you are evaluating a strategic acquisition of Toy Co. Inc. (the "target").

Industry Overview: The toys and games industry consists of a select group of global players. The $60 billion industry (excluding videos) is dominated by two US toy makers: Mattel (Barbie, Hot Wheels, Fisher-Price) and Hasbro (G.I. Joe, Tonka, Playskool). International players include Japan's Bandai Co. (Digimon) and Sanrio (Hello Kitty), as well as Denmark's LEGO Holding. Success in this industry is dependent on creating cross-culturally appealing brands backed by successful marketing strategies. Toy

---

[13]This problem was contributed by Professor Julia Plotts, University of Southern California.

Exhibit P7-10.1 **Planning Period Cash Flow Estimates**

Toy Co. Inc. ($ in Millions) Fiscal Year Ended	Projected Firm Free Cash Flows				
	12/31/07	12/31/08	12/31/09	12/31/10	12/31/11
Net Operating Income	$733.16	$757.63	$783.64	$799.32	$ 815.30
Less: Taxes	201.27	207.98	235.09	239.80	244.59
NOPAT	$531.90	$549.65	$548.55	$559.52	$ 570.71
Plus: Depreciation	183.58	186.21	191.80	195.64	199.55
Less: Capital Expenditures	(180.00)	(212.82)	(219.20)	(223.59)	(228.06)
(Increase) in Working Capital	(50.37)	43.54	(27.68)	(19.82)	(20.21)
Equals FCFF	**$485.11**	**$566.59**	**$493.47**	**$511.76**	**$ 521.99**
EBITDA	**$916.74**	**$943.84**	**$975.45**	**$994.95**	**$1,014.85**

---

companies achieve success through scoring the next big hit with their target consumers and unveiling the "must-have" toys (i.e. 2006 Mattel's T.M.X™ Elmo, LEGO's Harry Potter and the Chamber of Secrets, and Bratz Dolls from MGA Entertainment). Historically we have seen significant merger and acquisition activity and consolidation among brands in this industry.

Target Company Description: Toy Co. Inc. is a multi-brand company that designs and markets a broad range of toys and consumer products. The product categories include: Action Figures, Art Activity Kits, Stationery, Writing Instruments, Performance Kites, Water Toys, Sports Activity Toys, Vehicles, Infant/Pre-School, Plush, Construction Toys, Electronics, Dolls, Dress-Up, Role Play, and Pet Toys and Accessories. The products are sold under various brand names. The target designs, manufactures and markets

---

Exhibit P7-10.2 **Estimate a "Risk Appropriate" Discount Rate**

- Cost of debt—Estimated borrowing rate is 6.125% with a marginal tax of 27.29% results in an after-tax cost of debt of 4.5%
- Cost of equity—Levered equity beta for Toy Co. is .777; using the capital asset pricing model with a 10-year Treasury Bond yield of 4.66% and a market risk premium of 7.67% produces an estimate of the levered cost of equity of 10.57%.
- Other—Diluted Shares of Common Equity outstanding at 12/31/06: $422,040,500, Closing Stock Price $19.49; Debt Value Outstanding 12/31/06 $618,100,000
- Weighted average cost of capital (WACC)—Using the target debt to value ratio of 6.99% the WACC is approximately 10.14%.

a variety of toy products worldwide through sales to retailers and wholesalers and directly to consumers. Its stock price closed on 12/31/06 at $19.49 per share.

Valuation Assignment: Your task is to estimate the intrinsic value of Toy Co. Inc.'s equity (on a per share basis) at 12/31/06 using the Enterprise DCF Model; this will assist you with the determining what per share offer to make to Toy Co. Inc.'s shareholders. Treat all of the results/forecasts for the fiscal year ended 2007–2011 as projections. Your research on various historical merger and acquisition transactions suggest that comparable toy companies have been acquired at Enterprise Value/EBITDA multiples of 10.5×–11.5×. This is your assumption for a terminal value exit multiple at the end of the forecast period, 2011. Exhibit 1 includes the target's planning period cash flow estimates and Exhibit 2 provides market and other data for calculation of a weighted average cost of capital ("WACC") for a discount rate.

CHAPTER 8

Valuation in a Private Equity Setting[1]

Chapter Overview

This chapter takes the perspective of a private equity investor and applies the hybrid valuation methods developed in Chapter 7, which is particularly well suited to the types of investments made by private equity firms. These investment companies raise funds in limited partnerships with a relatively short life span of 7 to 10 years. They then invest in companies that span all stages of the life cycle of the firm—from venture capital to vulture capital. In all cases, however, their investments are of relatively short duration with targeted investment exit in four to six years. The short duration magnifies the importance of the terminal value component of the valuation, and since the exit often involves the public capital markets, market-based multiples are commonly used.

We consider two specific private equity valuation examples in this chapter. The first is the deal-structuring problem that arises when a venture capital firm makes an investment in a start-up firm. The second example is the valuation of a build-up leveraged buyout transaction by an LBO fund. In both cases private equity capital is the common denominator, although the purpose of the investment (providing start-up or growth versus restructuring capital) is quite different.

8.1 INTRODUCTION

Perhaps the most visible difference between how the valuation problems were approached in earlier chapters and the way private equity firms evaluate investments relates to the discount rate. Up to this point, our valuation problems used discount rates in the 8% to 12% range. However, most private equity investors claim to

---

[1] We would like to express our gratitude to J. William Petty for his many helpful insights in the preparation of this chapter.

require an internal rate of return in the 25% to 50% range and even higher for start-up investments. How do they justify such high required rates of return? There are four possible avenues that can be taken in this regard. The first avenue relates to the fact that these investments are quite risky. They involve risky investment propositions related to the financing of start-up firms, the provision of growth capital, or the restructuring of older firms. In the case of buyout firms they entail the use of substantial amounts of financial leverage. Moreover, investments in private equity funds do not benefit from the liquidity offered by public investments in stocks or bonds or mutual funds, and thus require a return premium over these alternative investments.

A second justification for the very high required rates of return is that these rates of return includes compensation to the private equity firm for more than just the use of money. It incorporates the value of the expertise that the private equity firm partners bring to the deal. The partners generally take a seat on the board of the firms in which they invest and provide advice to start-ups and actually control buyout investments.

The third justification for the very high required rates of return of private equity firms is that they generally evaluate what we referred to in Chapter 3 as "hoped for" cash flows rather than expected cash flows. Consequently, we might interpret the 25% to 50% required rates of return as hoped for returns rather than as expected rates of return.

Did you know?

How significant is the market for private equity?

The largest private equity firms now raise multi-billion dollar funds and so by participating in groups or clubs they are able to garner the billions needed to acquire some of the largest publicly held firms. For example, on September 15, 2006, four private equity firms (Blackstone Group Funds, Texas Pacific Group, Permira Group Funds, and the Carlyle Group) agreed to pay $17.6 billion for Freescale Semiconductor Inc. (Motorola's spin-off of its semiconductor operations).

Finally, it should be emphasized that the required rate of return on these investments is determined by the opportunity cost of capital, which means that when private equity firms have an abundance of good opportunities, and scarce capital, they can require very high rates of return. However, when there is abundant capital and fewer opportunities we expect required rates of return to decline.

There are some unique features of how the hybrid valuation approach is applied by private equity firms that we describe in this chapter. First, in most cases when a private equity firm makes an investment, it does not expect to receive significant cash flows in the initial planning period, so the valuation emphasis is on the (terminal) value of the enterprise at a future date when the private equity investor hopes to cash out of the investment. This value is generally estimated as a multiple of EBITDA. Second, the object of the valuation exercise generally focuses on the value of the investors' equity investment, rather than on the enterprise value of the company receiving funding. Neither of these features provides significant difficulties for the hybrid valuation approach, but they do give rise to some unique terminology and special adaptations of the tools developed in Chapter 7.

Up to this point we have focused our valuation approach on situations where we evaluate whether to invest a specified amount of cash in an investment opportunity that offers an uncertain set of future cash flows. From the perspective of the venture capitalist

INDUSTRY INSIGHT

Private versus Public Equity Investing

Private equity investing differs in four ways from public equity investing:

1. **Private equity investors make** *illiquid* **investments that cannot be sold either because of a lack of an organized market or investment restrictions.** The investment might take the form of equity or debt securities issued by a privately held firm or restricted shares of stock issued by a publicly held firm.[2] In either case, the investment cannot be easily sold. In contrast, mutual funds and other passive investors hold publicly traded debt and equity securities that can be bought or sold at any time.

2. **Private equity investors are** *active* **investors.** They generally take an active role in managing the companies in which they invest (for example, taking a seat on the board) or will serve as financial advisors to the firm's management. This contrasts with the "hands off" investment style followed by mutual funds and others who invest primarily in the public equity markets.

3. **Private equity investments are made for a** *finite* **period of time.** Traditional private equity investing involves ownership of limited partnership units that are part of a private equity fund. The partnership typically has a fixed life of 7 to 10 years, at which time the fund is liquidated and the proceeds are distributed to the partners. Mutual funds and other entities that invest in public equity have no set liquidation date and correspondingly can have a much longer investment horizon.

4. **Private equity investments are risky and illiquid and thus require high returns.** Since the failure rate can be quite high in some types of private equity investing and the investment is illiquid for years, private equity investors typically demand very high promised rates of return.

(VC), the investment problem is similar in that start-up firms typically require a specific amount of external funding in order to produce an uncertain set of future cash flows. However, the VC's problem is different in that he or she must not only evaluate the uncertain future cash flows but also negotiate the ownership fraction of the start-up's shares he or she must have in order to earn a desired return on the investment. Thus, the valuation problem for the VC is generally discussed in the context of deal structuring. Although this is a somewhat different problem from those we have addressed so far, we can solve it with a slight modification of our valuation methods.

---

[2]The restriction we refer to relates to the fact that the investor cannot sell his or her shares for a prescribed period of time.

This chapter is organized as follows: In Section 8.2 we provide a brief overview of the private equity and venture capital markets. Section 8.3 provides an overview of deal-structuring analysis as it is carried out by venture capital firms. In Section 8.4 we look at the valuation of an investment by a private equity firm. We close this section with an application of the APV model for a private equity investment. Finally, Section 8.5 contains summary comments.

8.2 OVERVIEW OF THE MARKET FOR PRIVATE EQUITY

Before we launch our discussion of the valuation of private equity investments, it is helpful to describe the market for private equity and to gain some perspective on the role of private equity finance in the U.S. economy. When we refer to a private equity firm, we are referring to a financial intermediary that is in the business of raising pools of capital (generally in limited partnerships) and using that capital to invest in companies that need financing. Essentially, private equity is an ownership stake either in a private company or in shares of a public company that are restricted such that they cannot be sold for some specified period of time.[3] In general, a private equity investor is an active investor who acquires some measure of control over the firms in which he or she invests, often by serving on the firm's board. The Industry Insight box (p. 319) summarizes the differences between public equity and private equity investing.

Market for Private Equity—Financial Intermediaries

Figure 8-1 summarizes the three parties involved in the private equity market. These include suppliers of funds (i.e., the investors in the private equity partnerships), the private equity investment companies, and the businesses that use private equity funds. Although it is difficult to know exactly how large the various components of the market are at any moment, it is generally believed that approximately 80% of the funds that flow into private equity come from public and private pension funds. The majority of these funds are then invested by the private equity firms in nonventure activities, which include meeting the expansion, recapitalization, and reorganization needs of companies, as well as acquiring large public firms (see the Industry Insight box "Biggest Buyout Deals of 2006" [p. 322]).

Investors—The Suppliers of Private Equity Finance

Most private equity firms are organized as *limited partnerships* that raise capital from a small number of sophisticated investors in a private placement. The investors in the fund include public and private employee pension funds, university endowment funds, wealthy families, bank holding companies, and insurance companies. The largest segment (as we noted above) is public and private pension funds, which contribute approximately 80% of all the funds in the private equity market.

---

[3]These investments are referred to as private investments in public equities or PIPEs.

Figure 8-1 The Market for Private Equity

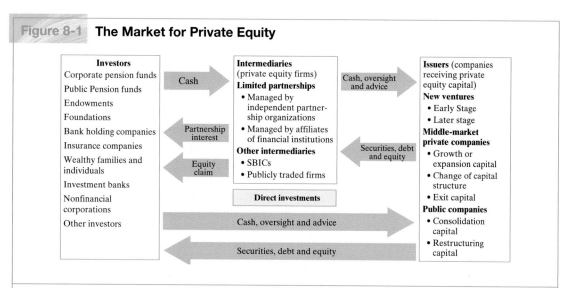

Private Equity Firms:

Limited Partnership—the standard vehicle for raising funds to invest in private equity is a limited partnership that typically has a fixed life of 10 years. The partnership's general partner makes investments, monitors them, and finally exits them for a return on behalf of the investors—limited partners.

SBIC—small business investment corporations were created in 1958. They are privately managed, for-profit investment funds formed to provide equity and/or debt capital to U.S. small businesses.

Categories of Private Equity Investments:

Seed and start-up capital—typically provided by angel investors (i.e., wealthy individuals), this type of capital is provided to develop a concept, create the initial product, and carry out the first marketing efforts. The company that seeks financing is typically very young (less than one year old) and has not produced a product or service for commercial sale.

First-stage capital—the money provided to an entrepreneur who has a proven product, to start commercial production and marketing. This is typically the earliest stage at which a venture capital firm will invest.

Second-stage capital—the capital provided to expand marketing and meet the growing working capital needs of an enterprise that has commenced production but does not have sufficient cash flows from its operations to fund its capital needs.

Expansion capital—the capital needed to fund the expansion of a profitable firm's operations where the growing firm is incapable of generating sufficient earnings internally to fund its needs for capital.

Bridge capital—a short-term loan that provides needed capital while the borrower arranges for more comprehensive longer-term financing.

Mezzanine capital—unsecured, high-yield, subordinated debt or preferred stock that represents a claim on a company's assets that is only senior to that of a company's shareholders. The term *mezzanine* comes from the fact that these forms of financing are somewhere between debt and equity in terms of the priority of their claim on the firm's earnings and assets in the event of default or bankruptcy.

Source: Based on Figure 3 in Stephen D. Prowse, "The Economics of the Private Equity Market," *Economic Review of the Federal Reserve Bank of Dallas,* 3rd Quarter, 1998, 21–34.

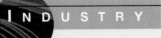

Biggest Buyout Deals of 2006

By far the largest fraction of all private equity investing involves nonventure, buyout financing. The following list contains the five largest buyout deals for 2006. Note that with only one exception, the investments involve multiple private equity firms. The reason for this relates to the magnitude of the investment being made and concerns by the private equity investors that they not let their investments become too concentrated in a small number of very large investments.

Date	Acquisition Target	Private Equity Buyer(s)*	Equity Value
May 29, 2006	Kinder Morgan Inc.	GS Capital Partners LP, AIG, Carlyle Group LLC, and Riverstone Holdings LLC	$27.4 billion
July 24, 2006	HCA Inc.	Bain Capital LLC, Kohlberg Kravis Roberts & Co., Merrill Lynch Global Private Equity Group, and Riverstone Holdings LLC	$32 billion
October 2, 2006	Harrah's Entertainment Inc.	Apollo Management LP and Texas Pacific Group Inc.	$25.8 billion
November 15, 2006	Clear Channel Communications, Inc.	Bain Capital Partners LLC and Thomas H. Lee Partners LP	$26.8 billion
November 19, 2006	Equity Office Properties Trust	Blackstone Group	$32.5 billion

Descriptions of the Private Equity Firms (from their web sites):

AIG Private Equity Ltd—a Swiss investment company that invests in a diversified portfolio of private equity funds and privately held operating companies.

Bain Capital LLC—Established in 1984, Bain Capital has approximately $40 billion in assets under management. Bain Capital's family of funds includes private equity, venture capital, public equity, and leveraged debt assets.

Blackstone Group—formed in 1987, the firm managed $28 billion through its Blackstone Capital Partners I, II, III, IV, and V and Blackstone Communications Partners funds.

Carlyle Group LLC—formed in 1987, the Carlyle Group is one of the world's largest private equity firms, with more than $46.9 billion under management with 46 funds across four investment disciplines including buyouts, venture and growth capital, real estate, and leveraged finance.

GS Capital Partners LP—makes private equity investments on behalf of Goldman Sachs and others. The firm's current fund, GS Capital Partners V, is an $8.5 billion fund, with about $2.5 billion committed by Goldman Sachs and its employees, with the remainder committed by institutional and individual investors. The firm invests in a range of industries in a variety of situations, including build-ups, leveraged buyouts, recapitalizations, acquisitions, and expansions.

Kohlberg Kravis Roberts & Co.—Established in 1976, KKR has completed over 140 transactions valued at approximately $226 billion. As of September 30, 2006, these transactions were valued at approximately $70 billion on $27 billion of invested capital. KKR's investors include corporate and public pension plans, financial institutions, insurance companies, and university endowments.

Merrill Lynch Global Private Equity Group—the private equity investment arm of Merrill Lynch provides capital to fund growth, financial restructuring, or change of control. MLGPE typically holds investments for the medium- to long-term (three to seven years).

Riverstone Holdings LLC—a $6 billion private investment firm founded in 2000. The firm has completed more than 20 transactions and is one of the largest private equity investors in the energy and power industry.

** Unless otherwise noted, these data are for 2006.

Investments—The Demand for Private Equity Finance

Although private equity funds invest in the full spectrum of businesses, individual private equity firms tend to specialize in a very narrow range of activities that coincide roughly with the life cycle of the firms in which they invest, as depicted in Figure 8-2. Seed capital for start-ups is typically supplied by wealthy individuals who are commonly referred to as "angel investors" or "business angels." This type of investing typically does not involve the use of an intermediary (i.e., it is a form of direct investing, as depicted at the bottom of Figure 8-1). Venture capitalists typically provide early stage financing for established start-up companies that can carry the companies up to the point where they need to access the public capital markets for their funding needs or where they are sold to another company (often a public company). This is typically the earliest stage in the firm's life cycle in which a venture capital firm will invest. See the Practitioner Insight box for a discussion of the thought process that goes into determining the size of a VC fund and the minimum level of investment in a portfolio company.

Growth and expansion capital is provided by a mixture of private equity firms, including some firms that consider themselves venture capitalists and others that fall into the buyout category. Finally, providing restructuring or reorganization capital is the domain of the buyout or LBO firm. The motive of the buyout firm can be to finance a reorganization that rationalizes and reconfigures the firm to become competitive or to break up and dissolve the firm's operations. In the latter case, the buyout firm is euphemistically referred to as a "vulture fund."

8.3 VALUING INVESTMENTS IN START-UPS AND DEAL STRUCTURING

When a successful new company grows at a pace that cannot be financed by the entrepreneur alone, the entrepreneur frequently seeks funding from a venture capital firm in exchange for partial ownership of the firm. In the negotiation process, a critical issue for the entrepreneur is, "How much of the company's equity will the outside investor demand in exchange for providing the needed capital?" The amount that the entrepreneur

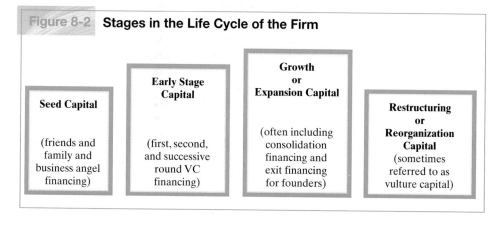

Figure 8-2   Stages in the Life Cycle of the Firm

Seed Capital

(friends and family and business angel financing)

Early Stage Capital

(first, second, and successive round VC financing)

Growth or Expansion Capital

(often including consolidation financing and exit financing for founders)

Restructuring or Reorganization Capital (sometimes referred to as vulture capital)

PRACTITIONER
INSIGHT
Determining the "Size" of VC Fund to Raise—An Interview with Venture Capitalist Joe Cunningham, MD*

Historically, venture capital (VC) funds that invest in early stage companies and start-ups have been relatively small when compared with buyout funds that buy mature businesses. However, in recent years venture capitalists have raised some very large funds. For example, Austin Ventures, which is located in Austin, Texas, has over $3 billion under management in nine funds with over a billion dollars raised in its fund VII, and Oak Investment Partners raised a $2.56 billion venture fund in 2006. However, the typical venture fund remains small in comparison with the gargantuan buyout funds raised in recent years.

To determine the size of the venture fund that we needed to raise, my two partners and I approached the problem by asking some basic questions and letting the answers guide our choice of a fund size:

1. *How large a portfolio of companies can we effectively manage?* ** Based on our experiences in founding and advising start-up companies in our target industry (medical technology and services), we estimate that we can each look after 5 companies for a total of 15.

2. *What is the nature of the typical exit and the value at exit for a startup company in our industry space?* To address this question we studied the exits of start-ups in the Medical Technology and Services industry for the last decade. We found that approximately 85% of these exits involved the sale of the start-up to a larger company, for a price between $100 million, to $200 million with only a half-dozen IPOs. We

---

**The answer to this question will vary from fund to fund depending upon the industry in which the fund invests (which determines its capital intensity), and the type of value proposition the VC brings to its portfolio companies. Value proposition refers to the level of VC contribution. For instance, simple monetary investment, or additional specialized industry knowledge, contacts, and that require more frequent involvement with the company.

---

must give up depends on the VC's assessment of the firm's value. This valuation, in turn, reflects the VC's evaluation of the firm's future prospects and the VC's target rate of return for the investment. Although the venture capital evaluation approach may appear unique, it is actually a variant of the hybrid valuation approach, presented in Chapter 7, which combines the methods of multiples and discounted cash flow.

The Cost of Capital for Venture Capital Financing

The venture capital evaluation approach, like any discounted cash flow (DCF) valuation method, requires two primary inputs: a discount rate and an estimate of future cash flows. Figure 8-3 (p. 327) reviews the two basic approaches that we have used to match cash flows and discount rates. The first is the traditional DCF approach to valuation, which discounts *expected* future cash flows using the *expected* rate of return concluded that we should make investments in firms that could be sold at our exit in the $100–$200 million range.

3. *What target return multiples (exit value/invested capital) should the fund use?* Given the risks and opportunities we saw in the industry we decided on a target exit multiple of 10 times our invested capital. Of course we realize that this multiple will be reached only for the most successful investments and the average for the fund will probably be around 5 times. Nonetheless, our target when making an investment is 10.

4. *How much money should we plan to invest in each start-up?* To get to a $100–$200 million exit value, with an exit value/invested capital ratio of 10 times, requires post-money valuations for the start-ups at the time we invest that are in the $10–$20 million range. Thus, if we invest $5 million in a start-up in return for 50% ownership of the firm, this is consistent with a post-money valuation of the firm's, equity of $10 million.*** Using the 10 times target exit multiple implies a valuation of the start-up's equity at exit of $100 million. Similarly, if we invest $10 million in the start-up company in return for half its equity, the post-money value of the startup will be $20 million and it will have an exit value of $200 million. Consequently, we anticipate investing from $5–$10 million in each start-up in two financing rounds.

Putting the answers to these questions together and assuming that we invest an average of $8 million in each of 15 companies, we determined that the optimal fund size for us was $120 million.

***Joe Cunningham, MD, is managing director for Santé Health Ventures, Austin, Texas.

***Post-money valuation is a commonly used term in the venture capital industry and it refers to the value of the start-up business that is implied by the amount of money invested by the VC fund in combination with the fraction of the start-up company's shares the VC acquires.

from a comparable-risk investment (i.e., the opportunity cost of capital). This DCF model is the de facto standard for most applications in finance and was the basis for most of our discussions in prior chapters. The second method is the optimistic or "hoped-for" DCF valuation approach.[4] This variant of the DCF model discounts optimistic or hoped-for cash flows back to the present using optimistic or "hoped-for" rates of return. We believe that the venture capital method falls into this latter category, although this terminology is not used by venture capitalists.

In general, the hoped-for cash flows used to value start-up firms are those that materialize in scenarios in which everything goes as planned. The optimism embedded

[4]There is yet a third variation of the DCF model that we did not include in Figure 8-3, and it is the certainty equivalent model. This model discounts *certainty equivalent* cash flows (i.e., risk adjusted to equal their certain equivalent) using the *risk-free* rate of interest. We will discuss this particular model later, when we consider futures and options.

Figure 8-3 Alternative DCF Valuation Approaches

Approach	Cash Flow	Discount Rate	Applications
Traditional DCF or expected-return valuation model	Expected cash flow	Expected rate of return on comparable-risk investment	Project and business valuation • Traditional WACC approach (Chapters 2 through 5) • Adjusted present value approach (Chapter 7)
Optimistic or "hoped-for" valuation approach	Optimistic cash flow	Optimistic or "hoped-for" rate of return	• Bond valuation (Chapter 4) • Venture capital valuation (Chapter 8) • LBO valuation (Chapter 8)

in these forecasts comes from the fact that entrepreneurs (who are generally very optimistic about the prospects for their businesses) are the primary source of these cash flow estimates. Venture capitalists like to encourage the enthusiasm of the entrepreneurs they fund, so rather than trim optimistic projections, they generally require rates of return that are high enough to offset the entrepreneurs' optimistic cash flow estimates, as well as compensate the venture capitalist for the risk of the venture. Besides, the venture capitalists can turn the entrepreneur's optimistic forecast into ambitious targets that the entrepreneur can be held to in the future.

Venture capital investor required rates of return (ROR) vary with the stage of the investment. For example, in the earliest stage of investment, referred to as the *seed* or *start-up stage,* venture capitalists typically require rates of return ranging from 50% to 100% (per annum!). As the firm progresses through the start-up phase into first- and second-round financings, the required rate of return drops, as the following table indicates.[5]

Stage of Investment[6]	Annual ROR (%)	Typical Expected Holding Period (years)
Seed and start-up	50–100% or more	More than 10
First stage	40–60	5–10
Second stage	30–40	4–7
Expansion	20–30	3–5
Bridge and mezzanine	20–30	1–3

[5]Jeffry Timmons and Stephen Spinelli, *New Venture Creation: Entrepreneurship for the 21st Century,* 6th edition, Irwin, 2004.
[6]See the legend to Figure 8-1 for definitions of each of the types of financing listed here.

Investing in Private Equity—An Interview with Jonathan Hook*

How do you think about rates of return you target for private equity investing?

The lack of liquidity in private equity investments is a critical consideration for anyone who considers making this type of investment. Investing in a private equity fund generally means you are tying up your money for several years. Consequently, as a general rule of thumb we require that private equity investments provide the opportunity to earn 4% to 5% more than the return we anticipate on the S&P 500.

How much of your endowment portfolio do you allocate to private equity?

A primary consideration for us is that we have a balanced and well-diversified portfolio, so we try not to get too overweighted in any one asset class. With private equity we target 15% of our portfolio, but with the flexibility to move this allocation up or down by 5% as opportunities present themselves.

*Jonathan Hook is Associate Vice President and Chief Investment Officer for the Baylor University Endowment Fund, Baylor University, Waco, Texas. For the three-year returns ended in 2006, the Baylor endowment fund tied for the seventh ranking with an 18.8% annual return (out of 656 U.S. colleges and universities).

Do venture capitalists actually realize these "hoped-for" returns? It is difficult to answer this question since the private equity funds are just that, "private," and do not report the performance of their funds on a regular basis. However, one recent study found that when fees are netted out buyout funds earn slightly less than the average return of the S&P 500 stock index.[7] The point here is that the average rates of return realized on both venture and nonventure investments are much lower than the required rates of return used in practice.

It is important to emphasize that these required rates of return reflect the opportunity cost of capital, which is in turn determined by the rate of return on alternative investments. See the Practitioner Insight box titled, "Investing in Private Equity–An Interview with Jonathan Hook. In the long run, we expect required rates of return to

---

[7]See Steven Kaplan and Antoinette Schoar, "Private Equity Performance: Returns, Persistence and Capital Flows," *Journal of Finance* 60, no. 4, pp. 1791–1823. Stephen D. Prowse, "The Economics of the Private Equity Market," *Economic Review of the Federal Reserve Bank of Dallas*, Third Quarter (1998), 21–34) provides similar results for earlier time periods as follows:

Partnerships Formed in:	Venture Capital	Nonventure Capital	Public Small-Company Stocks
1969–79	23.3%	—	11.5%
1980–84	10.0%	24.8%	15.3%
1985–89	15.2%	15.3%	13.4%
1990–91	24.1%	28.9%	15.6%

B E H A V I O R A L   I N S I G H T

Aligning Incentives among the Participants in the Private Equity Market

Asymmetric information is the norm for business dealings. Very simply, the parties to a transaction do *not* share the same information, and this allows one or both parties to take actions that are personally beneficial but detrimental to the other.

Two sets of relationships are of concern in our discussion of private equity finance. The first deals with the relationship between the more-informed general partners, who can potentially take advantage of the less-informed limited partners. The second relationship relates to the private equity partnership and the more-informed managers of the portfolio companies. The table below summarizes how partnerships try to limit the costs that arise from these information asymmetries by first performing extensive due diligence. They also control managerial behavior through the use of incentive-based contracts and by restricting access to partnership financing, since other financing sources are limited for the portfolio companies.

	Agency Relationship	
Means of Control	Limited Partners and General Partners in Private Equity Firms	Private Equity Firm and Portfolio Companies
Indirect: Performance Incentives (the "carrot")	■ Reputation of general partner affects future fund-raising ability ■ General partner compensation based on fund performance	■ Managerial ownership of company shares ensures a long-term interest in company performance ■ Managerial compensation tied to company performance
Direct: Contracts and Internal Controls (the "stick")	■ Covenants of the partnership agreement place boundaries on what the general partner can do and provide for limited partner intervention in extreme circumstances ■ Advisory boards (including limited-partner representation) provide direct oversight over general partner decisions	■ The private equity firm generally takes a board seat and can gain added seats if performance of the portfolio company falters ■ The fact that the private equity firm controls the portfolio company's access to additional financing provides a strong source of control over management of the portfolio companies

be determined by the risk factors discussed in Chapter 4. However, in the short run, the required rates of return on venture capital and other private equity investments are determined by the supply and demand for capital in this sector. When there is lots of capital chasing very few deals, required rates of return are likely to be relatively low. On the other hand, when capital is tight in this sector or when there are lots of opportunities, required rates of return are likely to be higher.

We offer one final point regarding the high required rates of return for venture capital financing, which relates to the fact that the relationship between a start-up firm and its venture capitalist often goes beyond acquiring financing. Frequently, the start-up firm receives valuable business advice and counsel as well as business connections from the venture capitalist who sits on their board. Since VCs typically focus their investing narrowly in a limited number of industries, this expertise and knowledge of the industry can prove essential to the future success of the start-up. The compensation for this nonfinancial source of value is wrapped up in the cost of VC financing, which also explains why VC financing looks so expensive.

Valuing a VC Investment and Structuring the Deal

In most cases, a venture capitalist provides funding to an entrepreneur in exchange for stock in his or her business. The key variable that determines the deal structure is the valuation that the venture capitalist places on the entrepreneur's business.

To illustrate how a venture capitalist values and structures a deal, consider the hypothetical case of Bear-Builders.com. The entrepreneur behind Bear-Builders .com started the business last year with an initial investment of $1 million and now needs an additional $2 million to finance the expansion of its already profitable operations. To raise the funds, the entrepreneur approaches Longhorn Partners, a venture capital firm located in Austin, Texas.

Investor Expectations

Longhorn believes the opportunity is good and is willing to provide the $2 million that Bear-Builders.com needs, in exchange for a share of the company's common equity. Now the key question is, "How much stock will the entrepreneur have to give up in the process of acquiring the needed funds?" Bear-Builders.com is seeking first-stage financing, so Longhorn Partners' required (i.e., hoped-for) rate of return is 50% per year. If Longhorn has a five-year investment horizon[8] and receives no cash distributions until the end of this period (which is frequently the case), then it needs to receive $15,187,500 at the end of five years in order to realize a 50% per annum rate of return. That is,

$$\$2,000,000(1 + .50)^5 = \$15,187,500$$

---

[8]The term "investment horizon" refers to the desired holding period for an investment. Since VC firms raise their capital with limited partnerships that have a limited life (normally five to seven years), they typically have a very short investment horizon when they invest.

Two variables determine whether the investor will actually receive $15,187,500 in five years: (1) the value of the firm at the end of the five years, and (2) the fraction of that value that belongs to the investor. Let's consider each of these factors in turn.

Valuing Bear-Builders.com's Equity

The VC's investment return from providing start-up capital to Bear-Builders.com is derived from the value of Bear-Builders.com's equity at the end of the VC's planned investment period (typically four to six years). The approach we take to value Bear-Builders.com's equity entails first estimating the firm's enterprise value and then deducting any interest-bearing debt the firm may have outstanding.

Estimating Enterprise Value at the End of the Planned Investment Period The first step in the valuation process is coming up with an estimate of enterprise value for Bear-Builders.com after five years, when the venture capitalist hopes to "harvest" or "exit" its investment by selling his or her shares. Venture capitalists typically calculate an estimate of the enterprise value of the firm on the harvest date by forecasting both the firm's ability to produce before-tax cash flows from operations, or EBITDA, and the appropriate multiple of EBITDA for valuing the firm. For example, if Bear-Builders.com's owners forecast the firm's EBITDA in five years to be $6 million, and the VC uses an EBITDA multiple of five, then Bear-Builders.com will be worth $30 million ($6 million × 5) when Longhorn Partners plans to harvest its investment in the firm.

Note that there are typically no interim equity cash flows to the VC (or the entrepreneur) prior to the VC's exit. This results from the fact that all available cash is either reinvested in the firm or used to service the firm's debt.

To recap quickly, the calculations used to estimate the enterprise value of Bear-Builders.com at the end of five years are as follows:

EBITDA in Year 5	$ 6,000,000
EBITDA multiple	× 5
Equals: Enterprise value	$ 30,000,000

Calculating Equity Value at the End of the Planned Investment Period Now that we have estimated the firm's enterprise value at the end of five years ($30,000,000), we can calculate the value of its equity as follows, i.e.,

$$\text{Equity Value} = \text{Enterprise Value} - \text{Interest-Bearing Debt} + \text{Cash}$$

or, where $\text{Net Debt} = \text{Interest-Bearing Debt} - \text{Cash}$

then $\text{Equity Value} = \text{Enterprise Value} - \text{Net Debt}$

Note that we subtract only interest-bearing debt from enterprise value, just as we did in Chapter 7. Moreover, to estimate equity value, we typically add in the projected amount of cash in the firm on the harvest (i.e., exit) date to our estimate of equity value. This assumes that the firm's cash balance can be viewed as excess cash and therefore is not reflected in the EBITDA multiple used to estimate enterprise value. For example, if we expect Bear-Builders.com to have $300,000 in cash at the end of five years, and if Bear-Builders.com is expected to have $3 million in interest-bearing debt in five years, the company's equity value would be $27.3 million, calculated as follows:

Enterprise value	$30,000,000
Less: Net debt (i.e., interest-bearing debt less cash)	(2,700,000)
Equals: Equity value	$27,300,000

Computing Ownership Interests—Defining the Deal Structure

Up to this point we have shown that if all goes as planned, the value of Bear-Builders.com's stockholder equity in five years will be $27.3 million. The venture capitalist requires $15,187,500 at that time in order to earn a 50% per annum rate of return on its $2,000,000 investment. Thus, to achieve this total return, the venture capitalist must own 56% of the firm's stock, computed as follows:

$$\frac{\text{Venture Capitalist's}}{\text{Ownership Percentage}} = \frac{\text{VC's Required Equity Value (in Year 5)}}{\text{Estimated Equity Value for the Firm (in Year 5)}}$$

$$= \frac{\$15,187,500}{\$27,300,000} = 56\%$$

Under this deal structure, the founder will own the remaining 44% of the common stock (100% − 56% = 44%), which would entitle him or her to shares worth $12,112,500 in five years.

Summing Up the Venture Capital Method

We have briefly described the process used by venture capitalists to evaluate an entrepreneurial company and structure a financing agreement. The methodology combines the method of multiples based on comparable transactions along with discounted cash flow. Very simply, the investor (venture capitalist) determines the fraction of the firm's ownership it must get in order to satisfy its return requirement as follows:

1. The investor first determines a rate of return that he or she hopes to realize from the investment ($k_{\text{Hoped-for VC Return}}$).

2. The investor's required rate of return is used to determine the dollar value that the investor hopes to realize at the end of the planned holding period, H years (typically four to seven), in order to justify making the initial investment in the firm plus cash less interest bearing debt i.e.,[9]

$$\left(\begin{array}{c} \text{Venture Capital} \\ \text{Investment}_{\text{Today}} \end{array} \right)(1 + k_{\text{Hoped-for VC Return}})^H = \left(\begin{array}{c} \text{Required Value} \\ \text{of the Venture Capital} \\ \text{Investment}_H \end{array} \right) \quad (8.1)$$

3. The investor next estimates the value of the firm's equity at the end of the planned holding period using a multiple of the firm's projected EBITDA in year H, i.e.,

$$\begin{array}{c} \text{Estimated Equity} \\ \text{Value}_H \end{array} = \text{EBITDA}_H \times \text{EBITDA Multiple}_H + \text{Cash}_H - \text{Debt}_H \quad (8.2)$$

4. Finally, the investor calculates the fraction of the firm's future value that will be needed to satisfy his or her total dollar required return (i.e., the initial investment compounded at the investor's "hoped-for" rate of return over the investment period), as follows:

$$\begin{array}{c} \text{Ownership} \\ \text{Share} \end{array} = \frac{\left(\begin{array}{c} \text{Required Value} \\ \text{of the Venture Capital} \\ \text{Investment}_H \end{array} \right)}{\text{Estimated Equity Value}_H} \quad (8.3)$$

Thus, the VC method results in an estimate of the VC's ownership share that generates the appropriate hoped-for rate of return.

Pre- and Post-Money Value of the Firm's Equity

We just pointed out that the venture capital approach focuses on the value of the firm at the future date when the venture capitalist plans to exit the investment. However, venture capitalists also estimate *the value today* for the businesses in which they invest. The implied value of the equity of the firm today is captured by something called the **post-money investment value.** For example, in the Bear-Builders.com

---

[9]This relationship holds only where the VC does not receive any interim cash flows, such as interest or preferred dividends in those cases where the firm issues debt or preferred stock. If interim cash flows are paid, then the right-hand side of Equation 8.1 is reduced by an amount equal to the future value of all such interim payments, compounded at the venture capitalist's "hoped-for" rate of return (e.g., where interim interest payments equal to Int_t are made each year up until year H):

$$\left(\begin{array}{c} \text{Venture Capital} \\ \text{Investment}_{\text{Today}} \end{array} \right)(1 + k_{\text{Hoped-for VC Return}})^H + \sum_{t=1}^{H} \text{Int}_t (1 + k_{\text{Hoped-for VC Return}})^{t-1}$$

$$= \left(\begin{array}{c} \text{Required Value} \\ \text{of the Venture Capital} \\ \text{Investment}_H \end{array} \right)$$

example, the VC gets 56% ownership for an investment of $2 million; this implies that the value of the firm's equity after (post) the VC firm's investment is $3,571,428. That is,

$$\begin{array}{l}\text{Post-Money} \\ \text{Investment Value} \\ \text{of the Firm's Equity}\end{array} = \frac{\text{Funding Provided by the VC Firm}}{\text{VC Firm's Ownership Interest (\%)}}$$

$$= \frac{\$2,000,000}{.56} = \$3,571,428$$

The post-money investment value is the focal point for negotiations between the entrepreneur and the VC. Basically, it provides a shorthand way to describe the structure of the VC deal.

Venture capitalists also use the term **pre-money investment value,** to refer to the difference between the post-money implied value of the firm's equity and the amount of money that the venture capitalist puts in the firm. In this case the pre-money investment value is $1,571,428, i.e.,

$$\begin{array}{l}\text{Pre-Money} \\ \text{Investment Value} \\ \text{of the Firm's Equity}\end{array} = \begin{array}{l}\text{Post-Money} \\ \text{Investment Value} \\ \text{of the Firm's Equity}\end{array} - \begin{array}{l}\text{Funding Provided} \\ \text{by the VC Firm}\end{array}$$

$$= \$3,571,428 - 2,000,000 = \$1,571,428$$

The critical elements of both post- and pre-money investment value have already been discussed, and the computations are straightforward. The importance of these terms to the financial analyst derives from their common usage among VC investors. The pre- and post-money investment values represent estimates, albeit crude ones, of the value of the firm's equity *on the date of* the financing.

Refining the Deal Structure

Entrepreneurs are often surprised and frustrated to learn how much of the firm they must give up to obtain VC financing. In this section we discuss how the entrepreneur might lower the rate of return required by the venture capitalist by assuming more of the risk of the venture. Although we cannot explicitly describe how this trade-off works, we can describe how the structure of the deal can be adjusted to reallocate risk and return between the entrepreneur and private equity investor. We consider two alternative ways to structure the venture capital investment. These include the use of *staged-financing* commitments and issuing a different type of security (e.g., preferred stock as opposed to common stock).

Using Staged-Financing Commitments
As we mentioned earlier, the rates of return required by venture capitalists are quite high because the investments are quite risky and the cash flow forecasts tend to be overly optimistic. Thus, anything that can be done to lower the venture capitalist's risks, and signal the entrepreneur's confidence, will result in lower required rates of return from the VC.

Because venture capitalists tend to be skeptical about cash flow forecasts and want to limit their risks, they generally make what is known as *staged-financing commitments*. Instead of providing the entrepreneur with all the required funding up front, the VC generally makes partial or staged investments as the firm meets predetermined performance milestones and as money is needed. This process gives the VC control over the firm's access to capital and thereby reduces the risk of the VC's investment. If the VC is not satisfied with the firm's progress, then the next installment is simply not made.[10]

Let's return to our Bear-Builders.com example to illustrate how staged financing can reduce the cost of financing to the entrepreneurial firm. In our original example, the entrepreneur needed $2 million, and the venture capitalist was willing to provide the funds in return for an annual rate of return of 50%. Thus the venture capitalist required that the value of its invested capital be worth $15,187,500 = $2,000,000 $(1 + .50)^5$ in five years. Since the firm's equity is estimated to be worth $27,300,000 at this time, we calculated that the venture capitalist must receive $15,187,500/ $27,300,000 = 56% of the equity of the firm.

Now let's consider a staged-investment alternative in which the venture capitalist invests $1 million initially (still requiring a 50% rate of return, since this is first-stage capital) but invests the second $1 million two years later, on the condition that the firm has achieved certain performance benchmarks. Since the second-stage investment is less risky than the first, we assume the VC requires only a 30% return on this second infusion of capital.

Using staged commitments, the venture capitalist requires the following dollar return at the end of five years (assuming the second-stage financing is forthcoming):

Financing Stages	Funding Provided	Return Required at the End of Year 5
First-stage investment	$1,000,000	$1,000,000 $(1 + .50)^5 = \$7,593,750$
Second-stage investment	$1,000,000	$1,000,000 $(1 + .30)^3 = \$2,197,000$
Total	$2,000,000	$9,790,750

The VC now requires only $9,790,750 for his or her $2,000,000 investment. This amount represents $9,790,750/$27,300,000 = 36% of the value of the firm's equity at the end of five years. This dramatic reduction (from 56% to 36%) represents the impact of two things: First, the VC firm pays only $1 million in capital for the first two years (not $2 million as before); second, the VC's required return in the second stage financing is only 30%.

Note that the above analysis assumes that the second-stage financing is provided with certainty. This, however, is not necessarily the case, since the VC has control over the decision to invest at the second stage and will only do so if the investment looks favorable at that time. In making a staged commitment, the VC has the "option" to invest at the second stage, rather than an obligation, and will choose not to invest more

---

[10]We will have more to say about staged financing later, when we discuss options.

money if the firm does not perform as planned. Since this option is valuable (as we discuss in Chapter 11), the venture capitalist is willing to provide financing at a lower rate.

It should be stressed that the entrepreneur gives up less of his or her business, but there is no free lunch here. The entrepreneur is required to take more risk. If the performance benchmarks are not met after two years, he or she will not be able to obtain the necessary funds to remain in business. But if the entrepreneur is very confident about meeting the benchmark, then the staged financing may be preferable. Similarly, a lack of willingness to accept a staged-financing commitment by an entrepreneur would send a negative signal to the VC.

Using Debt or Preferred Stock

A confident entrepreneur may also get more favorable financing by assuming more of the risk of the venture and limiting the VC's risk exposure by issuing debt or preferred equity securities. The VC's risk is reduced by virtue of the superior claim debt and preferred stock enjoy over common stock. Again, there is no free lunch here; the entrepreneur receives less costly financing by limiting the VC's risk exposure and in the process, bears more of the risk himself or herself.

To demonstrate how this works, we use the Bear-Builders.com example again. This time, instead of issuing common stock to the venture capitalist, the firm issues convertible preferred stock with a dividend rate of 8%, or an annual dividend of $160,000 ($2 million × .08 = $160,000). The preferred stock can be converted into the firm's common stock at the discretion of the VC. (There is generally no incentive on the part of the investor to convert early.) If the VC wants a 40% return and the investment horizon is 5 years, the cash flow stream to the VC consists of the following:

VC's "hoped-for" rate of return	40%					
VC's investment horizon	5					
Annual Interest/dividend payments	$ 160,000					
Financing provided by the VC	$ (2,000,000)					
	Year 0	**Year 1**	**Year 2**	**Year 3**	**Year 4**	**Year 5**
Dividends	$ (2,000,000)	$ 160,000	$ 160,000	$ 160,000	$ 160,000	$ 160,000
Conversion value in five years						$ 9,003,386
VC cash flows	$ (2,000,000)	$ 160,000	$ 160,000	$ 160,000	$ 160,000	$ 9,163,386

The key calculation we need to make is the required conversion value of the shares that will be realized in Year 5. It turns out that if the preferred shares can be converted into $9,003,386 worth of common stock, then the VC's $2 million investment will realize the VC's desired 40% annual rate of return. This, in turn, requires that the VC be given 32.98% of the firm's shares that were earlier valued at $27,300,000—a substantial savings over the 56% ownership share that was required when using common stock.

Over the last 25 years, we've seen seismic shifts in the way private equity investors generate investment returns. At the early part of this decade, we re-tooled our investment approach to account for changes in lending levels, and now seek to add value to our investments using three primary tools.

First, we follow a time-tested/proven investment strategy. We invest in under-managed, under-appreciated, or under-capitalized assets that can be transformed into much larger, more valuable companies by investing new capital and creating well-defined operating strategies. This investment approach allows us to generate value for investors by taking advantage of the price premium paid for large public companies compared to small, privately held companies. This strategy can be further simplified by focusing on specific sectors. HM Capital, for example, primarily invests in the energy, food, and media industries—sectors in which the firm has a long history of success and a broad network of contacts.

A recent example of this investment strategy is HM Capital's investment in Regency Energy Partners in December 2004. Prior to acquisition, Regency was a set of disparate natural gas gathering and processing assets in the Southwest. In just 14 months, HM Capital transformed Regency from a group of natural gas assets to a significant industry player, and took the company public. The IPO provided HM Capital with a means of returning all invested capital to investors, in a structure that allowed our investors to maintain a large stake in Regency.

The second tool we use is _Change Capital_. We transform our acquisitions through strategies designed to grow revenues, increase profits, and optimize assets. At HM Capital, we refer to these strategies and the activist role we play in transforming our investments as "_Change Capital_." We often acquire companies that have not been run as efficiently as we think is possible. This is sometimes due to the fact that the company is a division of a larger company that has been ignored by the management of the parent company. In other instances, the acquired company is being run by a management team that has little ownership in the company and minimal incentive to manage the company in a lean fashion. In either instance, our goal is to align management's interests with ours to reduce operating costs and create value for owners.

During our review of an investment opportunity, we identify the changes that will need to be implemented post-acquisition, and whether the right management team is in place to execute these strategies. We continue to work with management post-acquisition to further refine and implement our _Change Capital_ strategies.

Going back to the Regency example, HM Capital's investment thesis was that the company was an under-utilized midstream asset with attractive internal growth characteristics. Along with Regency management, HM Capital developed a _Change Capital_ plan to invest $140 million to expand Regency's transmission capacity and transform it from a natural gas gathering- and processing-focused business to a natural gas transmission business. This capital expenditure quadrupled Regency's pipeline capacity, doubled its cash flow, and helped position the company for an IPO.

The third tool at our disposal is the use of financial leverage as we engineer our capital structure. Much has been made over the amount of debt utilized by private equity firms. In fact, we were typically referred to as leveraged buyout (LBO) investors during the 1980s because we used high levels of debt to fund our acquisitions. Today, we utilize leverage to provide us with the financial flexibility needed to implement our *Change Capital* strategies and generate a higher rate of return on our investments. When used properly, financial leverage is simply an equity return accelerant that turns doubles into triples and triples into home runs.

The private equity industry has changed significantly since I first started in the business. Leverage is more optimally used to balance the debt and equity requirements of the capital structure, and the size of transactions has grown dramatically. It is not uncommon today to have private equity firms join forces to acquire public companies for $15 to $25 billion. In addition, the objective of today's private equity investor has evolved—take a company private, restructure its cost structure, and then take the firm back public or sell it to a private investor. Thus, the approach to making money has shifted from "break-ups" in the 1970s and 1980s to "buy and build" in the mid-1980s through the 1990s to "buy, restructure, and build." The more things change, the more they stay the same. Private equity as an asset class is as attractive as it has ever been.

About the Author. Jack D. Furst co-founded Hicks, Muse, Tate & Furst in 1989, renamed HM Capital Partners in 2006, and is now a Senior Advisor and member of the firm's Investment Committee. He also serves on the board of a number of portfolio companies and nonprofit institutions. Mr. Furst received his BS from the College of Business Administration at Arizona State University in 1981 and his MBA from the Graduate School of Business at the University of Texas in 1984.

About HM Capital. HM Capital Partners LLC is a Dallas-based private equity firm that leverages its sector expertise to acquire, change, and build strategically relevant business. HM Capital creates investment pools from investors (pension funds, financial institutions, and wealthy private investors) in the form of limited partnerships. The firm typically targets underperforming companies in specific niches (including cable TV, directories businesses, gas production and transmission, and branded foods), builds them up into strategically relevant businesses, and sells them to private investors or in the public markets.

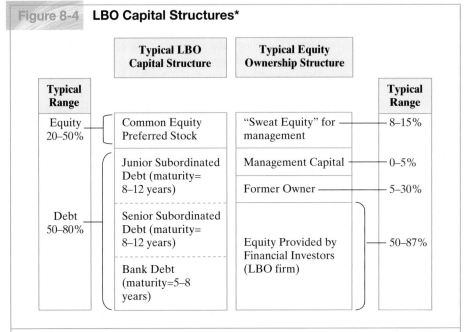

Figure 8-4   **LBO Capital Structures***

*Based on Scot Sedlacek, "Leveraged Buyouts: Building Shareholder Value through Capital Structure," Broadview International, LLC (April 2, 2003).

8.4 VALUING LBO INVESTMENTS

Leveraged buyouts or LBOs represent a business acquisition strategy whereby an investor group acquires all the equity of a firm and assumes its debts.[11] The acquisition is financed predominantly with debt—hence the term "leveraged" buyout. Figure 8-4 illustrates the proportion of the total financing that comes from debt and how it varies over time with market conditions, and typically constitutes 50–80% of the capital structure of the LBO.

The extreme use of financial leverage is a defining characteristic of LBOs when compared to firms' pre–LBO capital structures. Why is it that private equity investments are so highly levered? Perhaps private equity sponsors can more easily attract investors by providing highly levered returns rather than more modest unlevered returns. However, this "pure leverage" effect cannot create value on its own. Financial

---

[11]When the acquisition is made in conjunction with the firm's management, we refer to the transaction as a *management buyout* or *MBO*.

INDUSTRY INSIGHT

Leveraged Buyouts—Bust-ups to Build-ups

In the 1980s the term *leveraged buyout* or simply *LBO* became synonymous with corporate greed. Books and movies such as *Wall Street, Barbarians at the Gate,* and *Other People's Money* glamorized the process of buying a company using borrowed money to finance most of the purchase. Technically, an LBO is simply the acquisition of a company using lots of debt and very little equity. However, the extreme use of debt financing has important behavioral implications. The principal and interest requirements of the debt are usually so onerous so as to effectively bond the acquired firm's management to a strict regime of maximizing the cash flow potential of the firm. This can be a very important source of value for a firm that was not efficiently run prior to the LBO.

A popular form of LBO in the 1980s involved acquiring a target firm that was not performing up to its potential. The acquiring firm then would sell off excess capacity (productive assets) and lay off workers at the target firm to make the remaining assets more productive. This type of LBO became known as the "bust-up LBO."

In many cases, in a matter of years or sometimes only months, the LBO firm that made the acquisition realized a huge profit from the resale of the acquired firm. Most of the purchase price was financed by borrowing with very high credit risk *junk bonds,* and the interest and principal payments were made using the acquisition's future cash flows (a combination of the profits of the firm and the sale of assets in the case of "bust-up" LBOs). Thus, in a sense, the acquired company essentially paid for itself, while the managers of the LBO firm captured any increase in value of the firm as their profit.

More recently the "build-up LBO" has been utilized to consolidate firms in fragmented industries with large numbers of competitors and the potential for economies of size and scale of operations. The process entails first acquiring a "platform" or base company and then purchasing a number of related firms, so as to build a core firm of sufficient size to be sold in the public markets.

leverage also has an important bonding effect: By saddling their investments with a substantial amount of debt, private equity sponsors force managers to make the tough choices that may be necessary in turnaround situations. In addition, the fact that sophisticated financial institutions are willing to provide the debt for these highly levered entities should provide some comfort for the equity investors.

Alternative LBO Acquisition Strategies—Bust-ups and Build-ups

As the Industry Insight box (p. 339) describes, the use of the LBO acquisition strategy was very popular in the 1980s. Most buyouts in that era were known as "*bust-up*" LBOs. The term "bust-up" refers to the fact that once control of the acquired company is complete, the new owner sells off some (or all) of the firm's assets and uses the proceeds to repay the debt used to finance the acquisition. These acquisitions were also associated with efforts to increase efficiency in the operations of the remaining assets, which often entails reductions in the firm's workforce.

Beginning in the 1990s a different private equity strategy evolved that creates a large public company from the acquisition of an initial company (the "platform company"), followed by a series of smaller add-on acquisitions. This strategy, described in the Practitioner Insight box interview with Jack Furst (pp. 336–337), is generally referred to as the "*build-up*" strategy.

Example—Build-up LBOs

The build-up LBO is a special case of a roll-up merger strategy, where an acquiring firm purchases a group of firms in the same or very closely related businesses and then combines them into a single entity. For example, Hicks, Muse, Tate and Furst, a private equity firm in Dallas, Texas (and predecessor of HM Capital), purchased Berg Electronics from E. I. DuPont in 1993 for $370 million. The acquisition became the platform company to which over $100 million in acquisitions were added before Berg's initial public offering (IPO) in 1996.[12]

To illustrate the valuation issues involved in a build-up LBO, we consider a typical build-up transaction by a private equity partnership. The principals of our hypothetical private equity firm, Hokie Partners, LP, are considering the acquisition of PMG Foods, Inc., an electronics firm that manufactures printed circuit boards used in a wide variety of applications. PMG Foods is a wholly owned subsidiary of a large chemical company, which has decided the business is no longer critical to the firm's future success and seeks to sell PMG Foods to the highest bidder.

Acquisition data for PMG Foods found in Table 8-1 indicate that PMG Foods has current earnings before interest, taxes, depreciation, and amortization expense (EBITDA) of $100 million. The acquisition is expected to require a purchase price equal to five times the current level of EBITDA, or $500 million. In addition to the equity investment from Hokie Partners and its limited partners, the acquisition is financed with 75% debt that has an interest rate of 14%. The debt has covenants that require that all excess cash be used to retire principal, which means that the equity investors will not receive anything until Year 5, when the firm is sold. This requirement is commonly referred to as the *cash sweep*.

---

[12]For additional details, see S. Kaplan, J. Martin, and R. Parrino, Berg Electronics Corporation, http://ssrn.com/abstract=256107.

Table 8-1	PMG Foods, Inc., Acquisition Data ($ millions)		
Earnings Estimates		**Acquisition and Sale EBITDA Multiples**	
Current-year EBITDA (millions)	$100.00	Purchase multiple—Platform Company (PMG Foods)	5
Growth rate in EBITDA	10%	Purchase multiple—Add-on Company (Centex)	3
Planned holding period	5 years	Company sale (harvest) multiple	6
Corporate tax rate	35%		
Depreciable life of assets	10 years		
Depreciation expense (Year 0)	$ 40.00		
LBO Capital Structure			
Debt/Assets (book values)	75%		
Interest cost	14%		
Annual CAPEX	$ 50.00		

Hokie Partners projects that it can grow EBITDA at a rate of 10% per year for five years and then sell the firm, hopefully for six times EBITDA. When Hokie sells the firm, the firm's outstanding debt will be repaid and the remaining funds distributed to the equity investors.

Estimating Equity Returns for the Platform Company

In Table 8-2, we evaluate the equity free cash flows (EFCFs) and corresponding compound rate of return for the case where the estimates set out in Table 8-1 are realized. Recall the definition of EFCF from Chapter 2, which focuses on the cash flows to the common stockholder (as contrasted with the firm free cash flows).[13] Because of the cash-sweep requirement for the firm's debt, the EFCFs for each of the five years of the planning period are set to zero,[14] which implies that the projected principal payments on the firm's debt equal the amount of cash left over after meeting all the firm's required expenditures (including new capital equipment purchases).

Note that the transaction requires an investment of $500 million, and if all works as planned, it will produce an EBITDA of $161.05 million in five years. Under this scenario, Hokie Partners will sell PMG Foods for the projected six times EBITDA, which implies a value of $966.31 million and an equity value of $715.37 million (net of the outstanding debt in Year 5 of $250.93 million). Given these projections, the equity

---

[13]EFCF = Net Income + Depreciation Expense − Capital Expenditures (CAPEX) − Change in Net Working Capital − Principal Payments + New Debt Issued.

[14]Note that in Table 8-2 the EFCFs are forced to equal zero through the retirement of $3.13 million in debt in Year 1, thereby reducing the firm's debt from $375 million to $371.88 million; the retirement of $12.31 million in Year 2, which reduces the debt further to $359.57 million; and so forth.

Table 8-2 Estimating Equity Returns from the Acquisition of PMG Foods, Inc. ($ millions)

Panel a. Projected Net Income and EFCF

Pro Forma Income Statements	Year 0	Year 1	Year 2	Year 3	Year 4	Year 5
EBITDA		$ 110.00	$ 121.00	$ 133.10	$ 146.41	$ 161.05
Less: Depreciation		(45.00)	(50.00)	(55.00)	(60.00)	(65.00)
EBIT		$ 65.00	$ 71.00	$ 78.10	$ 86.41	$ 96.05
Less: Interest		(52.50)	(52.06)	(50.34)	(47.11)	(42.14)
Earnings before taxes		$ (12.50)	$ 18.94	$ 27.76	$ 39.30	$ 53.91
Less: Texas		(4.38)	(6.63)	(9.72)	(13.75)	(18.87)
Net income		$ 8.13	$ 12.31	$ 18.04	$ 25.54	$ 35.04
Calculation of EFCF						
Plus: Depreciation		$ 45.00	$ 50.00	$ 55.00	$ 60.00	$ 65.00
Less: CAPEX		(50.00)	(50.00)	(50.00)	(50.00)	(50.00)
Less: Principal payments		(3.13)	(12.31)	(23.04)	(35.54)	(50.04)
Equity free cash flow		$ —	$ —	$ —	$ —	$ —

	Year 0	Year 1	Year 2	Year 3	Year 4	Year 5
Outstanding loan	$375.00	$371.88	$359.57	$336.52	$300.98	$250.93

Panel b. Valuing the Platform Company LBO in Year 5 and the IRR on the Investment

	Year 0	Year 5
Debt	$ 375.00	$ 250.93
Equity	$ 125.00	$ 715.37
Firm	$ 500.00	$ 966.31
Internal rates of return (IRR)		
Equity (with debt—levered)	41.75%	
Equity (no debt—unlevered)	22.46%	

investor's original $125 million investment grows to $715.37 million in five years, which represents a compound annual rate of return of 41.75%.[15] This, of course, should be viewed as a hoped-for (rather than expected) return, based on a scenario where EBITDA grows quite quickly and the firm is sold for a higher multiple than was paid for it. The returns are also quite high because they represent the returns to a highly levered equity investment.

---

[15]$125 million$(1 + \text{IRR})^5$ = $715.37 million such that IRR is 41.75%.

To understand the effects of financial leverage on the equity return, we consider the *unlevered* returns on this investment given this same scenario. If the equity investor put up the full $500 million acquisition price, then the investment would have thrown off cash flows each year equal to the principal and after-tax interest. Again assuming the firm sells for $966.31 million after five years, the compound annual rate of return is only 22.46% per year.[16] This rate of return is still high, but much lower than the 41.75% levered-equity rate of return. Similarly, we can consider the returns on this investment under a much less favorable scenario where the EBITDA growth rate is 4% rather than 10% and the EBITDA multiple in Year 5 is only four instead of six times. In this scenario, the equity holders realize a value in five years of only $156.95 million, which implies a levered return of only 4.66%. In this less-favorable scenario, the unlevered return is 7.90%, which exceeds the levered return since the investment earns less than the interest rate on the debt. Financial leverage is truly a two-edged sword! It magnifies returns when outcomes are favorable, but decreases returns when outcomes are not favorable.

Analyzing the Returns from the Add-on Investment

The second stage of a build-up LBO involves the acquisition of one or more "add-on" investments. To illustrate how to evaluate these add-on acquisitions, we consider the acquisition details for Centex PowerPak Systems, Inc., found in Table 8-3.

This acquisition differs from the platform-company acquisition in two important respects. First, it is a much smaller company, with annual EBITDA of only $12 million in the current year. As discussed earlier in the Practitioner Insight box featuring Jack Furst, small companies are often acquired for lower price multiples, and we will

Table 8-3 **Acquisition Details for Centex PowerPak Systems, Inc. ($ millions)**

Current-year EBITDA	$12.00	EBITDA acquisition multiple	3 times
Growth rate in EBITDA	10%	Planning period	5 years
Corporate tax rate	35%	Annual CAPEX	$10.00
Depreciable life of assets	10 years	Depreciation expense (Year 0)	$ 3.00
LBO Capital Structure			
Debt/Assets	100%		
Interest cost (planning period)	14%		
Interest cost (post–planning period)	9%		

---

[16]The IRR to the equity investor who invests $500 million in return for the following cash flows (millions) is 22.46%. Note that in Year 5 the investor receives the annual equity cash flow of $77.43 million plus the anticipated sale value of the firm of $966.31 million (= $1,043.74 million).

Year 0	Year 1	Year 2	Year 3	Year 4	Year 5
$(500.00)	$37.25	$46.15	$55.77	$66.17	$1,043.74

assume that in this case Centex can be purchased at three times its current level of EBITDA, or $36 million. Adding the relatively cheap assets of the add-on firm to the more highly valued platform company and selling them for the higher multiple of the platform company in five years provides added value that private equity firms refer to as *multiples expansion.*

The second difference between the platform-company acquisition and the acquisition of the add-on company relates to financing. The add-on company's debt is generally guaranteed by the platform company, so it is difficult to determine exactly how much of the debt can be attributed to the add-on. In the particular example we are considering, the platform company finances the acquisition entirely with debt.

Once again, the initial EFCFs are set to zero since all of the firm's cash flow will be used to pay down its debt. However, the firm's initial cash flows are not sufficient to cover the debt service (interest) and CAPEX requirements (see Table 8-4), and so

Table 8-4   Analysis of the Add-on Acquisition of Centex PowerPak Systems, Inc. ($ millions)

	Year 0	Year 1	Year 2	Year 3	Year 4	Year 5
EBITDA		$ 13.20	$ 14.52	$ 15.97	$ 17.57	$ 19.33
Less: Depreciation		(4.00)	(5.00)	(6.00)	(7.00)	(8.00)
EBIT		$ 9.20	$ 9.52	$ 9.97	$ 10.57	$ 11.33
Less: Interest		(5.04)	(5.50)	(5.84)	(6.02)	(6.03)
Earnings before taxes		$ 4.16	$ 4.02	$ 4.14	$ 4.55	$ 5.30
Less: Taxes		(1.46)	(1.41)	(1.45)	(1.59)	(1.86)
Net income		$ 2.70	$ 2.61	$ 2.69	$ 2.96	$ 3.45
Plus: Depreciation		$ 4.00	$ 5.00	$ 6.00	$ 7.00	$ 8.00
Less: CAPEX		(10.00)	(10.00)	(10.00)	(10.00)	(10.00)
Less: Principal payments*		3.30	2.39	1.31	0.04	(1.45)
Equity free cash flows**	$ —	$ —	$ —	$ —	$ —	$ 74.36
	Year 0	Year 1	Year 2	Year 3	Year 4	Year 5
Debt	$36.00	$ 39.30	$ 41.68	$ 43.00	$ 43.04	$ 41.59

*Note that principal payments are subtracted, whereas additional borrowing is added. Thus in Year 1 it is necessary to borrow an added $3.3 million in order to meet the firm's cash flow needs.

**Since 100% of the purchase price is financed by borrowing, the equity investment in Year 0 is zero. Furthermore, in Year 5 Centex's EFCF includes the estimated value of the equity in the firm based upon the assumption that the firm is sold. Since there is no added equity investment in Year 0, the IRR for the add-on investment is undefined (translation — very large). If only 75% of the acquisition price were borrowed, as was the case for the platform company, the IRR would have been 57.88%, which is still quite high.

it will need to borrow more in Years 1 through 4. In Year 1, the cash flows fall short by $3.3 million, increasing the total debt for the Centex acquisition from $36 million to $39.3 million. Beginning in Year 5, the growth in operating income is sufficient to pay interest, cover CAPEX, and pay down the debt of the add-on investment by $1.45 million.

Table 8-4 presents an analysis of the projected earnings and equity cash flow from the Centex PowerPak add-on acquisition. In this case, the rate of return on equity will be determined by how much of the new debt that is issued to acquire the firm can be attributed to Centex PowerPak. If we had assumed 75% debt financing, just like the platform company, the IRR on the $9 million = 25% × $36 million investment in the add-on company would have been 57.88%, which is still very high.

Does the add-on make sense? If the platform company and the add-on companies are of like risk, and the platform company is deemed a good investment with its 41.75% rate of return on equity, the add-on with its much higher return is an even more attractive investment.

In Panel a of Table 8-5 (p. 346), we see that the combined (platform plus add-on acquisitions) EBITDA reaches $180.38 million by Year 5, which, based on the assumed harvest or sale multiple of six times EBITDA at the end of Year 5, implies an expected exit value of $1,082.26 million. Netting out the $292.53 million in debt still owed by the combined firms at the end of Year 5 generates an estimated equity value of $789.74 million. Comparing our initial equity investment of $125 million to this terminal value, we estimate a compound annual rate of return on the equity investment of 44.58%. In contrast, if no debt had been used and the combined purchase prices of $536 million had been raised through equity financing, the combined EFCFs for the platform and add-on investment would be the following:

	Year 0	Year 1	Year 2	Year 3	Year 4	Year 5
EBITDA		$ 123.20	$ 135.52	$ 149.07	$ 163.98	$ 180.38
Less: Depreciation expense		(49.00)	(55.00)	(61.00)	(67.00)	(73.00)
EBIT		$ 74.20	$ 80.52	$ 88.07	$ 96.98	$ 107.38
Less: Interest expense		—	—	—	—	—
EBT		$ 74.20	$ 80.52	$ 88.07	$ 96.98	$ 107.38
Less: Taxes		(25.97)	(28.18)	(30.83)	(33.94)	(37.58)
Net income		$ 48.23	$ 52.34	$ 57.25	$ 63.04	$ 69.80
Plus: Depreciation		49.00	55.00	61.00	67.00	73.00
Less: CAPEX		(60.00)	(60.00)	(60.00)	(60.00)	(60.00)
Less: Principal payments		—	—	—	—	—
EFCF	$ (536.00)	$ 37.23	$ 47.34	$ 58.25	$ 70.04	$ 1,165.06

The compound annual rate of return to the equity shareholders based on the EFCFs in the bottom row of the above table, then, is only 23.07%, which is quite high for an unlevered return.

Table 8-5 Analysis of the Build-up LBO ($ millions)

Panel a. Pro Forma Income Statements and EFCF

	Year 0	Year 1	Year 2	Year 3	Year 4	Year 5
EBITDA		$ 123.20	$ 135.52	$ 149.07	$ 163.98	$ 180.38
Less: Depreciation expense		(49.00)	(55.00)	(61.00)	(67.00)	(73.00)
EBIT		$ 74.20	$ 80.52	$ 88.07	$ 96.98	$ 107.38
Less: Interest expense		(57.54)	(57.56)	(56.17)	(53.13)	(48.16)
EBT		$ 16.66	$ 22.96	$ 31.90	$ 43.85	$ 59.21
Less: Taxes		(5.83)	(8.03)	(11.16)	(15.35)	(20.73)
Net income		$ 10.83	$ 14.92	$ 20.73	$ 28.50	$ 38.49
Plus: Depreciation		49.00	55.00	61.00	67.00	73.00
Less: CAPEX		(60.00)	(60.00)	(60.00)	(60.00)	(60.00)
Less: Principal payments*		0.17	(9.92)	(21.73)	(35.50)	(51.49)
EFCF**	$ (125.00)	$ —	$ —	$ —	$ —	$ —

	Year 0	Year 1	Year 2	Year 3	Year 4	Year 5
Debt	$ 411.00	$ 411.17	$ 401.25	$ 379.52	$ 344.02	$ 292.53

Panel b. Valuing the Build-up (Combined) LBO in Year 5 and the IRR on the Investment

Evaluation of IRR on the Platform Company Investment

	Year 0		Year 5
Debt	$ 411.00	$	292.53
Equity	$ 125.00	$	789.74***
Firm	$ 536.00	$	1,082.26

Internal rates of return (IRR)

Equity with debt (levered)	44.58%
Equity with no debt (unlevered)	23.07%

*Note that principal payments are subtracted, whereas additional borrowing is added. Thus in Year 1 it is necessary to borrow an added $3.3 million in order to meet the firm's cash flow needs.

**Since 75% of the purchase price for the platform company and 100% of the purchase price of the add-on are financed by borrowing, the equity investment in Year 0 is $125 million. Furthermore, in Year 5, Centex's EFCF includes the estimated value of the equity in the two acquisitions based upon the assumption that the firm is sold.

** Equity Value (Year 5) = Firm Value (Year 5) − Interest-bearing debt (Year 5) + Cash (Year 5)

thus,

Equity Value (Year 5) = $1,082.26 − 292.53 = $789.74

Where is the value creation from this strategy coming from? There are two possible sources of synergies that need to be considered in this strategy that can create what private equity professionals refer to as "multiples expansion." The first is the fact that the combined company (build-up LBO) will be larger and more liquid than the platform company or the individual add-ons it acquires. Consequently, the combined firm may sell for a higher multiple when it is sold in the public market. The second is that the combined company is more diversified, and will thus have a higher debt capacity, which can also result in a higher multiple.

A Limitation of the Industry Private Equity (LBO) Valuation Approach

A weakness of the private equity valuation approach illustrated in Figure 8-5 is that there are no direct comparisons of the risks associated with these investments. For example, the risk of the build-up acquisition strategy is an important determinant of whether the 44.58% anticipated return is sufficient to warrant engaging in the investment strategy.

Figure 8.5 Summary of the Industry Private Equity Valuation Method

Step 1: Estimate EBITDA at the end of the planned holding period by preparing pro forma income statements such as those found in Tables 8-4 and 8-5. This entails a careful analysis of the acquired firm's past performance and the planned changes the private equity firm has in mind.

Step 2: Estimate the enterprise value at the end of the planned holding period as the product of the predicted EBITDA for Year N and an appropriate EBITDA valuation multiple, $M_{\text{EBITDA Year } N}$.

$$\text{Enterprise Value}_{\text{Year } N} = M_{\text{EBITDA Year } N} \times \text{EBITDA}_{\text{Year} N} \qquad (8.4)$$

Step 3: Calculate the value of the equity of the acquired firm at the end of the planned holding period as follows:

$$\text{Equity Value}_{\text{Year } N} = \text{Enterprise Value}_{\text{Year } N}$$
$$- \text{Interest-Bearing Debt}_{\text{Year } N} + \text{Cash}_{\text{Year } N} \qquad (8.5)$$

We calculate the firm's outstanding interest-bearing debt at the end of the planned holding period (Year N) by substracting all the principal payments made during the holding period from the initial debt used to finance acquisition, plus any added borrowing up until Year N. Cash is added back under the assumption that it is not accounted for in the estimation of enterprise value and constitutes a non-operating asset.

Step 4: Calculate the IRR of the equity investment as follows:

$$\text{Equity Value}_{\text{Year } 0} = \frac{\text{Equity Value}_{\text{Year } N}}{(1 + \text{IRR})^{N}} \qquad (8.6)$$

This does not imply that the managers of private equity firms ignore risk and simply choose the investments with the highest projected rates of return. Indeed, it would not be unusual for a private equity firm to select an investment with a projected rate of return of 22% over an alternative investment with a projected rate of return of 28% if the latter were deemed to be much more risky. However, the point remains that the industry-based LBO valuation approach that we describe in this chapter does not explicitly account for risk.

Explicitly accounting for risk in these transactions is somewhat difficult because of the changing use of financial leverage over the life of the investment. The transactions are very highly levered at the outset, but due to the cash-sweep provision typically contained in the debt covenants, the debt ratio and the risk of the project decline over time (see Panel a of Table 8-5). In Chapter 7 we pointed out that the adjusted present value (APV) model provides an appropriate method to value businesses whose capital structures are not stationary over time but change in a predictable fashion. We consider this approach in the next section.

Valuing PMG Foods, Inc. Using the Hybrid APV Approach

This section applies the APV approach introduced in Chapter 7 and reviewed in Figure 8-6 to value PMG Foods, Inc. To implement this approach, we use the cash flow forecasts from Panel a of Table 8-6 for a five-year planning period (N), plus an estimate of the terminal value for the enterprise in Year N. Panel a of Table 8-6 provides estimates for both the unlevered operating cash flows (FFCFs) and interest tax savings for this acquisition. The FFCFs grow steadily over the planning period (N), from $37.23 million to $82.80 million, as a result of the planned growth in revenues. On the other hand, the interest tax savings decline from $20.14 million to $16.86 million as a result of the cash-sweep provision in the firm's debt agreement, which requires that the firm pay down the debt using all available cash flows.

In addition to the cash flows, we need estimates of three rates that we will use to discount the cash flows: First, we will need the firm's borrowing rate (k_d), which is used to discount the interest tax savings. Second, we will need the unlevered cost of equity, k_u, to discount the unlevered equity cash flows over the five-year planning period. Third, we need a cost of capital to discount the terminal value at the end of Year 5, which we will assume is also equal to the cost of equity. The borrowing rate we use to discount the interest tax savings is 14% (Panel b of Table 8-6). Finally, the unlevered cost of equity is 11.56%. Although the details are not shown here, we used the same procedure to estimate the unlevered cost of equity that we first demonstrated in Table 4-1.

We can now estimate the value of PMG Foods, Inc. *as of today* (not at the end of Year 5). Panel b of Table 8-6 contains the APV estimate of the value of PMG Foods, Inc. The terminal value contributes $626.28 million to the total estimated enterprise valuation of $898.97 million. Netting out the firm's initial debt of $411.00 million produces an estimated value of the private equity firm's equity investment of $487.97 million.

Figure 8.6   Review of the Hybrid Adjusted Present Value (APV) Model

Enterprise value is defined as follows:

$$\begin{array}{l}\text{Enterprise} \\ \text{Value (APV)}\end{array} = \begin{array}{l}\text{Present} \\ \text{Value}\end{array} \left(\begin{array}{c}\text{Planning} \\ \text{Period} \\ \text{Cash Flows}\end{array} \right) + \begin{array}{l}\text{Present} \\ \text{Value}\end{array} \left(\begin{array}{c}\text{Post--Planning} \\ \text{Period} \\ \text{Cash Flows}\end{array} \right) \quad (8.7)$$

where

$$\begin{array}{l}\text{Present} \\ \text{Value}\end{array} \left(\begin{array}{c}\text{Planning} \\ \text{Perioid} \\ \text{Cash Flows}\end{array} \right) = \sum_{t=1}^{N} \frac{\text{FFCF}_t}{(1 + k_u)^t} + \sum_{t=1}^{N} \frac{(\text{Interest}_t \times \text{Tax Rate})}{(1 + k_d)^t} \quad (8.8)$$

and

$$\begin{array}{l}\text{Present} \\ \text{Value}\end{array} \left(\begin{array}{c}\text{Post--Planning} \\ \text{Period} \\ \text{Cash Flows}\end{array} \right) = \frac{\text{Terminal (Enterprise) Value}}{(1 + k_u)^N} \quad (8.9)$$

Legend

FFCF = Firm free cash flow, which is the same as the unlevered equity free cash flow since its calculation does not entail deductions for either principal or interest. When FFCF is discounted to the present at the unlevered cost of equity capital (k_u), it represents the value of the unlevered equity of the firm.

Interest Expense$_t$ × Tax Rate = Interest tax savings, which represent the reduction in taxes owed that results from interest expense deductions.

Terminal (Enterprise) Value = Enterprise value estimated at the end of the planning period, which represents the present value of the post–planning period FFCFs. The terminal value is estimated as a multiple of earnings before interest, taxes, depreciation, and amortization (EBITDA) for year N (i.e., $M_{\text{EBITDA}} \times \text{EBITDA}_N$).

N = Planning period for which detailed estimates of cash flows are prepared (usually three to five years).

k_u = Unlevered cost of equity capital.

k_d = Cost of debt financing.

Is the proposed acquisition worthwhile? These numbers indicate that this is a great investment since it generates an equity value of $487.97 million on an equity investment of only $125 million. However, it should be emphasized that the estimated cash flows used in our analysis may correspond more closely to "hoped-for" cash flows than to expected cash flows, which suggests that one might want to use a much higher discount rate to value them. Consequently, before undertaking an investment of this magnitude, the private equity firm would be wise to engage in a wide range of

Table 8-6   **APV Valuation of the PMG Foods, Inc., Build-up LBO Transaction**

Panel a. Projected Firm Free Cash Flow (FFCF) and Interest Tax Savings

	Year 0	Year 1	Year 2	Year 3	Year 4	Year 5
EBITDA		$ 123.20	$ 135.52	$ 149.07	$ 163.98	$ 180.38
Less: Depreciation		(49.00)	(55.00)	(61.00)	(67.00)	(73.00)
EBIT		$ 74.20	$ 80.52	$ 88.07	$ 96.98	$ 107.38
Less: Taxes		(25.97)	(28.18)	(30.83)	(33.94)	(37.58)
NOPAT		$ 48.23	$ 52.34	$ 57.25	$ 63.04	$ 69.80
Plus: Depreciation		49.00	55.00	61.00	67.00	73.00
Less: CAPEX		(60.00)	(60.00)	(60.00)	(60.00)	(60.00)
FFCF		$ 37.23	$ 47.34	$ 58.25	$ 70.04	$ 82.80
Interest expense		$ 57.54	$ 57.56	$ 56.17	$ 53.13	$ 48.16
Interest tax savings		$ 20.14	$ 20.15	$ 19.66	$ 18.60	$ 16.86
Debt	$411.00	$ 411.17	$ 401.25	$ 379.52	$ 344.02	$ 292.53

Panel b. APV Valuation Analysis

Assumptions:

Terminal value multiple	6 times EBITDA$_{\text{Years 5}}$
Interest rate on debt	14%
Unlevered beta	1.19
Risk-Free rate	5.00%
Market equity risk premium	5.50%
Unlevered cost of equity	11.56%
Tax rate	35%

Hybrid APV Valuation ($ millions):

	Present Value of		
	Unlevered Equity Free Cash Flows (discount rate = $k_{\text{Unlevered}}$)	Interest Tax Savings (Discount rate = k_{d})	Total
Planning period cash flows	$206.48	$66.20	$272.69
Terminal value cash flow (discount rate = k_u)			$626.28
Enterprise value (Year 0)			$898.97
Less: Debt (Year 0)			(411.00)
Equals equity value (Year 0)			$487.97

sensitivity analyses of the key value drivers of the investment, following the procedures outlined in Chapter 3.

Private Equity Value Drivers

There are five drivers of value in the example just discussed. These are: (1) the estimate of the first year's EBITDA, (2) the anticipated rate of growth in EBITDA for each year of the planning horizon, (3) the level of capital expenditures required each year, (4) the EBITDA multiple used to estimate the terminal value in five years, and (5) the unlevered cost of capital. We will look at the sensitivity of the project outcome to each of these value drivers.

The simplest form of sensitivity analysis involves calculating the critical values of each of the five value drivers to determine the level of each required to produce an equity value for the investment equal to the $125 million investment. The results are as follows:

Value Driver (Variable)	Estimated Value	Critical Value	Margin of Error (Estimate − Critical)
Year 1 EBITDA	$123.20 = $110 + 13.20	$76.00	$47.20
EBITDA growth rate	10%	−3.65%	13.65%
CAPEX	$60 million/year	$181.32 million/year	$121.32 million/year
Harvest multiple	6 times EBITDA	2.523 times EBITDA	3.477 times EBITDA
Unlevered cost of equity	11.56%	26.81%	15.25%

Clearly, this investment creates value even in the face of very significant changes in the individual estimates of the key value drivers. For example, the initial year's projected EBITDA can drop from the projected $123.2 million to only $76 million, and the investment will still produce a value of $125 million.[17] Moreover, the growth rate in EBITDA (holding the other three value drivers at their prior levels) can drop to −3.65% before the value of the investment will drop below the $125 million in equity capital that is invested in the project. Capital expenditures (CAPEX) can increase to $181.32 million over the expected $60 million before the project NPV becomes negative. Similarly, the EBITDA (harvest) multiple at the end of Year 5 that is used to determine the terminal value of the firm can drop to 2.523 times, and the unlevered cost of equity could be as high as 26.81% before the project's value drops below the $125 million invested in the equity of the deal.

In the preceding analysis we analyzed only one value driver at a time. Such single-variable analysis can easily understate the true risks of the investment in cases where the value drivers vary together. For example, if both the initial EBITDA estimate and

---

[17]Note that in this analysis we assume that both the platform and add-on EBITDAs for Year 1 are changed simultaneously by the sensitivity parameter.

the growth rate in EBITDA are 20% higher than anticipated, and the CAPEX estimate is 20% lower than expected, then an exit multiple of EBITDA of 3.31 times generates an enterprise value just large enough to cover the debt payment, thereby leaving nothing for the equity holders. Although the above scenario may be unlikely, it illustrates the fact that this is a risky investment.

8.5 SUMMARY

Private equity firms are becoming an increasingly important source of capital for start-up firms as well as more mature firms that are going through some sort of transition. In most cases, private equity firms evaluate their investments using a variant of the hybrid valuation approach that was described in the previous chapter. Typically, the focus of the valuation is on the investor's equity investment, and since there are generally no planning period cash flows to the equity holders, the focus of the valuation is on the firm's terminal value, which is usually calculated as a multiple of EBITDA.

Another notable feature of the valuation approach used by private equity firms relates to their use of discount rates that are much higher than the rates considered in the previous chapters. These investments should have high expected rates of return, given their high risk and illiquidity. However, the discount rates required by private equity firms are high, even given the nature of these investments, and probably reflect the fact that they are used to discount cash flows that are likely to be overly optimistic.

We would again like to emphasize that there are reasons why, in practice, investors often evaluate optimistic or hoped-for cash flows. Because of this, the valuation approaches taken in practice often differ from those recommended by academics. We recommend that in situations where private equity investors have estimates of expected cash flows, rather than hoped-for cash flows, they evaluate the investment using the APV approach that we introduced in Chapter 7. Although this approach is not widely used in the private equity industry, we think it is appropriate, given that most of these transactions involve a substantial amount of initial debt that is paid down fairly quickly over the planning period.

In closing, we should point out that this chapter has considered a couple of investments which should really be viewed as options. First, in the venture capital example we consider staged financing, which involves an initial investment that gives the venture capitalist an option, not an obligation, to make additional investments in the firm when those investments look favorable. Second, in the LBO example we discussed the investment in a platform company that provides the option, and again, not the obligation, to acquire add-on companies in situations where doing so is favorable to the private equity firm. Over the past 20 years, financial economists have developed methods for explicitly valuing investments that include such options. These methods will be the subject of the chapters that conclude this book.

PROBLEMS

8-1 USING DEBT FINANCING TO ENHANCE EQUITY RETURNS Kimble Electronics is a small toy manufacturing company with total assets of $1.5 million. The company has the opportunity to do a leveraged recapitalization that would involve borrowing 30% to 50% of the firm's assets at a rate of 9% per year. Moreover, the firm's annual return on its total investment in assets varies from 4% to 15%.

Analyze the effects of financial leverage on the rate of return earned on Kimble's equity if the firm borrows 30% or 50% of its assets (i.e., complete the following table). (You may ignore taxes in your calculations.)

	15% Return on Assets	4% Return on Assets
30% debt to assets	?	?
50% debt to assets	?	?

8-2 VC VALUATION AND DEAL STRUCTURING Chariot.com needs $500,000 in venture capital to bring a new Internet messaging service to market. The firm's management has approached Route 128 Ventures, a venture capital firm located in the high-tech start-up mecca known as Route 128 in Boston, Massachusetts, which has expressed an interest in the investment opportunity.

Chariot.com's management made the following EBITDA forecasts for the firm spanning the next five years:

Year	EBITDA
1	−$175,000
2	75,000
3	300,000
4	650,000
5	1,050,000

Route 128 Ventures believes that the firm will sell for six times EBITDA in the fifth year of its operations, and that the firm will have $1.2 million in debt at that time, including $1 million in interest-bearing debt. Finally, Chariot.com's management anticipates having a $200,000 cash balance in five years.

The venture capitalist is considering three ways of structuring the financing:

1. Straight common stock, where the investor requires an IRR of 45%.
2. Convertible debt paying 10% interest. Given the change from common stock to debt, the investor would lower the required IRR to 35%.
3. Redeemable preferred stock with an 8% dividend rate plus warrants entitling the VC to purchase 40% of the value of the firm's equity for $100,000 in five years. In addition to the share of the firm's equity, the holder of the redeemable

preferred shares will receive 8% dividends for each of the next five years, plus the face value of the preferred stack in Year 5.

TERMINOLOGY

A *convertible* security (debt or preferred stock) is replaced with common stock when it is converted. The principal is not repaid. In contrast, the face value of a security with *warrants* is repaid, and the investor has the right to receive common stock shares by remitting the warrants.

Redeemable preferred stock is typically straight preferred with no conversion privileges. The preferred always carries a negotiated term to maturity specifying when it must be redeemed by the company (often the sooner of a public offering or five to eight years). The preferred shareholders typically receive a small dividend (sometimes none), plus the face amount of the preferred issue at redemption, plus a share of the value of the firm in the form of common stock or warrants.

a. Based on the offering terms for the first alternative (common stock), what fraction of the firm's shares will it have to give up to get the requisite financing?

b. If the convertible debt alternative is chosen, what fraction of the firm's ownership must be given up?

c. What rate of return will the firm have to pay for the new funds if the redeemable preferred stock alternative is chosen?

d. Which alternative would you prefer if you were the management of Chariot .com? Why?

8-3 VC VALUATION Southwest Ventures is considering an investment in an Austin, Texas–based start-up firm called Creed and Company. Creed and Company is involved in organic gardening and has developed a complete line of organic products for sale to the public that ranges from composted soils to organic pesticides. The company has been around for almost 20 years and has developed a very good reputation in the Austin business community, as well as with the many organic gardeners who live in the area.

Last year Creed generated earnings before interest, taxes, and depreciation (EBITDA) of $4 million. The company needs to raise $5.8 million to finance the acquisition of a similar company called Organic and More that operates in both the Houston and Dallas markets. The acquisition would make it possible for Creed to market its private-label products to a much broader customer base in the major metropolitan areas of Texas. Moreover, Organic and More earned EBITDA of $1 million in 2005.

The owners of Creed view the acquisition and its funding as a critical element of their business strategy, but they are concerned about how much of the company they will have to give up to a venture capitalist in order to raise the needed funds. Creed hired an experienced financial consultant, in whom they have a great deal of trust, to evaluate the prospects of raising the needed funds. The consultant estimated that the company would be valued at a multiple of five times EBITDA in five years, and that Creed would grow the combined EBITDAs of the two companies at a rate of 20% per year over the next five years if the acquisition of Organic and More is completed.

Neither Creed nor its acquisition target, Organic and More, uses debt financing at present. However, the VC has offered to provide the acquisition financing in the form of convertible debt that pays interest at a rate of 8% per year and is due and payable in five years.

a. What enterprise value do you estimate for Creed (including the planned acquisition) in five years?

b. If the VC offers to finance the needed funds using convertible debt that pays 8% per year and converts to a share of the company sufficient to provide a 25% percent rate of return on his investment over the next five years, how much of the firm's equity will he demand?

c. What fraction of the ownership in Creed would the venture capitalist require if Creed is able to grow its EBITDA by 30% per year (all else remaining the same) and the venture capitalist still requires a 25% rate of return over the next five years?

8-4 VC VALUATION AND DEAL STRUCTURING SimStar Manufacturing Co. needs $500,000 to fund its growth opportunities. The founder of the firm has approached Morningstar Ventures (a Phoenix-based venture capital firm), who has expressed an interest in providing the financing if acceptable terms can be worked out.

The venture capitalist asked SimStar's CFO to provide an EBITDA forecast for the next five years. The forecast found below and depict the rapid growth opportunities the firm anticipates:

Year	EBITDA
1	−$350,000
2	200,000
3	340,000
4	1,050,000
5	1,500,000

If the venture capitalist provides the needed funds, she will plan on an exit after five years, at which time the VC believes that the firm can be sold for six times EBITDA. Moreover, based on pro forma financials and the above projections, the VC estimates that SimStar will have approximately $1.2 million in debt outstanding, including $1 million in interest-bearing debt, at the end of the planned five-year investment. Finally, SimStar expects it will have $200,000 in cash at the end of five years.

The venture capitalist is considering three ways of structuring the financing:

a. Straight common stock, where the VC receives no dividends for a period of five years but wants 49% of the firm's shares.
b. Convertible debt paying 10% interest. Given the change from common stock to debt, the VC wants only 30% of the firm's equity upon conversion in five years.
c. Redeemable preferred stock with an 8% dividend rate plus warrants for 40% of the firm's equity in five years. Moreover, the exercise costs for the warrants total $100,000. Note that since this is "redeemable preferred," the investor not only receives an 8% dividend for each of the next five years plus the face value of the preferred stock, but also can purchase 40% of the firm's equity for $100,000.

Which of the alternatives would you recommend that SimStar's founder select? Explain your decision.

8-5 VC VALUATION AND DEAL STRUCTURING Brazos Winery was established eight years ago by Anna and Jerry Lutz with the purchase of 200 acres of land. The purchase was followed by a period of intensive planting and development of the grape vineyard. The vineyard is now entering its second year of production.

In March 2006, the Lutzs determined that they needed to raise $500,000 to purchase equipment to bottle their private-label wines. Unfortunately, they have reached the limits of what their banker can finance and have put all their personal financial resources into the business. In short, they need more equity capital, and they cannot provide it themselves.

Their banker recommended they contact a venture capital (VC) firm in New Orleans that sometimes made investments in ventures such as the Brazos Winery. He also recommended that they prepare for the meeting by organizing their financial forecast for the next five years. The banker explained that VCs generally target a five-year term for their investments, so it was important that they provide the information needed to value the winery at the end of five years.

After a careful analysis of their plans for the winery, the Lutzs estimated that earnings before interest, taxes, depreciation, and amortization (EBITDA) in five years will be $1.2 million. In addition to the EBITDA forecast, the Lutzs estimated that they would need to borrow $2.4 million by 2010 to fund additional expansion of their operations. Their banker indicated his bank could be counted on for $2 million in debt, assuming they were successful in raising the needed equity funds from the VC. Furthermore, the remaining $400,000 would be in the form of accounts payable. Finally, the Lutzs believe their cash balance would reach $300,000 at the end of five years.

The Lutzs were particularly concerned about how much of the firm's ownership they would have to give up in order to entice the VC to invest. The VC offered three alternative ways of funding the winery's $500,000 financing requirements. Each alternative called for a different ownership share:

■   Straight common stock that pays no dividend. With this option, the VC asked for 60% of the firm's common stock in five years.

- Convertible debt paying 10% annual interest and 40% of the firm's common stock at conversion in Year 5.
- Convertible preferred stock with a 10% annual dividend and the right to convert the preferred stock into 45% ownership of the firm's common stock at the end of Year 5.

a. If the VC estimates that the winery should have an enterprise value equal to six to seven times estimated EBITDA in five years, what do you estimate the value of the winery to be in 2010? What will the equity in the firm be worth? (*Hint:* Consider both the six and seven times EBITDA multiple.)

b. Based on the deal terms offered, what rate of return does the VC require for each of the three financing alternatives? Which alternative should the Lutzs select based on the expected cost of financing?

c. What is the pre- and post-money value of the firm based on the three sets of deal terms offered by the VC? Why are the estimates different for each of the deal structures?

d. How is the cost of financing affected by the EBITDA multiple used to determine enterprise value? Is it in the VC's best interest to exaggerate the size of the multiple or to be conservative in his estimates? Is it in the entrepreneurs' best interest to exaggerate the estimated EBITDA levels or to be conservative? If entrepreneurs are naturally optimistic about their firm's prospects, how should the VC incorporate this into his deal-structure considerations?

e. Discuss the pros and cons of the alternative sources of financing.

8-6 VC VALUATION AND DEAL STRUCTURING In 2005 Dub Tarun founded a firm using $200,000 of his own money, $200,000 in senior (bank) debt, and an additional $100,000 in subordinated debt borrowed from a family friend. The senior debt pays 10% interest, while the sub debt pays 12% interest and is convertible into 10% of the firm's equity ownership at the option of the investor, J Martin Capital. Both debt issues have 10-year maturities. In March 2006 the firm's financial structure appears as follows:

Dub Tarun, Inc., March 2006

Accounts payable	$100,000
Short-term notes	150,000
Total short-term debt	$250,000
Senior debt (10% interest rate)	200,000
Sub debt (12% interest rate, convertible into 10% stock)	100,000
Equity (Dub Tarun)	200,000
Total debt and equity	$750,000

Dub has determined that he needs an additional $250,000 if he is going to con-
tinue to grow his business. To raise the necessary funds, he intends to use an 8% convertible preferred stock issue.

Dub projects that the firm's EBITDA (earnings before interest, taxes, depreciation, and amortization) in five years will be $650,000. Although Dub isn't interested in
selling his firm, his banker recently told him that businesses like his typically sell for five
to seven times their EBITDA. Moreover, by March 2011 Dub expects that the firm will
have $300,000 in cash and the firm's pro forma debt and equity will be as follows:

Dub Tarun, Inc., Pro Forma Financial Structure, March 2011

Accounts payable	$ 200,000
Short-term notes	250,000
Total short-term debt	$ 450,000
Senior debt (10%)	400,000
Sub debt (12%, convertible into 10% of the firm's stock)	100,000
Equity (Dub Tarun)	800,000
Additional financing needed	250,000
Total debt and equity	$2,000,000

a. What would you estimate the enterprise value of Dub Tarun, Inc. to be on March
2011? (*Hint:* Enterprise value is typically estimated for private companies using
a multiple of EBITDA plus the firm's cash balance.) If the sub debt converts to
common in 2011, what is your estimate of the value of the equity of Dub Tarun in
2011?

b. If the estimated enterprise value of the firm equals your estimate in question a,
what rate of return does the sub debt holder realize if he converts in 2011?
Would you expect the sub debt holder to convert to common stock?

c. If the new investor were to require a 45% rate of return on his $250,000 pur-
chase of convertible preferred stock, what share of the company would he need,
based on your estimate of the value of the firm's equity in 2011? What is your
estimate of the ownership distribution of Dub Tarun's equity in 2011, assuming
the new investor gets what he requires (to earn his 45% required rate of return)
and the sub debt holder converts to common? What rates of return do each of
the equity holders in the firm expect to realize by 2011 based on your estimate of
equity value? Does the plan seem reasonable from the perspective of each of the
investors?

d. What would be Dub Tarun's expected rate of return if the EBITDA multiple
were five or seven?

e. What is the post-investment and pre-investment value of Dub Tarun's equity in
2006 based on the investment of the new investor?

8-7 LBO VALUATION Randy Dillingwater is the chief investment officer for Clearstone Capital. Clearstone is a private equity firm located in Orlando, Florida, which specializes in what Randy describes as "make-over" or "fixer-upper" investments. The firm tries to find privately held firms whose owners have tried to grow their business too fast and run into liquidity problems. Clearstone has been in this business for 11 years and has had reasonable success.

Clearstone is now completing the investment of its second fund and considering the acquisition of a local manufacturing and distribution company, Flanders, Inc. Flanders was founded by Mark Flanders 18 years ago and grew rapidly. Recently, however, the firm made a large acquisition of a competitor firm, and the problems the firm encountered when assimilating the acquisition led to financial difficulties for Flanders. The owner has recently voiced his interest in a buyout proposal to his local banker, who notified Randy (his next-door neighbor) of the opportunity.

Randy contacted Mark, and the two decided to open a dialogue about the possible acquisition of Mark's firm. After several meetings, Mark decided to solicit an offer from Clearstone. In response to Randy's request, Mark supplied him with the following set of pro forma income statements spanning 2007–2011:

Pro Forma Income Statements	2007	2008	2009	2010	2011
EBITDA	$11,000,000.00	$12,100,000.00	$13,310,000.00	$14,641,000.00	$16,105,100.00
Less: Depreciation	(3,900,000.00)	(4,300,000.00)	(4,700,000.00)	(5,100,000.00)	(5,500,000.00)
EBIT	$ 7,100,000.00	$ 7,800,000.00	$ 8,610,000.00	$ 9,541,000.00	$ 10,605,100.00
Less: Interest	(6,300,000.00)	(6,235,600.00)	(6,040,288.80)	(5,690,457.10)	(5,159,103.90)
Earnings before taxes	$ 800,000.00	$ 1,564,400.00	$ 2,569,711.20	$ 3,850,542.90	$ 5,445,996.10
Less: Taxes	(240,000.00)	(469,320.00)	(770,913.36)	(1,155,162.87)	(1,633,798.83)
Net income	$ 560,000.00	$ 1,095,080.00	$ 1,798,797.84	$ 2,695,380.03	$ 3,812,197.27

In addition, Randy asked Mark to estimate capital expenditures for each of the next five years. Mark indicated that he thought the firm would have to spend about $4 million a year and that the new capital would have a 10-year depreciable life. (Depreciation expense for 2006 is $3.5 million, such that the addition of $4 million in capital expenditures will add $400,000 in added depreciation expense for 2007.)

Mark indicated to Randy that his research suggested a five times EBITDA multiple would be appropriate. Randy, however, was not sure that Clearstone could afford to pay this much for the firm. He decided to do a quick analysis using the LBO method of valuation based on the following assumptions:

■ The firm can be purchased for five times the firm's 2006 EBITDA of $10 million, and resold in five years for the same multiple of the firm's Year 5 EBITDA.

■ Clearstone will finance 90% of the purchase price using debt that carries a 14% rate of interest. The debt will require a cash sweep such that all available cash flow will go toward the repayment of the note.

■ A tax rate of 30% is assumed in all calculations.

■ Capital expenditures (CAPEX) are estimated to be $4 million per year, and no net new investments in working capital are anticipated.

■ Flanders does not carry any excess cash and has no nonoperating assets.

a. What is the projected enterprise value of Flanders in five years? What is the estimated value of Clearwater's equity in the firm at the end of five years if everything works out as planned?

b. What rate of return should Clearstone expect on its equity in the acquisition under the projections made above?

c. After further review, Randy estimated that the firm's operating expenses could be shaved by roughly $1 million per year. How would this affect your answers to questions a and b?

8-8 LBO VALUATION USING THE APV MODEL *This problem utilizes information from Problem 8-7 but can be analyzed independently.* Randy Dillingwater wanted to perform a discounted cash flow analysis of the proposed acquisition of Flanders, Inc. However, the cash-sweep provision of the debt financing meant that the debt ratio was expected to change systematically over the five-year planned investment period used by Randy's firm (Clearstone Capital). This, Randy recalled, would make the traditional WACC model for valuing firms tough to use. Instead, he decided to use the adjusted present value (APV) model, which separates the valuation of operating and financial cash flows into two separate calculations.

In preparation for his analysis, Randy did some initial research to determine reasonable estimates of the capital market components of the CAPM. First, he noted that the 20-year long-term government bond yield was currently 5%, and the return premium of the equity market in excess of the long-term government bond yield had historically averaged about 5.5%. All that remained to do was estimate the unlevered beta coefficient for Flanders. To perform this analysis, Randy decided he needed to calculate the unlevered equity betas for a sample of similar firms and use the average of the sample as his estimate of Flanders' unlevered beta. He then collected the following information on four publicly traded firms that were deemed close substitutes for Flanders:

Company	Equity Betas	Debt	Equity Value	Debt to Equity	Marginal Tax Rate
Company A	1.400	$ 6.58 m	$ 22.1 m	29.77%	30%
Company B	1.750	11.34 m	25.8 m	43.95%	30%
Company C	1.450	3.42 m	10 m	34.20%	30%
Company D	1.230	6.59 m	25.2 m	26.15%	30%

The equity betas were what Randy referred to as "levered equity betas," for they were calculated using stock market returns, which in turn reflected the firm's use of debt in its capital structure. Consequently, Randy needed to unlever the equity betas. To perform this analysis, Randy decided to assume that the firm's debt had a zero beta such that the unlevered beta was defined as follows:

$$\text{Unlevered Equity Beta} = \frac{\text{Levered Equity Beta}}{1 + \text{Debt Ratio}(1 - \text{Tax Rate})}$$

a. What is your estimate of Flanders' unlevered equity beta? (*Hint:* refer back to Table 4-1.)

b. Using the CAPM, what is the required rate of return that Randy should use to value Flanders' operating cash flows?

c. What is the value of Flanders' estimated operating cash flows (based on Mark Flanders' original estimates from Problem 8-7) for the planning period (2007–2011)? What is the value of the firm's interest tax savings for the same period? (Recall that the firm's borrowing rate from Problem 8-7 was 14%.)

d. Randy decided to estimate the continuing or terminal value of the firm using a five times multiple of the firm's EBITDA (following the discussion from Chapter 7). What is the terminal value of the firm today using this procedure, with the terminal value discounted back to 2006 using the unlevered cost of equity capital? What is your estimate of the enterprise value of Flanders using the APV method (and your estimates from question c)? What is the estimated value of Clearstone's equity investment based on the APV estimate of enterprise value?

8-9 LBO VALUATION USING SIMULATION *This problem utilizes information from Problem 8-7 and requires that the LBO valuation model be constructed.* Randy was happy with the anticipated results from the acquisition of Flanders, Inc., but he wanted to do some exploratory analysis of the risks involved in the acquisition so that he might be able to anticipate the risks inherent in the investment. He planned to construct a spreadsheet model using the industry-standard LBO valuation model (using information from Problem 8-7), and then identify the key sources of risk in the model and construct what he felt were reasonable characterizations of the probability distributions for each of these variables. Specifically, Randy decided upon the following variables (value drivers) and distributional characterizations:

■ Mark Flanders estimated EBITDA growth to be 10% per year, but this rate is far from certain. Randy decided that he would set the most likely growth rate to be 10% but would use a triangular distribution with a minimum value of 0% and a maximum of 15% to characterize the annual rate of growth in EBITDA over the planning period. Moreover, Randy felt that the rate of growth each year would be related to what happened in the subsequent year, so he decided to impose a .80 correlation on the growth rates for successive years. That is, the correlation between the rate of growth in 2009 and 2008 is estimated to be .80, and so forth.

■   Another key determinant of the value of the Flanders acquisition is the exit multiple that Clearstone encounters in five years when it decides to sell the firm. Randy has estimated that they will be able to exit at the same multiple (five) at which they purchase Flanders, Inc.; however, this variable is subject to uncertainty. Based upon Clearstone's past experience, Randy estimates that there is a 10% chance that the exit multiple will be as low as three times EBITDA, a 20% chance it will be four, a 40% chance it will be five, a 20% chance it will be six, and a 10% chance the multiple will be as high as seven.

a. After incorporating Randy's two assumptions about the uncertainties in the acquisition of Flanders, Inc., what is the mean and median rate of return on Clearstone's investment in the firm's equity?

b. What is the probability that the Flanders acquisition will yield a rate of return to Clearstone that is below the firm's target of 40%?

CHAPTER 9

Earnings Dilution, Incentive Compensation, and Project Selection

Chapter Overview

In the long run, firms create value by implementing investment projects that have positive NPVs. However, at least in the short run, management decisions are influenced by the performance numbers that firms report to their stockholders. Indeed, in practice, managers tend to calculate the accounting implications of their investments as well as their NPVs, and it is not unusual for managers to pass up positive-NPV investments that would temporarily reduce their firm's earnings. Although there are important reasons for this focus on earnings, it nevertheless influences investment choices. To counter this tendency, firms have devised alternative performance measures and compensation programs that mitigate some of these biases.

9.1 INTRODUCTION

Up to this point, most of our focus has been on the cash flows that are expected to be generated by the investment being evaluated. In Chapter 6 we mentioned earnings (more precisely, EBITDA), but only as a proxy for the value of the firm at some future date (i.e., the terminal value) when cash flows are difficult to estimate. Our valuation approach completely ignores the actual earnings of the investment or the influence of the investment on the firm's reported earnings.

In reality, managers take their firm's earnings numbers very seriously, and are generally very aware of how a major investment influences their reported earnings in the short run as well as the long run. For example, CFO responses to a recent survey suggest that the pressures of the capital markets encourage decisions that at times sacrifice long-term value to meet earnings targets.[1] A startling 80% of the respondents indicated that they would reduce spending on research and development, advertising, maintenance, and hiring that was value enhancing in order to meet earnings benchmarks. Another indication of the importance of earnings numbers can be found in the growing evidence regarding the extremes to which some firms "manage" their reported earnings. The corporate scandals at Adelphia, Enron, Global Crossing, HealthSouth, Qwest, Rite Aide, Sunbeam, Waste Management, and WorldCom exemplify situations in which earnings management became earnings *manipulation* and even fraud. For the managers of these firms, it appears that reporting favorable earnings was sufficiently important that they were willing to risk criminal prosecution. Surely, if this is the case, concern about reported earnings will influence management's investment choices.

We start the chapter by explaining why positive-NPV investments sometimes reduce a firm's expected earnings per share (EPS) and why negative-NPV investments sometimes increase expected EPS. We first note that when managers evaluate investments by considering their effect on EPS, they are effectively basing their decision on an incorrect cost of capital. The effective cost of capital that is implicitly used with the EPS criteria is the return on cash for those projects financed with cash, the firm's cost of debt for those projects financed with debt, and the ratio of the firm's earnings to price for those projects financed with equity. For projects financed with internally generated cash or debt, the EPS criteria will generally lead to the acceptance of too many investment projects. For projects financed with equity, the EPS criteria can lead to the acceptance of either too many or two few investment projects, depending on the firm's earnings–price ratio.

A second problem arises because the cash flows of an investment are generally not evenly distributed over the life of a project. Many positive-NPV investments generate very little in the way of cash flows in their first few years, and as a result, these projects initially reduce or dilute earnings. In addition, many negative-NPV projects have very high initial cash flows, and as a result, temporarily boost EPS.

If the EPS criteria can lead managers astray, why don't managers simply ignore earnings when making investment choices? Perhaps they should, but unfortunately, the world is not so simple. As we will explain, the concern about earnings is an inevitable by-product of the practical realities of an environment where the quality of a firm and its management is judged from quarter to quarter. While managers ideally would *like* to manage for the long term, it is also important that they appear to be doing well now, which means that it is important that they report favorable earnings. As Jack Welch, ex-CEO of General Electric Corporation, so aptly put it,

---

[1] John R. Graham, Campbell R. Harvey, and Shiva Rajgopal, "The Economic Implications of Corporate Financial Reporting," *Journal of Accounting and Economics*, 40, Issue 1–3, December 1, 2005, 3–73.

"You can't grow long-term if you can't eat short-term."

"Anybody can manage short. Anybody can manage long. Balancing those two things is what management is." (*Source:* http://www.businessweek.com/1998/23/b3581001.htm)

Unfortunately, there are no simple formulas that will help managers determine the optimal trade-off between NPV, which measures the long-term influence of an investment on firm value, and EPS, which influences short-term value. However, this chapter should provide a framework that will help managers more thoughtfully consider this trade-off. We will also discuss alternative performance measures that have been designed to mitigate this disconnect between earnings and NPV. Arguably, the most prominent of these financial metrics is economic value added or EVA®, developed by Stern Stewart and Company.

The chapter is organized as follows: In Section 9.2 we begin by establishing the underlying rationale for managerial sensitivity to the firm's reported earnings. Next, in Section 9.3, we demonstrate how managerial concern for earnings affects project selection. We present examples that illustrate two shortcomings of earnings as an indicator of wealth creation. Section 9.4 reviews economic profit as an alternative to EPS when evaluating new investment proposals. We show that in many cases economic profit does provide signals that are consistent with the NPV criteria, but not always. Finally, Section 9.5 discusses the effective use of economic profit and Section 9.6 summarizes the chapter.

9.2 ARE REPORTED EARNINGS IMPORTANT?

An investment project that reduces the firm's earnings in the current or following year is referred to as **earnings dilutive.** Likewise, an investment that increases near-term earnings is referred to as **earnings accretive.** These concepts often are used to describe an investment's influence on the firm's total earnings, but for major investments that require the firm to issue new shares, managers are generally more interested in whether the investment is dilutive or accretive to the firm's earnings per share. In addition, there can be a time element to this concept. Managers may refer to projects that are dilutive in the first few years but are accretive thereafter. What this means is that the project has a negative effect on earnings in the first few years, but by taking the project, the firm is likely to have higher long-term earnings.

Why Managers Care about Earnings

There are a number of reasons why managers care about reported earnings. The most direct reason is that managers are often paid to care about earnings. Very simply, companies frequently tie short-term bonuses either directly or indirectly to the firm's operating performance, as reflected in its earnings.[2] In addition, long-term incentive

---

[2]Kevin Murphy, of USC, surveyed a broad sample of firms using proprietary data from Towers-Perrin and found that for industrial firms, 32 of 50 in his sample used earnings as their primary performance metric; 8 of 11 finance and insurance firms and 6 of 7 utilities did likewise.

compensation frequently involves the use of stock options and equity grants whose value, at least in the short run, is affected by corporate earnings. Finally, earnings (and their effect on share price) may affect the CEO's ability to operate without too much scrutiny from the board of directors, and perhaps even to keep his or her job.

Although it is easy to come up with selfish reasons for why managers care about earnings, earnings are also important to a selfless manager who is simply trying to do what is best for the shareholders. Since earnings communicate the financial viability of the firm to the external capital markets, favorable earnings numbers will positively influence a firm's stock price as well as its credit ratings. This is clearly important to a firm that plans to raise external capital in the near future, but may also be important even for firms with no need to raise capital, since earnings numbers also communicate information to a firm's nonfinancial stakeholders, such as their customers, employees, and suppliers. A negative earnings surprise, and the resulting stock price reaction, could have a negative effect on the firm's relation with these stakeholders, while positive earnings and a growing stock price could be critical in determining how these stakeholders view working for and partnering with the firm. In short, it's natural to want to do business with a winner, and in the corporate world, earnings and stock prices are how one keeps score. What this means is that both good and bad earnings can in a sense "snowball," harming the future prospects of firms that report bad earnings and helping the future prospects of firms that report good earnings.

The above discussion (also see the Practitioner Insight box) suggests that the focus on earnings in the corporate world is not something that is likely to change soon. The question we now address is how this focus on earnings influences managerial investment decisions, and whether it is possible to change the way that firms compensate their managers and communicate to shareholders so that this influence is mitigated.

9.3 PROJECT ANALYSIS—EARNINGS PER SHARE AND PROJECT SELECTION

The valuation analysis that we discussed in previous chapters is typically a major part of the analysis of large investments at most major U.S. corporations. However, as the above discussion suggests, for publicly held firms considering major investments, managers will also calculate how the project will affect the firm's financial statements over the following two to five years, and evaluate whether the project is earnings-accretive or earnings-dilutive. To illustrate how this is done in practice, we will evaluate hypothetical investment opportunities by considering both their NPV and their influence on earnings, with a particular focus on how these criteria can provide contradictory conclusions.

Our first example, which illustrates this contradiction, shows that the earnings criterion implicitly uses the wrong cost of equity capital to evaluate an investment. We refer to this as the **equity-cost problem.** Our second example considers a project whose earnings (and cash flows) are back-loaded, which means that the earnings (and

P R A C T I T I O N E R
I N S I G H T

Earnings and Future Cash Flows—
An Interview with Trevor Harris*

Question: In valuing a company, investors are primarily interested in the company's ability to produce future cash flows. In practice companies can't report what they think their cash flow is going to be for the next 10 years. Instead they report their earnings for the quarter and year just ended. This begs the question as to whether the reported earnings number should aim to provide a measure of current corporate performance that helps investors to predict future cash flows. Should investors focus their attention on operating cash flow to get a better sense of a company's future cash-generating capacity?

Trevor: As any corporate or Wall Street analyst will tell you, forecasting future earnings is very difficult. But what most people don't understand is that it's even harder to predict actual cash flows. Moreover, I would argue that reported operating cash flow is far easier for managers to manipulate than earnings. All you have to do is securitize some receivables one minute before your quarter ends, and you can significantly increase your reported operating cash flow. Or you can put off paying for trade receivables by one day—and unless you draw attention to these things, no one will have any idea what you've done. But neither of these things will affect operating earnings.

Question: Is there a better way of calculating earnings—one that would provide investors with a better sense of the company's future cash-generating capacity and provide a reliable measure of wealth creation?

Trevor: I believe that any single-period, flow-based summary statistic—regardless of whether you call it earnings, cash flow, or something else—is going to be a flawed, or at least an incomplete, measure of corporate value creation. Managers are making decisions today that will affect not only this year's results, but results for many years going forward. And there's no way that an accounting system can capture the effects on long-run value of these decisions in one number. If your business resembles a savings account where you put money in on schedule and accumulate value at a specified rate of interest, then I could come up with a measure of earnings that can be capitalized at a certain multiple to give you the right value. But, again, for virtually all companies with any degree of complexity, there is no single-period accounting measure that can serve that purpose in a reliable way.

*Managing Director at Morgan Stanley, where his main job is to help the firm's business units and clients with accounting and valuation problems. He is also co-director of the Center for Excellence in Accounting and Security Analysis at the Columbia University School of Business.

cash flows) that the project produces are negative in the early years of the project's life and increase over time. This situation is frequently encountered when a firm undertakes a *strategic investment* in new products or services that requires heavy promotional expenditures in the early years of the project's life. We will refer to this as the **back-loaded earnings problem.**

Example #1—Bad Project with Good Earnings Prospects: The Equity-Cost Problem

To illustrate the *equity-cost problem,* we will consider the case of Beck Electronics, which is evaluating an investment of $6,000,000 in the project described in Panel a of Table 9-1. The project is to be financed by drawing down $4,000,000 of the firm's cash reserves (the equity component) and $2,000,000 in new borrowing (the debt component).

To calculate the net impact of this project on the firm's EPS, managers first forecast the firm's EPS assuming that the project is not undertaken, and then compare this EPS forecast to the pro forma projections of EPS under the assumption that the project is taken. Panel b of Table 9-1 provides these estimates of the firm's EPS with and without the project. Note that to keep the example as simple as possible, we assume that both the firm and the new project have indefinite lives and that the firm and the project's revenues, expenses, and earnings are all level perpetuities.

Beck's management anticipates that without the new project, the firm will realize net income for the coming year of $2,928,000 and $1.46 a share (2 million shares outstanding). The analysis of Beck's post-project EPS (in Panel b of Table 9-1) reveals that the project is expected to generate earnings equal to $0.16 per share. However, since Beck will no longer have the $4,000,000 cash reserve that generated $160,000 or 4% in pre-tax interest income, the net gain in the firm's EPS is reduced by $0.064 per share, and the earnings attributable to the project is only $0.096 per share. Even so, the project increases the firm's EPS, and thus passes the EPS accretion test.

In general, we can express the effect on earnings or net income attributable to a new project as follows:

$$\text{Change in Net Income} = \left(\begin{array}{c} \text{Project} \\ \text{Operating} \\ \text{Income} \end{array} - \begin{array}{c} \text{Interest} \\ \text{Expense on} \\ \text{New Debt} \end{array} - \begin{array}{c} \text{Lost Interest Income} \\ \text{on Cash used to Fund} \\ \text{the Equity} \end{array} \right)(1 - \text{Tax Rate}) \quad (9.1)$$

It is useful to rearrange the terms as follows:

$$\text{Change in Net Income} = \underbrace{\left[\left(\begin{array}{c} \text{Project} \\ \text{Operating Income} \end{array} \right)(1 - \text{Tax Rate}) \right]}_{\textbf{Term \# 1}} - \underbrace{\left[\left(\begin{array}{c} \text{Interest Expense} \\ \text{on New Debt} \end{array} \right)(1 - \text{Tax Rate}) \right]}_{\textbf{Term \# 2}}$$

$$\underbrace{- \left[\left(\begin{array}{c} \text{Lost Interest Income} \\ \text{on Cash Used to Fund} \\ \text{the Equity} \end{array} \right)(1 - \text{Tax Rate}) \right]}_{\textbf{Term \# 3}} \quad (9.1a)$$

The first term on the right-hand side of Equation 9.1a represents the project's net operating profit after taxes, or NOPAT. The second term represents the after-tax cost of the debt used to finance the project, and the final term represents the after-tax opportunity cost of lost interest income on the cash used to fund the project. Substituting the values for each of these variables in the Beck project, we get the following estimate of the impact of the project on net income for the firm:

$$\text{Change in Net Income} = \$500,000(1 - .20) - \$2,000,000 \times .05(1 - .20)$$

$$- \$4,000,000 \times .04(1 - .20) = \$192,000$$

where the tax rate is 20%, the cost of debt is 5%, and the rate of interest earned on the firm's marketable securities (i.e., cash) is 4%.

Having established that the project is accretive, we now consider whether it has a positive NPV. The new investment is expected to contribute additional operating earnings (i.e., earnings before interest and taxes—EBIT) of $500,000 per year. The project also requires an expenditure of $600,000 per year on new capital equipment (CAPEX), which exactly equals the $600,000 in depreciation expenses. Thus, the project's after-tax free cash flows are estimated to be $400,000 per year:

Earnings before interest and taxes (EBIT)	$500,000
Less: Taxes (20%)	(100,000)
Equals: Net operating profit (NOPAT)	$400,000
Plus: Depreciation expense	600,000
Less: Capital expenditures (CAPEX)	(600,000)
Equals: Project free cash flow (PFCF)	$400,000

Assuming that the project's WACC is 8% (the same as that of the firm), the value of the project and its NPV can be calculated as follows:

$$\text{NPV} = \left(\begin{array}{c} \text{Present Value} \\ \text{of the Project's} \\ \text{Free Cash Flow} \end{array} \right) - \begin{array}{c} \text{Investment} \\ \text{in the Project} \end{array}$$

$$= \frac{\$400,000}{.08} - \$6,000,000 = \$5,000,000 - \$6,000,000 = (\$1,000,000)$$

Table 9-1 Example #1—Bad Project with Good Earnings (Beck Electronics) ($ thousands except for per share figures)

Panel a. Project Characteristics and Assumptions

Investment outlay	$6,000,000	Onetime expenditure
Project life	Infinite	Perpetual life asset
CAPEX = Depreciation expense	—	
Debt financing	2,000,000	Perpetual debt (never matures)
Equity (from retained earnings)	4,000,000	Raised using excess cash
Additional EBIT per year	500,000	Per year (level perpetuity)
Tax rate	20.0%	
T-bill yield	4.0%	
Borrowing rate (before tax)	5.0%	
Cost of equity	10.0%	
Cost of capital (WACC)	8.0%	WACC is the same for the firm and the project

Panel b. Pro Forma Income Statements

	Pre-Project Firm	Project	Firm + Project
EBIT	$4,000,000	$ 500,000	$4,500,000
Less: Interest expense	(500,000)	(100,000)	(600,000)
Plus: Interest income (equity financing)	160,000	0	0
EBT	$3,660,000	$ 400,000	$3,900,000
Less: Taxes	(732,000)	(80,000)	(780,000)
Net income	$2,928,000	$320,000,00	$3,120,000
Earnings per share	$1.464	$ 0.160	$ 1.560

Panel c. Cash Flow Analysis

	Pre-Project Firm	Project	Firm + Project
EBIT	$4,000,000	$ 500,000	$4,500,000
Less: Taxes	(800,000)	(100,000)	(900,000)
NOPAT	$3,200,000	$ 400,000	$3,600,000
Plus: Depreciation	2,400,000	0	2,400,000

Note—EPS increases if the project is accepted!

Less: CAPEX	(2,400,000)	0	(2,400,000)
FFCF	$3,200,000	$400,000	$3,600,000

Panel d. Firm and Project Valuation Analysis	**Project**	**Firm + Project**
Value of pre-project firm		$ 40,000,000
Less: Investment outlay	$ (6,000,000)	
Plus: Value of project cash flows	5,000,000	
Value of firm plus project		39,000,000
Net present value		$ (1,000,000)

But – The NPV of the project is negative!

Legend:
EBIT = earnings before interest and taxes
EBT = earnings before taxes
NOPAT = net operating profit after taxes
CAPEX = capital expenditures
FFCF = firm free cash flow

Note that the present value of the perpetual stream of project free cash flows of $400,000 per year, discounted at the project's 8% cost of capital, is $5,000,000, while the initial investment in the project is $6,000,000. This implies that the NPV is negative at –$1,000,000. Similarly, the IRR for the project is defined as follows:

$$NPV = \left(\begin{array}{c} \text{Present Value} \\ \text{of the Project's} \\ \text{Free Cash Flow} \end{array} \right) - \begin{array}{c} \text{Investment} \\ \text{in the Project} \end{array} = 0$$

$$= \frac{\$400,000}{\text{IRR}} - \$6,000,000 = \$0$$

$$\text{IRR} = \frac{\$400,000}{\$6,000,000} = .0667 = 6.67\%$$

Clearly, this is an unacceptable project since it earns a return of only 6.67%, while the cost of capital for the project is 8%.

How Can Projects with Negative NPVs Increase EPS?

How can it be that an investment is accretive to the firm's earnings but has a negative NPV? To understand this, it is useful to first remember that the discount rate that is used in the DCF analysis should be viewed as the opportunity cost of capital. This is the rate of return that the firm could earn on an alternative investment that has the same risk as the investment project under evaluation. In contrast, when we examined whether the Beck investment was accretive or dilutive we were, in effect, assuming that the opportunity cost equals the rate earned on the cash that is used to finance the project. In other words, we used a risk-free rate as the opportunity cost of equity capital, and thus ignored the fact that the investment project was risky. To better understand what we will refer to as the **equity-cost problem,** let's look more closely at Equation 9.1a:

$$\begin{array}{c} \text{Change in} \\ \text{Net Income} \end{array} = \underbrace{\left[\left(\begin{array}{c} \text{Project} \\ \text{Operating Income} \end{array} \right)(1 - \text{Tax Rate}) \right]}_{\textbf{NOPAT}}$$

$$\underbrace{- \left[\left(\begin{array}{c} \text{Interest} \\ \text{Expense on} \\ \text{New Debt} \end{array} \right)(1 - \text{Tax Rate}) + \left(\begin{array}{c} \text{Lost Interest Income} \\ - \text{on Cash Used to Fund} \\ \text{the Equity} \end{array} \right)(1 - \text{Tax Rate}) \right]}_{\textbf{Capital Cost}}$$

$$= \text{NOPAT} - \text{Capital Cost} \tag{9.1b}$$

The previous expression decomposes the equation for the change in net income resulting from the acceptance of a project into two components. The first term in brackets is net operating profit after taxes (NOPAT). The second term in brackets represents the dollar cost per year (after taxes) of the capital used to finance the project; this is the annual *capital cost* for the project.

An examination of the second term reveals that the only opportunity cost we include for the equity capital component of the employed capital is the lost after-tax income from the cash used to fund the equity in the project. In the Beck example, this was the 4% yield (3.2% after taxes) on short-term Treasury bills, which substantially understates the true opportunity cost of equity capital for the project.

The investment was accretive in this example because its internal rate of return of 6.67% exceeds the 4% risk-free return (3.2% after taxes). However, the project has a negative NPV since its IRR does not exceed the risk-adjusted opportunity cost of capital for the project, which is 8%.

Issuing New Equity: EPS Accretion/Dilution and the P–E Ratio

Up to this point we have assumed that the firm has sufficient cash from the retention of prior earnings to finance the equity component of its investments. Let's now consider how EPS is affected if Beck must finance the project by issuing new shares of stock. As the following discussion indicates, when firms do finance projects by issuing equity, a key factor that determines whether the project is accretive or dilutive is the firm's price to earnings (P–E) ratio.

To illustrate the importance of the P–E ratio, we will provide some additional information about Beck Electronics and consider a new investment opportunity that provides a 10% rate of return and that will require an equity issue. The investment provides added EBIT of $750,000 per year in perpetuity, which implies that the project is expected to produce an after-tax cash flow of $600,000 in perpetuity. The cost of this investment is $6,000,000, which implies a 10% IRR.

Specifically, as described in Case A of Table 9-2, we assume that both Beck and the new project are all-equity-financed, and that the cost of equity capital is 10% and Beck's P–E multiple is 10. The 10% cost of equity capital and P–E ratio of 10 reflect the fact that Beck pays out all of its earnings in dividends, and the equity holders anticipate no growth in the value of the firm's shares. (That is, the cost of equity is equal to the ratio of dividends to share price, which is the same as earnings to share price.) Note too that the project offers a zero NPV since the IRR is exactly equal to the cost of capital.

In this particular example, the project has *no effect* on the firm's EPS (it is neither accretive nor dilutive) and has an NPV equal to zero. Thus, EPS and NPV provide the same signal. As we will show, this occurs because the cost of equity capital in this example is equal to the reciprocal of the P–E ratio. In general, the cost of equity will not exactly equal $E \div P$ (the reciprocal of $P \div E$), which means that there are potential conflicts between the EPS and NPV criteria.

Table 9-2 Financing the Project by Issuing New Shares of Stock—EPS and NPV

Case A: ROE = 10% = $1/_{P-E}$ = E–P= 10%; <u>No-Growth Firm</u> (Cost of Equity = E–P = 10%)

Panel a. Pro Forma Income Statements	Pre-Project Firm	Project	Firm + Project
EBIT	$ 4,000,000	$ 750,000	$ 4,750,000
Less: Interest expense	0	0	0
Plus: Interest income (equity financing)	0	0	0
EBT	$ 4,000,000	$ 750,000	$ 4,750,000
Less: Taxes	(800,000)	(150,000)	(950,000)
Net income	$ 3,200,000	$ 600,000	$ 3,800,000
Earnings per share	$1.600	$0.253	$1.600

Panel b. Cash Flow Analysis	Pre-Project Firm	Project	Firm + Project
EBIT	$ 4,000,000	$ 750,000	$ 4,750,000
Less: Taxes	(800,000)	(150,000)	(950,000)
NOPAT	$ 3,200,000	$ 600,000	$ 3,800,000
Plus: Depreciation	2,400,000	600,000	3,000,000
Less: CAPEX	(2,400,000)	(600,000)	(3,000,000)
FFCF	$ 3,200,000	$ 600,000	$ 3,800,000

Panel c. Firm and Project Valuation Analysis	Project	Firm + Project
Value of pre-project firm		$ 32,000,000
Less: Investment outlay	$ (6,000,000)	
Plus: Value of project cash flows	6,000,000	
Value of firm plus project		32,000,000
Net present value		$ 0

> In Case A the firm's EPS is unchanged by the project's acceptance and the project has a zero NPV! However, in Case B, where the cost of equity capital is not equal to the reciprocal of the P–E ratio (i.e., the E–P ratio), the project's NPV is still zero but EPS increases.

To illustrate, let's alter the example and assume that Beck has significant growth prospects, as in Case B of Table 9-2, and as a result, its stock price is twice as high and

Case B: ROE = 10% > $1/_{P-E}$ = 5%; <u>Growth Firm</u> (Cost of Equity = 10% > $1/_{P-E}$ = 5%)

Panel a. Pro Forma Income Statements	Pre-Project Firm	Project	Firm + Project
EBIT	$ 4,000,000	$ 750,000	$ 4,750,000
Less: Interest expense	0	0	0
Plus: Interest income (equity financing)	0	0	0
EBT	$ 4,000,000	$ 750,000	$ 4,750,000
Less: Taxes	(800,000)	(150,000)	(950,000)
Net income	$ 3,200,000	$ 600,000	$ 3,800,000
Earnings per share	$1.600	$0.274	$1.737

Panel b. Cash Flow Analysis	Pre-Project Firm	Project	Firm + Project
EBIT	$ 4,000,000	$ 750,000	$ 4,750,000
Less: Taxes	(800,000)	(150,000)	(950,000)
NOPAT	$ 3,200,000	$ 600,000	$ 3,800,000
Plus: Depreciation	2,400,000	600,000	3,000,000
Less: CAPEX	(2,400,000)	(600,000)	(3,000,000)
FFCF	$ 3,200,000	$ 600,000	$ 3,800,000

Panel c. Firm and Project Valuation Analysis	Project	Firm + Project
Value of pre-project firm		$ 32,000,000
Less: Investment outlay	$(6,000,000)	
Plus: Value of project cash flows	6,000,000	
Value of firm plus project		32,000,000
Net present value		$ —

its P–E ratio is 20 instead of 10. With the higher stock price, Beck can fund the project by selling half as many shares of stock as before. The project itself has not changed.

However, because Beck's P–E ratio is now higher, initiating the investment dramatically increases the firm's EPS. Indeed, as long as the project returns more than 5%, it will be EPS-accretive.[3]

Generalizing the Earnings Accretion/Dilution Analysis

We can generalize the effects of project selection on a firm's EPS by analyzing the expected change in the firm's EPS that will result from the acceptance of a project or investment. *The key consideration in determining whether an equity-financed investment is accretive or dilutive is the relationship between the rate of return earned on the equity capital invested in the project (ROE) and the earnings to price ratio (i.e., E÷P or the reciprocal of the P–E ratio). If the project's ROE is greater than the E–P ratio, then it will be accretive to the firm's EPS. Similarly, if the ROE is less than the E–P ratio, the project will be dilutive to EPS.*

Figure 9-1 generalizes the relationship between the change in the firm's earnings, the project's ROE, and the E–P ratio. In Panel a the project's ROE is 10%, and this return produces earnings accretion as long as the E–P ratio is below 10%. In Panel b the project provides an ROE of 20%; so as long as the E–P ratio is below 20%, the project is accretive. In essence, holding new investments to the earnings accretion standard is equivalent to comparing the project's return on equity to the E–P ratio. This standard is appropriate only when the cost of equity for the project is equal to E÷P, which in general is not the case.

Which firms are most apt to take negative-NPV projects when using EPS accretion as a decision tool for project analysis? The answer, of course, is firms for which the E–P ratio most underestimates their true cost of equity financing. In general, these will be growth firms, which have high P–E ratios, because their earnings are likely to grow in the future.

Debt Financing and Earnings Dilution

The preceding example illustrates how the firm's P–E ratio influences whether the project is accretive or dilutive. However, this is only the case when the project is financed with new equity. When the project is financed with debt, a comparison of the project's IRR and the after-tax cost of the debt will determine whether the project is accretive or dilutive. For example, in the above example, the project is accretive if it is financed with debt with an after-tax cost that is less than 10%.

---

[3]The following numerical example may help illustrate this point: Without the project, the firm's EPS is $1.60 for each of the 2,000,000 shareholders. Based on a P–E ratio equal to 10, the share price is $16.00. Consequently, raising the $6,000,000 needed to fund the investment in the project will require the issue of $6,000,000/$16 = 375,000 additional shares. Based on the total shares outstanding after the issuance (2 million plus 375,000), the project's $600,000 annual earnings will increase EPS by $0.253. However, because the cost of equity is equal to E÷P or 10%, the combination of the firm and project has an EPS of $1.60—exactly the same EPS the firm has without the project. Suppose now that the P–E ratio is 20; the firms' share price would be $32 (20 × $1.60), which means that fewer shares (half, to be exact) would have to be issued to raise the $6 million needed to finance the project. The EPS of the project turns out to be $0.274 and the EPS of the combination is $1.737.

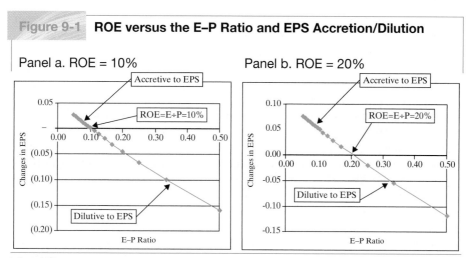

Figure 9-1   ROE versus the E–P Ratio and EPS Accretion/Dilution

Legend

Accretive to earnings per share (EPS)—the change in EPS is positive when the ROE exceeds the E–P ratio. When ROE is 10% (Panel a), the project is accretive where the E–P ratio is 10% or less. Similarly, when ROE is 20% (Panel b), the project increases firm earnings when the E–P ratio is 20% or less.

Dilutive to earnings per share (EPS)—the change in EPS is negative if the ROE is less than the E–P ratio.

Suppose that you are recommending a positive-NPV project that has an IRR of 8% and suggest that it be financed by issuing equity. Your firm's current P–E ratio is 10, which implies that this equity-financed project will be dilutive. Depending on the situation, your CEO may not like the idea of initiating a project that dilutes the firm's current EPS. What are your alternatives? One alternative is to simply abandon the project. A second alternative is to use sufficient debt financing so that the project is accretive rather than dilutive. Which is the preferred alternative? That depends on the NPV of the project and on the firm's ability to raise debt capital without jeopardizing its credit rating.

Example #2—Good Project with Back-Loaded Earnings Prospects

The second issue we discuss that can cause earnings accretion is the **back-loaded earnings problem.** By *back-loaded* we simply mean that the project generates little, if any, earnings in its early years, with most of its earnings occurring toward the end of the project's life.

Consider the situation faced by Dowser Chemical, which is about to launch a new product that involves an initial investment of $33,750,000 and is expected to generate revenues and earnings over a period of 10 years. In addition to the cost of plant and equipment, the new-product launch requires aggressive pricing and substantial expenditures for product promotion, which will severely reduce profits in the initial years.

As the new product gains acceptance in the marketplace, it will require a less generous promotional budget, and prices can be raised. The combined effects of these changes will boost both project cash flows and the firm's EPS.

Table 9-3 contains the accounting consequences of Dowser's investment project. Panel a contains pro forma balance sheets corresponding to the initial formation of the project in Year 0 and for Years 1 through 10. The initial balance sheet for Year 0 reveals an initial investment of $3,750,000 in current assets and an additional investment of $30,000,000 in property, plant, and equipment for total assets of $33,750,000. Dowser finances a portion of the firm's current assets with $1,250,000 in payables. The remainder of the project's financing needs is raised using long-term debt or bonds equal to $10,833,333, and $21,666,700 in equity, which total $32,500,000 in invested capital. Panel b contains pro forma income statements that indicate the project is expected to lose money in Year 1 of its operations but will be profitable in each year thereafter.

To estimate the NPV of the project, we convert the accounting pro forma income statements into estimates of project free cash flow in Panel a of Table 9-4 (pp. 382–383). This exercise reveals that the project will not produce positive cash flows until Year 5. Nonetheless, based on the project's 10 years of estimated cash flows and a discount rate of 12% (the project's weighted average cost of capital), we estimate the NPV of the project in Panel b of Table 9-4 to be $5,718,850. Consequently, based on the NPV estimate, we conclude that the project is a good prospect for the firm.

But what is the effect of the project's acceptance on the firm's earnings per share?

Earnings Effects—Accretion versus Dilution

Major projects like the one Dowser Chemical is considering can have a significant effect on the firm's reported earnings. To measure how the project affects EPS, we will again estimate the firm's EPS both with and without the project. In this case, we not only will look at how EPS is affected by the project in one year, but also will examine how EPS is affected over the next ten years. These projections, shown in Table 9-5 (p. 384), reveal that the project takes several years before it is accretive to EPS. As a result, during the first year the project reduces the firm's earnings by $758,000, thereby lowering EPS by ($0.42) in Year 1. The project continues to be dilutive for the next four years, and finally becomes accretive in Year 6 by $0.12 per share.

The dilemma faced by the manager, then, is the following: Should the firm adopt the project and suffer the earnings dilution effects over the next four years or avoid the project even though it has a positive NPV?

9.4 ECONOMIC PROFIT AND THE DISCONNECT BETWEEN EPS AND NPV

In the preceding section we demonstrated that there are two fundamental problems that arise when earnings accretion is used as a criterion for project selection. The first is the equity-cost problem, whereby the opportunity cost of equity is not properly accounted for in the calculation of EPS. The second is the back-loaded earnings problem, whereby projects produce a disproportionate amount of their earnings in the latter half of their life, which makes even positive-NPV projects' earnings dilutive in their early years. In both cases EPS accretion/dilution analysis can provide a faulty signal concerning the NPV of the project.

In the 1980s, financial consultants began recommending alternative performance measures and executive compensation programs to address the bias associated with the influence that EPS accretion/dilution analysis was having on management choices. The best known of these alternative "economic profit" measures was popularized by Stern Stewart and Company and is known as economic value added, or EVA®.

Economic Profit (aka, EVA®)

The accounting profession has long advocated the use of a modified accounting profit measure called residual income or economic profit to measure periodic firm performance. Stern Stewart and Company define economic profit, or EVA®, as follows:

$$\text{EVA}_t^{\circledR} = \begin{matrix} \text{Net Operating} \\ \text{Profit after} \\ \text{Taxes (NOPAT)}_t \end{matrix} - \begin{matrix} \text{Capital} \\ \text{Charge}_t \end{matrix} \qquad (9.2)$$

where

$$\text{NOPAT}_t = \left(\begin{matrix} \text{Earnings before} \\ \text{Interest and Taxes} \\ \text{(EBIT)}_t \end{matrix} \right) \times \left(1 - \begin{matrix} \text{Corporate} \\ \text{Tax Rate} \end{matrix} \right)$$

and

$$\begin{matrix} \text{Capital} \\ \text{Charge}_t \end{matrix} = \begin{matrix} \text{Invested} \\ \text{Capital}_{t-1} \end{matrix} \times \begin{matrix} \text{Weighted Average} \\ \text{Cost of} \\ \text{Capital (WACC)} \end{matrix}$$

Equation 9.2 looks very similar to Equation 9.1b, defined earlier in our discussion of the Beck example. However, the capital charge found in Equation 9.2 incorporates the true opportunity cost of equity, which is 8% in the Beck example rather than the after-tax yield on Treasury bills that is reflected in Equation 9.1b (4% yield,

Table 9-3   Pro Forma Financial Statements for a Proposed New Business by Dowser Chemicals

Panel a. Pro Forma Balance Sheets ($ thousands)

		Projected Sales Revenues			
	0	**1**	**2**	**3**	**4**
Sales		$30,000.00	$36,000.00	$43,200.00	$51,840.00
		Pro Forma Balance Sheets			
	0	**1**	**2**	**3**	**4**
Current assets	$ 3,750.00	$ 4,500.00	$ 5,400.00	$ 6,480.00	$ 7,776.00
Property, plant, & equipment	30,000.00	32,000.00	34,400.00	37,280.00	40,736.00
Total	$33,750.00	$36,500.00	$39,800.00	$43,760.00	$48,512.00
Accruals & payables	$ 1,250.00	$ 1,500.00	$ 1,800.00	$ 2,160.00	$ 2,592.00
Long-term debt	10,833.33	11,666.67	12,666.67	13,866.67	15,306.67
Equity	21,666.67	23,333.33	25,333.33	27,733.33	30,613.33
Total	$33,750.00	$36,500.00	$39,800.00	$43,760.00	$48,512.00
Invested capital	$32,500.00	$35,000.00	$38,000.00	$41,600.00	$45,920.00

Panel b. Pro Forma Income Statements ($ thousands)

	Years			
	1	**2**	**3**	**4**
Sales	$ 30,000	$ 36,000	$ 43,200	$ 51,840
Cost of goods sold	(12,000)	(14,400)	(17,280)	(20,736)
Gross profit	$ 18,000	$ 21,600	$ 25,920	$ 31,104
Operating expenses (excluding depreciation)	(15,000)	(16,800)	(18,960)	(21,552)
Depreciation expense	(3,000)	(3,200)	(3,440)	(3,728)
Net operating income	$ —	$ 1,600	$ 3,520	$ 5,824
Less: Interest expense	(1,083)	(1,167)	(1,267)	(1,387)
Earnings before taxes	$ (1,083)	$ 433	$ 2,253	$ 4,437
Less: Taxes	325	(130)	(676)	(1,331)
Net income	$ (758)	$ 303	$ 1,577	$ 3,106

Projected Sales Revenues

5	6	7	8	9	10
$62,208.00	$74,649.60	$89,579.52	$107,495.42	$128,994.51	$154,793.41

Pro Forma Balance Sheets

5	6	7	8	9	10
$ 9,331.20	$11,197.44	$13,436.93	$ 16,124.31	$ 19,349.18	$ 23,219.01
44,883.20	49,859.84	55,831.81	62,998.17	71,597.80	81,917.36
$54,214.40	$61,057.28	$69,268.74	$ 79,122.48	$ 90,946.98	$105,136.38
$ 3,110.40	$ 3,732.48	$ 4,478.98	$ 5,374.77	$ 6,449.73	$ 7,739.67
17,034.67	19,108.27	21,596.59	24,582.57	28,165.75	32,465.57
34,069.33	38,216.53	43,193.17	49,165.14	56,331.50	64,931.14
$54,214.40	$61,057.28	$69,268.74	$ 79,122.48	$ 90,946.98	$105,136.38
$51,104.00	$57,324.80	$64,789.76	$ 73,747.71	$ 84,497.25	$ 97,396.71

Years

5	6	7	8	9	10
$ 62,208	$ 74,650	$ 89,580	$ 107,495	$ 128,995	$ 154,793
(24,883)	(29,860)	(35,832)	(42,998)	(51,598)	(61,917)
$ 37,325	$ 44,790	$ 53,748	$ 64,497	$ 77,397	$ 92,876
(24,662)	(28,395)	(32,874)	(38,249)	(44,698)	(52,438)
(4,074)	(4,488)	(4,986)	(5,583)	(6,300)	(7,160)
$ 8,589	$ 11,907	$ 15,888	$ 20,665	$ 26,399	$ 33,278
(1,531)	(1,703)	(1,911)	(2,160)	(2,458)	(2,817)
$ 7,058	$ 10,203	$ 13,977	$ 18,506	$ 23,940	$ 30,462
(2,117)	(3,061)	(4,193)	(5,552)	(7,182)	(9,139)
$ 4,941	$ 7,142	$ 9,784	$ 12,954	$ 16,758	$ 21,323

Table 9-4 **Analysis of Project Cash Flow and NPV**

Panel a. Free Cash Flow Estimates ($ thousands)

	Years			
	1	2	3	4
Sales	$ 30,000	$ 36,000	$ 43,200	$ 51,840
Net operating income	0	1,600	3,520	5,824
Less cash tax payments	0	(480)	(1,056)	(1,747)
Net operating profits after taxes (NOPAT)	$ 0	$ 1,120	$ 2,464	$ 4,077
Plus: Depreciation expense	3,000	3,200	3,440	3,728
Less: Investments:				
In net working capital	(500)	(600)	(720)	(864)
In new capital (CAPEX)	(5,000)	(5,600)	(6,320)	(7,184)
Total net investment for the period	$ (5,500)	$ (6,200)	$ (7,040)	$ (8,048)
Project free cash flow (PFCF)	$ (2,500)	$ (1,880)	$ (1,136)	$ (243)

Panel b. NPV Analysis ($ thousands)

Project Valuation

Present value of free cash flows (12% cost of capital)	$ 6,859.72
Present value of invested capital Year 10	31,359.13
Present value of project cash flows	$ 38,218.85
Less: Initial invested capital in Year 0	(32,500.00)
Net present value	$ 5,718.85

		Years			
5	**6**	**7**	**8**	**9**	**10**
$ 62,208	$ 74,650	$ 89,580	$ 107,495	$ 128,995	$ 154,793
8,589	11,907	15,888	20,665	26,399	33,278
(2,577)	(3,572)	(4,766)	(6,200)	(7,920)	(9,983)
$ 6,012	$ 8,335	$ 11,122	$ 14,466	$ 18,479	$ 23,295
4,074	4,488	4,986	5,583	6,300	$ 7,160
1,037)	(1,244)	(1,493)	(1,792)	(2,150)	$ (2,580)
(8,221)	(9,465)	(10,958)	(12,750)	(14,899)	$ (17,479)
$ (9,258)	$ (10,709)	$ (12,451)	$ (14,541)	$ (17,049)	$ (20,059)
$ 828	$ 2,114	$ 3,657	$ 5,508	$ 7,729	$ 10,395

Table 9-5 Analysis of Earnings Dilution Effects ($ thousands except for per share information)

Analysis of Earnings Dilution Effects	1	2	3	4
Project net income	$ (758)	$ 303	$ 1,577	$ 3,106
Firm net income without the project	53,750	57,781	62,115	66,773
Total firm net income with the project	$ 52,992	$ 58,085	$ 63,692	$ 69,880
Total shares outstanding with the project	10,688.33	10,736.81	10,760.31	10,760.31
Combined firm and project earnings per share	$4.96	$5.41	$5.92	$6.49
Total shares outstanding without the project	10,000	10,000	10,000	10,000
Firm earnings per share without the project	$5.38	$5.78	$6.21	$6.68
Earnings (dilution)/accretion per share	$(0.42)	$(0.37)	$(0.29)	$(0.18)

or 3.2% after taxes).[4] Because the appropriate risk-adjusted capital charge is higher than the risk-free rate that is implicit in the analysis of earnings, the economic profits associated with this project will be much lower than the earnings attributable to the project.

---

[4]To see why this is the case we can rewrite the capital charge (cost) in Equation 9.1b as follows:

$$
\begin{aligned}
\text{Capital Charge} &= \left[\left(\begin{array}{c} \text{Interest Expense} \\ \text{on New Debt} \end{array} \right)(1 - \text{Tax Rate}) + \left(\begin{array}{c} \text{Lost Interest Income} \\ \text{on Cash Used to Fund} \\ \text{the Equity} \end{array} \right)(1 - \text{Tax Rate}) \right] \\[2ex]
&= \left[\frac{\left[\left(\begin{array}{c} \text{Interest rate} \\ \text{on New Debt} \end{array} \right) \times \text{Debt} \times \left(1 - \frac{\text{Tax}}{\text{Rate}} \right) + \left(\frac{\text{T-Bill}}{\text{Rate}} \right) \times \text{Equity} \times \left(1 - \frac{\text{Tax}}{\text{Rate}} \right) \right]}{\text{Debt} + \text{Equity}} \right] \times (\text{Debt} + \text{Equity}) \\[2ex]
&= \left(\begin{array}{c} \text{Weighted Average} \\ \text{of After-Tax Borrowing Rate} \\ \text{and the T-Bill Rate} \end{array} \right) \times (\text{Debt} + \text{Equity}).
\end{aligned}
$$

5	6	7	8	9	10
$ 4,941	$ 7,142	$ 9,784	$ 12,954	$ 16,758	$ 21,323
71,781	77,165	82,952	89,174	95,862	103,052
$ 76,722	$ 84,307	$ 92,736	$ 102,128	$ 112,620	$ 124,375
10,760.31	10,760.31	10,760.31	10,760.31	10,760.31	10,760.31
$7.13	$7.84	$8.62	$9.49	$10.47	$11.56
10,000	10,000	10,000	10,000	10,000	10,000
$7.18	$7.72	$8.30	$8.92	$9.59	$10.31
$(0.05)	$0.12	$0.32	$0.57	$0.88	$1.25

Using Economic Profit to Evaluate the Equity-Cost Problem

In Table 9-6 we apply the economic profit concept to the evaluation of the Beck investment introduced earlier in Table 9-1. The economic profit analysis found in Table 9-6 reveals that Beck's economic profit drops to $720,000, reflecting the −$80,000 economic profit of the project. This decrease reflects the fact that the project is not a value-creating investment (which is consistent with the negative NPV of −$1,000,000 that we calculated in Panel d of Table 9-1).

A further indication that economic profit provides the correct signal of the project's potential for creating shareholder value lies in the fact that the present value of all future economic profits is equal to the project's NPV. In the Beck Electronics investment example, where economic profit is a constant amount for all future years and the project is assumed to have an infinite life (i.e., the future economic profits are a level perpetuity), we can calculate the present value of all future economic profits as follows:

$$\text{Present Value of all Future Economic Profits} = \frac{\text{Economic Profit}}{\text{Cost of Capital}} = \frac{(\$800,000)}{.08} = (\$1,000,000)$$

The present value of all future economic profits is equal to what Stern Stewart refers to as the market value added (MVA) for the project (or firm), which is simply the project

Table 9-6	Using Economic Profit to Solve the Equity-Cost Problem—Beck Electronics, Inc.		
	Pre-Project Firm	**Project**	**Firm + Project**
EBIT	$ 4,000,000	$ 500,000	$ 4,500,000
Less: Taxes	(800,000)	(100,000)	(900,000)
NOPAT	$ 3,200,000	$ 400,000	$ 3,600,000
Less: Capital charge	(2,400,000)	(480,000)	(2,880,000)
Economic profit	$ 800,000	$ (80,000)	$ 720,000

Legend

EBIT = earnings before interest and taxes

NOPAT = net operating profit after taxes

Capital charge = invested capital times the weighted average cost of capital

Equity capital charge = equity capital times the cost of equity capital

Economic profit = NOPAT less the capital charge

NPV. We should point out, however, that the MVA used to rank company performance and reported in the popular financial press is not calculated as the present value of expected future economic profits (see the Technical Insight box titled "MVA and NPV").

TECHNICAL INSIGHT   MVA and NPV

Market value added, or MVA, has been calculated as the difference in the market value of the firm (share price times number of shares plus liabilities—often measured using book values) less an estimate of the capital invested in the firm at a particular point in time. The latter is basically an adjusted book value of the firm's assets taken from the most recent balance sheet. In this estimation of MVA, future economic profits are not estimated and discounted and the estimate of invested capital is not equal to replacement cost or the dollar amount that would be required to replicate the asset portfolio of the firm. Consequently, MVA as reported in the financial press (e.g., Stephen Taub, "MVPs of MVA," *CFO Magazine,* July 1, 2003) is not technically equal to the NPV of the firm but is an approximation based on a comparison of market value of the firm's outstanding securities (debt and equity) and the book value of the firm's assets (after making some key adjustments—See Chapter 5 in G. Bennett Stewart, III, *The Quest for Value,* HarperBusiness, 1991).

In this particular example, economic profit or EVA® provides a very useful tool for evaluating periodic performance in a way that is completely consistent with the NPV criterion. That is, since the project produces a constant stream of earnings and economic profit, a positive economic profit means the project has a positive NPV and a negative economic profit signals a negative NPV.

However, as we demonstrate using the Dowser Chemical example, economic profit does not automatically address the problems that arise when an investment's earnings are not stable or evenly distributed over the life of the project. Specifically, we consider two settings in which the distribution of earnings over the life of a project poses a problem. The first arises when earnings are concentrated in the latter years of a project's life; we have referred to this as the *back-loaded earnings problem*. In this case the project can have negative economic profits for one or more of the early years of its life and still provide a positive expected NPV. The second occurs when project earnings are concentrated in the early years of project life; we refer to this as the *front-loaded earnings problem*. In this situation the project may initially produce positive economic profits for one or more years that turn sufficiently negative in the latter years so that project has a negative NPV.

Using Economic Profit to Evaluate the Back- and Front-Loaded Earnings Problems

In the Beck Electronics example, the use of economic profit in place of EPS corrects a project selection error that can arise when EPS accretion or dilution is a critical decision variable. The Beck example illustrates that the EPS criterion implicitly uses the incorrect discount rate. Hence, to correct the problem, one uses an alternative performance measure that uses the correct discount rate. Unfortunately, economic profit does not directly address the issues associated with the back-loaded earnings problem illustrated in the Dowser Chemical example.

Back-Loaded Earnings

Panel a of Table 9-7 includes the economic profit calculations for each year of the Dowser Chemical problem introduced earlier. Although the project has a positive NPV, it has negative economic profits in Years 1 through 4 before becoming positive in Year 5.[5] As we mentioned earlier, the present value of all of the years' economic profits of an investment is equal to its NPV (see Panel b of Table 9-7). However, the fact that the sum of the present values of the annual economic profit measures is

---

[5]Note that two equivalent methods are used to calculate economic profit in Panel a of Table 9-7. The first is the conventional method defined in Equation 9.2. The second simply recognizes the fact that return on invested capital (ROIC) is equal to the ratio of NOPAT to invested capital and calculates economic profit multiplied by the difference in the ROIC and k_{WACC} invested capital.

Table 9-7	Using Economic Profit (or EVA®) to Evaluate the Dowser Chemical Example Introduced in Table 9-3

Panel a. Calculating Economic Profit ($000)

Method #1	Years			
	1	2	3	4
Sales	$ 30,000	$ 36,000	$ 43,200	$ 51,840
Operating income	0	1,600	3,520	5,824
Less: Cash tax payments	0	(480)	(1,056)	(1,747)
Net operating profits after taxes (NOPAT)	$ 0	$ 1,120	$ 2,464	$ 4,077
Less: Capital cost = Invested capital $\times k_{WACC}$	(3,900)	(4,200)	(4,560)	(4,992)
Economic profit = NOPAT − Capital cost	$ (3,900)	$ (3,080)	$ (2,096)	$ (915)

Method #2				
Return on invested capital (ROIC)	0.00%	3.20%	6.48%	9.80%
Cost of capital (k_{WACC})	12%	12%	12%	12%
Invested capital $(t-1)$	$ 32,500	$ 35,000	$ 38,000	$ 41,600
Economic profit = $(ROIC - k_{WACC})$ $\times$ Invested capital $(t-1)$	$ (3,900)	$ (3,080)	$ (2,096)	$ (915)

Panel b. Market Value Added (MVA) and Project NPV ($000)

Market Value Added = Present value of economic profits	$ 5,719
Plus: Invested capital	32,500
Project value	$38,219
NPV = Project value − Invested capital	$ 5,719

equal to NPV does not say that any particular year's economic profit reveals whether the project has a positive, negative, or zero NPV!

Front-Loaded Earnings

Table 9-8 contains an investment project that is similar to the Dowser example, except the pattern of earnings is reversed. In this example the project earns more in the early years and less in the later years of its life, implying that NOPAT as well as

		Years			
5	**6**	**7**	**8**	**9**	**10**
$ 62,208	$ 74,650	$ 89,580	$ 107,495	$ 128,995	$ 154,793
8,589	11,907	15,888	20,665	26,399	33,278
(2,577)	(3,572)	(4,766)	(6,200)	(7,920)	(9,983)
$ 6,012	$ 8,335	$ 11,122	$ 14,466	$ 18,479	$ 23,295
(5,510)	(6,132)	(6,879)	(7,775)	(8,850)	(10,140)
$ 502	$ 2,202	$ 4,243	$ 6,691	$ 9,629	$ 13,155
13.09%	16.31%	19.40%	22.33%	25.06%	27.57%
12%	12%	12%	12%	12%	12%
$ 45,920	$ 51,104	$ 57,325	$ 64,790	$ 73,748	$ 84,497
$ 502	$ 2,202	$ 4,243	$ 6,691	$ 9,629	$ 13,155

economic profits are higher in Year 1 than in any subsequent year.[6] The result is that for the front-loaded project, economic profits are positive for the first five years before

---

[6]Although we do not report it in Table 9-8, the project is also accretive to earnings in the first two years of its life before becoming dilutive in Years 3 through 10.

Table 9-8   Using Economic Profit (or EVA®) to Evaluate an Investment with Front-Loaded Earnings

Panel a. Calculating Economic Profit ($000)

Method # 1	Years			
	1	**2**	**3**	**4**
Sales	$ 80,000	$ 76,000	$ 72,200	$ 68,590
Operating income	12,632	11,600	10,620	9,689
Less: Cash tax payments	(3,789)	(3,480)	(3,186)	(2,907)
Net operating profits after taxes (NOPAT)	$ 8,842	$ 8,120	$ 7,434	$ 6,782
Less: Capital charge = Invested capital × k_{WACC}	(7,453)	(7,200)	(6,960)	(6,732)
Economic profit	$ 1,389	$ 920	$ 474	$ 50

Method #2				
Return on invested capital (ROIC)	14.24%	14.24%	13.53%	12.82%
Cost of capital (k_{WACC})	12%	12%	12%	12%
Invested capital	$ 62,105	$ 60,000	$ 58,000	$ 56,100
Economic profit	$ 1,389	$ 1,342	$ 889	$ 458

Panel b. Market Value Added (MVA) and Project NPV ($000)

Market Value Added = Present value of economic profits	$ (617)
Plus: Invested capital	62,105
Project value	$ 61,488
NPV = Project value − Invested capital	$ (617)

switching to negative in Years 6 through 10. In this example, the project has a negative NPV (see Panel b of Table 9-8), even though the EVA®s in the initial years are positive.

Summing Up

The fact of the matter is that the value of a multi-year project is a function of multiple cash flows, or analogously, multiple years of economic profit, and any one year's performance is generally not sufficient to evaluate the overall value of an investment project. This fact poses a very serious dilemma for the financial manager who would like to select positive-NPV investments, but is evaluated and paid based on the firm's

		Years			
5	**6**	**7**	**8**	**9**	**10**
$ 65,161	$ 61,902	$ 58,807	$ 55,867	$ 53,074	$ 50,420
8,805	7,964	7,166	6,408	5,687	5,003
(2,641)	(2,389)	(2,150)	(1,922)	(1,706)	(1,501)
$ 6,163	$ 5,575	$ 5,016	$ 4,485	$ 3,981	$ 3,502
(6,515)	(6,310)	(6,114)	(5,928)	(5,752)	(5,584)
$ (352)	$ (735)	$ (1,098)	$ (1,443)	$ (1,771)	$ (2,082)
12.09%	11.35%	10.60%	9.85%	9.08%	8.31%
12%	12%	12%	12%	12%	12%
$ 54,295	$ 52,580	$ 50,951	$ 49,404	$ 47,933	$ 46,537
$ 49	$ (341)	$ (712)	$ (1,065)	$ (1,400)	$ (1,719)

year-to-year performance. The problem is most serious when project value creation is uneven from year to year and takes place over many years.

9.5 PRACTICAL SOLUTIONS—USING ECONOMIC PROFIT EFFECTIVELY

We have demonstrated that if the cash flows of a positive-NPV project are back-loaded, the project can dilute economic profit as well as EPS. Similarly, a front-loaded project may be accretive to both economic profits and earnings even when its NPV is negative. In either case, there is a *horizon problem* that biases managers away from back-loaded projects even though they may have positive NPVs and toward front-loaded projects that may have negative NPVs.

Two approaches can be taken to resolve the horizon problem. The first involves refining how we calculate the performance measure. This means making adjustments to how the depreciation expense is calculated so that it more closely follows the actual changes in the value of the property, plant, and equipment over the life of the project rather than following an accounting rule such as straight-line depreciation. The second entails refinements to how managers are compensated. An example of the latter is something called a *bonus bank,* which effectively allows bonuses to reflect performance over longer time periods.

Modifying the Calculation of Economic Profit

When calculating economic profit, we typically use an accounting method for depreciating the cost of plant and equipment over the life of the investment. For example, using straight-line depreciation and no salvage value, we see that a $100,000 piece of equipment with a five-year depreciable life produces $20,000 per year in depreciation expenses. This means that the invested capital we assign to this equipment in Year 0 is $100,000, in Year 1 it is $80,000, and so forth. It would be highly unlikely that the actual value of the equipment declined in exactly this manner over time. In fact, for projects that have back-loaded earnings and cash flows, the value of the invested capital may actually increase during the early years of the project's life when the investment is being put in place. Similarly, for front-loaded projects, the value of the invested capital may decline very rapidly in the early years when the earnings are the greatest. This mismatch between standard methods of accounting for invested capital in depreciable assets and the actual pattern of change in value of those assets leads to the problems we noted in the previous section with regard to both earnings and economic profit.

Harold Bierman suggests a technical fix to this problem that utilizes what he refers to as either present value or economic depreciation to determine invested capital.[7] The key to Bierman's adjustment to the calculation of economic profit lies in the estimation of economic depreciation. Economic depreciation is simply the change in the present value of a project's expected future cash flows from year to year. To illustrate how this is done, Panel a of Table 9-9 presents an analysis of the back-loaded earnings investment faced by Dowser Chemical (this was introduced in Table 9-3 and its economic profits were analyzed in Table 9-7). The first step in the analysis involves estimating the IRR for the investment project, which is 13.73%. Next, we estimate the value of the project at the beginning of each year based on the present value of the project's future cash flows from that year forward using the IRR

---

[7]Harold Bierman, "Beyond Cash Flow ROI," *Midland Corporate Finance Journal* 5, No. 4 (Winter), 1988: 36–39.

as the discount rate. Thus, the value of the project's future cash flows in Year 0 equals the $32,500,000 invested in the project. In Year 1 the value of the invested capital equals the present value of the expected cash flows for Years 2 through 10, or $39,462,080, and so forth. The economic depreciation, then, is simply the change in value of the project from year to year such that for Year 1 the project depreciation is actually a positive $6,962,080, reflecting appreciation in the value of the project since the early period cash flows are actually negative, and the further we move out in time, the future cash flows consist of more positive (back-loaded) cash flows.

Our revised economic profit measure now reflects a revised NOPAT estimated as the sum of the project's original free cash flow (PFCF) plus the economic depreciation for the year. For Year 1, the revised NOPAT is equal to ($2,500,000) + $6,962,080, or $4,462,080. The capital charge for Year 1 (and all subsequent years) is also revised to reflect the economic value of the invested capital based on the present value of future cash flows for each year. Thus, for Year 1 the capital charge is equal to the invested capital of $32,500,000 × 12%, or $3,900,000. Subtracting the revised estimate of the capital charge from the revised NOPAT produces our revised economic profit for Year 1 of $562,080.

Recall that this example has a positive NPV of $5,718,850, but with the back-loaded earnings it produced negative economic profits in the early years of the project when we calculated economic profits in the conventional way in Table 9-7. Note that the revised economic profit measures are all positive if we use economic depreciation, which implies that this is a value-enhancing project.

Panel b of Table 9-9 provides an analysis of the front-loaded earnings project introduced earlier, in Table 9-8. Remember that this project had a negative NPV of ($617,100), but with front-loaded earnings, the economic profits for the early years of the project were positive. However, applying economic depreciation to the problem revises the economic profit measures, making them all negative for Years 1 through 10, which is consistent with the notion that the project destroys rather than creates wealth.

Stern Stewart offers additional recommendations that may mitigate the horizon problem. For example, they suggest that firms capitalize their R&D and advertising expenditures rather than expense them in the period in which the funds are spent. In addition, they recommend that the firm account for investment expenditure more slowly over time as the project comes on line and becomes productive (i.e., expensing the cost of capital equipment over time as the project starts to produce revenues). In this way the firm reduces the size of the capital charge in the early years of the project's life. These changes have the effect of making measured economic profits flow more evenly over time in the same way that switching to economic depreciation does.

Although these changes make sense, there is a real challenge in communicating any economic profit measure to the financial markets. Any profit measure that deviates from GAAP calculations is likely to be viewed as less credible, since management has the discretion to make those choices that describe their performance in the best possible light. What this means is that the firm will need a compelling argument, as well as credibility with the markets, to justify its economic profit calculations.

Table 9-9 **Revising Economic Profit to Reflect Economic Depreciation**

Panel a. Back-Loaded Earnings Example

	0	1	2	3	4
Project free cash flows	$(32,500.00)	$ (2,500.00)	$ (1,880.00)	$ (1,136.00)	$(243.20)
Internal rate of return on the investment	13.73%				
Present value of future cash flows (estimated invested capital)	$ 32,500.00	$ 39,462.08	$ 46,760.02	$ 54,315.93	$ 62,016.42
Economic depreciation = Change in present value of future cash flows		6,962.08	7,297.94	7,555.91	7,700.49
Revised NOPAT = PFCF + Economic depreciation		$ 4,462.08	$ 5,417.94	$ 6,419.91	$ 7,457.29
Revised capital charge = Revised invested capital $(t - 1) \times$ Cost of capital		(3,900.00)	(4,735.45)	(5,611.20)	(6,517.91)
Revised estimate of economic profit		$ 562.08	$ 682.49	$ 808.71	$ 939.38
NPV = MVA = Present value of all future economic profits (revised)	$ 5,718.85				

Panel b. Front-Loaded Earnings Example ($000)

	0	1	2	3	4
Project free cash flows	$ (62,105.26)	$ 10,947.37	$ 10,120.00	$ 9,334.00	$ 8,587.30
Internal rate of return on the investment	11.79%				
Present value of future cash flows	$ 62,105.26	$ 58,481.68	$ 55,258.16	$ 52,440.50	$ 50,037.27
Economic depreciation		(3,623.58)	(3,223.52)	(2,817.66)	(2,403.23)
Revised NOPAT = PFCF + Economic depreciation		$ 7,323.79	$ 6,896.48	$ 6,516.34	$ 6,184.07
Less: Revised capital charge		$(7,452.63)	$(7,017.80)	$(6,630.98)	$ (6,292.86)
Revised estimate of economic profit		$ (128.84)	$ (121.33)	$ (114.64)	$ (108.79)
MVA = Present value of all future economic profits (revised)	$ (617.10)				

As Bennett Stewart, interviewed in the Industry Insight box, indicates, managers in these situations are most likely to be credible in the financial markets if they can show that they are personally invested in their firms' long-term outcomes.

	5	6	7	8	9	10
	$ 828.16	$ 2,113.79	$ 3,656.55	$ 5,507.86	$ 7,729.43	$107,792.02
	$ 69,702.79	$ 77,158.83	$ 84,095.79	$ 90,133.84	$ 94,779.32	$ 0.00
	7,686.37	7,456.04	6,936.96	6,038.05	4,645.48	(94,779.32)
	$ 8,514.53	$ 9,569.83	$ 10,593.51	$ 11,545.91	$ 12,374.91	$ 13,012.71
	(7,441.97)	(8,364.34)	(9,259.06)	(10,091.49)	(10,816.06)	(11,373.52)
	$ 1,072.56	$ 1,205.50	$ 1,334.45	$ 1,454.42	$ 1,558.85	$ 1,639.19

	5	6	7	8	9	10
	$ 7,877.94	$ 7,204.04	$ 6,563.84	$ 5,955.64	$ 5,377.86	$ 50,038.95
	$ 48,060.00	$ 46,523.46	$ 45,445.92	$ 44,849.51	$ 44,760.54	$ 0.00
	(1,977.27)	(1,536.54)	(1,077.54)	(596.42)	(88.97)	(44,760.54)
	$ 5,900.67	$ 5,667.50	$ 5,486.30	$ 5,359.23	$ 5,288.90	$ 5,278.41
	(6,004.47)	(5,767.20)	(5,582.82)	(5,453.51)	(5,381.94)	(5,371.26)
	$ (103.81)	$ (99.70)	$ (96.52)	$ (94.28)	$ (93.04)	$ (92.86)

INDUSTRY INSIGHT

An Interview with Bennett Stewart, Jr.*

Question:
What should managers do when the NPV and earnings criteria come into conflict? Are managers sufficiently credible that investors will believe them when they say that earnings are temporarily lower because the firm has taken on investments that have positive NPVs but are temporarily dilutive?

Bennett:
Management can always communicate more information, such as the fact that a project has a ramp-up phase, or that an increase in research or marketing expense will temporarily depress earnings. When this occurs EVA® is a good framework for making such disclosures. However, I think that although all this is necessary, it is not a sufficient solution. The question for investors is: Why should we believe management? How do we know they are not manipulators just like Enron?

The best communication mechanism for a firm's management is this: They put their money where their mouth is. This can be accomplished using a combination of the following company policies: A bonus plan that is based on sharing the EVA® improvement over time; bonuses paid through the use of an *at risk* bonus bank; a requirement that managers hold significant illiquid equity in the company; a company share repurchase plan that times share repurchases to coincide with management's view of the market valuation of company stock; and restricting manager stock sales to programmatic sales (i.e., planned sales following a stated program).

*Founding partner of Stern Stewart and Company, New York, New York.

Modifying the Method Used to Pay Bonuses Based on Economic Profit

Stern Stewart recommends a number of practices that should lengthen the investment horizon of managers.[8] First, performance bonuses should be banked and paid out over time, and second, managers should participate in a leveraged stock option program. The "bonus bank" extends a manager's decision horizon because monies placed in the bonus bank are considered "at risk." The firm's performance over the term of the bonus bank influences the payout from the bank.

---

[8]The discussion in this section is based on J. Stern, B. Stewart III, and D. Chew, "The EVA® Financial Management System," *Journal of Applied Corporate Finance* 8, 2 (Summer 1995), pp. 32–46.

The typical bonus bank plan works as follows: Bonuses for the current year are determined based on firm performance (e.g., Stern Stewart recommends that bonuses be based on improvements in the firm's EVA®). One-third of the earned bonus is paid to the employees, while two-thirds is *banked* for later distribution. In the second year of the plan, the firm's performance is used to determine employee bonuses again. However, if the firm's performance deteriorates, the bonus is actually negative and is deducted from the employee's bonus bank account. If firm performance warrants the payment of a bonus in the second year, then the total bonus is equal to one-third of Year 1's bonus (from the bonus bank) plus one-third of the bonus earned in Year 2. The key factor here is that because the bonus bank is at risk, employees are discouraged from taking a very short-term view in their decisions. Taking actions in the current year to boost current period performance at the expense of the next two years (in a three-year plan) will come back to haunt the employee.

9.6 SUMMARY

In the classroom, financial economists drive home the notion that it is cash flows that determine value and that reported earnings should not be a matter of concern to investors. In reality, though, managers *do* care about the earnings their firm reports each quarter, and this concern has a significant effect on the investment projects that are chosen.

Are students being misinformed in the classroom when they are taught to focus on cash flow and disregard earnings? The answer is a qualified "no." Value is a function of cash flows received by investors. However, by ignoring reported earnings, the firm's management team subjects itself to the perils of misinterpretation by investors in the capital market. For this reason corporate executives not only look at wealth creation estimates for new projects based on net present value, but also frequently look at whether the project is accretive to earnings. Unfortunately, these competing investment criteria are not always consistent. As this chapter has demonstrated, projects that are accretive in their early years can produce negative NPVs, and projects that are initially dilutive can have positive NPVs.

Table 9-10 summarizes the performance measurement problems that arise when managerial performance is assessed periodically using earnings and when new projects are evaluated based on whether they are accretive or dilutive to firm earnings. The first is the *equity-cost problem,* which reflects the fact that EPS does not consider the appropriate opportunity cost of equity capital. Switching from earnings to economic profit resolves this problem by accounting for the opportunity cost of invested equity capital. The second problem relates to the timing of project earnings and cash flow. Specifically, projects that have *back-loaded earnings* can often be dilutive in their early years and still have a positive NPV. Similarly, bad projects that have *front-loaded earnings* can be accretive to earnings in the early years of project life and have negative NPVs. In both these cases the simplistic application of economic profit can lead to what we refer to as a "horizon problem." That is, managers who are paid

Table 9-10   Summary of the Managerial Horizon Problem—Solving the Measurement Problem

Distribution of Project Earnings/Cash Flows over Time	Source of Financing	Problem	Solution
I. Stable (i.e., neither front- nor back-loaded)	Internal equity	Economic profit assigns the proper equity cost to the project, whereas EPS assigns a cost for equity capital equal to the forgone interest income earned on excess cash by the firm.	Evaluate periodic performance using economic profit.
	External equity (sale of common stock)	If the cost of equity is not equal to the E–P ratio then the EPS dilution/(accretion) criterion is not consistent with NPV < 0 (> 0).	Evaluate periodic performance using economic profit.
	Debt financing	Economic profit assigns the proper cost of equity. However, projects financed with debt will be accretive so long as they earn more than the after-tax cost of debt.	Evaluate periodic performance using economic profit.
II. Back-loaded	Any	The annual economic profit in the early years of the project's life will be negative, even for positive-NPV projects.	Revise economic profit metric to reflect economic depreciation. Capitalize R&D and advertising expenses and amortize over project life. Use a bonus bank compensation plan to extend management's horizon.
III. Front-loaded	Any	The annual economic profit in the early years of the project's life can be positive, even for negative-NPV projects.	Revise economic profit metric to reflect economic depreciation. Capitalize R&D and advertising expenses and amortize over project life. Use a bonus bank compensation plan to extend management's horizon.

bonuses based on annual earnings or economic profits will have incentives to avoid back-loaded earnings projects and to undertake front-loaded earnings projects.

To address this horizon problem, firms need to compensate managers appropriately and communicate the long-term value of their investments to the capital markets. In other words, compensate managers in a way that provides incentives to take long-horizon projects with positive-NPVs and design economic profit measures that increase when firms undertake positive-NPV investments that have long horizons. While the solutions to the managerial horizon problem summarized in Table 9-10 make sense if the economic profit measures are used internally for compensation purposes, the real challenge lies in convincing the capital markets to believe that the numbers really capture the firm's true performance. The capital markets realize that managers always have an incentive to claim that their current earnings are low because they are making great investments that will pay off in the future. Essentially, the problem that a firm's management faces in this situation is one of trust and credibility with the outside investor community. There are no magic bullets or ready-made formulas that are available to create credibility. The real key involves taking the long view, where value-enhancing choices trump short-term earnings consequences.

PROBLEMS

9-1 EPS ACCRETION AND NPV The chapter demonstrated that the requirement that new projects be accretive to firm EPS sometimes results in accepting negative-NPV projects and rejecting positive-NPV projects. However, under more restrictive circumstances, requiring that new investments be accretive to earnings may be consistent with the NPV criteria. Are the following statements true or false? Defend your answer.

a. If project earnings are expected to grow at the same rate as the firm's earnings, an EPS-accretive project is a positive-NPV project.

b. The earnings-accretive criterion worked for conglomerates in the 1960s because they were able to take over low-P–E stocks that were earnings accretive.

9-2 ANALYZING A PROJECT WITH BACK-LOADED EARNINGS Hospital Services Inc. provides health care services primarily in the western part of the United States. The firm operates psychiatric hospitals that provide mental health care services using inpatient, partial hospitalization, and outpatient settings. In the spring of 2007, the firm was considering an investment in a new patient monitoring system that cost $6 million per hospital to install. The new system is expected to contribute to firm EBITDA via annual savings of $2.4 million in Years 1 and 2, plus $4.25 million in Year 3.

The firm's chief financial officer is interested in investing in the new system but is concerned that the savings from the system are such that the immediate impact of the project may be to dilute the firm's earnings. Moreover, the firm has just moved to an economic profit–based bonus system, and the CFO fears that the project may also make the individual economic profits of the hospitals look bad—a development that would generate resistance from the various hospital managers if they saw their bonuses being decreased.

a. Assuming that the cost of capital for the project is 15%, that the firm faces a 30% marginal tax rate, and that it uses straight-line depreciation over a three-year life for the new investment and that it has a zero salvage value, calculate the project's expected NPV and IRR.

b. Calculate the annual economic profits for the investment for Years 1 through 3. What is the present value of the annual economic profit measures discounted using the project's cost of capital. What potential problems do you see for the project?

c. Calculate the economic depreciation for the project and use it to calculate a revised economic profit measure following the procedure laid out in Table 9-8. What is the present value of all the revised economic profit measures when discounted using the project's cost of capital? (*Hint:* First, revise the initial NOPAT estimate from your answer to question a by subtracting the economic depreciation estimate from project free cash flow calculated in question a. Next, calculate the capital charge for each year based on invested capital less economic depreciation.)

d. Using your analysis in answering questions b and c, calculate the return on invested capital (ROIC) for Years 1 through 3 as the ratio of NOPAT for Year t to invested capital for Year $t - 1$. Compare the two sets of calculations and discuss how the use of economic depreciation affects the ROIC estimate for the project.

9-3 ANALYZING A PROJECT WITH FRONT-LOADED EARNINGS Wind Power Inc. builds and operates wind farms that generate electrical power using windmills. The firm has wind farms throughout the Southwest, including Texas, New Mexico, and Oklahoma. In the spring of 2007 the firm was considering an investment in a new monitoring system that cost $6 million per wind farm to install. The new system is expected to contribute to firm EBITDA via annual savings of $4.25 million in Year 1, $2.9 million in Year 2, and $1 million in Year 3.

Wind Power's chief financial officer is interested in investing in the new system but is concerned that the savings from the system are such that the immediate impact of the project is so accretive to the firm's earnings that the individual unit managers will adopt the investment even though it may not be expected to earn a positive NPV. Moreover, the firm has just moved to an economic profit–based bonus system, and the CFO fears that the project may also make the individual economic profits improve dramatically in the short term—a development that would provide an added incentive for the wind farm managers to take on the project.

a. Calculate the project's expected NPV and IRR assuming that the cost of capital for the project is 15%, the firm faces a 30% marginal tax rate, it uses straight-line depreciation for the new investment over a three-year project life, and that it has a zero salvage value.

b. Calculate the annual economic profits for the investment for Years 1 through 3. What is the present value of the annual economic profit measures discounted using the project's cost of capital? What potential problems do you see for the project?

c. Calculate the economic depreciation for the project and use it to calculate a revised economic profit measure following the procedure laid out in Table 9-8. What is the present value of all the revised economic profit measures when discounted using the project's cost of capital? (*Hint:* First, revise the initial NOPAT estimate from your answer to question a by subtracting the economic depreciation estimate from project free cash flow calculated in question a. Next, calculate the capital charge for each year based on invested capital less economic depreciation.)

d. Using your analysis in answering questions b and c, calculate the return on invested capital (ROIC) for Years 1 through 3 as the ratio of NOPAT for Year t to invested capital for Year $t-1$. Compare the two sets of calculations and discuss how the use of economic depreciation affects the ROIC estimate for the project.

9-4 EPS VERSUS ECONOMIC PROFIT Let's modify the Beck Electronics example found on page 368 as follows: First, we assume that *all* of the project's $6 million cost is funded through the use of excess cash (i.e., from equity, funded out of retained earnings). Moreover, assume that the market rate of interest earned on the $6 million in cash that will be invested in the project equals 12.5%. Note that the after-tax rate of return (given the 20% tax rate) is 10%, which is the cost of equity capital.

a. Evaluate the investment's impact on Beck's EPS.
b. What is the project's NPV?
c. What is the annual economic profit for the project?
d. What do the above calculations tell you about the project? Is it one that Beck should pursue? Why or why not?

9-5 ECONOMIC PROFIT AND NPV Steele Electronics is considering an investment in a new component that requires a $100,000 investment in new capital equipment, as well as additional net working capital. The investment is expected to provide cash flows over the next five years. The anticipated earnings and project free cash flows for the investment are found in the table.

a. Assuming a project cost of capital of 11.24%, calculate the project's NPV and IRR.
b. Steele is considering the adoption of economic profit as a performance evaluation tool. Calculate the project's annual economic profit using the invested capital figures found in the table.[9] How are your economic profit estimates related to the project's NPV?

---

[9]Recall that the invested capital in the project is equal to net fixed assets plus net working capital.

Project Pro Forma Income Statements

	2006	2007	2008	2009	2010
Revenues	$ 100,000	$ 105,000	$110,250	$115,763	$121,551
Less: Cost of goods sold	(40,000)	(42,000)	(44,100)	(46,305)	(48,620)
Gross profit	$ 60,000	$ 63,000	$ 66,150	$ 69,458	$ 72,930
Less: Operating expenses	(20,000)	(21,000)	(22,050)	(23,153)	(24,310)
Less: Depreciation expense	(20,000)	(20,000)	(20,000)	(20,000)	(20,000)
Net operating income	$ 20,000	$ 22,000	$ 24,100	$ 26,305	$ 28,620
Less: Interest expense	(3,200)	(3,200)	(3,200)	(3,200)	(3,200)
Earnings before taxes	$ 16,800	$ 18,800	$ 20,900	$ 23,105	$ 25,420
Less: Taxes	(5,040)	(5,640)	(6,270)	(6,932)	(7,626)
Net income	$ 11,760	$ 13,160	$ 14,630	$ 16,173	$ 17,794

Project Free Cash Flows

	2005	2006	2007	2008	2009	2010
Net operating income		$ 20,000	$ 22,000	$ 24,100	$ 26,305	$ 28,620
Less: Taxes		(6,000)	(6,600)	(7,230)	(7,892)	(8,586)
NOPAT		$ 14,000	$ 15,400	$ 16,870	$ 18,414	$ 20,034
Plus: Depreciation		20,000	20,000	20,000	20,000	20,000
Less: CAPEX	$ (100,000)	—	—	—	—	—
Less: Change in NWC	(5,000)	(250)	(263)	(276)	(289)	6,078
Project free cash flow	$ (105,000)	$ 33,750	$ 35,138	$ 36,594	$ 38,124	$ 46,112
Invested capital		$ 105,000	$ 85,250	$ 65,513	$ 45,788	$ 26,078

c. How would your assessment of the project's worth be affected if the economic profits in 2006 and 2007 were both negative? (No calculations required.)

9-6 EVA®, MVA, AND ENTERPRISE VALUATION Calculate the annual EVA®s for Years 1 through 4 using the Canton Corporation example described in Problem 7-1. Assuming that the EVA®s remain constant for Years 5 and beyond, calculate the present value of Canton's EVA®s. How is the present value of Canton's EVA®s related to enterprise value? What is Canton's enterprise value?

PART IV

Futures, Options, and the Valuation of Real Investments

Our focus throughout the first nine chapters has been on the valuation techniques that are widely used in practice. In particular, we have examined the discounted cash flow (DCF) approach, which first forcasts expected cash flows and then assigns a discount rate to each cash flow to determine its present value. Although we have emphasized what we consider cutting-edge industry practice, we have also pointed out a number of "disconnects" between industry practice and DCF theory.

One notable disconnect that we identified in Chapter 2 is that managers tend to propose cash flow forecasts that are overly optimistic. Specifically, their forecasts often represent what will happen if everything goes as planned rather than the expected cash flows called for in DCF theory. To counter this optimism, it is common business practice to use discount rates that are somewhat higher than the expected rates of return suggested by textbook DCF theory.

This is perhaps nowhere more apparent than in the cash flow forcasts made by naturally optimistic entrepreneurs in their business plans—which leads venture capitalists to use discount rates that are in the 30% to 40% range.

The second distinction between business practice and DCF theory is that firms often utilize a single discount rate to evaluate all their projects. This is at odds with DCF theory in two ways: First, risk differences across projects should be reflected in unique project discount rates. Second, using a single discount rate for all future cash flows is tantamount to assuming that the term structure of discount rates is a flat for all projects. In theory, there should be a matrix of discount rates, with time on one axis and project risk on the other. As we emphasized in Chapter 5, however, there are sound and very practical managerial reasons why firms use a limited number of discount rates to evaluate their investment projects.

In Part IV, we consider what is generally referred to as the real options approach to valuation. This approach, which is based on academic research from the mid-1980s, is widely used in the natural resource industries as well as by some technology companies. We believe, however, that some of the managerial issues that lead firms to use a single discount rate also have made firms relatively slow to adopt this approach to value investments more broadly. The slow adoption rate may also be due to the relative complexity of the approach and the fact that the real options approach can require a number of inputs. We hope that our discussion of this approach, along with software that can easily be adapted to these problems, will make it more accessible to managers and broaden its use.

The real options approach is based on two important ideas: The first is that financial markets often provide prices that can be used to value future cash flows. This is an idea we used previously in Chapter 6, where we discussed how one would use information from market values of publicly traded companies or recent transactions in the private markets to infer the value of a business's future cash flows. Similarly, in this part we consider how one can use transactions in the forward, futures, and options markets to value the future cash flows of investment projects.

The second idea that underpins the real option approach is that uncertainty and flexibility interact in ways that influence expected cash flows. We first introduced this concept in Chapter 2, where we described how simulation can be used to estimate expected cash flows. In this part we go one step further and discuss how these cash flows can be valued. In particular, we will discuss the concept of certainty equivalence, which was mentioned briefly in Chapter 2. The idea here is that instead of determining the expected value of a risky future cash flow, one determines the certain cash flow that has the same value as the risky cash flow. In other words, instead of adjusting for risk by using a higher discount rate, the cash flows themselves are adjusted for risk. The principal advantage of this approach, which we discuss in more detail in Chapter 10, is that certainty-equivalent cash flows are discounted at the risk-free rate, so the concerns about using different discount rates for different investments that we discussed in Chapter 5 are no longer an issue. However, in most cases, coming up with the certainty-equivalent cash flows is quite a challenge.

Our discussion in Chapter 10 focuses on what we call *contractual options,* which are options that are embedded in financial contracts. For example, as we will discuss, a levered equity investment provides the owners with the option to default on their debt obligations when the investment is doing poorly. Contractual options can be contrasted with *real options,* discussed in Chapter 11, which are options that are inherent in the nature of the physical investment. For example, almost all of the investments that a firm makes will provide the firm's management with some degree of flexibility in terms of when the investment is initiated, when and if the investment is abandoned, and how the investment is operated. All else equal, the more flexibility a project provides to management, the more valuable it will be. Real options analysis is used to quantify the value of this flexibility.

Finally, in Chapter 12, we analyze *strategic options*. These are options that arise from investments that improve the firm's capabilities or positions the firm in ways that can potentially generate value-enhancing investment opportunities in the future. For example, the contacts a firm establishes through an initial investment in a foreign country might generate lucrative opportunities in the future. An important part of corporate strategy is identifying investment opportunities that are not only value-enhancing on their own, but lead the firm in a direction that is likely to generate future opportunities.

Before proceeding, we should note that we will not go through all the technical details that are involved in the pricing of real options. Option pricing can get quite complicated, and valuation models that are used in practice are developed and implemented by individuals with PhDs in technical fields such as physics, mathematics, and computer science. These more technically inclined individuals generally collaborate with project sponsors and other less technical individuals who do not necessarily need to understand all the gory technical details. However, these less technical individuals need to be able to identify the options embedded in investment projects and to roughly gauge how those options contribute to an investment's value. This section of the book is designed to provide this level of expertise.

CHAPTER 10

Using Futures and Contractual Options to Value Real Investments

Chapter Overview

In this chapter we use the market prices of traded derivative securities, such as options, forwards, and futures contracts, to value real investment opportunities. These prices allow us to convert risky future cash flows into their certainty equivalents, which can then be discounted using the risk-free rate.

The chapter describes a three-step valuation process that is closely related to the three-step discounted cash flow (DCF) process described in earlier chapters. The following table summarizes the traditional DCF and the derivative securities approach to valuation and reveals that the relevant difference between the approaches lies in how we adjust for risk. In the traditional DCF approach we estimate expected cash flows and adjust for risk by using a risk-adjusted discount rate, whereas in the derivative securities approach we use market prices of publicly traded securities to estimate certainty-equivalent cash flows, which are then discounted using the risk-free rate. An important advantage of the derivatives approach is that it uses market forecasts based on market prices, whereas the traditional DCF approach relies on management's own price forecasts.

	Traditional DCF Approach to Valuation	Derivative Securities Approach to Valuation
Step 1	Forcast the amount and timing of future cash flows.	Forcast the amount and timing of future cash flows.
Step 2	Estimate a risk-appropriate discount rate.	Use observed market prices to estimate certainty equivalents of expected future cash flows.
Step 3	Discount the investment's expected cash flows using the risk-adjusted discount rate to find its present value.	Discount the certain equivalents of the cash flows of the investment to find its present value.

10.1 INTRODUCTION

Two important developments occurred in the spring of 1973 that had a profound effect on both the theory and practice of finance. The first was the April opening of the first organized exchange for trading stock options, the Chicago Board Options Exchange (CBOE).[1] The second development was the May publication of the Black-Scholes model, which provided a formula for valuing options.[2] In the ensuing three decades, we have seen the proliferation of a variety of financial markets that trade options as well as other **financial derivatives.**

Financial derivatives are securities whose value is *derived from* the value of another security or asset. The latter is commonly referred to as the underlying asset, which could be shares of stock, a commodity, or any other asset.[3] There are three principal types of derivative securities: options, forwards, and futures.[3a] An **option** contract provides the holder with the right, but not the obligation, to purchase (call option) or sell (put option) a specified asset (e.g., shares of common stock or a parcel of land) for a specified price (called the exercise or strike price) within a specified period of time. **Forward** contracts and **futures** contracts are similar to option contracts in that they also represent agreements to buy or sell an asset at a certain time in the future for a certain price. However, unlike options that do not obligate the holder to exercise the contract, forward and futures contracts do. For a review of specific differences between forward and futures contracts, see the Technical Insight box on page 410. In addition, Appendix A reviews the basics of options for those who want a brief refresher.

The development of markets for futures, forwards, and options is having an important influence on how investment projects are valued in practice. In this chapter we provide two examples to illustrate how this is done. The first example uses a technique commonly referred to as "pricing against the forward curve." Here we use forward market prices to estimate the certainty equivalence of future cash flows. The second example uses option prices to help value investment opportunities that have option-like features. In this example we show how option prices can be used to

---

[1]Derivative markets for futures contracts had long existed. For example, the Chicago Board of Trade (CBOT) was established in 1848 to allow farmers and merchants to contract for basic commodities.

[2]Fischer Black and Myron Scholes, "The Pricing of Options and Corporate Liabilities," *Journal of Political Economy* 81 (May–June 1973), 637–659.

[3]Swaps provide another important type of derivative contract that is widely used in hedging transactions; however, we will not utilize them in our examples. A **swap** is a derivative contract in which two counterparties exchange one stream of cash flows for another stream. These streams are called the "legs" of the swap. For example, take the case of a plain vanilla fixed-to-floating interest rate swap. Party A makes periodic interest payments to party B based on a variable interest rate, while party B makes periodic interest payments based on a fixed rate of interest. The payments are calculated using a notional amount. Swaps are over-the-counter (OTC) derivatives which mean that they are negotiated outside exchanges and cannot be bought and sold like securities or futures contracts, but are all unique.

capture the value of a firm's option to default on its debt obligations. Both of these examples illustrate the benefits of using market prices, whenever possible, when valuing risky investments.

Although the valuation approach used in this chapter is indeed somewhat different from the approaches used in earlier chapters, the similarities are really more important than the differences. In all cases, we are ultimately forecasting future cash flows that are discounted to the present; the difference comes from the method of coming up with the cash flows and the discount rate that is used. Moreover, using derivatives prices to value cash flows is also directly analogous to the use of comparables introduced in Chapter 6. However, instead of using another business as the comparable to value a stream of future cash flows, we use derivative prices as the appropriate comparable to value individual cash flows.

The techniques that we focus on in this chapter were originally designed for commodity-based businesses like mining, basic chemicals, and oil and gas exploration, where the cash flow risks are derived from commodity prices for which there are publicly traded derivatives. For this reason the examples we present in this chapter focus on extractive industries, with a particular focus on the oil and gas industry, where this approach is very popular. However, in Chapters 11 and 12 we describe how these techniques can be used more broadly to evaluate projects in a variety of industries.

Before we launch into the study of the derivatives approach to asset valuation, we want to emphasize a few important points that we hope will influence how you approach the material in this chapter:

■ Since this approach is newer than traditional DCF analysis, there is a tendency to think that this material represents "another approach" to the study of valuation. This conclusion is bolstered by the fact that much of the language used is different and we use different tools such as decision trees and the binomial lattice. The truth of the matter, however, is that we are still doing DCF analysis. The innovation in Chapter 10 is that we use observed market prices for derivative securities to *improve* our DCF analysis (not replace it).

■ The concepts developed in this chapter provide a critical building block to your understanding of Chapters 11 and 12, where we consider the value of flexibility and strategic options. So, if it has been a while since you studied derivatives or perhaps you have never done so, you will want to spend some extra time on Appendix A, where we provide a basic review of options and their payoffs. You may also find it helpful to visit one of the many excellent Web-based resources for a review of derivative contracts.[4]

■ Finally, in this chapter we use the binomial lattice for the first time. This will be a new tool for many readers. Consequently, you would do well to spend the time

---

[4]For example, see http://www.financialpolicy.org/dscprimer.htm.

A Primer on Forward and Futures Contracts

Forward contracts and futures contracts are similar in that they both represent agreements to buy or sell an asset at a specified time in the future for a specified price. The principal difference between a futures contract and a forward contract is that the *futures contract* is traded on an organized exchange and the forward is not. Instead, the *forward contract* represents a private or over-the-counter agreement between two financial institutions or between a financial institution and one of its corporate clients.

In addition to market differences, forward contracts usually have only one specified date for delivery of the commodity on which the contract is written, whereas a futures contract may offer a range of delivery dates. Still another important difference between forwards and futures is the method of settlement for the difference between the value of the underlying commodity and the agreed-upon future delivery price. For a forward contract, this difference is settled at the termination of the contract; in the case of a futures contract, it is settled *daily* through a procedure called *marking-to-market*. Finally, futures contracts, unlike forwards, are usually terminated or closed out prior to delivery; the physical commodity is not (usually) delivered.

The following exhibit summarizes the unique features of forward and futures contracts:

	Forward	Futures
Market	Private contract between two parties	Traded on an organized exchange
Contract	Not standardized	Standardized
Delivery	Generally on one delivery date	Range of delivery dates
Settlement	At the end of the contract	Daily (marked-to-market)
Termination	Delivery of commodity or final cash settlement	Generally, the contract is closed out prior to maturity

You might think that the market for immediate or current delivery of a commodity would be called the "current market," in contrast with the forward or futures market. However, this is not the case. This market is referred to as the *spot market*.

Each forward or futures transaction has a buyer and a seller. The party that agrees to buy the commodity at a future date is said to have a *long position*, whereas the party that agrees to sell the commodity in the future is said to have taken a *short position*.

you need to fully understand this tool, because it will also be used in the next two chapters.[5] The importance of understanding the use of this tool to the real options approach is analogous to the importance of understanding how to do time value of money calculations to DCF analysis, so "don't leave Chapter 10 without it"!

This chapter is organized as follows: Section 10.2 discusses the certainty-equivalence method for valuing risky future cash flows. This is one of the three discounted cash flow models discussed in earlier chapters and is commonly used in situations where derivative markets exist. Section 10.3 provides an example where we value a risky investment whose primary source of risk is that associated with the price of a commodity. As we show, the presence of forward market prices to hedge this risk greatly reduces the complexity of the task (if you are not familiar with the concept of financial hedging with forward and futures contracts or if you would benefit from a review, see the Technical Insight box entitled "Hedging Financial Risks"). Section 10.4 opens our discussion of options by providing an example of the valuation of an equity investment in a levered oil field. This example illustrates how firms can use options to capture the value of decision flexibility inherent in many investment opportunities. In the context of this example, we introduce the binomial option valuation technique, which is widely used to value financial options as well as real investments that have option-like components (Appendices B and C provide details for anyone who would like to understand the binomial model in more depth). Finally, Section 10.6 provides summary comments.

10.2 THE CERTAINTY-EQUIVALENCE METHOD

The approach that we will use to value investments in this chapter is a special case of the **certainty-equivalence (CE)** approach that requires that we first *risk-adjust* the risky future cash flows, creating what we call *certainty-equivalent* cash flows. A **certainty-equivalent** cash flow is defined as the certain cash flow that has the same value to the recipient as the uncertain cash flow that is being evaluated. For example, suppose the holder of a lottery ticket that is worth either $70 or $100 with equal probability is willing to accept a sure payment of $82 in exchange for the ticket. We can say that the certainty-equivalence of the uncertain cash flow to the lottery ticket is $82, which is lower than the $85 expected payoff (i.e., $85 = .5 \times $100 + .5 \times 70). The holder of the lottery ticket is willing to take less than the expected value because of his aversion to risk.

The certainty-equivalence approach is fundamentally the same as the traditional discounted cash flow (DCF) approach except that it adjusts the cash flows for risk rather than adjusting the discount rate. In most cases either adjustment is appropriate,

---

[5]If you find you need some extra help with this, see Chapter 10 in Robert L. McDonald, *Derivative Markets 2nd edition* (Boston, MA: Addison Wesley, 2006).

Hedging Financial Risks

Hedging is the process of reducing the firm's risk exposure by transferring part or all of it to another firm or entity. For some risks, such as the risk of fire or property damage to the firm's facilities, the hedge might entail the purchase of insurance. Other risks can be hedged in the financial derivatives market.

For example, a firm that sells its products and services to international clients who pay for them at a later date in a foreign currency is exposed to currency risk. Similarly, firms that need to borrow money in the future may be exposed to interest rate risk. Both the risk of adverse changes in foreign exchange rates and a rise in interest rates can be hedged using financial markets.

Consider how the hedging process would work using *forward contracts,* which represent agreements to buy or sell an asset at a certain time in the future for a certain price. To hedge, we combine a future commitment that the firm has to sell (buy) an asset with the acquisition (sale) of a forward contract. By locking in the price today that will be received (paid) in the future, the firm effectively eliminates its price risk.

but in general you should *not* risk-adjust *both* the cash flows *and* the discount rate. As it turns out, for the natural-resource valuation problems that we consider in this chapter, it is more convenient to risk-adjust the cash flows rather than the discount rate because forward prices can be used to help us make the risk adjustment.

Forward Prices as Certainty-Equivalent Cash Flows

The certainty-equivalence concept is quite useful in those situations in which the certainty-equivalent cash flow of an investment can be observed and calculated using observed market prices. Indeed, specifying the certainty equivalence of a future cash flow is preferred to specifying the expected cash flow, since the valuation of certainty-equivalent cash flows involves discounting at the risk-free rate and thus does not require an estimate of the appropriate risk-adjusted discount rate.

In some cases, managers can estimate the certainty equivalence of a cash flow more accurately than its expected value. This will generally be the case when the risk associated with a cash flow is closely related to the risk of securities traded in the derivative markets. To illustrate this, let's first consider the **forward prices** of commodities like oil, grains, or metals. The forward price of such a commodity is the price, which is set today, at which market participants are willing to buy and sell that commodity for delivery at some future date. In other words, it is the certain price today, which has the same current value as the uncertain price that will occur in the future. As such, forward prices can be viewed as the certainty equivalents of the uncertain prices that will be realized in the future.

To better understand this concept, consider an investment that generates 100,000 barrels of oil in one year. Since oil prices are uncertain, the cash flows from this investment are uncertain. However, suppose that there exists a forward market that allows you to buy or sell oil, for delivery in one year, for a price of $60/barrel. In this case, we would say that the certainty equivalence of the uncertain future oil price in one year is $60, and that the certainty equivalence of the investment's cash flow is $6 million ($60/barrel $\times$ 100,000 barrels). The owner of the oil can obtain this amount for certain by selling his or her oil in the forward market rather than facing the uncertain cash flow associated with the uncertain price of oil.

It should be stressed that the forward price is generally not equal to the expected price in the future. For example, suppose the price of oil next year is equally likely to be either $75/barrel or $55/barrel, implying that the expected price of oil is $65/barrel. If market participants have no aversion to risk, then this is also likely to be the forward price. However, if a sufficient number of risk-averse oil producers choose to hedge their oil price risk by selling forward contracts, the forward price will be below $65/barrel. The actual price that is realized in the forward market will be determined by supply and demand conditions that relate to the number of producers who want to hedge their oil price exposure by selling oil in the forward market, and the number of oil users (like airlines) and speculators (like hedge funds) that are willing to buy oil in the forward market. Although the equilibrium forward prices can, in theory, equal the expected price, in general this will not be the case.

Did you know?

Where Is the World's Largest Commodity Futures Market?

The New York Mercantile Exchange, Inc., or NYMEX, is the world's largest physical commodity futures exchange and a major trading forum for energy and precious metals. The exchange pioneered the development of energy futures and options contracts and offers options on all major futures contracts: light, sweet crude oil; Brent crude oil; heating oil; unleaded gasoline; natural gas; coal; gold; silver; platinum; copper; and aluminum. Also available are two crack spread options contracts, one for the differential, or the spread, between heating oil futures and light, sweet crude oil futures; and one on the New York Harbor unleaded gasoline/light, sweet crude spread.

Did you know?

How Does Southwest Airlines Avoid the High Cost of Jet Fuel?

Southwest Airlines's successful efforts to hedge the risk of rising jet fuel provide a classic example of the use of forward contracts. Specifically, the company used forward contracts to lock in the price of jet fuel for much of its expected fuel needs for 2005–2009. Southwest locked in 65% of its expected jet fuel needs in 2006 at $32 a barrel, more than 45% of its needs for 2007 at a maximum price of $31 per barrel, 30% of its planned 2008 fuel purchases at $33 per barrel, and 25% of its 2009 fuel needs at $35 per barrel.

(Source: http://money.cnn.com/2005/04/14/news/fortune500/southwest_oil/.)

10.3 USING FORWARD PRICES TO VALUE INVESTMENT PROJECTS

Natural resource investments, like oil and gas fields, illustrate how forward prices are used in discounted cash flow valuation. These investments entail an up-front commitment to explore and develop the hydrocarbon reserves, followed by several years of production. Since oil and gas are commodities that have well-developed forward and futures markets, managers in these industries can use prices from these markets to calculate certainty-equivalent cash flows.

Before valuing an investment with the certainty-equivalence approach, it is useful to first review how analysts value oil and gas investments using the traditional DCF approach. With the traditional method, expected cash flows are calculated by multiplying expected prices by expected quantities, and then discounting these cash flows using risk-adjusted discount rates. This traditional DCF method requires the analyst to make a number of estimates, including estimates of the underlying determinants of both the investment's expected cash flows (based on forecasted prices in combination with estimated extraction rates and operating costs) as well as the appropriate cost of capital to use in discounting the expected cash flows. In contrast, by utilizing information from the oil futures market, we can apply the certainty-equivalence method described in the previous section without having to forecast future oil prices or the appropriate discount rate, since all this information is impounded in forward prices. In the oil and gas industry this practice is referred to as "pricing against the forward price curve." The following example illustrates how this can be done.

Did you know?

What Fraction of an Underground Oil Reserve Is Recoverable?

Total oil reserves and recoverable reserves are not the same thing. For example, using standard recovery techniques, it is possible to extract no more than 15% to 20% of the total reserves found in the Austin chalk region near Giddings, Texas. However, using newly developed horizontal drilling and fracturing methods, the extraction percentage increases to about 50%.

Example

Cutter Exploration and Drilling Company is considering a promising opportunity to develop acreage in the Austin chalk region of central Texas. This area has been in production for many years, but has been plagued by recovery problems. Cutter has developed a new procedure for use in recovering oil from this type of geologic structure that has proven to be very successful in similar situations along the Louisiana Gulf Coast. The procedure is applicable for extracting oil from an oil lease Cutter is considering near Giddings, Texas. Let's see how we might use futures prices and the certainty-equivalence model to evaluate the investment.

Cutter's geologists are confident that the Giddings lease has 1,000,000 barrels of recoverable oil reserves, which can be extracted at a rate of 100,000 barrels per year over a period of 10 years using Cutter's new technology. To acquire this opportunity, Cutter will

Figure 10-1 **Forward Price Curve for Crude Oil**

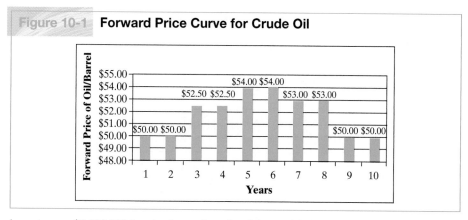

have to pay $7,000,000 for the lease (i.e., the right to drill for and produce the oil) and will incur drilling costs of $12,000,000. For simplicity, we assume that the total investment of $19,000,000 is spent at the beginning of the first year of the investment (i.e., at time $t = 0$) and that the cost of extracting and transporting the oil is $28 per barrel.[6]

Cutter's banker is willing to write a forward contract for the delivery of 100,000 barrels per year over the next 10 years. The "forward price curve" specified in this contract is found in Figure 10-1. Oil produced in Years 1 and 2 has a forward price of $50 per barrel, oil sold in Years 3 and 4 is priced at $52.50 per barrel, and so forth. Currently, the risk-free rate of interest on 10-year U.S. government bonds is 5%.

We can use the certainty-equivalence method to estimate the value of the investment to Cutter using the three-step process outlined in the Chapter Overview:

Step 1: Forcast the amount and timing of future cash flows. The most difficult part of this step has already been done in that the total production volume is assumed to be 100,000 barrels per year over the next 10 years.

Step 2: Use the forward price curve to calculate the certainty-equivalent future cash flows from the project.

Step 3: Discount the certainty-equivalent cash flows back to the present using the risk-free rate of interest.

Figure 10-2 depicts the cash flows generated by our simple investment example. Since the forward price for oil is equal to the certainty-equivalent price, the annual certainty-equivalent cash flow in Years 1 and 2 equals $50 – $28 = $22 per barrel times

Did you know?

What's the "Lingo" of the Forward Price Curve?

Forward price curves can be either upward sloping (i.e., forward prices for more distant periods are higher) or downward sloping. An upward-sloping forward curve is said to be in "**contango**," and a downward-sloping curve is said to be in "**backwardation**."

---

[6]Note that we assume that the quantity of oil to be extracted is known and that the costs of extracting it are fixed at $28 per barrel. These assumptions leave only the price of oil as a source of risk to the investment. We return to this point later in the chapter.

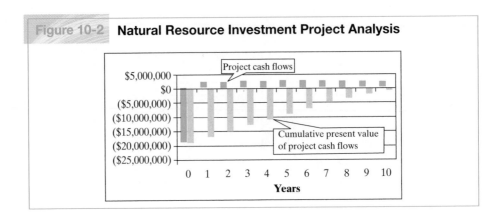

Figure 10-2   **Natural Resource Investment Project Analysis**

100,000 barrels, or $2,200,000. In Years 3 through 6, the annual cash flow rises because the forward price increases. By discounting these certainty-equivalent cash flows for Years 1 through 10 using the risk-free rate, we get a value for the project of $18,437,605. Subtracting the $12,000,000 cost of drilling and completing the well and the $7,000,000 cost of acquiring the lease from the $18,437,605 estimated value of the production during Years 1 through 10 generates a negative net present value for the property of ($562,395), found in Table 10-1. Since the NPV is negative, the analysis indicates that Cutter should reject the investment. In the next section we investigate the validity of this analysis more fully.

In the preceding Cutter example and for the balance of this chapter we will ignore the effects of taxes and the use of debt financing in order to simplify the analysis. For a discussion of the certainty-equivalence method including debt tax shields, see the Technical Insight box on page 418.

Convincing Your Skeptical Boss

Now suppose that you completed your analysis of Cutter's investment opportunity and delivered it to your boss. To your surprise, he strongly disagrees with your analysis. He believes that oil prices will average close to $60 per barrel over the next 10 years and believes that the forward prices you have used to forecast cash flows are not relevant to the project valuation because he does not plan to hedge the price of oil (that is, he does not plan to take up the bank's offer and commit to selling the production at the quoted forward prices). Based on his more optimistic forecast of $60 per barrel and a discount rate of 10%, he estimates that the project has a positive NPV of $662,615.[7]

---

[7]The annual cash flow is calculated as follows: 100,000 barrels($60/barrel − $28/barrel) = $3,200,000. Discounting these cash flows using the 10% cost of capital estimate provides a present value of $19,662,615. Subtracting the total investment costs of $19 million produces an NPV of $662,615.

	Table 10-1	**Project Cash Flows and Present Value**		

Year	Forward Price/Barrel[a]	Project Free Cash Flows[b]	Present Values[c]	Cumulative Present Values
0		($ 19,000,000)	($19,000,000)	($19,000,000)
1	$ 50.00	2,200,000	2,095,238	(16,904,762)
2	50.00	2,200,000	1,995,465	(14,909,297)
3	52.50	2,450,000	2,116,402	(12,792,895)
4	52.50	2,450,000	2,015,621	(10,777,274)
5	54.00	2,600,000	2,037,168	(8,740,106)
6	54.00	2,600,000	1,940,160	(6,799,946)
7	53.00	2,500,000	1,776,703	(5,023,242)
8	53.00	2,500,000	1,692,098	(3,331,144)
9	50.00	2,200,000	1,418,140	(1,913,004)
10	50.00	2,200,000	1,350,609	(562,395)[d]

[a]The prices in the forward price curve have been set through a contract with the bank.

[b]For Year 0 the project cash flow consists entirely of the $12 million cost of drilling plus the $7 million cost of acquiring the drilling lease (rights). In Year 1 the cash flow equals the difference in total revenues ($5 million = $50/barrel × 100,000 barrels), and the cost of extracting and transporting the oil ($28/barrel × 100,000 barrels = $2.8 million) or $2.2 million. Note that we assume a zero tax rate.

[c]Since the oil prices are hedged, they don't involve any future risk. Thus, we discount future cash flows using the risk-free rate of interest.

[d]Since these are cumulative present values, the value for Year 10 incorporates the present values of all 10 years of cash flows including the initial outlay such that this is the NPV. The present value of the cash flows for Years 1 through 10 is $18,437,605. Subtracting the initial outlay for the project of ($19,000,000), we get the NPV of ($562,395).

How should you convince him that his analysis is wrong and your analysis is correct? As we will show, because the derivatives valuation approach uses market prices, we can show that the market offers a better investment opportunity regardless of your boss's beliefs about future oil prices. By showing your skeptical boss that there exists a superior alternative investment opportunity, we should be able to convince him that the investment under evaluation is not attractive.[8] Specifically, we will devise an alternative investment strategy involving the purchase of a risk-free bond and a series of long positions in oil forward contracts that exactly replicates the cash flows

---

[8]Keep in mind, however, that by showing your boss that he is in error, you may be proven right, but also may find yourself working from a new office in one of the company's most obscure locations!

TECHNICAL

INSIGHT

The Certainty Equivalence Approach with Debt and Taxes

Accounting for an investment's debt tax shield is straightforward with the certainty-equivalence approach. If the free cash flows of an investment are calculated as certain equivalents they should be discounted using the risk-free rate for both the cost of equity and debt. Adjusting for the tax deductibility of interest costs results in an after-tax WACC equal to the following:

$$k_{WACC} = r_f - \left(\frac{Tax}{Rate}\right) r_f \left(\frac{Debt}{Value}\right) = r_f \left(1 - \left(\frac{Tax}{Rate}\right)\left(\frac{Debt}{Value}\right)\right)$$

where r_f is the risk-free rate of interest. For example, if the tax rate is 20%, the risk-free rate is 5%, and the debt-to-value ratio is 40%, then the WACC that would be used with the certainty-equivalence approach is calculated as follows: $5\%(1 - .2 \times .4) = 4.2\%$.

As we learned in Chapter 7, we can also calculate the debt tax shield using the APV approach, which separately values the unlevered or operating cash flows and the debt tax shield. When using this approach we recommend that the first component be valued by discounting the before tax certainty equivalent free cash flow at the risk-free rate of interest. We do not, however, recommend calculating the certainty equivalence of the interest tax savings component; these should be calculated and discounted at the cost of debt, as described earlier in Chapter 7.

of the oil investment project over the next 10 years. As we will show, this investment costs less than the $19 million required to make the oil investment, but generates identical cash flows.

Here's how you can construct the alternative investment: First, the company purchases a portfolio of risk-free bonds that generate annual cash flow equal to the project's certainty-equivalent cash flows. For example, you could purchase ten zero coupon bonds with maturity values that are equal to the 10 annual cash flows found in Table 10-1. This portfolio would cost an amount equal to the present value of the 10 annual cash flows, or $18,437,605. In addition to buying the portfolio of bonds, the company also enters into a series of forward contracts with the bank, in which the bank agrees to purchase 100,000 barrels of oil to be delivered at the end of each of the next 10 years at the prices found in the forward price curve in Figure 10-1. The profit (or loss) on these contracts will be the difference between the uncertain future market price that is realized at those delivery dates and the forward price per barrel specified in the contract.

To see how this works, let's assume your boss is right, and the price per barrel of oil climbs to $60, so that the oil field generates a cash flow for Year 1 equal to $3,200,000.

Cash Flow$_1$ = ($60/Barrel − $28/Barrel) × 100,000 Barrels = $3,200,000

Alternatively, if we had invested in the bond and the forward contracts, our bond payment would be $2,200,000 (the Year 1 cash flow based on the forward price of $50/barrel) and the profit from our forward contract would be ($60 − $50)/barrel × 100,000 barrels = $1,000,000. Added together, the Year 1 cash flow from the bond investment and the forward contract is $3,200,000, which is identical to the cash flow from the oil investment. Panel a of Table 10-2 contains the calculations for both the replicating strategy (i.e., bond plus forward contracts) and the actual project, where the price of oil is expected to equal $60/barrel every year.

Now consider a different scenario for Year 1: Let's assume that OPEC falls apart and crude oil prices drop to only $35/barrel. In this scenario, owning the well generates cash flow of only $700,000, i.e.:

Cash Flow$_1$ = ($35/Barrel − $28/Barrel) × 100,000 Barrels = $700,000

From our alternative investment, we would earn $2,200,000 from the bond payment and lose ($1,500,000) = ($35/barrel − $50/barrel) × 100,000 barrels from our forward contracts, netting the identical $700,000 cash flow. Panel b of Table 10-2 contains the cash flows for both the replicating strategy (using bonds and forward contracts) and the actual project under the assumption that the price of crude equals $35/barrel in each of the next 10 years.

What this simple example illustrates is that we *can* replicate the cash flow stream from the risky oil drilling investment using risk-free bonds and forward contracts to purchase oil. Note the key difference between the two alternatives, however: The upfront cost of the replicating strategy using the forward market to purchase oil and investing in a risk-free bond is equal to the cost of the bond, or $18,437,605, since the forward contracts have no cost associated with them at the time they are initiated. On the other hand, it costs $19,000,000 to purchase and develop the oil field investment. Clearly, the replicating strategy dominates investing in the Giddings project as it generates *identical* annual cash flows, yet the replicating strategy costs $562,395 less (which is the negative NPV loss associated with making the investment).

10.4 USING OPTION PRICES TO VALUE INVESTMENT OPPORTUNITIES

The investment considered in the previous section was quite simple. The buyer did not use any debt financing, and the implementation of the investment required no managerial choices beyond the initial decision to undertake the investment. The key insight we gained from our analysis was that we could value the investment using market prices from the forward price curve for oil.

Table 10-2   Replicating Project Cash Flows Using Forward Contracts

Panel a. Expected Price of Oil Equal to $60/Barrel

	(A)	(B)	(A + B)	
Year	Bond Payouts	Gain/Loss on Forwards	Replicating Cash Flows	Actual Project Cash Flows
1	$2,200,000	$ 1,000,000	$3,200,000	$3,200,000
2	2,200,000	1,000,000	3,200,000	3,200,000
3	2,450,000	750,000	3,200,000	3,200,000
4	2,450,000	750,000	3,200,000	3,200,000
5	2,600,000	600,000	3,200,000	3,200,000
6	2,600,000	600,000	3,200,000	3,200,000
7	2,500,000	700,000	3,200,000	3,200,000
8	2,500,000	700,000	3,200,000	3,200,000
9	2,200,000	1,000,000	3,200,000	3,200,000
10	2,200,000	1,000,000	3,200,000	3,200,000

Panel b. Expected Price of Oil Equal to $35/Barrel

	(A)	(B)	(A + B)	
Year	Bond Payouts	Gain/Loss on Forwards	Replicating Cash Flows	Actual Project Cash Flows
1	$2,200,000	($1,500,000)	$700,000	$700,000
2	2,200,000	(1,500,000)	700,000	700,000
3	2,450,000	(1,750,000)	700,000	700,000
4	2,450,000	(1,750,000)	700,000	700,000
5	2,600,000	(1,900,000)	700,000	700,000
6	2,600,000	(1,900,000)	700,000	700,000
7	2,500,000	(1,800,000)	700,000	700,000
8	2,500,000	(1,800,000)	700,000	700,000
9	2,200,000	(1,500,000)	700,000	700,000
10	2,200,000	(1,500,000)	700,000	700,000

TECHNICAL
INSIGHT   **Option Terminology**

The type of option contract—put or call. A *call* (*put*) option gives its owner the right, but not the obligation, to buy (sell) a specified asset at a contractually agreed upon price (commonly referred to as the option's *exercise price*) within a specified period of time. Appendix A provides a brief review of option contract payoffs.

The underlying asset. The *underlying asset* is the common stock, tract of land, etc., that the owner of the option contract buys or sells if the contract is exercised. We say the option is *written* on the underlying asset.

The expiration date of the option. Options have a finite life during which they can be exercised. The final date on which the option can be exercised is referred to as its *expiration date.*

The exercise (or strike) price. The *exercise* (*strike*) price is the price at which the option owner may buy or sell the underlying asset on which the option is written. We will use the symbol K to refer to the option's exercise price.

The terms of exercise—American or European. A *European option* provides the holder with the right to exercise the option only on its expiration date. The *American option* allows the holder to exercise the option at any time up through the expiration date.

For an in-depth review of option contracts, refer to Appendix A.

This section illustrates how a similar process can be used to value investment opportunities that have option-like components. Specifically, we show how companies can use **financial options** (i.e., options that are traded in financial markets) to replicate investment cash flows and to value investments in much the same way that we used forward contracts in the earlier example.

We will start our discussion by considering the **default option** embedded in debt contracts. This is an example of what we refer to as a **contractual option,** which is an option that arises because of the design of the contract that defines the terms of an investment. To illustrate the importance of the default option, we will consider an investment that is financed with *nonrecourse debt,* or debt that is collateralized only by the specific assets being financed, with no separate guarantee by the firm. When a firm uses nonrecourse debt to finance an investment, it has the option to default on the debt and simply walk away from the investment if it is doing especially poorly. As we will show, observed option prices can sometimes be used to determine the value of the firm's equity investment in such a project.

Option Value and Nonrecourse Financing

To illustrate the importance of incorporating information from the prices of financial options in the evaluation of productive investments, consider the following investment opportunity:

- For a price of $5 million, you have the opportunity to purchase the equity of the Cotton Valley oil field that contains five million barrels of reserves. Note that the oil field investment will be partially financed by borrowing, so this is a levered investment.
- The oil can be extracted in one year at a cost of $12 per barrel, for a total cost of $60 million = $12/barrel × 5 million barrels. For simplicity, we assume that the extraction costs are paid at the end of the year and at the time the oil is produced.
- The current owner borrowed $200 million to finance the purchase of the field. If you purchase the equity you will assume this debt, which requires a onetime payment at the end of the year of $220 million (including interest of 10%).
- The debt is *nonrecourse*, which means that the debt holders cannot lay claim to the acquiring firm's other assets if it defaults on the debt payments. They can only lay claim to the oil field. As an equity investor, your firm has the option not to repay the loan and to walk away from the investment if it is in your financial interest to do so. If you chose to do so, you would forfeit any rights of ownership to the oil field, which would transfer to the lender. For example, this would be the case if the revenues generated by the oil field at the end of the year turn out to be worth less than $280 million—the $220 million needed to retire the note plus the $60 million needed to develop the property and produce the oil. Note that the $280 million "breakeven" point equals $56/barrel = $280 million/5 million barrels.
- The forward price of oil to be delivered in one year is $54.17, and the price of a call option to purchase one barrel of crude oil in one year, at an exercise price of $56/barrel, is $1.75.

Valuing the Investment Using Forward Prices

Before proceeding with our formal analysis of the default option, we begin by explaining why the approach from section 10.3 that used forward prices is not appropriate in this case. In the previous example we valued the investment by assuming that oil price risk is hedged or sold in advance in the forward market. However, in this particular case if the oil from the field is sold today for the forward price of $54.17, the equity investment will have no value. To understand this, note that if the investor sells the crude oil forward for $54.17/barrel, this will guarantee revenues of $270,850,000 = 5,000,000 barrels × $54.17/barrel. The equity cash flow at the end of one year for the hedged investment is then:

$$\text{Equity Cash Flow} = \text{Revenues} - \text{Extraction Costs} - \text{Note Payoff}$$
$$= \$270,850,000 - 60,000,000 - 220,000,000 = (\$9,150,000)$$

Hence, if the oil is sold forward, the equity investment generates a negative cash flow of ($9,150,000) if the investor chooses not to default. As a result, the equity investor will in fact default on his debt obligation, so the actual cash flow to the equity holders is zero.

Because of this option to default, the investment in the project's equity has a higher value if the oil price risk is not hedged. Indeed, when we value this investment opportunity in a way that incorporates the option to default on the debt, we will see that the equity investment does have a positive value when the oil price risk is not hedged.

Analyzing Equity Value with the Default Option—Managing the Project

We begin our analysis by showing that the payoff to the equity in the project is identical to an investment in a one-year call option on five million barrels of oil with an exercise price of $56/barrel (i.e., the cost of extracting a barrel of oil from the oil field in one year).

- If the price of oil exceeds $56/barrel, the option will be exercised and will generate a profit equal to the price of oil times five million barrels minus $280 million, (the $56 exercise price per barrel times five million barrels). This profit is identical to the profit from the equity investment, which also generates cash flows equal to the price of oil times five million minus $280 million (the sum of the $60 million in extraction costs plus the $220 million needed to retire the note).
- If oil prices fall below $56/barrel, the option expires worthless. When this is the case, the equity investor defaults on the debt and walks away from the investment.

Just as having forward prices simplified the analysis of Cutter Exploration Company in the example discussed earlier, having observable option prices simplifies the valuation of this equity investment. In this case, the **tracking portfolio,** that is the portfolio of traded securities that replicate the real investment cash flows, for the oil investment consists of a portfolio of call options on five million barrels of crude oil with an exercise price of $56/barrel. If these call options have a price of $1.75/barrel, then the tracking portfolio is worth $8.75 million = $1.75 per barrel × 5 million barrels of oil. Since the equity investment in the project has the same cash flows as the tracking portfolio, it, too, is worth $8.75 million. Given that the equity of the Cotton Valley oil field investment can be acquired for $5 million, this seems like a pretty good investment. Indeed, the NPV of the investment is $3.75 million = $8.75 million − $5 million.

Convincing Your Skeptical Boss

Again, since this kind of analysis is relatively new, we might expect to encounter a skeptical boss reluctant to accept the valuation of the equity in the project using the option-pricing approach. Since this is a positive-NPV investment, we cannot create a better transaction using derivatives, as we did earlier using risk-free bonds

TECHNICAL INSIGHT

Settlement Differences in Forward versus Option Contracts and Discounting

The cash flows associated with forward and option contracts change hands at different times. When a forward contract is initiated, no cash changes hands until the contract delivery date. Consequently, when forward prices are used to calculate the certainty equivalent of future project cash flows, we discount the resulting cash flows back to the present using the risk-free rate to determine their value. However, when the market prices of options are used to value an investment, we do not discount them. The reason for this difference is that with options, the buyer of an option pays up front—i.e., the option price we observe is the discounted value of the certainty-equivalent payoff of the option.

and forward contracts in the Cutter example. Instead, to convince the skeptical boss to take the investment, we should show her how to use the derivative market to hedge the risk associated with this investment and thereby guarantee that the NPV of the investment is realized.

To lock in the positive NPV associated with this investment, we acquire the equity position in the oil property for $5 million, and at the same time, write (sell) call

Table 10-3   Locking in a Positive NPV Using Options—Cutter Example

Year	Hedging Strategy	Cash Flows
0	(1) Sell call options on 5 million barrels of crude oil for $1.75 each	$8.75 million
	(2) Purchase the oil investment	$ (5 million)
	(3) Net cash flow for Year 0	**$3.75 million**

		Cash Flows for Alternative Crude Oil Prices	
		$60/barrel	$ 56/barrel
1	(1) Payoff (loss) from sale of call options	($4) × 5 million = ($20 million)	$0.00
	(2) Payoff (loss) from the oil investment	$300 million − $280 million = $20 million	$0.00
	(3) Net cash flow for Year 1	**$0.00**	**$0.00**

options on five million barrels of oil for $1.75 per barrel. Since the option transaction generates a total cash inflow of $8.75 million = 5 million $\times$ $1.75, the combination of these two transactions nets $3.75 million in the current period. As we illustrate in Table 10-3, despite this initial cash inflow, the combination of these two investments generates no cash outflows in the following year since the cash flows of the two investments exactly offset each other.

10.5 CAVEATS AND LIMITATIONS—TRACKING ERRORS

Most of our discussion up to this point has assumed that it is possible to construct a portfolio of traded financial securities whose cash flows are a *perfect match* for the cash flows of the real investment we are trying to value. In practice it is not always possible to match cash flows perfectly with the payoffs to traded financial securities. As a consequence, the value of the tracking portfolio will differ from that of the investment. Figure 10-3 illustrates the problem of tracking error. The black line depicts the true value of the project over time, and the blue one reflects the value of the tracking portfolio over a period of time. Obviously, the greater the difference between the two lines, the less precise the valuation of the investment using the value of the tracking portfolio.

There are three fundamental reasons why the cash flows of the tracking portfolio will deviate from those of the investment being analyzed. The first relates to the reliability of market prices for derivatives. The second relates to what we will refer to as *omitted project risks,* which are simply sources of risk in the investment's cash flows that are not captured in the cash flows of the tracking portfolio. Finally, there is something that derivatives traders refer to as *basis risk,* which arises out of differences in the specific nature of the assets underlying the derivative contracts and the assets

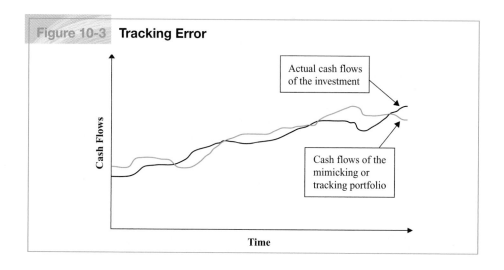

Figure 10-3   Tracking Error

that underlie the real investment being evaluated. We describe each of these sources of tracking error in some detail below.

How Liquid Are Futures, Forward, and Option Markets?

If derivative markets are very illiquid, the market prices may not provide a reliable estimate of the certainty-equivalent prices. Our analysis assumes that the investor can, in fact, transact at the quoted financial market prices. For example, suppose we are considering a project to extract two billion barrels of oil over a five-year period (a bit more than one million barrels per day). Although the derivative markets have sufficient depth to hedge multi-billion-dollar oil price exposures, it may not be possible to hedge such a huge exposure without significantly affecting forward prices. Because of this, large oil producers tend to hedge very little, and as a result, they do not believe the derivatives approach is applicable for their investments and prefer to use the traditional DCF approach. Although they may use futures prices as a guide to their estimates of expected oil prices, they also use their own judgment about expected future oil prices.

Uncertain Quantities and Operating Costs

Our second caveat has to do with project risks that have been omitted from our analysis. Here tracking errors arise from sources of variation in cash flows that cannot be known in advance and consequently cannot be used to determine the tracking portfolio. Specifically, although the tracking portfolio procedure can be extremely valuable in dealing with the commodity price risks in capital investments, typically there are other sources of risk that affect an investment's cash flows that are not driven by commodity prices. Two important sources of noncommodity price risk are the quantity of the commodity produced and the operating costs associated with extracting and processing the commodity.

In our oil and gas examples, you may have noted that we assumed that the quantity of oil and the cost of extraction were both known with certainty, so that the only source of risk was the uncertain price of crude oil. In practice, valuing an oil field (or any investment in a commodity industry) requires estimates of the quantity of oil produced and the costs of extracting the oil. To accommodate the effects of uncertain production quantities, managers may opt for conservative estimates of those quantities to adjust for this source of uncertainty.[9] One might also use relatively conservative estimates of extraction costs (i.e., costs on the high end of what is expected) for the same reason.

---

[9]However, one would not want to use quantity estimates that are substantially lower than expected quantities, because the quantity of oil that is produced is not likely to be correlated with the aggregate economy. In other words, quantity is likely to be a low or zero beta risk.

Basis Risk

The final source of tracking error that we consider is something analysts refer to as **basis risk,** which, as we noted earlier, arises out of differences in the specific nature of the assets underlying the derivative contracts and the assets that underlie the real investment being evaluated. We will discuss three sources of such differences: product quality, geographic location, and contract terms.

Differences in Product Quality

Although the list of traded derivatives on commodities is quite lengthy, it is not encyclopedic. This means that the analyst will often have to use a surrogate commodity contract since a derivative contract for the exact commodity that underlies the risks of the investment being analyzed may not exist. For example, if the investment involves the production of heavy crude oil, the analyst might use derivative contracts based on light, sweet crude since this is the contract that is traded on the New York Mercantile Exchange (NYMEX). The problem is that the price of light, sweet crude is imperfectly correlated with the price of other forms of crude oil. Consequently, the resulting valuation of the investment using the light, sweet crude contracts will differ from the true value of the investment because of the differences in the *quality of the products* underlying the investment and the derivative contract.

Differences in Geographic Locations

Basis risk also arises out of *geographic differences*. For example, crude oil futures are priced for delivery in Cushing, Oklahoma, and natural gas futures are priced for delivery at Henry Hub in Louisiana. Obviously, differences in the physical location of crude oil or natural gas from the standard locations used in the option contracts give rise to tracking errors. In this instance, the tracking error is due to delivery costs.

Although the problem of tracking errors due to geography can be resolved by considering delivery costs, the problem is not inconsequential. Delivery costs vary with supply and demand conditions, and in some extreme instances the costs can become prohibitive. For example, during the California energy crisis in 2000, the costs of delivering electric power to the residents of the state rose to astronomical levels as the power grid became overloaded.

Differences in Contract Terms

These are cases where the match between traded options and the option component of the investment that is being valued is far from perfect. For example, suppose we can find prices of call options on oil with an exercise price of $50, but there are no traded options with an exercise price of $56, which is the price we need to solve our valuation problem. An even more common problem is that the analyst is evaluating an investment that offers cash flows distributed over many years, whereas traded options have maturities extending out only one year. In such cases, we will need an option pricing model to value the investment, which is the topic we discuss in the next section.

The Relation between Tracking Error and Imperfect Comps

The astute student of finance will recognize that the problem of finding an appropriate tracking portfolio is analogous to the problem of finding appropriate comparison firms that can be used to value a business. As we mentioned in earlier chapters, it is generally impossible to find comparable companies that provide a perfect match when we are trying to identify either the appropriate valuation multiple or the appropriate risk-adjusted cost of capital. In general, managers consider a variety of comps, and then use their judgment to come up with a weighted average that provides discount rates and multiples that are appropriate in their judgment.

Identifying the appropriate tracking portfolio to determine the certainty-equivalent cash flows is also an imperfect procedure, but no more so than the procedures that are used to identify appropriate valuation ratios and discount rates. We again need to stress that there are inherent uncertainties in valuing future cash flows whether we use the traditional DCF model (which focuses on the estimate of risk-adjusted discount rates) or the real options approach (which focuses on identifying a tracking portfolio), and both approaches require sound judgment on the part of the user.

Using an Option Pricing Model to Value the Investment

In the Cotton Valley oil example, the financial options exactly matched the investment that was being evaluated. Unfortunately, as our discussion in the last section indicates, in even the best cases there is likely to be some basis risk, and in other cases there may be no traded option that even remotely resembles the option embedded in the investment being valued. As we will show in this section, when you cannot match an investment's cash flow with a traded option, you *may* be able to price the option component of the investment using information from forward prices. However, this requires an option pricing model, along with assumptions about the distribution of oil prices in the future.

In this section we illustrate how to estimate the value of a call option on oil using a single-period **binomial option pricing** model, which makes the assumption that the future oil price follows a **binomial distribution** (see the Technical Insight box titled "Probability Trees and the Binomial Distribution"). In our re-examination of the Cotton Valley oil field investment we make assumtion about the distribution of oil prices. Specifically, as we illustrate in Figure 10-4, we assume that oil prices

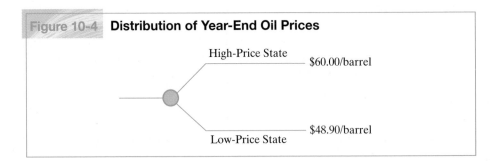

Figure 10-4   **Distribution of Year-End Oil Prices**

High-Price State ————— $60.00/barrel

Low-Price State ————— $48.90/barrel

Probability Trees and the Binomial Distribution

The idea behind a probability tree is not new to most students of finance. Very simply, a *probability tree* specifies the outcomes of an uncertain event such as the price of a pound of copper at the end of next year and the probabilities associated with each of the possible prices. If there are only two possible outcomes, the probability tree is a binomial tree, if there are three possible outcomes it is a trinomial tree, and so forth. For our purposes we will stick to the simplest case, the binomial probability tree.

To illustrate the construction of a binomial tree consider the binomial distribution of oil prices at the end of one year that are found in Figure 10-4. The high and low price of oil at the end of one year are calculated in terms of the forward price of oil observed today for oil delivered at the end of Year 1, $F_{0,1}$:[10]

$$\text{High Price} = F_{0,1}u \text{ where } u = e^{+\sigma} \quad \text{and} \quad \text{Low Price} = F_{0,1}d \text{ where } d = e^{-\sigma}$$

To calculate these prices we need the forward price of oil to be delivered in one year $F_{0,1} = \$54.17$ and the standard deviation in annual oil price changes, $\sigma = .10232$. Therefore, $u = e^{+\sigma} = e^{.10233} = 1.10775$ and $d = .9027$ which, implies that at the end of one year the price of oil will be either

$$\text{High Price} = F_{0,1}u = \$54.17 \times 1.10775 = \$60.00$$

or

$$\text{Low Price} = F_{0,1}d = \$54.17 \times .9027 = \$48.90$$

The single-period binomial model can be extended to multiple periods with a few slight modifications. We demonstrate this procedure in Appendix B.

in the next period will be equal to a high price of $60.00/barrel or a low price of $48.90/barrel.

The first step in the investment valuation process is to identify the cash flows that accrue to the equity holder under each of the crude-oil-price scenarios. The cash flows equal the revenue generated by five million barrels of production sold for either $60.00/barrel or $48.90/barrel minus the $12/barrel cost of extracting the oil, plus the $20.0 million due on the note. Thus, the summary information for the oil-field investment is as follows.[11]

---

[10]There are other ways to characterize the distribution of prices in a binomial lattice. However, we follow the approach taken by Robert L. McDonald, *Derivative Markets,* 2nd edition (Boston, MA: Addison Wesley, 2006).

[11]This is an existing note that has a $200 million face value, however given the assumptions in this example its market value would be less.

Continuous Time Discounting

In the option literature, the standard convention is to use continuous time compounding/ discounting. Consequently, the future value of $1.00 compounded using continuous compounding at a rate of 10% for one year is equal to $e^{.10}$, which is equivalent to discrete time compounding using an annual rate of 10.517%, i.e., $(1 + .10517)$.

- The oil price next year will be either $48.90 or $60.00 per barrel, as illustrated in Figure 10-4.
- Extraction and transportation costs are known and equal $12 per barrel.
- The risk-free interest rate is 8%.
- The forward price for oil observed today for delivery in one year is $54.17/barrel.
- A total of five million barrels of oil can be extracted from the property, and the entire amount can be extracted next year.
- The oil field serves as the sole collateral for a $200 million note that is due at the end of next year that requires 10% interest compounded annually.
- The owner of the oil field has offered to sell his equity for $5 million, and the buyer will assume the $200 million note, which is secured by the property.

The question, then, is this: Is the offer a good one?

The decision trees found in Panels a and b of Figure 10-5 provide a convenient way to illustrate graphically how the decision process unfolds over time. The circle nodes represent uncertain events, such as different oil prices possibilities, and the square nodes represent decision events, for example, whether or not to drill. The numbers found in the square nodes are used to keep track of the particular decision that is to be made as part of the decision problem (e.g., investment) being described.

Panel a of Figure 10-5 presents a detailed analysis of the cash flows that are realized from an uncertain future price of crude oil if the firm does not sell the oil in the forward market. If oil prices increase to $60.00/barrel, the investment revenues will be $300 million = 5 million barrels × $60.00/barrel, leaving a profit of $20 million after paying the extraction costs ($60 million) and retiring the debt ($220 million). If oil prices at year-end equal the low price of $48.90/barrel, the investment will lose $35.5 million after extraction costs and repayment of the debt. Since the loan is nonrecourse, the investor will default when oil prices are low, making the cash flow to equity equal to zero.

As Figure 10-5 illustrates, the payoff to the equity investors is identical to the payoff from holding a call option to buy five million barrels of oil with an exercise price of $56/barrel. In both cases, the investment pays $20 million (if oil prices turn out to be $60/barrel) and nothing (if oil prices are $48.90/barrel).

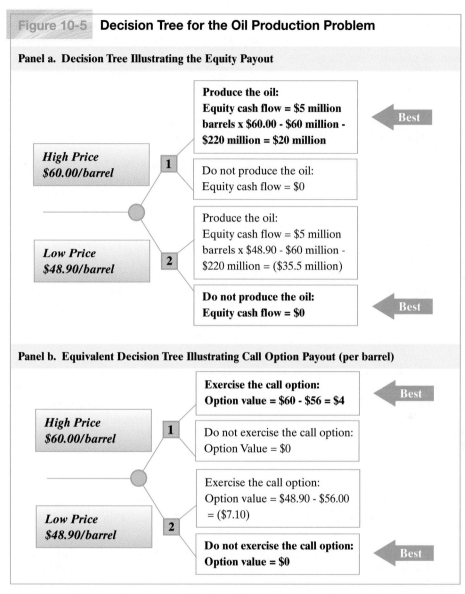

Figure 10-5   Decision Tree for the Oil Production Problem

Panel a. Decision Tree Illustrating the Equity Payout

High Price $60.00/barrel

1

> **Produce the oil:**
> **Equity cash flow = $5 million**
> **barrels x $60.00 - $60 million -**
> **$220 million = $20 million**   ◀ Best

> Do not produce the oil:
> Equity cash flow = $0

Low Price $48.90/barrel

2

> Produce the oil:
> Equity cash flow = $5 million
> barrels x $48.90 - $60 million -
> $220 million = ($35.5 million)

> **Do not produce the oil:**
> **Equity cash flow = $0**   ◀ Best

Panel b. Equivalent Decision Tree Illustrating Call Option Payout (per barrel)

High Price $60.00/barrel

1

> **Exercise the call option:**
> **Option value = $60 - $56 = $4**   ◀ Best

> Do not exercise the call option:
> Option Value = $0

Low Price $48.90/barrel

2

> Exercise the call option:
> Option value = $48.90 - $56.00
> = ($7.10)

> **Do not exercise the call option:**
> **Option value = $0**   ◀ Best

Again, it is worth noting that the traditional DCF approach would require (1) estimating the possible cash flow outcomes for the option in the high and low crude-oil-price states, (2) calculating the expected cash flow by weighting these cash flows using the probabilities of the high- and low-price state, and (3) then discounting the expected cash flow at an appropriate risk-adjusted discount rate. The alternative that is used in practice is to calculate the option's certainty-equivalent cash flow rather than its expected cash flow, and to discount this value at the risk-free rate.

The advantage of this approach is that we do not need to know the *actual* probabilities of the two oil-price scenarios. Instead, we calculate what is referred to as **risk-neutral probabilities.** Specifically, the *risk-neutral probabilities are hypothetical probabilities that make the forward price equal the expected price of oil next year.* We can solve for the risk-neutral probabilities using Equation 10.1 as follows:

$$\text{Forward Price for Oil}_{\text{Year }t} = \left(\text{High Price for Oil}_{\text{Year }t}\right) \times \left(\text{Risk-Neutral Probability}_{\text{High Price}}\right)$$
$$+ \left(\text{Low Price for Oil}_{\text{Year }t}\right) \times \left(\text{Risk-Neutral Probability}_{\text{Low Price}}\right) \quad (10.1)$$

Substituting values from our current example, we solve for p, which represents the risk-neutral probability that the $60.00 price will prevail, as follows:

$$\$54.17 = p \times \$60.00 + (1 - p) \times \$48.90,$$

where $(1 - p)$ is the corresponding risk-neutral probability that the $48.90 price will prevail. By solving the above equation we see that the risk-neutral probability of the high price occurring is 47.44%, which leaves a 52.56% risk-neutral probability for the low price.[12]

Using the risk-neutral probabilities, we see that the risk-neutral expected value or certainty equivalence of the option payoff at its expiration date in one year is .4744 × $4.00 + .5256 × $0.00 = $1.90. Discounting this certainty-equivalence payoff using the 8% risk-free rate provides an estimate of the value of the call option today. Thus, the value of one call option to acquire a barrel of oil via the investment just described is $1.75 = 1.90e^{-.08}$, which is what we assumed earlier, and the value of an option to acquire five million barrels is $8.75 million.[13]

How Does Volatility Affect Option Values?

How is the value of this equity position affected if uncertainty increases? In our discounted cash flow analysis, we learned that an increase in risk, other things remaining

---

[12]As we discussed in Section 10.2, forward prices need not equal the expected value of future spot prices because hedging pressure from market participants may cause forward prices to be either higher or lower than the expected future prices. This in turn implies that risk-neutral probabilities, which make the forward price equal to its certainty-equivalent value, will not generally equal actual probabilities. For example, if the forward price is lower than the expected price in the future, the risk-neutral probability of the high-price state will be lower than the actual probability, and the risk-neutral probability of the low-price state will be higher than the actual probability.

[13]The astute reader will notice that we have not presented anything that might be construed as an *option pricing model* in the traditional sense. Instead we valued the call option simply using the certainty-equivalent DCF model that we have been using throughout this chapter. We were able to do this because we can observe forward prices for the underlying asset. In Chapter 11 we tackle situations in which forward prices are not observable.

the same, led to an increase in the discount rate and a corresponding decrease in the present value of expected future cash flows. However, as we now illustrate, this is not necessarily the case for investments with option components.

Consider the case where the forward price stays at $54.17/barrel, but the oil price when the economy is strong is increased to $66.00/barrel and the price when the economy is weak is decreased to $44.50/barrel. In this case, the risk-neutral probabilities can be computed using Equation 10.1 to be 45% for the high-price state and 55% for the low-price state.[14] Since the equity position has value only when the price of oil is $66.00, the value of the equity in Year 1 is calculated as follows:

$$\frac{.45 \times (\$66/\text{barrel} \times 5 \text{ million barrels} - \$280 \text{ million})}{1.08} = \$20.833 \text{ million}$$

This is a substantial increase from the $8.75 million value calculated with the lower volatility.[15]

This result may seem odd since we normally associate greater uncertainty with higher risk, not higher value. However, the equity investor benefits from the increased volatility, which leads to the possibility of both higher and lower future oil prices, because higher *and* lower oil prices have an asymmetric effect on cash flows. Although higher oil prices always generate higher revenues, the loss associated with lower oil prices has a floor. Since the investor has the option to walk away from the investment, the investor cannot lose more than her original investment no matter how much oil prices decline.

Calibrating Option Pricing Models

It is often the case that traded options exist that resemble the embedded option being valued, but the basis risk is quite large. When this is the case, financial analysts infer information from the best available option and forward prices and use this information in combination with an *option pricing model* to value the options under consideration. Specifically, analysts use observed option prices to back out the volatility (or equivalently, the spread between the price in the high and low state) of the price of the underlying commodity. For example, if the prices of traded options on oil are relatively high, they infer that oil prices are expected to be relatively volatile, which means that a higher volatility should be used to value the options embedded in an oil field. This process of using observed option prices to infer the parameters that are used for a model is known as *calibrating* the model. Appendix C contains an illustration of this process using the binomial option pricing model.

---

[14]Where the forward price remains $54.17, the risk-neutral probability of the high price state, p, is calculated as follows:

$$\$54.17 = p \times \$66.00 + (1 - p) \times \$44.50$$

[15]Most of the gain in value of the equity is due to a reduction in the value of the outstanding debt.

10.6 SUMMARY

The central point of this chapter is that the observable market prices of derivative contracts (forwards, futures, and options prices) provide information that can be used to value real investment projects. For example, forward prices provide the information needed to calculate certainty-equivalent cash flows, which can be easily valued by discounting them using the risk-free rate of interest. This approach should not be viewed as an alternative to DCF analysis. Indeed, a key learning point of this chapter is that observed prices of traded derivatives can be used to facilitate DCF valuation.

How useful are the methods described in this chapter for valuing real investment opportunities? In reality, it is unlikely that an investment's cash flows can be exactly replicated with publicly traded financial derivatives. However, this problem is no different from the problem of finding comparable firms for implementing relative valuation, as discussed in Chapter 6, or the problem of estimating a project's risk-adjusted cost of capital, as discussed in Chapters 4 and 5. When this problem arises in a valuation analysis, and it almost always does regardless of the method being used, financial analysts must exercise their professional judgment to come up with combinations of futures and/or options that track the investment cash flows as closely as possible.

In some cases managerial judgment may be used to select derivative prices for a traded commodity that is closely related to the commodity that underlies the project cash flows. For example, if an investment's cash flows are derived from the production and sale of heavy oil from Alberta, the analyst may use the West Texas crude oil futures price, adjusted for the typical $4 per barrel difference in prices of the two sources of crude. In other cases, more complex transformations are required. For example, if the terms of the traded option contracts do not match the specific attributes of the option embedded in the investment being valued, an option pricing model, such as the binomial option pricing model introduced in this chapter can be used. To apply such a model you should use information from the prices of traded options that have attributes that closely resembles the real options being valued.

As we mentioned at the outset of this chapter, we have illustrated the derivative valuation approach with examples of oil investments. The techniques that we have described were originally developed to value oil, gas, and other natural resource investments. However, as we illustrate in chapters 11 and 12, the approach that we have described is currently being extended to value a wide range of investments in an expanding variety of industries.

PROBLEMS

10-1 USING DERIVATIVES TO ANALYZE A NATURAL GAS INVESTMENT Morrison Oil and Gas is faced with an interesting investment opportunity. The investment involves the exploration for a significant deposit of natural gas in southeastern Louisiana near Cameron. The area has long been known for its oil and gas production, and the new opportunity involves developing and producing 50 million cubic feet (MCF) of gas. Natural gas is currently trading around $14.03 per MCF; the price next year, when the gas would be produced and sold, could be as high as $18.16 or as low as $12.17. Furthermore, the forward price of gas one year hence is currently $14.87. If Morrison acquires the property, it will face a cost of $4.00 per MCF to develop the gas.

The company trying to sell the gas field has a note of $450 million on the property that requires repayment in one year plus 10% interest. If Morrison buys the property, it will have to assume this note and responsibility for repaying it. However, the note is nonrecourse: If the owner of the property decides not to develop the property in one year, the owner can simply transfer ownership of the property to the lender.

The property's current owner is a major oil company that is in the process of fighting off an attempted takeover; thus, it needs cash. The asking price for the equity in the property is $50 million. The problem faced by Morrison's analysts is whether the equity is worth this amount.

   a. One possible response to the valuation question is to estimate the value of the project where the price risk of natural gas is eliminated through hedging. Estimate the value of the equity in the project where all the gas is sold forward at the $14.87 per MCF price. The risk-free rate of interest is currently 6%.

   b. Alternatively, Morrison could choose to wait a year to decide on developing it. By delaying, the firm chooses whether or not to develop the property based on the price per MCF at year-end. Analyze the value of the equity of the property under this scenario.

   c. The equity in the property is essentially a call option on 50 MCF of natural gas. Under the conditions stated in the problem, what is the value of a one-year call option on natural gas with an excessive price of 13.90 MCF worth today? (*Hint:* Use the binomial option pricing model.)

10-2 VALUING AN ENERGY INVESTMENT USING OIL OPTIONS The Pampa Oil Company operates oil and gas exploration throughout the panhandle of Texas. The firm recently was approached by a wildcatter named William "Wild Bill" Donavan with the prospect to develop what he thought was a sure thing. Wild Bill owned the lease and wanted to sell it to Pampa to meet some rather pressing gambling debts.

The exploration would involve efforts expended over the period of one year and cost $600,000 (which for simplicity we assume is paid at the end of the year). Wild Bill is extremely confident that there are 20,000 barrels of oil to be found, and he has engineering and geological reports to support his view. The value of the proposition hinges on the price of oil, the cost of exploration, and the cost of extracting the oil. Pampa Oil is very familiar with exploration and production in the area and is confident about its cost estimates. Pampa Oil estimates that the exploration would involve efforts expended over the period of six months and cost $600,000 (which for simplicity we assume is paid at the end of the year). Pampa Oil also feels confident that the cost of extracting oil will be no more than $8 a barrel. However, oil prices have been very volatile, and the experts in the economy predict that oil prices might hit $50 a barrel by year-end or drop back to $35 depending upon progress made in securing a lasting peace in the Middle East. Pampa Oil is, therefore, considering the possibility of deferring development of the oil field for six months. Waiting for six months will place Pampa Oil in a better position to determine whether to go ahead with exploration or not. The risk-free rate of interest is currently 5%, and the forward price of oil one year in the future is now trading at $40 a barrel. What should the investment proposal be worth to Pampa (you may assume a zero income tax rate)?

10-3 THE LOGIC OF HEDGING Morrison Oil Company's (from Problem 10-1) chief financial analyst is Samuel (Sam) Crawford. Sam completed his analysis suggesting that the investment was indeed a good one for the company and presented it to the firm's executive committee. The executive committee consists of the firm's CEO, CFO, and COO. The CFO thought Sam's analysis was on target, but the COO and CEO were concerned about the fact that the hedging strategy would not work for the investment. In fact, they wondered why hedging the investment was such a good idea. Sam thought for a second or two before responding and decided how to best explain why the project was a good one and involved hedging the investment cash flows using one-year call options on natural gas. These call options, which have a $13.90 per MCF strike price, were selling for $1.86 per MCF. Show how selling call options on 50 MCF of gas today and undertaking the investment provides Morrison with a hedged (i.e., risk-free) investment.

10-4 VALUING A COPPER MINING PROJECT USING FORWARD PRICES Harrington Explorations Inc. is interested in expanding its copper mining operations in Indonesia. The area has long been noted for its rich deposits of copper ore, and with copper prices at near-record levels, the company is considering an investment of $60 million to open operations into a new vein of ore that was mapped by company geologists four years ago. The investment would be expensed (a combination of depreciation of capital equipment and depletion costs associated with using up the ore deposit) over five years toward a zero value. Since Harrington faces a corporate tax rate of 30%, the tax savings are significant.

The company's geologists also estimate that the ore will be of about the same purity as existing deposits such that it will cost $150 to mine and process a ton of ore containing roughly 15% pure copper. The company estimates that there are 75,000 tons of ore in the new vein that can be mined and processed over the next five years at a pace of 15,000 tons per year.

Harrington's CFO asked one of his financial analysts to come up with an estimate of the expected value of the investment using the forward price curve for copper as a guide to the value of future copper production. The forward price curve for the price per ton of copper spanning the next five years when the proposed investment would be in production is as follows:

2008 $7,000/ton
2009 $7,150/ton
2010 $7,200/ton
2011 $7,300/ton
2012 $7,450/ton

In a study commissioned by the CFO last year, the firm's cost of capital was estimated to be 9.5%. The risk-free rate of interest on five-year Treasury bonds is currently 5.5%.

a. Estimate the after-tax (certainty-equivalent) project free cash flows for the project over its five-year productive life.
b. Using the certainty-equivalent valuation methodology, what is the NPV of the project?
c. Assume now that the analyst estimates the NPV of the project using the certainty-equivalent methodology, and it is negative. When the firm's CFO sees the results of the analysis, he suggests that something must be wrong because his own analysis using conventional methods (i.e., expected cash flows and the firm's weighted average cost of capital) produces a positive NPV of more than $450,000. Specifically, he estimates that the price of copper for 2008 would indeed be $7,000 per ton but that this would increase by 12% per year over the five-year life of the project. How should the analyst respond to the CFO's concerns?

10-5 VALUING A GOLD INVESTMENT OPPORTUNITY Jim Lytle, a financial advisor, recommends that his clients invest in gold. Specifically, he is advising a client to invest $100,000 to purchase 175 ounces of gold bullion, with the expectation of holding the gold for a period of one year before selling it. The client points out that the futures price for 175 ounces of gold to be delivered in one year is $104,000, which represents a 4% return on the $100,000 investment, while the one-year Treasury yield is currently 5%. "Wouldn't it be better," he asks, "if I sold 175 ounces of gold today for $100,000 while purchasing a forward contract to purchase the gold in one year at a price of $104,000? I could then invest the $100,000 in 5% Treasury bonds maturing in one year."

a. Analyze the returns to the investor's proposed strategy. What is your recommendation?
b. Why might the two alternatives offer different returns?

10-6 VALUING GOLD RECLAIMED FROM OLD PERSONAL COMPUTERS A number of industrial products include gold and silver as a component since they have very good conductive properties. The S&M Smelting Company engages in the recovery of gold from such products and is considering a contract to begin extracting the gold from the recycling of personal computers. The project involves contracting with the state governments of three Midwestern states to dispose of their PCs. The project will last for five years, and the contract calls for the disposal of 200,000 PCs per year. Three tons of electronic scrap contains approximately one Troy ounce of gold. Moreover, each PC contains approximately 6 pounds of electronic scrap, and the processing cost involved in extracting the gold is $67.50 per ton of scrap. In addition, the current (spot) price of gold is $592.80 and the forward price curve for the price per ounce of gold spanning the next five years is as follows:

2008: $679.40/ounce
2009: $715.10/ounce
2010: $750.60/ounce
2011: $786.90/ounce
2012: $822.80/ounce

S&M estimates that the firm's cost of capital is 10.5%, and the risk-free rate of interest on five-year Treasury bonds is currently 5.0%. In addition, S&M faces a 30% tax rate and the entire investment of $450,000 made in the project in 2007 will be depreciated using straight-line depreciation over five years with a zero salvage value.

a. Estimate the after-tax (certainty-equivalent) project free cash flows for the project over its five-year productive life.
b. Using the certainty-equivalent valuation methodology, estimate the NPV of the project.
c. If we assume that gold prices will increase at a rate of 7% per year over the next five years, what is the NPV of the project using the traditional WACC method of analysis based on expected project free cash flows, where the WACC is estimated to be 10.5%? What rate of growth in gold prices is required to produce the same NPV using the traditional WACC approach as with the certainty-equivalent approach used in part b?

Option Basics—A Quick Review

This appendix is targeted toward the reader whose knowledge of options and their payoffs is either limited or just rusty from years of nonuse. Our objective is to develop a platform from which to build an understanding of the use of options throughout this chapter and the two that follow.

What Is an Option?

An **option** gives its owner the right, but not the obligation, to buy or sell a specified asset at a contractually agreed-upon price (the option's *exercise price* or *strike price*) within a specified period of time. A **call** option gives the owner the right (but again, not the obligation) to buy the asset at the exercise price. A **put option** gives the owner the right (but again, not the obligation) to sell the asset at the exercise price. In either case, the option owner can walk away if it is not in his or her best interest to buy or to sell.

Option contracts come in two basic types depending upon *when* they can be exercised: The **European option** provides the holder the right to exercise the option *only* on its expiration date; the **American option** allows the holder to exercise it at *any time* up until the expiration date of the option.

How Can We Characterize the Payoffs to Option Contracts?

Consider the economic consequences of owning a call option on a share of stock. The payoff to the holder of the option at maturity (i.e., date T when the option expires) can be represented graphically using the position diagram in Figure 10A-1. The expiration date payoff to owning the call option (or being long in the call) is represented by the 45° line moving up and to the right beginning at the exercise price, K, of $30. If the stock price, $P(T)$, is, say, $50 and the exercise price, K, is $30, then on the day the option expires it has a value of $P(T) - K = \$50 - 30 = \$20$. However, if on the expiration date of the option the stock price falls below $30, the option is worthless. For example, if the stock price on the expiration day were only $25, then the holder would not exercise the option because it has no value. (Who would pay $30 to exercise an

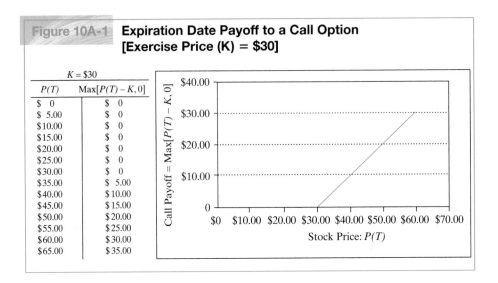

Figure 10A-1 **Expiration Date Payoff to a Call Option [Exercise Price (K) = $30]**

$P(T)$	Max$[P(T) - K, 0]$
$ 0	$ 0
$ 5.00	$ 0
$10.00	$ 0
$15.00	$ 0
$20.00	$ 0
$25.00	$ 0
$30.00	$ 0
$35.00	$ 5.00
$40.00	$10.00
$45.00	$15.00
$50.00	$20.00
$55.00	$25.00
$60.00	$30.00
$65.00	$35.00

option to buy a share of stock that one could purchase in the market for only $25?) Thus we want to own call options when we expect that prices of the underlying asset are going to increase.

Defining Call Option Payoffs

Analytically, we write the payoff to the call option as max$[P(T) - K, 0]$, which is read "the maximum of $P(T) - K$ or zero." When the option payoff is positive (i.e, $P(T) > K$), the option is said to be "in the money." Similarly, when $P(T) = K$, the option is at the money and when $P(T) < K$, the option is "out of the money." Consequently, for a call option there are two critical states at expiration—the stock price is either greater than the exercise price or it is not—that are summarized in Equation 10A.1:

$$\begin{matrix} \text{Call Option} \\ \text{Payoff at} \\ \text{Expiration } (T) \end{matrix} = \text{Max}\,[P(T) - K, 0] = \begin{cases} P(T) - K \text{ if } P(T) > K \\ 0 \text{ if } P(T) \le K \end{cases} \quad (10A.1)$$

If $P(T) > K$, then the call option has value equal to $P(T) - K$. Otherwise, the call expires worthless.

Figure 10A-1 represents the expiration day payoff to *the owner of a call option* with an exercise price, K, of $30. What does the payoff look like for the *person who sold the call option*? The answer is straightforward. For every dollar the owner of the call option makes, the seller loses a dollar. For example, if the price of the stock is $50, the owner of the call owns a security that is worth $20. (She can purchase a share of stock worth $50 by exercising the call option for $30.) However, the issuer of the call option is obligated to deliver the share of stock worth $50 in the market for the exercise

Figure 10A-2 **Expiration Date Payoff to the Seller of a Call Option [Exercise Price (K) = $30]**

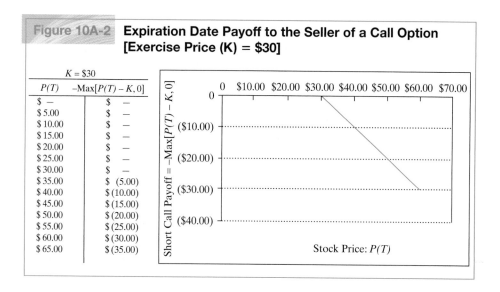

$K = \$30$	
$P(T)$	$-Max[P(T) - K, 0]$
$ —	$ —
$ 5.00	$ —
$ 10.00	$ —
$ 15.00	$ —
$ 20.00	$ —
$ 25.00	$ —
$ 30.00	$ —
$ 35.00	$ (5.00)
$ 40.00	$ (10.00)
$ 45.00	$ (15.00)
$ 50.00	$ (20.00)
$ 55.00	$ (25.00)
$ 60.00	$ (30.00)
$ 65.00	$ (35.00)

price of $30 (a loss of $20). Therefore, the payoff to selling (shorting which is referred to as writing) the call option, shown in Figure 10A-2, is the mirror, or inverse, image of Figure 10A-1. Analytically, the payoff to shorting a call is the negative of the payoff to owning (being long in) the call, that is, $-max[P(T) - K, 0]$.

Defining Put Option Payoffs

A put option gives its owner the right, but not the obligation, to sell an asset at a prescribed exercise price and within a specified time period. Thus, we want to own put options when we expect that prices of the underlying asset are going to fall. This is because the put option has value when the price of the underlying asset falls below the stated exercise price.

Consider the put option payouts in Figure 10A-3, where the put option has an exercise price of $30. If the price of the underlying asset on which the put is written has a price of $25, then the holder of the put can exercise the option to sell the stock for the $30 exercise price. However, if the price of the stock is $40, the put will expire worthless since the stock can be sold in the market for $40, while the put exercise price is only $30.

You can think of a put option contract like an insurance policy. That is, in the event that the value of the underlying asset drops below some threshold level, then we are protected since the payoff to the put increases dollar for dollar with any further decline in the value of the underlying asset. Similarly, in the event your home burns down, a homeowner's insurance policy provides you with the right to sell the home to the insurance company for the value of the insured damage.

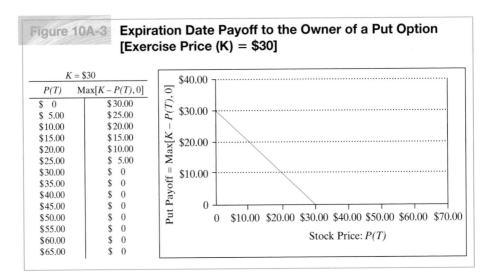

Figure 10A-3 **Expiration Date Payoff to the Owner of a Put Option [Exercise Price (K) = $30]**

$P(T)$	$Max[K - P(T), 0]$
$ 0	$30.00
$ 5.00	$25.00
$10.00	$20.00
$15.00	$15.00
$20.00	$10.00
$25.00	$ 5.00
$30.00	$ 0
$35.00	$ 0
$40.00	$ 0
$45.00	$ 0
$50.00	$ 0
$55.00	$ 0
$60.00	$ 0
$65.00	$ 0

Analytically, we can express the payoff to owning the put option (a long position) as $max[K - P(T), 0]$. That is, the put has positive value equal to $[K - P(T)]$ only when the price of the stock falls below the exercise price, K. Equation 10A.2 captures the payoff structure of the put option on date T:

$$\text{Put Option Payoff at Expiration } (T) = Max\,[K - P(T), 0] = \begin{cases} K - P(T) \text{ if } P(T) \le K \\ 0 \text{ if } P(T) > K \end{cases} \quad (10A.2)$$

Once again, the payoff to the seller of the put option is the mirror (or inverse) image of the payoff to the one who buys it (i.e., the owner), as Figure 10A-4 illustrates.

If the stock price is $25, the put option is worth $5 to the holder of the option. Correspondingly, the person who sold the put (commonly referred to as the *put writer*) is obligated to pay the exercise price of $30 for the share of stock that is worth only $25 in the market and consequently faces a loss of $5.

Risk and the Valuation of Options

An important feature of most option contracts is that their value is higher when the underlying asset becomes more volatile or risky. For example, stock options are more valuable when the volatility of the stock is higher. The intuition that supports this statement is straightforward. For most investments, volatility is viewed negatively because the increased probability of achieving very high returns is offset by a

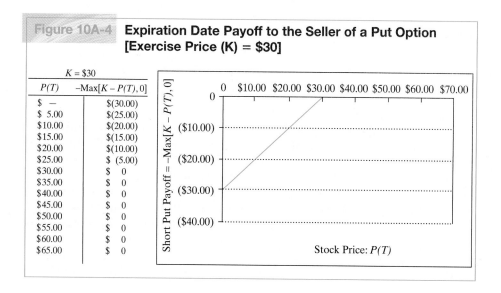

Figure 10A-4 **Expiration Date Payoff to the Seller of a Put Option [Exercise Price (K) = $30]**

P(T)	−Max[K − P(T), 0]
$ —	$(30.00)
$ 5.00	$(25.00)
$10.00	$(20.00)
$15.00	$(15.00)
$20.00	$(10.00)
$25.00	$ (5.00)
$30.00	$ 0
$35.00	$ 0
$40.00	$ 0
$45.00	$ 0
$50.00	$ 0
$55.00	$ 0
$60.00	$ 0
$65.00	$ 0

higher probability that very negative returns will be realized. However, the expected payoff of an option generally increases as the volatility of the underlying investment increases. This is because higher volatility increases the probability that the option payoff will be very high, but since the maximum loss on an option contract is fixed, the increase in the upside potential is not completely offset by increases in downside risk.

Valuing Call Options Using the Black-Scholes Model

To this point we have restricted our discussion to the expiration date payoff of the option or the value of the option on the day it expires. Valuing options prior to the expiration date provides a much more challenging problem and perhaps the best-known valuation model is the one developed by Fisher Black and Myron Scholes. Their model can be used to value options that can be exercised only at expiration (i.e., European options). Another significant difference between their model and the binomial option pricing model that we discuss in Appendix C of this chapter is that the distribution of stock prices in the Black-Scholes model is assumed to be continuous rather than binomial. However, the basic approach to the derivation of the pricing model is the same. By buying shares of stock and simultaneously selling options on the stock, the investor can create a risk-free payoff. The resulting option pricing equation for a call option on a stock whose current price is P_{Today} and which expires in period T can be written as follows:

$$\text{Call}(P, T, K) = P_{\text{Today}} N(d_1) - K e^{-r_f T} N(d_2) \qquad (10A.3)$$

where K = the option's strike price, r_f = the risk-free rate of interest,

$$d_1 = \frac{\ln\left(\dfrac{P_{\text{Today}}}{K}\right) + \left(r_f + \dfrac{\sigma^2}{2}\right)T}{\sigma\sqrt{T}}, \quad \text{and} \quad d_2 = d_1 - \sigma\sqrt{T}.$$

$N(d_i)$ is the probability that a value less than d could occur under the standard normal distribution (i.e., mean zero and standard deviation equal to 1); σ^2 is the annualized variance in the returns (continuously compounded) on the stock, i.e., $\ln[P(t+1)/P(t)]$; and all the remaining terms retain their previous definitions.

To illustrate the use of the Black-Scholes formula, let us consider the following example: The current price of the stock on which the call option is written is P_{Today} = $32.00; the exercise price of the call option K = $30.00; the maturity of the option is T = 90 days or .25 years; the (annualized) variance in the returns of the stock is σ^2 = .16; and the risk-free rate of interest is r_f = 12% per annum. To estimate the value of the call option using Equation 10A.3, we must first solve for d_1 and d_2 as follows:

$$d_1 = \frac{\ln\left(\dfrac{P_{\text{Today}}}{K}\right) + \left(r_f + \dfrac{\sigma^2}{2}\right)T}{\sigma\sqrt{T}} = .572693$$

and

$$d_2 = .1432 - .4\sqrt{.25} = .372693$$

Now, using Equation 10A.3 and the table of areas under the standard normal distribution (found in any standard statistics book), we calculate the value of the option by substituting the appropriate values into Equation 10A.3, i.e.,[16]

$$\text{Call}(P, T, K) = P_{\text{Today}}\, N(d_1) - K e^{-r_f T}\, N(d_2)$$

$$\text{Call}(P, K, T) = \$32\,(.716574) - \$30\, e^{-.12(.25)}(.645311) = \$4.1437.$$

Note that the option's value is $4.14 even though the current $32 price of the stock is only $2.00 greater than the exercise price of $30. This premium arises because there is the potential for the value of the call option to go up even higher if the stock price should rise over the next 90 days. In fact, if the term to maturity of the option was six months rather than three months, the value of the option would be to $5.58.

---

[16]We can use the Normsdist (d_1) function in Excel to calculate $N(d_1)$ directly.

Multiperiod Probability Trees and Lattices

In the chapter we introduced the binomial tree to characterize the outcomes of uncertain future oil prices. In this appendix we extend the single-period tree to multiple periods using forward prices. There are multiple ways to construct a binomial tree and the method we describe here develops a forward tree.[17]

Figure 10B-1 produces a three-year binomial lattice for the price of crude oil with a volatility (σ) estimate of .10 for the annual changes in oil prices. We calculate the high and low price for Year 1 based on today's forward price for oil to be delivered at the end of Year 1 ($F_{0,1}$) as follows:

$$\text{High Price (for Year 1)} = F_{0,1} \, u$$

where $u = e^{+\sigma}$ and σ is the volatility in oil price changes, and

$$\text{Low Price (for Year 1)} = F_{0,1} \, d$$

where $d = e^{-\sigma}$.

Given a \$52.04 per barrel forward price for crude oil at the end of Year 1 and an estimated volatility in annual price changes (σ) equal to .10 we calculate the high and low prices for Year 1 as follows:

$$\text{High Price (for Year 1)} = F_{0,1} \, u = \$52.04 \, e^{.10} = \$57.51$$

and

$$\text{Low Price (for Year 1)} = F_{0,1} \, d = \$52.04 \, e^{-.10} = \$47.09$$

The formulas used to calculate the possible prices in the binomial lattice for Years 2 and 3 are based on the forward prices for each year and are found just below the price in each node of the lattice.

The binomial tree found in Figure 10B-1 is a recombining binomial tree or lattice. The practical importance of this is that the resulting tree utilizes fewer price nodes.

---

[17]See Robert McDonald, *Derivative Prices*, 2nd edition, (Boston, MA: Addison Wesley, 2006).

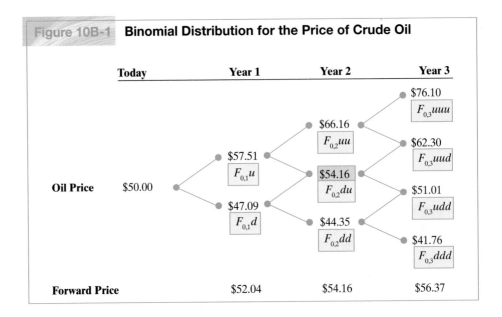

Figure 10B-1 **Binomial Distribution for the Price of Crude Oil**

For example, consider the middle node found in Year 2 of Figure 10B-1 equal to $54.16. This price can be achieved by a sequence of one high price in Year 1 followed by a low price in Year 2, or a low price in Year 1 followed by a high price in Year 2. This shared price node feature of the recombining binomial tree or lattice means that there are fewer price nodes to deal with in the tree.

Summing Up

We close our brief overview of the construction of the binomial lattice with a few key observations:

- First, we construct a special form of binomial tree, known as a recombining tree or lattice, in which up moves and down moves are restricted to be symmetrical. This restriction facilitates the computation of large multiperiod trees.
- Second, the source of uncertainty in future values contained in the lattice is determined by the underlying volatility in the annual price changes.
- Third, the technique we use to construct the binomial lattice is designed to be consistent with observed forward prices.
- Finally, although the examples we use in this chapter all use annual periods. However, the length of each time step is not restricted to one year. We simply adjust the risk-free rate and annualized volatility to correspond to the length of one *time step* in the lattice. Note that by using multiple time steps per year, we greatly expand the number of data points (value estimates) per year, thereby improving the precision with which we are able to replicate the distribution of end-of-year values.

Calibrating the Binomial Option Pricing Model

This chapter introduces a valuation approach that employs information from the financial derivatives markets to value real investment opportunities. This approach, like all valuation approaches, makes a number of simplifying assumptions. In some cases these assumptions are reasonable, but in other cases they are more troublesome.

This calibration and valuation process involves three steps:

Step 1: Select an option pricing model that provides a reasonable description of option prices. For our purposes, we will use the binomial model.

Step 2: Calibrate the option pricing model by determining which model parameters do the best job of describing observed option prices. Most of the model parameters, including contract terms and the risk-free interest rate, are observable. The key unobservable variable is the volatility of the future commodity prices. In the binomial model, this is the spread between the price in the high and low states. The volatility that best explains observed option prices is generally referred to as the volatility that is implied by observed option prices (i.e., the **implied volatility**).

Step 3: Finally, we substitute the contract terms for the option we are trying to value along with the implied volatility from the observable options into the binomial option pricing model and estimate the value of the option.

To illustrate how this calibration to observed market prices can be done, consider the problem we face if we need to know the value of a call option on a barrel of crude with one year to maturity and an exercise price of $52. If options with exercise prices of $50 and $54 were publicly traded, you might be tempted to simply interpolate these option values and use an average of the two observed values as our estimate of the value of the $52 option. However, as the Technical Insight box on page 448 illustrates, the relationship between exercise prices and option value is not linear, and such an interpolation could provide a very poor estimate of the value of the option with a $52 exercise price.

Figure 10C-1 contains the binomial distribution of prices used to derive this option value. What we want to do now is to use the information reflected in the valuation of the option with the $56 exercise price to value the new option.

TECHNICAL
INSIGHT

Option Values and
Exercise Prices

When trying to value a call option with an exercise price that is not observed in the option market, we may be tempted to try to simply interpolate a price using observed market prices and their exercise prices. Unfortunately, interpolation (which involves the use of a linear approximation) does not work well with option prices since, as the following graph indicates, the relationship between option values and exercise prices is not linear:

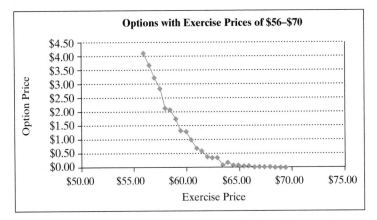

Options with Exercise Prices of $56–$70

The option prices represent call options on crude oil, with exercise prices ranging from $56.00 to $70.00 at a time when the price of crude was around $55.00 a barrel. The nonlinearity in option prices is very pronounced, suggesting that any use of linear interpolation will be fraught with estimation error.

Panels b and c of Figure 10C-1 describe the option valuation process for the single-period binomial option pricing model. In panel b we define the call option payoff for each of the two price states to be $8 [=Max($60 − 52, 0)] for the high-price state and $0 [=Max($48.90 − 52, 0)] for the low-price state. We would like to estimate the value of a call option with an exercise price of $52. However, what we can observe in the option market is a call option for crude oil with a one-year maturity and a $56 exercise price that sells for $1.75.

Solving for the implied volatility, we estimate that $\sigma = .10232$. We use the implied volatility to calculate the risk-neutral probability of the high price of oil as follows:

$$P = \frac{e^r - e^{r-\sigma}}{e^{r+\sigma} - e^{r-\sigma}} = 0.4744$$

| Figure 10C-1 | **Using the Binomial Option Pricing Model** |

Panel a. The Price Distribution for Crude Oil in One Year

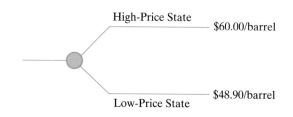

High-Price State — $60.00/barrel

Low-Price State — $48.90/barrel

Panel b. Option Valuation Using the Binomial Option Pricing Model

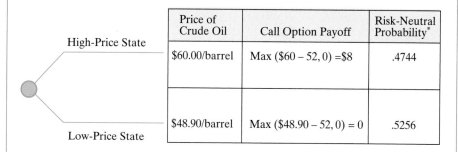

High-Price State

Low-Price State

	Price of Crude Oil	Call Option Payoff	Risk-Neutral Probability*
	$60.00/barrel	Max ($60 – 52, 0) =$8	.4744
	$48.90/barrel	Max ($48.90 – 52, 0) = 0	.5256

*The forward price of crude oil for the end of Year 1 is equal to the current price, $50.00, compounded one year at the risk-free rate of 8% or 50e^{.08}$ = $54.17. Risk-neutral probabilities are the probabilities that we apply to both the high- and low-price states for crude to obtain an average equal to the forward price of crude oil.

Panel c. Calculate the Value of the Call Option

Call Option (Exercise Price = $52.00, 1 Year to Maturity)
$$= (\$8.00 \times .4744 + \$0.00 \times .5256) \, e^{-.08}$$
$$= \$3.80 \times .9231 = \$3.51$$

We are now ready for Step 3 (see Panel c in Figure 10C-1) in the three-step calibration process. Using the $52 exercise price, and the risk-neutral probability of .4744, we get the option price estimate of $3.51.

In this brief appendix we have demonstrated how observed market price information can be incorporated into an option pricing model to calibrate a model that can be used to value options that are not publicly traded. The simple example we used involved the estimation of an option with an exercise price that is not observed in the market. However, we could also have estimated the value of an option with a maturity not represented in the market or even estimated the value of an option for a particular commodity for which options are not traded but which is closely related to another commodity, whose option prices are available.

CHAPTER 11

Managerial Flexibility and Project Valuation: Real Options

Chapter Overview

This chapter considers situations where management has flexibility in the implementation of investment projects. Specifically we consider cases where managers have flexibility regarding the timing of an investment's implementation as well as when it is shut down. In addition, we consider embedded real options that present themselves before an investment has been initiated. For example, an investment project can be designed to provide management with flexibility with respect to the products the firm produces or the inputs it uses. To value investments that benefit from managerial flexibility we utilize (1) decision trees in combination with binomial lattices, (2) a real option pricing formula, and (3) simulation analysis.

11.1 INTRODUCTION

In the last half of the previous chapter we evaluated an equity investment that could be characterized (and valued) as an option on a debt-financed investment. There we learned that the option to default on the debt and walk away from the investment added significant value to the equity investment. In this chapter we extend our analysis to consider optionality that is *embedded* within the very nature of investment opportunities. These embedded options, which are generally referred to as *real options*, exist for any investment in which managers have the ability to exercise discretion. This discretion may involve timing issues such as determining when to initiate a new project or shut down an old one. In addition, managerial discretion can be exercised over how an existing investment is operated. For example, managers can respond to changing product demand by altering the mix of products and can respond to changing input prices by changing the mix of inputs they use. They can also speed up or slow down production of existing products, decide to extend existing product lines to incorporate new products, and implement a myriad of other choices that enable the firm to adapt to changing circumstances. Consequently, when we value real options, we are in a sense determining the value that an *active management team* can add when it responds in a dynamic way to a changing environment.

Consider, for example, an investment in a copper-mining operation. An important feature of copper ore is that it does not spoil or otherwise lose value when it is left in the ground. Consequently, if the price of copper drops below the cost of extracting, processing, and shipping the ore, management may choose to slow down production or temporarily shut down operations until market conditions improve. Similarly, if a real estate developer purchases land that is well suited for developing office property, and the market for office space weakens due to a slowdown in the local economy, the developer may decide to delay the build-out of the property until the market begins to turn around or may consider other uses for the property. In both these examples, a key contributor to investment value is the embedded *flexibility* of the investment opportunities.

In the first half of this chapter we will continue to illustrate concepts relating to real options within the context of oil field examples, which build on the ideas developed in the last chapter. For example, we will consider an oil field example that provides its owner with the option to extract oil if oil prices are high and to keep the oil in the ground if oil prices are low. We will also continue to apply the binomial valuation model introduced in the last chapter.

In more realistic settings, the relevant options can be exercised at multiple dates, making their valuation quite complicated. In these cases, the valuation problem resembles the problem of valuing an American-style stock option, which is an option that can be exercised at any time prior to its expiration date. However, these real options are more difficult to value than stock options, because the underlying assets have uncertain payouts (analogous to dividends on a stock) and, in general, the exercise date is uncertain.

We demonstrate three approaches to solving the kinds of real option problems that are likely to arise in practice. The first is the binomial lattice, which is a multiperiod extension of the binomial option pricing model introduced in Chapter 10. We apply this approach to value an oil investment. The second approach applies an option pricing formula developed for use in valuing American call options that have infinite lives. We illustrate the use of this formula to value a real estate investment and a chemical plant. Finally, we use simulation to analyze operating options that arise when producers have the flexibility to choose between multiple modes of operation.

Since the analysis of real options is relatively new, we are aware of a number of different mistakes that are made in its application. To help our readers avoid these mistakes, we close our discussion of real options by identifying some common mistakes that analysts often make. Many of these errors arise out of the differences between options on financial assets (i.e., securities) and options on real investments.

11.2 TYPES OF REAL OPTIONS

Real options contribute to an investment's value whenever the following two conditions hold: (1) the environment is uncertain, and (2) managers can respond to changing circumstances by altering the way the investment is implemented and/or managed. It is useful to think about real options in terms of choices that are made *before* an investment has been launched, and choices that are available to the managers who oversee the operations of an *ongoing business venture*. In either case the availability of embedded optionality provides management with opportunities to exercise discretion that can have an important effect on the value of the project.

Real Options to Consider Before an Investment Launch

Before an investment is launched, the firm's focus is generally on timing issues and design-for-flexibility issues. The company grapples with questions such as the following:

Staged-investment options. In most cases, investments are made in stages. As we discussed in Chapter 8, venture capital investments are generally made in stages. For example, a pharmaceutical start-up may invest in research in the first stage, which provides the firm with *an option* to develop and market a new drug if the research turns out favorably and if market conditions are promising. Another example is the acquisition of undeveloped land, which gives the owner *the option* to construct an office building, condos, or whatever is appropriate, given future market conditions and zoning restrictions. Similarly, the acquisition of an undeveloped oil field gives the owner *the option* to develop the field and extract the oil. In each of these examples, we can think of the initial investment in the project as the *cost of a call option to invest in the next stage*.

Timing options. *Timing options* arise when it is possible to postpone the implementation date of an investment. The benefit of deferring an investment comes from the fact that the value of the investment is uncertain and some of this uncertainty will be resolved in the future.

Operating options. The fundamental problem here is how best to design or structure an investment so that it provides the firm with the operating flexibility necessary to respond to changes in the environment. The investment is more valuable if it is designed in a way that allows management to make choices that can capitalize on changing circumstances and the opportunities they bring.

Real Options to Consider after an Investment Launch

After an investment has been launched, the firm generally faces a different set of issues. In general we refer to these as *operational issues*, and they too give rise to optionality that can enhance the value of the investment. Some examples where real options contribute to value include the following:

Growth options. This type of option includes the opportunity to expand both the scale and the scope of an investment. Expanding the *scale* of the investment refers to growing the specific project output through increased volume of production. Growing the *scope* of an investment includes such things as follow-on projects. These options are sometimes called *strategic options.* They often are used to justify investing in what appear to be negative-NPV projects if the project opens the door for a sequence of future investments.

Shutdown options. Almost all businesses have both good and bad times. Clearly, the business will be more valuable if management has the flexibility to shut it down during bad times and to operate it when the business is profitable.

Abandonment options. If a business is currently unprofitable and is expected to remain unprofitable in the future, it may make sense to abandon or sell it. The decision to abandon is not only influenced by the current profitability of the investment but also by the amount the firm could get for the business if it were to be sold.

Switching options—outputs. The ability to vary the output mix to reflect the relative value from alternatives can be a very valuable source of managerial flexibility.

Switching options—inputs. The ability to switch between two or more inputs provides managers with the opportunity to minimize input costs.

Even a cursory examination of the list of real options enumerated above suggests that most real investments contain some degree of optionality or discretion for the managers who design, implement, and operate the investment. The simple truth is that most investment projects are not the static opportunities that are frequently characterized in traditional discounted cash flow analysis; it is therefore critical that when the investments are valued, consideration be given to the inherent flexibilities that each investment opportunity offers.

11.3 VALUING INVESTMENTS THAT CONTAIN EMBEDDED REAL OPTIONS

This section opens our discussion of real option analysis with some simple examples that provide a framework for analyzing the importance of real options to project valuation. We then move progressively toward more complex examples that better illustrate how these valuation problems are solved in practice. Where it is possible to do so, we utilize the valuation procedure outlined in Chapter 10; that is, we combine traded options into a tracking portfolio that mimics the payout of the real investment. In most cases, however, this is not possible and we will need to develop an approach to value the embedded options directly.

**Applications of Option Pricing
Methods to Energy Investments—
A Conversation with Vince Kaminski, PhD***

We used option pricing methods extensively in the energy industry to value physical assets and long-term contracts. In general, any source of flexibility in quality, time of delivery, and so forth can be modeled as an option. Moreover, every source of rigidity in a contract contains embedded option components that can be modeled as interactive, multi-layer options.

Traditional valuation methods for energy investments depend on estimates of future prices and these forecasts are subject to the inherent limitations and biases of the individuals making the projections. Consequently, one advantage of the option valuation approach is that it relies on market prices that reflect the consensus across a wide range of traders. A second advantage of the option approach is that it relies on mathematical algorithms that were developed for use in valuing financial derivatives.

A very common example of the application of option valuation methods to physical assets is the valuation of a natural gas power plant. This investment can be viewed as a portfolio of short-term spread options on the difference between electricity prices and natural gas prices (adjusted for thermal efficiency, referred to commonly as "the heat rate" of the plant). However, there are complications that have to be incorporated into the modeling of such a plant. The plant operator faces physical constraints in the form of start-up costs, ramp-up and ramp-down costs, and added maintenance resulting from the wear and tear associated with switching the plant on and off in response to the demand for electricity. If these costs are ignored, then the estimated value of the plant (i.e., the spread options) will be biased upwards.

Yet another example of the application of option valuation methods in the energy industry involves the valuation of natural gas storage facilities. Depleted oil fields are often used to store natural gas produced during the summer months so that it can be sold during the winter months when the price of gas is higher. In this instance the gas storage facility creates value as a calendar spread option. Salt domes can serve the same function. However, since the gas can be refilled and extracted from the salt dome much more quickly than from a depleted oil field, this type of storage facility provides the opportunity to respond much more frequently to short-term gas price spikes.[1] Consequently, this latter type of storage facility is often referred to as a "peaker storage facility."

*Vince Kaminski has had extensive industry experience related to the development of option valuation, price, and credit risk management models for energy trading. He has been a managing director of research groups at Citigroup Commodities (Houston, TX), Sempra Energy Trading (Stamford, CT), Citadel Investment Group (Chicago, IL), as well as director of research for Enron Corp (Houston, TX). He is currently a professor in the Jesse H. Jones Graduate School of Management, Rice University, Houston, TX.

---

[1]Although these salt dome facilities can be abandoned salt mines they often are not. After locating a salt deposit within a layer of relatively impervious rock a hole is drilled into the formation, water is used to dissolve the salt, and the solution is pumped out to form the storage facility.

The Option to Invest: Staged Investments

In this section we use an oil field investment example to illustrate the use of options for valuing a staged investment. In this particular case, the firm acquires an oil lease in the first stage that provides it with the opportunity to extract oil in later stages, depending on market conditions. To illustrate the value of this option to extract oil now or at a later date, we consider the investment opportunity faced by Master Drilling Company, which is considering the purchase of an oil lease costing $450,000. The lease provides Master Drilling Company with the opportunity to develop oil reserves on a specified piece of property during the next year (later we relax this assumption and use a two-year lease). Because this particular lease is on property adjacent to a producing oil field, the company geologists are very confident about the quantity of oil that will be produced. Consequently, the primary concern that Master Drilling's management has about the venture relates to the price at which the oil will be sold.

Did you know?

Texas Hold 'em is a game of options

There is a great analogy that can be drawn between the game of Texas Hold 'em and real options. To see the connection, let's review how the game is played. Initially players receive two down cards as their personal hand (hole cards), after which there is a round of betting. Each player must decide whether to match the highest bet, which buys her the option to continue to play or fold at the next round of betting. If a player decides not to bet, then she is choosing to abandon the hand. Next, three board cards are turned simultaneously (called the "flop") and another round of betting occurs, followed by two more board cards turned one at a time, with a round of betting after each card. Each round of betting provides the players with the opportunity to match or raise the highest bet or fold. The winner is the one who forms the highest-ranking five-card hand using the hole cards plus community cards. Clearly, Texas Hold 'em is a game of deciding when to acquire the option to stay in the game (betting) and when to exercise the abandonment option (folding).

Valuing an Oil Lease

To demonstrate the value of the option to delay the decision to develop the property, we will initially assume that by purchasing the lease, the company is committed to start developing immediately, and will extract the oil the following year. This requires an initial expenditure of $300,000 and an expenditure of $45 per barrel for each of the 100,000 barrels of oil extracted the following year. The following table summarizes the investment opportunity:

Today (Year 0)	Year 1
Master Drilling	Master Drilling
a. Purchases the lease for $450,000	**a.** Produces 100,000 barrels of oil at a cost of $45 per barrel
b. Spends $300,000 to develop the property in preparation to extract the oil in one year	**b.** Sells the oil at the prevailing market price in one year

In addition, we make the following assumptions concerning the Master Drilling Company lease:

- The current forward price for the delivery of oil in one year is $50/barrel.
- An option to deliver a barrel of oil in one year with an exercise price of $45 per barrel can be bought or sold today for $8.50 per barrel.
- The risk-free rate of interest is 5%.

Traditional (Static) DCF analysis of the lease To evaluate the decision to acquire the lease (assuming we begin development immediately and extract and sell the 100,000 barrels of oil in one year) using a traditional DCF analysis, we compute the NPV of the investment, as expressed in Equation 11.1 as follows:

$$
\text{NPV}_{\text{Oil Lease}} = \frac{\left(\begin{array}{c} \text{Expected Price} \\ \text{of Oil per Barrel}_{\text{Year 1}} \end{array} - \begin{array}{c} \text{Extraction Cost} \\ \text{per Barrel of Oil} \end{array} \right) \times \begin{array}{c} \text{Barrels of} \\ \text{Oil Produced}_{\text{Year 1}} \end{array}}{\left(1 + \begin{array}{c} \text{Risk-Adjusted} \\ \text{Discount Rate} \end{array} \right)}
$$
$$
- \left(\begin{array}{c} \text{Cost of Acquiring} \\ \text{and Developing the Oil Lease} \end{array} \right) \tag{11.1}
$$

Substituting for the values and estimates that we already know leaves the following:

$$
\text{NPV}_{\text{Oil Lease}} = \frac{\left(\begin{array}{c} \text{Expected Price of} \\ \text{Oil per Barrel}_{\text{Year 1}} \end{array} - \$45.00 \right) \times 100,000 \text{ barrels}}{\left(1 + \begin{array}{c} \text{Risk-Adjusted} \\ \text{Discount Rate} \end{array} \right)} - \$750,000
$$

Thus, to solve for the project's NPV, we need to estimate an expected price for crude oil one year hence and also a risk-adjusted discount rate that is appropriate to the risks of developing the oil lease.

Certainty-equivalent analysis—using the forward price to value the lease As we learned in Chapter 10, the lease can also be valued with the certainty-equivalent approach using the observed forward price of oil. Specifically, for the price of oil we substitute the forward price, which is also the certain equivalent price. Since the resulting cash flow is now the certain equivalent of the risky future cash flow, we can calculate its present value by discounting with the risk-free rate as shown in Equation 11.2, i.e.,

$$
\text{NPV}_{\text{Oil Lease}} = \frac{\left(\begin{array}{c} \text{Forward Price} \\ \text{of Oil per Barrel}_{\text{Year 1}} \end{array} - \begin{array}{c} \text{Extraction Cost} \\ \text{per Barrel of Oil} \end{array} \right) \times \begin{array}{c} \text{Barrels of} \\ \text{Oil Produced}_{\text{Year 1}} \end{array}}{\left(1 + \begin{array}{c} \text{Risk-Free} \\ \text{Rate} \end{array} \right)}
$$
$$
- \left(\begin{array}{c} \text{Cost of Acquiring} \\ \text{and Developing the Oil Lease} \end{array} \right) \tag{11.2}
$$

Substituting for the forward price of oil in one year and the risk-free rate of interest, we calculate the NPV of developing the oil lease using Equation 11.2 as follows:

$$NPV_{Oil\ Lease} = \frac{(\$50.00 - 45.00) \times 100,000}{(1 + .05)} - \$750,000$$

$$= \$476,191 - 750,000 = (\$273,810)$$

Clearly, under the assumption that Master Drilling must begin immediate development and commits to the production and sale of the oil reserves at the end of Year 1, the lease has a negative NPV! However, the typical, lease *does not* commit the acquirer of the lease to produce and sell the oil reserves, but gives the buyer the right, but not the obligation, to do so. In other words, the lease can be viewed as a call option on 100,000 barrels of crude oil that can be produced at a cost of $45 per barrel and sold one year hence.

Dynamic analysis—valuing the lease as an option to produce Oil Up to now, we have assumed that when Master Drilling Company makes the investment to acquire the lease it is obligated to develop and produce the reserves in the oil field. As the decision tree in Figure 11-1 illustrates, the firm has the option but not the obligation to produce the oil reserves and will extract the oil *only* if the revenue from selling the oil exceeds the $45 per barrel cost of extraction, and will let the lease expire otherwise.

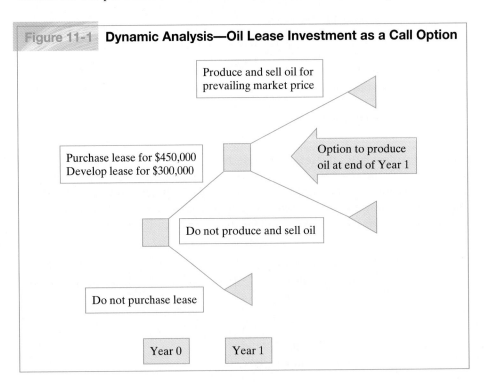

Figure 11-1   Dynamic Analysis—Oil Lease Investment as a Call Option

Produce and sell oil for prevailing market price

Purchase lease for $450,000
Develop lease for $300,000

Option to produce oil at end of Year 1

Do not produce and sell oil

Do not purchase lease

Year 0   Year 1

We assumed earlier that an oil option with a $45 per barrel exercise price currently has a price of $8.50 per barrel. Hence, the lease should have the same value as 100,000 of these call options, or $850,000. The relatively high price of the oil options in the derivatives market suggests that oil prices are relatively uncertain, and having the option to walk away from the lease without producing, or producing only when the price of oil exceeds extraction costs, is quite valuable.[2] This value exceeds the sum of the $450,000 acquisition price of the lease plus the initial $300,000 development costs, indicating that acquiring the lease and developing the oil field for possible production in one year (at a total cost of $750,000) is a positive-NPV investment (i.e., NPV = $850,000 − 750,000 = $100,000).

Valuing the option to delay or wait In our preceding example, we analyzed the value of the lease as an option to either extract oil in the following year or not at all. However, like many other investments, oil leases also contain timing options that allow the owner to choose *when* to extract the oil. To illustrate the timing option, we continue with the Master Drilling Company example, but with a minor twist. We now assume that the lease allows Master Drilling two years to develop and produce the oil and we are now sitting at the end of the first year after having purchased the lease and spent the $300,000 required to develop the property. In other words, the company is prepared to produce the oil at the end of Year 1 and must decide whether to do so now or to wait a year until the end of Year 2. The revised investment opportunity is illustrated in Figure 11-2, where we now have three decisions to make, as indicated by the decision nodes (squares) in the figure: (1) Should the company purchase the lease or not in Year 0? (2) If the answer to the first question is yes, then should the company produce and sell the oil reserves at the end of Year 1 or wait until the end of Year 2? (3) If the answer to the second question is to wait until Year 2 (i.e., do not produce in Year 1), then should the company produce and sell the oil at the end of Year 2 or abandon the lease?

Let's assume that the observed (spot) price of oil at the end of Year 1 is $50/barrel, which exceeds the $45 cost of extracting the oil. Consequently, the option to drill is *in the money*. However, Master Drilling's management now realizes they have an additional option. They can extract the oil today, or wait one more year and consider

---

[2]Using the binomial option pricing relation presented in Chapter 10, we can evaluate just how volatile the future price of oil must be to warrant an option price of $8.50 per barrel where the exercise price is $45 per barrel. For example, assume that the price of oil in one year can be one of two prices: a high price of $62.85 per barrel or a low price of $37.15 per barrel. Using the forward price of $50, we can calculate the implied risk-neutral probabilities of the two prices to both be 50% (i.e., $50 = $62.85 × Risk-Neutral Probability of the High Price + $37.15 × Risk-Neutral Probability of the Low Price). The payoff to an option for one barrel of oil with an exercise price of $45 then is either $62.85 − 45 = $17.85 for the high price or $0 if the low price occurs. We calculate the value of the option today as the risk-neutral probability weighted average payoff to the option (i.e., it's certain-equivalent payoff), discounted at the risk-free rate of interest, i.e.,

$$\frac{\text{Call Option}}{\text{Value}_{\text{Today}}} = \frac{\$17.85 \times .50 + \$0.00 \times (1 - .50)}{(1 + .05)} = \$8.50.$$

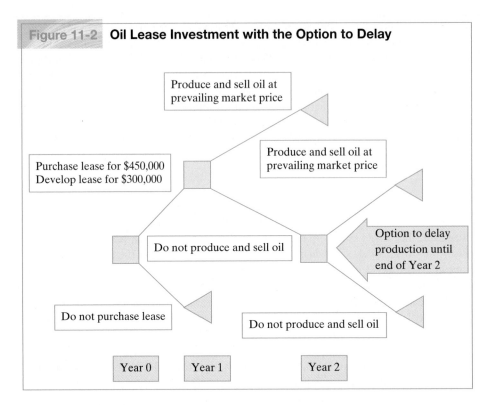

Figure 11-2   **Oil Lease Investment with the Option to Delay**

extracting the oil then. If they do not extract the oil at the end of this second year, the lease will expire worthless. In addition to assuming that the price of oil is now $50/barrel, we will assume that the one-year forward price (for Year 2) is also $50 and that the value of an option to acquire oil one year hence (in Year 2), with a $45 exercise price still sells for $8.50/barrel.

Since the price of oil at the end of Year 1 is $50/barrel, extracting the oil immediately generates $5 million in oil revenues. Subtracting the extraction costs of $4.5 million = $45/barrel × 100,000 barrels of oil, generates a net profit of $500,000. Note that this calculation did not consider the $450,000 cost of acquiring the lease or the $300,000 spent to develop the oil field and prepare it for production. These expenditures were made in Year 0 and as such represent sunk costs that do not influence the extraction decision. Consequently, the relevant comparison is between the $500,000 cash flow from extracting the oil today and the discounted value of the expected cash flow from waiting and having the option to extract the oil at the end of Year 2.

Let's first ignore the option associated with the Year 2 extraction choice and consider the certainty-equivalent profits if the owner extracts the oil at the end of Year 2 of the original lease contract. Since the forward price is $50/barrel for Year 2, the certainty-equivalent profit one year hence (at the end of Year 2) is the same as it was at the end of Year 1, or $500,000, which has a present value (discounted at the risk free rate) of $476,191 at the end of Year 1. In this particular case, since the spot price for Year 1 and the forward price for Year 2 are equal (both are $50 per barrel), the difference between the value of extracting now and extracting in the future arises solely because of the *time value of money*.[3]

Let's now consider how uncertainty and the flexibility to pass up the investment in the future affects the incentive to wait. As we have already shown, if an option to buy oil in the financial markets is valued at $8.50 per barrel, and if we extract the oil in one year *only when oil prices exceed extraction costs,* the oil lease is worth $850,000. This exceeds the $500,000 value realized from extracting the oil immediately. Hence, the gains from waiting to develop the field only when oil prices are high more than offsets the effect of the time value of money, which makes it optimal to wait before investing.

Hedging the Price Risk of Delaying the Decision to Invest

You may find it counterintuitive to wait to invest when the environment is very uncertain. After all, if you delay the decision to drill, you face the risk of a declining oil price that can potentially make your lease expire worthless. Would it, instead, make sense to take a sure positive-NPV investment today rather than wait and hope for a higher-NPV investment in the future?

This intuition may have merit when the project's risks cannot be hedged. When no hedge is available, the investor's risk aversion may be an important factor in the decision problem.[4] However, if the Master Drilling Company can sell call options on oil with a strike price of $45 per barrel, it can hedge these risks and lock in the gains associated with waiting to invest. Table 11-1 describes the payoffs per barrel of oil associated with maintaining the option to extract the oil in the following year, and hedging the uncertainty by selling call options on 100,000 barrels of oil with an exercise price of $45 per barrel at the current market price of $8.50 per barrel. As the numbers in the table indicate, the waiting-and-hedging strategy locks in a gain of $8.50 per barrel, which exceeds the gain from extracting the oil immediately.

If the price of oil drops below $45 per barrel, then both the project and the call options that the firm sold are worthless. Similarly, if the price of oil were to rise to $60 per barrel, then the project payoff is $60 per barrel − $45 per barrel = $15 per barrel, which again is exactly equal to the payout Master Drilling must pay to the holders of the call options it sold. In both cases, the payoff from the hedged position is simply the $8.50 per barrel proceeds from the sale of the options.

---

[3]It should also be noted that the slope of the forward curve also provides an incentive to either produce now or wait. If forward prices in the future are much higher than the current spot price, this offsets the effect of the time value of money and increases the incentive to delay production. For example, if the forward price of oil was $55/barrel rather than $50, it would clearly pay to wait.

[4]In theory, risk aversion should not enter the decision of a publicly traded firm. However, in reality risk-averse managers may not want to delay positive-NPV investments that may need to be abandoned in the future. Also, as we discussed in Chapter 9, accounting issues may influence the decision to delay an investment.

Table 11-1	Hedging the Option to Delay with Call Options		
		Price of Oil	
		$45.00 or below	$ 60.00
Project earnings per barrel (= Price/Barrel − Extraction Costs)		$ 0.00	$ 15.00
Minus Call Payoff per Barrel (= Max[Price/Barrel − $45, 0])		$ 0.00	$(15.00)
Call Price per Barrel		$ 8.50	$ 8.50
Total		$ 8.50	$ 8.50

More Complicated Options and the Incentive to Wait

The preceding example indicates that price uncertainty provides an incentive for firms to delay their investments. This example is easy to evaluate because the risks associated with oil price uncertainty can be hedged, providing the firm with the opportunity to lock in the gains associated with waiting. However, the option to delay should be viewed broadly, and one should not conclude that realizing the value to delay requires that the risks be hedged. The general principal, that the value of the option to delay comes from the opportunity to learn more about the investment's prospects, can be applied to almost any investment. By learning more, the firm may decide to configure the investment in a different way or to simply expand or contract the scale of the investment in light of what it learns during the delay.

One straightforward example arises in the context of undeveloped land, which can be viewed as an option to acquire a building at the cost of construction. When there is only one type of building that can be built, the option is a simple call option, just like the oil lease. However, the owner of the land may have the opportunity to build a number of different types of structures on the land, such as condos, a hotel, or an office building. When this is the case, the investor's options are somewhat more complicated, making them more difficult to value and hedge. However, the intuition is still the same: Greater uncertainty makes the options more valuable and increases the incentives to wait to invest. In general, *when the options provide more flexibility, they are more valuable, and the benefits from waiting are greater.* Intuitively, when you have more choices, it pays to wait to see how uncertainty unfolds to make sure that you are making the best choice.

Do Firms Delay Optimally?

For a variety of reasons, managers may not be as willing to delay the initiation of positive-NPV investments as the real options model suggests that they should. Our introductory finance classes may be partially to blame since they tend to place too much emphasis on the static NPV rule, which suggests that firms should undertake all projects with positive NPVs. However, these same textbooks also say that positive-NPV investments may be passed up when there exist other *mutually exclusive* investments with even higher NPVs.

In essence, whenever an investor has discretion as to the timing of an investment, this creates mutually exclusive alternatives. For example, Project 1 is taking the project immediately, and Project 2 is waiting and taking the same project at a future date. It may be the case that Project 1 has a positive NPV, but Project 2, which requires waiting (and of course cannot be implemented if Project 1 has already been implemented), may have a higher NPV and would therefore be preferred.

We should also stress that this tendency to initiate positive-NPV investments too early relative to the specification of the real options model may not simply be a mistake. Managers may be reluctant to wait on a positive-NPV investment for a number of good reasons:

1. *In reality, we cannot perfectly hedge the real option by selling financial options.* As a result, waiting is risky.
2. *The investor may be credit constrained or may face very high borrowing costs.* Credit constraints can have the effect of speeding up some investments and slowing down others. For example, an investor may extract oil more quickly than he otherwise would if doing so provides capital that can be invested in positive-NPV investments that could not be funded otherwise. However, if speeding up extraction requires new capital, then having limited access to financial markets to raise the capital can delay the investment.
3. *Initiating the project may generate information that would be useful to the firm's managers in evaluating future investments.* For example, the quantity of oil that is extracted may provide information about the potential amount of oil in similar regions. In this instance, the information gleaned from early exercise provides the firm with valuable information about future prospects. In essence, exercising one option may increase the value of a firm's other options.
4. *It may be important to signal to outside investors the fact that the firm does indeed have a positive-NPV investment.* If outside investors are not as well informed as the firm's management, it may be important that the firm periodically provide signals related to its ability to generate positive-NPV projects. For example, to show investors that they have the best geologists, an oil firm may need to develop some of its oil fields. Once again, early exercise may provide extra value and benefits to the firm and its future projects. If, for example, the firm is about to enter the capital markets to raise additional financing, revealing information about the prospects of new investments could lead to a higher stock price and a lower cost of capital. These benefits may overshadow the lost value from delayed exercise.
5. *Managers may undertake early initiation for personal reasons.* The compensation practices of firms that reward current-period performance (see the discussion in Chapter 9) can provide very strong incentives for managers to exercise their investment options too early. These practices tend to reward executives for

immediate performance; and penalize long-term investments that have too detrimental an impact on current-period performance.

Option to Abandon

Financial analysts have long recognized the value of the option to abandon an investment that is not performing as planned. For example, if you own a widget factory that is generating very low cash flows, you may be better off closing the factory and selling the property to a real estate developer who wants to convert the space for loft apartments. Moreover, if the cash flows are negative, you might want to abandon the factory even if the property has no alternative use.

The abandonment option has an important timing component that is very much in the same spirit as the "option to defer or delay" that we considered earlier. Just as option theory implies that there is an incentive to defer a positive-NPV investment, there may also be an incentive to continue operating a money-losing investment. Intuitively, the combination of uncertainty and flexibility should make decision makers more cautious about making irreversible decisions to either initiate a project or abandon a project. The key assumption that drives this conclusion is that the decision to permanently shut down or abandon an investment is irreversible.

Stripper-Well Example

To illustrate the shutdown or abandonment option, we analyze the decision to shut down a **stripper well,** which is an oil well that produces relatively low volumes of oil each year and frequently is just barely profitable. Prior to 1998, there were a number of stripper wells in Texas that had annual production volumes of 1,000 barrels of oil or less. Because these wells produced very little, their operating costs per barrel of oil were relatively high, which means that although they can be quite profitable when oil prices are high, many operate at a substantial loss when oil prices are low.

At the end of 1998 oil prices fell to close to $10 per barrel, making most of the Texas stripper wells unprofitable. Because of their operating losses, a number of the wells were closed in 1999, without the possibility of being reopened.[5] Oil prices subsequently increased substantially, making the stripper wells that had not been shut down quite profitable. With the benefit of hindsight, one can argue that the decision to shut down the wells at the end of 1998 was a mistake. What we need to understand here is whether shutting down the wells was a wise, or at least defensible, decision in 1999, given the information that was available at that time.

To illustrate how we might use real option analysis to evaluate the option to abandon these wells, we will consider a regional oil producer with 100 stripper wells that can produce 100,000 barrels both this year and next year before depleting their

---

[5]The problem encountered in shutting down production is that the formation may collapse or otherwise stop the flow of oil. This, in turn, means that for practical purposes the decision to shut down production is tantamount to abandoning the well.

reserves. The cost of operating the wells and transporting the oil is $14 per barrel, and the wells can be shut down either now or at the beginning of next year. The current price of oil is $10 per barrel, and the forward price for delivery in one year is also $10 per barrel. However, since oil prices are extremely volatile, an option to buy oil in one year for an exercise price of $14 a barrel sells for $4.50 today.

Given the current oil price and the forward price in one year, we can evaluate the current value of the 100 stripper wells, assuming that we will operate the wells this year and next year. We again assume a risk-free rate of 5%:

$$PV = 100{,}000 \text{ barrels}(\$10/\text{barrel} - 14/\text{barrel})$$

$$+\frac{100{,}000 \text{ barrels}(\$10/\text{barrel} - 14/\text{barrel})}{(1.05)} = (\$400{,}000) + (\$380{,}952) = (\$780{,}052)$$

This analysis indicates that if our *only* alternative is to operate the well for the next two years, it is best to shut the wells down, since the investment has a large negative NPV. However, if the owner of the wells has the *option* to shut down the wells next year *if* oil prices continue to be low (illustrated in Figure 11-3), it may, in fact, make sense to continue operating the wells this year at a loss of ($400,000), since shutting them down now eliminates the option to produce next year. If the loss from *producing now* is less than the *value of the option to produce next year*, it makes sense to continue to operate the wells.

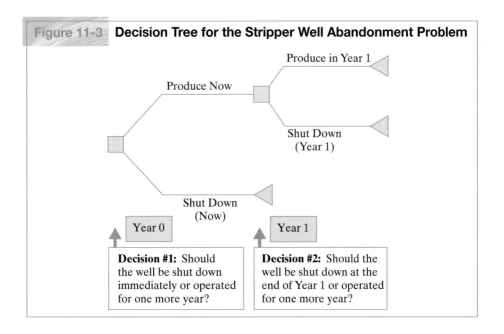

Figure 11-3 **Decision Tree for the Stripper Well Abandonment Problem**

Produce in Year 1

Produce Now

Shut Down
(Year 1)

Shut Down
(Now)

Year 0

Year 1

Decision #1: Should the well be shut down immediately or operated for one more year?

Decision #2: Should the well be shut down at the end of Year 1 or operated for one more year?

In this particular example, we see that an option to buy oil at $14 per barrel generates the same cash flow as the stripper wells in one year. If oil prices recover and rise above $14, the wells will produce per barrel profits equal to the oil price minus the $14 per barrel extraction costs. This net cash flow is exactly the same as the payoff on the option contract in this situation. If, however, oil prices stay below $14 per barrel, the options will expire worthless, and the oil wells will be shut down and will also generate no revenue. Hence, the *real* option to extract oil in the next year has the same value as the financial option to purchase oil for $14 per barrel, which we earlier assumed could be bought and sold for $4.50 per barrel.

In a sense, by continuing to produce this year, the investor acquires an option to produce next year. When prices are very volatile, having the right, but not the obligation, to produce in the following year can be very valuable, and this option may exceed the loss incurred by operating the wells in Year 1. So, what is the value of continuing to operate the stripper wells? The total value equals the sum of the profits from extracting the oil this year, which is a negative number, plus the value of the option to extract next year. Our analysis indicates that the stripper wells should not be shut down because the loss suffered from operating the wells in the current year is more than offset by the value of the option to extract 100,000 barrels next year. That is:

$$
\begin{pmatrix} \text{Value of the} \\ \text{Stripper} \\ \text{Well} \end{pmatrix} = \begin{pmatrix} \text{Value} \\ \text{of Operating} \\ \text{in Year 0} \end{pmatrix} + \begin{pmatrix} \text{Value of the} \\ \text{Option to Operate} \\ \text{in Year 1} \end{pmatrix}
$$

$$
= 100{,}000 \text{ barrels}(\$10/\text{barrel} - \$14/\text{barrel}) + \$4.50 \times 100{,}000 \text{ barrels}
$$
$$
= (\$400{,}000) + \$450{,}000 = \$50{,}000
$$

Hence, there is positive value from operating the stripper wells this year that is derived from the fact that by operating the wells the firm obtains the option to operate them next year. Consequently, it is best not to shut down the wells.

Note that in the preceding example we assumed that there was no cost of shutting down the stripper wells immediately beyond the loss of value derived from the option to produce in the second year. In many types of investments, however, there *are* costs incurred to shut down or decommission an investment, and these costs are sometimes so large that they dominate the decision. For example, refineries and chemical plants can face large cleanup costs when they are shut down. These cleanup costs may be so massive that the opportunity to delay incurring them may be a primary reason for keeping an old plant operating.

11.4 ANALYZING REAL OPTIONS AS AMERICAN-STYLE OPTIONS

The previous discussion presented very simple examples that included, at most, two possible drilling or abandonment dates. Our objective in these examples was to develop a framework that would help build intuition for how analysts and firms solve these problems in practice. Unfortunately, there are no simple formulas (nor even any complicated ones) that we can use for realistic valuation problems involving real options. In this section, to provide more insight about how these problems are solved in practice, we introduce a bit more complexity by means of another oil example that is more realistic than the examples discussed previously.

Evaluating National Petroleum's Option to Drill

National Petroleum, a small exploration and production (E&P) company, has a lease that provides the company with an option to drill on the property within a period of three years. If National drills and finds oil, it has the option to extract oil on the property until the reservoir is depleted, which is estimated to be 10 years after drilling is initiated. Specifically, the property is expected to produce oil at the rate described in Figure 11-4, where Year 0 is the drilling date. If, however, the company chooses not to drill within the allotted three-year period, the lease and the option to drill will expire.

Hedging Oil Price Risk

National Petroleum estimates the cost of drilling to be $38 million and the extraction and delivery costs to be $28 per barrel. Once again, our problem is to place a value on the lease. To establish a base value for the property, we assume that drilling begins immediately and that all of the production is sold forward at the forward prices found in Table 11-2. This strategy, as we learned in Chapter 10, effectively hedges the price risk of the project cash flows and locks in the profits based on these forward prices.[6] Since the resulting profits are now hedged (i.e., risk free) we can value the project by discounting the future cash flows using the risk-free rate of 6%.

Figure 11-4   Production Volume for the National Petroleum Lease

Year 0	0 barrels
Year 1	400,000 barrels
Year 2	300,000 barrels
Year 3	200,000 barrels
Years 4–10	100,000 barrels

---

[6]Again, recall that this assumes that we know the quantity that will be produced. This is an important caveat since profits depend upon both oil prices *and* the volume of oil produced. Thus, our ability to hedge the risk associated with our profits depends on both price and production volume.

Table 11-2 **Calculation of Project Revenues Using Forward Prices for Oil**

Year	Forward Price	Volume (barrels)	Revenue	Extraction Cost	Net Cash Flow
1	$59.00	400,000	$23,600,000	$(11,200,000)	$12,400,000
2	$60.00	300,000	18,000,000	(8,400,000)	9,600,000
3	$61.00	200,000	12,200,000	(5,600,000)	6,600,000
4	$62.00	100,000	6,200,000	(2,800,000)	3,400,000
5	$62.00	100,000	6,200,000	(2,800,000)	3,400,000
6	$63.00	100,000	6,300,000	(2,800,000)	3,500,000
7	$63.00	100,000	6,300,000	(2,800,000)	3,500,000
8	$63.00	100,000	6,300,000	(2,800,000)	3,500,000
9	$63.00	100,000	6,300,000	(2,800,000)	3,500,000
10	$63.00	100,000	6,300,000	(2,800,000)	3,500,000
PV (6%) =	$42,034,394				
Drilling cost =	(38,000,000)				
NPV =	$ 4,034,394				

Table 11-2 presents the hypothetical forward prices for the next 10 years, in addition to volumes, revenues, extraction costs, and the resulting free cash flows for the investment. We have evaluated the NPV of drilling today using the forward price curve to hedge oil price risk and found the NPV to be $4,034,394. However, National does not have to drill immediately according to the terms of the lease. In fact, the forward price curve may be such that drilling at the end of Year 1 and producing in Years 2 through 11 might be even more valuable. Similarly, National could initiate drilling at the end of Year 2 or even Year 3. If we know the forward prices for oil in Years 11 through 13, we can use the same hedging strategy to value the opportunity to drill in each of these three years and then select the best time to drill. If the forward price curve remains flat at $63 a barrel in Years 11 through 13, then the decision today to commence drilling in each of the next three years produces the following NPVs:

Commence Drilling in Year	NPV (Present values as of Year 0)
0	$4,034,394
1	$4,642,831
2	$5,024,001
3	**$5,197,453**

Clearly, given this forward price curve, National should *not* drill immediately, since the firm can lock in the highest value by committing to drill in three years and hedging the oil price risk. Note however, that the above analysis *presumes* that National commits *today* to a drilling program that does not begin until the end of Year 3. In reality, National has the option to drill at the end of Year 2 if it chooses not to drill in Year 1, so we should view the NPV calculated above as a very conservative estimate of the value of the oil field. If we consider the fact that National has the option to defer the decision to initiate the drilling operation for as long as three years, the lease becomes even more valuable.

Considering the Option to Delay

Figure 11-5 uses a decision tree to illustrate the options available to National during the three-year period of the oil lease. This decision tree has as its basis the binomial model that specifies oil prices, discussed in Chapter 10, along with an illustration of the decisions that can be made. Recall that the circles indicate a random event (in this case, whether the price of oil will be the high price or the low price) and squares indicate that a decision must be made. For example, assume that at the end of Year 1

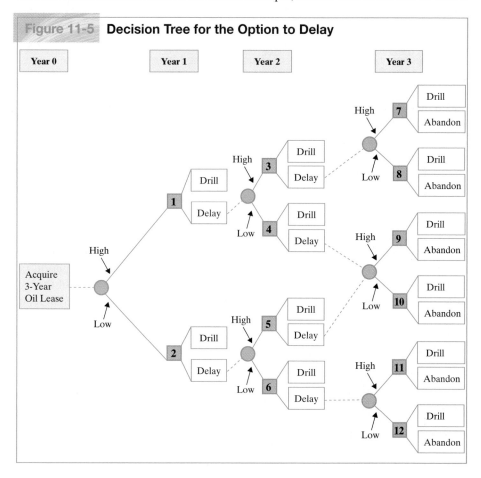

Figure 11-5   Decision Tree for the Option to Delay

the price of oil is equal to the high price.[7] National's management now faces decision node #1 and will have to decide whether it is best to drill now or delay until Year 2. If the decision is made to drill (i.e., exercise the option to drill), then that is the end of that branch of the decision tree. However, if the decision is made to delay until Year 2, then we follow the dotted line to the appropriate probability node for Year 2, where we learn whether the price of oil will be high or low, leading to decision nodes #3 and #4, respectively. Note that if National has not exercised its option to develop the property by the end of the three-year lease term, it effectively abandons the investment opportunity.

To this point, we have not described how the decision should be made with regard to drilling now versus delaying the decision to drill. Incorporating the option to defer drilling for up to three years into our analysis requires that we evaluate the investment opportunity as follows: To determine whether the option to drill should be exercised, we compare the value of the oil field today minus drilling and development costs, with the value of the option to drill and develop the well in the future. When the value of the option to drill in the future exceeds the value of drilling immediately, it is better to wait, and vice versa.

In this particular case, National Petroleum has the option to drill at any time up to the expiration of the three-year lease, which provides the firm with what is analogous to an American call option on a stock. That is, National Petroleum with what is equivalent to an option to acquire a producing oil well at an exercise price that equals the cost of drilling. To value the lease, we would like to find the market price of a traded option that exactly matches the option that we are trying to value. However, since, it is unlikely that there exists a publicly traded option on a producing oil well that exactly matches the option associated with this particular oil field, we will need a model to value the option. Such a model requires estimates of several key inputs, which are analogous to the inputs needed to value an American stock option on a share of stock. Table 11-3 summarizes the analogy between the American call option problem and the option to extract oil problem.

Valuing the option to drill is substantially more difficult than solving a typical American stock option valuation problem, though. This is true primarily because the input that determines the expected change in the value of the developed well—the *convenience yield* (the counterpart to the dividend yield)—changes from period to period as the prices in the forward curve change. In addition, the *volatility* of the returns to investing in the producing well is likely to change over time and is difficult to estimate.

Valuing American Options Using a Binomial Lattice

In practice, analysts frequently use a multiperiod version of the binomial option pricing model discussed in Chapter 10 to evaluate American-style real options. To show

---

[7]To simplify our exposition, we assume that decisions are made annually and that the time step used to define the binomial lattice is also one year.

Table 11-3	**Comparing Real Options with American Stock Options**

Inputs for Valuing American Stock Options	**Oil and Gas Field Counterparts**
1. Stock Return volatilities	*Volatility* of the value of the producing field
2. Value of underlying stock	The present value of the cash flows from the producing wells
3. Dividend yield	The *convenience yield* is the benefit associated with the physical ownership of the commodity*
4. Expiration date	The *expiration date* on the lease
5. Exercise price	The *cost of drilling*

*When the convenience yield is high, the benefit from having the commodity today is higher, which means that the price today is high relative to the expected price in the future. The convenience yield is important because it determines the expected rate at which the commodity will appreciate, and is related to the slope of the forward curve minus the risk-free rate.

how this works, we will apply such a model to the valuation of the drilling investment opportunity faced by the National Petroleum Company. Since National has the option to initiate drilling at any time until the end of a three-year period, the problem National faces is to value a three-year American call option.

Earlier we estimated the value of the drilling opportunity to be $42,034,394 if drilling begins immediately. However, this value does not reflect the added value that might be captured if the firm exercises its option to delay drilling until a later period when oil prices might be more favorable. To value this option, we start by constructing the multiperiod binomial lattice found in Figure 11-6. This lattice, which is based on the oil prices described in the decision tree in Figure 11-5, describes the possible values that the drilling opportunity might have in each of the next three years (the life of the American call option we wish to value.)

We can think of the values at each node of the binomial lattice as the discounted values of future project cash flows based on the forward curve of oil prices as they evolve through time. The actual future values of the developed oil field that are specified in the binomial lattice can be somewhat arbitrary, and may depend on the judgment of the decision marker. (We address this issue in more detail in the Appendix). But first, let's walk through the valuation process *assuming* that we know the value of developing the oil field at each node of the binomial lattice.

Four values are listed at each node of the binomial lattice in Figure 11-6. We will refer to them as valuations #1 through #4 and they represent (from top to bottom):

1. *Valuation #1: The value of the developed field*—the estimated value of initiating the development of the undeveloped oil field on this date, which is equal to the DCF

Figure 11-6   Binomial Tree Describing the Possible Values of the Drilling Opportunity (in millions)

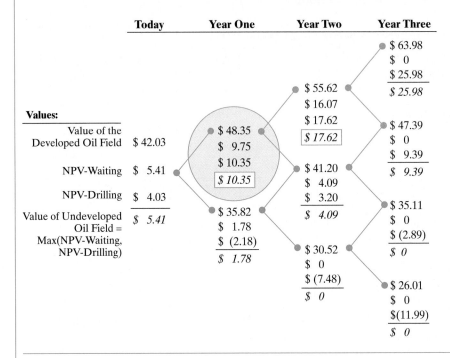

Definitions

a. *Value of the developed field* = present value of future cash flows from the oil field spanning a period of 10 years from the date of the valuation—for example, in the circled node at the end of Year 1 this value is equal to $48.35 million = The present value of the oil field if developed at the end of Year 1 and if evaluated using the forward price curve for oil produced in Years 2 through 11. Technically, this is the way to think about the value of the oil field if drilling and development commences during Year 1. However, the forward curve that will exist at the end of Year 1, where the high-price state occurs, is not observable today when we are performing our analysis. Consequently, we model the price distribution for the value of the oil field using the binomial process described in the Appendix to this chapter.

valuation based on the forward price curve for this period and the assumption that drilling begins in this year and production follows in the subsequent 10-year period.

2. *Valuation #2: The NPV of waiting to drill*—the expected value of the undeveloped field if the option to drill is not exercised this period.[8]

[8]For example, the NPV of waiting until the end of Year 1 is equal to the present value of the undeveloped oil field at the end of Year 1. That is, it is the present value of the probability-weighted values of the undeveloped oil field at the end of Year 1, which are equal to $10.35 million or $1.7822 million.

b. *Risk-neutral probabilities.* In Chapter 10 we calculated the risk-neutral probability using the forward price of oil. This method can be translated into the following calculation to get the risk-neutral probability of the high-price state (P) using the following relationship:

$$P = \frac{e^{(r-\delta)} - e^{(r-\delta)-\sigma}}{e^{(r-\delta)+\sigma} - e^{(r-\delta)-\sigma}}$$

where r is the risk-free rate of interest, δ is the convenience yield, and σ is the volatility of the returns to the oil field investment. As discussed in the Appendix, we assume $r = 6\%$, $\delta = 7\%$, and $\sigma = 15\%$. These values imply that $P=0.4626$.

c. *NPV of waiting*= present value of exercising the option to drill at a later date—for the circled node at the end of Year 1 this is equal to $9.75 million = the present value of the risk-neutral probability-weighted expected value of the call option in Year 2, i.e.,:

$$\begin{aligned}\text{NPV of Waiting to Drill} &= e^{-.06}[\$17.62 \text{ million} \times .4626 + \$4.09 \text{ million} \times (1 - .4626)] \\ &= \$9.75 \text{ million}\end{aligned}$$

Note that the payoff to the option to wait to drill (evaluated at circled node at the end of Year 1) is based on the maximum of the NPV of waiting until Year 2 to decide whether to drill or not for each potential node (i.e., for the high-price node the payoff to waiting until Year 2 is max($16.71 million, $17.62 million). For the low-price node the payout to waiting is equal to max($4.09 million, $3.2 million). The risk neutral probability of the high-value state was defined in (b) above.

d. *NPV of drilling now*= Value of developed oil field cash flows if drilling takes place in the current period [item (a) above] minus the cost of drilling = $10.35 million for the circled node in Year 1—is calculated as follows: NPV of drilling now (circled node) = Value of the developed field (circled node)—Cost of developing the field, i.e.,

$$\$10.35 \text{ million} = \$48.35 \text{ million} - \$38 \text{ million}$$

e. *Value of the undeveloped oil field* = The maximum of the NPV associated with waiting to exercise the option to drill [(c) above] and the NPV of exercising the option in the current period [(d) above]. This is analogous to the value of an American call option on the value of developing the oil field—$10.35 million=maximum of the NPV of waiting and the NPV of drilling now:

$$\begin{aligned}\text{Value of the Undeveloped Oil Field} &= \text{Max}(\{e^{-.06}[\$17.62 \text{ million} \times .4626 + \$4.09 \text{ million} \times (1 - .4626)]\}, \\ &\quad \{\$48.35 \text{ million} - \$38 \text{ million}\}) \\ &= \text{Max}(\$9.75 \text{ million}, \$10.35 \text{ million}) = \$10.35 \text{ million}\end{aligned}$$

3. *Valuation #3: The NPV of drilling now*—that is, the value of the oil field if developed this period (valuation #1 above) less the $38 million cost of drilling and developing the field.

4. *Valuation #4: The value of the undeveloped oil field*—this valuation is analogous to that of an American call option, which is equal to the maximum of either the

NPV of waiting until the next period to drill (valuation #2 above) or the NPV of drilling in the current period (valuation #3 above).

Solving for the value of the undeveloped oil field   To value the option associated with owning the undeveloped field, we must work backwards in the binomial lattice, beginning in Year 3 (the year in which the option expires). This procedure is commonly referred to as *rolling back the branches of the decision tree*. The analysis for Year 3 proceeds as follows: The value of the option to drill in Year 3 is the maximum of the NPV of drilling in Year 3 (i.e., the value of the developed oil field minus the $38 million development cost) or zero. For example, if the value of the developed field is $63.98 million in Year 3 (the highest value node), then the value of the undeveloped oil field equals

$$\text{Max(\$63.98 million} - \$38 \text{ million}, 0) = \$25.98 \text{ million}$$

In this particular node, it is optimal to develop the field; however, this is not always the case. For example, if the value of the developed oil field in Year 3 were equal to the lowest node in the lattice, which is $26.01 million, the value of the undeveloped field is zero, since the NPV of drilling at this node is negative (i.e., $26.01 million − $38 million = −$11.99 million).

After evaluating all the Year 3 nodes of the lattice, we now consider the nodes for the end of Year 2. In the highest-value node for Year 2, where the value of the developed oil field is equal to $55.62 million. The NPV of waiting is equal to the present value of the certainty-equivalent payoff[9] from the option to begin drilling in Year 3, i.e.,:

$$\begin{array}{l} \text{NPV of Waiting} \\ \text{to Drill} \end{array} = e^{-.06}[\$25.98 \text{ million} \times .4626 + \$9.39 \text{ million} \times (1 - .4626)]$$

$$= \$16.07 \text{ million}$$

The NPV of drilling at the end of Year 2 is $17.62 million, calculated as the value of the developed property minus the $38 million drilling cost. Since the NPV of drilling exceeds the NPV of waiting to drill, the optimal decision is to drill if this node in the lattice occurs. Hence, the value of the undeveloped oil field is defined as follows:

$$\begin{array}{l} \text{Value of the} \\ \text{Undeveloped} \\ \text{Oil Field} \end{array} = \text{Max(NPV of Exercising Now, NPV of Waiting to Exercise)}$$

---

[9]Recall from Chapter 10 that the certainty-equivalent payoff from the option is equal to the weighted-average payoff where the weights are the risk-neutral probabilities. In the binomial lattice found in Figure 11-6 the risk-neutral probabilities of up and down prices are equal to .4626 and (1 − .4626), respectively.

where "exercising" refers to the initiation of drilling and production of the field. Substituting for the appropriate values needed to evaluate the option in the highest-value node for Year 2,

Value of the
Undeveloped = Max{\$55.62 million − \$38 million,
Oil Field $\quad e^{-.06}$[\$25.98 million × .4626 + \$9.39 million × (1 − .4626)]}

= Max(\$17.62 million, \$16.07 million) = \$17.62 million

Note that when we evaluate the option to wait at the end of Year 1, the value that we use for Year 2 to calculate the certainty-equivalent value is the maximum of the NPV of the field if it is developed in Year 2 (i.e., \$17.62 million in the example calculation above) and the value of waiting until Year 3. The latter is the present value of the expected NPV of drilling or waiting for each of the two value nodes connected to the top node in Year 2. That is, for the high-value node in Year 3 we already determined that the maximum of the NPVs of drilling and waiting (abandoning the opportunity since the lease expires) is to drill for a NPV of \$25.98 million. Similarly, if the next lower node (the low-value state compared to the high-value node in Year 2 that we are analyzing) occurs then the maximum NPV for the investment entails drilling and this opportunity has a NPV of \$9.39 million.

We now have all the information we need to determine the optimal exercise strategy for developing the three-year lease of the oil field. Specifically, reviewing the completed binomial lattice found in Figure 11-6, we see that exercising the option immediately in Year 0 has a positive NPV of \$4.03 million = \$42.03 million − \$38 million. The value of waiting to implement the investment at a later date is \$5.41 million. Therefore, National should not begin drilling immediately but should wait until the end of Year 1 and reevaluate. If at the end of Year 1 the undeveloped oil field is worth \$48.35 million, it will be better to exercise the option to drill and develop the property. Put another way, the value of waiting until the end of Year 2 is worth only \$9.75 million, while the NPV of developing the oil and gas reserves at the end of Year 1 is \$10.35 million. If, however, at the end of Year 1 the value of the undeveloped oil field is equal to \$35.82 million (the lower node in Year 1), then the field should not be developed since the NPV of waiting is worth \$1.78 million, while the NPV realized by implementing the development process at the end of year 1 is negative (i.e., −\$2.18 million).

Constructing the binomial lattice for the developed oil field In Figure 11-6 in the preceding example we provided the valuations of the oil field investment in each node at the end of Years 1, 2, and 3. In practice, the analyst would not be given these values but would have to estimate them. Since this estimation process, which is referred to as "calibrating the model," is quite complex, we will briefly summarize how it is done in practice. (Calibration was introduced in Appendix C in Chapter 10, and is discussed in more detail in the Appendix at the end of this chapter.) We will not delve into the specifics of the calibration process here for that is where much of the "heavy lifting" occurs in modeling commodity prices, and it can be quite technical.

The first step in the estimation process is to specify a binomial tree that illustrates the distribution of future oil prices. Since it takes 10 years to produce the oil field's reserves and production may not commence for three years we need to specify the distribution of crude oil prices for the next 13 years. The price distribution should be chosen so that the expected future prices at each date are equal to forward prices for crude oil that we observe in the financial markets. In addition, the discounted values of option payoffs calculated from the binomial lattice should equal the option prices that are observed in the financial markets. In the next step, one can calculate the value of the producing oil field at each node of the binomial tree by discounting the value of the cash flows that will be generated, given the oil prices that are realized in successive branches of the tree.

While this is somewhat more complicated than simply plugging in observed option prices from the financial derivatives markets for their real counterparts, it accomplishes the same thing. By calibrating the model we are effectively using prices in the financial markets to determine real option values.

Real Option Valuation Formula

Since the Black-Scholes option pricing formula is so well known and can be programmed into handheld calculators, there is a temptation to apply the formula to real option problems. In most cases, the Black-Scholes formula is completely inappropriate for real option problems because it assumes that the options have a fixed maturity date, that they can only be exercised at the maturity date, and that the underlying investment has no cash payouts.

In this section we provide an option pricing formula that we think is much more appropriate for valuing real options. This formula, which was developed by McDonald and Siegel (1986) based on earlier work by Samuelson and McKean (1965),[10] is based on similar assumptions as the Black-Scholes formula, except for the fact that it assumes that the underlying investment does have cash payouts and that the option can be exercised at any time and never matures. In other words, this is a formula for pricing an infinite life American option. The derivation of the option pricing formula requires an understanding of stochastic calculus, so we present it here without further discussion.

The infinite life option pricing model can be used to value real options in much the same way that the Black-Scholes formula (see Appendix A in Chapter 10) is used to value European options. Although the formula looks complicated, it is simple to

---

[10]Robert L. McDonald and D. Siegel, 1986, "The Value of Waiting to Invest," *Quarterly Journal of Economics* 101 (4), 707–727, and Paul A. Samuelson and H. P. McKean, Jr., 1965, "Rational Theory of Warrant Pricing," *Industrial Management Review*.

put into a spreadsheet and requires relatively few inputs. You can use it to calculate an initial value of a real option, and perform sensitivity analysis to develop your intuition about what determines real option values.

Under these assumptions, the following equation describes the value of an American-style call option:

$$\text{Real Option Value} = (V^* - I)\left(\frac{V}{V^*}\right)^{\beta} \tag{11.3}$$

where each of the terms is defined as follows:

- V^* is the value of the underlying investment that "triggers" exercise of the real option. Note that this variable is an *output* of the model, rather than an input. The threshold value (V^*) is defined by

$$V^* = \frac{\beta}{(\beta - 1)}I \tag{11.4}$$

TECHNICAL
INSIGHT

Comparing the Black-Scholes and Infinite Life Option Pricing Models

Like the Black-Scholes formula, the infinite life option pricing model formula assumes that the value of the underlying asset is unpredictable and that the volatility of the returns earned by the underlying investment and the interest rate are fixed. However, there are three important differences between the assumptions underlying this formula and the assumptions that are the basis of the Black-Scholes model:

- The first is that this model assumes that the option never expires, which should be contrasted to the Black-Scholes assumption that the option has a predetermined expiration date.
- The second difference is that the Black-Scholes formula assumes that the underlying investment pays no dividends. In contrast, the real option valuation formula takes into account the fact that real investments generally generate cash flows that reduce the value of call options written on the investment. However, the model requires that cash flows from the investment are always proportional to the value of the investment and that this proportion does not change over time.
- The final difference is that the Black-Scholes formula assumes that the option is a European-style option that can be exercised only on the option's maturity date. In contrast, the real option valuation formula found in Equation 11.3 assumes that the option can be exercised at any time (is an American-style option), and that the option never expires.

where

$$\beta = \frac{1}{2} - \frac{r_f - \delta}{\sigma^2} + \sqrt{\left(\frac{r_f - \delta}{\sigma^2} - \frac{1}{2}\right)^2 + \frac{2r_f}{\sigma^2}} \tag{11.5}$$

- I is the initial cost of making the investment. Hence, $V^* - I$ is the net present value that triggers the exercise of the real option. This difference is also sometimes referred to as the NPV hurdle, since it measures how high the NPV must be before the investment is initiated.
- V is the current value of the underlying investment.
- The risk-free rate of interest is r_f.
- The cash flow yield or cash distribution as a fraction of the value of the investment is represented by δ, which is assumed to remain constant over the life of the investment.
- σ is the standard deviation, or the *volatility* of the rate of return of the underlying investment.

We warned you that this formula looks complicated. However, as with the Black-Scholes model, we can learn from using this formula without understanding all its mathematical intricacies. For example, from this formula, we can show that increased volatility increases real option values and, in addition, increases the NPV hurdle; that is, the minimum NPV required before the investment is triggered. Similarly, an increase in an investment's cash flow yield will decrease the option's value, since it implies that the investment's value appreciates at a slower rate.

Real Estate Development Option

To illustrate the use of this real option valuation model, we start with a simple example involving the purchase of 50,000 square feet of land that can be used to develop a 60,000-square-foot office building at a cost of $10 million ($I$ in Equation 11.3). It is currently not economical to initiate development since the current value of such a building is only $9 million ($V$ in Equation 11.3). However, existing buildings in the area can be leased to yield (after taxes and all expenses) an 8% rate of return to the owner (δ in Equation 11.5). These buildings have volatilities (i.e., standard deviations $-\sigma$) in their annual rates of return of 10%. The risk-free rate, r_f, is assumed to equal 6%.

Note that if the property were developed today, it would have a value of only $9 million but would cost $10 million to develop, so we would lose money developing this property at the current time. However, the land has substantial value since it provides the owner with the *option to build* in the future. Substituting into Equation 11.3, we estimate that this property, which provides the owner with the option to build the above-described building, has a value of about $287,667, i.e.,

$$\text{Real Option Value} = (V^* - I)\left(\frac{V}{V^*}\right)^\beta$$

$$= (\$11{,}732{,}501 - \$10{,}000{,}000)\left(\frac{\$9{,}000{,}000}{\$11{,}732{,}501}\right)^{6.772} = \$287{,}667$$

where β is calculated using Equation 11.5 as follows:

$$\beta = \frac{1}{2} - \frac{r_f - \delta}{\sigma^2} + \sqrt{\left(\frac{r_f - \delta}{\sigma^2} - \frac{1}{2}\right)^2 + \frac{2r_f}{\sigma^2}}$$

$$= \frac{1}{2} - \frac{.06 - .08}{.01} + \sqrt{\left(\frac{.06 - .08}{.01} - \frac{1}{2}\right)^2 + \frac{2 \times .06}{.01}} = 6.772$$

Consequently, as a speculator, you would be willing to pay up to \$287,667 for the right to develop this property.

The model also provides information about what we call the *trigger point*—in other words, how high the value must be before it makes sense to commence construction. Using Equation 11.4,

$$V^* = \left(\frac{\beta}{\beta - 1}\right)I = \left(\frac{6.772}{6.772 - 1}\right)\$10{,}000{,}000 = \$11{,}732{,}501$$

This calculation indicates that we should not begin construction until the value of the developed property exceeds \$11,732,501. Once the property value reaches this *trigger point,* the option to develop should be exercised.

How Do Changes in Model Parameters Affect Real Option Values?

It is useful to examine how the value of the option to develop the vacant land is affected by changes in the parameter estimates. For example, if the volatility parameter is increased to 15%, the option to develop the land calculated using Equation 11.3 increases to \$669,762. If we reset the volatility to 10% but increase the dividend yield to 9%, the value of the option to develop the vacant land is reduced to \$191,225. Higher payouts make options less attractive relative to the underlying investments, since the owner of the building receives a payout on his or her investment, while the owner of vacant land (i.e., the option holder) receives nothing.

Extensions of the Model

The real option valuation model in Equation 11.3 can be extended in a number of ways without too much difficulty. For example, suppose that the land is not completely vacant and is currently being used as a parking lot that generates income of \$100,000 per year. We can account for this complication by simply determining the value of the parking lot and adding this to the construction costs. For example, in the earlier example we assumed that the cost of constructing the building was \$10 million. To account for the loss of parking lot revenues valued at, say, \$1.8 million, we simply increase the development costs to $11.8 million. In the same way, one can account for taxes on the land, which would generate a positive cost associated with holding the land.

Applying the Model to a Chemical Plant

We now apply the model to the valuation of the real options associated with building a manufacturing plant. Suppose that DuPont has an ethylene plant that currently produces 10,000 tons of ethylene per year. The plant is old and inefficient, but it still shows a fairly stable profit of $1 million per year. DuPont is considering an opportunity to convert this facility to make dyethelyne, which is a specialty chemical that will be substantially more profitable. DuPont's analysts estimate that the conversion will cost $90 million and will generate an initial cash flow next year of $10 million. The analysts expect these profits to increase 2% per year for the foreseeable future, and the standard deviation of the returns to the investment is estimated to be 15% per year. Under the assumption that these profit changes are random and that the discount rate is constant at 12% per year, we can estimate the value of the plant with a simple growth model, i.e.:

$$\text{Value of the Plant} = \frac{\text{Cash Flow(Year 1)}}{(\text{Discount Rate} - \text{Growth Rate})} = \frac{\$10 \text{ million}}{.12 - .02} = \$100 \text{ million}$$

Under these assumptions, the investment has a value of $100 million, and a corresponding payout rate of 10%.

In order to evaluate this opportunity, one must also value the ethylene plant, since part of the cost of building the new plant is the opportunity cost associated with liquidating the old plant. We will assume that the old plant has a value of $8.5 million, which is the capitalized value of the plant's cash flow at a 12% discount rate, i.e., $1 million ÷ .12 = $8.5 million. The total opportunity cost of building the new plant is equal to the $90 million direct cost of converting the old plant to produce the new product plus the $8.5 million opportunity cost associated with closing the old plant, for a total of $98.5 million. Consequently, the new plant has a net present value of $1.5 million, which equals the estimated value of the new plant ($100 million) less the opportunity loss associated with closing the old plant and the cost of building the new plant ($98.5 million), or NPV = $100 million – $98.5 million = $1.5 million.

Although the investment has a positive NPV, the NPV is quite small compared to the value of the investment (i.e., 1.5%). Hence it might be the case that the project would be worth more if we delay the investment. To analyze this possibility, we value the project using the real option valuation formula found in Equation 11.3, with inputs as follows: the risk-free rate is 6%, the dividend yield is 10%, and the volatility of the underlying investment is 15%. Using Equation 11.3, we estimate that the chemical plant should not be converted until the new plant has a value of $120,284,902. Under this conversion strategy, the option to convert has a value of $7,857,267. That is,

$$\text{Real Option Value} = (V^* - I)\left(\frac{V}{V^*}\right)^\beta$$

$$= (\$120,284,902 - \$98,500,000)\left(\frac{\$100,000,000}{\$120,284,902}\right)^{5.5215}$$

$$= \$7,857,267$$

where β is calculated using Equation 11.5 as follows:

$$\beta = \frac{1}{2} - \frac{r_f - \delta}{\sigma^2} + \sqrt{\left(\frac{r_f - \delta}{\sigma^2} - \frac{1}{2}\right)^2 + \frac{2r_f}{\sigma^2}}$$

$$= \frac{1}{2} - \frac{.06 - .10}{.0225} + \sqrt{\left(\frac{.06 - .10}{.0225} - \frac{1}{2}\right)^2 + \frac{2 \times .10}{.0225}} = 5.5215$$

such that

$$V^* = \left(\frac{\beta}{\beta - 1}\right)I = \left(\frac{5.5215}{5.5215 - 1}\right)\$98,500,000 = \$120,284,902$$

Limitations of the Model

We need to emphasize that this model makes a number of strong assumptions, which affect the accuracy of the value estimates that it provides. For example, the valuation model assumes that interest rates and volatilities are fixed for the life of the options. Clearly, that will not be the case in the real world. The model also requires payouts to be a fixed percentage of the investment's value and assumes that the investment opportunity lasts forever or never expires. However, as restrictive as this final assumption may sound, we can modify the model to accommodate deterioration in the value of the option due to the effects of competition by assuming the value of the opportunity deteriorates at a fixed rate (say, 2% per year) over time. In essence, we assume that the growth rate in the value of the investment is negative.

It should also be noted that in the real estate and chemical plant examples considered in this section, no financial options correspond with the options that are being valued. Consequently, managers have much more leeway in how these investments can be valued than they would if their assumptions were constrained by the values that are observed in financial markets. Given this fact, it is imperative that when doing valuations like these, managers perform a sensitivity analysis that examines the extent to which the investment value is sensitive to the choice of the various parameters of the model.

11.5 USING SIMULATION TO VALUE SWITCHING OPTIONS

Three basic approaches are used to evaluate real options: the binomial lattice, the real option formula for options with an infinite maturity, and simulation. In this section we illustrate the latter.

Simulation is commonly used to solve very complex real option problems that involve multiple and interactive sources of uncertainty. To illustrate how simulation can be used, we will consider the valuation of an investment with a switching option which provides managers with the flexibility to alter operations as economic conditions change. For example, in response to changes in demand for their products, managers generally have the flexibility to speed up or slow down production as well as shift the mix of products they produce and sell. In addition, if the cost of inputs changes over time, managers often can switch to a lower-cost alternative input.

The type of *switching option* that we focus on in this section is the option to exchange one input for another, specifically, the option to switch between natural gas and fuel oil to fire an electric power plant. Another form of switching option is the option to exchange one output for another. For example, a toy manufacturing plant that produces stuffed animal toys might switch between teddy bears and stuffed lions in response to perceived changes in demand. Designing a plant in a way that allows for such switching can be costly, so it is important to be able to value this option to switch.

Option to Switch Inputs

To illustrate the value derived from switching options, we consider the CalTex Power Company, which is considering the installation of a large electric power plant and has three alternative technologies under consideration: a natural gas–fired plant, a fuel oil–fired plant, and a co-fired or flexible plant that has the capability of switching between fuel oil and natural gas depending on which is the cheaper power source. The gas and oil-fired plants each cost $50 million to build, while the flexible plant costs $55 million.

All three plants can produce the same amount of electricity and are expected to run at full capacity every year of their 10-year life. Table 11-4 summarizes the expected revenues and costs of operating all three plant alternatives. To simplify the analysis, we assume the following:

■ Plant revenues equal $32,550,000 in Year 1 and grow at a rate of 5% per year.
■ All three plant technologies incur two costs of operations: fuel costs and fixed operating expenses.
■ There are no costs associated with switching between the fuel alternatives with the flexible plant.[11] Moreover, the costs of the two fuels change only once per year, at the end of each year.

---

[11]In practice, there are often setup or changeover costs that will deter a firm's willingness to switch from one mode of operation to another.

Table 11-4 Static DCF Analysis of the Gas-Fired, Oil-Fired, and Flexible (Gas or Oil)-Fired Power Plants

Year	Expected Cost of Fuel/Btu[a]		Expected Fuel Costs[b]		Other Expenses	Revenues[c]	Expected Free Cash Flow[d]		
	Gas	Fuel Oil	Gas	Fuel Oil			Gas	Fuel Oil	Flexible[e]
0							$(50,000,000)	$(50,000,000)	$(55,000,000)
1	$7.94	$7.32	$(27,803,125)	$(25,602,500)	$(800,000)	$32,550,000	3,946,875	6,147,500	6,147,500
2	8.14	7.64	(28,498,203)	(26,754,613)	(800,000)	34,177,500	4,879,297	6,622,888	6,622,888
3	8.35	7.99	(29,210,658)	(27,958,570)	(800,000)	35,886,375	5,875,717	7,127,805	7,127,805
4	8.55	8.35	(29,940,925)	(29,216,706)	(800,000)	37,680,694	6,939,769	7,663,988	7,663,988
5	8.77	8.72	(30,689,448)	(30,531,457)	(800,000)	39,564,728	8,075,281	8,233,271	8,233,271
6	8.99	9.12	(31,456,684)	(31,905,373)	(800,000)	41,542,965	9,286,281	8,837,592	9,286,281
7	9.21	9.53	(32,243,101)	(33,341,115)	(800,000)	43,620,113	10,577,012	9,478,998	10,577,012
8	9.44	9.95	(33,049,179)	(34,841,465)	(800,000)	45,801,119	11,951,940	10,159,654	11,951,940
9	9.68	10.40	(33,875,408)	(36,409,331)	(800,000)	48,091,175	13,415,767	10,881,844	13,415,767
10	9.92	10.87	(34,722,293)	(38,047,751)	(800,000)	50,495,733	14,973,440	11,647,983	14,973,440

	Gas	Oil	Flexible
NPV[f]	$ (503,157)	$462,277	$(528,142)
IRR	9.81%	10.19%	9.81%

[a]The expected cost of fuel per Btu for gas and fuel oil is estimated from the current costs and the expected rate of inflation. For example, the current cost of natural gas is $7.75 per Btu, and the anticipated rate of inflation is 2.5%. Thus, the expected price of gas in one year is equal to $7.94/Btu = $7.75/Btu × (1 + .025).

[b]The expected cost of fuel equals the product of the total fuel (measured in Btus) consumed by the plant to produce 500,000 kWh of electricity times the fuel cost per Btu from either gas or fuel oil. We calculate the total fuel required to produce electricity using the heat rate for the plant, which differs if the plant is being run with natural gas (assumed to be 7) or fuel oil (assumed to be 7.25). The heat rate equals the ratio of total fuel consumed in Btus divided by the total kWh of electricity produced.

[c]Plant revenues are the same for each of the three plant alternatives and are expected to grow at a rate of 5% per year.

[d]Free Cash Flow = Revenues − Expected Fuel Cost − Other Expenses. We assume there are no taxes or salvage value for any of the plant alternatives.

[e]The fuel cost incorporated in the calculation of the expected free cash flow for the flexible plant is equal to the lower of the expected fuel cost using natural gas or fuel oil for each year.

[f]Net present value is calculated using a 10% cost of capital for each plant alternative.

485

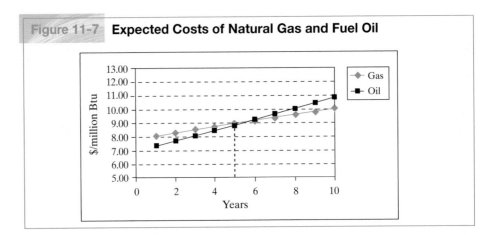

Figure 11-7 **Expected Costs of Natural Gas and Fuel Oil**

- The current price of natural gas is $7.75 per million Btu, and this cost is expected to rise at a rate of 2.5% per year. The price of fuel oil is currently $7.00 per million Btu, and it is expected to rise at a rate of 4.5% per year.[12]
- There are no income taxes.
- The plants are assumed to have no salvage values at the end of Year 10.

The question that we will address is whether the added cost of the flexible power plant is worthwhile. Very simply, is the option to switch fuel sources worth the added $5 million it would cost?

Static NPV Analysis of the Plant Choices

Traditionally, DCF analysis calculates and discounts the cash flows that arise, given the *expected* outcome scenario. We refer to this as **the static DCF analysis.** The results of the static analysis are presented in Table 11-4 for each of the three power plant alternatives. This analysis is static in that it assumes that the oil versus gas choice for the flexible plant is determined in advance based on the most likely scenario or, equivalently, the expected cost of the fuel at each future date. As we illustrate in Figure 11-7, the expected cost of oil is less than that of gas for Years 1 through 5, but then rises above it, triggering a switch from fuel oil to natural gas in Year 6.

Although the cash flows from these plants are not necessarily equally risky, and the risk of the switching plant may change over time as the preferred fuel changes, we will initially value these plants assuming a constant 10% discount rate. As we show in Table 11-4, with this discount and the assumed cash flows, the fuel oil plant is the preferred alternative and the flexible plant has a negative NPV. Based on this static analysis, it appears that the flexible plant does not offer sufficient expected fuel cost savings to warrant spending an additional $5 million.

---

[12]Note that the prices of natural gas and fuel oil have been standardized in terms of the cost per million Btu of energy they are expected to produce. This allows us to compare the costs of the two fuel sources in terms of a common unit that can be related directly to the production of electric power.

Our static NPV analysis, however, ignores an important benefit associated with the flexible plant: It assumes that the fuel input is predetermined based on the expected cost of the alternative fuels, and thus ignores the possibility that management can alter its choice of fuel throughout the life of the flexible plant, using gas in those years in which gas is less expensive and oil in those years in which oil offers the better alternative. Since the costs of natural gas and fuel oil are uncertain, there is a benefit to having the flexibility to respond to future market conditions that cannot be known at the time the analysis is being done. As we demonstrate below, the value of this flexibility can be estimated with a simulation model that incorporates the dynamic effects of having the option to switch fuel sources so as to minimize the cost of fuel.

Dynamic Analysis—Valuing the Option to Switch Fuel Sources

In our static analysis we established that the fuel oil–fired plant is preferred to the natural gas–fired plant. Now we must determine whether adding the option to switch between fuel oil and natural gas using the flexible plant is worthwhile. Consequently, we want to value the fuel cost savings that would accrue to the owner of the flexible plant when compared to those of the fuel oil–fired plant.

Modeling future oil and gas prices Although this problem is somewhat more difficult to solve than the problems that we described up to now, the overall process is very similar. The basic idea is to specify a price process for the commodities that are the value drivers for the power plant projects. In this case, we have two value drivers: the prices of natural gas and fuel oil per Btu, so we must specify a price process for both commodities. By this we mean the process that describes their volatilities and how these volatilities change over time. Up to now we have assumed that commodities are like stocks and follow a random walk, which means that price changes in any given time period are independent of the previous price changes. This assumption simplifies option pricing problems, but for most commodities it is not realistic. Commodity prices are generally assumed to be mean-reverting, which means that if prices increase a lot in one year, they are likely to fall in the following year. In the Technical Insight box titled "Modeling Natural Gas Prices

---

Did you know?

Origins of Brownian Motion

Studying the random behavior of pollen particles suspended in water, the Scottish scientist Robert Brown is credited with identifying the phenomenon we now refer to as Brownian motion. Many years later Albert Einstein developed the mathematical properties of Brownian motion that are commonly used today.

The sad truth, however, is that Louis Bachelier (1870–1946) in his 1900 dissertation, *Theorie de la Spéculation* (and in his subsequent work, especially in 1906, 1913), anticipated the ideas behind the random walk of financial market prices, Brownian motion, and martingales (*Note:* all before both Einstein and Wiener!) His innovativeness, however, was not appreciated until it was rediscovered in the 1960s.

(http://cepa.newschool.edu/het/profiles/bachelier.htm.)

Using Geometric Brownian Motion and Mean Reversion," we will provide more detail about the price processes that analysts use to describe oil, gas, and other commodity prices.

We will again use observed prices from the financial markets to value the option to switch between natural gas and fuel oil, but in this case we cannot simply plug in the prices of traded derivatives. Instead we must first specify a price process for natural gas and fuel oil and then calibrate the process so that it generates values for observed forward and option prices that are consistent with the prices observed in the financial markets. We will not provide the technical details of such a calibration process, but will assume that from such a process we arrive at the following set of parameter estimates:

	Rate of Reversion in Prices*	Mean Reversion Price = Forward Price**	Standard Deviation of Price Changes
Natural gas	1.0	$7.75/Btu	30%
Fuel oil	0.6	$7.00/Btu	20%

*Historical estimates of the rate of reversion to the mean for natural gas have been faster than for oil prices.
**This is also the initial price of each commodity in the current period (Year 0).

We have one final attribute that we need to estimate. Note that since we have two commodity prices (natural gas and fuel oil) that must be considered when valuing the switching option, it is also necessary that we estimate the correlation between the prices of natural gas and fuel oil per Btu. If the prices of natural gas and fuel oil are very highly correlated, the option to switch will be less valuable. Intuitively, the gain from switching is much less if fuel oil prices are likely to be high whenever natural gas prices are high. Since fuel oil and natural gas are frequent substitutes, high demand for one is likely to put pressures on the price of the other, which does make the two commodities positively correlated. However, the correlation is not particularly high, and for our purposes we assume a positive correlation of 0.25.

> **Did you know?**
>
> **What's a Wiener process?**
>
> The increment to Brownian motion defined by Equation 11.7 is often referred to as a *Wiener process*, named after the American mathematician Norbert Wiener (1894–1964).

We must again note that since the simulated price process has been calibrated using derivative prices, the resulting prices that we estimate using Equation 11.6 are not the actual expected prices, but instead are *risk-adjusted* expected prices or certainty-equivalent prices. Consequently, the expected cash flows that we calculate from this *calibrated price process* are certainty-equivalent cash flows that can be valued by discounting them at the risk-free rate.

Modeling Natural Gas Prices Using Geometric Brownian Motion and Mean Reversion

Brownian motion without mean reversion has been compared to the path that a drunk might take home after a night out on the town. We can think of the path marked by the staggering steps of the drunken man as he wanders toward home as a representation of Brownian motion. Based on this analogy, Brownian motion is sometimes referred to as a random walk.

Now consider the possibility that the drunken man takes his faithful dog, Sparky, to the bar. Since Sparky doesn't drink, he can lead his master home. With Sparky along to guide him, the man staggers along aimlessly until the dog's leash tugs him back toward the direct path taken by Sparky. The path of the drunken man as he staggers along behind Sparky's lead provides a rough approximation of Brownian motion with mean reversion. The leash, like mean reversion, keeps the drunken man from wandering too far from the path home.

Stock prices are generally modeled as Brownian motion without mean reversion, that is, as a random walk. However, the prices of a commodity, like natural gas, are generally modeled as Brownian motion with mean reversion, which means that if prices tend to get too far away from a long-term equilibrium price, they tend to gravitate towards that price, which is usually governed by the cost of production and the level of demand.

We can mathematically express this price process in Equation 11.6, which defines the price of natural gas at the end of Year 1, $P_{\text{Gas}}(1)$, as the sum of the observed price of natural gas today, $P_{\text{Gas}}(0)$, plus the change in the price of gas over the coming year, $\Delta P_{\text{Gas}}(1)$:

$$P_{\text{Gas}}(1) = P_{\text{Gas}}(0) + \Delta P_{\text{Gas}}(1) \tag{11.6}$$

Next, for a mean reverting geometric Brownian motion process, $\Delta P_{\text{Gas}}(1)$ can be defined by the following equation:

$$\Delta P_{\text{Gas}}(1) = P_{\text{Gas}}(0)[\text{Predictable Component } (\mu) + \text{Unpredictable Component } (\sigma_{\text{Gas}} \varepsilon)]$$
$$\Delta P_{\text{Gas}}(1) = P_{\text{Gas}}(0)[\mu + \sigma_{\text{Gas}} \varepsilon], \tag{11.7}$$

where the predictable component $\mu = \alpha_{\text{Gas}}[\ln(L) - \ln(P_{\text{Gas}}(0))]$ and α_{Gas} is the rate at which gas prices revert back to the mean price, L_{Gas}. For example, a reversion rate of two would suggest that prices would revert to the mean price in half a period (six months in our example). The unpredictable component is described by ε, which is a normal random variable with mean zero and unit standard deviation, and σ_{Gas}, which represents the volatility of the logarithm of natural gas price changes. The unpredictable component is the source of randomness in the price path.

Substituting Equation 11.7 into Equation 11.6, we see that the price of gas next year is

$$P_{\text{Gas}}(1) = P_{\text{Gas}}(0)[1 + \alpha_{\text{Gas}}[\ln(L) - \ln(P_{\text{Gas}}(0))] + \sigma_{\text{Gas}} \varepsilon] \tag{11.8}$$

Using simulation to value the flexibility option At this point we have made all the assumptions and forecasts we need to characterize the future prices of natural gas and fuel oil and are ready to value the option to switch between the two sources of fuel. To solve for the value of this flexibility option, we use the simulation process that we previously discussed in Chapter 3. This process requires the following three steps (refer back to Chapter 3 for a more thorough review):

■ *Step 1: Identify the sources of uncertainty, characterize the uncertainty using an appropriate probability distribution, and estimate the parameters of each distribution.* In this instance the sources of uncertainty associated with the value of the option to switch fuel sources are the costs of natural gas and fuel oil for each of the next 10 years. We have modeled the prices of natural gas and fuel oil per Btu using Equation 11.6.

■ *Step 2: Define the summary measure that we are attempting to estimate.* In this instance, our objective is to evaluate the present value of the expected fuel cost savings for Years 1 through 10 if the flexible plant is constructed.

■ *Step 3: Run the simulation.* We use 10,000 iterations or trials in the simulation of fuel prices. The iterations begin with the cost of fuel per Btu observed in Year 0. Then the change in price is simulated using Equation 11.7 (one for natural gas and one for fuel oil) and added to the cost/Btu for Year 0 to get the simulated price for Year 1. The process is repeated to obtain fuel prices for Years 2 through 10. The simulated prices for gas and oil form a single price path for each of the fuels. We repeat this process a total of 10,000 times to form 10,000 price paths for oil and, likewise, 10,000 price paths for natural gas. These simulated costs of gas and oil per Btu are then used to calculate the annual fuel cost savings that accrue to the flexible plant alternative. Since we are analyzing the value of the flexible plant compared to the fuel oil plant alternative, the flexibility option creates savings only when the cost of natural gas falls below the price of fuel oil.

Once we have identified the distributions of fuel cost savings from the simulation, we calculate the value of these expected annual savings by discounting them using the risk-free rate of 6%.

The column titled "Average Annual Fuel Savings" in Panel a of Table 11-5 contains the average annual cash flow savings that are expected to accrue to the flexible plant when it always selects the lower-cost fuel source. Discounting these savings back to the present using the risk-free rate of interest produces a value of $22,252,213, which when compared to the $5 million added cost of building the flexible plant provides an NPV of $17,252,213. Based on this analysis, CalTex should select the flexible plant technology.

Panel b of Table 11-5 contains a histogram of the values generated from each of the simulations for the flexibility option. We will not engage in a full sensitivity analysis using the simulated distribution here (see Chapter 3) but will point out that the discounted value of the simulated cash flows associated with the switching option was at least equal to the $5 million additional investment in 94.88% of the simulation trials.

11.6 MISTAKES MADE IN REAL OPTION VALUATION

Real options, in general, are much more difficult to value than stock options and other options on financial claims. Perhaps the most obvious difference between real and financial options is the fact that real option values are often determined by the values of other assets that are not actively traded. For example, in contrast to a stock, which might be traded every minute, factories, buildings, and other real assets are bought and sold very rarely. This fact makes it difficult to estimate how their returns are distributed and makes it impossible to hedge the risk associated with the real option by buying or selling the underlying asset.

A second difference between real and financial options is that the exercise choices are much more complicated with real options. With a stock option, one simply decides whether to buy the stock at some prespecified price. For real options, the decisions can be much more complicated. For example, a land owner must decide more than just whether to build on his land. He must decide what to build and how quickly to construct the building. In addition, he must consider the effect of changing construction costs (that is, an uncertain exercise price) and uncertainty about the value of the building. For example, the developer may want to design the building so that it can be more easily expanded to accommodate the potential for growth in demand in the future.

Because of the difficulties associated with valuing real options, it is no surprise that it is very easy to make mistakes in the valuation process. Some of the more common mistakes include the following, which we discuss in the remainder of the chapter:

1. Trying to fit the problem into the Black-Scholes model.
2. Using the volatility of a commodity price rather than the volatility of the underlying investment to value a natural resource investment.
3. Assuming that the exercise price of the real option is fixed.
4. Overestimating flexibility.
5. Double-counting risk.
6. Failing to understand how investment choices affect price volatility.
7. Abusing real option analysis to justify "strategic investments."

Trying to Fit the Problem into the Black-Scholes Model

There is a natural tendency to use financial formulas even when the underlying assumptions upon which the models were developed are not consistent with the realities of the situation. This tendency has led many analysts to "force-fit" the Black-Scholes option pricing formula to real option problems in cases where the model is not even remotely appropriate.

Table 11-5 Dynamic Analysis of the Option to Switch Fuels—Comparing the Fuel Oil–Fired Plant and the Flexible Plant

Panel a. Certain Equivalent Expected Annual Fuel Cost Savings

Year	Average Annual Fuel Savings
1	2,518,650
2	3,215,166
3	3,180,391
4	3,094,741
5	3,138,945
6	3,121,089
7	3,038,148
8	3,012,766
9	3,001,547
10	2,972,366

Risk-free rate	6.0%	
Value switching option (fuel savings)	$ 22,252,213	
Less: Cost of option	(5,000,000)	
NPV (switching option)	$ 17,252,213	

These savings correspond to the benefits of having the option to switch between fuel sources compared to the fuel oil–fired plant. The latter was determined to be the better alternative where the natural gas and fuel oil–fired plants were compared.

To get an idea of the potential problems with applying the Black-Scholes formula, consider just a few of its underlying assumptions: (1) The option can be exercised only at maturity, (2) the payoff to the option is contingent on the value of just one underlying risky investment, (3) the underlying investment generates no cash flow over the term of the option, (4) the market price of the investment is both observable and the process it follows over time is known, and (5) the exercise price of the option is a known constant. Reflecting upon the attributes of the investments we have analyzed in this chapter, you should see that the Black-Scholes assumptions are not at all appropriate for most real option investments.

As we discussed earlier, real options should generally be viewed as American options that can be exercised at any time. In addition, in most cases, the underlying investment generates cash flows, and these cash flows, like dividends on a share of

Panel b. Distribution of Flexible Option Values (Crystal Ball Output)

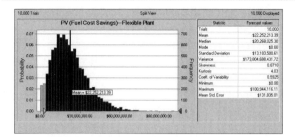

PV(Fuel Cost Savings) = present value of the cost of reduced fuel consumption due to switching fuel to low cost source.

Fuel cost savings = the difference in the total annual fuel cost of fuel oil and natural gas where natural gas is cheaper than fuel oil.

Certainty = Percent of the 10,000 iterations where the present value of the fuel cost savings exceeded the $5 million added cost of the flexible plant.

Panel c. Distribution of the Number of Switches over 10 Years (Crystal Ball Output)

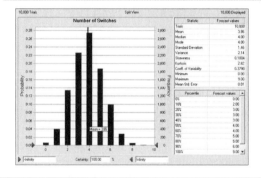

Definitions:
- A fuel switch occurs whenever the cost of fuel can be lowered by changing over from one fuel to another.
- The number of switches equals the number of times within the 10-year plant life.

stock, affect the value of the investment and consequently the value of any options based on the investment's value. Finally, the exercise prices of real options are typically unknown.

Using the Wrong Volatility

Analysts often use the wrong volatility when valuing natural resource investments with embedded options. In particular, the volatility of the price of the commodity is erroneously used rather than the volatility of the value of the appropriate underlying asset. For example, as we described earlier, the volatility of the value of a producing oil field is the appropriate volatility that should be used to value a lease that gives the holder the option to extract oil. However, in practice, it is difficult to determine this volatility, so analysts sometimes take the shortcut of using the volatility of oil prices. This shortcut would produce the correct answer if oil prices were like stock prices and followed a random walk (that is, price changes were serially uncorrelated). However, oil prices, like most commodity prices, tend to be mean-reverting, which means that a very large positive price change is more likely to be followed by a drop in price than by another increase. When this is the case, the volatility of commodity prices will be greater than the volatility of investments that generate cash flows that depend on the commodity prices. This will, in turn, lead to an overvaluation of options.

Assuming That the Exercise Price of the Real Option Is Fixed

Unlike financial or contractual options, the exercise price of a real option is generally not fixed. For example, your firm may have the option to undertake a project today at a cost of $8 million or to delay the investment for another year. However, if over the year the price of the project's output increases significantly, it is likely that the cost of initiating the project may have also risen. For example, when housing prices increase, we often see a building boom, which drives up the costs of lumber and other building materials. In general, a high correlation between an investment's value and the cost of implementing the investment has the effect of lowering the value of the option to invest.

Overestimating the Value of Flexibility

The fundamental source of the value of real options comes from optimally taking advantage of flexibility. However, to capture this value the firm's management must be both willing and able to exercise the options when conditions warrant doing so. In reality, managers tend not to ruthlessly exercise real options as the theory suggests. For example, management may fail to act to shut down a facility when it is optimal to do so because of loyalties to employees, suppliers, or customers. Furthermore, even absent conflicting motives, management may not have the incentives or the ability to exercise real options in an optimal fashion. The message here is that one should not place much value on options that can be exercised *in theory* but are unlikely to be exercised *in reality*.

Double-Counting Risk

In our analysis of the value of embedded options in oil fields, we used forward prices to calculate "certainty-equivalent" cash flows and discounted these cash flows at the risk-free rate of interest. This analysis *correctly* associates a risk-free discount rate to certainty-equivalent cash flows. However, industry applications sometimes mistakenly use forward prices to represent expected prices, which are then used to calculate what are erroneously *assumed* to be expected cash flows, which are then discounted at a risk-adjusted rate. Hence, the analyst ends up adjusting both the cash flows and the discount rate for risk, which will result in a conservative estimate of value.

Failing to Understand How Investment Choices Affect Price Volatility

Essentially, this mistake is a direct result of failing to understand that a firm's actions can have feedback effects on the environment in which it operates. For example, electric utilities own what are referred to as "peaker plants," which can be *turned on* and *off* in response to peak-load demands for power. Peaker plants can be extremely profitable since they are operated only when there are spikes in the price of electricity, which happen on very hot days when air conditioners (and power plants) are operating at capacity.

Unregulated energy companies value peaker plants as an option to deliver electricity when the price is high. In the late 1990s, power companies acquired a large number of these plants. In doing so, they were partly motivated by very high real option values that were calculated based on very volatile electric power prices. However, the introduction of more peaker plants to meet peak demand had the effect of increasing the available capacity during spikes in demand, thereby dampening fluctuations in electricity prices. In other words, the presence of peaker plants, which were designed to give the unregulated power companies the flexibility to exploit the volatility in electricity prices, had the effect of reducing volatility to a level where the plants were no longer profitable. The message here is that the inputs into the real options formulas are not simply numbers that can be estimated from past history. One needs to combine estimates from past history with managerial judgment that accounts for more recent and anticipated industry trends.

Abusing Real Option Analysis to Justify "Strategic Investments"

An often-heard complaint about real option analysis is that it makes it too easy for a project sponsor to justify pet projects. One simply specifies a multitude of options that arise from the initial investment and argues that the project has "strategic value." When your VP in charge of international development suggests an investment in a golf course in Tahiti based on options created to do business throughout Asia, you may want to scrutinize his analysis. One should not lose sight of the fact that real option analysis, like any valuation model, is only as good as its inputs.

11.7 SUMMARY

The growth in the use of real option analysis over the last decade can largely be attributed to its broad-based appeal as a tool to communicate and estimate the value that flexibility can add to real investments. The examples in this chapter illustrate that there can be a substantial increment to project value whenever managers have the flexibility to act opportunistically when managing real investments in an uncertain environment.

Surveys of business practice indicate that MBA programs have been very successful in ingraining the use of static discounted cash flow analysis into hoards of newly minted MBAs. However, this success has had an unfortunate side effect—static DCF analysis has supplanted some of the commonsense business analyses used in years past that recognized the importance of operational flexibility. This has meant that the early adherents of a more quantitative approach to project analysis based on static DCF analysis may have underestimated the extent to which flexibility is a source of value. The computational power of computer spreadsheets, simulation software, and specialized option valuation software on the desks of analysts today makes real option analysis a practical reality. However, as we learned with the adoption of quantitative techniques like static DCF, change takes time, so it may be years before the real option approach to project valuation is as prevalent as static DCF. But we believe this is the direction of the future.

In this chapter we presented three approaches that can be used to value investments with real options:

■ The first approach we discussed is the binomial lattice approach. This, and related approaches, are used extensively on Wall Street to value financial options, and because of its success there, it has been adopted in some settings to value real investments.

■ The second approach is the application of a real option formula, which to our knowledge is not really used in industry. We presented this formula because, like the Black-Scholes formula, it is simple to program and provides a rough estimate of real option values. Like the Black-Scholes formula, this formula provides estimates that are a bit too simple and too rough to use for a final valuation of a major investment. However, it may provide a useful starting point to determine whether a more refined analysis is warranted.

■ The final tool that we discussed is simulation analysis. This is becoming increasingly more important for valuing investments, and we think that this is the tool of the future. Simulation is capable of handling the most complicated investments in a way that does not require a great deal of technical sophistication from the analyst. In reality, major investments often contain many sources of managerial flexibility as well as a number of sources of uncertainty, and simulation is the only available tool that is capable of dealing with this level of complexity.

The application of real option analysis varies across industries and even firms within industries. For example, real option analysis is used extensively in the energy and natural resource industries where commodity markets are active and derivative prices are readily observable. We hasten to point out, however, that although the complexity of the analysis presented in this chapter is greater than in prior chapters, the real option valuation approaches that are actually used in practice can be even more complicated. However, since these industry approaches are generally based on either the simulation approach or the binomial approach described in this chapter, an understanding of this material provides the foundation for understanding the most complicated valuation approaches used in industry.

In other industries real options are evaluated with approaches that are less sophisticated than the approaches described in this chapter. For example, although flexibility plays a very important role in real estate development, real estate investors typically do not use explicit valuation models to value real estate development options. In addition, while managers do understand the value of timing options, which exist for almost any major investment project, they tend to use relatively simple and intuitive approaches for valuing the option to wait as well as the option to abandon.

Why are real option valuation approaches more popular in energy and natural resource industries than in other industries? In these industries, the payoffs between the real options and the options that are traded in the financial markets are quite close, allowing managers to value the investment without having to use a lot of judgment. In other cases, such as the valuation of land with development opportunities, there are no financial option prices that are directly analogous to the development option being valued. In these cases, real option analysis is viewed less favorably, since the manager must substitute his or her judgment about the future distribution of the relevant values for the financial option prices that do not exist in this case. While the need to exercise judgment in a valuation problem is not unique to the application of real option models, it is natural for managers to be more reluctant to exercise judgment in the application of tools they are less familiar with, and thus to be less confident about their judgment. As we have emphasized earlier, in those cases where more managerial judgment is required, it is important that the valuation analysis also include a detailed sensitivity analysis.

In the next chapter we evaluate investment strategies, which we will define as the potential for a *series* of investment opportunities. For example, when Toyota considers an assembly plant to build pickup trucks in Texas, it is considering a single investment. However, when the company considers whether it makes sense to assemble cars in Eastern Europe where the company does not currently build automobiles, it is evaluating an investment strategy that can eventually lead to assembly plants in multiple locations for a variety of cars and trucks. The fact that both flexibility and uncertainty are inherent in all investment strategies implies that some sort of option analysis is required for a disciplined approach to evaluating the strategy.

PROBLEMS

11-1 ANALYZING AN OIL LEASE AS AN OPTION TO DRILL FOR OIL Suppose you own the option to extract 1,000 barrels of oil from public land over the next two years. You are deciding whether to extract the oil immediately, allowing you to sell the oil for $20 per barrel, or to wait to extract the oil next year and sell it then for an uncertain price.

The extraction costs are $17 per barrel. The forward price is $20, and you know that oil prices next year will be either $15 per barrel or $25 per barrel depending on demand conditions. Are you better off extracting the oil today or waiting one year? Explain how your answer might be different if prices next year are either more or less certain but have the same mean.

11-2 CONCEPTUAL ANALYSIS OF REAL OPTIONS Huntsman Chemical is a relatively small chemical company located in Port Arthur, Texas. The firm's management is contemplating its first international investment, which involves the construction of a petrochemical plant in Sao Paulo, Brazil. The proposed plant will have the capacity to produce 100,000 tons of the plastic pellets that are then used to manufacture soft drink bottles. In addition, the plant can be converted over to produce the pellets used in the manufacture of opaque plastic containers such as milk containers.

The initial plant will cost $50 million to build, but its capacity can later be doubled at a cost of $30 million should the economics warrant it. The plant can be financed with a $40 million nonrecourse loan provided by a consortium of banks and guaranteed by the Export Import Bank. Huntsman's management is enthusiastic about the project, as its analysts think the Brazilian economy will continue to grow into the foreseeable future. This growth, in turn, may offer Huntsman Chemical many additional opportunities in the future as the company becomes better known in the region.

Based on a traditional discounted cash flow analysis, Huntsman's analysts estimate that the project has a modest NPV of about $5 million. However, when Huntsman's executive committee members review the proposal, they express concern about the risk of the venture based primarily on the fact that the Brazilian economy is also very uncertain. Toward the close of their deliberations, the company CEO turns to the senior financial analyst and asks him whether he has considered something he had recently read about called "real options" in performing his discounted cash flow estimate of the project's NPV.

Assume the role of the senior analyst and provide your boss with a brief discussion of the various options that may be embedded in this project, and very roughly sketch out how these options can add to the value of the project. (*Hint:* No computations are required.)

11-3 OPTION TO ABANDON Newport Mining has a lease with two years remaining in which it can extract copper ore on a remote island in Indonesia. The company has completed the exploration phase and estimates that the mine contains five million pounds of ore that can be extracted. The ore deposit is particularly rich and contains 37.5% pure copper.

Newport can contract with a local mining company to develop the property in the coming year at a cost of $1.2 million. Three-fourths of the cost of development must be paid immediately and the remainder at the end of one year. Once the site is developed, Newport can contract with a mine operator to extract the ore for a cash payment equal to $0.60 per pound of ore processed or $1.60 per pound of copper produced.[13] The total cost must be paid in advance at the beginning of the second year of operations. This amounts to a cash payment in one year of $3 million.

At the end of one year, Newport can contract to sell the copper ore for the prevailing spot price at that time. However, since the spot price at the end of the year is unknown today, the proceeds from the sale of the refined copper are uncertain.

The current price is $2.20 per pound, and commodity analysts estimate that it will be $2.50 a pound at year-end. However, since the price of copper is highly volatile, industry analysts have estimated that it might be as high as $2.80 or as low as $1.20 per pound by the end of the year. The price of copper is expected to stay at $2.80 or as low as $1.20 throughout the second year. As an alternative to selling the copper at the end-of-year spot price, Newport could sell the production today for the forward price of $2.31 and eliminate completely the uncertainty surrounding the future price of copper. However, this strategy would require that the firm commit today to producing the copper. This, in turn, means that Newport's management would forfeit the option to shut down the plant should the price be less than the cost of producing the copper.

Given the risk inherent in exploration, Newport requires a rate of return of 25% for investments at the exploration stage but requires only 15% for investments at the development stage. The risk-free rate of interest is currently only 5%.

a. What is the expected NPV for the project if Newport commits itself to the development, extraction, and sale of the copper today and sells the copper in the forward market?

b. What is the NPV of the project if the production is *not* sold forward and Newport subjects itself to the uncertainties of the copper market?

c. Using the decision tree on page 498, construct a diagram that describes Newport's payoff from the investment that includes the option to extract the ore at the end of one year.

d. What is the lease worth to Newport if it exercises its option to abandon the project at the end of Year 1? Should the firm proceed with the development today?

e. If Newport decided to extract the ore itself, how could it use the copper call options to hedge the risk of mining for the copper? The price of a European call option on one pound of copper with an exercise price of $1.68 and maturity of two years is $0.70.

---

[13]Since the ore contains 37.5% copper and there are five million pounds of ore in the mine, the total is 1.875 million pounds of copper to be produced at a cost equal to $0.60 × 5 million pounds of ore, or $3.0 million. Thus, the cost per pound to produce the ore is $3.0 million/1.875 million pounds, or $1.60 per pound.

Newport's Options to Develop and Produce a Copper Mine

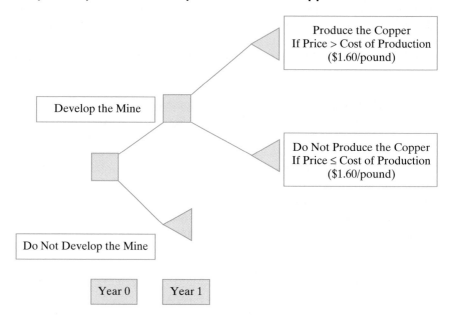

11-4 VALUING AN AMERICAN OPTION J&B Drilling Company has recently acquired a lease to drill for natural gas in a remote region of southwest Louisiana and southeast Texas. The area has long been known for oil and gas production, and the company is optimistic about the prospects of the lease. The lease contract has a three-year life and allows J&B to begin exploration at any time up until the end of the three-year term.

J&B's engineers have estimated the volume of natural gas they hope to extract from the leasehold and have placed a value of $25 million on it, on the condition that explorations begin immediately. The cost of developing the property is estimated to be $23 million (regardless of when the property is developed over the next three years). Based on historical volatilities in the returns of similar investments and other relevant information, J&B's analysts have estimated that the value of the investment opportunity will evolve over the next three years as shown in the figure on page 499.

The risk-free rate of interest is currently 5%, and the risk-neutral probability of an uptick in the value of the investment is estimated to be 46.26%.

a. Evaluate the value of the leasehold as an American call option. What is the lease worth today?

b. What is your recommendation to J&B as to when it should begin drilling?

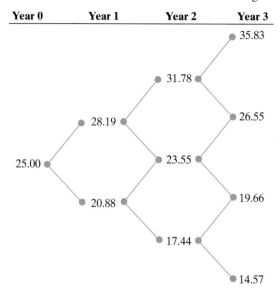

Year 0	Year 1	Year 2	Year 3

11-5 OPTION TO SWITCH INPUTS—CRYSTAL BALL EXERCISE The Central and Southeast Power Company of Mobile, Alabama, is considering a new power plant that will allow it to switch between gas and oil. The company has a contract to provide it with gas for $8 that is sufficient to produce one unit of electric power. (The numbers are standardized to one unit for ease of computation.) However, the plant can also be run using fuel oil. The price of fuel oil is uncertain, and the firm's analysts believe the uncertain future price can be characterized as a triangular distribution with a minimum value of $2, a most likely value of $7, and a maximum value of $12. Next year the plant is expected to produce one standard unit of electrical power that can be sold for $10.

a. What is the expected cash flow from the power plant for next year, if the cost of fuel is set equal to the minimum of the expected costs of gas and oil? (*Hint:* There are no taxes, and the only expenses that the plant incurs are for fuel.)
b. Construct a simple Crystal Ball simulation model for the plant's cash flow using a triangular distribution for the cost of fuel oil and selecting the minimum-cost source of fuel to run the plant. What is the expected cash flow from the power plant based on your simulation?
c. If the cost of capital for the plant is 10% and the cash flows for the plant are expected to be constant forever, what is the value of the plant?

11-6 REFINERY WITH THE OPTION TO SWITCH OUTPUTS—CRYSTAL BALL EXERCISE The Windsor Oil Company is considering the construction of a new refinery that can process 12 million barrels of oil per year for a period of five years. The cost of constructing the refinery is $2 billion and it will be depreciated over five years toward a zero salvage value. The plant can produce either gasoline or jet fuel and the product can be changed once each year based on the prices of the two products. The refinery can convert 44 gallons (per barrel) of crude into 90% of this quantity of gasoline or 70% if jet fuel is produced. The residual can be sold but for no net profit.

Windsor's analysts characterize the distribution of gasoline prices for next year and each of the next five years using a triangular distribution that has a minimum value of $1.75 per gallon, a most likely value of $2.50, and a maximum of $4.00. They characterize the price per gallon of jet fuel using a triangular distribution with a minimum value of $2.50 per gallon, a most likely value of $3.25, and a maximum value of $5.00 a gallon. The price of crude is fixed via forward contracts over the next five years at $25 per barrel. Windsor also estimates that the cost of refining is equal to 35% of the selling price of the particular product being produced.

Windsor faces a 30% tax rate on its income and uses a cost of capital of 10% to analyze refinery investments. The risk-free rate is 5.5%.

a. What is the NPV of the refinery if it produces only jet fuel (since the revenues under this alternative are higher based on the most likely price)?
b. Construct a simulation model for the refinery that makes the price of gasoline and jet fuel random variables with the triangular distribution described above. What is the NPV of the refinery investment if the firm selects the higher-valued product to produce based on the realized prices of gasoline and jet fuel?

11-7 CONCEPTUAL ANALYSIS OF REAL OPTIONS Highland Properties owns two adjacent four-unit apartment buildings that are both on 20,000 square feet of land near downtown Portland, Oregon. One of the properties is in very good condition and the apartments can be rented for $2,000 per month. The units in the other property require some refurbishing and in their current condition can only be rented for about $1,500 per month.

Recent zoning changes, combined with changes in market demand, suggest that both lots can be redeveloped. If they are redeveloped, the existing units would be torn down and new luxury apartment buildings would be built on the site, each with 10 apartment units. The cost of the 10-unit buildings is estimated to be about $1.5 million, and each of the 10 apartment units can be rented for $2,500 per month under current market conditions. Similar properties that have been refurbished are selling for 10 times their annual rentals.

a. Identify the real option(s) in this example.
b. What are the basic elements of the option(s) (i.e., the underlying asset on which the option is based, the expiration date, and the exercise price)?
c. Estimate the value of the option to develop the property. (*Hint:* Make any assumptions you need to arrive at an estimate.)

11-8 CONCEPTUAL ANALYSIS OF REAL OPTIONS The destruction that Hurricane Katrina brought to the Gulf Coast in 2005 devastated the city of New Orleans, as well as the Mississippi Gulf coast. Notably, the burgeoning casino gambling industry along the Mississippi coast was nearly destroyed. CGC Corporation owns one of the oldest casinos in the Biloxi area, and it was not destroyed by Katrina's tidal surge since it was located several blocks off the beach. Because of the near-total destruction of many of the gambling properties located along the beach, CGC is considering the opportunity to make a major renovation in its casino. The renovation would transform the casino from a second-tier operation into one of the top attractions along the Mississippi Gulf coast. The question that the firm faces involves placing a value on the opportunity to renovate the property.

CGC's analysts estimate that it would cost $50 million to do the renovation. However, based on the uncertainties associated with the redevelopment of the region, the firm's financial analyst estimated that the casino, under the current conditions, would only be valued at $45 million. Alternatively, CGC could continue to operate the casino, in which case it expects to realize an annual rate of return of 10% on the value of the investment. Moreover, the estimated return of 10% is highly uncertain. In fact, the volatility (standard deviation) in this rate of return is probably on the order of 20%, while the risk-free rate of interest is only 5%.

   a. What is the NPV of renovation of the property if undertaken immediately?
   b. What is the value of having the option to renovate in the future? (*Hint:* You can assume that the option never expires.)

APPENDIX

Constructing Binomial Lattices

The binomial option pricing model utilizes a binomial tree to specify the evolution of the value of the underlying asset through time. The tree begins with the current value of the underlying asset equal to S_0. In one period the value is equal to either uS_0 or dS_0. Moreover, to ease the computational problem involved in evaluating the tree, where there are many periods it is now standard practice to restrict the price changes in the tree to be symmetrical such that u equals $1/d$. This means that in the next period the possible values are reduced to three: u^2S_0, udS_0, and d^2S_0. This version of the binomial tree is called a *recombining binomial tree* or a *binomial lattice*.

When the risk-neutral valuation approach is used to value options, we construct what is referred to as a risk-neutral binomial lattice, in which the expected return to the underlying asset is the risk-free rate, r, but the asset's volatility, σ, is the same as that of the risky asset.

To illustrate how u and d are determined, let's first assume that the asset is risk free. In this setting the value of the asset appreciates at the risk-free rate less any payout over the period. For example the value of a share of stock will appreciate at the risk-free rate less the dividend yield, δ. So, if the stock were worth $10.00 at the beginning of the period and the risk-free rate is 6% and the dividend yield is 4%, then the value of the stock at the end of one period will be $\$10e^{.06 - .04} = \$10.20$.[14] Thus, in the absence of uncertainty, we can now define u as follows:

$$S_1 = S_0 e^{r - \delta}$$

Now we introduce uncertainty into S_1 using the annualized volatility of the returns to the asset, σ:

$$uS_0 = S_0 e^{r - \delta} e^{\sigma} = S_0 e^{r - \delta + \sigma} \quad \text{and} \quad dS_0 = S_0 e^{r - \delta - \sigma}$$

---

[14]For a commodity such as oil held in the tanks of a refinery or cattle in the feed lots of a meatpacker, the payout is referred to as a *convenience yield* since owning the physical commodity has value to the holder (e.g., it meets an inventory need) that is lost with the passage of time.

Multiple Time Steps per Year

To this point we have assumed that one period equals one year; however, this need not be the case. If, for example, one period equals one month, then the risk-free rate, payout, and annual volatility have to be adjusted to reflect one-twelfth of a year, i.e., the monthly volatility would be $\sigma\sqrt{\frac{1}{12}}$ and S_1 would become

$$uS_0 = S_0 e^{(r-\delta)(\frac{1}{12})+\sigma\sqrt{\frac{1}{12}}} \quad \text{and} \quad dS_0 = S_0 e^{(r-\delta)(\frac{1}{12})-\sigma\sqrt{\frac{1}{12}}}$$

More generally, if there are n time steps per year such that each *time step* is of length $1/n$th of a year, we define the value of the underlying asset at the end of one time step as follows:

$$uS_0 = S_0 e^{(r-\delta)(\frac{1}{n})+\sigma\sqrt{\frac{1}{n}}} \quad \text{and} \quad dS_0 = S_0 e^{(r-\delta)(\frac{1}{n})-\sigma\sqrt{\frac{1}{n}}}$$

Building the Binomial Lattice for the National Petroleum Oil Field Investment

To implement the binomial option pricing model to value the National Petroleum Company's investment opportunity, we must first determine the future values of the drilling opportunity specified in the binomial lattice. We will specify these values using the procedure just discussed. To do so we need the following information:

    a.   The starting point for the value of the oil field investment opportunity today, which is $42.034 million.

    b.   The risk-free rate of interest (r) is 6%.

    c.   The convenience yield (δ) is 7%.

    d.   The standard deviation (volatility) of the annual returns to the drilling investment (σ) is assumed to be .15.

Given this information, we can calculate the binomial distribution of values for the oil development project at the end of the first year as follows:

$$\text{High Value} = S_0 u \quad \text{where} \quad u = e^{r-\delta+\sigma}$$

or

$$\text{Low Value} = S_0 d \quad \text{where} \quad d = e^{r-\delta-\sigma}$$

Substituting for the determinants of u and d, we calculate

$$u = e^{r-\delta+\sigma} = e^{.06-.07+.15} = 1.1503 \quad \text{and} \quad d = .852$$

such that the two possible values for National's drilling opportunity at the end of Year 1 are

$$S_0 u = \$42.03 \text{ million} \times 1.1503 = \$48.35 \text{ million}$$

and

$$S_0 d = \$42.03 \text{ million} \times .852 = \$35.82 \text{ million}$$

At the end of Year 2, there are three possible valuations for the drilling opportunity corresponding to the following sequence of events:

$$S_0 uu = \$42.03 \text{ million} \times 1.1503 \times 1.1503 = \$55.62 \text{ million}$$

$$S_0 ud = S_0 du = \$42.03 \text{ million} \times 1.1503 \times .852 = \$41.20 \text{ million}$$

$$S_0 dd = \$42.03 \text{ million} \times .852 \times .852 = \$30.51 \text{ million}$$

In Year 3, the number of nodes expands to four, corresponding to $S_0 uuu$, $S_0 uud$, $S_0 udd$, and $S_0 ddd$. Figure 11-6 contains the completed binomial lattice for the National Petroleum drilling opportunity.

Strategic Options:
Evaluating Strategic
Opportunities

Chapter Overview

This chapter offers three important lessons for corporate managers. First, when evaluating individual projects, the analyst should always be aware of the project's role in the firm's overall business strategy. What this means is that firms may not want to pass up what might at first appear to be a negative-NPV investment, if the investment can be viewed as the first stage of a very promising strategy. Second, although the evaluation of a firm's business strategy requires considerable judgment on the part of senior management, strategic decisions are not purely qualitative. Indeed, as we will show, the quantitative tools we have used to evaluate individual investment projects are also useful for evaluating investment strategies. And third, not all organizations have the same capabilities regarding the exercise of strategic options. Prior to embarking on a strategy with valuable embedded options, executives must determine, as best they can, whether their organizations will have the financial flexibility and the managerial wherewithal to appropriately exercise the options when the time comes.

12.1 INTRODUCTION

Faced with a saturated market for burgers in the United States, McDonald's Corporation changed its growth strategy in the 1990s to focus on global markets, and now has restaurants in over 100 countries. Changing demographics produced another shift of focus in the 1990s toward developing new types of restaurants for the U.S. market, including the acquisition of the Chipotle Mexican food restaurant chain in

1998.[1] Under McDonald's ownership, Chipotle grew to more than 450 restaurants in 22 states, when in January 2006 McDonald's spun off a significant portion of Chipotle's equity in an initial public offering.

McDonald's, like most successful companies, follows a flexible strategy that allows it to adapt to changing business conditions. Does this sound familiar? It should. McDonald's' flexible strategy entails the exercise of important options that are embedded in the investments that it makes. Indeed, the original Chipotle acquisition included an important option to abandon the strategy, if it proved to be unsuccessful, as well as options to speed up or slow down the rollout of new restaurants in the chain. The strategy could also have included options to redesign the restaurants, moving them upscale by expanding the menu to include more expensive items or moving them downscale by offering more affordable menu items.

In Chapter 11 we focused on the analysis of well-defined individual investment projects. In this chapter we consider the murkier concept of corporate strategy. More specifically, we will discuss the evaluation of strategic opportunities. Such opportunities are less straightforward to evaluate than well-defined projects because the actual investments materialize out of initiating strategies that cannot be precisely defined and involve investments that take place in the distant future. For example, DuPont may want to expand its presence in the specialty chemical business in Brazil, or Toyota may decide that there are long-term opportunities to sell heavy-duty trucks in South America. These strategies have as their components individual investment projects (e.g., individual chemical plants or truck assembly plants) that can be evaluated as we did in the previous chapters. However, in addition, companies must evaluate these investments within the context of an *overall* strategy that includes investments that may or may not take place in the future.

We begin the chapter with a brief discussion of the origins of positive-NPV investments. Up to this point we have taken the characteristics of the investments as given. The evaluation of an investment strategy, however, must examine the extent to which investment choices position the firm in ways that allow it to exploit investment opportunities in the future. In other words, we must consider not only the NPV of the individual investment, but also the extent to which the investment creates future opportunities, or options, to invest in the future.

To illustrate these ideas and to demonstrate how the value of these future opportunities can be quantified, we will consider a detailed example of an investment strategy involving the construction of a series of coal-fired power plants. The plants utilize a "green" strategy in the form of a new clean-burning technology for controlling plant emissions. The initial plant is a negative-NPV project, but it enables the firm to launch what may be a promising strategy of building successive plants, which may become profitable as the technology and construction methods are perfected. Within the context of this example, we will show how companies can use the real option analysis developed in the last chapter to evaluate a business strategy.

---

[1]Sandra Guy, "McDonald's Plans Big Chipotle Boost," *Chicago Sun Times* (May 24, 2002).

12.2 WHERE DO POSITIVE-NPV INVESTMENTS COME FROM?

Good investment opportunities do not simply fall from the heavens. In fact, projects with positive NPVs all share one common characteristic: They leverage some type of *comparative advantage* that the investing firm has over its competitors. The advantage for the firm could be, among others, the ability to produce a product more cheaply, exclusive access to customers, or strong brand recognition that allows the firm to charge a premium for its products and services. Whatever the source, every project must be founded on some type of comparative advantage in order to be successful.

But where do these capabilities come from? One possibility is that they come from more capable managers, which is of course a correct, but not particularly helpful, observation. Alternatively, we can view these capabilities as synergies with the firm's existing businesses that arise because the firm's organization has developed better know-how and better business relationships from past experiences. In other words, opportunities today are likely to have arisen from investment choices that were made in the past. Viewed from this perspective, we can define a good strategic opportunity as *an investment that enhances a firm's capabilities*, generating comparative advantages that create positive-NPV investment opportunities in the future.

If positive-NPV investments do, in fact, come from capabilities that are developed

> ### Did you know?
>
> **Who is the largest automaker?**
>
> Since establishing manufacturing operations in the United States, Toyota (soon to be the number one automaker in the world) has steadily increased its market share while the U.S. automakers have lost market share. Specifically, Toyota's market share in 1990 was 7.6%; it was 12.2% by the end of 2004. By year-end 2006 GM barely clung to its top position with 9.17 million units sold in 2005, while Toyota projects it will sell 9.42 million vehicles in 2007.
>
>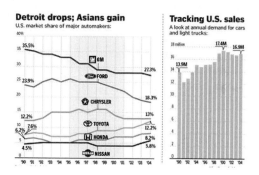
>
> *Sources: Christine Tierney, Detroit News (January 5, 2005), and Malcolm Berko, "GM Clings to Its Ranking as World's Top Automaker," BeaconNewsOnline.com, http://www.suburbanchicagonews.com/beaconnews/business/*

as a result of prior investments, then it is important that when evaluating an investment opportunity, we account for two factors: (1) how the investment contributes directly to the firm's cash flows, as well as (2) how the investment contributes to the firm's capabilities. For example, does the investment provide access to new markets that can be exploited in other ways? Does the investment allow the firm to build business relationships or create alliances that are likely to be valuable in the future? Does the investment generate new technologies that can be applied to other businesses in the future?

It is not difficult to come up with examples of investment projects that create capabilities that are likely to be exploited in subsequent projects. This is frequently true whenever a firm enters a new market. For example, when Toyota initially started assembling its Camry line of automobiles in the United States (the plant was located in Georgetown, Kentucky, and opened production in 1988), significant costs made the start-up assembly plant very costly. However, this initial experience made it easier for Toyota to get permits and attract workers as it added an additional 11 plants by 2005. Moreover, Toyota's expanded presence in the United States, and the fact that Toyota was employing U.S. workers, may have enhanced the Toyota brand in the U.S. market, making it easier for Toyota to sell cars there—even cars built in Japan. In summary, the original Kentucky plant contributed to the value of Toyota by enhancing the firm's capabilities in a way that allowed it to initiate subsequent positive-NPV investments.

A second example is Wal-Mart's foray into the grocery business. One should first note that Wal-Mart's ability to enter this business would not have been possible if it had not first acquired the expertise to mass-market merchandise from its years as a discount retailer. However, despite Wal-Mart's expertise, it is unlikely that its initial investment in the grocery business was a positive-NPV investment if viewed in isolation. Rather, the initial investment was probably viewed as a learning experience that gave the organization the expertise to pursue a much larger investment in this business if the opportunity looked sufficiently attractive. In other words, the initial stores could be viewed as an investment that gave Wal-Mart the option, but not the obligation, to enter a very large grocery market.

> **Did you know?**
>
> **How does Wal-Mart rank as a grocer ?**
>
> Wal-Mart began selling groceries in its stores in 1988 and by 2002 became the nation's leading grocer with more than $53 billion in grocery sales.
>
> *Source: Patricia Callahan and Ann Zimmerman, "Wal-Mart, after remaking discount retailing, now nation's largest grocery chain," Wall Street Journal (May 31, 2003).*

12.3 VALUING A STRATEGY WITH STAGED INVESTMENTS

It is useful to start our discussion by looking at the movie business and considering an important difference between romantic comedies and superhero action movies. Although these movie genres differ along a number of dimensions, from our perspective, the relevant difference is that successful superhero movies (for example, those featuring Spiderman, Batman, and Superman) result in sequels, but romantic comedies generally do not. Hence, a romantic comedy can be evaluated as a single investment with traditional DCF analysis. However, if you want to evaluate the script of, say, a Ratman action movie (e.g., a bizarre lab experiment creates a super-strong and intelligent rat that fights crime, trades options, and gets the girl), then you must evaluate an overall strategy, since in the unlikely event that the movie is successful, there will be sequels, cartoons, toys, etc. What this means is that a studio may be willing to produce the Ratman movie even if its NPV is negative, because by producing the movie, the studio is in effect buying an option on a series of projects.

The example that follows illustrates the distinction between a single investment and an investment strategy and demonstrates that in some situations companies should take on negative-NPV projects, because doing so allows them to initiate a positive-NPV strategy. This example also illustrates three of the most important characteristics of a good investment strategy:

- First, the strategy allows the firm to develop relatively unique capabilities that cannot be easily replicated by competitors.
- Second, the strategy can be abandoned in later stages if economic conditions turn out to be unfavorable.
- Finally, the strategy can be scaled up in later stages if economic conditions turn out to be favorable.

Description of Vespar's New Coal Technology

Vespar Energy, Inc., is a (hypothetical) Houston-based diversified energy company that has acquired a new "green" technology for generating electricity using high-sulfur-content coal that pollutes substantially less than other coal-burning technologies. Typically, coal-fired plants that use low-quality soft coal must have very expensive anti-pollution equipment, called *scrubbers*, to reduce the pollutants they emit into the atmosphere. Vespar's proprietary technology promises to reduce these costs dramatically.

However, since the technology is new, Vespar anticipates it will not be able to capture the cost savings potential of the new technology in the first plant it builds. Instead, the company will need to develop capabilities and knowledge that it will acquire through the construction and operation of multiple plants over several years. In fact, by Vespar's calculations, the first plant clearly has a negative NPV when viewed in isolation. However, the company wants to view this plant as part of a larger strategy, and the challenge facing management is the evaluation of this larger strategy. Let's look at the analysis first in isolation and then as part of an overall strategy.

Stand-Alone Project Analysis of the Initial Plant

Panel a of Table 12-1 presents Vespar's estimates of the revenues, expenses, and cash flows of the initial power plant. An analysis of the present value of the plant's cash flows based on an 8% cost of capital indicates that the plant should be valued at $320 million. However, the company's analysts have estimated that the cost of building the

Table 12-1 NPV Analysis of Building the First Coal-Fired Power Plant

Panel a. Cash Flow Projections

	1	2	3	4	5	6	7	8	9	10
Revenues	$ 500,000,000	$ 507,500,000	$ 515,112,500	$ 522,839,188	$ 530,681,775	$ 538,642,002	$ 546,721,632	$ 554,922,456	$ 563,246,293	$ 571,694,988
Operating and maintenance (includes fuel)	(434,671,731)	(431,843,463)	(429,015,194)	(426,186,926)	(423,358,657)	(420,530,388)	(417,702,120)	(414,873,851)	(412,045,582)	(409,217,314)
Fixed operating expenses	(95,000,000)	(95,000,000)	(95,000,000)	(95,000,000)	(95,000,000)	(95,000,000)	(95,000,000)	(95,000,000)	(95,000,000)	(95,000,000)
EBIT	$ (29,671,731)	$ (19,343,463)	$ (8,902,694)	$ 1,652,262	$ 12,323,118	$ 23,111,614	$ 34,019,512	$ 45,048,605	$ 56,200,711	$ 67,477,674
Less: Taxes	8,901,519	5,803,039	2,670,808	(495,679)	(3,696,936)	(6,933,484)	(10,205,854)	(13,514,582)	(16,860,213)	(20,243,302)
NOPAT	$ (20,770,212)	$ (13,540,424)	$ (6,231,886)	$ 1,156,583	$ 8,626,183	$ 16,178,130	$ 23,813,659	$ 31,534,024	$ 39,340,498	$ 47,234,372
Plus: Depreciation expense	45,000,000	45,000,000	45,000,000	45,000,000	45,000,000	45,000,000	45,000,000	45,000,000	45,000,000	45,000,000
Less: CAPEX	(5,000,000)	(5,075,000)	(5,151,125)	(5,228,392)	(5,306,818)	(5,386,420)	(5,467,216)	(5,549,225)	(5,632,463)	(5,716,950)
Firm free cash flow	$ 19,229,788	$ 26,384,576	$ 33,616,989	$ 40,928,191	$ 48,319,365	$ 55,791,710	$ 63,346,442	$ 70,984,799	$ 78,708,035	$ 86,517,422
Present value of firm free cash flows	$ 320,000,000									
Less: Construction costs	(450,000,000)									
Net present value	$ (130,000,000)									

Panel b. Breakeven Sensitivity Analysis

Value Driver (variable)	Requisite Change to Make NPV = 0 (holding all else constant)
Cost of capital (8%)	Reduce by 71% to 2.33%.
Operating and maintenance expenses	Decrease to 93.47% of projected totals.
Annual rate of decrease in operating and maintenance expenses	Increase the rate of decline in operating and maintenance expenses through time by a factor of three.
Fixed operating expenses	Decrease to $27.677 million from $95 million per year.
Revenues	Increase the level of revenues across all years by 5%.

first plant is approximately $450 million, which means that the NPV of the initial plant turns out to be negative (i.e., −$130 million).

Panel b of Table 12-1 shows sensitivity analysis of the several key drivers of the project's NPV. This analysis suggests that very dramatic changes in the anticipated values of the key value drivers are needed to produce even a zero NPV for the plant. For example, the cost of capital would have to be reduced from 8% to 2.33% (about 71%) before the project would offer a zero NPV. Alternatively, a zero NPV can be achieved if the variable operating expenses are reduced to 93.47% of their expected value.

The key observation we can make at this point is the following: As a stand-alone project, the clean coal–fired plant is clearly unacceptable. But what if the project is viewed as the first stage of an investment strategy?

Analyzing Projects as a Part of a Strategy

The Vespar executives proposing the plant argue that the firm should take the investment, despite its negative NPV, for *strategic* reasons. They maintain that by being an early mover with this technology, Vespar will achieve significant cost advantages relative to its competitors, and with these cost advantages, the firm will be very well positioned to generate significant profits in the future if market conditions change in a way that favors coal-generated electricity. The CEO finds this strategic argument somewhat convincing, but would like to see a more quantitative analysis of the strategic rationale for taking a negative-NPV project. He likes the story, but is unwilling to invest several hundred million dollars based only on an analysis that, although plausible-sounding, is not backed up by hard numbers.

In response to the CEO's request, the managers proposing the project develop a more detailed strategic analysis. Specifically, they explicitly consider the possibility of constructing a series of power plants over the next four years, beginning with the initial plant this year. As the managers explain, each year can be viewed as a separate phase of the strategy's rollout since the firm will reevaluate its plans annually before launching the construction of more plants. The plan recognizes that at the end of each of the next four years, the firm has the option, but not the obligation, to continue with its strategy. As we will see, the value created by this strategy comes from these options.

Details of the Plan

When evaluating an investment strategy, analysts need to make a number of assumptions. For example, the analysts know that the costs of building the plants are likely to decline significantly as they gain experience but are unlikely to know exactly how much the cost per plant is likely to decline. They also know that they will be able to ramp up the building process, but this is also a function of unknown economic conditions that are difficult to predict. The "art" of evaluating a strategy is in the initial stage of analysis, where the analysts make certain assumptions that allow them to evaluate the investment strategy.

Table 12-2   Vespar's Power Plant Rollout Strategy

Rollout Phase of the Strategy (construction beginning in Year x)	Estimated Cost of Plant Construction (per plant)	Number of Plants to Be Built
Phase I (Year 0)	$450 million	1 plant
Phase II (Year 1)	$375 million	2 plants
Phase III (Year 2)	$350 million	2 plants
Phase IV (Year 3)	$320 million	6 plants
Phase V (Year 4)	$320 million	6 plants

Vespar's executives must first make assumptions about the firm's ability to build these plants in the future. Specifically, based on discussions with their engineers, they assume that the engineering staff will have their hands full designing and constructing one plant in the first year (Year 0) of the strategy. However, when this plant is completed, the engineers believe that they can build two plants simultaneously in Year 1, two more plants in Year 2, and by Year 3 they can ramp up to build six plants per year. Moreover, the analysts estimate that with the benefit of their greater experience, as well as economies of scale associated with building multiple plants, the cost of constructing each successive plant will decline over time. The assumed per plant construction costs are summarized in Table 12-2.

Note that the cost estimates for the plants are based on the assumption that all plants are built in sequence. It is through the learning that takes place in constructing and operating the plants that the cost of construction is driven down over time.

The investment strategy described in the above table can be evaluated in terms of a sequence of options using the following four-step procedure:

Step 1	Use simulation to model the underlying uncertainty in power plant values (i.e., volatility).
Step 2	Use the estimated volatility to construct a binomial lattice of power plant values spanning the strategic planning horizon.
Step 3	Determine when the strategy should be abandoned and when it should be continued.
Step 4	Assess the value of the strategy.

Step 1: *Use simulation to model the underlying uncertainty in power plant values (i.e., volatility).* The first step is to estimate how the values of power plants are expected to evolve over time. To do this, we will use simulations, as described earlier in Chapter 3, to estimate distributions of possible power plant values. In our analysis we assume that primary value drivers come from external forces that impact the value of a coal-fired electric power plant. Examples of these

value drivers include (1) coal and alternative energy prices, (2) pollution laws that affect the costs of competing technologies, (3) economic conditions that affect the overall demand for electrical power, and (4) the entrance of potential competitors who might be developing similar technologies.

The goal of this exercise is to identify the value drivers, determine their volatility, and then determine how the volatility of the value drivers translates into the volatility of power plant values. Although the process used to simulate these values can be quite detailed, the general procedure can be summarized as follows.

First, we specify a model of power plant cash flows that incorporates consideration for the various sources of uncertainty. We then take the initial values of these uncertain variables and calculate the value of a power plant, as we did in our estimate of the first power plant in Table 12-1. We then simulate how these economic variables may change over time, and the way these changes will affect how the value of the power plants evolves over the next four years. By running 10,000 iterations of the simulation experiment, we can estimate the volatility of the year-to-year changes in power plant values.

Step 2: *Use the estimated volatility to construct a binomial lattice of power plant values spanning the strategic planning horizon.* We use the volatility estimate and the procedure discussed earlier in the appendix to Chapter 11 to construct a binomial lattice that summarizes the value of a power plant at the end of each year in the planning horizon. Intuitively, what we are doing is taking a relatively complex distribution of future values and summarizing it with a simpler distribution, which will be easier to work with. The objective of our analysis at this point is to develop a binomial lattice that provides a reasonable representation of the uncertainty in the value of future power plants.

Step 3: *Determine when the strategy should be abandoned and when it should be continued.* We calculate the NPV of constructing a new plant at each node in the lattice as the difference between the value of a plant and the cost of constructing it. The value of continuing the strategy is the value of building the new plant plus the expected value of continuing the strategy until the next period. The expected value of continuing the strategy is never negative, since the firm always has the option to abandon the strategy in the future if it has a negative value. This means that one will never turn down a positive-NPV project for strategic reasons. The interesting cases that we will consider are ones where the current plants have negative NPVs, but the strategy has a positive expected value.

Step 4: *Assess the value of the strategy.* Once we have analyzed each node in the decision tree to determine when it is optimal to abandon, we are ready to place a value on the investment strategy.

We will not provide the details of the simulation described in Step 1, but instead will focus on the end product of this exercise described in Step 2, which consists of the expected present values of the power plant cash flows (i.e., estimated plant values) in each node in the binomial lattice. These estimates, described in Panel a of Table 12-3, illustrate that these values are quite uncertain over the four-year planning

CHAPTER 12 ■ Strategic Options: Evaluating Strategic Opportunities

Table 12-3 Naïve Analysis of Vespar's Investment Strategy

Panel a. Present Values of Future Plant Cash Flows ($ Millions)

	Years				
	0	**1**	**2**	**3**	**4**
					$ 467.93
				$ 425.52	
			$ 386.96		398.74
		$ 351.89		362.61	
	$ 320.00		329.75		339.79
		299.86		308.99	
			280.99		289.55
				263.31	
					246.74

The number in each node represents the present value of the expected future cash flows resulting from building and operating a single power plant in that year.

Panel b. Net Present Values of Each Phase of the Investment Strategy[a] ($ Millions)

	Years				
	0	**1**	**2**	**3**	**4**
					$ 887.59
				$ 633.14	
			$ 73.92		472.47
		$ (46.22)		255.65	
	$ (130.00)		(40.51)		118.73
		(150.28)		(66.04)	
			(138.02)		(182.71)
				(340.16)	
					(439.58)

The number found at each node represents the sum of the NPVs of all the plants constructed in each year. The present values of the future cash flows for each plant in each phase are found in panel a above, and the number of plants built and the cost of each are found below, e.g., for the highest-value node in Year 4:

$$\text{NPV} = (\$467.93\text{ m} - \$320\text{ m}) \times 6$$
$$= \$147.93\text{ m} \times 6 = \$887.59\text{ m}$$

	0	1	2	3	4
Number of plants to be built	1	2	2	6	6
Cost of constructing each plant	$ 450	$ 375	$ 350	$ 320	$ 320
Expected NPVs for each phase[b]	$ (130.00)	$ (98.25)	$ (36.28)	$ 107.73	$ 144.96
PV (Year 0) of annual expected NPVs[c]	$ (130.00)	$ (90.97)	$ (31.10)	$ 85.52	$ 106.55
Value (naïve estimate) of the strategy[d]	**$ (60.01)**				

Notes:

[a]The NPV at each node in the tree is calculated as follows:

$$\text{NPV} = \begin{pmatrix} \text{Value of} & & \text{Cost of} \\ \text{Plant Future} & - & \text{Constructing} \\ \text{Cash Flows} & & \text{a Plant} \end{pmatrix} \times \begin{array}{c} \text{Number of} \\ \text{Plants Built} \\ \text{in the Period} \end{array}$$

[b]The expected NPV for each year is calculated as a weighted average of the possible NPVs using the estimated probability of an up or down value for the future cash flows. In this instance management estimates the probability of an up and down move in value of project cash flows to equal 50%. Thus, for Year 2 the expected NPV = .5 × ($46.22 m) + .5 × ($150.28 m) = ($98.25 m). The probabilities associated with each node in the tree are found below:

		Years			
0	**1**	**2**	**3**	**4**	
				6.25%	
			12.50%		
		25.00%		25.00%	
	50.00%		37.50%		
100.00%		50.00%		37.50%	
	50.00%		37.50%		
		25.00%		25.00%	
			12.50%		
				6.25%	
100%	100%	100%	100%	100%	

[c]PV of the annual NPVs equals the present value today of the expected NPVs of the five phases of the investment strategy (e.g., for phase I the present value is equal to ($98.25 m)/$(1.08)^1$ = ($90.97 m).

[d]The value of the strategy is equal to the sum of the present values of all the NPVs for each of the five phases of the strategy rollout corresponding to Years 0 through 4.

horizon. For example, in the most favorable node in Year 4, the present value of the expected cash flows generated from clean-coal plants is $467.93 million. However, this is clearly a very rosy case, and nodes where power prices are low and the clean-coal plants have values less than $300 million are also quite possible.

A Naïve Static Analysis of the Value of Vespar's Strategy

Before carrying out Steps 3 and 4 of our valuation procedure, we first calculate the NPV of the strategy with the traditional ("naïve") approach. This approach assumes that the strategy cannot be abandoned, which means that if it is initiated in Year 0, it will be carried out in all nodes of the binomial lattice. The relevant cash flows in this NPV analysis are the average, across nodes, of the NPVs of the power plants that are built in each year (averaged across all possible nodes). Intuitively, we are valuing the strategy as if Vespar sells the power plants after they are built for the present values of their cash flows, thereby generating a cash flow to Vespar equal to the NPVs of the power plants. These "cash flows" are then discounted to the present to determine the NPV of the strategy in Year 0.

Panel b of Table 12-3 calculates the NPVs of the power plants that are built in each node by subtracting the plant construction costs from the present values of the plant's future cash flows, and multiplying this difference by the number of power plants built each year. Based on these numbers, we can calculate the NPV that we expect to generate in each year of the strategy. The expected NPVs in each year are calculated by weighting the NPVs of the power plants in each node by the probability of reaching that node, and calculating the weighted average. We assume that at each node, the probability of moving either up or down in value is 50% (see footnote b in Table 12-3). For example, in Year 1 the expected NPV is −$98.25 million, which represents a probability-weighted average of the two possible NPV outcomes for that year.

From Table 12-3 we see that in the initial years of the strategy's rollout, the expected NPVs are negative. However, over time, as the cost of developing the plants declines, the NPVs become positive. Specifically, we see that the expected values in Years 0 through 4 are −$130 million, −$98.25 million, −$36.28 million, $107.73 million, and $144.96 million, respectively. In Year 3 the NPV becomes positive. However, discounting these expected NPVs back to the present using the 8% cost of capital that Vespar uses for projects of this type yields an estimated value for the naïve strategy of a negative $60.01 million. This large negative NPV indicates that if the strategy is inflexible, as the above analysis assumes, the company should not undertake it.

An Option Pricing Approach for Evaluating Vespar's Strategy

We learned in Chapter 11 that the option to abandon an investment can provide an important source of value. The naïve analysis that we just did accounted for the fact that the scale of the project could be increased (in fact it assumed that the scale increased regardless of the value of the plant in the future). However, the analysis ignored the possibility that the strategy could be abandoned in situations where the outlook was especially unfavorable. In this section we will explicitly consider this abandonment option.

To value the option to abandon the strategy, we must first determine *when* the strategy should, in fact, be abandoned. Our analysis of this decision closely follows our analysis of the abandonment decision in Chapter 11. As a first step, we change the probabilities of reaching each node in the binomial tree found in Panel a of Table 12-3 from the actual probabilities to the risk-adjusted (i.e., risk-neutral) probabilities, so that we can calculate certainty-equivalent rather than expected cash flows. Let's assume that the risk-neutral probability for the up state is 0.48, and the probability for the down state is 0.52. Note that increasing the probability of the low state and decreasing the probability of the high state converts the expected cash flows to certainty equivalent cash flows that should be discounted using the risk-free rate of interest of 5%, rather than the 8% risk-adjusted rate that was used in the last section.

To value the strategy at the current date, we must first determine the value of the strategy at each node in the binomial lattice, as we did in Chapter 11, by solving the tree backwards, step by step: We start by calculating the values of the strategies at each of the nodes at the end of Year 4, and work back to today. Panel a of Table 12-4 contains these values. For example, in Year 4 the value of the strategy generated by the six power plants built in that year is simply the sum of the NPVs of the power plants built at that date if the NPV is positive, and is zero otherwise (since at the last date negative-NPV power plants will not be built). Hence, as we see in Panel a of Table 12-4, the strategy generates positive values in the three highest-value nodes in Year 4, but generates zero value in the two lower-value nodes in which the NPVs of constructing the plants are negative (Panel b of Table 12-3). Given these Year 4 values, we can now calculate the values of the strategy for each node in Year 3.

The value of the strategy at each node in Year 3 is equal to the sum of the NPVs of the plants built in Year 3 plus the present value of the payoffs to the strategy in Year 4. For example, consider the highest-value node in Year 3, where the value of the strategy equals \$1,272.11 million. This value is calculated as follows:

$$
\begin{pmatrix} \text{Value of the Investment} \\ \text{Strategy in Highest-Value} \\ \text{Node of Year 3} \end{pmatrix} = \begin{pmatrix} \text{NPV of Plants} \\ \text{Built in} \\ \text{Year 3} \end{pmatrix} + \begin{pmatrix} \text{Present Value} \\ \text{of Certainty-Equivalent} \\ \text{Value of NPVs in Year 4} \end{pmatrix}
$$

$$
= \$633.14 \text{ million} + e^{-.05}(\$887.59 \text{ million} \times .48 + \$472.47 \text{ million} \times .52) = \$1,272.11 \text{ million}
$$

Obviously, the investment in the six new plants *should* be made at the end of Year 3 if the highest-value node is reached.

Let's now consider the lowest-value node found in Year 3. In this node the NPV of building six new plants (Panel b of Table 12-3) is negative (that is, −\$340.16 million). Consequently, the only way that Vespar should build these plants is if the discounted value of the certainty-equivalent NPVs in Year 4 is greater than \$340.16 million. However, the possible NPVs for investments in Year 4, following a realization equal to the lowest-value node in Year 3, are both negative. Consequently, Vespar should abandon the strategy if this low-value node is reached in Year 3. One can similarly show that the strategy should be optimally abandoned in the second-to-lowest node in Year 3, and as a consequence of the abandonment in these two lowest nodes in Year 3, the strategy should also be abandoned in the lowest node in Year 2.

Table 12-4   Dynamic Analysis of Vespar's Investment Strategy

Panel a. Value of Continuing to Invest ($ Millions)

	Years				
	0	1	2	3	4
Each node contains the discounted value of investing in the subsequent period (weighted by the risk-neutral probability of each node) plus the NPV of investing in that current period.					$887.59
				$1,272.11	
			$916.97		472.47
		$472.15		530.10	
	$85.59		201.53		118.73
		0		0	
			0		0
				0	
					0
					0

Panel b. Net Present Values of Each Phase of the Investment Strategy[a] ($ Millions)

Phase of the Strategy Rollout	I	II	III	IV	V
Year	0	1	2	3	4
The value in each node is the NPV of investing in the plants built in that period or zero if continuing to invest is not optimal. The nodes in which the strategy is abandoned are determined in panel a.					$887.59
				$633.14	
			$ 73.92		472.47
		($46.22)		255.65	
	($130.00)		(40.51)		118.73
		0		0	
			0		0
				0	
					0
Expected NPVs of initiated plants	($130.00)	($23.11)	($1.77)	$175.01	$218.11
PV of annual NPVs (Year 0)[a]	(130.00)	(20.03)	(1.33)	113.91	123.04
Value of the strategy (Year 0)	$85.59				

Panel c. Sensitivity of the Value of the Investment Strategy to the Discount Rate

Discount Rate (k_{WACC})	Value of the Strategy in Year 0
10.0%	$127.99 million
15.0%	88.34 million
20.0%	55.97 million

[a]The discount rate used here is 15.39% and is calculated as the rate that, when used to discount the expected NPVs of all five phases of the strategy back to the present, results in a value of $85.59 (the value estimated using the binomial option valuation method). Since the discount rate cannot be known until we have estimated the value of the strategy using the option pricing approach, the DCF analysis is strictly a tool for presenting the strategy valuation to company executives using a methodology they are familiar with.

The middle node in Year 2 deserves special attention. In this node the NPV of the plants that are built in Year 2 is negative $40.51 million (Panel b of Table 12-3). However, as we will see, because there is a possibility of building very high-NPV plants in the future, the firm should not abandon the strategy in this situation. Following the procedure used earlier to analyze the highest-value node for Year 3, we estimate the value of the strategy at this node (i.e., the NPV of the plant investments plus the present value of the certainty-equivalent value of the plant NPVs built in Year 3) to be $201.53 million (Panel a of Table 12-4):

$$
\begin{pmatrix} \text{Value of the Investment} \\ \text{Strategy for Middle Node} \\ \text{in Year 2} \end{pmatrix} = \begin{pmatrix} \text{NPV of Plants} \\ \text{Built in} \\ \text{Year 2} \end{pmatrix} + \begin{pmatrix} \text{Present Value} \\ \text{of Certainty-Equivalent} \\ \text{Value of NPVs in Year 3} \end{pmatrix}
$$

$$
= (\$40.51 \text{ million}) + e^{-.05}(\$530.1 \text{ million} \times .48
$$
$$
+ \$0 \text{ million} \times .52) = \$201.53 \text{ million}
$$

After rolling back all the branches of the decision tree, we find that the value of the investment strategy at the current date (i.e., in the Year 0 node) is $85.59 million. Consequently, the strategy has significant value, even though the plants built today and in Year 1 (phases I and II) all have negative NPVs. The negative NPVs associated with the initial investments can be viewed as the cost of buying an option to continue a strategy that can potentially create significant value in the future. The strategy will not generate positive-NPV investments with certainty. In some future nodes the NPVs are very negative and the strategy will be abandoned. Indeed, this option to abandon the strategy is what generates its positive value. Without the abandonment option the strategy has a negative $60.01 million value, as we calculated using the naïve or static analysis (as shown in Panel b of Table 12-3), but with the option it has a positive value of $85.59 million calculated using the dynamic analysis (as shown in Table 12-4).

Recapping the Analysis of the Vespar Strategy

It is useful to momentarily step back and reconsider the four-step procedure that we just described. We started by simulating the cash flows under a wide variety of scenarios to estimate the volatility of future "green" coal-fired plant values. We then used this volatility estimate to form a binomial lattice that summarizes the future distribution of these values. Reducing the number of scenarios to those specified in the binomial lattice made it easier for us to describe the underlying uncertainty in the value of a coal-fired plant, which in turn allowed us to determine the scenarios in which it would be optimal to abandon the strategy. After determining the situations in which the strategy is abandoned, we work back through the binomial tree to solve for the value of the strategy.

Using DCF Analysis to Estimate the Value of Vespar's Strategy

To clarify our analysis, it is generally useful to translate the options-based analysis of Vespar's strategy into the language of traditional DCF analysis. In addition to making it easier to communicate the analysis to other executives, it may facilitate a comparison with other strategies. To do this, we recommend that the analyst use the dynamic analysis as a guide to determine conditions under which the strategy should be abandoned. Given these prespecified abandonment nodes, we can then estimate the expected NPV of the power plants that are built in each year by computing the average of the NPVs found in each node where the strategy is not abandoned and setting the NPVs to zero in those nodes where the strategy is abandoned. Once the expected NPVs for each year have been calculated, we can estimate the value of the strategy by discounting them back to the present using an appropriate discount rate.

The DCF approach thus requires that an appropriate discount rate be specified. We earlier suggested that the appropriate cost of capital for building one power plant is 8%, and used this same 8% to discount the cash flows of the naïve strategy. This implicitly assumes that the risks of the strategy and the individual power plants are equivalent, which is quite unlikely. Clearly, an investment strategy that involves building multiple plants over several years is much riskier than an 8% discount rate would suggest. For example, in Panel b of Table 12-4 we see that the rollout phases I and II of the strategy (in Years 0 and 1) call for the commitment of $1.2 billion for the construction of three power plants,[2] all of which have negative NPVs, in the hope that in Year 2 a favorable outcome will occur.

Panel b of Table 12-4 provides a DCF analysis of the proposed investment strategy, which assumes that management has specified that the investment strategy be abandoned *in exactly those nodes* where our option pricing analysis indicates that the strategy should optimally be abandoned. The expected NPV of the plants built in each phase of the strategy are found in Panel b of Table 12-3. For example, these NPVs take on two values in Year 1 (phase II), ($46.22) million and $0.00, each with a 50% probability, which implies that the expected NPV generated in Phase II is ($23.11).[3] Similarly, we can calculate the expected values generated in Phases III through V as ($1.77) million, $175.01 million, and $218.11 million, respectively.

To calculate the NPV of the entire strategy, we must specify an appropriate discount rate. In Panel c of Table 12-4 we calculate the NPV of the strategy using discount rates of 10%, 15%, and 20%. In each case, we find that the NPV of the strategy

---

[2]The plan calls for one plant in Year 1 costing $450 million and two plants in Year 2 that cost $375 million each, for a total of $1.2 billion.

[3]The probability tree reflecting actual binomial probabilities of 50% is found below:

		Years		
0	**1**	**2**	**3**	**4**
				6.25%
			12.50%	
		25.00%		25.00%
	50.00%		37.50%	
100.00%		50.00%		37.50%
	50.00%		37.50%	
		25.00%		25.00%
			12.50%	
				6.25%
100.00%	100.00%	100.00%	100.00%	100.00%

is significantly positive. In addition, we can calculate the discount rate that makes the discounted sum of the expected NPVs for each of the phases of the rollout of the strategy equal the $85.59 million value we estimated in Panel a using the option valuation method. The discount rate that solves this problem is 15.39%, which means that the option pricing approach implicitly assumes that the appropriate discount rate for evaluating the strategy is 15.39%, which seems about right given the risk of the strategy.

The Anatomy of Vespar's Power Plant Strategy

Since this analysis required a number of assumptions, most executives would not approve the strategy based on the preceding analysis without considerable sensitivity analysis. However, before doing the sensitivity analysis, it is useful to step back and consider the features of the power plant strategy that make it attractive. The strategy is clearly very risky, but Vespar has the flexibility to alter the strategy in ways that make the uncertainty an advantage rather than a disadvantage. First, the strategy can be abandoned in those unfavorable scenarios where present and future investment alternatives are not likely to be attractive. Second, the strategy is scalable. Since Vespar can scale up its development efforts and build up to six new power plants in those scenarios where it is attractive to do so, it generates very high NPVs in the most favorable nodes in Years 4 and 5. We use sensitivity analysis to investigate the economic importance of these features.

Sensitivity Analysis of Vespar's Power Plant Strategy

Our analysis of Vespar's strategy for investing in clean-burning coal-fired power plants is based on a number of assumptions that ultimately determine whether the firm should proceed. Consequently, the next stage in the analysis involves an investigation of the impact of the individual assumptions on the final decision to commit to the investment strategy. We explore these assumptions in much the same way that we did earlier for the single-plant investment: In the next section, we perform breakeven sensitivity analysis for each of the key value drivers individually. We follow that with the construction and analysis of a simulation model that incorporates multiple sources of uncertainty simultaneously.

Sensitivity Analysis of the Strategy One Variable at a Time

The first driver to consider involves the *timing* of the investment strategy. What will happen if the planned "ramp-up" of the strategy cannot be accomplished in the four-year time frame?[4] Specifically, we will consider the possibility that Vespar reduces the

---

[4]Recall that the cost estimates for the plants deliberately assume that all plants are built in sequence, because it is through the learning that takes place in constructing and operating the plants that the cost of construction is driven down over time and the costs of operations decline. For example, if this were not the case, Vespar would reject the building of the initial plant or either of the plants in Year 1, since all three plants have negative NPVs.

number of plants that can be built in Years 3 and 4 from six and six to three and four, respectively. If this is the case, the value of the strategy drops dramatically, from $85.59 million to a negative $9.71 million—a decline of $95.3 million![5] Obviously, it is critical that Vespar be able to achieve the planned number of new plants by Years 3 and 4, when the strategy becomes value-enhancing.

A second consideration that is potentially very important to the analysis is the *cost* of constructing each new plant at each phase of the rollout process. Up until this point in our analysis, we treated these construction costs as if they were known. To gain some perspective on the importance of uncertainty about these costs, we consider how big a cost overrun the strategy could withstand before the value of the strategy drops to zero. To do this, we consider the possibility that the cost of constructing plants throughout the rollout of the strategy is increased by 5%. When this is the case, the value of the strategy declines to negative $25.7 million. If we solve for the breakeven cost-overrun percentage, we find that the costs of construction for all of the plants can rise by only 3.98% before the value of the strategy becomes negative. Obviously, the value of the strategy is quite sensitive to the costs of constructing the new plants. Consequently, the expenditure of time and resources refining these estimates is probably warranted.

The remaining value driver we consider in our sensitivity analysis is the *distribution of future plant values*, which were described in the binomial lattice found in Panel a of Table 12-3. Specifically, we consider how the value of the strategy changes if uncertainty about future plant values changes. The plant values specified in our original binomial tree reflect a volatility estimate of .08.[6] If this volatility drops to .0462, the NPV of the investment strategy drops to zero, and if the volatility drops to .04, the value of the strategy declines to a negative $15.56 million. However, if the volatility of plant values is increased to .10, the value of the strategy rises to $139.64 million. Once again, the sensitivity of the strategy's value to the volatility measure suggests that significant time and energy be spent in evaluating this estimate. The key insight here is that higher volatility significantly increases the upside potential for the investment strategy but, because of the option to abandon, has much less of an effect on the downside.

---

[5]This analysis assumes that Vespar undertakes the investment and discovers only at the end of the second year that it can build a maximum of three and four plants in the final two years of the strategy. Of course, if Vespar were aware today of the restrictions on the number of plants that could be built in Years 3 and 4, then the valuation of the strategy would suggest that the plan be abandoned before any investments are made, thus producing a strategy valuation of zero.

[6]We assume a risk-free rate (r) of 5% and a convenience yield (δ) of 3.5%. Using the simulation procedure described in Step 1 and Step 2, we estimate the volatility parameter (σ) as 8%. Given these values, the up move is computed as $u = e^{r-\delta+\sigma} = 1.0997$ and the down move as $u = e^{r-\delta-\sigma} = 0.9370$. It follows that the risk-neutral probability, given by

$$P = \frac{e^{(r-\delta)} - e^{(r-\delta)-\sigma}}{e^{(r-\delta)+\sigma} - e^{(r-\delta)-\sigma}},$$

is equal to 0.48 in the up state.

Simulation Analysis of the Strategy

We learned in Chapter 3 that breakeven sensitivity analysis provides a useful tool for evaluating the importance of changes in key value drivers when taken one at a time. However, if we want to take a broader view of the underlying uncertainty in the outcome of the strategy, we need to construct a simulation model that simultaneously captures the uncertainties surrounding several value drivers.

Table 12-5 presents the underlying assumptions and forecasts used to construct a simulation model of the value of the strategy. Panel a of Table 12-5 defines the two value drivers (construction costs and the present value of future cash flows) and the assumptions that underlie the simulation. Briefly, to capture the uncertainty about the cost of constructing new plants, we consider a multiplicative cost-overrun factor, which is drawn from a triangular distribution with a most likely value of 1, indicating no cost overrun, as well as a minimum and a maximum value.[7] (The specific parameter values are described in Panel a of Table 12-5.) The simulated cost-overrun factors are assumed to be positively correlated over time with a correlation coefficient equal to .90. This means that the simulation accounts for the fact that if there is a cost overrun for plants built in Year 1, there is a very good chance that the costs in later years will also be higher than projected.

The value of the plants at each future date is modeled using the binomial lattice found in Panel a of Table 12-3. However, as we noted in our breakeven sensitivity analysis, the uncertainty underlying these values is captured by the volatility of the returns to the plant investments, which we have assumed to be equal to .08. To incorporate the effects of uncertainty about this estimate, we use a triangular distribution with parameter values of .06, .08, and .15, representing the minimum, most likely, and maximum values of the distribution of the volatility measure.[8]

Each of the iterations of the simulation process calculates a value for the strategy just as we did earlier using the option valuation method. However, with each iteration of the simulation process, we sample different values of each of the value drivers based on their assumed distributions as defined in Panel a of Table 12-5, which leads to a different estimate of the value of the strategy.

The simulation focuses on the NPV of Vespar's strategy based on the assumption that Vespar commits to implementing the strategy by constructing the initial plant in Year 0. Then, after one year, Vespar can decide whether it will construct the second plant depending on market conditions (i.e., the estimated value of the plant cash flows at the end of Year 1), and so forth.

Panel b of Table 12-5 contains the distribution of simulated values for the investment strategy based on 10,000 iterations. Note that a wide range of values for the strategy is generated with this simulation, and in over 73% of them the value is positive. This, of

---

[7]In other words, the cost of constructing a new plant in Year t = Estimated Cost of Constructing a Plant in Year $t \times$ (1 + Percent Cost-Overrun).

[8]Note that since the volatility in power plant prices cannot be inferred from traded financial derivatives, so we have to estimate it using other means. Because there is estimation error in the volatility measure, we incorporate this measure as one of the value drivers in the simulation analysis.

Table 12-5   Simulation Analysis of Vespar's Investment Strategy

Panel a. Assumptions

Value Drivers	Assumptions Underlying the Simulation

Plant Construction Costs

Example: Plant construction cost in Year 0

    $450 million × Cost-overrun Factor

Cost-overrun factor has a triangular distribution with a minimum value of .99, a most likely value of 1.00, and a maximum value of 1.05.

Distribution of Cost-Overrun Factors

Assumption—Triangular (parameters below)[a]

	Year 0	Year 1	Year 2	Year 3	Year 4
Min	0.99	0.95	0.92	0.90	0.87
Most Likely	1.00	1.00	1.00	1.00	1.00
Max	1.05	1.10	1.15	1.20	1.25

Value of Future Plant Cash Flows

The volatility of the annual rates of return to investing in the coal-fired power plants is the primary driver of the present value of future power plant cash flows.

Distribution of Volatility

Assumption—Triangular (parameters below)

Min = .06, Most likely = .08, and Max = .15

Distribution of the # of Plants for Years 3 and 4

Assumption—Discrete (same for both years)[b]

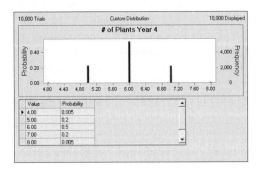

---

[a]The cost-overrun factors are assumed to be highly correlated with a coefficient of .90 from year to year.

course, means that in 26.26% of the simulation trials the strategy generates a negative NPV, with the maximum negative NPV being −$152 million. However, the maximum NPV of $539.47 million is even more impressive. Again, the takeaway message from this analysis is that although the NPV of the strategy is positive given our *best* assumptions, we can envision plausible sets of assumptions under which the strategy generates a negative NPV as well as other plausible sets of assumptions under which the NPV is very large.

    Panel c of Table 12-5 presents a tornado chart, a tool used for organizing information from a sensitivity analysis that we introduced in Chapter 3. The tool shows the sensitivity of the strategy's valuation to changes in each of the assumptions

Table 12-5 (continued)

Panel b. Simulated Distribution of Strategy Values for Today

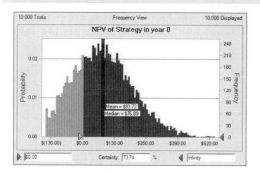

The "certainty" box contains the percentage of the area under the distribution of NPV that lies above 0. Correspondingly, the likelihood that the NPV of the strategy would be negative is equal to 26.26% or (1 − 73.74%).

The mean NPV of the strategy is not equal to the value calculated earlier for two reasons: First, the simulation incorporates distributions for some value drivers whose expected values differ slightly from the expected values used in the prior analysis. Second, we incorporate consideration for correlation among the value drivers that was not incorporated into the earlier analysis.

Panel c. Sensitivity Analysis—Tornado Chart

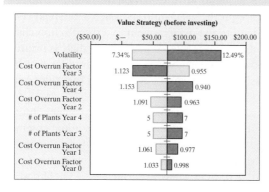

The tornado chart contains estimates of the value of the strategy today (NPV [Year 0]), where each assumption or value driver (listed down the left-hand side of the chart) is set equal to its 10th- and 90th-percentile value, respectively. The assumptions that have the greatest impact on the value of the strategy are placed at the top of the chart (e.g., the volatility metric), followed by each of the assumptions in decreasing order in terms of their effect on the value of the strategy.

[b]The number of plants constructed in Year 4 is assumed to be highly correlated (correlation = .90) with the number that can be built in Year 3.

underlying the valuation. Specifically, the tornado chart contains estimates of the value of the strategy today (NPV in Year 0), measured on the horizontal axis at the top of the chart, where each assumption or value driver (listed down the left-hand side of the chart) is set equal to its 10th- and 90th-percentile value from their own distributions, respectively. For example, if the volatility measure equals its 90th-percentile value (which is 12.49%), while holding all other variable values constant, then the value of the strategy is equal to $159.88 million. Correspondingly, if the cost-overrun factor for Year 3 were equal to its 10th-percentile value (which is .955), then the value of the strategy rises to $118.64 million. The next most influential variable in the analysis is the cost-overrun variable in Year 4, and so forth.

Consequently, we can see from the tornado chart that the key value drivers in the analysis (based on the parameter estimates used by Vespar's analyst) are the volatility in the changes in the present value of plant cash flows, followed by the costs of building the plants in Years 3 and 4, and so forth. This type of analysis can help managers determine where to focus their efforts—both in terms of forecasts made prior to undertaking the investment, and of monitoring efforts made after the investment strategy has been initiated.

12.4 STRATEGIC VALUE WHEN THE FUTURE IS NOT WELL DEFINED

The Vespar case provides a structured example where the future investments that comprise the strategy can be identified with a high degree of certainty. In cases such as this we have shown that a quantitative options type of analysis can be very useful. However, it is often the case that it is quite difficult to identify the relevant strategic options in advance—a fact that makes a quantitative valuation much more difficult. Who knew, for example, that Dell's foray in the 1980s into the sale of personal computers directly to the end user would lead to the development of a distribution channel that could be adapted to the sale of computer-related peripherals such as printers and even flat-panel television sets today? Similarly, when Apple Computer first began developing its handheld digital assistant, who could have guessed that this would lead to the iPod phenomenon?

The point here is that strategic investments often end up creating valuable future investment opportunities that are simply not knowable at the time the initial commitment to the strategy is made. What, then, can the analyst hope to do when looking for valuable strategic options? This is clearly a difficult question, however, we believe that there are some key value drivers that, if present, suggest an increased likelihood of valuable strategic options. Recognizing the situations where strategic options are likely to be found is the first step in attempting to incorporate consideration their value in the analysis of new investment proposals.

Which Investments Generate Strategic Options?

To illustrate how strategic options can be both very valuable and difficult to define in advance, let's consider the move by Heinz, Inc., into India in 1994. At this time, the market potential in India was expected to be large but highly uncertain and undeveloped. India had close to 350 million urban middle-class consumers, who were increasingly demanding more variety in processed food products. Only 2% of food output consisted of processed food at this time, suggesting that the country was ripe for more investments in food processing. However, despite this potential, it was difficult to precisely define an initial investment project that could be viewed as having a positive NPV when viewed in isolation. Any particular project faced a high likelihood of failure, but with time and experience, the Heinz management felt confident the initial investment would lead to valuable follow-on investment opportunities.

Heinz made its strategic entry into Indian markets by acquiring the consumer-products division of Glaxo (India). Although some of the acquired consumer-product brands were profitable, the strategy did not produce the market penetration in India that Heinz had hoped to achieve. However, based on what it learned from its failures, Heinz changed its strategy to offer smaller package sizes called *sachets* that had low unit prices that appealed to lower-income buyers. This strategy was successful in helping attract new customers who had been unwilling to try the products earlier.

We can generalize from Heinz's initial experiences in the Indian market to identify three primary drivers of strategic option value.

Driver #1: *High uncertainty combined with strategic flexibility is a potent formula for value creation.* Heinz's entry into the Indian market offered highly uncertain but potentially very profitable results. This situation illustrates the following point. To the extent that higher uncertainty implies greater upside potential, it increases the value of a multi-stage investment strategy. Very simply, if the implementation of the strategy is flexible, the firm can limit the costs associated with bad outcomes and capitalize on the benefits of good outcomes.

Driver #2: *The strategy creates relatively unique capabilities.* Since projects with high NPVs can arise only when there is limited competition, firms should develop capabilities that distinguish them from their competitors. Heinz had an internationally recognized brand, but needed to tailor it to local tastes. By getting into India early and developing a reputation for product quality, Heinz might expect to develop a brand within India that can be used in a wide range of products. In other words, developing a brand can be viewed as the first stage of an investment strategy that can lead to a multitude of positive-NPV investments in the future.

Driver #3: *The acquired capability leads to investment opportunities that are scalable.* We have already stressed that uncertainty creates value only when it is linked to flexibility, and perhaps the most important flexibility is the flexibility to expand. Given the size and growth potential of the Indian market, it was clear that the Heinz investment was clearly scalable.

How Does Corporate Structure Affect Strategic Option Value?

Up to this point in our discussion we have focused on strategic investment opportunities without analyzing the firm itself. Indeed, positive-NPV investment opportunities arise as a result of a marriage between opportunity and the firm's capability to capitalize on those opportunities. As we discuss below, capability is likely to be related to characteristics of the firm's financial structure, its workforce, and its past investment choices.

Choice #1: *Financial flexibility.* A good credit rating can enhance the value of a firm's strategic options for a couple of reasons. First, a firm with a good credit rating may be better positioned to quickly take advantage of opportunities when they are presented, without having to find financial backers. Moreover, a firm with financial resources is less likely to be pressured to invest too soon, when the option to wait is valuable.

Although financial flexibility increases the value of a firm's strategic options, this does not mean that firms should not use debt financing. Indeed, as we discussed in Chapter 4, because of the tax deductibility of interest expenses, a firm's WACC declines as it includes more debt in its capital structure. In addition, financial flexibility may allow a poorly managed firm to make bad choices that reduce a firm's value. Indeed, financial distress, which severely limits a firm's flexibility, can sometimes enforce a discipline on a firm that makes it more likely that the firm will exercise its options to abandon bad projects in a timely manner.

Choice #2: Workforce flexibility. Firms with more flexible labor forces can move quickly to capitalize on opportunities as they become available, and can more easily abandon underperforming investments when it is optimal to do so. Firms with highly flexible workforces will offer affirmative responses to the following questions: Do individuals rotate through different jobs as part of their training so that they can later be redeployed to where they can be of greatest value? Do employees have a broad education that allows them to pick up new skills, or do they tend to have relatively narrow skills that limit their flexibility? Does the firm have flexible work rules? Inflexible work rules imposed either by unions or government regulations are likely to limit a firm's ability to optimally exercise its strategic options. Along this dimension, a U.S. firm, which generally has more flexible work rules, is likely to be better positioned to optimally exercise strategic options than a French or Italian firm, which is likely to be subject to more governmental and regulatory restrictions.

Choice #3: Diversification. A large and growing literature discusses the advantages and disadvantages of diversification. For the most part, this literature discusses a trade-off between the benefits of reducing risk through diversification and the costs associated with managers getting involved in investments that may be outside their areas of expertise. To the growing list of plusses and minuses of diversification, we would like to add the possibility that a diversified firm may have increased flexibility that allows its management to exercise valuable strategic options.

To illustrate the issues surrounding firm diversification and strategic options, consider the situation involved with both real estate and oil and gas investments. In these cases, diversification allows the firm to move resources to where they are most productive. The oil and gas firm will concentrate more of its efforts on producing oil when oil prices are high and more of its efforts on producing natural gas when gas prices are high. Similarly, a firm that develops real estate in both Dallas and Los Angeles has the option to concentrate its efforts in Dallas when the Dallas economy is doing well and then concentrate its efforts in Los Angeles when Los Angeles is doing well. The manufacturing firm can also benefit from flexibility, by shifting production to those facilities that have the lowest costs; but it will not want to completely shut down a high-cost facility because it will want to maintain the option to shift production back to the facility if the situation changes.

It should be stressed that these gains from diversification arise only when the businesses are closely enough related that resources can indeed be shifted between them. Unrelated diversification, such as Mobil Oil Corporation's acquisition of the department store Montgomery Ward, would be difficult to justify based on this type of analysis. It should also be stressed that the benefits of diversification require high-quality management with the incentives to optimally exercise these options to shift resources. Indeed, some have argued that diversification destroys value because of the tendency of management to perversely exercise these options: subsidizing badly performing businesses with the profits of the best performers.

Management Incentives, Psychology, and the Exercise of Strategic Options

In our earlier analysis, we assume that managers exercise their strategic options optimally. However, in reality managers may deviate from optimal exercise depending on how they are compensated, the organizational structure, and managerial psychology.[9]

Since the options to expand and abandon are so crucial to determining the value of an investment strategy, they deserve extra attention. Managers may be reluctant to abandon a strategy, and may even want to prematurely expand a strategy. One reason is that a decision to expand or abandon a strategy may convey information to investors that will affect the firm's stock price. For example, the decision to abandon a strategy may convey negative information about a firm's outlook, and can thus lead to a reduction in its stock price even when the decision itself is a good decision that benefits shareholders. Because of this potential for a negative stock price reaction, management may be reluctant to abandon a value-destroying strategy.

As we discussed in Chapter 8, depending on its circumstances, a firm's management may be more or less concerned about the firm's stock price. If, for example, the firm is likely to be raising external capital in the near future, or alternatively, if managers have stock options that are close to expiration, managers are likely to be very concerned about making announcements that are likely to be viewed negatively. Hence, in these situations they may be reluctant to optimally abandon what may have initially looked like a good strategy, but has since turned sour.

The second reason for not exercising an abandonment option optimally is closely related to the first, and arises because of the information it reveals within an organization. The problem arises when the individuals who originally approved a strategy are also responsible for determining when to abandon it. In this case, abandonment may be viewed as an admission that the original decision was a mistake. When the decision to

---

[9]Recall from our discussion in Chapter 11 that managers may have valid reasons for exercising too early even when the option to delay suggests otherwise. Similarly, managers may find it difficult to exercise the abandonment option for valid reasons or for reasons that are personally optimal but not necessarily best for the firm (recall our discussion of earnings management in Chapter 9).

abandon reflects poorly on the decision maker, perhaps influencing his or her promotion opportunities and bonus, the decision maker has a clear incentive to interpret market conditions much more favorably than warranted, in the hope that conditions will turn around in a way that makes the strategy profitable.

For example, in Panel a of Table 12-4, we can see that it is optimal to abandon the strategy in the lowest-value node in Year 2 (i.e., the value of the strategy is negative). However, to protect his personal reputation, the project manager may argue that if things turn around in Year 3, it is still possible for the strategy to generate a positive NPV; indeed, a sequence of two consecutive positive changes in the value of the plants in Years 3 and 4 would make the value of the strategy $118.73 million. If higher-level executives can be convinced that this is a likely event, then they may choose to allow the strategy to continue.

The final reason that managers sometimes do not optimally exercise the option to abandon a strategy is psychological and arises because of what psychologists call *cognitive dissonance*, which means that individuals tend to selectively observe information that supports their decisions. The basic idea is that individuals want to avoid information that makes them question their own abilities. The benefit of this psychological tendency is that it allows individuals to remain more confident about their abilities, even in the face of mistakes in judgment. Having confident managers is likely to have some benefits to the organization, but it has the obvious disadvantage of potentially generating bad decisions. In particular, one cannot rely on the project team that originally championed a strategy to objectively evaluate whether the strategy should be abandoned.

The important thing to note from the above discussion is that even with the best of intentions, managers may not optimally exercise the abandonment option. This suggests that simply tinkering with compensation to encourage managers to recognize their mistakes may not be sufficient. It is very difficult to provide incentives for managers to do the "right thing" if managers already think they are doing the right thing. Hence, one might want to be cautious about implementing a strategy that has a value that is quite sensitive to exercising abandonment options optimally.

The factors that make managers reluctant to optimally abandon an investment strategy are likely to be most relevant for strategies that are the most ambiguous to describe and evaluate. This bias against making decisions based on ambiguous information is a documented behavioral phenomenon known as the Ellsberg Paradox (see the Behavioral Insight box).

To understand how ambiguity influences the abandonment choice, contrast the Vespar example in this chapter to the examples in Chapter 11, where the owner of an oil field has an option to develop the field within a set number of years. In the oil field example, the decision to abandon is based mainly on oil prices. Because oil prices are both easy to observe and known to be difficult to predict, the incentive and behavioral issues associated with the abandonment decision are likely to be less important. Specifically, the economics of the choice are relatively straightforward to analyze (the project should be abandoned if oil prices fall), and because oil prices are difficult to predict,

BEHAVIORAL INSIGHT

Decision Making with Ambiguity—The Ellsberg Paradox

Daniel Ellsberg became famous during the Vietnam War for leaking sensitive government documents known as the Pentagon Papers. He is also known for identifying a very important attribute of human behavior that has come to be called the *Ellsberg Paradox*.* The idea behind the paradox is that people tend to be averse to making choices based on ambiguous information.

To illustrate this behavioral trait, Ellsberg asked participants in his experiment to select a ball from one of two urns, which each contained 100 balls. In one urn we know that 50 balls are red, and the rest are black. In the other urn the number of red and black balls is unknown, i.e., ambiguous. If the individual selects a red ball, he or she is paid $50, but he or she is paid nothing if a black ball is selected.

Ellsberg found that when posed with this dilemma, individuals overwhelmingly chose the urn with the *known* proportions of red and black balls. If the individual chose the first urn, with known proportions, then the experimenter would state the following: "So you think that the likelihood of selecting a red ball from the 50-50 urn is higher than by selecting from the urn with unknown proportions." The experimenter then asked the individual to draw another ball but was told that if a black ball was drawn from one of the two urns, he or she would receive $50. Faced with this new choice, the experimental subjects overwhelmingly selected the 50-50 urn again! Once again the subjects of the experiment preferred the urn for which the probability of selecting a black or red ball was known (less ambiguous).

The natural bias against making decisions involving ambiguity provides a major challenge for managers evaluating investments with potential strategic value. There might be a reluctance to move forward on an investment based on future opportunities that are vague and difficult to quantify. Similarly, ambiguity aversion can lead managers to be too slow to exercise the option to abandon a strategy, when the unfavorable information is vague and difficult to quantify. Indeed, some have speculated that Daniel Ellsberg believed that because of a lack of concrete information, the United States was reluctant to exit Vietnam, (i.e., we were slow to exercise our abandonment option), and he leaked the Pentagon Papers to provide additional clarity.

*Daniel Ellsberg, "Risk, Ambiguity, and the Savage Axioms," *Quarterly Journal of Economics* 75 (1961), 643–649.

deterioration in the value of the oil property is less likely to be viewed as a negative reflection on the individual who originally chose to invest in the project.

The economics of the Vespar strategy, however, are much more ambiguous and thus more difficult for an outsider to evaluate. The initiation of the project must be based on a number of subjective variables that require managerial judgment. What this means is that the abandonment choice must also be based on subjective information, and may thus reflect on management's prior judgment. This suggests that behavioral and incentive problems are more likely to influence the abandonment choice in the Vespar example.

12.5 SUMMARY

Throughout this book, we have described approaches for evaluating individual investment projects. In this chapter we step back from our focus on individual projects to think more broadly about a firm's investments as part of an overall strategy. From this analysis we arrived at three important "lessons." First, most major projects should be viewed as components of broader investment strategies, and should be evaluated as such. Second, although the evaluation of a firm's business strategy rests heavily on the judgment of the firm's senior management, strategic choices do have financial consequences that should be estimated, even if crudely. The final lesson is that not all firms are created equally when it comes to their organization's ability to capitalize on strategic investment opportunities. Organizational structure, financial structure, and the way in which the firm has chosen to diversify all play roles in the firm's ability to optimally exercise strategic options.

Throughout this book we have made the case for taking a disciplined, quantitative approach to the evaluation of investment opportunities. In addition to bringing more precise information to bear on the decision problem, a quantitative valuation process tends to take organizational politics out of the investment choice, making it easier to evaluate an investment based on its economic attributes rather than on the persuasiveness and power of the project sponsor. The advantage of using a more disciplined quantitative approach is especially relevant for the evaluation of investment *strategies,* since by their very nature, investment strategies are much more ambiguous, and hence, more susceptible to the biases associated with organizational politics.

Because strategy tends to be ambiguous, it is much more difficult to apply a quantitative approach to the evaluation of investment strategies than it is for individual investment projects. Although this is clearly a daunting task, real options analysis provides management with a framework as well as the necessary tools for quantifying strategic value. Managers will note that the suggested approach requires that the analyst make numerous assumptions. However, if managers are not making the assumptions explicitly in a quantitative analysis, they are, by default, making them implicitly when using more qualitative forms of analysis. Indeed, although real option analysis still requires considerable managerial judgment, it allows managers to apply their intuition and judgment in a disciplined way. For example, with a real option approach the analyst can conduct a sensitivity analysis to determine how each assumption affects the valuation of the investment strategy, thereby allowing the analyst to home in on the assumptions that are most important to the success of the strategy.

A final point to stress is that the approach presented here goes beyond the valuation of investment strategy and into the realm of optimal implementation. To be more precise, we have introduced an approach that not only values options but provides guidance as to when they should be optimally exercised. For example, our approach can be used to determine when a strategy should be expanded ("Should we build five rather than three power plants?"), as well as when a strategy should be abandoned. In addition, our approach provides some insights about how firms should be organized to extract the most value from their investment strategies. The key word here is *flexibility*. When firms design their organizations and determine their financial structures, it is critical that they be mindful of the benefits of being flexible in an uncertain environment.

PROBLEMS

12-1 OPTIONALITY AND STRATEGIC VALUE You have been retained by a major entertainment company to evaluate the purchase of land near one of its new amusement parks in Australia. The land will not be developed immediately but will later be developed for either high-density or low-density hotels, depending on the success of the amusement park.

Describe a strategy for developing the land and the approach you would take to value the strategy. Comment on the merits of this approach to evaluating the value of the land (no computations required).

12-2 ANALYZING A STRATEGY USING OPTION ANALYSIS Reliable Industries is considering the construction of a power plant investment in India. Reliable's analysts calculate that the cost of building the plant is $600 million, and the IRR of the plant is 13%. The analysts also estimate that given the experience of building the first plant, a second plant can be built for $550 million, and additional plants can be built for about $500 million each.

a. How would you go about evaluating whether or not to build this power plant in India?
b. Are you evaluating a project or a strategy?
c. How does the risk associated with the power plant strategy compare with the risk associated with the individual power plants?

12-3 THOUGHT PROBLEM Many financial analysts are very skeptical of the use of strategic considerations to justify a project. This opinion is largely based on the observation that some of the biggest investment disasters were undertaken based on a "strategic" rationale. However, this type of mind-set can lead to a form of managerial myopia in which the only projects that can survive the firm's acceptance hurdle are those for which future cash flows can be easily identified and forecast. Comment on the validity of this statement (no computations required).

12-4 VALUING A BUSINESS STRATEGY Vespar's senior management team was poised to undertake the clean-burning coal power plants when they received a call from the chief engineer for the contractor who had been selected to build the initial plant. The engineer had the following proposed change to the plan: Instead of building two power plants each in Years 1 and 2, the engineer suggested that the firm consider building only one plant per year and that additional funds be spent on R&D so that the learning that was expected to be accomplished by the building of multiple plants could be accomplished. The cost of plants plus the increased cost of R&D in Years 1 and 2 would rise to $400 million and $385 million, respectively. Vespar's management found the proposal intriguing and decided to revisit the economic analysis based on the reduced number of plants and higher total cost per plant.

When Vespar's financial analyst in charge of the original strategy evaluation was told of the need to reanalyze the strategy, he noted that this was probably a good idea because of recent events in the energy market. In fact, he felt that the volatility of the coal-fired strategy was substantially higher than when the original analysis had been done. He estimated the present values of the individual plants ($ millions) built over the next four years would now be as follows:

		Years		
0	**1**	**2**	**3**	**4**
				$534.30
			$450.77	
		$449.58		395.82
	$379.30		394.78	
$320.00		333.06		346.65
	280.99		292.46	
		246.74		256.81
			216.66	
				190.25

All the other information regarding the strategy remains the same except that the risk-neutral probability of a positive shift in the value of a new plant is now estimated to be 46.26%. (The actual probabilities remain 50-50.)

a. What is the expected value of the investment strategy in which the abandonment option is ignored and all the plants are built, regardless of their NPV? For purposes of this analysis, assume that the appropriate discount rate for the strategy is 13.77%.

b. What is the expected value of the investment strategy in which the option to abandon is optimally exercised?

c. How much more can the plants cost in Years 1 and 2 before the revised strategy is no longer preferred to the initial strategy? Assume that the same cost inflation factor applies to each plant in Years 1 and 2 and that the net present value lattice applies.

12-5 SIMPLE INVESTMENT STRATEGY—STAGED INVESTMENTS You have been retained to evaluate a major investment for a technology company. The cost of the project is $100 million. If the project is successful, it will generate expected profits of $15 million per year forever, which has a present value of $150 million. However, there is a 50% chance that the project will be a complete failure, in which case it will generate no cash flows. Moreover, if the project is successful there will be a follow-on project that can be initiated the following year. The follow-on project will have a cost of $1 billion, and if things go well it will generate expected cash flows of $150 million per year that last forever and result in a value of $1.5 billion (in Year 1 dollars). If the follow-on project is not successful, it will result in a stream of cash flows with a present value of $900 million. Should the initial project be taken? Explain your recommendation in commonsense terms to your boss, who is not a "techie."

Epilogue

In preparing to write this book, we reviewed the academic literature on valuation theory, corporate finance, and behavioral economics and interviewed corporate managers, consultants, and investment bankers. This dual-track process not only helped solidify our understanding of valuation theory and industry practice, but also identified a number of situations where there is a substantial disconnect between the two. To conclude the book, we will revisit these disconnects along with our explanations for why each exists. In addition, we will use this recap as an opportunity to discuss how we think industry practice is likely to evolve in the future.

ESTIMATING FUTURE CASH FLOWS

The first source of disconnect that we observe relates to the tendency of managers to provide cash flow forecasts that are biased estimates of expected cash flows. These biases, depending on the situation, can be either positive or negative. For example, positive biases tend to arise from the fact that cash flow estimates are frequently based on what the analyst believes is a *likely* scenario. These estimates tend to be optimistic, rather than expected, cash flows, since there is a tendency for optimistic project champions to focus on scenarios in which the project succeeds. However, this focus on likely scenarios may also result in a downward bias, because it can lead the analyst to ignore the benefits of project flexibility. The latter is especially problematic when the investment presents opportunities for scaling up when it is doing well and scaling down when it is doing poorly.

It should also be noted that in practice, cash flow forecasts are often used for more than project evaluation. A venture capitalist, for example, is generally quite happy to fund an entrepreneur based on the entrepreneur's optimistic cash flow forecasts. To understand why, you should first note that venture capitalists, who are aware of the optimistic bias in the entrepreneur's cash flow forecast, easily address it by requiring very high rates of return. Consequently, the ultimate investment decision is not necessarily biased. You should also note that the venture capitalist uses the entrepreneur's cash flow forecasts as cash flow targets for the entrepreneur. As a result, the optimistic cash flow estimates provide higher targets that may serve to motivate the entrepreneur and provide the venture capitalist with bargaining power in the future, if realized cash flows fail to meet the entrepreneur's projections.

As we noted above, cash flow estimates are sometimes biased downward if significant sources of project flexibility are unrecognized. The fact that analysts often ignore the effects of project flexibility may simply be due to the complexity associated with accounting for the inherent flexibility of most projects. Indeed, our chapters on real options and the valuation of flexibility are probably the most complex in this book. For a variety of reasons, executives believe that complexity can lead to mistakes since complicated problems are more difficult to solve than simple problems, and may require hidden assumptions that the financial analyst does not completely understand. In addition, as we discuss in Chapter 5, internal political problems (what we call *influence costs*) in more complex decision problems can provide decision makers with the leeway to make assumptions that make their pet projects look more favorable. When more complicated valuation approaches are used, project champions who are cleverer, more articulate, and politically more adept are more likely to get their projects approved, even though the projects they champion may not necessarily be the best ones for the firm.

ESTIMATING DISCOUNT RATES

Anecdotal evidence suggests that firms tend to use hurdle rates substantially higher than what most academics would consider to be appropriate risk-adjusted discount rates, and more importantly, they often use the same discount rate to evaluate investments with very different levels of risk. As we mentioned above, the higher discount rate may be used to offset overly optimistic cash flow forecasts, and it may also serve as a higher hurdle to motivate project sponsors to bargain for the best deals possible with supplies, employees, etc. The use of a single discount rate rather than more appropriate risk-adjusted discount rates tailored to each project is probably a function of the complexity of the task and the role that influence costs play.

EARNINGS DILUTION AND ACCRETION

Perhaps the most important disconnect between theory and practice that we identified has to do with the importance of reported accounting earnings. Most valuation textbooks provide very little discussion of the accounting implications of project selection, however, in practice managers often devote as much time evaluating whether an investment is earnings accretive or earnings dilutive as they spend on estimating the NPV of the project. As we discuss in Chapter 9, managers are likely to be concerned about the earnings impact of an investment project as long as their performance and the overall performance of the firm are evaluated on the basis of accounting earnings.

NARROWING THE GAP—FUTURE DIRECTIONS

Although we believe that the gap between theory and practice will never be eliminated entirely, it is narrowing over time and should continue to shrink in the future. This will partly come about as theory changes to account for the realities of operating in a diverse business organization that is populated by managers with multiple objectives and recognized behavioral biases. More importantly, business practice is changing, as managers come to recognize the costs associated with failures to adjust properly for optimism bias, to account for project flexibility, and to use an appropriate discount rate.

As the magnitude of these costs becomes more apparent, we expect firms to make changes that counter the organizational difficulties that arise when firms implement more complex valuation tools suggested by theory. We believe that these organizational difficulties can be substantially mitigated if firms set up truly independent control groups, whose sole purpose is the evaluation of major investment projects and who have no incentive to either accept or reject investments. Because of their unbiased nature, these groups can reduce incentive problems, which in turn will allow the firm to use more sophisticated valuation approaches. From our casual observations, we find that firms with such evaluation groups do tend to use more sophisticated valuation approaches; however, this may reflect the more sophisticated nature of the organizations themselves.

Finally, we believe that the gap between theory and practice will narrow with time as valuation approaches that initially appear to be very complex begin to appear more intuitive. The development of valuation software will contribute to this trend by making the somewhat more complicated academic solutions easier to implement in practice. Indeed, we hope that this book plays a role in hastening this process as well.

Credits

Chapter 3   Pages 115, 116, 117: All Crystal Ball Professional Edition software screenshots, © 2007 Decisioneering, Inc. Used by permission. http://www.crystalball.com

Chapter 4   Page 143: Source: Ibbotson Associates *SBBI 2006 Yearbook.*; Page 169: Source: Adapted from Moody's Investor's Service, Default and Recovery Rates of Corporate Bond Issuers: 2000, Global Credit Research (February 2001), Exhibit 42, Page 47. © Copyright 2007 Moody's Investors Service.

Chapter 6   Pages 271, 272: Source: FactSet Research Systems; as of 10/14/02. © FactSet Research Systems Inc. 2000–2007.

Chapter 8   Page 323: Source: Based on Figure 3 in Stephen D. Prowse, 1998, The Economics of the Private Equity Market, *Economic Review of the Federal Reserve Bank of Dallas*, 3rd Quarter, 1998, 21–34.; Page 340: Source: Based on Scott Sedlacek, "Leveraged buyouts: Building Shareholder Value through Capital Structure," Broadview International, LLC (April 2, 2003).

Chapter 12   Page 507: Sources: Christine Tierney/ Detroit News (January 5, 2005) and Malcolm Berko, "GM clings to its ranking as world's top automaker," BeaconNewsOnline.com

Index